The Princeton Review®

AP® EUROPEAN HISTORY

PREMIUM PREP

24th Edition

The Staff of The Princeton Review

PrincetonReview.com

Penguin Random House

The Princeton Review
110 East 42nd Street, 7th Floor
New York, NY 10017
princetonreview.com
penguinrandomhouse.com

Published in the United States by Penguin Random House
LLC, New York.

ISBN: 978-0-593-51849-6
eBook ISBN: 978-0-593-51850-2
ISSN: 2690-5426

Editor: Meave Shelton
Production Editors: Liz Dacey and Becky Radway
Production Artist: Jason Ullmeyer
Content Contributor: Brandon Bub

Manufactured in the United States of America

10 9 8 7 6 5 4 3 2 1

24th Edition

EU Contact:
Penguin Random House Ireland
32 Nassau Street
Dublin D02 YH68
https://eu-contact.penguin.ie

The Princeton Review Publishing Team
Rob Franek, Editor-in-Chief
David Soto, Senior Director, Data Operations
Stephen Koch, Senior Manager, Data Operations
Deborah Weber, Director of Production
Jason Ullmeyer, Production Design Manager
Jennifer Chapman, Senior Production Artist
Selena Coppock, Director of Editorial
Aaron Riccio, Director, Editorial Admissions Content
Orion McBean, Senior Editor
Meave Shelton, Senior Editor
Chris Chimera, Editor
Patricia Murphy, Editor
Laura Rose, Editor
Isabelle Appleton, Editorial Assistant

Penguin Random House Publishing Team
Tom Russell, VP, Publisher
Alison Stoltzfus, Senior Director, Publishing
Emily Hoffman, Managing Editor
Mary Ellen Owens, Assistant Director of Production
Suzanne Lee, Senior Designer
Eugenia Lo, Publishing Assistant

For customer service, please contact
editorialsupport@review.com,
and be sure to include:

- full title of the book
- ISBN
- page number

Eugene Black's testimony is used with the kind permission of the
Black family and the Holocaust Survivors' Friendship Association.

Acknowledgments

A very special thanks to Brandon Bub for his updates to this edition. Thanks also to Jason Ullmeyer, Liz Dacey, and Becky Radway for their careful attention to every page.

Contents

Get More (Free) Content
at **PrincetonReview.com/prep**

As easy as **1·2·3**

1 Go to PrincetonReview.com/prep or scan the **QR code** and enter the following ISBN to register your book:
9780593518496

2 Answer a few simple questions to set up an exclusive Princeton Review account. *(If you already have one, you can just log in.)*

3 Enjoy access to your **FREE** content!

Access Your Online Test Practice

Your AP Prep book comes with new interactive practice exams to help you prepare for digital test-taking! Find these tests in your online Student Tools, provided in at least one of the following formats:

- Fully digital versions with a timer option to simulate the exam experience
- Downloadable interactive PDFs with digital features like clicking your answer and typing your free-responses

Check back often as we continue to update the included AP Student Tools.

PLUS, IN YOUR ACCOUNT YOU CAN:

- Get valuable advice about the college application process, tips for essay writing, and financial aid info
- Use our searchable rankings to learn more about your dream school

- Access comprehensive study guides, digital flashcards, key terms, timelines, and more
- Check whether there have been any updates or corrections to this edition

Look For These Icons Throughout The Book

 ONLINE PRACTICE TESTS

 ONLINE ARTICLES

 OTHER REFERENCES

 APPLIED STRATEGIES

 PROVEN TECHNIQUES

 ONLINE VIDEO TUTORIALS

Learn From the Best

Part I
Using This Book to Improve Your AP Score

- Preview: Your Knowledge, Your Expectations
- Your Guide to Using This Book
- How to Begin

PREVIEW: YOUR KNOWLEDGE, YOUR EXPECTATIONS

Your route to a high score on the AP European History Exam depends a lot on how you plan to use this book. Start thinking about your plan by responding to the following questions.

1. What is your level of confidence about your knowledge of the content tested by the AP European History Exam?

   A. Very confident—I know it all
   B. I'm pretty confident, but there are topics for which I could use help
   C. Not confident—I need quite a bit of support
   D. I'm not sure

2. If you have a goal score in mind, circle your goal score for the AP European History Exam.

   5   4   3   2   1   I'm not sure yet

3. What do you expect to learn from this book? Circle all that apply to you.

   A. A general overview of the test and what to expect
   B. Strategies for how to approach the test
   C. The content tested by this exam
   D. I'm not sure yet

YOUR GUIDE TO USING THIS BOOK

This book is organized to provide as much—or as little—support as you need, so you can use it in whatever way will be most helpful to improving your score on the AP European History Exam.

Scoring Worksheets
We've included a scoring worksheet for each of the Practice Tests. Remember that these worksheets are meant to serve as a rough guideline only. AP Exam scores are weighted according to a statistical process that varies slightly every year based on how students perform on the exam. But you can use the worksheets to approximate your score!

- The remainder of **Part I** will provide guidance on how to use this book and help you determine your strengths and weaknesses.

- **Part II** of this book contains Practice Test 1, its Diagnostic Answer Key, detailed answers and explanations, and a scoring guide. (Bubble sheets can be found in the very back of the book for easy tear-out and online in your Student Tools.) We strongly recommend that you take this test before going any further in order to realistically determine:

  o your starting point right now
  o which question types you're ready for and which you might need to practice
  o which content topics you are familiar with and which you should carefully review

  Once you have nailed down your strengths and weaknesses with regard to this exam, you can focus your test preparation, build a study plan, and be efficient with your time. Our Diagnostic Answer Key will assist you with this process.

- **Part III** of this book will:

  o provide information about the structure, scoring, and content of the AP European History Exam

  o help you to make a study plan

  o point you toward additional resources

- **Part IV** of this book will explore various strategies:

  o how to tackle multiple-choice questions

  o how to write effective essays for document-based questions (DBQs) and thematic essay questions

  o how to manage your time to maximize the number of points available to you

- **Part V** of this book covers the content you need for the AP European History Exam.

- **Part VI** of this book contains two additional practice tests, along with their answers and explanations. If you skipped Practice Test 1, we recommend that you take all three (with at least a day or two between them) so that you can compare your progress from one to the next. Additionally, this will help to identify any external issues. If you get a certain type of question wrong each time, you probably need to review it. If you get it wrong only once, you may have run out of time or been distracted by something. In either case, this will allow you to focus on the factors that caused the discrepancy in scores and to be as prepared as possible on the day of the test.

- **Online Resources** contain three additional practice tests. Follow the study guide found there based on the amount of time you have to study for the exam.

Take Your Digital Tests Online
Register your book at PrincetonReview.com/prep to access Practice Tests 4, 5, and 6 via your Student Tools. Two of these tests are available in a fully digital format to give you a feel for the exam interface.

You may choose to use some parts of this book over others, or you may work through the entire book. Your approach will depend on your needs and how much time you have. Now let's look at how to make this determination.

HOW TO BEGIN

1. Take Practice Test 1

Before you can decide how to use this book, we recommend that you take a practice test. Doing so will give you insight into your strengths and weaknesses, and the test will also help you make an effective study plan. If you're feeling test-phobic, remind yourself that a practice test is a tool for diagnosing yourself—it's not how well you do that matters but how you use information gleaned from your performance to guide your preparation.

So, before you read further, take Practice Test 1 starting on page 9 of this book. Be sure to do so in one sitting, following the instructions that appear before the test.

2. Check Your Answers

Using the Diagnostic Answer Key on page 43, follow our three-step process to identify your strengths and weaknesses with regard to the tested topics. This will help you determine which content review chapters to prioritize when studying this book. Don't worry about the explanations for now, and don't worry about why you missed questions. We'll get to that soon.

3. Reflect on the Test

After you take your first test, respond to the following questions:

- How much time did you spend on the multiple-choice questions?

- How much time did you spend on each essay?

- How many multiple-choice questions did you miss?

- Do you feel you had the knowledge to address the subject matter of the short-answer questions and essays?

- Do you feel you wrote well-organized, thoughtful short-answer responses and essays?

4. Read Part III of this Book and Complete the Self-Evaluation

Part III will provide information on how the test is structured and scored. It will also set out areas of content that are tested.

As you read Part III, reevaluate your answers to the questions above. At the end of Part III, you will revisit and refine the questions you answered above. You will then be able to make a study plan, based on your needs and time available, that will allow you to use this book most effectively.

5. **Engage with Parts IV and V as Needed**

Notice the word *engage*. You'll get more out of this book if you use it intentionally than if you read it passively, hoping for an improved score through osmosis. In other words, focus on what you need as a learner.

Strategy chapters in Part IV will help you think about your approach to the question types on this exam. This part opens with a reminder to think about how you approach questions now and then closes with a reflection section asking you to think about how/whether you will change your approach in the future.

Content chapters in Part V are designed to provide a review of the content tested on the AP European History Exam, including the level of detail you need to know and how the content is tested. You will have the opportunity to assess your understanding of the content of each chapter through test-appropriate questions.

6. **Take Another Test and Assess Your Performance**

Once you feel you have developed the strategies you need and gained the knowledge you lacked, you should take Practice Test 2, which starts on page 369 of this book. You should do so in one sitting, following the instructions at the beginning of the test.

When you have taken the test, check your answers to the multiple-choice section with the correct responses on page 402. Then, see whether a teacher will read your short answers and essays and provide feedback for your improvement.

Got a Question?
For answers to test-prep questions for all your tests and additional test-taking tips, subscribe to our channel at YouTube.com/ThePrincetonReview

Once you have checked your answers, reflect on what areas you still need to work on, and revisit the chapters in this book that address those deficiencies. You have additional practice tests that you can use to prepare, so space those out as you complete your content review. Part VI includes Practice Tests 2 and 3, and three more practice tests can be found online in your Student Tools. Through this type of reflection and engagement, you will continue to improve.

7. **Keep Working**

As we'll discuss in Part III, there are other resources available to you, including a wealth of information at AP Students, which is the AP section of the College Board's website. You can continue to explore areas that can stand improvement and engage in those areas right up to the day of the test. For updates and information on the AP European History Exam, as well as free practice, check out its home page: https://apstudents. collegeboard.org/courses/ap-european-history.

Part II
Practice Test 1

- Practice Test 1
- Practice Test 1: Diagnostic Answer Key and Explanations
- How to Score Practice Test 1

Practice Test 1

AP® European History Exam

At a Glance

Time
55 minutes
Number of Questions
55
Percent of Total Score
40%

DISCLAIMER: The official AP European History Exam will be administered digitally. Instructions for the digital exam may differ from this practice test.

Instructions

Section I, Part A has 55 multiple-choice questions and lasts 55 minutes.

Each question in this part is followed by four suggested answers. Select the best answer to each question.

Indicate all of your answers to the multiple-choice questions on the answer sheet. Give only one answer to each question.

Use your time effectively, working as quickly as you can without losing accuracy. Do not spend too much time on any one question. Go on to other questions and come back to the ones you have not answered if you have time.

Your total score on the multiple-choice section is based only on the number of questions answered correctly. Points are not deducted for incorrect answers or unanswered questions.

At a Glance

Time
40 minutes
Number of Questions
3
Percent of Total Score
20%
Questions 1 and 2
Mandatory
Question 3 or 4
Choose one question

Instructions

Section I, Part B has 3 short-answer questions and lasts 40 minutes.

In this part, answer Question 1 and Question 2 and **either** Question 3 **or** Question 4.

In your responses, be sure to address **all** parts of the questions you answer. Use complete sentences; an outline or bulleted list alone is not acceptable.

You may pace yourself as you answer the questions in this part, or you may use these optional timing recommendations:

It is suggested that you spend an equal amount of time, approximately 13 minutes, on each question.

For this practice test, use scratch paper for notes and planning as well as writing your responses.

GO ON TO THE NEXT PAGE.

**AP EUROPEAN HISTORY
SECTION I, Part A
Time—55 minutes
55 Questions**

Directions: Each of the questions or incomplete statements below is followed by four suggested answers or completions. Select the one that is best in each case.

Questions 1 through 3 refer to the following.

"The vegetable kingdom affords no food more wholesome, more easily procured, or less expensive, than the Potatoe (sic). It is well known with what resources it furnished the Irish in 1740; many families would have been swept away without this supply: the eagerness with which children devour it, the preference which they give it to the chesnut [sic], would seem to show that it is well adapted to the constitution of man: persons of all ages and temperaments feed upon it without experiencing the slightest inconvenience. In the last German war these roots were the resource of many soldiers, who happening to be separated from the main body of the army, would have fallen sacrifices to fatigue and hunger, if they had not met with Potatoes, which they eat in excessive quantities after simple boiling, and with no other seasoning than a good appetite: gratitude induced several of them to import the plant into their own country, where it was unknown: they cultivated it with skill, and set an example which was soon imitated. At present there is scarce an elegant repost where Potatoes are not introduced with emulation in various disguises; and the great consumption in the Capital, proves that they are no longer despised there.

THE excessive price to which grain has been advanced of late years, forms a remarkable area at which the beneficial qualities of Potatoes have begun to be tried in many places. …

IF we consider all the properties of Potatoes, we shall be forced to acknowledge, that if there really exists a medicinal food, it is to be found in these roots."

Source: Antoine Augustine Parmentier, French pharmacist and agronomist, *Observations on Such Nutritive Vegetables as May Be Substituted in the Place of Ordinary Food, in Times of Scarcity*, 1781

---

1 ☐ Mark for Review

The historical development referenced in the second paragraph most directly led to which of the following in France in the late 1700s?

(A) Strict price controls and government rationing to control the price of grain

(B) Tax cuts and deregulation of businesses to spur job creation

(C) Mass civil rebellion culminating in the overthrow of the government

(D) The creation of a military dictatorship

---

2 ☐ Mark for Review

Which of the following is most directly a cause of the presence of the crop in Europe alluded to in the first paragraph?

(A) A global exchange of plants, animals, and diseases between the Old and New Worlds

(B) The establishment of plantation economies in European colonies

(C) Innovations in banking and finance promoting the growth of urban financial centers

(D) Primitive agricultural practices and land-owning patterns

---

GO ON TO THE NEXT PAGE.

3 ☐ Mark for Review

Which of the following best describes the author's purpose in writing the excerpt?

- Ⓐ To warn European policymakers of the danger of the overreliance on a single crop

- Ⓑ To advocate for the interests of small landowners who risked losing their land due to enclosure

- Ⓒ To criticize government policies that forbade the cultivation of new crops

- Ⓓ To encourage the French to take advantage of a crop already well-regarded by rival states

GO ON TO THE NEXT PAGE.

Questions 4 through 8 refer to the following.

<u>Orders concerning infected Houses, and Persons sick of the Plague</u>

"Notice to be given of the Sickness
        The master of every House, as soon as anyone in his House complaineth, either of Botch, or Purple, or Swelling in any part of his Body, or falleth otherwise dangerously Sick, without apparent Cause of some other Disease, shall give knowledge thereof to the Examiner of Health within two hours after the said Sign shall appear.

Sequestration of the Sick
        As soon as any man shall be found by this Examiner, [Surgeon], or Searcher to be sick of the Plague, he shall the same Night be sequestered in the same House. And in case he be so sequestered, then though he afterwards die not, the House wherein he sickened shall be shut up for a Month, after the use of the due Preservatives taken by the rest.

Airing the Stuff
        For Sequestration of the Goods and Stuff of the Infected, their Bedding, and Apparel, and Hangings of Chambers, must be well aired with Fire, and such Perfumes as are requisite within the infected House, before they be taken again to use; This to be done by the Appointment of the Examiner."

Source: *A Collection of Very Valuable and Scarce Pieces relating to the Last Plague in the Year 1665*
No attributed author. Published in London, 1721.

---

4 ☐ Mark for Review

A historian could best use this excerpt to study which of the following about Europe in the 1600s?

(A) Methods that municipal governments used to stem the spread of infectious disease

(B) The adoption of new technologies and innovations that successfully reduced the presence of the Plague

(C) The effect that widespread disease had on European wages

(D) How responses to the spread of the plague differed by socioeconomic status

---

5 ☐ Mark for Review

Diseases such as those referenced in the excerpt were most strongly affected by which of the following in nineteenth-century Europe?

(A) The invention of penicillin

(B) Rapid improvements in public sanitation

(C) Global reduction in rat populations

(D) A European population with increased immunity

---

6 ☐ Mark for Review

The actions described in the excerpt reflect what intellectual development of the 1600s?

(A) The continued influence of the humoral theory of disease

(B) Skepticism of the institutional authority of the Catholic Church

(C) The understanding of the human body as an integrated system

(D) The use of alchemy and astrology as tools to understand a predictable universe

---

GO ON TO THE NEXT PAGE.

7 🔖 Mark for Review

All of the following resulted from diseases such as the one described in the excerpt largely subsiding in Europe in the 1600s EXCEPT

(A) population levels largely recovering to pre-Black Death levels across the continent

(B) larger influxes of migrants to cities in search of new economic opportunities

(C) a shift away from agriculture as the dominant European livelihood

(D) uneven price increases and increases in the prices of agricultural commodities

8 🔖 Mark for Review

From a socioeconomic perspective, the Great Plague of 1665 resulted in

(A) more casualties among the poor than among the wealthy, who could afford to leave London

(B) the return of Royalists to the city at the end of the Commonwealth

(C) the hasty construction of plague pits for the dead

(D) the development of the plague doctor costume, with a bird-like beak mask, gloves, boots, and a wide-brimmed hat

GO ON TO THE NEXT PAGE.

Questions 9 through 11 refer to the following.

Alfred Choubrac, Moulin Rouge poster, 1896

Events such as the one referenced in the image were facilitated most directly by all of the following EXCEPT

(A) new efficient methods of transportation such as streetcars and bicycles

(B) mass marketing increasing both production and demand of new consumer goods

(C) the growth of the middle class as industrialization created new sources of wealth and leisure

(D) the adoption of new methods by corporations and governments to manage volatile business cycles

Art created in the period referenced in the image tended to most commonly emphasize which of the following themes?

(A) Materialism and bourgeois sensibility

(B) Ennui and subjectivism

(C) Passion and reason

(D) Religiosity and high art

GO ON TO THE NEXT PAGE.

11 🔖 Mark for Review

The poster would most likely have been intended for which of the following audiences in France in the late 1800s?

- Ⓐ A member of the industrial bourgeoisie

- Ⓑ A Parisian factory worker

- Ⓒ A member of the French royal family

- Ⓓ A high-ranking member of the Catholic Church

GO ON TO THE NEXT PAGE.

Questions 12 through 15 refer to the following.

"Nothing is easier than to admit in words the truth of the universal struggle for life, or more difficult at least I have found it so than constantly to bear this conclusion in mind. Yet unless it be thoroughly engrained in the mind, I am convinced that the whole economy of nature, with every fact on distribution, rarity, abundance, extinction, and variation, will be dimly seen or quite misunderstood. We behold the face of nature bright with gladness, we often see superabundance of food; we do not see, or we forget, that the birds which are idly singing round us mostly live on insects or seeds, and are thus constantly destroying life; or we forget how largely these songsters, or their eggs, or their nestlings are destroyed by birds and beasts of prey; we do not always bear in mind, that though food may be now superabundant, it is not so at all seasons of each recurring year."

Source: Charles Darwin, *On the Origin of Species*, 1859

12 ☐ Mark for Review

The passage best reflects which of the following concepts or periods?

(A) The scientific era

(B) The Enlightenment

(C) Neoclassicism

(D) Neoplatonism

13 ☐ Mark for Review

Which of the following best describes a claim made in the excerpt?

(A) The strong in society naturally dominate the weak.

(B) Birds struggle to find food because they fail to adapt to their environment.

(C) Science alone provides knowledge rather than faith.

(D) The struggle to survive is shared among all living creatures.

14 ☐ Mark for Review

The ideas expressed in the passage would have been most strongly rejected by which of the following?

(A) A believer in European racial and cultural superiority in the 1800s

(B) A high-ranking member of the Catholic Church in the 1500s

(C) A scientist working in a university in the 1900s

(D) A nineteenth-century philosopher who emphasized the irrationality of human society

15 ☐ Mark for Review

Which of the following rationales for imperialism in the late 1800s contrasts most strongly with the ideas presented in the passage?

(A) Colonies were needed as sources of raw materials and markets for manufactured goods.

(B) Colonization was a tool that would allow for the *Mission Civilisatrice* or Civilizing Mission.

(C) European races were naturally more fit to rule over non-European races.

(D) European national rivalries fostered expansion and competition for colonies.

GO ON TO THE NEXT PAGE.

Questions 16 through 19 refer to the following.

Anthony van Dyck, *The Lomellini Family*, Genoa, Italy, 1623

16 ☐ Mark for Review

In seventeenth-century Italy, such aristocratic families typically lived in

(A) sprawling estates in the farmlands

(B) spacious *palazzi* in the cities

(C) rustic chateaus in the mountains

(D) ornate apartments in suburban areas

17 ☐ Mark for Review

One common way for Italian families to enter the upper classes was through

(A) bravery in warfare

(B) exemplary achievement in the arts

(C) ecclesiastical promotion

(D) amassing a fortune

GO ON TO THE NEXT PAGE.

18 ☐ Mark for Review

Which of the following describes the most likely purpose that the family portrayed had in commissioning this piece of art?

- Ⓐ To support the development of a burgeoning artistic movement

- Ⓑ To promote their own power and stature

- Ⓒ To challenge the perceptions of women and their place in public life

- Ⓓ To cement alliances with rival states

19 ☐ Mark for Review

All of the following features of the Italian Renaissance are reflected in the painting EXCEPT

- Ⓐ the use of geometric perspective

- Ⓑ admiration for Greek and Roman political institutions

- Ⓒ emphasis on artistic naturalism

- Ⓓ artistic portrayal using classical form

GO ON TO THE NEXT PAGE.

Questions 20 through 23 refer to the following.

"Theresa inherited [her mother's] wealth of hair, but with more colour in it—bright golden colour. Beneath its coils and curls her forehead no longer looked disproportionately high. Her mother's blue eyes were in keeping with the flower-like beauty of her youth. Theresa's eyes were grey, though with gleams of blue in them—eyes so full of sparkle that they seemed to give out light rather than reflect it.

Though deficient as yet in physical strength, there was no doubt of the vigour of her mental powers…. But she had an inborn aptitude for observation, reflection, and logical reasoning. Save in the sphere of religion, where she had been led to believe that inquiry was deadly sin, she proved quite capable of thinking for herself, of taking direct, unbiased views of things, and of forming her own opinions of the social and political worlds of her day in so far as she was acquainted with them. Her will was strong."

Source: English author Mary Maxwell Moffat, *Maria Theresa*, 1911

20 ☐ Mark for Review

The author's reference to "the sphere of religion" is best interpreted as

(A) an expression of twentieth-century agnosticism

(B) an overt attack upon the Protestant ruling elite of Austria-Hungary

(C) a cautious judgment of Maria Theresa's neutrality during the Wars of Religion

(D) a subtle criticism of the Catholic Church for its doctrine of infallibility

21 ☐ Mark for Review

All of the following are true; which of the following policies would most contradict the account of Maria Theresa described in the excerpt?

(A) Her establishment of new educational institutions and reform of Austria's primary school system

(B) Her creation of a unified legal system under the Hapsburg government

(C) Her institutionalized system of censorship of books and education considered harmful to the state

(D) Her promotion of inoculation as a means of stemming epidemic disease

22 ☐ Mark for Review

For women, the type of mentality described in the passage was most easily expressed in which of the following eighteenth-century institutions?

(A) Dutch universities

(B) Parisian salons

(C) English scientific societies

(D) Italian coffeehouses

23 ☐ Mark for Review

In the context of the book's publication, the author was most likely most influenced by which of the following in the early twentieth century?

(A) The movement for women's suffrage

(B) The use of popular nationalism to strengthen the state

(C) Imperialist expansion as Europeans claimed racial and cultural superiority

(D) Realist literary attitudes drawing attention to social problems

GO ON TO THE NEXT PAGE.

Questions 24 through 27 refer to the following.

Source: J.F. Horrabin, "Germany after the Peace Treaty of 1919," from H.G. Wells,
The Outline of History: Being a Plain History of Life and Mankind, London, 1923

---

24 ☐ Mark for Review

Which of the following represents a limitation of the map in portraying how German territory changed after 1919?

(A) It does not indicate where the German capital was moved after the war.

(B) It fails to show German colonial holdings outside of Europe and how they changed hands.

(C) It does not portray Allied Powers including Great Britain.

(D) It does not indicate what languages were spoken in the various territories.

25 ☐ Mark for Review

All of the following new technologies characterized the conflict referenced in the map EXCEPT

(A) nuclear weapons

(B) submarines

(C) poison gas

(D) airplanes

GO ON TO THE NEXT PAGE.

26 ▣ Mark for Review

The map best illustrates which of the following historical developments after 1919?

(A) The conflicting goals of peace negotiators pitted diplomatic idealism against the desire to punish Germany.

(B) The Versailles settlement's war guilt provisions hindered Germany's ability to create a stable and legitimate economic system.

(C) The dissolution of the Ottoman Empire created a strategic interest for European powers in the Middle East and its oil.

(D) Wilsonian notions of self-determination transformed the imperial balance of power through the establishment of the League of Nations.

27 ▣ Mark for Review

Which of the following 1930s developments in Germany represents the most direct violation of the peace terms illustrated in the map?

(A) The Nazi-Soviet Non-Aggression Pact

(B) The Annexation of Austria

(C) The Remilitarization of the Rhineland

(D) The Munich Agreement

GO ON TO THE NEXT PAGE.

Questions 28 through 31 refer to the following.

"The Union shall set itself the following objectives: - to promote economic and social progress which is balanced and sustainable, in particular through the creation of an area without internal frontiers, through the strengthening of economic and social cohesion and through the establishment of economic and monetary union, ultimately including a single currency in accordance with the provisions of this Treaty; ...

The Community shall have as its task, by establishing a common market and an economic and monetary union and by implementing the common policies or activities referred to in Articles 3 and 3a, to promote throughout the Community a harmonious and balanced development of economic activities, sustainable and non-inflationary growth respecting the environment, a high degree of convergence of economic performance, a high level of employment and of social protection, the raising of the standard of living and quality of life, and economic and social cohesion and solidarity among Member States."

Source: The Maastricht Treaty, ratified in 1992, Netherlands

---

28 ☐ Mark for Review

The document is best understood in the context of which of the following developments in the late twentieth century?

(A) Increased immigration into Europe altered Europe's religious make-up, causing debate and conflict over the role of religion in social and political life.

(B) New communication and transportation technologies multiplied connections across space and time, transforming daily life and contributing to globalization.

(C) The collapse of the USSR ended the Cold War and led to the establishment of capitalist economies throughout Eastern Europe.

(D) European states began to set aside nationalist rivalries in favor of economic and political integration.

---

29 ☐ Mark for Review

All of the following would likely express skepticism of the ideas expressed in the first paragraph EXCEPT

(A) a proponent of the British policy of Brexit

(B) a member of the World Trade Organization

(C) a candidate of the French National Front

(D) a supporter of the Austrian Freedom Party

---

30 ☐ Mark for Review

Which of the following best describes a cause of the creation of the economic alliance alluded to in the passage?

(A) Efforts to contain communism through military alliances based on collective security

(B) Nationalistic tariff policies and depreciated currencies due to overproduction

(C) Policies to spur economic recovery in the wake of wartime destruction

(D) Resistance to indigenous nationalist movements and a reluctance to relinquish imperial control

---

31 ☐ Mark for Review

The ideas expressed in the second paragraph represent the strongest refutation of which of the following earlier political and economic systems?

(A) Capitalism

(B) Mercantilism

(C) Communism

(D) Imperialism

GO ON TO THE NEXT PAGE.

Questions 32 through 34 refer to the following.

"If anyone says that the New Testament does not provide for a distinct, visible priesthood; or that this priesthood has not any power ... but is only an office and bare ministry of preaching and gospel ... let him be anathema...

If anyone says that in the Catholic Church there is not a hierarchy instituted by divine ordination, consisting of bishops, priests, and ministers, let him be anathema...

In order that the faithful may approach and receive the sacraments with greater reverence and devotion of mind, this holy Council enjoins on all bishops that ... they shall first explain, in a manner suited to the capacity of those who receive them, the efficacy and use of those sacraments ... even in the vernacular tongue, if need be ...

[Those] who undertake the office of bishop should understand what their portion is, and comprehend that they are called, not to their own convenience, not to riches or luxury, but to labors and cares, for the glory of God ... the rest of the faithful also will be more easily excited to religion and innocence if they shall see those who are set over them not fixing their thoughts on the things of this world, but on the salvation of souls and on their heavenly country ... It strictly forbids them, moreover, to strive to enrich their own kindred or domestics out of the revenues of the Church."

Source: The Council of Trent,1545–1563

---

32 ☐ Mark for Review

All of the following groups would likely disagree with the idea presented in the <u>first paragraph</u> EXCEPT

(A) supporters of English King Henry VIII

(B) followers of theologian John Calvin

(C) members of the Society of Jesus

(D) Puritan settlers living in the New England colonies

---

33 ☐ Mark for Review

The source best illustrates which of the following continuities in European History from previous centuries?

(A) The religious doctrine that salvation is mediated by faith alone

(B) The Catholic Church's political dominance as an institution across the continent

(C) The institutional Church's strong efforts to root out corruption among its ranks

(D) Church officials' insistence on exclusive control over the administration of sacraments and religious teaching

---

34 ☐ Mark for Review

Which of the following Church policies most directly contradicts the principles expressed in the last two paragraphs?

(A) Support for mystic preachers such as St. Theresa of Avila

(B) The establishment of the Roman Inquisition

(C) The use of Jesuits to establish missions abroad in the Americas and Asia

(D) Relaxations on the restrictions of translations of the Bible

GO ON TO THE NEXT PAGE.

Questions 35 through 39 refer to the following.

"I was thus lost to my dear indulgent parents and relations, and they to me. All my help was cries and tears, and these could not avail; nor suffered long, till one succeeding woe, and dread, swelled up another. Brought from a state of innocence and freedom, and, in a barbarous and cruel manner, conveyed to a state of horror and slavery: This abandoned situation may be easier conceived than described. From the time that I was [kidnapped] and conducted to a factory, and from thence in the brutish, base, but fashionable way of traffic, consigned to Grenada, the grievous thoughts which I then felt, still pant in my heart; though my fears and tears have long since subsided. And yet it is still grievous to think that thousands more have suffered in similar and greater distress, under the hands of barbarous robbers, and merciless taskmasters; and that many even now are suffering in all the extreme bitterness of grief and woe, that no language can describe the cries of some, and the sight of their misery, may be seen and heard afar; but the deep sounding groans of thousands, and the great sadness of their misery and woe, under the heavy load of oppressions and calamities inflicted upon them, are such as can only be distinctly known to the ears of Jehovah Sabaoth."

Source: Ottabah Cugoano (a.k.a. John Stuart), *Thoughts and Sentiments on the Evil and Wicked Traffic of the Slavery and Commerce of the Human Species*, London, 1787

35 ☐ Mark for Review

Which of the following best contextualizes the system described by the author in the excerpt?

- (A) The expansion of trade in enslaved Indigenous persons in the Americas

- (B) The use of Social Darwinism to justify European subjugation of Africa

- (C) The growth of plantation-based economies in European Caribbean colonies

- (D) The promotion of the Civilizing Mission as a means to spread Christianity to non-Europeans

36 ☐ Mark for Review

The excerpt could best be used to support which of the following arguments against slavery in the 1700s?

- (A) Slavery constituted a moral evil.

- (B) Slavery was an outmoded system due to industrialization.

- (C) Slavery undercut the labor of free white people.

- (D) Slavery was too expensive a system to maintain due to uprisings and rebellions.

37 ☐ Mark for Review

Which of the following likely constituted the author's audience?

- (A) Members of the British Parliament

- (B) The English monarch

- (C) Plantation owners

- (D) Managers of textile factories

38 ☐ Mark for Review

Resistance to the institution described in the excerpt best highlights the continued influence of which of the following intellectual movements?

- (A) The Enlightenment

- (B) The Reformation

- (C) The Renaissance

- (D) The Scientific Revolution

GO ON TO THE NEXT PAGE.

39 ▢ Mark for Review

Changes to the labor system described in the passage parallel what other major change in Europe in the 1800s?

Ⓐ The expansion of the electoral franchise to unpropertied men

Ⓑ The proliferation of urban industrial factories

Ⓒ The creation of cash crop plantations in colonies such as the Congo

Ⓓ The elimination of serfdom in eastern European states such as Russia

GO ON TO THE NEXT PAGE.

Questions 40 through 43 refer to the following.

1. Immediately after the publication of the present decree, all suspects within the territory of the Republic and still at large, shall be placed in custody.

2. The following are deemed suspects:

1 – those who, by their conduct, associations, comments, or writings have shown themselves partisans of tyranny or federalism and enemies of liberty;

2 – those who are unable to justify, in the manner prescribed by the decree of 21 March, their means of existence and the performance of their civic duties;

3 – those to whom certificates of patriotism have been refused; ...

5 – those former nobles, together with husbands, wives, fathers, mothers, sons or daughters, brothers or sisters, and agents of the émigrés [those who fled France], who have not constantly demonstrated their devotion to the Revolution;

Source: *The Law of Suspects*, passed September 1793, France

---

40 ☐ Mark for Review

All of the following represent causes of the political situation referenced in the source EXCEPT

(A) bourgeois grievances against an unrepresentative government structure

(B) shortages of staple foods such as bread

(C) French support for Enlightenment-inspired revolutions such as the American war against Britain

(D) nationalist-inspired rebellion against royal authority

---

41 ☐ Mark for Review

Which of the following would likely be most supportive of the policies shown in the excerpt?

(A) A government official of the Jacobin republic

(B) A member of the Society of Republican Revolutionary Women

(C) A signatory of the Declaration of the Rights of Man and Citizen

(D) A supporter of the restoration of the French monarchy

---

42 ☐ Mark for Review

Which of the following describes the most likely purpose of the laws shown in the excerpt?

(A) To stabilize the tumultuous economy by fixing prices and wages

(B) To enforce the principles of the Constitution of 1791

(C) To weaken political factions that rivaled the Committee of Public Safety

(D) To allow Napoleon to seize control of the French state

---

43 ☐ Mark for Review

Laws such as the ones described were most likely to be enacted in which of the following?

(A) Poland in the 1990s

(B) Russia in the 1930s

(C) Germany in the 1920s

(D) Spain in the 1910s

GO ON TO THE NEXT PAGE.

Questions 44 through 48 refer to the following.

When war has ceased and o'er the minds of men
Another lucid interval breaks in light
When Peace once more sits throned in splendor bright,
And Labour, God-beloved, returns again:
What thing in all its devilish blackness then
Shall stand out monumental in its fright?
A Christian nation fighting for its Might
With hell's munitions more than sword and pen.
Ah Germany, we little dreamed that thou
Wert leagued with hell, with all its powers enthralled,
And that thy friends were Heaven's own enemies!
England had shrunk from war I do avow,
Had she but known that thou had had'st installed
A private wire with Mephistopheles*.

Source: William Dowsing, "Burning Fire," 1916

The Alliances in World War I: Resources of 1913

| | TERRITORY | | | GDP IN 1990 PRICES | |
	Population, millions	million sq. km	hectares per capita	$ billion	$ per capita
Allies					
November 1914					
Allies, total	793.3	67.5	8.5	1,096.5	1,382
UK, France, and Russia only	259.0	22.6	8.7	622.8	2,405
November 1916					
Allies, total	853.3	72.5	8.5	1,213.4	1,422
UK, France, and Russia only	259.0	22.6	8.7	622.8	2,405
November 1918					
Allies, total	1,271.7	80.8	6.4	1,760.5	1,384
UK, France, and Russia only	182.3	8.7	4.8	876.6	4,809
Central Powers					
November 1914					
Central Powers, total	151.3	5.9	3.9	376.6	2,489
Germany and Austria-Hungary only	117.6	1.2	1.0	344.8	2,933
November 1915					
Central Powers, total	156.1	6.0	3.8	383.9	2,459

*Mephistopheles was a demonic folk character in German mythology.

GO ON TO THE NEXT PAGE.

44 ☐ Mark for Review

The second sentence of the first source is most likely a reference to which of the following?

(A) The desire of Christian nations to win at all costs

(B) The deadly military technology being used for the first time in WWI

(C) The power of the written word compared with the power of weaponry

(D) The belief in an afterlife even for those who commit the worst war atrocities

45 ☐ Mark for Review

According to the last three lines of the poem, the author would most likely agree with which of the following claims?

(A) England wouldn't have become involved in the war if it had known how forceful the Germans would become.

(B) The military's use of private telephone lines meant the difference between winning and losing.

(C) England had initially avoided war to fulfill its political vows.

(D) Germany had been painted as a demonic character by English propaganda efforts.

46 ☐ Mark for Review

Data from the table best prove that which of the following was an important factor in the Allied victory?

(A) The presence of France in the alliance

(B) Wise and strategic leadership

(C) Overall population and industrial production

(D) Ratio of territory to gross domestic product

47 ☐ Mark for Review

The change in population in the UK, France, and Russia from 1914 to 1918 most likely led to which of the following?

(A) The development of new technologies that changed traditional military strategies

(B) The decision of the United States to enter the war

(C) The creation of the League of Nations

(D) The Versailles settlement's provisions of German war guilt

48 ☐ Mark for Review

The change in GDP of the Allied powers between 1914 and 1918 is best explained by

(A) the success of Russian industrialization during the war

(B) more large industrial powers joining the side of the Allies such as the United States

(C) major increases in government spending stimulating European economies

(D) the seizure of German colonies as part of the war settlement

GO ON TO THE NEXT PAGE.

Questions 49 through 52 refer to the following.

Source 1

"We have shewed before that it is God that does appoint kings, who chooses them, who gives the kingdom to them: now we say that the people establish kings, puts the scepter into their hands, and who with their suffrages approves the election. God would have it done in this manner, to the end that the kings should acknowledge, that after God they hold their power and sovereignty from the people, and that it might the rather induce them, to apply and address the utmost of their care and thoughts for the profit of the people, without being puffed with any vain imagination, that they were formed of any matter more excellent than other men, for which they were raised so high above others; as if they were to command our flocks of sheep, or herds of cattle. But let them remember and know, that they are of the same mould and condition as others, raised from the earth by the voice and acclamations, now as it were upon the shoulders of the people unto their thrones, that they might afterwards bear on their own shoulders the greatest burdens of the commonwealth."

Source: Hubert Languet, French diplomat, *A Defense of Liberty Against Tyrants*, 1579
Translator unknown, 1689

Source 2

"As there is not a thing so necessary to be known by the people of any land, next the knowledge of their God, as the right knowledge of their allegiance according to the form of government established among them, especially in a monarchy (which form of government, as resembling the divinity, approacheth nearest to perfection, as all the learned and wise men from the beginning have agreed upon, unity being the perfection of all things), so hath the ignorance and (which is worse) the seduced opinion of the multitude, blinded by them who think themselves able to teach and instruct the ignorants, procured the wrack and overthrow of sundry flourishing commonwealths and heaped heavy calamities threatening utter destruction upon others."

Source: King James I of England, *The True Law of Free Monarchies*, 1598

49 ☐ Mark for Review

Which of the following is a claim that both authors would agree with?

(A) Kings are no different from the people that they rule.

(B) Chaos ensues when power is taken from the king.

(C) Kings must be bound by laws just like their subjects.

(D) Monarchy exists to benefit the people the king rules over.

50 ☐ Mark for Review

In the second passage, King James I argues for

(A) hereditary monarchy

(B) the divine right of kings

(C) constitutionalism

(D) absolute monarchy

GO ON TO THE NEXT PAGE.

51 ☐ Mark for Review

A supporter of the principles discussed in Source 1 would most likely agree with which of the following concepts?

(A) State management of economic resources

(B) Social contract theory

(C) Free market capitalism

(D) Freedom of religious worship

52 ☐ Mark for Review

In England, the conflict described between the two passages was finally resolved with

(A) the execution of Charles I

(B) Oliver Cromwell's Commonwealth

(C) the Restoration era

(D) the abdication of King James II and the Glorious Revolution

GO ON TO THE NEXT PAGE.

Questions 53 through 55 refer to the following.

"Fundamental in the problems facing Spain, no matter what the political form of its State, is its unsolved agrarian revolution. Agriculture, involving more than half the population, accounting for half of its income, has never been freed from feudal fetters. And without that freedom, growth of any kind, not to say social progress, is impossible. Until the group of the feudal landlords is broken, the peasantry cannot become free citizens of a democratic Republic. The soil remains, then, as the permanent breeding ground of reactionary landlordism, the aristocracy, and the hope of monarchical restoration. The terrible subjection of the country population continues.

Without a solution of the agrarian question Spain cannot also solve its national question, the striving for national autonomy of the Basque, Galicia, and Catalonia. So long as the land question remains unsettled, it acts as an anchor on the aspirations of the modern proletariat in Spain. Industry, no matter how relatively advanced, still remains subordinated to the backwardness of the countryside. Capitalism, placed over feudalism like a thick plaster of cosmetic on a corpse, is subordinated to the semi-feudal nature of agriculture."

Source: Harry Gannes and Theodore Repard, *Spain in Revolt*, 1936

53 　Mark for Review

The source is best understood in the context of which of the following?

(A) The use of guerrilla warfare to resist French occupation of Spain

(B) The collapse of Spain's overseas empire

(C) The emergence of authoritarianism in alliance with fascist governments

(D) The establishment of a Catalan Republic

54 　Mark for Review

The political situation in Spain described in the first paragraph is most similar to which of the following European states in the early part of the twentieth century?

(A) Germany

(B) Italy

(C) France

(D) Russia

55 　Mark for Review

Which of the following historical developments would best modify the claim made by the author in the second paragraph?

(A) The Irish nationalist movement increasingly adopted terrorist tactics to resist British authority in the late 1900s.

(B) In the mid-twentieth century, the French government was heavily weakened over relinquishing control of its colonies in Asia and Africa.

(C) The dissolution of Yugoslavia in the 1990s led to ethnic cleansing of groups like Albanian and Bosnian Muslims.

(D) The Basque ETA evolved into a violent paramilitary group in the late 1900s.

GO ON TO THE NEXT PAGE.

AP EUROPEAN HISTORY
SECTION I, Part B
Time—40 minutes

Directions: Answer Question 1 **and** Question 2. Answer **either** Question 3 **or** Question 4.

In your responses, be sure to address all parts of the questions you answer. Use complete sentences; an outline or bulleted list alone is not acceptable.

Question 1 refers to the following.

"The British Empire comprises some 13 million square miles of territory, with a population of over 400 millions. Of this the territory of the United Kingdom forms less than a hundredth part, and its population is approximately ten percent of the total. The inhabitants of the more or less self-governing Colonies account for, say, a further four percent (although, of course, of these there are many who do not enjoy complete political freedom), the Colonies without self-government constitute something less than two percent; and the remainder, that is about eighty-four percent or some 350 millions, are members of the subject races, the bulk of whom are practically ruled by the officials of the dominant race.

This rule is arbitrary; it is commonly supposed to be benignant; and it is not unfrequently referred to as 'benevolent despotism.' This adjective may be taken to express that apology which, it seems to be intuitively felt, government by an alien race demands…. Naked despotism is repugnant to [the average Englishman], but 'benevolent' despotism—when exercised by a superior race, such as that to which he belongs—sounds reassuring."

Source: John George Godard, *Racial Supremacy, Being Studies in Imperialism*, 1905

1 ☐ Mark for Review

Using the excerpt, respond to parts A, B, and C.

A. Using a specific example, analyze one reason that England used to justify its control of its colonies.

B. Using a specific example, describe how one colony rejected Godard's "benevolent despotism" by throwing off British rule after 1905.

C. Using a specific example, explain one long-term effect of colonialism.

GO ON TO THE NEXT PAGE.

Question 2 refers to the following.

James Gillray, British printmaker and satirist, *Politeness*, 1780

The text at the bottom reads, "With Porter Roast Beef and Plumb Pudding well cram'd, Jack English declares that Monsieur may be Damned. The soup Meagre Frenchman such Language don't suit, So he grins indignation and calls him a Brute."

---

2 ☐ Mark for Review

Using the image, respond to parts A, B, and C.

    A. Identify one point of view expressed about the relationship between England and France before 1815.

    B. Identify and explain one piece of evidence not explicitly mentioned in the excerpt that could be used to support the point of view expressed in the cartoon before 1815.

    C. Identify and explain one change in the relationship between England and France in the twentieth century.

GO ON TO THE NEXT PAGE.

Question 3 <u>or</u> 4

Directions: Answer **either** Question 3 **or** Question 4.

3. Respond to parts A, B, and C.

      A. Describe one significant <u>change</u> that occurred to education during the Italian Renaissance.

      B. Analyze one significant <u>consequence</u> of the changes that occurred to education during the Italian Renaissance.

      C. Explain one significant change that occurred to the fine arts during the Italian Renaissance.

4. Respond to parts A, B, and C.

      A. Identify one democratic successor state that emerged in Europe after the First World War.

      B. Identify and explain one change to a European democratic successor state in the second half of the twentieth century.

      C. Identify and explain one effect of a change to a European democratic successor state in the second half of the twentieth century.

3-4   ⬓ Mark for Review

Choose a question to answer before you start writing.

○   **Answer Question 3**

○   **Answer Question 4**

END OF SECTION I

GO ON TO THE NEXT PAGE.

AP® European History Exam

At a Glance

Total Time
1 hour, 40 minutes
Number of Questions
2
Percent of Total Score
40%
Question 1 (DBQ): Mandatory
Suggested Reading and Writing Time
60 minutes
Reading Period
15 minutes. Use this time to read Question 1 and plan your answer. You may begin writing your response before the reading period is over.
Suggested Writing Time
45 minutes
Percent of Total Score
25%
Question 2, 3, or 4 (Long Essay): Choose ONE Question
Answer either Question 2, 3, or 4
Suggested Time
40 minutes
Percent of Total Score
15%

DISCLAIMER: The official AP European History Exam will be administered digitally. Instructions for the digital exam may differ from this practice test.

Instructions

Section II has 1 document-based question (DBQ) and 1 long essay question, and lasts 1 hour and 40 minutes.

In this section, answer Question 1 (the DBQ) and **either** Question 2 **or** Question 3 **or** Question 4. After reviewing Questions 2, 3, and 4, choose the question that you are best prepared to answer. This section of the exam requires answers in essay form. Use complete sentences; an outline or bulleted list alone is not acceptable.

You may pace yourself as you answer the questions in this section, or you may use these optional timing recommendations:

For Question 1 (DBQ), it is suggested that you spend approximately 15 minutes reading the question and planning your answer, and then 45 minutes writing your essay. The suggested writing time for the long essay question is 40 minutes.

For this practice test, use scratch paper for notes and planning as well as writing your responses.

GO ON TO THE NEXT PAGE.

AP EUROPEAN HISTORY
SECTION II
Total Time—1 hour, 40 minutes

Question 1 (Document-Based Question)
Suggested reading and writing time: 1 hour

It is suggested that you spend 15 minutes reading the documents and 45 minutes writing your response.

Note: You may begin writing your response before the reading period is over.

Directions: Question 1 is based on the accompanying documents. The documents have been edited for the purpose of this exercise.

In your response, you should do the following:

- Respond to the prompt with a historically defensible thesis or claim that establishes a line of reasoning.
- Describe a broader historical context relevant to the prompt.
- Support an argument in response to the prompt using at least four documents.
- Use at least one additional piece of specific historical evidence (beyond that found in the documents) relevant to an argument about the prompt.
- For at least two documents, explain how or why the document's point of view, purpose, historical situation, and/or audience is relevant to an argument.
- Demonstrate a complex understanding of a historical development related to the prompt through sophisticated argumentation and/or effective use of evidence.

GO ON TO THE NEXT PAGE.

1 ▢ Mark for Review

Evaluate the extent to which the First World War contributed to the collapse of the Austro-Hungarian Empire.

Document 1

Source: G.E. Mitton, British editor and guidebook writer, *Austria-Hungary*, 1914.

At the present time Austria and Hungary are governed by Francis Joseph, Emperor of Austria and King of Hungary. The two countries are united for the purposes of Defence, Foreign Affairs, and Finance, including the Post Office, but have separate Houses of Parliament.... It is the tie of the Royal House alone which unites them, and it is expediency only which dictates the amalgamation of the military power and finance in the two countries.... The inhabitants of the two countries are not men of one blood and one tongue as the English and the Scots are, but are separated by lines of deep cleavage. And this main cleavage is repeated in numerous smaller fractures, so that the kingdom is split and cracked in many directions.

There are no less than eleven languages in this polyglot country, and over all rules the one German-speaking monarch.

Document 2

Source: Map, Austro-Hungarian Empire, 1910.

GO ON TO THE NEXT PAGE.

Document 3

Source: Photo, Archduke Franz Ferdinand of Austria, shortly before his assassination in 1914.

GO ON TO THE NEXT PAGE.

Document 4

Source: *Austria-Hungary*, by Geoffrey Drage, 1909.

As regards religion, although the lack of religious unity has deprived Hungary of what might be a unifying influence, yet the religious differences have not, except as between Croat and Serb, been a cause of much dissension….

In Hungary there is now perfect legal equality among all recognized religions…. Each has the independent administration of its own affairs, and this principle has, on the whole, been loyally respected….

Document 5

Source: Wolf von Schierbrand, *Austria-Hungary: The Polyglot Empire*. 1917.

[Food conditions] are vastly better in Hungary than in Austria, Hungary being largely an agricultural country, whereas in Austria industrial interests predominate…. If the foodstuffs of both Hungary and Austria were put into a joint pool, so to speak, and the people of the whole monarchy fed out of it evenly, there would be no serious difficulty. But Hungary is a sovereign state, just as much as is Austria, and Hungarians do not propose to stint themselves to please the people of the other half of the Dual Monarchy.

During September and October, 1916, the poor in Vienna had to go without potatoes; and bread, their only other staple, was sold in but insufficient bulk….

Document 6

Source: *Should Austria-Hungary Exist?* by Charles Pergler, 1918.

Conditions among the non-German nationalities in Austria were bad enough in times of peace. Today after three years of war, they beggar description. The meager right to use the Bohemian language in administrative offices in Bohemia has been abolished, and German has been established as the official language. On the railroads the humblest laborer cannot obtain any position unless he has a command of the German language. A conversation in Czech is treated as a gross breach of discipline.

When we come to the Hungarian part of Austria we meet a condition which, if anything, is still worse. For three million Slovaks, there does not exist in Hungary a single adequate Slovak school conducted in the Slovak language.

Document 7

Source: Memorandum written to the Allied forces by Tomas Masaryk, an activist for Czechoslovak independence, 1915.

Austria owes her origin to the invasions of the Turks, and previously of the Huns (Magyars); Austria means the Eastern Empire, the German provinces, Bohemia and Hungary joined in a federation against Turkey. With the fall of the Turks Austria falls also; Austria lost her ruling idea, and is unable to find a positive idea. So Austria falls from step to step. The Austrian-Spanish Empire was dissolved. Austria lost the greater part of Silesia and was driven by Prussia to abandon Germany; in 1848, saved by Russia, she lost in 1859 the Italian provinces; in 1866 she was beaten by Prussia. Since then she exists only as the vassal of Berlin, being divided into Austria and Hungary; it is to Berlin that both the Germans and Magyars owe their dominating position in Austria.

END OF DOCUMENTS FOR QUESTION 1

GO ON TO THE NEXT PAGE.

Question 2, 3, or 4 (Long Essay)

Suggested writing time: 40 minutes

Directions: Answer Question 2 **or** Question 3 **or** Question 4.

In your response, you should do the following:

- Respond to the prompt with a historically defensible thesis or claim that establishes a line of reasoning.
- Describe a broader historical context relevant to the prompt.
- Support an argument in response to the prompt using at least two pieces of specific and relevant evidence.
- Use historical reasoning (e.g., comparison, causation, continuity or change) to frame or structure an argument that addresses the prompt.
- Demonstrate a complex understanding of a historical development related to the prompt through sophisticated argumentation and/or effective use of evidence.

2. Evaluate the most significant effect of the Reformation between 1517 and 1650.

3. Evaluate the most significant effect of industrialization in Europe between 1750 and 1914.

4. Evaluate the most significant effect of the Cold War between 1945 and 2000.

2-4 ☐ Mark for Review

Choose a question to answer before you start writing.

○ **Answer Question 2**

○ **Answer Question 3**

○ **Answer Question 4**

WHEN YOU FINISH WRITING, CHECK YOUR WORK ON SECTION II IF TIME PERMITS.

STOP

END OF EXAM

Practice Test 1:
Diagnostic
Answer Key and
Explanations

PRACTICE TEST 1: DIAGNOSTIC ANSWER KEY

Let's take a look at how you did on Practice Test 1. Follow the three-step process in the diagnostic answer key below and go read the explanations for any questions you got wrong, or you struggled with but got correct. Once you finish working through the answer key and the explanations, go to the next chapter to make your study plan.

 Check your answers and mark any correct answers with a ✔ in the appropriate column.

Section I, Part A: Multiple Choice							
Q #	Ans.	✔	Chapter #, Chapter Title	Q #	Ans.	✔	Chapter #, Chapter Title
1	C		**5,** Monarchical States to Napoleon	29	B		**7,** Global Wars to Globalization
2	A		**5,** Monarchical States to Napoleon	30	C		**7,** Global Wars to Globalization
3	D		**5,** Monarchical States to Napoleon	31	B		**5,** Monarchical States to Napoleon
4	A		**4,** The Renaissance to the Wars of Religion	32	C		**4,** The Renaissance to the Wars of Religion
5	B		**6,** Age of Revolutions to World War I	33	D		**4,** The Renaissance to the Wars of Religion
6	C		**4,** The Renaissance to the Wars of Religion	34	B		**4,** The Renaissance to the Wars of Religion
7	C		**4,** The Renaissance to the Wars of Religion	35	C		**5,** Monarchical States to Napoleon
8	A		**5,** Monarchical States to Napoleon	36	A		**5,** Monarchical States to Napoleon
9	C		**6,** Age of Revolutions to World War I	37	A		**6,** Age of Revolutions to World War I
10	B		**6,** Age of Revolutions to World War I	38	A		**5,** Monarchical States to Napoleon
11	A		**6,** Age of Revolutions to World War I	39	D		**6,** Age of Revolutions to World War I
12	A		**5,** Monarchical States to Napoleon	40	D		**5,** Monarchical States to Napoleon
13	D		**6,** Age of Revolutions to World War I	41	A		**5,** Monarchical States to Napoleon
14	B		**4,** The Renaissance to the Wars of Religion	42	C		**5,** Monarchical States to Napoleon
15	B		**6,** Age of Revolutions to World War I	43	B		**7,** Global Wars to Globalization
16	B		**4,** The Renaissance to the Wars of Religion	44	B		**7,** Global Wars to Globalization
17	C		**4,** The Renaissance to the Wars of Religion	45	A		**7,** Global Wars to Globalization
18	B		**4,** The Renaissance to the Wars of Religion	46	C		**7,** Global Wars to Globalization
19	B		**4,** The Renaissance to the Wars of Religion	47	D		**7,** Global Wars to Globalization
20	D		**5,** Monarchical States to Napoleon	48	B		**7,** Global Wars to Globalization
21	C		**5,** Monarchical States to Napoleon	49	D		**4,** The Renaissance to the Wars of Religion
22	B		**5,** Monarchical States to Napoleon	50	B		**4,** The Renaissance to the Wars of Religion
23	A		**6,** Age of Revolutions to World War I	51	B		**5,** Monarchical States to Napoleon
24	B		**7,** Global Wars to Globalization	52	D		**4,** The Renaissance to the Wars of Religion
25	A		**7,** Global Wars to Globalization	53	C		**7,** Global Wars to Globalization
26	A		**7,** Global Wars to Globalization	54	D		**7,** Global Wars to Globalization
27	C		**7,** Global Wars to Globalization	55	A		**7,** Global Wars to Globalization
28	D		**7,** Global Wars to Globalization				

Section I, Part B: Short Answer			
Q #	Ans.	✔	Chapter #, Chapter Title
1	See Explanation		**6,** Age of Revolutions to World War I
2	See Explanation		**5,** Monarchical States to Napoleon
3	See Explanation		**4,** The Renaissance to the Wars of Religion
4	See Explanation		**7,** Global Wars to Globalization
Section II: DBQ			
1	See Explanation		**7,** Global Wars to Globalization
Section II: Long Essay			
2	See Explanation		**4,** The Renaissance to the Wars of Religion
3	See Explanation		**6,** Age of Revolutions to World War I
4	See Explanation		**7,** Global Wars to Globalization

 Tally your correct answers from Step 1 by chapter. For each chapter, write the number of correct answers in the appropriate box. Then, divide your correct answers by the number of total questions (which we've provided) to get your percent correct.

CHAPTER 4 TEST SELF-EVALUATION

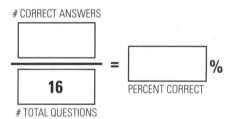

CORRECT ANSWERS

16

TOTAL QUESTIONS

= ___ % PERCENT CORRECT

CHAPTER 6 TEST SELF-EVALUATION

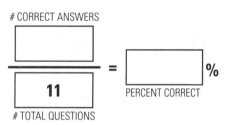

CORRECT ANSWERS

11

TOTAL QUESTIONS

= ___ % PERCENT CORRECT

CHAPTER 5 TEST SELF-EVALUATION

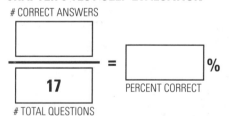

CORRECT ANSWERS

17

TOTAL QUESTIONS

= ___ % PERCENT CORRECT

CHAPTER 7 TEST SELF-EVALUATION

CORRECT ANSWERS

19

TOTAL QUESTIONS

= ___ % PERCENT CORRECT

 Use the results above to customize your study plan. You may want to start with, or give more attention to, the chapters with the lowest percents correct.

PRACTICE TEST 1: ANSWERS AND EXPLANATIONS

Section I, Part A: Multiple Choice

1. **C** The second paragraph mentions "the excessive price to which grain has been advanced of late years," which means food was getting more expensive. This is one of the chief causes of the French Revolution. While the French revolutionary government did try to regulate the price of grain, that happened after the revolution actually began, so it's not a direct connection. Eliminate (A). The same goes for the military dictatorship, which wasn't created until later in the revolution. Eliminate (D). Tax cuts and deregulation are associated with free market capitalism, something not common in Europe until the 20th century. Eliminate (B). Choice (C) is the best answer because it has the strongest connection to the text.

2. **A** The crop being alluded to in the first paragraph is potatoes, which were not brought to Europe until settlers discovered them in the Americas during the 1500s. While potatoes are a crop, they were not associated with plantation-based agriculture. Eliminate (B). Banking and finance did help spur international exploration and colonization, but the fact remains that the crops were found in the Americas, not Europe. Eliminate (C). Primitive agricultural practices and land-owning patterns were still common across much of agrarian Europe, but that's not relevant to what the question is asking. Eliminate (D). Choice (A) is the best answer because it most accurately describes the Columbian Exchange, which this question references.

3. **D** The sourcing info says the author was a pharmacist and agronomist, so it's safe to assume the author is someone who is relatively well-educated and high up in French society. The text extols the benefits of the potato but doesn't describe the risks of relying on other crops; eliminate (A). While small landowners often did lose their land due to enclosure, that's not pertinent to what's happening in France at the end of the 1700s; eliminate (B). There's nothing to indicate that the government was explicitly banning potatoes either, so eliminate (C). Choice (D) is the best answer because in the source, the author points out that German states had already adopted potato cultivation, and he wants France to emulate their success.

4. **A** The source talks about procedures that local London officials used in case of plague outbreak in the 1600s. The text primarily focuses on quarantining the sick and preventing the disease from spreading, but there's little mention of technology being used to stem the spread of plague. Eliminate (B). The outbreak of the Black Death in earlier centuries had strong effects on European wages and displacing feudalism, but that's not relevant to this text, so eliminate (C). There's no indication in the source about how the rich or poor were affected by these policies differently; eliminate (D). Choice (A) is the best answer because it most closely aligns with the text's subject matter.

5. **B** The 19th century created Europe's modern public health infrastructure. It saw many improvements in public sanitation, such as the end of public pit toilets that contaminated sources of drinking water. It wasn't just the plague, either: typhus, cholera, yellow fever—all of which had spread

quickly in the crowded streets of Europe—were reduced. Choice (A) occurred in the 20th century, and there is no evidence to support (C) or (D).

6. **C** The strategies being used to prevent the spread of plague here involve quarantining the sick and disinfecting their possessions. While germ theory had not yet been codified in the 1600s, there seems to be an implicit understanding that plague spreads from person to person, a major advance in scientific understanding of the body. Humoral theory is an outdated view of illness that was later discredited; eliminate (A). The source doesn't reflect anything in particular about the government's relationship to the Catholic Church; eliminate (B). Alchemy and astrology also represent branches of science that remained popular during the Scientific Revolution that were later discredited; eliminate (D). Choice (C) makes the most sense because the understanding of the disease here reflects a stronger understanding of the human body and disease.

7. **C** This question asks for all of the following EXCEPT, which means it is asking for the incorrect answer. By the 1600s, population levels in Europe had largely recovered to pre-Black Death levels, so eliminate (A). The subsiding of the Black Death had also made urban centers more appealing, so eliminate (B). The price revolution meant that prices largely did increase for agricultural commodities, so eliminate (D). Choice (C) is the correct answer because agriculture would remain the dominant way that Europeans made a living until the Industrial Revolution.

8. **A** The answer should reflect divisions among social classes. Wealthy supporters of King Charles II were able to escape London during this epidemic, either to their country homes or to the houses of relatives elsewhere. As a result, the deaths were almost entirely among the lower classes, who couldn't afford to leave. Choice (B) is political, and (C) only hints at class divisions. Choice (D) describes attire that was used primarily in Italy and France. Note: unlike plagues, fires burn equally, and the Great Fire of London—which occurred just a few years later—devastated the middle and upper classes.

9. **C** The picture shows a poster from Paris at the end of the 1800s, and the Moulin Rouge is a famous venue for dance and music performances. Streetcars and bicycles were popular forms of transportation in cities at the turn of the century, but that's not a direct reason why events like this could happen; eliminate (A). The poster itself seems like an effective form of marketing, but it's not an ad for a consumer good but rather a leisure activity; eliminate (B). Corporations certainly did become very wealthy during the industrial era, but that's also not as pertinent to what's being shown; eliminate (D). Choice (C) is the correct answer because events like these were geared for members of the middle class, who now had more money and time to entertain themselves.

10. **B** *Ennui* is a feeling of listlessness and dissatisfaction that arises from a lack of meaningful purpose or excitement. *Subjectivism* refers to the belief in the absence of absolute moral truths—in other words, the sense that nothing exists outside of our own selves. Both of these ideas were very much in keeping with the end-of-the-century wariness and anxiety, and as a result, the French people occupied themselves with parties and pleasures of the flesh, which Choubrac's posters (as well as other posters of the time) reflect.

11. **A** In question 9, it was clear that this was an ad intended to target the middle class. Factory workers would not have the time or money to enjoy leisure activities like this; eliminate (B). By the turn of the century, France had completely eliminated its monarchy, so any attempts to reach out to them would be ahistorical; eliminate (C). Religious officials would likely be scandalized by the types of shows seen at the Moulin Rouge; eliminate (D). Choice (A) is the correct answer because *bourgeoisie* is another word for the middle class, the exact audience for this image.

12. **A** The excerpt is part of Darwin's *On the Origin of Species*, which is associated with his theory of evolution, a major scientific breakthrough. The Enlightenment is closely related to and overlaps with the Scientific Revolution, but its focus is more explicitly on political behavior and institutions. Eliminate (B). Neoclassicism represents an artistic movement based around inspiration from Greco-Roman influence, but Darwin is not an artist; eliminate (C). Neoplatonism is a philosophical tradition that heavily influenced medieval Christianity (for instance, Thomas Aquinas), but Darwin is not writing about religion. Eliminate (D). Choice (A) is the best answer because even though the Scientific Revolution began more in the 1600s, Darwin's ideas are closely linked to it.

13. **D** This question requires reading the source to determine Darwin's central claim. While Social Darwinism and the idea of the "survival of the fittest" grew popular among some elites in the late 1800s, Darwin himself never actually used the phrase "survival of the fittest" and it's not an accurate summation of what's being discussed here. Eliminate (A). Birds are used as an example in the passage, but it never says that they fare worse in finding food than other animals; eliminate (B). Many scientists might have felt that scientific reasoning was superior to faith, but Darwin never says this in the passage either; eliminate (C). Choice (D) is the best answer because it most accurately summarizes a point made throughout the paragraph by the author.

14. **B** In the passage, Darwin talks about the struggle for existence and implies that humans are just as much part of the natural environment as animals. Many supporters of European cultural superiority adopted a version of Darwin's line of reasoning to support policies like eugenics, so they would not reject Darwin's reasoning; eliminate (A). By the 1900s, Darwin's theories had become mainstream, so scientists in most universities would likely support them; eliminate (C). Modernist philosophy in the 19th and 20th centuries often emphasized the irrationality of human behavior, and they would be unlikely to take issue with any of Darwin's claims here. Eliminate (D). Choice (B) is the best answer because the Catholic Church in the 1500s roundly rejected major scientific theories such as the heliocentric universe that challenged the assumption that humanity was at the center of nature.

15. **B** Darwinism and Social Darwinism were important theoretical frameworks for the growth of European imperialism in the late 1800s. In the excerpt, Darwin highlights competition as a major factor in natural behaviors. Industrial titans often argued that businesses needed raw materials from colonies in order to survive, very consistent with Darwinian thinking. Eliminate (A). European racists often argued that nonwhite races were genetically or culturally inferior and therefore they had a right to rule over their subjects, a variation of this kind of thinking. Eliminate (C). European

empires competed with each other for dominance and used colonies as a tool for this competition, another example of the struggle to survive. Eliminate (D). Choice (B) is the best answer because the idea of the Civilizing Mission was framed as a benign one; though still racist in application, supporters of the concept of the "White Man's Burden" argued that colonies gained nothing from ruling over subjects and cast it as a moral imperative, which would fly in the face of Darwinian thought.

16. **B** In 17th-century Europe, the rise of the middle class had just begun, and the aristocrats were still in power across the continent. The nobility maintained their wealth and their power through an ancient feudal arrangement: the nobles owned and occupied large tracts of rural land, surrounded by peasants whom they permitted to farm the earth. Italy, however, was the lone exception to this rule—the aristocrats of the Italian peninsula were urbanized. They typically lived in large city mansions *(palazzi)*, many of which have been converted into museums today.

17. **C** Bravery in battle (A) was celebrated, and so was painting or carving something extraordinary (B), but neither of these accomplishments was a ticket to the upper classes. In fact, those pursuits were done *in service to* the upper classes. The nobility had achieved their position the old-fashioned way: either by inheriting it (quite common) or by seeing a family member achieve a high rank in the Church (such as cardinal, or even pope). Choice (D), *amassing a fortune*, was by itself not enough to enter the aristocracy—remember that European nobility always looked down upon the "new money" of the merchant class, the *nouveau riche*.

18. **B** In the 1600s, commissioning a family portrait such as this from a professional artist would have been extraordinarily expensive, so only the elite of society would undertake such an expenditure. While wealthy Italians were common patrons of the arts, they were hardly doing it out of the goodness of their own hearts and mostly had interests beyond art for art's sake. Eliminate (A). The painting does show a woman prominently in the painting, but the woman does not seem to be explicitly challenging any gender roles of the time; eliminate (C). It might be tempting to think that since the painter has a Dutch surname and the subjects were Italian that this might be something diplomatic, but there's no indication that the painter has any kind of ties to the Dutch state, so this is a red herring; eliminate (D). Choice (B) is the best answer because promotion of power and stature is usually the most common reason any wealthy people of the Renaissance sought to have their portraits done, and this is no exception.

19. **B** The painting is broadly representative of the typical forms seen in Renaissance art. There is strong attention to geometric perspective in the arrangement of the subjects; eliminate (A). The painter is clearly interested in artistic naturalism by painting the subjects in a manner as close to reality as possible; eliminate (C). The classical form is evident in the painter's interest in depicting the human form, as often seen in classical style; eliminate (D). Choice (B) is the correct answer because nothing in the painting indicates any particular admiration for Greek or Roman political institutions.

20. **D** Moffat writes: *Save in the sphere of religion, where she had been led to believe that inquiry was deadly sin….* Then recall that Maria Theresa was a Habsburg, the very Catholic ruling family of not only Austria but also Spain and the Netherlands. From that you can deduce that she was speaking about the Catholic doctrine of infallibility, (D), which is the Catholic Church's belief in the perfection of its own theology.

21. **C** The account of Maria Theresa is very complimentary, and emphasizes in particular her "aptitude for observation, reflection, and logical reasoning" as well as "thinking for herself." Establishing a system of education is very much keeping in this spirit, so eliminate (A). Unifying Austria's legal system is another innovation that sounds like it would fit in well with the author's flattering portrait; eliminate (B). Inoculation was a novel innovation in the 1700s when Maria Theresa ruled, so her championing of it would also show her to be logically minded; eliminate (D). However, censorship of books and education considered harmful to the state is not in keeping with the relatively progressive reforms of the other answer choices, so pick (C).

22. **B** In an age when feminism was basically unheard of, any woman with a strong mind who wished to express herself typically made her way to the salon scene in Paris. Usually held in private homes of wealthy individuals, the salons were staples of Enlightenment thinking, with logic, wit, and equal opportunity on full display. Many of the hosts of the salons were in fact women.

23. **A** The sourcing info says that this source is written by an author who is a woman and British at the turn of the 20th century. Popular nationalism is not really an ideology as closely tied to Great Britain at the time as it was to rival states like Germany; eliminate (B). There is nothing in the source that explicitly or implicitly connects to imperialism; eliminate (C). Realist literary attitudes drawing attention to social problems are more closely tied to novelists and fiction writers (such as Dickens in the 1800s); eliminate (D). Choice (A) is the best answer because the author focuses on the political accomplishments of Maria Theresa likely in support of allowing other women to participate in politics based on her example.

24. **B** The map displays changes to German territorial holdings after the First World War. The location of the German capital has little to do with changes in Germany territory; eliminate (A). Great Britain is not shown on the map, but that would have little to do with German territorial control as Germany did not cede any of its European territory to Britain. Eliminate (C). Language speaking patterns also would tell us little about territorial control. Eliminate (D). Choice (B) is the best answer because the map only shows German territory in Europe and does not indicate anything about German colonies in Africa being given over to France and Britain.

25. **A** The question is asking about new technologies that affected how World War I was fought. Submarines were used by the Germans (U-boats) as a new innovation; eliminate (B). Soldiers had to carry gas masks to deal with the threat of poison gas on the battlefield; eliminate (C). Though a brand-new technology, European armies did rely on planes for the first time for limited fighting in the war; eliminate (D). Choice (A) is the correct answer because nuclear technology did not exist until World War II.

26. **A**   All of these statements are true developments that characterize the Versailles treaty. War guilt and its effect on the German economy can't accurately be shown in this map; eliminate (B). The Ottoman Empire is not depicted on the map; eliminate (C). Self-determination might be seen in the establishment of Poland as a democratic successor state on the map, but the League of Nations isn't broached in the map; eliminate (D). Choice (A) is the correct answer because there are several examples on the map of the Allied powers trying to punish Germany (such as the demilitarization of the Rhineland, visible in the map key).

27. **C**   This question asks about a later development and how it violates the terms of peace as articulated in the map. There is nothing in the Versailles treaty that bars the Germans from making treaties with the Soviets; eliminate (A). The annexation of Austria was controversial, but it happened without military invasion; eliminate (B). The Munich Agreement was negotiated by the very same powers in Europe that negotiated the Versailles treaty in the first place (such as Britain); eliminate (D). Choice (C) is the correct answer because the map explicitly says that regions such as the Rhineland were to be internationalized, so remilitarizing it is a clear violation of the peace treaty's terms.

28. **D**   The excerpt is from the Maastricht Treaty, which is the document that formally established the political entity known as the European Union. Increased immigration into Europe has led to political controversy, but this is something that has largely happened after the creation of the EU; eliminate (A). The EU is a strong example of globalization, but its connection to communication and transportation technologies is more indirect; eliminate (B). The new governments created at the end of the Cold War largely did not join the EU until the 00's or later; eliminate (C). Choice (D) is the best answer because the EU is an example of internationalism in politics in contrast to the nationalism that characterized the early 20th century.

29. **B**   The first paragraph talks about the creation of a political system with no "internal frontiers" and "a single currency." Proponents of Brexit were highly skeptical of the EU and ultimately voted to have the United Kingdom leave it; eliminate (A). The French National Front, led by Marine Le Pen, is very Euro-skeptic and has challenged France's position in the union; eliminate (C). In a political sense, the Austrian Freedom Party is similar to the French National Front: eliminate (D). Choice (B) is the correct answer because the World Trade Organization has sought to increase trade ties between countries and would likely support the goals highlighted in the first paragraph.

30. **C**   This question asks about a reason for why the EU was created in the first place. It was preceded by the European Coal and Steel Community which was created after World War II. Western European nations did try to contain communism, but that was a policy more closely tied to military alliances like NATO; eliminate (A). Nationalistic tariff policies are one of the factors behind the Great Depression, which preceded World War II; eliminate (B). Many European states did resist relinquishing imperial control, but the EU and organizations like it were not as explicitly concerned with this phenomenon; eliminate (D). Choice (C) is the correct answer because the ECSC and EEC were designed to spur postwar economic recovery.

31. **B** The second paragraph talks about "economic and social cohesion and solidarity among member states." The EU is closely associated with capitalism, still the primary economic system in Europe today; eliminate (A). The EU was created after the fall of communism in Europe thanks to the Cold War, so at this point they likely had little reason to refute it; eliminate (C). Imperialism was often tied to competition between European states, but it's not a system that the writers of this document were particularly concerned with as they were more interested in the domestic situation in Europe; eliminate (D). Choice (B) is the correct answer because mercantilism is an economic system based on a zero-sum theory of wealth in which cooperation between states is discouraged.

32. **C** This excerpt is from the Council of Trent, which was convened in response to the Protestant Reformation by the Catholic Church to reaffirm its core teachings. Supporters of Henry VIII likely would have supported his break with the Catholic Church; eliminate (A). John Calvin was a major figure in the Protestant Reformation who disagreed strongly with Church authority; eliminate (B). Puritan settlers in New England followed Calvin's teachings; eliminate (D). Choice (C) is the correct answer because the Society of Jesus was an order of Catholic priests created by Ignatius of Loyola and would likely agree with the hierarchy of the Church.

33. **D** The doctrine that salvation is mediated by faith alone is a Protestant teaching, not a Catholic one; eliminate (A). The time period when this document was written was one when the Catholic Church's political dominance was faltering thanks to the emergence of rival Protestant states; eliminate (B). While the Council of Trent was interested in rooting out corruption, the medieval Church had little interest in that goal; eliminate (C). Choice (D) is the correct answer because the document reaffirms the centrality of the Church's hierarchy.

34. **B** The last two paragraphs focus on the Church trying to make the faith more accessible to new groups. Support for mystic preachers was a relatively new development during this period and would be directly in keeping with the sentiments of the passage. Eliminate (A). Trying to convert new followers with Jesuit missionaries also represents these same tactics. Eliminate (C). The text explicitly mentions that preaching in the vernacular tongue can be acceptable in some circumstances so that would make translating the Bible less controversial. Eliminate (D). Choice (B) is the best answer because the Roman Inquisition was more tied to the Church protecting its own ranks and cracking down on supposed faith violations than being more open.

35. **C** The author is describing his life as a slave during the age of the Trans-Atlantic slave trade. As the author was an African slave, he was not indigenous to the Americas; eliminate (A). Social Darwinism was a philosophy used to justify imperialism in Africa, but that was in the 1800s after this was written. Eliminate (B). The civilizing mission was also used to justify the spread of Christianity and imperial influence, but that too was a later development. Eliminate (D). Choice (C) is the correct answer because Caribbean colonies primarily relied on African slavery to operate.

36. **A**   The author is clearly an abolitionist who opposes slavery, and he focuses on how it is "barbarous" and "cruel." He does not mention anything about the economics of slavery; eliminate (B). His argument has nothing to do with how slavery affects free white people; eliminate (C). He never discusses the politics of administering slavery by states; eliminate (D). Choice (A) is the correct answer because he frames slavery as an evil that needs to be eliminated.

37. **A**   The author wrote this in 1787 while living in London. His main interest was abolishing slavery, so he likely wanted to communicate to an audience that could have made that possible. By the late 1700s, the English monarchy had little formal legislative power compared to Parliament; eliminate (B). Plantation owners would have had no interest in eliminating a system on which their livelihood was dependent; eliminate (C). Managers of textile factories might not have owned slaves themselves, but in the 1800s they often depended on cotton cultivated by slave labor, so this argument might have had little support from them; eliminate (D). Choice (A) is the correct answer because Parliament had the strongest power to outlaw slavery and eventually did by abolishing the slave trade a few decades later.

38. **A**   Opposition to slavery in the late 1700s was often couched in the language of liberty and human rights. The reformation greatly diminished the power of the Church, but few Reformation theologians were interested in challenging the system of slavery; eliminate (B). The Renaissance is too far removed historically to be connected to the abolitionist movement; eliminate (C). The Scientific Revolution was more concerned with understanding the natural world than natural rights; eliminate (D). Choice (A) is the correct answer because abolitionists in the 1700s and 1800s often borrowed the concepts of the Enlightenment in their protests against the institution.

39. **D**   The 1800s saw European states such as Britain formally abolish the slave trade and slavery within their empires. Britain did gradually expand the franchise to unpropertied men in this time, but these men had not been slaves; eliminate (A). Urban industrial work was challenging, and indeed some Marxists began to refer to it as "wage slavery;" eliminate (B). Cash crop plantations in many ways came to resemble systems of forced labor, especially on rubber plantations in the Belgian Congo, which would be the opposite of eliminating forced labor; eliminate (C). Choice (D) is the correct answer because in the same way that the African slave trade came to be eliminated, so too did many eastern European states eliminate serfdom throughout the 1800s.

40. **D**   The law was passed in France in 1793, which is exactly the time period of the Reign of Terror. Members of the middle class were upset about France's unrepresentative government which is why they created the National Assembly in the first place; eliminate (A). Bread shortages were a major factor in motivating peasants to support the revolution; eliminate (B). French support for the American revolution was a key event in the timeline of the lead-up to the French Revolution; eliminate (C). Choice (D) is correct because nationalism as a political philosophy developed more as a result of the French Revolution than as a cause of it.

41. **A** The policies shown in the excerpt are examples of the radical phase of the French Revolution. The Society of Republican Revolutionary Women (of which Olympe Des Gouges was a member) was ultimately banned by the revolutionary government as they were accused of being unsupportive of the revolution; eliminate (B). The Declaration of the Rights of Man and Citizen was created during the moderate phase of the revolution, and many of those signatories likely would not have endorsed these laws. Eliminate (C). Supporters of the restoration of the French monarchy would be most likely to be targeted by this law; eliminate (D). Choice (A) is the correct answer because Jacobins were the group most tied to these laws.

42. **C** The revolutionary government did attempt to fix prices and wages, but that is not broached in this excerpt; eliminate (A). The Constitution of 1791 was a liberal document based on Enlightenment principles, but these policies are far more radical; eliminate (B). Napoleon would not seize power several years later; eliminate (D). Choice (C) is the best answer because laws like these were designed to allow the Committee of Public Safety to maintain its grip on power by targeting political opponents.

43. **B** The laws shown in the excerpt are examples of repressive government authoritarianism. Poland in the 1990s had emerged from the Cold War with a newly liberalized government after decades of communist rule; eliminate (A). The Nazis had not yet seized control of Germany in the 1920s as it was still under Weimar rule; eliminate (C). Spain in the 1910s was still decades away from being taken over by Franco; eliminate (D). Choice (B) is correct because in the 1930s, Stalinism took its strongest hold in Russia and saw significant crackdowns on rival communist factions.

44. **B** The entire line reads *A Christian nation fighting for its Might/With hell's munitions more than sword and pen*. The Christian nation fighting for its might is Germany, and *the hell's munitions* is a reference to the brand-new efficient killing technology used in World War I, such as mustard gas, armored tanks, and fighter planes. This is in contrast to the way that conflicts used to be waged—with swords on horseback, or merely with the written word.

45. **A** Mephistopheles was a demonic folk character in German mythology, and the implication of the *private wire* is that the German army was consulting with demons for military advice. *England had shrunk from war I do avow* can be translated into the more modern *I swear that England would have avoided the war*, so it's clear that Dowsing and other English citizens had been stunned by the power of the German military. The other three choices have all been misinterpreted.

46. **C** The table clearly shows that the Allied powers enjoyed an overwhelming advantage in population, territory, and gross domestic product. In fact, this is a commonly explored theme among WWI historians—how during the early 20th century, success in warfare came not from strategy and leadership but from sheer volume of production and population. France is irrelevant, as is wise and strategic leadership, so eliminate (A) and (B). While territory and gross domestic product are both listed in the table, there is no evidence that the ratio between them is a factor; eliminate (D).

47. **D** According to the table, the UK, France, and Russia's combined population was 259 million in 1914, 259 million in 1916, and 182.3 million in 1918, a dramatic decrease. New technologies like machine guns and chemical weapons were almost certainly a cause of this population drop, not the other way around; eliminate (A). The United States did enter the war toward the end, but this had more to do with reasons specific to that country's interests than trying to avenge the deaths of the Allies; eliminate (B). The League of Nations was created to try to avert future wars, but the idea was pushed more by the Americans than by European states; eliminate (C). Choice (D) is correct because the scale of British and French death made the Allies even more interested in punishing Germany for its role in the war.

48. **B** Between 1914 and 1916, the Allies' GDP increases a bit, but it increases dramatically between 1916 and 1918. Russia's time during the war was disastrous, eventually precipitating the Communist Revolution; eliminate (A). European countries did have to spend a lot of money to fight the war, but that doesn't necessarily mean it was an economic boon for them; eliminate (C). The Allies did seize several of Germany's colonies, but any change in GDP would not have shown up immediately in the data in 1918 before the peace settlement had been signed; eliminate (D). Choice (B) is correct because the data is partially misleading; the United States was a huge industrial economy, and by joining the side of the Allies in 1917, it would likely show up as a perceived increase in GDP as shown here.

49. **D** The author of Source 1 seems to argue that kings are of the same sort as the people they rule, but King James would not agree with that sentiment; eliminate (A). King James endorsed the idea of keeping the king's power, but the first source seems more amenable to placing limits on the king's power; eliminate (B). The first source is a major defense of the idea that kings must be bound by laws, but this is not something that King James would support; eliminate (C). Choice (D) is correct because both authors at least share an assumption that monarchs are a legitimate form of government and exist for the benefit of the people, even if they disagree on what kinds of limits those monarchs should have.

50. **B** King James I specifically writes *monarchy (which form of government, as resembling the divinity...)*. Traditional royalists such as himself and, earlier, Richard II, argued that a monarch's power came directly from God. There is definitely no constitutionalism present here, so eliminate (C). And while James I certainly believed in the idea of hereditary monarchy (and quite possibly absolute monarchy as well), there is no evidence supporting those ideas in this passage. Eliminate (A) and (D).

51. **B** The first author is primarily interested in sources of political legitimacy and does not explicitly discuss his views on economics; eliminate (A). Similarly, it's hard to get a sense of how the author would feel about capitalism, especially when that economic system did not yet exist; eliminate (C). Freedom of worship was an Enlightenment era concept, but the author does not discuss explicitly whether or not he thinks this is a right worth protecting; eliminate (D). Choice (B) is correct because the author is arguing that the king has an obligation to the people he rules and the sovereignty comes from the people, a key part of social contract theory.

52. **D**   The conflict contained within and around the English Civil War took nearly a century to resolve. It started with the arrival of King James I in 1603, at the very beginning of the 17th century, and culminated in Charles II's forced abdication in 1688. At the end of that turbulent period, English society finally confirmed the primacy of Parliament (representing the people) over the royal crown via the passage of the English Bill of Rights (1689). The other three answer choices were important events during this period, but none of them resolved the conflict.

53. **C**   The source is about Spain in 1936, exactly the time during which it was fighting a civil war between republican forces and fascist-allied ones. Spain's resistance to French occupation was part of the Napoleonic wars a century prior; eliminate (A). Spain's overseas empire had already collapsed by the end of the 1800s with their loss of the Philippines; eliminate (B). The Catalan Republic was established briefly in the mid-1600s, way before this source was written. Eliminate (D). Choice (C) is correct because this source fits exactly within the context of Franco's seizure of control of Spain.

54. **D**   The first paragraph emphasizes Spain's agrarian and feudal nature. In the early part of the 20th century, Germany had successfully industrialized and unified; eliminate (A). Italy's political situation was very similar to Germany's after its unification in the late 1800s; eliminate (B). Feudalism in France had largely been destroyed by the French Revolution; eliminate (C). Choice (D) is correct because Russia's various revolutions in the early 1900s were all in direct reaction to its largely under-industrialized and mostly feudal political situation, most similar to what is shown in the excerpt.

55. **A**   The author's claim in the second paragraph is that Spain would be unable to solve the issue of nationalist movements among groups like the Catalonians and Basques without first reforming its feudal-esque land system, which the author believes to be unique among other European states. While France's politics were heavily disrupted due to wars in Vietnam and Algeria, these were wars that involved the control of colonies, not France's European territory, making this answer largely irrelevant; eliminate (B). Yugoslavia's dissolution did lead to conflicts and ethnic cleansing attempts among national groups, but these national groups had existed long before Yugoslavia was established in the early 20th century, and if anything this example further goes to support the author's claim; eliminate (C). Terrorist attacks by the ETA also largely support the author's claim given that the ETA was founded under Franco's rule of Spain, supporting the idea that Spain had failed to resolve issues of nationalist opposition; eliminate (D). Choice (A) is the correct answer because Britain had long moved past feudalism by the time of the 20th century; the fact that a violent nationalist campaign would begin in a state like Britain complicates the author's claim because the author implies that such conflicts would be less likely in a fully industrialized state like the UK.

Section I, Part B: Short Answer

Question 1

A. The official record of the British Empire, and the boots-on-the-ground history of the people absorbed into the empire, are two very different things. Your answer for part A could include some of the following ideas:

- Officially, the British arrived in foreign lands looking merely for trading partners. Joint-stock companies such as the British East India Company were examples of this.
- However, as time went on, local "instability"—whether real or imagined—supposedly forced the British to take over the government of the foreign land, converting a former trading partner into an outright colony. Over the centuries, the Royal Navy grew in power, becoming the greatest fleet in the world, all to reinforce this political "goodwill."
- The outright racism evidenced by Godard was typical of its time, and it can be seen as the British Empire's method of justifying its own imperialism. A famous American poem of the era, "The White Man's Burden," by Rudyard Kipling, exemplified this idea and would be appropriate to mention here.
- Given that England invaded and/or colonized so many regions of the world in the 18th and 19th centuries, you have a wide array of specific examples to analyze. One obvious one, however, would be India, the so-called "jewel in the crown" of the British Empire, which England first approached as traders looking for resources. Another is Australia, which England first used as a distant prison for its worst criminals. Others include Jamaica (in which a native revolt was brutally put down through mass slaughter) and the United States.

B. Godard wrote the passage in 1905, which was the very height of the British Empire. This meant that his point of view was one of supreme confidence in England's abilities to maintain an empire. But if there's one thing we know from history, it's that change is inevitable. As the 20th century carried on, many of its colonies began to divest themselves from the crown as England's ability to maintain its empire was cast into doubt.

Therefore, for part B your answer could include the emancipation process involved in any of many colonies or dominions that won independence. Here's a list of some of those colonies/nations:

- India
- Egypt
- Ireland
- Canada
- South Africa
- Zimbabwe
- Palestine
- Iraq
- Singapore
- Sudan

This isn't the place to analyze each in detail, but here is a broad picture: early in the 20th century, England resisted some of these independence movements, while later in the century it granted independence much more easily. After all, maintaining a global empire is a very expensive undertaking, and in the years after World War II, England was flat broke. (Food was rationed for more than a decade following the end of the war.)

For example, India's independence process would be an easy one to discuss, since it involves a name that everybody knows: Gandhi, whose leadership on the Indian National Congress and nonviolent techniques led to his own imprisonment, to a hunger strike, and eventually to independence in 1947. At that time, England simultaneously granted independence to India and created the nation of Pakistan in an event known as the Partition.

Another prominent example is Egypt, which England had occupied since 1882 (though it wasn't technically a colony). Of special note would be the Suez Canal crisis in 1956, in which England tried an unsuccessful invasion of Egypt in a vain attempt to maintain control of the canal, since it allowed easy access for British ships carrying oil to pass from England to the Middle East and vice versa. The defeat was humiliating, and it marked the end of the British Empire.

C. It will probably be easier to describe some of the negative long-term effects of colonial rule. These include environmental degradation, resource depletion, lack of industrialization, dependence on a cash crop economy, the rise of ethno-religious conflict, corruption among government officials, and the emotional effects of post-slavery society.

Possible specific examples might include the following:

- Nigeria. The British favored certain ethnic groups in the country, which made interethnic rivalries much worse than they had been in the past. This continued after the departure of the British.
- Barbados. This Caribbean island is a former British slave colony that was dedicated for centuries to sugar cultivation. It accepted the second-greatest number of African slaves in the region after Jamaica and even served as a slave breeding ground for the Carolinas. In 2023, its prime minister, Mia Mottley, asked King Charles III of England for nearly $5 trillion in reparations to replace the wealth that the people of the island lost during the centuries of slavery under colonial rule.
- India. During the Partition of India (the division of the region that accompanied independence in 1947), millions of people were displaced, millions more died, and the entire region became segregated by religion. All Hindus went to India and Muslims went to Pakistan.

Question 2

A. According to the source, this author is a British satirist, which means there is likely irony present in the cartoon. The character on the left is a caricature of a British man, giving a very dirty look to the man on the right, who is supposed to be French (and it appears he returns the favor). The text seems to show both men exchanging epithets with one another, and the fact that this cartoon was created in 1780 all lend credence to the idea that the cartoonist was highlighting the poor state of relations between the two countries. A good answer would explain that the cartoon suggests that Britain and France in the late 18th century had a strained or conflictual relationship with one another.

B. The poor state of the relationship between England and France throughout the 18th century was expressed through their more or less constant warfare. During the 18th century, the two nations waged a seemingly endless series of wars with one another. These conflicts had many different causes, including:

- The War of the League of Augsburg (1688–1697). Louis XIV of France attempted to seize more land along the French border in order to create a solid line of defense. (Yes, that was the official explanation.) He was opposed by an entire European alliance, which included England, Spain, Austria, and others. This conflict also saw France funding or supporting revolts inside Scotland and Ireland against the English crown.

- The War of Spanish Succession (1702–1713). Spain's king, Charles II, was going to die childless, so he bequeathed the monarchy of Spain to Philip, grandson of Louis XIV of France. Alarmed at the possibility of a politically united France and Spain, England moved to fight them. The conflict lasted for more than a decade until Philip, on the Spanish throne, gave up rights to the French throne.
- The Seven Years' War (1756–1763). The first global war. England and France fought one another on three different continents, including North America (where it was called the French and Indian War). England's win is considered foundational to its future success as an empire.
- The Anglo-French War (1778–1783). This was the European side of the American Revolutionary War. France sent support to the colonists; England sent support and soldiers to the Royalists. Also, often using allies or proxies, England and France fought for dominance in the Mediterranean, the Indian Ocean, and the West Indies.
- The War of the First Coalition (1791–1812). These 21 years of more or less continuous warfare included the period of the French Revolution, during which England stirred up civil unrest affecting its rival. France actually declared war on England while its own country was erupting into civil violence.
- · Napoleon Bonaparte was frustrated by England; it was the only European country he didn't conquer. So he attempted an economic war against Britain instead, creating the continental system, which is a code term for an embargo against England. Meanwhile, England pursued military action against French troops in Portugal and Spain.

C. Numerous devastating events of the 20th century brought the two countries closer than they'd ever been.

- The Entente Cordiale of 1904 settled various questions of boundaries, especially on the open seas and with regard to fishing. This formally brought the two nations into close allyship.
- That agreement happened just in time, since World War I forced them to cooperate in their fight against the Axis Powers.
- A short two decades later, the two countries faced an even worse common opponent, in the form of Adolf Hitler and Nazi Germany in World War II. British troops helped free France from Nazi troops.
- Both countries founded NATO (North Atlantic Treaty Organization), a mutual defense pact among Western countries.
- In the second half of the century, the two empires experienced a period of decolonization at the same time.
- In the 20th century, both countries exhibited a fierce defense of democracy.

Question 3

A. To answer this part fully, you need to first describe education on the Italian peninsula in the medieval era.

- Medieval education in Italy was dominated by the Catholic church, particularly in monastic schools and in cathedral schools. There were some independent tutors, however, for the wealthier people.
- Medieval education centered upon deductive reasoning, in which general principles are used to deduce equally general conclusions. Some of these could verge on the ridiculous. See the famous medieval scholastic debate *How many angels can dance on the head of a pin?*

With the arrival of new texts, new philosophies, new teachers, and new schools, the Italian Renaissance changed education immensely. Here are a few examples:

- The Italian peninsula borrowed old ideas from antiquity that were new to them, such as Protagoras's famous quote that "Man is the measure of all things." This is the modern definition of humanism.
- The translation and study of classic works of ancient Greece and Rome, as urged by Petrarch, the main founder of Renaissance humanism.
- The *studia humanitatis.* Today called the humanities, this course of study consisted of the trivium (grammar, logic, and rhetoric) and the quadrivium (arithmetic, astronomy, music, and geometry). These courses were studied at new schools called gymnasiums, which were designed essentially as liberal arts schools for wealthy boys.
- Neoplatonism rose in popularity. This was an arcane branch of knowledge that included mysticism, numerology, and even alchemy. Its chief proponent was Marsilio Ficino.

B. The consequences of this sea change in education were enormously transformative.

- Italians began forming their young men to become well-rounded civic leaders, or men of *virtu* (meaning "virtue").
- Because of this, learning how to conduct oneself in the court of a ruler became important. Baldassare Castiglione wrote a handbook called *The Courtier* for this reason. *The Prince* by Niccolo Machiavelli could be relevant here as well.
- Their ideas about education began to be exported to northern Europe via book traders and traveling tutors. This dissemination of information stimulated the questioning of orthodoxy, which led to the principled resistance of figures such as Sir Thomas More. Consequently, northern European figures such as Erasmus and Luther kickstarted the most important event in the last thousand years of European history, the Protestant Reformation.

C. There are many techniques and innovations that you could write about in the field of painting, sketching, and sculpture. Here are a few:

- Linear perspective. An imaginary point on the horizon serves as a focal point against which the size, shape, and positions of all objects are measured.
- Proportion. The dimensions of a composition and the relationship between the height, width, and depth.
- A shift from abstract themes to representational themes. In other words, there was a greater emphasis on the particular details of individuals.
- Foreshortening. The technique of producing the illusion of depth or projection into space.
- *Sfumato.* The gradual shading of tones and colors into one another, which creates softness and haziness.
- *Chiaroscuro.* The contrasting use of light and shade.

Question 4

A. This question only requires us to identify a successor state (which means little is needed in the way of explanation). Several new successor states were created in Europe after the Versailles settlement. Some of the best examples would be the following:

- Poland
- Czechoslovakia
- Hungary
- Yugoslavia

B. For this question, we can either use the democratic successor state we chose in part A, or use one of the other ones, depending on what is easier. Here are a few examples of how the question could be answered based on each one:

- Poland struggled to maintain its independence in the years after its independence. Germany invaded it in 1939, which set off the European front of World War II. After World War II ended, the Soviet Union sought to expand its sphere of influence to Poland, installing a communist government there and guaranteeing communism would take root there for much of the rest of the century.
- In 1938, the Nazis annexed the Sudetenland from Czechoslovakia as part of the Munich agreement, further emboldening the Nazis to expand their reach across Europe. After the war, Czechoslovakia fell under Soviet influence and aligned itself with the Eastern Bloc during the Cold War.
- In the interwar period, Hungary established itself as an independent republic after splitting from Austria. A fascist government took root there in the interwar period that allied itself with Hitler. After World War II, the Soviet Union sought to expand communism to Hungary as it became a Soviet satellite state.
- Yugoslavia was invaded by the Axis powers during World War II. After the war, Yugoslavia developed a socialist government but sought to distance itself from the Soviet Union, in hopes of positioning itself between both Cold War superpowers.

C. For this question, we can either use the democratic successor state we chose in part B, or use one of the other ones, depending on what is easier. Here are a few examples of how the question could be answered based on each one:

- As the Cold War dragged on, many in Poland grew dissatisfied with communist rule, which culminated in the Solidarity independent trade union movement in the 1980s and eventually Poland's democratic elections in 1989.
- Czechoslovakia had a fraught relationship with the Soviet Union, and in 1968, the Prague Spring attempted to reform the government, which led to a Soviet invasion that continued political repression there until the end of the Cold War.
- Hungarians upset over Soviet political repression led a revolution in 1956, but it was crushed by a strong-handed Soviet military response. The attack cemented much anti-Soviet feeling across Europe in the decades after.
- Yugoslavia struggled to maintain a stable government that could rule over the various ethnic groups that comprised it, and the rise of nationalist movements in the late 20th century ultimately led to the violent breakup of the country in the 1990s.

The breakup of Yugoslavia is an immensely complicated topic, so don't worry if you don't quite have a handle on it. This is a short answer—it is highly doubtful that you would ever be asked to write anything longer on the topic!

Section II: Document-Based Question (DBQ)

The document-based question (DBQ) section begins with a 15-minute reading period. During those 15 minutes, you should 1) come up with some information not included in the given documents (from your outside knowledge), 2) get an overview of what each document means and the point of view of each author, 3) decide what opinion you're going to argue, and 4) write an outline of your essay.

The DBQ in Practice Test 1 is concerned with the extent to which World War I caused the collapse of Austria-Hungary. You should be prepared to discuss the empire's formation, its many weaknesses, its few strengths, and the particulars of the war. You should also remember the famous PERSIA method of organizing characteristics of any historical time period—Political, Economic, Religious, Social, Intellectual, and Artistic. The first three tend to be more useful than the last three, so try to at least remember PER.

BEFORE YOU LOOK AT THE DOCUMENTS, first brainstorm for a minute or two. Try to list everything you know (from class, leisure reading, or informational documentaries) about the history of Austria and Hungary and especially the two of them together. This list will serve as your reference to the outside information you must provide to earn a top grade.

Next, read over the documents. As you read them, take notes on your scratch paper, including which passages you are certain you will use in your essay. Make note of the opinions and position of each document's author. If a document helps you remember a piece of outside information, add that outside information to your brainstorming list. If you cannot make sense of a document, or if it argues strongly against your position, relax! You do not need to mention every document to score well on the DBQ.

Here is what you might assess in the time you have to look over the documents.

The Documents

Document 1

This is a factual explanation of how fractured the Austro-Hungarian Empire was at the dawn of World War I. As the first document, it will be easy to use as background for the dangerously unbalanced conditions in which Austria-Hungary found itself at the beginning of the war.

Document 2

This map gives specific names and concrete visual proof of the fracturing of Austria-Hungary along ethnic lines. Obviously it can be used to argue that multiethnic states are a weakness. After all, Italy was similarly broken into many different city-states, but they were able to unify.

Document 3

The photo of Archduke Franz Ferdinand is meant to stimulate outside knowledge about the role that his assassination played in the start of World War I. As the nephew of Emperor Franz Josef, he was a major figure in Austria. This is your opportunity to discuss the system of entangling alliances, and to explain Serbia's alliance with Russia, among other things.

Document 4

This is the only document that supports a unified Austria-Hungary, specifically pointing out that there were surprisingly few religious tensions in the empire, either from a legal or a social standpoint.

Document 5

In this document, Schierbrand seems to be blaming the Hungarians for not sharing their bountiful harvest with Austrians during the war. (Note his Germanic last name as an instance of potential bias.) Refusal to share basic resources, such as food, is another strong reason for the war to have accelerated the end of the empire.

Document 6

The impossibility of finding a shared language is offered in this document. It provides evidence that one more reason for the fractured empire was linguistic—if all the people don't speak at least one common language, then the people cannot unify.

Document 7

In this document from 1915, Masaryk (who is something of a folk hero to the Czech people today) points out that Austria had been falling apart for a very long time prior to the start of World War I. He opines that Austria-Hungary only arose to counter the Ottoman Empire, and that without this common enemy, it would collapse. (This is exactly what happened a few years later—very prescient!) He points out that Austria-Hungary *exists only as the vassal of Berlin*, meaning that the power of Germany and the German-speaking people are the only things keeping the empire propped up.

Outside Information

We have already discussed more than you could include in a 45-minute essay. Do not worry. You will not be expected to mention all of what we have covered in the section above. You will, however, be expected to include some outside information—that is, information not directly mentioned in the documents. Here are some examples of outside information that you might incorporate in your essay:

- Though they exist outside the bounds of this question, 18th-century Austrian rulers could be namedropped as examples of the long history of German-speaking people's domination of the Holy Roman Empire (which was a forerunner to Austria-Hungary). For example, you could mention the

Pragmatic Sanction, which guaranteed the Habsburgs' right to bind together the region by passing on their inheritance to their daughter, Maria Theresa, and afterward to her son, Joseph II.

- The philosophy of nationalism was the invisible presence throughout these documents. You could link anything from that movement (philosophers, revolutions, etc.) to conditions inside Austria-Hungary.

- Austria-Hungary boasted a single monarch for almost its entire official existence, Emperor Franz Joseph, head of the Habsburg dynasty (also spelled Hapsburg). Dominating its politics from 1848 (before it even officially became the Austro-Hungarian Empire) to 1916 (just before it collapsed), he was the third-longest reigning monarch in European history.

- The Austro-Hungarian Compromise of 1867 was the official agreement that formally ended the Austrian Empire and replaced it with the dual monarchy of Austria-Hungary. In this agreement, the Habsburgs joined forces with Hungarian elites by granting them greater autonomy, such as their own parliament, the Diet of Hungary, separate from the Austrian one. However, the Habsburgs kept the title of *Emperor* for Franz Joseph, and also insisted that he be given the title of King of Hungary. Confused yet?

- Franz Josef annexed Bosnia and Herzegovina in 1908. This precipitated the Bosnian Crisis, during which Austria-Hungary's Balkan neighbors complained angrily about Austrian interference. This diplomatic conundrum indirectly laid the groundwork for the reaction to the assassination of Archduke Franz Ferdinand (Document 3) in Sarajevo. As a result, it became the inciting incident of World War I.

- It could be worth mentioning Austria-Hungary's official role in starting World War I. After Ferdinand's assassination, Austria-Hungary declared war on Serbia, which was an ally of Russia. This was the match that started the fire, the very first formal step in the series of entangling alliances that led to the most destructive war in the history of the world at that time.

- The effect of the Bolshevik Revolution is also very important. It was viewed as a cry for nationalism, which stirred the minorities in the Austro-Hungarian Empire to demand political rights for themselves too.

Choosing a Thesis Statement

A wishy-washy thesis—meaning taking both sides—is usually a good way to organize your response to any essay featuring the words *to what extent*. In other words, it's quite easy to argue that World War I did in fact accelerate the destruction of Austria-Hungary, BUT that the seeds of their destruction had already been present for many years. Choosing such a thesis allows a lot of wiggle room.

The proportion of evidence, however, is up to you. It's probably not possible to do a fifty-fifty type of essay for this prompt, just because most of the documents support the war hypothesis, and most students probably don't have the depth of outside knowledge to be able to argue the preexisting conditions. Therefore, the best proportion of evidence to use here would be 75% war, 25% preexisting conditions.

Planning Your Essay

Unless you read extremely quickly, you probably will not have time to write a detailed outline for your essay during the 15-minute reading period. However, it is worth taking several minutes to jot down a loose structure of your essay because it will actually save you time when you write. First, decide on your thesis and write it down on your scratch paper. Then, take a minute or two to brainstorm all the points you might put in your essay. Choose the strongest points and number them in the order you plan to present them. Lastly, note which documents and outside information you plan to use in conjunction with each point. If you organize your essay before you start writing, the actual writing process will go much more smoothly. More importantly, you will not write yourself into a corner, suddenly finding yourself making a point you cannot support or heading toward a weak conclusion (or, worse still, no conclusion at all).

This particular DBQ doesn't offer a whole lot of room for interpretation. It's clear from the documents that World War I severely stressed out an already teetering Austro-Hungarian Empire. The only exception to this is Document 4, which notes that religious tolerance was one of the empire's strong points. This is your best (and only) option to show the other side, called a counterargument.

The most obvious way to organize this essay would be using PERSIA. Your grouping of documents might look like this:

<u>Political</u>
Document 1
Document 3
Document 7

<u>Economic</u>
Document 5

<u>Religious</u>
Document 4

<u>Social/Linguistic</u>
Document 2
Document 6

An easy way to organize this essay would be to devote one paragraph to each category. The Economic paragraph would serve nicely as the counterargument, and can be placed anywhere—beginning, middle, or end. However, Document 1 would do best at the beginning of the essay, since it lays out the background of the Austro-Hungarian Empire.

Notice also that the above organization uses all the documents! Typically it's not recommended, but the general uniformity of this particular DBQ offers a greater opportunity to use all of the sources. After all, 6 of the 7 documents support the same view of the issue, and a couple of them even overlap in theme. So if there's ever a time to swing for the fences, it's here.

There are other ways to organize, but this way is the most obvious—and with only 45 minutes to write, it's often better to go the obvious route. Once you choose one of these structures, go down your list of outside information and think of ways to integrate each one into the essay. It won't always be possible, but every outside idea you can add will lend weight to your essay, as long as you can fit it into your thesis statement. Remember that an obvious, desperate stretch will only hurt your score. However, history is by nature intricate, and the readers of your exam want to see that you respect the intrinsic complexity behind many historical events.

Section II: Long Essay

Because you have only 40 minutes to plan and write this essay, you will not have time to work out an elaborate argument. That's okay; nobody is expecting you to read three questions, choose one, remember all pertinent facts about your subject, formulate a brilliant thesis, and then write a perfect essay. Here is what you should do. First, choose your question; next, brainstorm for two or three minutes, and edit your brainstorm ideas. Then, number those points you are going to include in your essay in the order you plan to present them, just as you did for the DBQ. Last, think of a simple thesis statement that allows you to discuss the points your essay will make.

Question 2—The Reformation (Option 1)

2. Evaluate the most significant effect of the Reformation between 1517 and 1650.

About the Structure of Your Essay

The prompt asks about the "most significant effect of the Reformation," which implies that there is more than one effect. The easiest way to organize this essay is to try to write multiple body paragraphs about each effect of the Reformation you can think of, but also, in one of those body paragraphs, to make a claim as to why one of the effects is more significant than the others. Merely describing the different effects is not going to be enough. Remember that a successful AP European History essay always argues for something over something else.

Some of the major effects of the Reformation that you could focus on in your body paragraphs include the following:

- The Reformation helped many new sects of Christianity flourish, including Lutheranism and Calvinism. These branches of Christianity competed with Catholicism's influence by offering a different theology more amenable to Europe's growing merchant classes. For instances, Calvinists argued that wealth accumulation was actually a sign of God's favor and not something to be restricted as the Catholic Church had long done in Europe with its efforts to restrict banking.

- The Reformation challenged the centrality of the Catholic Church's role in European politics. In England, for instance, King Henry VIII broke away from the Church in favor of establishing the Church of England. Monarchs in Europe used the Reformation as a way to further centralize their rule and consolidate control of state affairs such as taxation and control of the army.

- The Reformation was a major impetus behind European colonization of the Americas. The Catholic Church sought new ways to maintain its status, and one way to do that was by seeking new converts in regions such as Asia and Africa. As the Spanish and Portuguese empires sought new colonies abroad, the Catholic Church sponsored missions by Jesuit priests to spread their faith to all new regions in order to challenge Protestant rivals.

This is a partial list. Try to come up with enough effects to be able to write about 2 to 3 body paragraphs and make sure that your claim is supported with clear and specific evidence.

Question 3—Industrialization (Option 2)

3. Evaluate the most significant effect of industrialization in Europe between 1750 and 1914.

About the Structure of Your Essay

The prompt asks about the "most significant effect of industrialization," which implies that there is more than one effect. The easiest way to organize this essay is to try to write multiple body paragraphs about each effect of industrialization you can think of, but also, in one of those body paragraphs, to make a claim as to why one of the effects is more significant than the others. Merely describing the different effects is not going to be enough. Remember that a successful AP European History essay always argues for something over something else.

Some of the major effects of industrialization that you could focus on in your body paragraphs include the following:

- Industrialization exacerbated major class inequalities across much of Europe. In industrialized states such as England and Germany, capitalists and factory owners accumulated vast amounts of wealth, and the bourgeoisie grew wealthier with lots of new ways to spend their money on things like leisure activities. At the same time, factory workers often enjoyed few labor protections and struggled to make ends meet.

- Industrializing states sought colonies both as sources of raw materials and markets for finished goods. In the 1800s, European states sought control of states in Africa for access to raw materials such as rubber to support factory growth. At the same time, they also used economic imperialism to make inroads in places like China after the Opium Wars to sell large amounts of finished goods.

- Industrialization bred new movements for reform. Abolitionists seized on industrialization to push the case for abolishing slavery in European empires abroad, while workers began organizing into labor unions to push for the inspection of factories and wage protections on the job. Radical reformers such as Karl Marx wrote ideological tracts such as *The Communist Manifesto*, pushing for worker control of the factors of production.

This is a partial list. Try to come up with enough effects to be able to write about 2 to 3 body paragraphs and make sure that your claim is supported with clear and specific evidence.

Question 4—The Cold War (Option 3)

4. Evaluate the most significant effect of the Cold War between 1945 and 2000.

About the Structure of Your Essay

The prompt asks about the "most significant effect of the Cold War," which implies that there is more than one effect. The easiest way to organize this essay is to try to write multiple body paragraphs about each effect of the Cold War you can think of, but also, in one of those body paragraphs, to make a claim as to why one of the effects is more significant than the others. Merely describing the different effects is not going to be enough. Remember that a successful AP European History essay always argues for something over something else.

Some of the major effects of the Cold War that you could focus on in your body paragraphs include the following:

- The Cold War led to competing military alliances among European states. In the West, states found themselves forming military alliances with the United States through the creation of NATO, whereas Eastern European states joined the Warsaw Pact. Both the United States and Soviet Union sought to use diplomacy and military pressure to influence the politics of their allied states.

- The Cold War motivated many states in Europe to form closer economic ties in an effort to rebuild after the destruction of World War II. Western European states initially formed the European Coal and Steel Community, which eventually developed into the European Economic Community and finally the EU in the 1990s, increasing economic and political integration between member states.

- The Cold War fostered dissatisfaction among many Eastern European satellite states, who resisted Soviet influence through protest and rebellion. In Hungary, the Prague Spring movement of the 1960s sought to introduce economic reforms, and in the 1980s, the Solidarity independent trade union movement in Poland challenged the communist government's iron grip on political affairs, culminating in Poland's 1989 elections.

This is a partial list. Try to come up with enough effects to be able to write about 2 to 3 body paragraphs and make sure that your claim is supported with clear and specific evidence.

HOW TO SCORE PRACTICE TEST 1

Section IA: Multiple Choice

_____ × 1.090 = _____
Number Correct   Weighted
(out of 55)   Section I Score
                                  (Do not round)

Section IB: Short Answer

Question 1:   _____   × 3.3333 =   _____
                  (out of 3)   (Do not round)

Question 2:   _____   × 3.3333 =   _____
                  (out of 3)   (Do not round)

Question 3 or 4: _____   × 3.3333 =   _____
                  (out of 3)   (Do not round)

AP Score Conversion Chart European History	
Composite Score Range	AP Score
107–150	5
90–106	4
73–89	3
56–72	2
0–55	1

Section II: Document-Based Question

Question 1:   _____   × 5.3571 =   _____
                  (out of 7)   (Do not round)

Section II: Long Essay

Question 2, 3, or 4: _____   × 3.750 =   _____
                  (out of 6)   (Do not round)

Composite Score

_____ + _____ + _____ + _____ = _____
Weighted   Weighted   Weighted   Weighted   Composite Score
Section IA   Section IB   DBQ Score   Long   (Round to the
Score   Score   Essay   nearest whole
                                       Score   number)

Note: This score sheet is to help you estimate your approximate score for the official exam, not your actual score.

Part III
About the
AP European
History Exam

- The Structure of the AP European History Exam
- The AP European History Exam Is Fully Digital
- How the AP European History Exam Is Scored
- Overview of Content Topics
- How AP Exams Are Used
- Other Resources
- Designing Your Study Plan

THE STRUCTURE OF THE AP EUROPEAN HISTORY EXAM

The AP European History Exam is 3 hours and 15 minutes long and broken up into two sections, each of which consists of two parts. Your performance on these four parts, outlined in the table below, is compiled and weighted to find your overall exam score.

	Question Type (#)	Time
Section I	Part A: Multiple Choice (55 questions)	55 minutes
	Part B: Short Answer (3 questions)	40 minutes
Section II	Document-Based Question (1 question)	60 minutes (includes a reading period with a suggested time of 15 minutes)
	Long Essay (1 question chosen among three different periods)	40 minutes

Here's what to expect in each of these parts:

- **Multiple Choice:** Questions will be grouped into sets of two to five and based on a primary or secondary source, including excerpts from historical documents or writings, images, graphs, maps, and so on. Each set of questions will be based on a different piece of source material. You'll have 55 minutes to answer 55 multiple-choice questions. This section will test your ability to analyze and engage with the source materials while recalling what you already know about European history.

- **Short Answer:** This section consists of three questions that will be based on a primary source, a secondary source, and no source. There will be two questions you must answer, and then you can choose between two others. All questions will ask you to identify and analyze historical evidence. The time allotted for this section is 40 minutes, which means you'll have a little more than 13 minutes for each question. You must answer the first two questions and then you can choose between either question 3 or question 4.

- **Document-Based Question (DBQ):** Here you'll be presented with a variety of historical documents that are intended to show the complexity of a particular historical issue. You will need to develop a thesis that responds to the question prompt and to support that thesis with evidence from both the documents and your knowledge of European history. To earn the best score, you should incorporate outside knowledge and be able to relate the issues discussed in the documents to a larger theme, issue, or time period. The 60-minute time frame for this section includes a suggested 15-minute reading period so that you can familiarize yourself with the question and documents.

- **Long Essay:** You'll be given a choice of three essay options that cover three different periods of the course (1, 2–3, 3–4) and you must choose one. (See page 74 for more on these historical periods.) The long essay is similar to the DBQ in that you must develop a thesis and use historical evidence to support your thesis, but there will not be any documents on which you must base your response. Instead, you will need to draw upon your own knowledge of topics you learned in your AP European History class. You'll have 40 minutes to write this essay.

THE AP EUROPEAN HISTORY EXAM IS FULLY DIGITAL

Both the multiple-choice and free-response sections of the AP European History Exam are administered and completed digitally via the College Board's Bluebook testing app. To take the exam, you must have access to the testing app, available for Window and Mac laptops/desktops, iPads, tablets, and Chromebooks. If your computer or tablet is owned or managed by your school, then a school official will likely have to install this app for you if it is not already on it. The test cannot be taken on a smartphone.

The Bluebook app allows you to annotate and highlight texts, eliminate answers, and flag questions for review later. You will also have access to scratch paper to plan responses to essay questions. Unlike other digital exams (like the SAT), the digital AP Exam will NOT be adaptive: this means that the difficulty of questions will not change depending on how well you do on earlier sections of the test.

With this change, it is important to note that the digital exam includes the same number of sections, number and types of questions, and timing as the paper exam. This means the strategies used for success on paper versions of the AP European History Exam are just as applicable to the digital version. So don't worry; the practice tests in this book will still prepare you for test day.

For the latest information regarding the digital AP Exams and testing accommodations, visit the College Board website at apcentral.collegeboard.org/exam-administration-ordering-scores/digital-ap-exams.

We've Got You Covered!
For more information on strategy and testing features for the digital AP Exam, please see our "How to Approach Digital Testing for AP Students" PDF online via your Student Tools.

HOW THE AP EUROPEAN HISTORY EXAM IS SCORED

Each of the four parts is weighted differently to determine your overall score.

Test Section	Percentage of Overall Score
Multiple Choice	40%
Short Answer	20%
DBQ	25%
Long Essay	15%

As you can see, the writing portions of the exam count a little more heavily toward your total score (a combined total of 60 percent) than the multiple-choice section (40 percent). The DBQ and long essay are scored according to separate rubrics. You can earn a maximum of 7 points on the DBQ and 6 points on the long essay. In Chapter 2 we'll show you a complete breakdown of how to earn points for both types of free-response essay.

The score report that you receive sometime around early July will give you a 1- to 5-point score rating your performance. Here is the distribution of scores among test-takers for the 2024 exam administration.

Score	2024 Percentage	Credit Recommendation	College Grade Equivalent
5	13.1%	Extremely Well Qualified	A
4	33.3%	Well Qualified	A–, B+, B
3	25.2%	Qualified	B–, C+, C
2	20.7%	Possibly Qualified	–
1	7.7%	No Recommendation	–

Scores from the May 2024 test administration. Data taken from the College Board website.

OVERVIEW OF CONTENT TOPICS

The AP European History course is organized into **nine units** aligning with **four major chronological periods**.

Chronological Period	Units
Period 1 c. 1450 to c. 1648	1. Renaissance and Exploration
	2. Age of Reformation
Period 2 c. 1648 to c. 1815	3. Absolutism and Constitutionalism
	4. Scientific, Philosophical, and Political Developments
	5. Conflict, Crisis, and Reaction in the Late 18th Century
Period 3 c. 1815 to c. 1914	6. Industrialization and Its Effects
	7. 19th-Century Perspectives and Political Developments
Period 4 c. 1914 to the present	8. 20th-Century Global Conflicts
	9. Cold War and Contemporary Europe

Similarly, we've divided our content review (Part V) into four chapters corresponding with the four periods shown above and covering the same two to three units each. (Further, we've included sidebars detailing the exact unit number and subtopic associated with each section.)

In addition, the course focuses on **seven major themes**, the goal of which is to help you to think conceptually about—and understand how—these themes manifest throughout European history. The questions on the exam will also be rooted in these seven themes. The following table highlights some topics that will likely be addressed. Note that this list is *not* comprehensive nor is it in chronological order. It is merely a sampling of the kinds of topics that fall under these thematic umbrellas.

Theme	Relevant Course Topics
1. Interaction of Europe and the World	• commercial and religious motivations to interact with the world • competition for trade • commercial rivalries • Christianity • social Darwinism • mercantilism; slave-labor system; expansion of slave trade • slave revolt and Haitian independence • national self-determination • extreme nationalist political parties • increased immigration into Europe, anti-immigrant policies • Woodrow Wilson's political/diplomatic idealism • causes of World War I • Columbian exchange • Marshall Plan • 1929 stock market crash • Cold War outside Europe • responses to imperialism • diplomacy and colonial wars
2. Economic and Commercial Developments	• industrialization; Second Industrial Revolution • French Revolution • Russian reform and modernization • world monetary and trade systems • European economic and political integration • baby boom • the putting-out system • Agricultural Revolution and population growth • mechanization; the factory system • migration from rural to urban areas • critiques of capitalism • evolution of socialist ideology • Russian Revolution • Lenin's New Economic Policy; Stalin's economic modernization • fascism • the Great Depression • green parties; revolts of 1968 • labor laws and reform programs

Theme	Relevant Course Topics
3. Cultural and Intellectual Developments	• revival of classical texts • invention of the printing press • Renaissance art • scientific method • rational thought • theories of Locke and Rousseau • humanism • romanticism • fascist nationalism
4. States and Other Institutions of Power	• English Civil War • French Revolution • wars of Napoleon • Enlightenment principles • Congress of Vienna • social contract • post-1815 revolutions • nation-building • industrialization • Russian Revolution • constitutionalism • rise of the Nazis • mass media and propaganda • total war • post-1945 nationalist/separatist movements • genocide • imperialism • colonial independence movements • League of Nations • collapse of communism
5. Social Organization and Development	• gender roles and marriage patterns • hierarchy and social status • urban expansion; rise of commercial and professional groups • family economy • Napoleon and meritocracy • industrialization and class • destructive effects of technology • religious minorities • social Darwinism

Theme	Relevant Course Topics
6. National and European Identity	• new class identities • ethnic cleansing • national self-determination • transnational identities • European integration • conflict between religious groups • continued influence of local identities • separatist movements • decolonization • radical political thought • rise of Zionism • mass politics • worker movements
7. Technological and Scientific Innovation	• golden age of Dutch advances: telescope, microscope, etc. • 1st Industrial Revolution (18th century): spinning jenny, steam engine, steamboat, etc. • 2nd Industrial Revolution (19th century) o electric motors, electric railways, telegraph o internal combustion engine, automobile o medical technology such as scalpel, stethoscope, aspirin, anesthesia, smallpox vaccine, Louis Pasteur's germ theory of disease • 20th century o less European innovation as America increased in power o Einstein and the theory of relativity o color photography by the Lumière brothers o warfare technology used in WWI: mustard gas, barbed wire, tanks, fighter planes o media: radio, television o medical: penicillin, antibiotics, electron microscope

Finally, the AP European History course emphasizes key **historical thinking skills**, which will also be tested on the exam in how you grasp the source material presented throughout the test, as well as how you demonstrate your ability to make historical connections in writing for the DBQ and long essay. The historical thinking skills that you develop in the course will be tested in the exam. These skills are grouped into SIX areas:

1. Developments and processes
2. Sourcing and situations
3. Claims and evidence in sources
4. Contextualization
5. Making connections
6. Argumentation

These skills are tested across all units.

Stay Up to Date!
For late-breaking information about test dates, exam formats, and any other changes pertaining to AP European History, make sure to check the College Board's website at apstudents.collegeboard.org/courses/ap-european-history/assessment

HOW AP EXAMS ARE USED

Different colleges use AP Exams in different ways, so it is important that you go to a particular college's website to determine how it uses AP Exams. The three items below represent the main ways in which AP Exam scores can be used:

More Great Books

For more information on colleges, you might want to check out some of our guide books, which include *The Best 391 Colleges, Paying for College,* and many more!

- **College Credit**. Some colleges will give you college credit if you score well on an AP Exam. These credits count toward your graduation requirements, meaning that you can take fewer courses while in college. For those who pay for college per credit or course, rather than per semester or year, this could be quite a benefit, indeed.

- **Satisfy Requirements.** Some colleges will allow you to "place out" of certain requirements if you do well on an AP Exam, even if they do not give you actual college credits. For example, you might not need to take an introductory-level course, or perhaps you might not need to take a class in a certain discipline at all.

- **Admissions Plus**. Even if your AP Exam will not result in college credit or even allow you to place out of certain courses, most colleges will respect your decision to push yourself by taking an AP course or even an AP Exam outside of a course. A high score on an AP Exam shows proficiency with more difficult content than is taught in many high school courses, and colleges may take that into account during the admissions process.

OTHER RESOURCES

There are many resources available to help you improve your score on the AP European History Exam, not the least of which are your **teachers**. If you are taking an AP class, you may be able to get extra attention from your teacher, such as obtaining feedback on your essays. If you are not in an AP course, reach out to someone who teaches European history and ask if they will review your essays or otherwise help you with content.

Looking to Guarantee a 5?

We now offer one-on-one tutoring for a guaranteed 5 on the AP European History Exam. For information on rates and availability, visit PrincetonReview.com/college/ap-test-prep

Another wonderful resource is **AP Students**, the official site of the AP Exams. The scope of the information at this site is quite broad and includes:

- the course description, which provides details on what content is covered and sample questions
- free-response prompts from previous AP European History Exams, along with scoring guidelines
- access to AP Classroom if you are enrolled in a course (teacher assistance required)
- exam practice tips

The AP Students web page is apstudents.collegeboard.org.

NOTE: Late-breaking updates to the course and exam can be released after the publication of this book, so we highly recommend visiting this website often!

Finally, The Princeton Review offers tutoring for the AP European History Exam. Our expert instructors can help you refine your strategic approach and add to your content knowledge. For more information, call 1-800-2REVIEW.

DESIGNING YOUR STUDY PLAN

As part of the Introduction, you identified some areas of potential improvement. Let's now delve further into your performance on Practice Test 1, with the goal of developing a study plan appropriate to your needs and time commitment.

Read the answers and explanations associated with the multiple-choice questions (starting on page 46). After you have done so, think about the following items:

- Which areas in the Overview of Content Topics do you feel confident about and in which do you need further review?

- How many days/weeks/months away is your AP European History Exam?

- What time of day is your best, most focused study time?

- How much time per day/week/month will you devote to preparing for your AP European History Exam?

- When will you do this preparation? (Be as specific as possible: Mondays and Wednesdays from 3:00 to 4:00 P.M., for example.)

- Based on the answers above, will you focus on strategy (Part IV), content (Part V), or both?

- What are your overall goals in using this book?

Prep Like a Pro
Need some help devising a plan of action? Look no further than our AP Euro study guides. Also check out our digital flashcards of the key terms you'll need to know on test day. To access your free online content, see page viii or scan the QR code below.

Part IV
Test-Taking Strategies for the AP European History Exam

- Preview
1 How to Approach Multiple-Choice Questions
2 How to Approach Short Answers and Essays
3 Using Time Effectively to Maximize Points

PREVIEW

Review your responses to the first three questions on page 4 of Part I and then respond to the following questions:

- How many multiple-choice questions did you miss even though you knew the answer?

- On how many multiple-choice questions did you guess randomly?

- How many multiple-choice questions did you miss after eliminating some answers and guessing based on the remaining answers?

- Were you able to complete all short-answer questions within the allotted 40 minutes?

- Did you create an outline before you wrote each essay?

- Did you find any of the essays easier/harder than the others—and, if so, why?

HOW TO USE THE CHAPTERS IN THIS PART

Before you read the following Strategy chapters, think about your current approach to the different question types. As you read and engage in the directed practice, be sure to appreciate the ways you can change your approach. At the end of Part IV, you will have the opportunity to reflect on how you will change your approach.

Chapter 1
How to Approach Multiple-Choice Questions

THE BASICS

The multiple-choice portion of this exam is organized in sets of two to five questions, each set centering upon a primary or secondary source. Expect to see primary texts in translation, texts by contemporary historians, cartoons, paintings, charts, graphs, and tables. Unlike several other AP Exams, there are only four answer choices for each multiple-choice question.

The good news is that you'll be tested primarily on that source material, along with a certain amount of outside knowledge. The bad news is that you'll be responsible for understanding the grand sweep of European history—causes and effects, continuity and change, comparing and contextualizing.

The exam seeks to achieve a measure of balance between the period from the High Renaissance to Napoleon and the period after 1815. Also, note that equal emphasis is placed on political and diplomatic history, cultural and intellectual questions, and social and economic themes. Remember this as you study.

Let's Get Digital

Remember that you will be taking the AP European History Exam in the Bluebook app. The test will be administered at your school on a desktop or laptop computer that has the Bluebook app installed. To prepare for this, it's best if you practice as much as you can in a digital environment so that you will be used to the look and feel of the test. Head to your online Student Tools at PrincetonReview.com/prep and register your book to access a digital practice test.

TYPES OF QUESTIONS

The majority of questions in the multiple-choice section will ask you to choose the response that is *most correct*. Here is an example. (Answers to the sample questions are on page 95.)

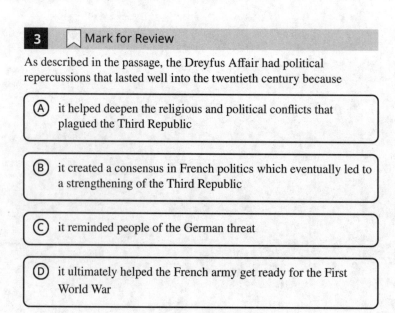

3   🔖 Mark for Review

As described in the passage, the Dreyfus Affair had political repercussions that lasted well into the twentieth century because

(A) it helped deepen the religious and political conflicts that plagued the Third Republic

(B) it created a consensus in French politics which eventually led to a strengthening of the Third Republic

(C) it reminded people of the German threat

(D) it ultimately helped the French army get ready for the First World War

Sometimes, the College Board makes the questions a little trickier. One way it does this is by phrasing a question so that you are actually looking for the answer choice that is *incorrect*. We call these questions "NOT/EXCEPT" questions because they usually contain one of those words (in capital letters, so they're harder to miss). Look at the following example:

---

6 ⬚ Mark for Review

The author indicates that all of the following led to the Russian Revolution of 1917 EXCEPT

(A) the outbreak of World War I

(B) the failure of autocratic government

(C) growing disenchantment of the intellectual class

(D) a decline in the rate of industrialization in the decade leading up to 1917

The answer choices will occasionally rely upon the source material, but at other times will bring in outside information that may not even be from the period discussed in the question. When that happens, understand that the College Board is testing you on your knowledge of themes that recur throughout European history—rise of the middle class, end of religion as an organizing force, and so on. It doesn't necessarily mean that the answer choice is wrong.

Here is an example:

Political cartoon in the London Daily Mail, June 23, 1941

42 ⬚ Mark for Review

The political cartoon implies that

(A) Hitler broke his promise not to destroy the German Communist Party

(B) Hitler betrayed his 1939 nonaggression pact with Stalin

(C) Stalin was warned by the Western Allies that Hitler was dangerous

(D) a nonaggression pact with Germany was fraught with problems

Other types of primary source materials will be statistical in nature. Be sure to read any chart carefully. If there are easily observed trends, note them on your scratch paper using up arrows, down arrows, bell curves, and so on.

Here's an example:

Rate of Industrial Production in Great Britain
(percentage increase per decade)

1800 to 1810	22.9
1810 to 1820	38.6
1820 to 1830	40.8
1830 to 1840	47.2
1840 to 1850	37.4
1850 to 1860	39.3
1860 to 1870	27.8
1870 to 1880	33.2
1880 to 1890	17.4
1890 to 1900	17.9

13 ☐ Mark for Review

Which of the following conclusions can be drawn from the information presented in the chart?

(A) The rate of increase of industrial production in the 1860s was due to the American Civil War.

(B) The rate of industrial production remained steady throughout the century.

(C) By the last decades of the century, the increase in industrial production was in an irreversible decline.

(D) The period between 1830 and 1860 witnessed the greatest increase in industrial production.

No Military History and No Trivial Pursuit

Here's some good news. The AP European History Exam doesn't ask specifically about military history. You will *never* see a question on the AP Exam like the one below:

16 ☐ Mark for Review

During the First World War, the Battle of Passchendaele

(A) was a British defeat due to the weakening of their right flank at a critical time

(B) ended with a German counterattack and breakthrough of the British lines

(C) was a British defeat due to insufficient artillery support

(D) witnessed the last attempt by the British to blast their way through the German lines without the element of surprise

Although the British assault on German positions at the Battle of Passchendaele serves as an important example of the foolhardiness of Britain's military leadership, you won't be asked about it on the test. The AP European History Exam does not ask about military strategy per se. When it asks about war, the questions concern the political or social implications of a war or the introduction of new technology rather than strategic questions. Reminder: answers to the sample questions are on page 95.

The Big Picture

The questions and answers are designed to illustrate **basic principles** of European history. Multiple-choice questions will NOT ask about exceptions to historical trends; the test ignores these, because the test-writers are trying to determine whether you have a complete understanding of the important generalizations that can be drawn from history. They do not want to know whether you have memorized your textbook (they already know that you haven't).

Therefore, you should always keep the **big picture** in mind as you take this exam. Even if you cannot remember the specific event or concept being tested, you should be able to answer the question by remembering the general social and political trends of the era.

Let's look at this illustrative example, which would be accompanied by a passage on the actual exam:

---

48 ☐ Mark for Review

As evidenced by the last paragraph of the excerpt, John Calvin argued that from the beginning of time, God

(A) allowed humans to select their own path to salvation, provided that it included some degree of faith

(B) knew few would be granted salvation unless they performed charitable works

(C) selected those who would be saved and those who would be condemned, and that human actions play no role in this

(D) operated as the divine creator but played no real role in the daily workings of this world

Here's How to Crack It

Using general knowledge of the Protestant Reformation can potentially help you as much as, or sometimes even more than, analyzing the text closely. For example, this question is really asking whether you understand the fundamentals of John Calvin's theology. Calvin believed God selected only a very few individuals to be saved. Nothing these individuals did affected their own ultimate salvation, because to imply they had a role in it would mean that God's authority was not total, something Calvin did not accept. Choices (A) and (B) are thus incorrect, as both imply some measure of human free will. Choice (D) could not be correct; it represents the Deist point of view dating from the 18th century Enlightenment and bears little resemblance to what a 16th-century theologian like Calvin would have believed. The correct answer is (C), which illustrates a "big picture" principle, the primacy for Protestants of faith over works.

Process of Elimination and Guessing

There will be times, however, when you can eliminate one or more clearly wrong answers and still have more than one reasonable answer choice left over. You may not be able to decide which one is right. When this happens, you should guess. Does this advice take you by surprise? Lots of students think that they should never guess on an exam. But even the College Board will tell you that's not true. AP Exams do not have any sort of "guessing penalty" for every incorrect answer. Instead, students are assessed only on the total number of correct questions. A lot of AP materials, even those you receive in your AP class, may not include this information. It is really important to remember that if you are running out of time, you should try to answer every question before the time for the multiple-choice section is up. Even if you don't plan to spend a lot of time on every question, and even if you have no idea what the correct answer is, you need to fill something in. We don't recommend random guessing as an overall strategy, but taking smart guesses at the right time can substantially increase your raw score on the multiple-choice section of the test.

Let's see exactly how guessing can help you. There are four answer choices for each multiple-choice question. If you cannot eliminate any answer choices at all, random odds say that you would get one-fourth of the questions correct. That's about 13 or 14 out of 55 questions. If you were able to eliminate just one wrong answer for each question on the entire multiple-choice section, random odds say that you would get one-third of the questions correct. That's about 18 out of 55. And so on. What does that mean for you when you take the test? It means that you should take your best guess, period—no matter how many answer choices you can eliminate. However, you will rarely be faced with a question for which you can't eliminate at least one of the answer choices. In many cases, you will be able to eliminate two or even three incorrect answers. Whenever you eliminate one or two answers but can go no further, you *must* guess from among the remaining answer choices.

Guess Actively
Because you don't lose points for incorrect answers, you should always guess on questions you don't know—no matter how many answer choices you can eliminate. Be assertive.

If it seems that we are focusing more on eliminating incorrect answers than on finding the correct answers, it's because this is the most efficient way to take a multiple-choice exam. Use **Process of Elimination** to whittle down the answer choices to one on every question except the ones you find easiest (on those questions, the correct answer will be obvious), because incorrect answers are much easier to identify than the correct one. When you look for the correct answer among the answer choices, you may have a tendency to try to justify how each answer *might* be correct. You'll adopt a forgiving attitude in a situation in which tough assertiveness is rewarded. Eliminate incorrect answers with extreme prejudice. If you have done your job well, only the correct answer will be left standing at the end.

This all probably sounds pretty harsh to you. It is. The fact is, a ruthless attitude pays on this test. Sift through the answer choices, toss incorrect answers into the bin, guess without remorse, and prowl the test searching for questions you can answer—all with the tenacity and ruthlessness of a shark. Okay, maybe that overstates the case a *little*, but you get the point.

Common Sense Can Help

Sometimes, an answer on the multiple-choice section contradicts common sense. Eliminate those answers. Common sense works on the AP European History Exam. Which of the answer choices to the question below don't make sense?

---

26 ⬜ Mark for Review

During the period when England was a republic (1649–1660), which of the following applied to Ireland?

(A) Ireland became primarily Protestant.

(B) Ireland won its independence.

(C) Ireland obtained extensive military assistance from the French.

(D) An army led by Cromwell invaded Ireland and solidified English control.

Here's How to Crack It

Common sense should allow you to eliminate (A) immediately, since you are probably aware that all of Ireland has never been primarily Protestant. Choice (B) can be eliminated because independence came for the Republic of Ireland only in the early 20th century. If (C) actually occurred, then perhaps (B) would have taken place, but that was not what happened. That leaves (D) as the only correct answer.

Context Clues

If the question compares periods or themes in history, there will be context clues or even vocabulary words that will help lead you to the correct answer or eliminate an incorrect answer. Take a look at the following question:

Helpful Hints

Key words in the question and answer choices will often guide you to the correct answer. In this question, the book title contains a helpful hint: "Consequences" suggests that the work is critical, so look for the choice that aligns with this idea.

---

54 ☐ Mark for Review

In his *Economic Consequences of the Peace* (1919), John Maynard Keynes contradicts the author's statement when he

(A) supported the reparations payments by the Germans as a necessary evil

(B) argued that the reparations amount was too low to seriously compromise the German economy

(C) charged that by punishing the Germans with a large reparations bill, the entire European economy was threatened

(D) urged that the issue of reparations be postponed for a decade so that the postwar economies could adjust to peace

---

Here's How to Crack It

Again, you are dealing with a book and an author that you might be less than familiar with, but don't panic—the question itself contains a major clue. The word *consequences* in the title of Keynes's work provides you with the hint that Keynes was possibly critical of the reparations component of the Treaty of Versailles. This bit of information allows you to eliminate (A), (B), and (D), because these answers indicate at least some level of support by Keynes for reparations. The one that stands out from the others is (C); it alone seems to be critical of the very concept of German reparations.

SKILL TYPES

Read the following passage closely. As you work through the four questions that follow it, be sure to read the commentary before and after each question. Each contains a description of a type of multiple-choice question that you're sure to encounter. Because it's good to know your enemy, it's recommended that you commit these four question types to memory.

"Presently two other figures caught our eye: a man in a long cape to the tops of his boots, made of sheepskin, the wool inside, the outside decorated with bright-coloured wools, outlining crude designs. The black fur collar was the skin of a small black lamb, legs and tail showing, as when stripped off the little animal. The man wore a cone-shaped hat of black lamb and his hair reached to his shoulders. He smoked a very long-stemmed pipe with a china bowl, as he strolled along. Behind him a woman walked, bowed by the weight of an immense sack. She wore boots to the knees, many full short skirts, and a yellow and red silk head-kerchief. By her head-covering we knew her to be a married woman. They were a farmer and his wife! Among the Magyars the man is very decidedly the peacock; the woman is the pack-horse. On market days he lounges in the sunshine, wrapped in his long sheepskin cape, and smokes, while she plies the trade. In the farmers' homes of southern Hungary where we passed some time, we, as Americans, sat at table with the men of the house, while wife and daughter served. There was one large dish of food in the centre, into which every one dipped! The women of the peasant class never sit at table with their men; they serve them and eat afterwards, and they always address them in the second person as, "Will your graciousness have a cup of coffee?" Also they always walk behind the men. At country dances we have seen young girls in bright, very full skirts, with many ribbons braided into the hair, cluster shyly at a short distance from the dancing platform in the fair grounds, waiting to be beckoned or whistled to by one of the sturdy youths with skin-tight trousers, tucked into high boots, who by right of might, has stationed himself on the platform. When they have danced, generally a czardas, the girl goes back to the group of women, leaving the man on the platform in command of the situation! Yet already in 1897 women were being admitted to the University of Budapest. There in Hungary one could see woman run the whole gamut of her development, from man's slave to man's equal."

Source: Emily Burbank, *Woman as Decoration,* 1917

A Note on Primary-Source Content
You may spot some outdated and possibly offensive language and perspectives in primary sources. We do not endorse this content but include it to accurately reflect what you may encounter on the AP European History Exam.

Chronological Reasoning

The first and most common type of question you'll see is about causes and effects, how things have stayed the same or changed over time, and awareness of the various periods of European history. These are habits of mind that historians have when they approach the past in a critical way.

Try this one.

1 ☐ Mark for Review

In the passage, the author primarily describes

Ⓐ a pair of Magyars representing all those who had survived the horrors of World War I

Ⓑ the fundamental injustice shown toward women of the European peasant classes

Ⓒ the traditional role of women in Europe that the feminist movement had just begun to change

Ⓓ the dress and carriage of the inhabitants of an unusual corner of eastern Europe

Here's How to Crack It

While (A) places World War I in the correct time period, it incorrectly assumes that this is relevant to the passage, or that the people in the passage actually experienced the war. You can eliminate it. Because this author is describing the habits of only the rural Magyar people, you have to eliminate (B), which is both too broad and too negative. Choice (D) is out because we don't know that this was unusual for this part of eastern Europe. By Process of Elimination, (C) is correct, and it uses a word ("feminist") that was not present in the text. Your job is to associate that movement with the themes of the passage. Note also the year of the passage's publication, 1917. You should remember that the feminist movement had significant early successes in that decade.

Comparison and Contextualization

In these various types of questions, you'll be asked to compare similar themes across different time periods and societies. For example, recall the attempts at reform in Russia, Prussia, and Austria under the enlightened monarchs of the mid-18th century. Each ruler pursued similar yet different courses of action. Each ruler succeeded and failed to different degrees.

You could also be asked to view the same event from different perspectives, because people have vastly different viewpoints on life depending upon their place of birth, class, education, and so on.

Let's use the Magyar passage again.

---

2 ☐ Mark for Review

The author's surprise at the traditional customs of the Magyar community is at least partly attributable to

(A) the more modern behaviors exhibited by women in other parts of the Austro-Hungarian Empire

(B) the nearly uniform adherence to these strict gender roles within the community that she had visited

(C) the expectations that she had developed according to her knowledge of customs in the capital city of Budapest

(D) her background as an American, where the women were already more liberated from traditional gender roles

Here's How to Crack It

Choice (A) is possible but unsupported by any evidence in the passage. Choice (B) also could be true, but it's unclear that the uniform adherence was what caused her surprise. Choice (C) is similarly unsupported; we don't know how much she'd studied about Hungarian traditions. Choice (D) is the remaining answer, and in this case, it's the only one actually supported by the passage. Recall those two small words "as Americans." This indicates her own background, and it's quite conceivable—given the year of publication, the name of her book, and the final sentence of the passage—that she was a proto-feminist.

Creating and Supporting a Historical Argument

The test-makers also want to see that you can support a thesis with evidence. Clearly, this is evident on all of the essays; however, it can also occur on multiple-choice questions, where it will take the form of identifying a piece of evidence that would (or would NOT) support an idea that was present in the text.

Here's an example:

---

3 ☐ Mark for Review

In the passage, Emily Burbank argues that women were on a trajectory that led them from "man's slave to man's equal." What evidence would NOT support this idea?

(A) The passage of various women's suffrage laws in the decade of publication

(B) Photos of working-class women protesting the violent attacks upon public property that were committed by Emmeline Pankhurst in the name of feminism

(C) A letter from a department store manager describing his new squadron of female employees as cooperative, efficient, and punctual

(D) A political cartoon mocking the cult of domesticity

Here's How to Crack It

Notice that none of these answer choices are actually present in the passage. Of the four answer choices, three of them demonstrate that the old view of women was rapidly receding, to be replaced by the more modern equalist view. The correct answer, (B), describes the public reaction against violent tactics used by the more extreme wing of the feminist movement.

———————○———————

Historical Interpretation and Synthesis

The document-based question (DBQ) is the undisputed king of this type of question. However, multiple-choice questions can also, in a general way, test your ability to synthesize information from various parts of your studies.

Here's an example:

———————○———————

4 ☐ Mark for Review

By the 1990s, the idea of women leading lives independent of men, as implied in the passage, had undergone what type of change?

(A) The idea gradually grew more accepted, though slightly dampened by the economic fallout from World War II.

(B) The idea was gradually weakened by a renewed interest in conservative lifestyles.

(C) The idea came to be regarded with suspicion by many of the new immigrants who had arrived in Europe from developing nations.

(D) The idea was entirely supplanted by new ways of looking at gender relations.

Here's How to Crack It

Choice (A) is correct here, as evidenced by present-day daily life of millions of European women, as well as the large number of female heads of state in Europe. However, it depends almost entirely upon your knowledge of everything you've learned about women's history—in your classwork, reading, exams, conversation, even personal experience of Europe (if you've visited).

———————○———————

Finally, here are the answers to the questions that appear in the first part of this chapter:

3: (A)

6: (D)

42: (B)

13: (D)

16: (D)

Chapter 1 Summary

o   Familiarize yourself with the different types of questions that will appear on the multiple-choice section. Be aware that you will see almost an even split between questions on political and diplomatic history, cultural and intellectual trends, and social and economic themes. Tailor your studies accordingly.

o   Look for "big picture" answers. Correct answers on the multiple-choice section confirm important trends in European history. The test will not ask you about weird exceptions that contradict those trends. It also will not ask you about military history. You will not be required to perform miraculous feats of memorization; however, you must be thoroughly familiar with all the basics of European history. There are a lot of them! See our history review in Part V.

o   The multiple-choice questions accompanying a passage do not necessarily have to be about the same time period of the passage. Given the College Board's desire to emphasize general trends rather than specific factoids, there is a lot of "weaving" between eras.

o   Practice. Practice a lot.

Chapter 2
How to Approach
Short Answers
and Essays

THE BASICS

There are three types of essay questions on the AP European History Exam. The first are the short-answer questions. There are three of these (two you must answer and two you can choose between), and they require you to use historical-thinking skills to respond to a primary source, a historian's argument, secondary sources such as data or maps, or general propositions about European history. No thesis is necessary. You have 40 minutes to complete them, and they count for 20 percent of your score.

The second type of essay question is the document-based question (DBQ), which requires you to answer a question based on approximately seven source documents and whatever outside knowledge you have about the subject. There are no choices for this section, besides selecting which documents you will address in your essay. You have 60 minutes, which includes a suggested 15-minute reading period. It counts for 25 percent of your score.

The third type is the long essay. This is more like a typical essay on a history exam in your class. For this essay, you are given three choices, all from different time periods. You are required to pick one and are given 40 minutes to write it. This counts for 15 percent of your score.

We will discuss each of these question types in greater detail in the rest of this chapter. First, let's talk about the basics of writing a successful long AP essay.

WHAT ARE THE AP ESSAY-GRADERS LOOKING FOR?

In conversations with those who grade AP European History Exams, it is clear that what they want above all else is for you to address the question. In some of your classes, you may have gotten into the habit of throwing everything but the kitchen sink into an essay without truly addressing the question at hand. Do not try to fudge your way through the essay. The graders are all experts in history, and you will not be able to fool them into thinking you know more than you actually do.

> **Essay Rule #1**
> Answer the question! Writing down every fact you know won't help you unless your facts address what the question is asking.

It is also very important to focus on the phrasing of the question. Some students are so anxious to get going that they start writing as soon as they know the general subject of the question, and many of these students lose points because their essays do not answer the question being asked. Take, for example, an essay question that asks you to discuss the effects of fascism on the daily life of the average German in the 1930s. If you are an overanxious test-taker, you might start rattling off everything you know about German fascism—the reasons for its electoral success in the years leading up to 1933, the personality cult around Adolf Hitler, the Holocaust, and so on. No matter how well this essay is written, you will lose points for one simple reason—not answering the question!

> **Essay Rule #2**
> Don't just rattle off facts—show that you understand and can effectively analyze historical developments in a clear, cohesive way.

Second, a good essay does more than rattle off facts. Just as the multiple-choice questions seek to draw out certain general principles or the "big picture" of European history, the essay questions seek to do the same. The readers are looking to see that you understand some of the fundamental issues in European history and that you can successfully discuss this material in a coherent manner.

If all this sounds intimidating, read on! There are a few simple things you can do to improve your grade on the AP essays.

REASONS TO BE CHEERFUL

AP graders know that you are given very little time to write the DBQ and the long essay. They also know that there is not enough time to cover the subject matter tested by the question. The fact is, any subject that can appear on the DBQ and free-response question has been written about in numerous very long books.

For the exam, students are expected to write an essay that has a well-developed thesis, provides support for the thesis with specific examples, addresses all parts of the question, and is generally well organized. Therefore, expressing good ideas and presenting valid evidence in support of those ideas are important. Making sure you mention every single relevant piece of historical information is not so important.

Download free-response questions from past exams and sample responses from exam-takers at apcentral. collegeboard.org/courses/ ap-european-history/ exam/past-exam- questions

Also, you should remember that graders are not given a lot of time to read your essays. When they gather to read the exams, each goes through more than 100 per day. No one could possibly give detailed attention to all points in your essay when they are reading at such a fast clip. What they can see in such a brief reading is whether you have something intelligent to say and whether you have the ability to say it well. As many teachers and professors will tell you, when you read several bad essays (and there will be quite a few, even among AP students), you tend to give those that are not completely awful more credit than they possibly deserve. The good news is that you'll get some points just for being prepared and addressing the prompt.

THINGS THAT MAKE ANY ESSAY BETTER

There are two essential components to writing a successful timed essay. First, plan what you are going to write before you start writing! Second, use a number of tried-and-true writing techniques that will make your essay appear well organized, well thought out, and well written. This section is about those techniques.

Before You Start Writing

Read the question carefully. Make note of key words and dates. Then, brainstorm for one or two minutes. Write down everything that comes to mind on your scratch paper. Look at your notes and consider the results of your brainstorming session as you decide what point you will argue in your essay; that argument is going to be your thesis. Tailor your argument to your information, but by no means choose an argument that you know is wrong or with which you disagree. If you do either of these things, your essay might not be the top-scorer you know it can be. Finally, sort the results of your brainstorming. Some of what you wrote down will be "big picture" conclusions, some will be historical facts that can be used as evidence to support your conclusions, and some will be…well, some things are better left unsaid.

Next, make an outline. You should plan to write five paragraphs for each of the essay questions and intend to go into special detail in each of the paragraphs on the DBQ. (Remember: you will have the documents and your outside knowledge to discuss on the DBQ. Plus, you will have more time.) Your first paragraph should contain your thesis statement, in which you directly answer the question in just a few sentences. Your second, third, and fourth paragraphs should each contain one argument (for a total of three) that supports that statement, along with historical evidence to support those arguments. The fifth paragraph should contain your conclusion and reiterate your answer to the question.

Before you start to write your outline, you will have to decide what type of argument you are going to make. Here are some of the classics.

1. Make Three Good Points

This is the simplest strategy. Look at the results of your brainstorming session, and pick the three best points supporting your position. Make each of these points the subject of one paragraph. Make the weakest of the three points the subject of the second paragraph, and save the strongest point for the fourth paragraph. If your three points are interrelated and there is a natural sequence to arguing them, then by all means use that sequence, but otherwise, try to save your strongest point for last. Begin each paragraph by stating one of your three points, and then spend the rest of the paragraph supporting it. Use specific, supporting examples whenever possible. Your first paragraph should state what you intend to argue. Your final paragraph should explain why you have proven what you set out to prove.

2. Make a Chronological Argument

Many questions lend themselves to a chronological treatment. Questions about the development of a political, social, or economic trend can hardly be answered any other way. When you make a chronological argument, look for important transitions and use them to start new paragraphs. A five-paragraph essay about the events leading up to the French Revolution, for example, might start with an introductory discussion of France and the role of royal absolutism. This is also where you should state your thesis. The second paragraph might then discuss the economic crisis that led to the calling of the Estates General. The third paragraph could deal with concern among members of the Third Estate that their interests might not be represented at Versailles, despite the vital economic role they played in 18th-century France. The fourth paragraph could be concerned with the events leading up to and including the king's agreement to meet the three estates as a National Assembly. Your conclusion in this type of essay should restate the essay question and answer it. For example, if the question asks whether the French Revolution was inevitable, you should answer "yes" or "no" in this paragraph.

3. Identify Similarities and Differences

Some questions, particularly on the long essay, ask you to compare events, issues, and/or policies. Very often, the way the question is phrased will suggest the best organization for your essay. Take, for example, a question asking you to compare the impact of three events and issues on the decision to execute the English monarch Charles I in 1649. This question pretty much requires you to start by setting the historical scene prior to the three events/issues you are about to discuss. Continue by devoting one paragraph to each of the three, and conclude by comparing and contrasting the relative importance of each. Again, be sure to answer the question in your final paragraph.

Other questions will provide options. If you are asked to compare Italian and Northern humanism during the Renaissance, you might open with a thesis stating the essential similarity or difference between the two. Then, you could devote one paragraph each to a summary of certain trends and authors, while in the fourth paragraph, you could point out the major similarities and differences between Italian and Northern humanism. In the final paragraph, you could draw your conclusion (for example, "their similarities were more significant than their differences," or vice versa).

Or, using another angle altogether, you might start with a thesis and then use the body of your essay to discuss three pertinent philosophical, religious, or political issues. Then, you might address how Italian humanists dealt with such questions, then discuss the Northern humanists, and ultimately wrap up with an overview of your argument as a conclusion.

4. Use the Straw Man Argument

In this essay-writing technique, choose a couple of arguments that someone taking the position opposite yours would take. State their arguments and then tear them down. Remember that proving your opposition wrong does not mean that you have proved you are correct; that is why you should choose only a few opposing arguments to refute. Summarize your opponent's arguments in paragraph two, dismiss them in paragraph three, and use paragraph four to make the argument for your side. Or, use one paragraph each to summarize and dismiss each of your opponent's arguments, and then make the case for your side in your concluding paragraph. Acknowledging both sides of an argument, even when you choose one over the other, is a good indicator that you understand the complexity of historical issues and that they can be interpreted in more than one way, which is something that teachers and graders like to see.

Conclusion

No matter which format you choose, remember to organize your essay so that the first paragraph addresses the question and states how you are going to answer it. (That is your thesis.) The second, third, and fourth paragraphs should each be organized around a single argument that supports your thesis, and each of these arguments must be supported by historical evidence. Your final paragraph ties the essay up into a nice, neat package. Your concluding paragraph should also answer the question. And remember, stay positive!

Writing Wins
If you follow the guidelines and strategies highlighted in this chapter, you'll be on your way to a high-scoring essay!

As you are writing, observe the following guidelines:

- **Keep sentences as simple as possible.** Long sentences get convoluted very quickly.

- **Throw in a few big words.** But don't overdo it. Remember that good writing does not have to be complicated; some great ideas can be stated simply. *Never* use a word if you are unsure of its meaning or proper usage. A malapropism (misuse of a word) might cost you points.

- **Define your terms.** Most questions require you to use terms that mean different things to different people. One person's "liberal" is another person's "conservative," and yet another person's "extremist." What one person considers "expansionism," another might call "colonialism" or "imperialism." The folks who grade the test want to know what *you* think these terms mean. When you use them, define them. Take particular care to define any such terms that appear in the question. Almost all official College Board materials emphasize this point, so do not forget it. Be sure to define any term that you suspect can be defined in more than one way.

- **Use transition words to show where you are going.** When continuing an idea, use words such as *furthermore*, *also*, and *in addition*. When changing the flow of thought, use words such as *however* and *yet*. Transition words make your essay easier to understand by clarifying your intentions. Better yet, they indicate to the graders that you know how to make a coherent, persuasive argument.

Key Words
Using transition words (such as *however* and *furthermore*) and structural indicators (such as *first, second,* and *finally,* for example) in your essay is a great way to organize your writing and give the reader a sense of where your essay is headed. This will also make your writing seem more coherent and persuasive.

- **Use structural indicators to organize your paragraphs.** Another way to clarify your intentions is to organize your essay around structural indicators. For example, if you are making a number of related points, number them (First…Second…Last…). If you are writing a compare/contrast essay, use the indicators *on the one hand* and *on the other hand*.

- **Stick to your outline.** Unless you get an absolutely brilliant idea while you are writing, do not deviate from your outline. If you do, you risk winding up with an incoherent essay.

- **Try to prove one "big picture" idea per paragraph.** Keep it simple. Each paragraph should make one point and then substantiate that point with historical evidence.

- **Back up your ideas with examples.** Yes, we have said it already, but it bears repeating: do not just throw ideas out there and hope that you are right. You will score big points if you substantiate your claims with facts.

- **Make sure your first and last paragraphs directly address the question.** Nothing will cost you points faster than if the graders decide you did not answer the question. It is always a safe move to start your final paragraph by answering the question. If you have written a good essay, that answer will serve as a legitimate conclusion.

- **Always place every essay into a historical context.** For example, if you are given an essay asking you to compare and contrast Newton's and Einstein's ideas on the universe, don't make it an essay on science. Instead, show how each of these men was a product of his respective time period, and show how their ideas influenced their contemporaries as well as future generations.

- **Take up space.** An overly short essay will hurt you more than one that is overly long.

- **Type efficiently.** Because you will be typing your essay responses on the digital exam, it is important to pay close attention to what you are typing. Re-read your sentences as you type. If you are making any changes, make sure to delete the right word or sentence before you submit your response and move on to the next question.

SHORT-ANSWER QUESTIONS

The short-answer part of Section I involves answering three short-answer questions: the first two will be required, and the last will offer you a choice between two possible prompts. Each question always has three parts (A, B, and C), and the questions always proceed in the following order:

Question 1: Secondary Source Analysis. You will be given either a single secondary source or a set of two secondary sources, generally written by a professional historian. You will be required to read and understand the historical claims in the passage and then come up with some kind of outside evidence to support or refute the claims.

Question 2: Primary Source Analysis. You will be given a primary source, which can be textual or visual. For this part, you will have to answer a series of questions analyzing the source, usually that involve putting the source in context, analyzing its audience, discussing the purpose, or making a claim about the point of view of the source.

Question 3 and 4: No Stimulus. You may choose to answer either question 3 or question 4 (it does not matter which one you choose, and they will be equivalent in difficulty). Each question will focus on a different time period, but the question stems will likely look similar. You will likely need to use one of the historical reasoning processes (comparison, causation, or change/continuity over time) to answer the question.

Time Crunch

Probably the biggest challenge you will have in answering the short-answer questions is the time allotment. You have a total of 40 minutes to answer three different 3-part prompts, which gives you about 13 minutes total for each question (the question without the stimulus will probably take you less time since there is no source you need to analyze for it). Plan on taking about 3 minutes to brainstorm and 10 minutes to answer each one. The name "short-answer question" is well-chosen on this section because your answer should be exactly that: short. This is not a time to develop a thesis-driven essay. Each part of the short-answer question should be answerable in one to two sentences.

Here are the steps you should follow for the short-answer section:

1. **Choose.** It does not matter in what order you answer these short-answer questions. Remember, the first two are required, but you are given all the questions at once. It's best to preview the questions and see which set is easiest for you to answer first. All of them are worth the same number of points, so if you answer the stuff you know first, you will maximize your points.

2. **Analyze.** You need to spend some time analyzing the question to come up with a response. This will be more time-consuming for the questions that have a stimulus like a reading or image attached to them, but even the ones without a stimulus still require some kind of analysis to answer them correctly. Note, in particular, what time period the questions specify. If they ask you for a piece of evidence within a certain time period and yours is even one year outside of what was assigned, you won't be given credit for it.

3. **Write.** Unlike the essay sections, there is very little pre-writing to be done here. Use the question stem to formulate your response, and then include the specific evidence you need to answer the question. The College Board prefers that you label each part of your answer with an A, B, and C to make it clear which part of the question you're referring to. It is not advised to write your response in para- graph form. However, the question always specifies that you must write using complete sentences; bullet points will not be sufficient.

Strategy for the Short-Answer Questions

Every short-answer question is worth a total of 3 points, and you are required to answer 3 of them, totaling to 9 points between all the questions. Even though there are 4 possible ques- tions, you do not get extra points for answering an extra question (and you likely wouldn't have space to do this anyway).

The scoring guide determined by the College Board for each short-answer question is 0 to 3 points:

*   3 points: Response accomplishes all three tasks set by the question
*   2 points: Response accomplishes two of the tasks set by the question
*   1 point: Response accomplishes one of the tasks set by the question
*   0 points: Response accomplishes none of the tasks set by the question

It is important to note that for each part of the question (A, B, and C), there is no partial credit. You either earn the point for the task or you don't.

Many of these questions will resemble the example shown below.

"In England the legal method of executing a witch was by hanging; after death the body was burnt and the ashes scattered. In Scotland, as a rule, the witch was strangled at the stake and the body burned, but there are several records of the culprit being sentenced to burning alive. In France burning alive was the invariable punishment. In cases where popular fury, unrestrained by the law, worked its own vengeance on individuals, horrible scenes occurred; but these were the exception, and, examining only the legal aspect of the subject, it will be found that witches had a fair trial according to the methods of the period, and that their punishment was according to the law."

Source: Margaret Alice Murray, *The Witch-Cult in Western Europe*, 1921

Using the excerpt, respond to parts A, B, and C.

A. Briefly explain two factors that led to a change in the way suspected witches were punished.

B. Briefly explain one thinker who most likely opposed the burning of witches for intellectual reasons.

C. Briefly explain one legal reform that later addressed the excesses and abuses mentioned in the passage.

Here's How to Crack It

1. **Choose**. Most students know about the Salem witch trials (usually through Arthur Miller's *The Crucible*), but those took place in North America. In AP European History, you'll have to connect this subject with something you learned in your course. Possible areas of connection include legal systems, reason, religious traditions, reason versus superstition, and many others. It would make sense to bring in anything related to the Enlightenment, specifically thinkers who emphasized reason. You could connect the Napoleonic Code, since it was a legal framework based on reason. You could also connect it with Francis Bacon, and the contrast between inductive and deductive thought. You might even touch on the Catholic Church's role in this type of activity, pointing at the Church's support of the Spanish Inquisition.

Apply the Strategy!

2. **Analyze**. Make sure you understand what the question is asking. In this case, part A is asking for reasons why the punishment of witches ended. A few would include the jettisoning of custom in favor of reason, the reworking of legal codes in Europe as it moved into the modern era, and the decline of both religion and superstition, especially in the 20th century. Part B asks for a person who would've disapproved of irrational religious customs: take your pick from a variety of Enlightenment thinkers, such as Voltaire or Descartes or David Hume. Part C asks for a legal reform (one that presumably outlawed the punishment of witchcraft), and the obvious one here would be the Napoleonic Code, based on individual civil rights as laid out by John Locke and others.

3. **Write**. Here is a sample response using some of the ideas outlined above, formatted in the way the College Board would prefer you to answer:

> A. Many factors account for a change in the way that witches were punished in European life. One would be the ascendancy of reason as an organizing principle in daily European life, which is evidenced by the power of Enlightenment thinkers such as Rene Descartes and John Locke. Another would be the decline of religion, especially in the nineteenth and twentieth centuries—the Catholic Church had been responsible for a lot of superstitious beliefs over the years.
>
> B. David Hume, a Scottish philosopher of the Enlightenment, often said that he didn't believe in anything except what his five senses told him. To him, this type of input was the only way we could learn anything, which was a belief he called positivism. It would stand to reason that since he couldn't sense evidence of a witch working her black magic upon somebody, he probably wouldn't support her punishment.
>
> C. The Napoleonic Code was enacted in the early nineteenth century in France by the famous dictator Napoleon Bonaparte. It removed the patchwork of medieval legal systems that dotted the French land, ones that had been based on Catholic or local custom. This code replaced them with a consistent universal legal framework based on individual civil liberties. This was the first modern revamping of the law in European history, and it would almost certainly give no support to prosecuting people who supposedly engaged in witchcraft.

THE DOCUMENT-BASED QUESTION (DBQ)

What Is the DBQ?

DBQ stands for "document-based question," an essay question that requires you to interpret primary source documents. (There are typically no more than seven documents in a DBQ.) These documents might come from newspaper articles and editorials, letters, diaries, speeches, excerpts from legislation, political cartoons, charts, or graphs. The documents will *not* include excerpts from current textbooks. Occasionally, one or two of the documents will be taken from something "classic" that you may have seen previously, but generally, the documents will be new to you. However, they will discuss events and ideas with which you should be familiar. All of the documents will pertain to a single subject. The average document is about six lines long, although occasionally you will see something longer.

The 60-minute DBQ is the first part of Section II of the exam. The DBQ session begins with a suggested 15-minute reading period, during which you are allowed to read the documents and take notes on your scratch paper. It is suggested that you spend 15 minutes reading the documents and 45 minutes writing your response. However, you may begin writing your response before the reading period is over.

To give you an idea of what you can expect on your DBQ, let's look at what appeared on a previous test. The question asked students to discuss and evaluate problems in the relationship between the English and Irish in the period from 1800 to 1916. The documents included excerpts from the following:

- A quote from English Prime Minister William Pitt, the creator of the Act of Union of 1801, in which he states that "Ireland must be governed in the English interest"

- A parliamentary speech by a Protestant Irish leader dating from 1805 demanding the continuation of exclusive Protestant political rights within the United Kingdom

- A poem written in 1842 by an Irish Nationalist that speaks of the commonality of interests between Irish Protestants and Catholics

- An article in the English Conservative Party newspaper from 1848 that claims that anything good in Ireland is due to the influence of England, while the Irish have only themselves to blame for all their problems

- A declaration of principles from 1879 by the National Land League that states that the "land of Ireland belongs to the people of Ireland"

- A piece of writing from 1900 by Maud Gonne, founder of the Daughters of Ireland, in which she declares that her organization wants to help establish Irish independence in part through a revival of indigenous Irish culture

- A map showing the distribution in 1901 of Protestants and Roman Catholics in the Irish population

Although you may not know much about the authors of these documents, the tensions between England and Ireland might be familiar to you. In other words, you will not be starting from square one, even when the documents are new to you.

Is There a "Right" Answer to Each DBQ?

No. DBQs are worded in such a way that you can argue any number of positions. In the previous example, the documents provide evidence for various issues that stand at the heart of the Irish-English conflict, such as religious bigotry and questions concerning Home Rule. As long as you support your argument with evidence, you can argue whatever thesis you want.

Graders are supposed to take into account the strength of your argument and the evidence you offer in support of it. In other words, if you forget to mention a good, illustrative historical event but manage to back your point up in some other way, you will not be penalized.

However, the best DBQ responses will contain relevant **outside information**. As you can see from the rubric below, you cannot get the maximum number of points for this essay unless you incorporate outside evidence and knowledge.

Using the Documents *and* Your Knowledge of the Subject

"Your knowledge of the subject" is the outside information. It includes historical facts and ideas that are relevant to the question but that are not mentioned in the DBQ documents. For example, in the England and Ireland DBQ described earlier, any information offered about the writers' backgrounds would count as outside information, as would information concerning, for example, Charles Stuart Parnell and the Land League. Some students make the mistake of throwing everything they know about a subject into their essays, whether or not it pertains to the question. That type of information receives partial credit at best.

HOW IS THE DBQ SCORED?

You can earn up to 7 points on the DBQ. Here's a breakdown of how to do it.

DBQ Scoring Rubric		
Task	**Points Possible**	**Description**
Thesis/Claim	1	To earn this point, the thesis must make a claim that *responds* to the prompt rather than restating or rephrasing the prompt. The thesis must consist of one or more sentences located in one place, either in the introduction or the conclusion.
Contextualization	1	To earn this point, the response must relate the topic of the prompt to broader historical events, developments, or processes that occur before, during, or continue after the time frame of the question. This point is not awarded for merely a phrase or reference.

DBQ Scoring Rubric		
Task	**Points Possible**	**Description**
Evidence	3 total	***Evidence from the Documents*** To earn **1 point**, the response must accurately describe—rather than simply quote—the content from **at least 3 of the documents** to address the **topic** of the prompt. To earn **2 points**, the response must accurately describe—rather than simply quote—the content from **at least 4 documents.** In addition, the response must use the content of the documents to support an **argument** in response to the prompt.
		Evidence Beyond the Documents To earn **1 point**, the response must describe, using more than a phrase of reference, **at least 1 additional piece of specific historical evidence** beyond that found in the documents. This additional evidence must be relevant to an argument about the prompt AND different from the evidence used to earn the point for contextualization.
Analysis and Reasoning	2 total	To earn **1 point**, the response must explain how or why (rather than simply identifying) the document's point of view, purpose, historical situation, or audience is relevant to an argument about the prompt **for each of at least 2 documents sourced**.
		To earn **1 point**, a response must demonstrate a complex understanding of the historical development that is the focus of the prompt, using evidence. This can be accomplished in a variety of ways, such as: • Explaining the nuance of an issue by analyzing multiple variables • Explaining both similarity and difference, or explaining both continuity and change, or explaining multiple causes, or explaining both cause and effect • Explaining relevant and insightful connections within and across periods • Effectively using seven documents to support an argument that responds to the prompt; OR • Explaining how the point of view, purpose, historical situation, and/or audience of at least four documents supports an argument that responds to the prompt; OR • Using documents and evidence beyond the documents effectively to demonstrate a sophisticated understanding of different perspectives relevant to the prompt. A response may demonstrate a complex understanding through effective use of evidence relevant to an argument that addresses the prompt. This may be done in a variety of ways, such as: • Effectively using seven documents to support an argument that responds to the prompt; OR • Explaining how the point of view, purpose, historical situation, and/or audience of at least four documents supports an argument that responds to the prompt; OR • Using documents and evidence beyond the documents effectively to demonstrate a sophisticated understanding of different perspectives relevant to the prompt. This understanding must be part of the argument, not merely a phrase or reference.

Maximum Points: 7

Getting the Points

Here are concrete ways to earn the points for each of the DBQ tasks.

- Study the question carefully; make sure you are writing about what the question is actually asking. Misinterpreting the question is the most common mistake students make and results in a zero on the essay. Also, be careful to provide a thesis that is not a regurgitation of the exam question. Failure to come up with your own thesis will also result in a zero.

- Try to use every document, but no worries if that isn't possible. To earn both evidence points, you only need to use four of the seven—but of course you should always aim for more than that. A good practice is to try to cite all documents minus one. There's almost always one source that will confuse you!

- Show your reader that you understand the basic meaning of the documents. This doesn't mean that there won't possibly be a number of ways of interpreting the document, but make it clear that you understand the connection of your document to the topic at hand.

> **Tone**
> Don't forget about the importance of tone when analyzing the documents, particularly in regard to point of view. Tone can also present a point of view: for example, outrage, contempt, or concern.

- Try to organize your documents into groups and then write each of your body paragraphs about one of your document groups. Start off with a topic sentence and write an analysis of the information drawn from the documents in that group. Use quotes or examples to support your analysis. Just quoting for the sake of quoting is a common error among students. Do not assume that quotations can simply stand on their own without any elaboration. Be sure to show the graders that you understand what the quotation means and use the quote in a manner that furthers your argument.

- The documents may not be fact; they may be opinions. Write the essay in such a way that this is made clear to the reader.
  - Make a big effort to find point of view. Before you read the document, look at who the author is and when they made this statement. Why did the author have this particular point of view? What about the author's background or the time, place, or historical circumstance shaped the writer's outlook on life? Is there an ulterior motive behind the statements made? Do not hesitate to use logic. For example, if the DBQ is about the various views on German unification in the 1860s, why would a German poet, the Italian Foreign Minister, and Otto von Bismarck support unification, while an ethnically French citizen of Alsace-Lorraine, a French socialist politician, and Napoleon III all oppose it?
  - Demonstrate that you are aware that certain documents are more credible than others. A document giving statistics from a government census, for example, is considered more credible than claims made by an editorialist for a party newspaper.

- Have three or more groupings. A group cannot contain just one document, and it's safest to use more than two (in case one is used incorrectly). It is fine to use a document more than once.

- The thesis is not simply restating the question. It must also answer the question and indicate the various groupings into which the essay is divided.

How to Group Documents

How to group will vary according to the question. Some DBQs, for example, may ask you to show how various segments of society view a particular issue; some will ask how views on a particular issue have changed over time. Find the documents that have similar points of view and write about those views; in other words, pro versus con, German versus French, liberal versus conservative, 19th century versus 20th century.

You may group according to the reasons and motives behind the arguments. Your groups might be, for example, individuals influenced by nationalist idealism, individuals representing the power politics of the era, and groups representing the internationalism promoted by Karl Marx.

- Use attribution as much as possible. Attribution means that you give credit to the authors of the statements used. It is also useful to cite the document you are quoting. For example, you might write "British Prime Minister William Gladstone stated in his address to Parliament 'blah-blah-blah' (Document 7)." (Citing the document is not mandatory, but it makes it easier for the reader to see which documents you used.) Never write an essay that says, "In Document 7, such-and-such is said, which is contradicted by Document 5." Your essay is not about the documents; it is about the opinions of the people quoted in the documents.

- To earn the maximum number of points on the DBQ, you now need to bring in outside examples into your essay. This shows a greater historical understanding, so be sure to spend some time during the 15-minute reading period brainstorming a couple examples that go beyond the scope of the documents.

GETTING STARTED ON THE DBQ: READ THE QUESTION

Start by reading the question. Students miss the question because they get anxious during the exam. They panic. They think they are going too slowly. In an effort to speed up, they read half the question, say to themselves, "A-ha! I know what they're going to ask!" and stop reading. Do *not* make this mistake! The question is probably the shortest thing you have to read on the DBQ. Take your time; savor it. Explore its nuances. Essays that address the question fully earn huge bonuses; those essays that ignore parts of the question are doomed to get lower scores.

Here's a sample question:

---

1 ☐ Mark for Review

Using the documents and your knowledge of European history, evaluate the reasons why the year 1848 brought about an explosion of revolutionary activity throughout Europe.

As you look over the question, you should ask yourself two questions.

- Do I have an opinion about this subject?
- What must I discuss in order to write a successful essay?

Of the two questions, the second is much more important. You can construct a position later, after you have gathered the information you want to include in your essay. First, you need to figure out what issues you must address and what data you will use in your discussion.

To begin, you might want to break down the question in a variety of ways. Perhaps focus first on economic issues, such as the economic downturn of the 1840s, a decade that some referred to as the "hungry forties." Then move on to critical political issues, such as a backlash against the repressive nature of politics in the decades after 1848, or the role of nationalism in the revolutions of 1848. Others might find it more useful to discuss events in 1848 on a nation-by-nation basis, beginning with the collapse of the Orléans monarchy in France and moving on to the revolutionary movements in places such as the German states, the Austrian Empire, Italy, and so on. Finally, you must include a discussion of the given documents and your outside knowledge in the essay.

However you decide to approach the question, it is essential that you take your time. Read carefully to make sure that you understand what issues must be addressed in your essay. Then, determine how to organize the information you plan to collect from the documents and from memory for inclusion in the essay.

Organizing Your Essay: Use Grids and Columns

Many DBQs ask you to draw comparisons. For those questions, you can always organize your thoughts about a DBQ in a grid. Drawing a grid helps in seeing all sides of an argument, which is important because DBQ graders will reward you for acknowledging arguments other than your own.

For the DBQ on the revolutions of 1848, you may find it useful to create a grid like the one shown below. Such a grid will allow you to see the complexity of the events of 1848 and how economics, domestic politics, and nationalism all played a role in fanning the flames of revolution across Europe.

	Economics	Politics	Nationalism
France			
Prussia			
Austria			
Italian States			

If a grid doesn't seem to work for a question, you can instead set up column headings. Because every DBQ can be argued from at least two different positions, you can always set up two (or more) columns, designating one for each position. Consider the DBQ about Ireland, which we discussed at the beginning of the chapter. You could create one column, entitled "England," where you can provide examples of English justification for holding onto Ireland. A second column, labeled "Unionist," will give the Unionist argument for remaining part of the United Kingdom, and a third, labeled "Nationalist," can provide their argument for creating an independent Irish state, free from British domination. You might even want a fourth column, for information that you know belongs in your essay but that you cannot yet classify (give that the title "To be classified").

Set Up a Grid
As you remember appropriate outside information and as you read the documents, take notes in the appropriate boxes. When it comes time to write your essay, you might find this to be a good way to compare and contrast because your information will already be organized in a way that makes similarities and differences more obvious.

Good essays do not just flow out of you by accident. They happen when you know what you are going to say before you start writing. Although you can't prepare your entire DBQ essay before you begin writing, given the time constraints, pre-organization and a good outline will get you much closer to that goal.

A Sample Question

Let's take a look at another possible DBQ.

---

1 🔖 Mark for Review

Using the documents and your knowledge of European history, discuss whether Napoleon was a supporter of the ideas espoused in the eighteenth-century Enlightenment or whether he was an enemy of individual liberty.

Your essay will have to show whether you understand certain basic tenets of the Enlightenment and also show your knowledge of the period of Napoleon's domination over France (1799–1815). You will, of course, have to include both analysis of the documents and outside information. Since the question is asking for a basic comparison, you might want to make a simple three-column grid like the one below:

Ideals of Enlightenment	Napoleon pro	Napoleon con

Once you have created your grid, begin organizing information for your essay. At this point, you are probably anxious to start reading the documents. Resist the temptation. You have one more important job to do before you start reading.

Gather Outside Evidence

Most students read the DBQ documents first and *then* try to think of outside evidence and examples to supplement their essays. This is a mistake. The reason? The power of suggestion. Once you have read the documents—a chore that can take from six to eight minutes—those documents will be on your mind. If you read the provided passages and *then* brainstorm outside information, you will invariably think of things you *just* read about, rather than things you *have not* read about.

Plus, reading and processing the documents is a big task. Once you have accomplished that, you should immediately start organizing and writing your essay while the documents are fresh in your mind. So, brainstorm outside evidence *before* you read the documents.

Here's what you should do. Look at your grid or columns and brainstorm. In a separate blank space on your scratch paper (*not* in your grid/columns), write down everything you can think of that relates to the question. Spend just two or three minutes on this task, and then look at what you have written. Enter the useful information into your grid/columns in the appropriate spaces.

Chances are that some of the outside evidence you think of will be mentioned in the documents, which means that it will not be outside information any more. That is no big deal. In fact, you should think of it as something good. If some of what you remembered shows up in the documents, that means you are on the right track toward answering the question!

This is what a brainstorming grid for the Napoleon question might look like.

Ideals of Enlightenment	Napoleon pro	Napoleon con
religious tolerance	• extended religious freedom throughout the empire • concordat	
rational government	• Napoleonic Code • increased centralization of government	
equality of individuals	• favored meritocracy	• created imperial title and a new aristocracy • placed relatives on foreign thrones
freedom from repression		• created secret police censorship • jailed and executed political opponents

Brainstorming Grid
Before you even read the documents, spend 2–3 minutes writing down everything you can think of relating to the question. This mini-brainstorming session will help you organize your thoughts before you begin writing, as well as provide you with some relevant outside information to use in your response.

Read the Documents

After you have gathered outside evidence and examples to include in your essay, you are ready to read the documents. As you read, keep the following things in mind:

- **The order in which documents appear may be helpful.** The documents in the DBQ may appear in chronological order, which could indicate that you are expected to trace the historical development of the DBQ subject. On such questions, you do not have to write an essay that adheres strictly to chronological order, but chronology should play an important part in the development of your thesis. When the documents appear in an order other than chronological, they are usually organized so that you can easily compare and contrast different viewpoints on a particular event or issue. On these questions, one of your main goals should be to draw those same comparisons.

- **Watch for inconsistencies within and among the documents.** The documents will not necessarily agree with one another. In fact, they are almost certain to present different viewpoints on issues, and almost as certain to present conflicting accounts of a historical event. Some documents might even contradict themselves! This is intentional. The exam is testing your ability to recognize these contradictions. You are expected to resolve these conflicts in your essay. To do so, you will have to identify the sources of the documents. (See below.)

- **Identify the sources of the documents.** Why do two accounts of the same event contradict each other? Why do two historians, looking at the same data, come up with dissimilar interpretations of their significance? Is it because the people giving these accounts—the sources of the documents—have different perspectives? Identify the sources and explain why their opinions differ. As you explain these differences, look for the following differences among sources:

  - political ideology
  - class
  - race
  - religion
  - gender

Consider the question on Napoleon. A supporter of the exiled Bourbons would offer a very different point of view on this question than a member of Napoleon's inner circle. The graders will be looking specifically to see if you have tried to explain those differences.

- **Look for evidence that could refute your argument.** Once you have decided what your thesis will be, look through the documents for evidence to support your argument. Not all the documents will necessarily back you up. Some may appear to contradict your argument. Do not simply ignore those documents! As you read them, try to figure out how you might incorporate them into your argument.

Don't Discount Counter-Evidence

Let's consider the Napoleon DBQ. Suppose you argue that Napoleon was a supporter of the ideals of the Enlightenment. Now suppose that one of the documents presents evidence that Napoleon kidnapped a Bourbon prince living in exile in one of the German states and then had him killed. You might be tempted to pretend that the document does not exist. However, you will be better off if you incorporate the document into your essay. By doing this, you are acknowledging that this historical issue, like all historical issues, is complex. This acknowledgment is good. AP essay-graders are instructed to look for evidence that you understand that history has no simple answers, and to reward you for it.

As you read the documents, be aware that each one holds a few morsels of information for your essay. Do not fixate on any one document, but at the same time, do not ignore any. Also, as you read the documents, take note of any outside information that the document reminds you of and enter it into your grid/columns.

DRILL

Below is a "mini-DBQ" (it has only four documents, which is fewer than you will see on the actual exam). Read through the documents, taking notes on your scratch paper.

---

1 ⚑ Mark for Review

Using the documents and your knowledge of European history, evaluate the roles of women in the religious conflicts of the sixteenth century.

Document 1

Source: A printed pamphlet, circa 1525, addressed to Katharina von Bora, the wife of Martin Luther.

Woe to you, poor fallen woman, not only because you have passed from light to darkness, from the cloistered holy religion into a damnable shameful life, but also that you have gone from the grace to the disfavor of God, in that you have left the cloister in lay clothes and have gone to Wittenberg like a chorus girl. You are said to have lived with Luther in sin.

Document 2

Source: Letter written in 1523 by Argula von Grumbach, the daughter of a Bavarian noble, to the faculty of the University of Ingolstadt after they had forced a young member of the teaching staff to recant his belief in Luther's theology.

What have Luther and Melanchthon taught save the Word of God? You have condemned them. You have not refuted them. Where do you read in the Bible that Christ, the apostles, and the prophets imprisoned, banished, burned, or murdered anyone? You tell us that we must obey the magistrates. Correct. But neither the pope, nor the Kaiser, nor the princes have any authority over the Word of God.

Document 3

Source: Examination of Elizabeth Dirks before a Catholic court in 1549 on the charge of being an Anabaptist.

Examiner: We understand that you are a teacher and have led many astray. We want to know who your friends are.

Elizabeth: I am commanded to love the Lord my God and honor my parents. Therefore I will not tell you who my parents are. That I suffer for Christ is damaging to my friends.

Examiner: What do you believe about the baptism of children, seeing that you have had yourself baptized again?

Elizabeth: No my Lords, I have not had myself baptized again. I have been baptized once on my faith, because it is written, "Baptism belongs to believers."

Document 4

Source: *The Way of Perfection* by St. Teresa of Avila (1515–1582), a prominent Catholic reformer and author of spiritual books.

At about this time there came to my notice the harm and havoc that were being wrought in France by these Lutherans and the way in which their unhappy sect was increasing. I felt that I would have laid down a thousand lives to save a single one of all the souls that were being lost there. And, seeing that I was a woman, and a sinner, I determined to do the little that was in me—namely, to follow the evangelical counsels as perfectly as I could, and to see that these few nuns who are here should do the same.

Here's How to Crack It

Here you are provided with four different examples of the ways in which women participated in the religious disputes of the 16th century.

Document 1 may initially look somewhat confusing until you take a moment to think about the source: it is a pamphlet addressed to the wife of Martin Luther. If you forgot about the story of Katharina von Bora and her marriage to Luther, you're in luck, since the document provides you with some background. You should be aware, however, that the position taken in the pamphlet is entirely hostile to both Katharina and Martin Luther. Therefore, it does not take much of a leap of faith to conclude that the document was written by a Catholic who was horrified by Katharina's leaving the cloistered life and by her marriage to Luther.

Document 2 reveals another side of the participation of women in the religious debates of the Reformation. It is from a woman who actively participated in such questions by championing a young Lutheran teacher. The author, Argula von Grumbach, will probably not be a familiar name to you, but you can see from the document that she was fully aware of the major issues of the conflict, such as Luther's emphasis on the Bible as the sole source of faith and his rejection of papal authority. Challenging the authorities on behalf of this young man is an interesting example of open defiance, something not usually expected from women in the 16th century.

Document 3 is part of a transcript of a trial of a woman who was accused of being an Anabaptist. Don't panic if you have forgotten what the Anabaptists believed in, since the document explains that Anabaptists believed in adult baptism. As the accused woman Elizabeth Dirks says, "Baptism belongs to believers," implying that it's not appropriate for unaware infants. There are other things that you can pull from this document. One of the accusations that the Catholic authorities mentioned is that she was a teacher, albeit one who was leading people astray. Considering that women were rarely literate in this age, her profession is something to be noted, as should her intense loyalty to her friends, whom she refuses to betray by revealing their presence at her rebaptism. She must have been aware that such a refusal would bring her additional torture, the typical means of extracting a confession.

Document 4 can be compared with Document 2, because, once again, a woman actively threw herself into the religious debates of the period. This time, however, our author, St. Teresa of Avila, used her pen not to challenge the Catholic Church but to defend it. She revealed that she found herself as a defender of the Church in response to Lutheranism taking root in France. She also grappled with the question of how, as a woman, she could best serve her church. She would have liked, if the opportunity arose, to "have laid down a thousand lives to save a single one of all the souls that were being lost there," but since that cheery prospect was not open to her, she had to find some other outlet for her anger. So she organized the nuns who still remained in the monastery and recommitted them to the Catholic Church.

That's it for the documents. Now, formulate a thesis, figure out how and where to fit all your information into your argument, and write an essay. Relax. It is easier than it sounds.

Develop a Thesis

Before you decide on your thesis, *go back and read the question one more time!* Make sure that your thesis addresses all the pertinent aspects of the question. Your thesis should not simply restate the prompt; it also needs to answer the question and pose an argument or position.

For this sample question, your thesis might read as follows:

> Women played an active role in the religious debates of the sixteenth century, both as supporters of a break with Rome and as defenders of the Catholic Church.

You can then bring in the variety of experiences revealed in the four sources to buttress this thesis.

Create an Outline

Need More Help on Essays?
We've got just the book for that! *How to Write Essays for Standardized Tests* contains advice and examples of best practices on an assortment of AP Exams, plus the ACT and others!

At this point, you should still have time left in the suggested 15-minute reading period. Create an outline with one Roman numeral for each paragraph. Decide on the subject of each paragraph and the information you will include in each paragraph. Do not rely on your grid/columns if you do not have to. The grid/columns are good for organizing your information but are less efficient for structuring an essay.

Write Your Essay

The most important advice when writing your essay is to stay confident. Everyone else taking the test, all across the country, is at least as nervous about it as you are.

THE LONG ESSAY QUESTION

What Is the Long Essay?

The long essay consists of three questions, and you must choose *one* to answer. The long essay is found in Section II, immediately following the DBQ. It's the final portion of the exam, and you do not get a break before it begins. You'll have 40 minutes to write this essay.

The long essay, like the DBQ, has no single "correct" answer. Unlike the DBQ, though, the questions are not accompanied by documents; *everything* you include in your essay response will be outside information. Also, because you have less time to plan and write the long essay, it will likely be shorter than your DBQ response. A clear, relevant thesis, accompanied by an organized essay laying out supporting evidence and solid examples, should earn a good score. Here are examples of the types of questions you might see on this section.

---

2   ☐ Mark for Review

Evaluate the extent to which Renaissance humanism and its effects on the concept of the individual can be considered a pivotal point in European history.

3 ⬚ Mark for Review

Evaluate the extent to which the growth of industrialization in Great Britain in the first half of the nineteenth century C.E. can be considered a pivotal point in European history.

As you can see, the long essay allows you to expound upon the themes and topics you learned in the course to craft a historical argument.

Long Essay Scoring Rubric		
Task	**Points Possible**	**Description**
Thesis/Claim	1	To earn this point, the thesis must make a claim that responds to the prompt (rather than restating or rephrasing the prompt) with a historically defensible thesis/claim that establishes a line of reasoning. The thesis must consist of one or more sentences located in one place, either in the introduction or the conclusion.
Contextualization	1	To earn this point, the response must relate the topic of the prompt to broader historical events, developments, or processes that occur before, during, or continue after the time frame of the question. This point is not awarded for merely a phrase or reference.
Evidence	2 total	To earn **1 point**, the response must identify specific historical examples of at least **two pieces** of evidence relevant to the topic of the prompt. To earn **2 points**, the response must use at least **two pieces** of specific and relevant examples of historical evidence to support an **argument** in response to the prompt.
Analysis and Reasoning	2 total	To earn **the first point**, the response must demonstrate the use of historical reasoning (e.g., comparison, causation, and change and/or continuity over time) to frame or structure an argument, although the reasoning might be uneven or imbalanced. To earn **the second point**, a response must demonstrate a complex understanding of the historical development that is the focus of the prompt, using evidence. This can be accomplished in a variety of ways, such as: • Explaining the nuance of an issue by analyzing multiple variables • Explaining both similarity and difference, or explaining both continuity and change, or explaining multiple causes, or explaining both cause and effect • Explaining relevant and insightful connections within and across periods • Explaining how multiple pieces of specific and relevant evidence (at least **four**) support a nuanced or complex argument that responds to the prompt; OR • Using evidence effectively to demonstrate a sophisticated understanding of different perspectives relevant to the prompt. A response may demonstrate a complex or nuanced understanding through effective use of evidence relevant to an argument that addresses the prompt. This may be done in a variety of ways, such as: • Explaining how multiple pieces of specific and relevant evidence (at least four) support a nuanced or complex argument that responds to the prompt; OR • Using evidence effectively to demonstrate a sophisticated understanding of different perspectives relevant to the prompt. This understanding must be part of the argument, not merely a phrase or reference.

Maximum Points: 6

You can earn a total of 6 points on the long essay. Here's the breakdown:

Which Question to Choose

Choose the question about which you know the most specific details, *not* the one that looks easiest at first glance. The more you know about the subject, the better your final grade will be.

How to Write the Essay

Since we have already covered this information earlier in this chapter, here are brief directions for how to structure your essay.

- Read the question and analyze it.
- Assess your information and devise a thesis.
- If you have time, write a quick outline.
- Write your essay.

A Final Note

This section is short, not because the long essay question is unimportant, but because we have already discussed in this chapter what you need to know to write successful AP essays. Many students are tempted to ease up when they finish the DBQ because (1) it's so challenging, (2) they're tired, and (3) the test is three-fourths of the way over. Do not make that mistake. Reach down for that last bit of energy like a long-distance runner coming into the home stretch. After all, this is where you can truly shine—with no stimulus material whatsoever, the more you recall, the more you will shine. You can take it easy *after* you finish this final essay.

Chapter 2 Summary

The Basics

- Read questions carefully. Be sure you are answering the question that is asked. You must answer the question in order to get full credit.

- Do not start writing until you have brainstormed, chosen a thesis, and written an outline. Follow your outline. Stick to one important idea per paragraph. Support your ideas with historical evidence.

- Do not write in long, overly complex sentences. Toss in a couple of big words you know you will not misuse. When in doubt, stick to simple syntax and vocabulary.

- Use transition words to indicate continuity of thought and changes in the direction of your argument.

- Provide a strong historical context. You may be faced with questions focusing on science, economics, philosophy, literature and art, religion, and other disciplines. Always remember this is a history exam.

- Remember also that this is a European history exam (not an American history exam). So, for example, if you get a question on technological changes in the 19th century, you should focus on Marconi, Siemens, or Bessemer, not on Edison or Bell. Similarly, on Cold War questions, don't avoid the United States, but have your answer reflect Europe's situation as much as possible.

- Study the question. Make sure you understand what it is asking you to write about. Address all parts of the questions. If it asks for "social, political, and economic changes," make sure you discuss all three. If you cannot address the whole question, either choose another question or try your best with the knowledge you have. If you don't know anything about the social impact, then try to use logic—how would something like this affect society?

- Try for at least two or three concrete facts to support each of your themes or assertions.

Short Answers

o The short-answer questions follow the multiple-choice questions in Section I. Spend a few minutes reading the questions carefully, and answer them based on the order of how well you understand them.

o For Questions 3 and 4, choose the topic that is easier for you to answer. The graders won't be more impressed if you pick a tougher question.

o Make sure your responses are clear, succinct, and fully address all parts of the questions. Do NOT write full paragraphs here, and label each part of your answer. Wasted words are wasted time on this section.

o Be mindful of your time. You will only be able to answer this section after the multiple-choice part has ended, and before the essays have begun, meaning you cannot split time for this section with any other part of the exam. If you are spending more than 15 minutes on a single question, it is time to move on to another.

The DBQ

o The DBQ consists of an essay question and approximately seven historical documents. Most likely, the documents will not be ones that you have seen before, but they will all relate to major historical events and ideas you should be familiar with. You'll have 60 minutes to prepare and write your essay. It is suggested that you spend 15 minutes reading the documents and 45 minutes writing your response.

o There is no single "correct" answer to the DBQ. DBQs are framed so that they can be successfully argued from many different viewpoints.

o Read the essay question carefully. Make note of important words and phrases. Once you understand the question, create a grid or columns in which to organize your notes on the essay.

o Before you start reading the documents, brainstorm about the question. This way, you will gather additional evidence before you immerse yourself in the documents.

○ Read the documents. Pay attention to contradictions and connections within and among the documents, and also notice who is speaking and what sociopolitical tradition they represent. If you have decided on a thesis, keep an eye out for information that might refute your thesis, and be prepared to address it in your essay.

○ Decide on a thesis; then write an outline for your essay.

○ Use the provided historical background sparingly in your essay.

○ Your introductory paragraph should set the historical scene and include a thesis that takes a position on the issue posed by the question.

○ Try to include as many of the documents as you can in your essay.

○ When you write the essay, do not be concerned with literary merit. Be sure your essay is logically organized, easy to understand, and always focused on the thesis.

○ Stay positive. Do not panic. Everyone else is as nervous as you are.

The Long Essay Question

○ The long-essay portion of the exam consists of three prompts. You must answer one of them.

○ Choose the question about which you know the most specific details, not the one that looks easiest.

○ Study each question carefully. Make sure you are answering the question exactly. If you misinterpret a question and write about something other than what the prompt asks, you will receive a 0 for that question.

○ Note all key words. Consider the dates given; they are clues to what you are to write about. Suppose a question asks, "How did the nature of the Soviet regime change after 1924?" The question is in fact asking you to show the differences between the leadership and policies of Lenin and Stalin.

○ Do not ignore any part of the question. If a question asks you to "Compare and contrast the different personalities and leadership styles of Charles V, Holy Roman Emperor, and his son Philip II, King of Spain, and how these influenced the methods they used to counter the Protestant movement," be sure to address personalities, leadership styles, and the ways these influenced policy toward the

Reformation. If you find yourself in a situation in which you do not know enough to answer a part of the question, do not ignore that part. Use the historical knowledge you have, combined with logic, to guess at the answer.

o Decide on a thesis, and then write an outline for your essay.

o Follow your outline. Stick to one important idea per paragraph. Provide concrete examples to support the point you are making. We recommend at least two examples per issue.

o Stay focused on the question, and don't go off on tangents. Write only about what the question asks, and carefully choose the evidence to support it. You have very little time to throw together these essays. Do not spend time including information that isn't directly relevant.

o Your introductory paragraph is more than just your thesis statement. It should also set the historical scene (time, place, historical situation) so that the reader can more clearly understand what your essay is about. In your thesis, do not simply restate the question; be sure to also *answer* the question. The thesis tells the reader what the main points of your essay are.

o Do not be concerned with literary merit. Be sure your essay is logically organized, easy to understand, and *always focused on the thesis*. Each paragraph should have a topic sentence, and the essay should close with a concluding paragraph.

o Keep a close watch on the time. Remember that 40 minutes for an essay is less time than you may think. Be sure to pace yourself by taking no more than 5 minutes to brainstorm and outline, and by working steadily through the essay. Remember that the style of the sentences is less important than the quality of the ideas.

o Stay positive. Do not panic. Everyone else is at least as nervous as you are.

Chapter 3
Using Time Effectively to Maximize Points

BECOMING A BETTER TEST-TAKER

Very few students stop to think about how to improve their test-taking skills. Most assume that if they study hard, they will test well, and if they do not study, they will do poorly. Most students continue to believe this even after experience teaches them otherwise. For example, have you ever studied really hard for an exam and then blown it on test day? Have you ever aced an exam for which you thought you weren't well prepared? Most students have had one, if not both, of these experiences. The lesson should be clear: factors other than your level of preparation influence your final test score. This chapter provides some insights that will help you perform better on the AP European History Exam as well as on other tests.

PACING AND TIMING

A big part of scoring well on an exam is working at a consistent pace. The worst mistake made by inexperienced or unsavvy test-takers is that they come to a question that stumps them, and rather than just skip it, they panic and stall. Time stands still when you're working on a question you cannot answer, and it is not unusual for students to waste five minutes on a single question (especially a question involving a graph or the word EXCEPT) because they are too stubborn to cut their losses. It is important to be aware of how much time you have spent on a given question and on the section you are working. There are several ways to improve your pacing and timing for the test:

- **Know your average pace**. While you prepare for your test, try to gauge how long you take on 5, 10, or 20 questions. Knowing how long you spend, on average, per question will help you identify how many questions you can answer effectively, and how best to pace yourself for the test.

- **Have a clock-checking strategy.** The Bluebook testing app provides a count-down clock that you can view or hide. We recommend that you keep it hidden as your default, because constantly checking the clock is, in itself, a waste of time and can be distracting. Devise a plan. Try checking the clock after every 15 or 20 questions to see if you are keeping the correct pace or whether you need to speed up; this will ensure that you're cognizant of the time but will not permit you to fall into the trap of dwelling on it.

- **Know when to move on.** Since all questions are scored equally, investing an appreciable amount of time on a single question is inefficient and can potentially deprive you of the chance to answer easier questions later on. If you are able to eliminate answer choices, do so; but don't worry about picking a random answer and moving on if you cannot find the correct answer. Remember: tests are like marathons; you do best when you work through them at a steady pace. You can always come back to a question you don't know. When you do, very often you will find that your previous mental block is gone, and you will wonder why the question perplexed you the first time around (as you gleefully move on to the next question). Even if you still don't know the answer, you will not have wasted valuable time that you could have spent on questions that you found easier.

- **Be selective.** You don't have to do any of the questions in a given section in order. If you are stumped by an essay or multiple-choice question, skip it or choose a different one. In the section below, you will see that you may not have to answer every question correctly to achieve your desired score. Select the questions or essays that you can answer, and work on them first. This will make you more efficient and give you the greatest chance of getting the most questions correct.

- **Use Process of Elimination on multiple-choice questions.** Many times, one or more answer choices can be eliminated. Every answer choice that can be eliminated increases the odds that you will answer the question correctly. The chapter on multiple-choice questions addresses strategies to find these incorrect answer choices and increase your odds of getting the question correct.

Remember: when all the questions on a test are of equal value, no one question is that important; your overall goal for pacing is to answer the most questions correctly. Finally, you should set a realistic goal for your final score. In the next section, we will break down how to achieve your desired score.

GETTING THE SCORE YOU WANT

Depending on the score you need, it may be in your best interest not to try to work through every question. Check with the schools to which you are applying to see what score you need to earn credit.

AP Exams in all subjects no longer include a "guessing penalty" for every incorrect answer. Instead, students are assessed only on the total number of correct answers. It is really important to remember that if you are running out of time, you should answer every question before the time for the multiple-choice section is up. Even if you don't plan to spend a lot of time on every question and even if you have no idea what the correct answer is, you need to fill something in.

TEST ANXIETY

Everybody experiences anxiety before and during an exam. To a certain extent, test anxiety *can* be helpful. Some people find that they perform more quickly and efficiently under stress. If you have ever pulled an all-nighter to write a paper and ended up doing good work, you know the feeling.

However, *too much stress* is definitely a bad thing. Hyperventilating during the test, for example, almost always leads to a lower score. If you find that you stress out during exams, here are a few preemptive actions you can take.

- **Take a reality check**. Evaluate your situation before the test begins. If you have studied hard, remind yourself that you are well prepared. Remember that many others taking the test are not as well prepared, and (in your classes, at least) you are being graded against them, so you have an advantage. If you didn't study, accept the fact that you will probably not ace the test. Make sure you get to every question you know something about. Don't stress out or fixate on how much you don't know. Your job is to score as high as you can by maximizing the benefits of what you do know. In either scenario, it is best to think of a test as if it were a game. How can you get the most points in the time allotted to you? Always answer questions you can answer easily and quickly before you answer those that will take more time.

- **Try to relax.** Slow, deep breathing works for almost everyone. Close your eyes, take a few slow, deep breaths, and concentrate on nothing but your inhalation and exhalation for a few seconds. This is a basic form of meditation, and it should help you to clear your mind of stress and, as a result, concentrate better on the test. If you have ever taken yoga classes, you probably know some other good relaxation techniques. Use them when you can. (Obviously, anything that requires leaving your seat and, say, assuming a handstand position won't be allowed by any but the most free-spirited proctors.)

- **Eliminate as many surprises as you can.** Make sure you know where the test will be given, when it starts, what types of questions are going to be asked, and how long the test will take. You don't want to be worrying about any of these things on test day or, even worse, after the test has already begun.

The best way to avoid stress is to study both the test material and the test itself. Congratulations! By buying or reading this book, you are taking a major step toward a stress-free AP European History Exam.

REFLECT

Respond to the following questions:

- How long will you spend on multiple-choice questions?

- How will you change your approach to multiple-choice questions?

- What is your multiple-choice guessing strategy?

- How much time will you spend on the DBQ? The long essay? The short-answer questions?

- What will you do before you begin writing an essay?

- How will you change your approach to the essays?

- Will you seek further help outside of this book (such as a teacher, tutor, or AP Students) on how to approach multiple-choice questions and essays, or determine a pacing strategy?

Part V
Content Review for the AP European History Exam

HOW TO USE THE CHAPTERS IN THIS PART

You may need to come back to the following content chapters more than once. Your goal is to obtain proficiency with the content you are missing, and a single read of a chapter may not be sufficient. At the end of each chapter, reflect on the following questions to help you determine whether or not you truly have grasped the content of that chapter:

Don't forget your digital flashcards!

Scan the QR code below to register your book and access digital flashcards of select Key Terms from each chapter in this section.

- For which content topics discussed in this chapter do you feel you have achieved sufficient understanding to answer multiple-choice questions correctly?

- For which content topics discussed in this chapter do you feel you have achieved sufficient understanding to discuss effectively in an essay or short answer?

- For which content topics discussed in this chapter do you feel you need more work before you can answer multiple-choice questions correctly?

- For which content topics discussed in this chapter do you feel you need more work before you can discuss effectively in an essay or short answer?

- What parts of this chapter are you going to re-review?

- Will you seek further help outside of this book (such as a teacher, tutor, or AP Students) on any of the content in this chapter—and, if so, on what content?

Chapter 4
Units 1–2:
The Renaissance
to the Wars
of Religion
(c. 1450–1648)

THE RENAISSANCE: AN OVERVIEW

Intellectuals and artists of the 15th and 16th centuries believed that they were part of a new golden age. **Georgio Vasari**, a 16th-century painter, architect, and writer, used the Italian word *rinascita*, meaning **"rebirth,"** to describe the era in which he lived. Vasari and other artists and intellectuals believed that their achievements owed nothing to the backwardness of the Middle Ages and instead were directly linked to the glories of the Greek and Roman world. History tells us that they were kidding themselves. The **Renaissance** artisans owed far more to the cultural and intellectual achievements of the medieval world than they cared to acknowledge. Nevertheless, the Renaissance was a time in which significant contributions were made to Western civilization, with particular gains in literature, art, philosophy, and political and historical thought. Our modern notion of **individualism** was also born during the Renaissance, as people sought to receive personal credit for their achievements, opposed to the medieval ideal of all glory going to God.

CED Alignment
Throughout Part V, look for sidebars indicating the unit number and topic from the Course and Exam Description (CED) associated with each section.

These intellectual and artistic developments first took place in the vibrant world of the Italian **city-states**. Eventually, the invention of the **printing press** in the mid-15th century allowed these cultural trends to spread to other parts of Europe, which resulted in the creation of the **Northern Renaissance** movement. The Italian Renaissance writers were primarily interested in secular concerns, but in the north of Europe, the Renaissance dealt with religious concerns and ultimately helped lay the foundation for the movement known as the **Protestant Reformation**.

THE ITALIAN CITY-STATES

CED 1.2
Italian Renaissance

The city-states of Renaissance Italy were at the center of Europe's economic, political, and cultural life throughout the 14th and 15th centuries. During the Middle Ages, the towns of northern Italy were nominally under the control of the **Holy Roman Empire.** Residents, however, were basically free to decide their own fate, which resulted in a tremendously vibrant—and at times violent—political existence. The old nobility, whose wealth was based on land ownership, often conflicted with a new class of merchant families who had become wealthy in the economic boom times of the 12th and 13th centuries. Both groups had to contend with an urban underclass, known as the *popolo*, or "the people," who wanted their own share of the wealth and political power.

In Florence in 1378, the *popolo* expressed their dissatisfaction with the political and economic order by staging a violent struggle against the government that became known as the **Ciompi Revolt**. The revolt shook Florence to its very core and resulted in a brief period in which the poor established tenuous control over the government.

This struggle reverberated in the other city-states throughout Italy. In Milan, the resulting social tensions led to the rise of a tyrant, or *signor*, and the city eventually came to be dominated by the family of a mercenary *(condottiero)* named Sforza. Florence and Venice remained republics after the revolt, but a few wealthy families dominated them. The most noteworthy of these families, the **Medici**, used the wealth gained from banking to establish themselves first as the behind-the-scenes rulers of the Florentine republic and later as hereditary dukes of the city.

The Italian States During the Renaissance

The internal tensions within the city-states were matched by external rivalries as the assorted city-states were engaged in long-term warfare among themselves. By the mid-15th century, these external wars had effectively narrowed the numerous city-states of the medieval age to just a few dominant states—Florence, Milan, and Venice in the north, the **papal states** in central Italy, and the Kingdom of Naples in southern Italy.

In addition to every city-state's internal and external tensions that may have helped stir the creative energy that was so important to the Renaissance, economic factors were also a significant energy-creating agent. The Italian city-states were generally more economically vibrant than the rest of western Europe, with merchants carrying Italian wool and silk to every part of the continent, and with Italian bankers providing loans for money-hungry European monarchs. Wealthy Italian merchants became important **patrons** of the arts and insisted on the development of secular art forms, such as portraiture, that would represent them and their accumulated wealth to the greatest effect.

Geography also played a role in the vibrant cultural life of the Italian Renaissance. Italy's central location in the Mediterranean was ideal for creating links between the Greek culture of the East and the Latin culture of the West. Additionally, southern Italy had been home to many Greek colonies and later served as the center for the Roman Empire. In essence, classical civilization had never totally disappeared from the Italian mainland, even following the collapse of the western half of the Roman Empire in the 5th century.

HUMANISM

"Man is the measure of all things."
—proto-humanist Protagoras,
5th century B.C.E.

Humanism is a highly debated term among historians. Most would characterize it not as representing a particular philosophical viewpoint but rather as a program of study, including rhetoric and literature, based on what students in the classical world (c. 500 B.C.E. to 500 C.E.) would have studied. **Francesco Petrarch** (1304–1374) is often considered the founder of humanism. Petrarch became dissatisfied with his career as a lawyer and set about to study literary classics. It was Petrarch who coined the phrase **"Dark Ages"** (c. 400–900) to denote what he thought was the cultural decline that took place following the collapse of the Roman world in the 5th century.

The Italian Renaissance and the Greek Revival

The revival of ancient Greek culture is one of the most important aspects of the Italian Renaissance. It allowed Westerners to become acquainted with that part of the classical heritage that had been lost during the Middle Ages—most significantly the writings of the ancient Greek philosopher Plato (427–348 B.C.E.). In particular, these writers were fascinated by Plato's belief that ideals such as beauty and truth exist beyond the ability of our senses to recognize them, and that we can train our minds to make use of our ability to reason to get beyond the limits imposed by our senses. This positive Platonic view of human potential is found in one of the most famous passages from the Renaissance, **Pico della Mirandola's** *Oration on the Dignity of Man*. In addition, the **Florentine Platonic Academy**, sponsored by Cosimo d'Medici, merged platonic philosophy with Christianity to create **Neoplatonism**. A closely related school of thought was hermeticism, a pantheistic philosophy stating that God is in everything and that humans were created divine but chose to live in a material world. It was associated with astrology, alchemy, and the Kabbalah—all important parts of Italian Renaissance intellectual life.

While literate in *medieval* Latin from his study of law, Petrarch learned *classical* Latin as preparation to study these important literary works. In a task that was to become exceedingly important during the Renaissance, Petrarch sought classical texts that had been largely unknown during the Middle Ages. It was common in the Middle Ages to become familiar with classical works not by directly reading the original manuscripts but rather by reading secondary commentaries about the works. Petrarch set out to read the originals and quickly found himself engaged with such works as the letters of Cicero, an important politician and philosopher whose writings provide an account of the collapse of the Roman Republic. Cicero was a brilliant Latin stylist. To write in the Ciceronian style became the stated goal of Petrarch and those humanists who followed in his path.

Although his contemporaries accused him of turning to the pagan culture of ancient Greece and Rome, Petrarch—despite his fascination with classical culture—did not reject Christianity. Instead, he argued for the universality of the ideas of the classical age. Petrarch contended that classical works, although clearly written by pagans, still contained lessons that were applicable to his own Christian age.

Petrarch's work served as inspiration to a group of wealthy young Florentines known as the **civic humanists**. They viewed Cicero's involvement in political causes as justification to use their own classical education for the public good. They did this by serving Florence as diplomats or working in the chancellery office, where official documents were written. They also went beyond Petrarch's achievements by studying a language that had almost been completely lost in western Europe—classical Greek.

Renaissance humanist scholarship branched out in a number of different directions. Some writers strove to describe the ideal man of the age. In **Castiglione's** *The Courtier* (1528), such a person would be a man who knew several languages, was familiar with classical literature, and was also skilled in the arts—what we might label today as a "Renaissance Man" (or *l'uomo universale*). Other contributions were made in the new field of critical textual analysis. **Lorenzo Valla** was one of the critical figures in this area. Working in the Vatican libraries, he realized that languages can tell a history all their own. In 1440, he proved that the *Donation of Constantine*, a document in which Constantine, the first Christian Emperor, turned control of the western half of his empire over to the papacy, could not have been written by Constantine. Valla noticed that the word *fief* was used by Constantine in describing the transfer of authority to the pope, a word that Valla knew was not in use until the 8th century, around four hundred years after Constantine's death. In another work that influenced the humanists in northern Europe, Valla took his critical techniques to the Vulgate Bible, the standard Latin Bible of the Middle Ages, and showed that its author, Jerome, had mistranslated a number of critical passages from the Greek sources.

Women were also affected by the new humanist teachings. Throughout the Middle Ages, there were women, very often attached to nunneries, who learned to read and write. During the Renaissance, an increasing number of wealthy, secular women picked up these skills. The humanist scholar **Leonardo Bruni** even went so far as to create an educational program for women, but tellingly left out of his curriculum the study of rhetoric or public speech, critical parts of men's education, because women had no outlet to make use of these skills. **Christine de Pisan**, an Italian who was the daughter of the physician to the French King Charles V, received a fine humanist education. She wrote *The City of Ladies* (1405) to counter the popular notion that women were inferior to men and incapable of making moral choices. Pisan wrote that women have to carve out their own space or move to a "City of Ladies" in order for their abilities to be allowed to flourish. (Virginia Woolf would later espouse this idea in her early 20th-century work, *A Room of One's Own*.)

RENAISSANCE ART

It is arguably in the area of fine arts that the Renaissance made its most notable contribution to Western culture. A number of different factors drove Renaissance art. In a reflection of the shift toward individualism, Renaissance artists were now considered to be important individuals in their own right, whereas in the Middle Ages they toiled as anonymous craftsmen. These artists sought prestige and money by competing for the patronage of secular individuals such as merchants and bankers. These wealthy individuals wanted to sponsor art that would glorify their achievements rather than tout the spiritual message that was at the heart of medieval art.

Classical Motifs in Renaissance Art
In architecture, one can see the increasing influence of classical motifs, such as the use of simple symmetrical decorations and classical columns. Perhaps the most noteworthy architectural achievement of the Early Renaissance period was **Filippo Brunelleschi's** dome over the Cathedral of Florence, the first dome to be completed in western Europe since the collapse of the Roman Empire.

These patrons demanded a more naturalistic style, which was aided by the development of new artistic techniques. These included the rejection of the old practice of hierarchical sealing, in which figures in a composition were sized in proportion to their spiritual significance. In the Middle Ages, painting consisted of **fresco** on wet plaster or tempera on wood. In the 15th century, oil painting, which developed in the north of Europe, became the dominant method in Italy. Artists also began to make use of *chiaroscuro*, the use of contrasts between light and dark, to create three-dimensional images. Perhaps the most important development was in the 1420s with the discovery of **single-point perspective,** a style in which all elements within a painting converge at a single point in the distance, allowing artists to create more realistic settings for their work.

The end of the 15th century marked the beginning of the movement known as the **High Renaissance.** During the High Renaissance, the center of the Renaissance moved from Florence to Rome. Florence had experienced a religious backlash against the new style of art, while in Rome, a series of popes (most notably **Michelangelo**'s great patron **Julius II**) were very interested in the arts and sought to beautify their city and their palaces. The High Renaissance lasted until around the 1520s, when art began to move in a different direction. We sometimes label this art as Late Renaissance, or **Mannerism**. This art that showed distorted figures and confusing themes may have reflected the growing sense of crisis in the Italian world due to both religious and political problems.

There are three major High Renaissance artists with whom you should be familiar: Leonardo da Vinci, Raphael, and Michelangelo.

Leonardo da Vinci

Fun Fact
Leonardo da Vinci's famous sketchbooks are now owned by none other than Bill Gates.

While it is a bit of a cliché to label **Leonardo da Vinci** (1452–1519) as a Renaissance man, the label is accurate. Leonardo was a military engineer, an architect, a sculptor, a scientist, and an inventor whose sketchbooks reveal a remarkable mind that came up with workable designs for submarines and helicopters. Recent reconstructions of his sketches show that he even designed a handbag. Oh yes, he was also a painter, as the hordes of tourists snaking their way through the Louvre to see the *Mona Lisa* will attest to.

Raphael

In an age of artistic prima donnas, **Raphael** (1483–1520), a kindly individual, stands out for not being despised by his contemporaries. He came from the beautiful Renaissance city of Urbino and died at the early age of 37, but in his brief life, he was given some very important commissions in the Vatican palaces. Besides his wonderfully gentle images of Jesus and Mary, Raphael links his own times and the classical past in *The School of Athens*, which shows Plato and Aristotle standing together (in a crowd that also features the images of Leonardo and Michelangelo) in a fanciful classical structure and uses the deep, single-point perspective characteristic of High Renaissance style.

Michelangelo

Like Leonardo, **Michelangelo** (1475–1564) was skilled in numerous areas. His sculptural *David* was commissioned by Michelangelo's native city, Florence, as a propaganda work to inspire the citizens in their long struggle against the overwhelming might of Milan. Four different popes commissioned works from him, most notably the warlike Julius II, who gave Michelangelo the task of creating his tomb. Julius II also employed Michelangelo to work on the **Sistine Chapel** in the Vatican, a work that Julius II began to have doubts about as he rushed to have the revealing anatomy of some of the figures covered up with fig leaves, much to the anger of its creator. Michelangelo, who enjoyed a very long life, lived to see the style of art in Italy change from the harmony and grace of the High Renaissance to the more tormented style of the Late Renaissance, exemplified in his final work in the Sistine Chapel, the brilliant yet disturbing *Final Judgment*.

THE NORTHERN RENAISSANCE

By the late 15th century, Italian Renaissance humanism began to affect the rest of Europe. Although the writers of the Italian Renaissance were Christian, they thought less about religious questions than their northern counterparts. In the north, questions concerning religion were paramount. Christianity had arrived in the north later than in the south, and northerners at this time were still seeking ways to deepen their Christian beliefs and understanding, and display what good humanists they were. They believed they could achieve this higher level by studying early Christian authors. In this sense, the Northern Renaissance was a more religious movement than the Renaissances in Italy. Eventually, northern writers such as Erasmus and More, often referred to as **Christian Humanists**, criticized their mother church. To their horror, they found that more extreme voices of dissent—for example, that of Martin Luther—had not used their methodology to find ways to better the Catholic Church, but to show why the Church had strayed from the will of God.

> **CED 1.3**
> Northern Renaissance

Erasmus and Sir Thomas More

The greatest of the northern humanists was **Desiderius Erasmus** (1466–1536). You can thank Erasmus the next time you use such tired clichés as "Where there's smoke, there's fire," because he collected this and many other ancient and contemporary proverbs in his *Adages*. Erasmus's *In Praise of Folly* used satire as a means of criticizing what he thought were the problems of the Church. His *Handbook of the Christian Knight* emphasized the idea of inner faith as opposed to the outer forms of worship, such as partaking of the sacraments. Erasmus's Latin translation of the New Testament also played a major role in the 16th-century movement to better understand the life of the early Christians through its close textual analysis of the *Acts of the Apostles*. Erasmus was at first impressed with Luther's attacks on the Church and even initiated a correspondence with him. Eventually, however, the two men found that they had significant disagreements. Unlike Luther, Erasmus wanted to reform the Church, not abandon it, and he could never accept Luther's belief that humans do not have free will.

> It is often said that "Erasmus laid the egg that Luther hatched."

Another important northern humanist was the Englishman **Sir Thomas More** (1478–1535). A friend of Erasmus, he wrote the classic work *Utopia* (1516). More was critical of many aspects of contemporary society and sought to depict a civilization in which political and economic injustices were limited by having all property held in common. More, like Erasmus, was highly critical of certain practices of his church, but in the end he gave his life for his beliefs. In 1534, Henry VIII had More, who was serving the king as his chancellor, executed for refusing to take an oath recognizing Henry as Head of the Church of England.

Northern Renaissance Culture

The Northern Renaissance also represented more than simply the Christian humanism of individuals such as More and Erasmus. Talented painters from the north, while clearly influenced by the artists of the Italian Renaissance with whom they often came into contact on visits to the Italian peninsula, also created their own unique style. This is seen, for example, in the work of **Albrecht Dürer**, a brilliant draftsman, whose woodcuts powerfully lent support to the doctrinal revolution brought about by his fellow German Martin Luther: the illiterate peasants were moved more by Dürer's art than by Luther's texts.

The greatest achievement in the arts in northern Europe in the 16th and early 17th centuries took place in England, a land that had, up until then, been a bit of a cultural backwater, with the notable exception of **Geoffrey Chaucer**, whose *Canterbury Tales* were based on *The Decameron* by **Boccaccio** (both works written during the 14th century). There is perhaps no way to explain the emergence of the sheer number of men possessing exceptional talent during the reign of Queen Elizabeth, because providing her with much credit for this cultural awakening seems to be unwarranted. In fact, much of what we refer to as the **Elizabethan Renaissance** occurred during the reign of her cousin and heir, James I.

Although **Christopher Marlowe** and **Ben Jonson** are both writers of significant repute, the age produced an unrivaled genius in **William Shakespeare** (1564–1616). Though little is known of Shakespeare's life and the question of the provenance of his plays will never be answered to the satisfaction of all, this man, who received little more than a primary school education, apparently was able to author plays such as *Hamlet* and *King Lear*, works that reveal an unsurpassed understanding of the human psyche as well as a genius for dramatic intensity.

The Printing Press

The search for new ways to produce text became important in the late medieval period, when the number of literate individuals rose considerably as the number of European universities increased. The traditional method of producing books, via a monk working dutifully in a monastic scriptorium, was clearly unable to meet this heightened demand. **Johannes Gutenberg**, from the German city of Mainz, introduced movable type to western Europe. Between 1452 and 1453, Gutenberg printed approximately 200 Bibles and spent a great deal of money making his Bibles as ornate as any handwritten version. He eventually went broke. The significant increase in literacy in the 16th century supports the theory that few inventions in human history have had as great an impact as the printing press. It is hard to imagine the Reformation spreading so rapidly without the books that informed people of the nature of the religious debate.

Power of the Printing Press

Historians consider the printing press to be one of the most culturally significant inventions in all of human history. The ability to rapidly disseminate printed material almost certainly led to the spread of the Reformation, among other historical events.

THE PROTESTANT REFORMATION

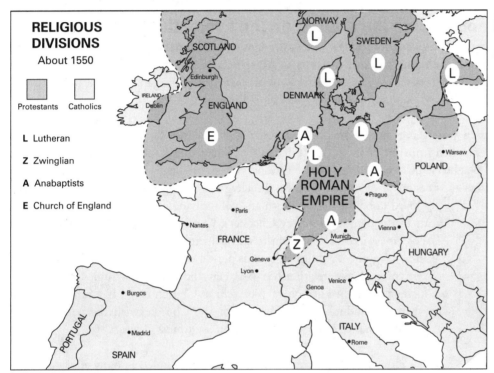

Religious Divisions Around 1550

In western Europe in the year 1500, the simple declarative sentence, "I went to church on Sunday," could mean only one thing, as only one church existed in the West. At the top of this hierarchical church sat the pope in Rome, to whom all of Europe looked for religious guidance. Several decades later, the **Protestant Reformation** movement resulted in the great split in Western Christendom, which displaced the pope's status as the single religious authority in Europe. Although it took several decades, eventually there was a Catholic response to this challenge known as the **Catholic Reformation**.

In part, the Reformation of the 16th century was a reflection of the ways in which Europe was changing. The humanism of the Renaissance, particularly in the north of Europe, had led individuals to question certain practices, such as the efficacy of religious relics and the value to one's salvation of living the life of a monk. In addition, the printing press had made it possible to produce Bibles in ever greater number, which made the Church's exclusive right to interpret the Scriptures seem particularly vexing to those who could now read the text themselves.

The rise of powerful monarchical states also created a situation in which some rulers began to question why they needed to listen to a distant authority in Rome or Vienna.

> One important thing to keep in mind is that on the AP European History Exam, you are not looking for absolute religious truths. So, when dealing with religious questions, leave your personal beliefs at the door and think as a historian.

Problems Facing the Church on the Eve of the Reformation

It is important for the student of the 16th-century Reformation to remember that the Reformation is far more than just the story of **Martin Luther** (1483–1546). While Luther is a central figure in the story, to reduce it simply to his own struggles against the Catholic Church oversimplifies what is actually a complex and compelling story.

The Church was facing significant problems on the eve of the Reformation. Some of these problems resulted from the crisis of the 14th century, when the **Black Death,** a ferocious outbreak of plague, struck the population of Europe. These problems included a growing **anti-clericalism**—a measure of disrespect toward the clergy, stemming in part from what many

During the **Great Schism** of the early 15th century, there were three different popes at the same time—and all were trying to excommunicate one another!

perceived to be the poor performance of individual clergymen during the crisis years of the plague. Geoffrey Chaucer's *The Canterbury Tales* and Boccaccio's *The Decameron* reveal some of the satirical edge with which literate society now greeted clergymen. Additionally, this period witnessed a rise in **pietism**, or the notion of a direct relationship between the individual and God, thereby reducing the importance of the hierarchical Church based in Rome. The 14th century was undoubtedly a disaster for the Church, with the papacy under French dominance in the city of Avignon for almost 70 years.

Other problems on the eve of the Reformation included a poorly educated lower clergy. Peasant priests, who in many cases knew just a bit of Latin, proved to be unable to put forward a learned response to Luther's challenge to their church. **Simony**, the selling of church offices, was another considerable problem, as was the fact that some members of the clergy held multiple positions, thus making them less than effective in terms of ministering to their flocks.

In response to some of these problems, a number of movements arose in the late Middle Ages that would be declared heretical by the Church. In England, **John Wycliffe** (1329–1384) questioned the worldly wealth of the Church, the miracle of transubstantiation, the teachings of penance, and, in a foretaste of the ideas of Luther, the selling of indulgences. Wycliffe urged his followers (known, for unclear reasons, as the **Lollards**) to read the Bible and to interpret it themselves. To aid in this task, Wycliffe translated the Bible into English.

In Bohemia (the modern-day Czech Republic), **Jan Hus** (1369–1415) led a revolt that combined religious and nationalistic elements. Hus, the rector of the University of Prague, argued that it was the authority of the Bible and not the institutional church that ultimately mattered. Like Wycliffe, he was horrified by what he saw as the immoral behavior of the clergy. This antagonism toward the clergy and its special role in administering the sacraments led Hus to argue that the congregation should be given the cup during the mass as well as the wafer, something that only clergymen were allowed. Hus was called before the Council of Constance in

1415 by Pope Martin V, and although he was promised safe passage, he was condemned as a heretic and burnt at the stake. In response, his followers in Bohemia staged a rebellion, which took many years to put down.

Martin Luther

The initial issue that first brought attention to Martin Luther (1483–1546) was the debate over indulgences. The **selling of indulgences** was a practice that began during the time of the Crusades. To convince knights to go on crusades and to raise money, the papacy sold indulgences, which released the buyer from purgatory. Eventually, long after the crusading movement had ended, the Church began to grant indulgences as a means of filling its treasury. In 1517, **Albert of Hohenzollern**, who already held two bishoprics, was offered the Archbishopric of Mainz. He had to raise 10,000 ducats, so he borrowed the money from the great banking family of the age—the Fuggers. To pay off his debt, the papacy granted him permission to raise money from the preaching of an indulgence, with half of the money going directly to Rome, where the papacy was in the midst of a program to finally complete St. Peter's Basilica. **Johann Tetzel**, a Dominican friar, was sent to preach the indulgence throughout Germany with the famous phrase "As soon as gold in the basin rings, right then the soul to heaven springs."

Luther was horrified by the behavior of Tetzel and tacked up his *95 Theses* on the Castle Church at **Wittenberg**, which was the medieval way of indicating that an issue should be debated. Part of Luther's complaints dealt with German money going to Rome. Another major point involved control over purgatory. If the pope had control over it, Luther wondered, why didn't he allow everyone out? Luther believed that a pope could remit only those penalties that he himself had placed on someone. Therefore, the pope had no right to sell misleading indulgences.

In a reflection of the power of the printing press, the *95 Theses* were quickly printed all over Germany. At first, the papacy was not concerned. **Pope Leo X** reportedly said he was not interested in a squabble between monks. The Dominicans wanted to charge Luther with heresy, but Luther soon found himself with a large number of supporters.

Luther began to move in a more radical direction. In part, a great deal of his attack on the Church was based on his own fears that he was unworthy of salvation. Back in 1505, he was caught in a thunderstorm and a bolt of lightning struck near him. He cried out, "St. Anne help me; I will become a monk." Luther kept his promise and joined the Augustinian order. However, Luther was dissatisfied leading the life of a monk. In later years, he claimed that if any monk could have been saved by what he termed "monkery," it was he:

> Though I lived as a monk without reproach, I felt that I was a sinner before God with an extremely disturbed conscience. I could not believe that He was placated by my satisfaction. I did not love, yes, I hated the righteous God who punishes sinners, and I was angry with God.

Still troubled, Luther went on to be appointed Professor of Scriptures in Wittenburg in Electoral Saxony (northern Germany).

CED 2.2
Luther and the Protestant Reformation

Luther and Indulgences
One of Martin Luther's main criticisms of the Catholic Church was the selling of indulgences, which the papacy claimed released the buyer from purgatory into heaven. Luther pointed to this practice as a sign of the Church's corruption. The term "preaching an indulgence" refers to a practice of ministers by which they would peddle the sale of indulgences in their sermons.

Following the publication of his *95 Theses*, Luther engaged in a public debate on these issues in Leipzig, where John Eck, a prominent theologian, challenged him. Eck then called Luther a Hussite, while Luther claimed that Hus had been unjustly condemned at the Council of Constance. After this debate, Luther spent the year 1520 writing three of his most important political tracts.

1) In his *Address to the Christian Nobility*, he urged that secular government had the right to reform the Church.

2) In *On the Babylonian Captivity of the Church*, Luther attacked other teachings of the Church, such as the sacraments.

3) Finally, in *Liberty of a Christian Man*, he hit on what would become the basic elements of Lutheran belief: grace is the sole gift of God; therefore, one is saved by faith alone, and the Bible is the sole source of this faith.

In response to these works, Pope Leo X finally decided he had to act. He issued a papal bull (an official decree) that demanded that Luther recant the ideas found in his writings or be burnt as a heretic. In a highly symbolic gesture, Luther publicly burned the bull to show that he no longer accepted papal authority. In turn, the pope excommunicated Luther.

Luther was fortunate in that, unlike Hus, he had some important patrons. Some North German princes, such as Frederick the Elector of Saxony, were either sympathetic to Luther's ideas or at least wanted him to be given a public hearing. To that end, in 1521 Luther appeared before the **Diet of Worms**, a meeting of the German nobility. In one of the most famous scenes in history, Luther was asked by **Charles V, the Holy Roman Emperor**, "Do you or do you not repudiate your books and the errors they contain?" Luther began to answer with a quivering voice but then gathered his courage and said:

> Unless I am convicted by Scripture and plain reason—I do not accept the authority of popes and councils, for they have contradicted each other—my conscience is captive to the Word of God. I cannot and I will not recant anything, for to go against conscience is neither right nor safe. God help me. Amen.

In response, Luther was placed under the ban of the Empire but was safely hidden over the next year in Wartburg Castle by the Elector of Saxony. In the castle, Luther continued to write prolifically and finished some of his most important works, including a translation of the Bible into German.

Since he now considered papal authority to be a human invention, Luther and his friend Philip Melanchthon decided to form a new church based on his revolutionary ideas free from papal control. Instead of the seven sacraments of the Catholic Church (Marriage, Ordination, Extreme Unction, Confirmation, Penance, Communion, Baptism), he reduced them to two—baptism and communion. Luther changed the meaning of the latter (also called the Holy Eucharist) by rejecting the Catholic idea of **transubstantiation**, the miraculous transformation of the bread and wine into the flesh and blood of Christ, an act that could be performed only by an ordained priest. Instead, Luther claimed that Christ was already present in the sacrament. Luther also did away with the practice of monasticism and the insistence on the celibacy of the clergy. He himself went on to have a happy marriage with Katharina von Bora, a former nun with whom he had several children.

Why Did the Reformation Succeed?

Within three decades after Luther posted his *95 Theses*, **Protestantism** had spread to many of the states of northern Germany, Scandinavia, England, Scotland, and parts of the Netherlands, France, and Switzerland. There are a number of possible explanations for its phenomenal success.

Luther and the church that he founded were socially conservative and therefore not a threat to the existing social order. Luther's conservatism can be seen clearly in the **German Peasants' Revolt** of 1525. The revolt was the result of the German peasants' worsening economic conditions and their belief, articulated in the Twelve Articles, that Luther's call

> ### The Origins of the Term *Protestantism*
> The term today is used very broadly and means any non-Catholic or non-Eastern Orthodox Christian faith. Initially, it referred to a group of Lutherans who in 1529 attended the Diet of Speyer in an attempt to work out a compromise with the Catholic Church and ended up "protesting" the final document that was drawn up at its conclusion.

for a **"priesthood of all believers"** was a message of social egalitarianism. It certainly was not. The revolt and the distortion of his ideas horrified Luther. He published a violently angry tract entitled "Against the Robbing and Murderous Hordes of Peasants," in which he urged that no mercy be shown to the revolutionaries.

Another reason Luther's movement was allowed to grow was that Luther was willing to subordinate his church to the authority of the German princes. As his response to the Peasants' Revolt shows, political questions were not of great importance to Luther, who felt that what occurred on this Earth was secondary to what truly mattered—the Kingdom of Heaven. He was not critical of the German princes who created state churches under their direct control. Luther also encouraged German princes to confiscate the lands of the Catholic Church, and many rulers did not have to be asked twice, in part because one-quarter of all land in the Holy Roman Empire was under Church control.

Political issues within the Holy Roman Empire produced turmoil. When the Emperor Maximilian died in 1519, his grandson and heir **Charles V** was caught in a struggle with the French King Francis I to see who would sit on the imperial throne. Although Charles V was able to muster enough bribe money (borrowed from the Fuggers) to convince the rulers of the electoral states to select him, he was ultimately unable to effectively control his empire. Also, as ruler of a vast multinational empire that included Spain and its possessions in the Western Hemisphere, the Netherlands, southern Italy, and the Habsburg possessions in Austria, Charles had huge commitments. He was unable to deal with the revolt in Germany for several critical decades because he was involved in extended wars with France as well as with the powerful **Ottoman Empire** to the east.

In the 1540s, the **Schmalkaldic War** was fought between Charles and some of the Protestant princes. While for a time Charles had the upper hand, by 1555 he was forced to sign the **Peace of Augsburg**. This treaty granted legal recognition of Lutheranism in those territories ruled by a Lutheran ruler, while a Catholic ruler ensured that the territory remained Catholic.

The Empire of Charles V

Radical Reformation

CED: 2.3
Protestant Reform
Continues

Historians sometimes use the term **Radical Reformation** to describe a variety of religious sects that developed during the 16th century, inspired in part by Luther's challenge to the established Church. Many felt that Luther's Reformation did not go far enough in bringing about a moral transformation of society.

Fun Fact
The modern-day Amish and Mennonite religious sects are direct descendants of the early Anabaptists.

One such group was the **Anabaptists**, who denied the idea of infant baptism. Instead they believed that baptism works only when it is practiced by adults who are fully aware of the decision they are making. Eventually, rebaptism, as the practice became known, was declared a capital offense throughout the Holy Roman Empire, something on which both the pope and Luther heartily agreed. Attacks against Anabaptists became even worse following the Anabaptist takeover of the city of Munster in 1534, during which time they attempted to create an Old Testament theocracy in which men were allowed to have multiple wives. Following the capture of Munster by combined Catholic and Protestant armies, Anabaptism moved in the direction of pacifism under the leadership of Menno Simons.

Besides Anabaptists, other groups such as the **Antitrinitarians**, who denied the scriptural validity of the Trinity, were part of the Radical Reformation. Both Catholics and Lutherans hunted down those who held such beliefs.

Zwingli and Calvin

Shortly after the appearance of Luther's *95 Theses*, **Ulrich Zwingli's** (1484–1531) teachings began to make an impact on the residents of the Swiss city of Zurich. Like Luther, Zwingli accused monks of indolence and high living. In 1519, Zwingli specifically rejected the veneration of saints and called for the need to distinguish between factual and fictional accounts of their lives. He announced that unbaptized children were not, in fact, damned to eternal hellfire. He questioned the power of excommunication. His most powerful statement, however, was his attack on the claim that tithing (the required donation of one-tenth of one's income to the church) was a divine institution. Unlike Luther, however, Zwingli was a strict sacramentarian in that he denied all the sacraments. To him, the Holy Communion was simply a memorial of Christ's death. It did not entail *transubstantiation* (the actual presence of Christ's flesh) as it did for the Catholic Church. Zwingli was also a Swiss patriot in ways that Luther could not be called a German patriot. Zwingli was far more concerned with this world and called for social reform. He died leading the troops of Zurich against the Swiss Catholic cantons in battle.

John Calvin (1509–1564) was born in France, although he eventually settled in Geneva, Switzerland. His main ideas are found in his *Institutes of the Christian Religion*, in which he argued that grace was bestowed on relatively few individuals, and the rest were consigned to hell. This philosophy of predestination was the cornerstone of his thought, and one that does not make any room for free will. This was contrary to everything that the Catholic Church taught about death. Although many of the Catholic Church's practices, such as the sale of indulgences, were extremely corrupt, the Church also taught that people have the ability to save their souls following death. Calvin preferred for his followers to focus on correct living in earthly matters. He was a strict disciplinarian who did his best to make Geneva the new Jerusalem. He closed all the taverns and inflicted penalties for such crimes as visiting a fortune-teller.

Calvinism began to spread rapidly in the 1540s and 1550s, becoming the established church in Scotland, while in France—where the Calvinists were known as **Huguenots**—only a significant minority joined. In many ways, it can be said that Calvinism saved the Protestant Reformation. In the mid-16th century, it was a dynamic Calvinism—rather than the increasingly moribund Lutheranism—that stood in opposition to a newly aggressive Catholic Church during the Catholic Counter-Reformation. It's also worth noting that it was a group of English Calvinists (who were called Puritans) who grew tired of religious harassment from the mainstream Anglican church and fled England to Holland. In the shipbuilding capital of Europe, they saved enough money to build a pair of ships, which they used to sail across the Atlantic Ocean, where they established a new colony in Massachusetts based on religious freedom. Yes, these were the pilgrims.

Calvin also stands as a good example of the way that city governments became "moral police" during this period. In Geneva, Calvinists eventually took over the city government, creating a small theocracy. There, singing crude lyrics in a song could result in a forced tongue piercing. Other sins could result in excommunication from the city, and blasphemy could be punished by death. This phenomenon was replicated in varying degrees all over northern Europe. Where Protestants gained power, city governments often shut down taverns, restricted prostitution, and ended carnivals.

THE ENGLISH REFORMATION

The English Reformation was of a different nature—a political act rather than a religious act as in other parts of Europe. **Henry VIII** (r. 1509–1546), the powerful English monarch, was supportive of the Catholic Church. He even criticized Martin Luther in a pamphlet that he wrote, ***The Defence of the Seven Sacraments***. Henry was never comfortable with Protestant theology. He did not believe in salvation by faith and saw no need to limit the role of the priest. The story of the English Reformation begins with what became known as the "King's Great Matter," which involved King Henry VIII's attempt to end his marriage to his Spanish wife, **Catherine of Aragon**. Henry had grown concerned that he did not have a male heir, and he began to question whether Catherine's failure to produce sons (a man of his times, he blamed his wife) was a sign of God's displeasure at his marriage to Catherine, who had earlier been married to Henry's deceased older brother. Because the Catholic Church did not recognize divorce, Henry would have to go through the process of getting an annulment. During this time, Henry fell in love with a young woman at his court, **Anne Boleyn**, who refused to sleep with him unless he made her his queen.

When the papacy showed no signs of granting the annulment, primarily because Catherine was the aunt of the powerful Charles V, Henry decided to take authority into his own hands. Starting in November 1529 and continuing for seven years, he began what became known as the **Reformation Parliament**, which Henry used as a tool to give him ultimate authority on religious matters. This parliament would become very useful, because by 1533, Henry was on a short timetable. He had bribed Anne Boleyn into joining him in bed. Three months later she was pregnant and had secretly married Henry, although Henry was still married to Catherine as well. If Henry was to be saved from bigamy, and if his child was to be legitimate, he had only eight months to end his marriage to Catherine. Henry decided the only way to do this was by cutting off the constitutional links that existed between England and the papacy. In April 1533, Parliament enacted a statute known as the Act in Restraint of Appeals, which declared that all spiritual cases within the kingdom were within the king's jurisdiction and authority and not the pope's. A month later, Henry appeared before an English church tribunal headed by the man he selected to be Archbishop of Canterbury. The tribunal declared that his marriage to Catherine was null and void and that Anne Boleyn was his lawfully wedded wife. That September, a child was born, but it was a baby girl, **Elizabeth Tudor**, instead of the boy Henry so desperately wanted. Eventually, Henry would marry a total of six times; his third wife, **Jane Seymour**, gave birth to a son, Edward. In 1534, the English Reformation was capped off by the **Act of Supremacy,** which acknowledged the King of England as the Supreme Head of what became known as the Church of England.

While Henry may have been merely interested in creating what we might call Catholicism without the pope—in that he wanted to keep all the aspects of Catholic worship without acknowledging the primacy of the pope—it proved to be difficult to stem the tide of change. Henry himself played a role in this by closing all English monasteries and confiscating their lands. The brief reign of his son **Edward VI** (r. 1547–1553) saw an attempt to institute genuine Protestant theology into the church that Henry had created.

During the similarly short reign of Edward's half-sister **Mary Tudor** (r. 1553–1558), the daughter of Catherine of Aragon and wife of the fanatically Catholic Philip II of Spain, there was an attempt to bring England back into the orbit of the Catholic Church. While succeeding in restoring the formal links between England and the papacy, Mary found that many still held to their Protestant beliefs. To end this heresy, she allowed for several hundred Englishmen to be burnt at the stake, thus earning her the sobriquet "**Bloody Mary.**" It was only during the long, successful reign of her half-sister Elizabeth (r. 1558–1603), the daughter of Anne Boleyn, that a final religious settlement was worked out, one in which the Church of England followed a middle-of-the-road Protestant course.

THE COUNTER-REFORMATION

Although it took several decades to be effective, eventually there was a Catholic response to the Protestant Reformation. Initially, historians referred to this move-ment as the **Counter-Reformation**, although today it is more commonly known as the **Catholic Reformation**. To a certain extent, both labels are appropriate. It was a Counter-Reformation in the sense that the Catholic Church was taking steps to counteract some of the successes of the Protestant side. Among these steps was the creation of the notorious **Index of Prohibited Books**, including works by writers such as Erasmus and Galileo. Also, the medieval institution of the **papal Inquisition** was revived, and individuals who were deemed to be heretics were put to death for their religious beliefs. The term Catholic Reformation is also apt in that the Catholic Church has a long tradition of adjusting to changed conditions, whether it was the papal Reform Movement of the 11th century or, more recently, the Second Vatican Council of the 1960s.

> **CED 2.5**
> The Catholic Reformation

The centerpiece of the Catholic Reformation was the **Council of Trent** (1545–1563). Unlike the medieval conciliar movement, which sought to place the papacy under the control of a church council or parliament, the Council of Trent was dominated by the papacy and, in turn, enhanced its power. The council took steps to address some of the issues that had sparked the Reformation, including placing limits on simony, the selling of church offices. Recognizing that the poorly educated clergy was a major problem, the council mandated that a seminary for the education of clergy should be established in every diocese. The Council of Trent refused to concede any point of theology to the Protestants. Instead they emphatically endorsed their traditional teachings on such matters as the sacraments, the role of priests, the belief that salvation comes from faith as well as works, and that the source for this faith was the Bible and the traditions of the Church. Although it is incorrect to say that the council created the idea of the **baroque** style of art, the council was critical of what it deemed to be the religious failings of the mannerist style. It urged that a more intensely religious art be created, something that did play a role in the development of the early baroque.

Perhaps the greatest reason for the success of the Catholic Reformation was the founding of the **Society of Jesus (Jesuits)** organized by **Ignatius Loyola** (1491–1556), a Spanish noble who was wounded in battle and spent his recuperation time reading various Catholic tracts. After under-going a religious conversion, he attempted, not unlike Luther, to reconcile himself to God through austere behavior. He became a hermit but still felt that something was amiss. While Luther, in his search for spiritual contentment, decided that the Bible was the sole source of faith, Loyola believed that even if the Bible did not exist, there was still the spirit.

Loyola's ideas are laid out in his *Spiritual Exercises*; one passage in particular states his belief in total obedience to the Church:

> To arrive at complete certainty, this is the attitude that we should maintain: I will believe that the white object I see is black if that should be the desire of the hierarchical church, for I believe that linking Christ our Lord the Bridegroom and His Bride the church, there is one and the same Spirit, ruling and guiding us for our souls' good. For our Holy Mother the church is guided and ruled by the same Spirit, the Lord who gave the Ten Commandments.

This total and complete loyalty is why the Jesuit order, although at first under suspicion by a cautious papacy uncomfortable with Loyola's mysticism, would be accepted as an official order of the Church in a papal bull in 1540. The Jesuits began to distinguish themselves as a teaching order and also worked as Catholic missionaries in places where Lutheranism had made large inroads. Poland served as a strong example of where Catholicism was re-proselytized.

THE PORTUGUESE AND SPANISH EMPIRES

CED 1.6
Technological Advances and the Age of Exploration

If geography is destiny, then it is not surprising that the Portuguese would look to the sea. Living in a land that was not well suited to farming, the Portuguese had always looked to distant lands for sources of wealth. In 1415, **Prince Henry the Navigator**, a younger son of the King of Portugal, participated in the capture of the North African port of Ceuta from the Muslims. This conquest spurred his interest in Africa. It also inspired him to sponsor a navigational school in Lisbon and a series of expeditions, crewed mainly by Italians, which aimed not only to develop trade with Africa, but also to find a route around Africa to India and East Asia, thereby cutting out the Italian go-between.

In 1487, a Portuguese captain, **Bartholomew Dias**, sailed around the **Cape of Good Hope** at the tip of Africa. A decade later, in 1498, **Vasco da Gama** reached the coast of India. The Portuguese defeated the Arab fleets that patrolled the Indian Ocean by being the first to successfully mount cannons on their ships and also by deploying their ships in squadrons rather than individually, which gave them a huge tactical advantage. The Portuguese established themselves on the western coast of India and for a while controlled the lucrative spice trade.

It's often said that Portugal built an empire mostly by sea, while Spain built an empire mostly by land. Portugal also kept looser control over its properties, while Spain maintained a tighter grip over its tributary empire. And Portugal lost its holdings quickly, to the British and Dutch who developed faster ships and more powerful weapons, whereas the Spanish maintained its overseas properties until the 19th century.

With the Portuguese having a head start on the African route to the Indian Ocean, the Spanish decided to try an Atlantic route to the East. **Christopher Columbus**, a sailor from Genoa, Italy, set sail on August 2, 1492, certain that he would find this eastern route. Although Columbus was not unique in insisting that the world was round, he did believe he would fulfill medieval religious prophesies that spoke of converting the whole world to Christianity. After a 33-day voyage from the Canary Islands, Columbus landed in the eastern Bahamas, which he insisted was an undeveloped part of Asia. He called the territory the "Indies" and the Indigenous population

"Indians," and noted ominously in his diary that they were friendly and gentle, and therefore easy to enslave.

Columbus's failure to locate either gold or spices during his voyages was a disappointment. However, within a generation, others were able to build on Columbus's discoveries. The most important of the journeys was undertaken by **Ferdinand Magellan** in 1519, who set out to circumnavigate the globe. Although Magellan did not live to see the end of his voyage (he died in the Philippines), he did prove that the territory where Columbus landed was not part of East Asia. Rather, it was an entirely unknown continent, a continent that the Spanish planned to conquer.

In 1519, **Hernán Cortés** landed on the coast of Mexico with a small force of 600 men. He had arrived at the heart of the **Aztec Empire**, a militaristic state, which through conquest had carved out a large state with a large central capital, **Tenochtitlán** (modern-day Mexico City). The Aztecs were less than popular with the people they conquered, primarily because they practiced human sacrifice to appease their gods. These conquered people felt no loyalty to the Aztec state and were willing to cooperate with the Spanish.

The Aztecs viewed the Spaniards, who were riding on horses (unknown at this time in North and South America), wearing armor, and carrying guns, as gods. At first, Montezuma, the Aztec ruler, tried to appease them with gifts of gold. Unfortunately for the Aztecs, this just further whetted the appetite of the Spanish, who seized the capital city and took Montezuma hostage. He died mysteriously while in Spanish captivity. While rebellions against Spanish rule continued, the Aztec ability to fight was sapped by smallpox and other European diseases foreign to the Indigenous peoples. By 1521, Cortés declared the former Aztec Empire to be New Spain.

The Spanish also succeeded in destroying another great civilization, the **Inca Empire of Peru**. Like the Aztecs, the Incas had carved out a large empire by conquering and instigating harsh rule over many other tribes. In 1531, **Francisco Pizarro**, a Spanish soldier, set out for Peru with a tiny force of approximately 200 men. Pizarro, following Cortés's brutal example, treacherously captured the Inca Emperor Atahualpa, who then had his subjects raise vast amounts of gold for ransom. By 1533, Pizarro had grown tired of ruling through Atahualpa, and he had him killed. Once again, Western technology and diseases harmed the Indigenous population's ability to fight back. While it took longer for the Spanish to secure their hold over the Inca territories, by the 1560s, they had stamped out the last bit of resistance.

> **New Toys For New Empires**
>
> The **magnetic compass** gave sailors the power to check their position at any time, in any weather. Also used for navigation, the **sextant** measured the angle between an object in the sky and the horizon. A **Mercator projection** was a new map, designed specifically for sailors, that standardized all courses of bearing as straight segments. The **caravel** was a small but agile Portuguese ship that could approach very close to land and even sail up rivers.

The impact of this age of exploration and conquest was immense, not just for Europe but for the entire globe. The Spanish set out to create *haciendas*, or plantations, to exploit both the agricultural and mineral riches of the land. Indigenous people, compelled to work under a system of forced labor called *encomienda*, continued to die at an incredible pace from both disease and overwork. So to provide labor for their estates, the Spanish and Portuguese began to take captured Africans from their homeland to serve on the farms and in the mines of the so-called **"New World."** It has been estimated that by the time the slave trade ended in the early 19th century, almost 10 million Africans were abducted from Africa, with countless numbers dying as a result of the inhumane conditions on the difficult overseas passage.

The European powers relied upon the Catholic Church to justify their atrocious overseas behavior. In fact, the Catholic Church was the single most important institution in Latin America. Its mission was twofold. One, it used thousands of missionary priests such as the Jesuits to convert Indigenous peoples to its Christian cause. This mission to save souls was often cited as a reason for the European expansion into the New World. Two, the Catholic Church also acquired massive amounts of land, or haciendas, in the New World. It sold these holdings to the European landowning classes via preferential loans, becoming the mortgage holder for the indebted hacienda owners.

CED 1.8
Colonial Expansion and
Columbian Exchange

Another consequence of the Spanish and Portuguese empires in the New World was what became known as the **Columbian Exchange**—the transatlantic transfer of animals, plants, diseases, people, technology, and ideas among Europe, the Americas, and Africa. As Europeans and Africans crisscrossed the Atlantic, they brought the Old World to the New and back again. From the European and African side of the Atlantic, horses, pigs, goats, chili peppers, and sugarcane (and more) flowed to the Americas. From the American side, squash, beans, corn, potatoes, and cacao (and more) made their way back east. Settlers from the Old World carried bubonic plague, smallpox, typhoid, influenza, and the common cold into the New and then carried Chagas and syphilis back to the Old. Guns, Catholicism, and enslaved people also crossed the Atlantic. Never before had so much been moved across the oceans, as ship after ship carried the contents of one continent to another.

Mercantilism had a strong effect on European governance. Far from *laissez-faire*, the practitioners of mercantilism believed that the government needed to actively regulate the economy of its population. In this way, the rulers could maintain a favorable balance of trade, monitor the import and export of raw materials and finished goods, and fund the pursuit of precious metals that supported much of the national wealth.

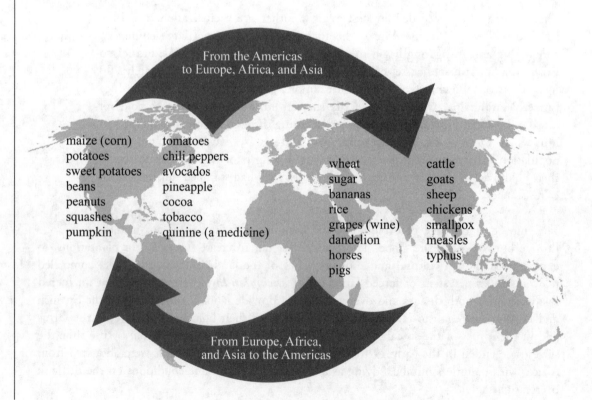

As a result of the Mediterranean region's growing trade with the Arab world, Italian bankers grew wealthy and powerful as they financed the Spanish exploration of the New World. Together with prosperous merchants, both groups influenced city politics as never before. The wheels of commerce turned faster in northern Europe as well, particularly in Prussia and the German-speaking states. In France, the new "nobles of the robe" bought and sold their government positions as easily as trading for candy.

CED 1.5
New Monarchies

THE DEVELOPMENT OF MONARCHICAL STATES

Tools of statecraft, such as permanent embassies in foreign lands, were first developed in the city-states of Renaissance Italy. Large, unified **nation-states** began to develop in northern Europe during the early modern period. These city-states ultimately came to dominate the Italian peninsula and contributed to the transition away from the medieval notion of feudal kingship. Prior to the 16th century, the king was not an absolute ruler; instead he had to rule with the consent of his great vassals. In the age of the new monarchical state, it was deemed that monarchical power was God-given and therefore by its very nature absolute. In the Middle Ages, parliamentary institutions developed throughout Europe as a means of placing limits on kings. However, in the early modern period, thought shifted. The 16th-century French philosopher Jean Bodin wrote of this new style of monarchy:

> It is the distinguishing mark of the sovereign that he cannot in any way be subject to the commands of another, for it is he who makes law for the subject, abrogates laws already made, and amends absolute law.

The French monarchy is the most important example of how this power shift came about. It was not an easy victory for the French monarchy, which had to deal with assorted aristocratic and religious conflicts that threatened to destroy the state. Eventually, under Louis XIV, France created a centralized monarchy in which the power of the king was absolute. However, it came at a high price as it helped pave the way for the late 18th-century French Revolution. England serves as a very different model. In England, the Stuart monarchs, who reigned for most of the 17th century, were interested in adopting French-style royal absolutism but found that the English Parliament stood in their way. Eventually, England became embroiled in what one historian has labeled as a "century of revolution," which eventually resulted in the supremacy of Parliament over the monarchy.

Be aware of these important characteristics of the new nation-states:

1. Growing Bureaucratization

Across Europe, salaried officials began to depend on the monarchy for their livelihood. In France, the monarchy established the new office of intendant, which employed individuals to collect taxes on behalf of the monarch. Corruption was still a part of this system, as was the practice of buying and selling royal offices to satisfy the short-term financial needs of the monarch. England was the exception to this trend. In England, the older system of cooperation between the crown and its leading subjects continued.

2. Existence of a Permanent Mercenary Army

In the late medieval/early modern periods, a revolution in warfare came about. In the 14th century, Swiss mercenary infantry soldiers lined up in a phalanx of 6,000 men and used their pikes to kill aristocratic riders. By the end of the century, gunpowder further eroded the dominance of the mounted knight and made feudal castles far easier to conquer. The rising cost of warfare, most particularly the need to provide for an army on an annual (as opposed to occasional) basis, played into the hands of the developing monarchical state, which alone could tap into the necessary resources. Again, England was the exception, because it did not establish a permanent army until the end of the 17th century when it was firmly under parliamentary control.

3. Growing Need to Tax

This is an instance in which 1 + 2 = 3. Countries like France basically faced a vicious circle: monarchs were in constant need of taxes to pay for their permanent armies, while it was the army that the monarchy needed to ensure control over a rebellious peasantry who resented the high rate of taxation. Traditionally, medieval monarchs were supposed to live off their own incomes, although in the early modern period this was becoming impossible because of the Price Revolution and the increased costs of managing a centralized state.

ITALY

Not every part of Europe followed this process of national consolidation under a centralizing monarchy. The Italian peninsula remained divided throughout this period, and thus it became an easy target for ambitious monarchs of centralized states, such as France and Spain.

The **Treaty of Lodi** (1454) had provided for a balance of power among the major Italian city-states. It created an alliance between long-term enemies Milan and Naples, and also included the support of Florence. Their combined strength was enough to ensure that outside powers would stay out of Italian affairs. This system came to an end in 1490, when **Ludovico il Moro**, upon becoming despot of Milan, initiated hostilities with Naples, and then four years later invited the French into Italy to allow them to satisfy their long-standing claims to Naples. **Charles VIII**, the King of France, didn't have to be asked twice; he immediately ordered his troops across the Italian Alps.

Charles and his forces crossed into Florence, where a radical Dominican preacher, **Savonarola** (1452–1498), had just led the Florentine population in expelling the Medici rulers and then had established a puritanical state. This complete religious and political transformation of the city marked the end of Florence's leading role in Renaissance scholarship and art. Eventually, by 1498, Ludovico il Moro recognized the folly of what he had wrought and joined an anti-French Italian alliance that ultimately succeeded not only in expelling the French but also in restoring the Medici in Florence. The Medici promptly burnt Savonarola at the stake with the support of the papacy, which hated the Dominican friar because of his pre-Lutheran call for a complete overhaul of the Church, including the institution of the papacy.

The damage to the independence of the Italian city-states had already been done. Throughout the 16th century, Italy became the battlefield in which Spain and France fought for dominance. The collapse of Italian independence was the historical context in which **Niccolò Machiavelli** wrote what is generally seen as the first work of modern political thought, *The Prince* (1513). Machiavelli had happily served his beloved Florentine Republic as a diplomat and official in the chancellery. When the Republic was overthrown by the Medici, Machiavelli was forced into exile to his country estate. *The Prince* is a résumé of sorts in which Machiavelli tried to convince the Medici to partake of his services. Although some scholars have debated whether he was serious about his ideas, it does appear that Machiavelli was genuinely horrified by the increasing foreign domination of the Italian peninsula and believed that only a strong leader using potentially ruthless means could unify Italy and expel the foreigners.

ENGLAND

The Tudors

England had achieved a measure of unity under a centralized monarchy in the medieval period, well before its continental counterparts. The 15th-century **Wars of the Roses** (commonly known to us, although a bit inaccurately, through the plays of Shakespeare) were not aristocratic attempts to break the power of the monarchy but rather a series of civil wars to determine which aristocratic faction, York or Lancaster, would dominate the monarchy. In the end, it was a junior member of the Lancastrian family, **Henry Tudor (Henry VII)**, who won central authority in England when he established the **Tudor dynasty** following his defeat of Richard III in 1485 at the battle of Bosworth Field.

Following the death of his autocratic father in 1509, Henry VIII became king and maintained his father's policies to strengthen the crown. The near total decimation of aristocratic opponents during the Wars of the Roses and an expanding economy, which benefited the Tudor dynasty throughout the 16th century, helped the King to restore royal authority. Henry created a small but efficient bureaucracy that made the King's intentions known throughout the land. Henry, however, believed that his sovereignty would not be manifest so long as England was under the religious leadership of the papacy. In 1534, he made a political—not a religious—decision when he broke with Rome and created the Church of England. Although their tenures on the throne were short and full of religious tension, Henry VIII's children, Edward VI and Mary Tudor, enjoyed the benefits of the restored prestige of the monarchy, which resulted from the efforts of Henry VII and Henry VIII.

The greatest of all the Tudors was **Queen Elizabeth** (r. 1558–1603), Henry VIII's daughter with Anne Boleyn. Elizabeth had been educated in the Italian humanist program of classical studies; she was intelligent and a diligent worker, with excellent political instincts like her father. Also like her father, Elizabeth knew how to select able ministers who would serve the crown with distinction—men such as William Cecil (Lord Burghley)—but she always kept herself as the ultimate decision maker in the land. Elizabeth used the prospect of marriage as a diplomatic tool, and she allowed almost every single ruler in Europe to imagine that he could possibly marry her—a powerful way to build alliances whenever the need arose. Whether she truly was the **"Virgin Queen"** is a question that no one—not even the wise folks who write the questions for the AP Exam—could ever answer. She did seem to regard marriage as incompatible with her sovereignty. Yet by staying single, she exposed England to the risk of religious war, because as long as she remained unmarried, the Catholic **Mary Stuart**, the ruler of Scotland, was her legal heir. (Mary Stuart's paternal grandmother, Margaret Tudor, was the sister of Henry VIII.)

The relationship between England and Scotland was a complex affair that continued to plague both lands throughout the 16th and 17th centuries. For years, Mary lived as Elizabeth's prisoner, following a rebellion by Scottish nobles that forced her from the throne. Elizabeth treated Mary as the rightful ruler of Scotland and the probable heir to the English crown, though she kept her under house arrest because she feared that Mary was plotting against her. Only after Mary conspired with Philip II of Spain did Elizabeth decide to settle relations with the Scots and distance herself from Mary. In the Treaty of Berwick (1586), she entered into a defensive alliance with Scotland. She recognized James, Mary's son who was being raised as a Protestant, as the lawful king, gave him an English pension, and—while she never specifically said so—let it be known that James was the heir to her throne. In 1587, Elizabeth finally took a step that she had been reluctant to take: she ordered the execution of **Mary, Queen of Scots**.

The year 1588 brought the greatest moment in Elizabeth's reign—the defeat of Philip II's **Spanish Armada**, which ensured that England would remain Protestant and free from foreign dominance. Although at least part of Elizabeth's authority gradually eroded as she grew older and people began to look beyond her reign to the future, the decades that followed the Armada conquest were also a period of an incredible cultural flourishing. This was the age of Shakespeare, Christopher Marlowe, Ben Jonson, and Edmund Spenser; and while Elizabeth may not have been a significant direct patron of this English Renaissance, the stability that she provided England during her reign allowed it to take place.

SPAIN

Prior to the 15th century, Spain was divided into several Christian kingdoms in the north, while the south had been under Islamic control since the 8th century. The 1469 marriage of **Ferdinand, King of Aragon**, and **Isabella, Queen of Castile**, laid the groundwork for the eventual consolidation of the peninsula, with the final stage of the *Reconquista* taking place in 1492, when their armies conquered the last independent Islamic outpost in Spain—the southern city of Grenada. The same year also marks the beginning of a new wave of religious bigotry, as the ardently Catholic Ferdinand and Isabella began to demand religious uniformity in their lands, and formally expelled the Jewish population that had been established in Spain since the time of the Roman Empire. The Jews and Moors who converted so that they could remain in Spain were later hounded by the **Spanish Inquisition**, an effective method that the Spanish monarchy would later use to root out suspected Protestants.

Through a series of well-planned marriages, Ferdinand and Isabella's grandson, **Charles V,** eventually controlled a vast empire that dominated Europe in the first half of the 16th century. His Spanish possessions were the primary source of his wealth and also supplied him with the tough Castilian foot soldiers who were the best in Europe. When Charles V—exhausted from his struggles to destroy Protestantism in the Holy Roman Empire—abdicated in 1556, he gave his brother Ferdinand (whom he disliked intensely) the troublesome eastern Habsburg lands of Austria, Bohemia, and Hungary, as well as his title of Holy Roman Emperor. Charles's son **Philip** (r. 1556–1598) received the more valuable part of the empire: Spain and its vast holdings in the New World, along with southern Italy and the Netherlands.

Philip gained a vast wealth from the New World's silver mines. Yet surprisingly, Philip spent most of his reign in debt, as he used his riches to maintain Spanish influence. In the Mediterranean, the Spanish fought for supremacy against the Ottoman Empire and won a notable success against that eastern power at the **Battle of Lepanto** in 1571. In northern Europe, however, Philip was caught in a quagmire when he attempted to put down a revolt in the Netherlands. This revolt—which combined religious and nationalistic ideas (as did the whole Reformation)—began in 1568 following an attempt by Philip to impose the doctrines of the Council of Trent and the Inquisition in a land where Calvinism had made significant inroads, particularly among key members of the aristocracy. For the next several decades, Philip expended huge amounts of money to try to restore Spanish control. Inquisition-based efforts such as the Duke of Alva's **Council of Troubles** (a.k.a. the "Council of Blood") failed, as did the effort of military hero **Don Juan**. It was for this reason that Philip launched the great **Spanish Armada** in 1588 as an attempt to conquer England, which, under Queen Elizabeth's rule, was aiding the Dutch rebels. By 1609, an exhausted Spain conceded virtual independence to the northern provinces of the Netherlands (while still maintaining control over the southern part of the country), and in 1648, formally acknowledged their independence.

Golden Age in Spain

The 16th and early 17th centuries were a cultural golden age that featured the writings of **Cervantes** (1547–1616), possibly Spain's greatest writer, whose masterpiece, *Don Quixote*, bemoans the passing of the traditional values of chivalry in Spain. It was also a period of remarkable Spanish painters such as the Greek-born **El Greco** (1541–1614). His magnificent yet somber works reveal much about a Spain that appeared to have it all, only to find it could not maintain its preeminent European position. In fact, the golden age of Spain did prove to be short-lived. The constant wars, the effects of the Price Revolution (more on this in Chapter 5), and the economic collapse of the Castilian economy led to a decline in Spain's power by the end of the 17th century.

THE HOLY ROMAN EMPIRE

The Holy Roman Empire, a large "state" that straddled central Europe, can be said to date back to 962, when the Saxon King Otto I was crowned emperor in Rome by the pope. In the late 10th and 11th centuries, the Empire was the most powerful state in Europe, but it was eventually weakened as a result of a series of conflicts with the papacy. While lacking the soldiers to stem the ambitions of the Holy Roman emperors, successive popes were able to find support among the German nobility, who chafed under strong imperial leadership. By 1356, the practice of electing the emperor was formally defined in the **Golden Bull** of **Emperor Charles IV**. This document, which granted to seven German princes the right to elect an emperor, made it clear that the emperor held office by election rather than hereditary right. The electors usually chose weak rulers who would not stand in the way of their own political ambitions.

Despite its name, the Holy Roman Empire was neither holy nor Roman nor an empire!

In the ensuing centuries, the empire continued to splinter into numerous semiautonomous territorial states so that by 1500 it consisted of more than 300 semiautonomous entities over which the emperor ruled but had very little actual authority. Charles V, the powerful Habsburg ruler who was elected emperor in 1519, attempted to establish genuine imperial control over the state. He soon found that the Lutheran Reformation provided a new weapon for those German princes and cities that wanted to avoid losing their independence.

The **Peace of Augsburg** (1555) signified the end of the religious wars in the time of Charles V, who now agreed to adhere to the basic principle that the prince decides the religion of the territory. The treaty, however, did not grant recognition to Calvinists, thus creating a problem when **Frederick III** converted to Calvinism in 1559. (Frederick III was the ruler of the Palatinate, a region in southwest Germany.) What further complicated the situation was that as the ruler of the Palatinate, Frederick was one of the seven electors of the Holy Roman Emperor.

Within the next two decades, several other German princes followed Frederick's lead and aggressively challenged the religious status quo achieved by the Peace of Augsburg. The tremendous success of the Catholic Counter-Reformation in Southern Germany further stoked religious tensions in Germany.

In areas such as Bavaria, all traces of Protestantism were stamped out as Jesuits were invited to take charge of Bavarian schools and universities. Although Charles V failed in his attempt to create a unified German state, the dream would continue. The **Thirty Years' War** (1618–1648), a struggle that combined political and religious issues, marked one final attempt within the Holy Roman Empire to make that dream a reality.

CED 2.4
Wars of Religion

The Thirty Years' War (1618–1648)

Are You a Visual Learner?
Consider looking at our *ASAP* books, available for some AP subjects. These handy guides present the most-tested content in a friendly, illustrated fashion. For example, in *ASAP European History*, you'll find a concise, informative chart outlining each country's involvement in the Thirty Years' War.

The Thirty Years' War began in **Bohemia** (the modern-day Czech Republic), where in 1617 Ferdinand of Styria, an avid Catholic, was crowned King of Bohemia. The majority of Bohemians were Protestant, and they were angered with their new King Ferdinand's intolerance toward their religious beliefs. In May of 1618, a large group of Bohemian Protestant nobles surrounded two of Ferdinand's Catholic advisors and threw them out of a window (the second Defenestration of Prague). They survived by landing in a dung heap. The next year, Matthias, the Holy Roman Emperor, passed away, and his cousin Ferdinand, the King of Bohemia, was elected Emperor in his stead. A few hours after being elected, Ferdinand learned to his horror that rebels in Bohemia had deposed him and elected **Frederick**, the **Calvinist Elector of the Palatinate**, as their king. Since he did not have an army, Ferdinand had to turn to the Duke of Bavaria, who agreed to lend his support in exchange for the electoral right enjoyed by the Palatinate. At the Battle of White Mountain, the Bavarian forces won a major victory, and Frederick became known as the Winter King because he held onto the Bohemian throne for only that season. By 1622, he had lost not only Bohemia but also the Palatinate.

The question now arises as to why the Thirty Years' War didn't end in 1622 (and force historians to give it a different name). Part of the problem was that there were still private armies throughout the Empire that wanted to fight to keep earning a living. The perceived threat to Protestants in Germany drew outsiders, such as the King of Denmark, into the fight. Additionally, both Catholic and Protestant rulers were concerned that the traditional constitution of the Holy Roman Empire had been dramatically altered when the Palatinate's electoral vote was given to Bavaria. Taking away this vote from the Palatinate was deemed an attack on what contemporaries called "German liberties," by which they meant the independence and political rights enjoyed by territories within the Holy Roman Empire.

This issue of liberties also came to the foreground when Emperor Ferdinand confiscated defeated Protestant princes' land in the north and created the genuine opportunity to forge a unified state under Habsburg control. Given this opportunity, Ferdinand first had to find a new army, because he could no longer rely on the Duke of Bavaria, who began to fear Habsburg domination. He turned to a Bohemian noble by the name of **Albrecht von Wallenstein** for this second phase of the war, who promised to create a vast mercenary army. By 1628, Wallenstein controlled an army of 125,000 and had won a series of major victories in the north.

The high-water mark for Habsburg success in the Thirty Years' War came with the **Edict of Restitution** of 1629. The edict outlawed Calvinism in the empire and required Lutherans to turn over all property seized since 1552—16 bishoprics, 28 cities and towns, and 155 monasteries and convents. This led the King of Sweden, **Gustavus Adolphus,** to enter the war, triggering a third phase. Although he claimed that he became involved to defend Protestant rights in Germany, Adolphus was also interested in German territory along the Baltic. To make matters even more confusing, the French government financially supported the Swedish army, because France's chief minister, **Cardinal Richelieu**, was concerned about the increase of Habsburg strength in Germany. Clearly this skirmish had ignited far beyond a religious war.

The Swedes rolled back the Habsburgs until 1632, when Adolphus died in battle. The next year, Wallenstein was murdered on orders of the emperor, because Ferdinand began to fear that his general was negotiating with his opponents. The final phase of the war consisted of the French and Swedes fighting against the Austrian Habsburgs and their Spanish allies. This was the most destructive phase of the war. German towns were decimated, and a general agricultural collapse and famine ensued. By the end of the war in 1648, the Empire had eight million fewer inhabitants than it had in 1618.

> **The Cost of War**
> By the end of the Thirty Years' War in 1648, the Empire's population had decreased by about eight million.

The **Peace of Westphalia** (1648) marked the end of the struggle. Thirty years of war had brought about very little. The Holy Roman Empire maintained its numerous political divisions, and the treaty ensured that the Emperor would remain an ineffectual force within German politics. The treaty also reaffirmed the Augsburg formula of each prince deciding the religion of his own territory, although the new formula now fully recognized Calvinism.

FRANCE

By the end of the reign of the powerful **Francis I**, it appeared as if the struggle between the feudal aristocracy and the monarchy had been settled in favor of the newly powerful centralized monarchy. However, the **French Wars of Religion** (1562–1598) revealed that the struggle was not quite over. Although ostensibly concerned with religious ideas, this series of civil wars was part of a long tradition,

> **French Calvinists**
> In France, Calvinists were known as Huguenots.

dating back to the very roots of French history, in which the aristocracy and monarchy battled each other for supremacy.

In part because Calvin himself was French, Calvinism had made early inroads in France. Religious conflicts rose to the surface following the French monarch Henry II's 1559 death, when his eye was pierced with a lance in a jousting accident while celebrating the end of the wars between the Habsburgs and the French Valois monarchs. On Henry's death, his sickly 15-year-old son Francis II came to the throne. Francis was to be replaced the next year by his brother, who reigned as Charles IX (r. 1560–1574) and then 14 years later by a second brother, the last of the Valois kings, Henry III (r. 1574–1589). All three boys would be influenced by their mother, one of the most remarkable women of the age, **Catherine de' Medici**.

Behind the scenes of the French monarchy, a power struggle began to emerge among three prominent families. The rise of the nation-state in France had contributed to a decline in the power of the old aristocratic families. These three families hoped that, with a weak monarch on the throne, they could reverse this trend. The **Guises**, the most powerful of the three, turned toward a militant, reactionary form of Catholicism. Meanwhile, partly through religious convictions and partly out of political opportunism, **Admiral Coligny**, the leader of the Montmorency family, and the **Prince of Conde**, the leading Bourbon, both converted to Calvinism.

The Wars of Religion began in 1562 when the Duke of Guise was infuriated to see a group of Huguenots worshiping in a barn and had them killed. After 10 years of combat, in which both the Duke of Guise and the Prince of Conde were killed, the Huguenots had the upper hand. As a sign of this Calvinist ascendancy, **Henry of Navarre**, a young Bourbon prince, married King Charles IX's sister. The political eclipse of the Valois family greatly concerned Catherine de' Medici, who, although not the religious bigot of legend, constantly sought to balance out the power of the aristocratic families to protect the interest of her sons. When the cream of the Huguenot aristocracy gathered in Paris in 1572 to celebrate the wedding, Catherine encouraged her son the king to set in motion the **St. Bartholomew's Day Massacre,** in which an estimated 3,000 died in Paris. Possibly 20,000 Huguenots in total were killed in organized attacks throughout France. Admiral Coligny was killed, but Henry of Navarre's life was spared when he promised to return to Catholicism.

In 1574, Henry III, the last of the Valois kings, turned to the Huguenots to defeat the powerful Catholic League that the Guise family had formed to serve their interests. He eventually made Henry of Navarre his heir, who became **King Henry IV** in 1589 following his assassination, thus beginning the **Bourbon dynasty** that would rule France up to the time of the French Revolution. Above all else, the new king wanted peace in his kingdom. Henry was faced with a struggle with Spain, a nation that sought to keep France both politically weak and Catholic. Because of these pressures, and also because most Parisians remained fiercely Catholic, Henry IV—having switched numerous times for political reasons between Calvinism and Catholicism—in 1593 converted permanently to Catholicism. He marked this occasion with these noteworthy words: "Paris is worth a Mass."

In many ways, Henry's actions instigated a new way of thinking in France, the idea of the *Politique*, putting the interests of France before the goal of religious unity. Although his Calvinist allies and the Anglican Queen Elizabeth were horrified by Henry's final religious conversion, he did not forget them. In 1598, he issued the **Edict of Nantes**, granting the Huguenots freedom of worship and assembly as well as the right to maintain fortified towns for their protection.

CHAPTER 4 TIMELINE

Just before the Review Questions at the end of each chapter, you'll find a timeline of events for the relevant period. The timeline below includes events not only mentioned in this chapter, but also events discussed in the next chapter. This is due to the overlap in time frames between chapters. Use the timelines as quick reviews of key events; don't obsess over memorizing every date.

Year(s)	Event
1341	Petrarch crowned Poet Laureate in Rome
1378	Ciompi Revolt
1378	Black Death hits Europe
1387	Chaucer starts *The Canterbury Tales*
1397	Establishment of the Medici Bank
1403	Alberti begins work on the doors of the baptistery in Florence
1405	Christine de Pisan's *City of Ladies*
1406	Florence conquers Pisa
1415	Burning at the stake of Jan Hus at the Council of Constance
1415	Prince Henry the Navigator participates in the capture of Ceuta in northwestern Africa
1417	Great Schism comes to an end
1420s	Development of single-point perspective
1440	Lorenzo Valla's *On the Donation of Constantine*
1440s	Donatello's *David*
1452	Gutenberg prints Bible
1453	End of the Hundred Years' War
1453	Fall of Constantinople
1454	Treaty of Lodi
1469	Marriage of Ferdinand of Aragon to Isabella of Castile
1485	Henry VII begins Tudor dynasty following Battle of Bosworth
1486	Pico's *Oration on the Dignity of Man*
1487	Bartholomew Dias sails around Cape of Good Hope
1490	Ludovico il Moro becomes despot of Milan
1492	Columbus leaves Spain for what he believes will be Asia
1492	Expulsion of the Jews from Spain
1492	*Reconquista* of Spain completed
1492	Lorenzo de Medici dies
1494	King Charles VIII of France invades Italy
1494	The Treaty of Tordesillas divides the discoveries in the New World between Spain and Portugal

Year(s)	Event
1498	Vasco da Gama reaches the coast of India
1498	Burning of Savonarola
1501	Michelangelo's *David*
1503	Leonardo's *Mona Lisa*
1509	Raphael's *School of Athens*
1513	Machiavelli writes *The Prince*
1515	Erasmus's *In Praise of Folly*
1516	More's *Utopia*
1517	Luther's *95 Theses*
1519	Charles V becomes Holy Roman Emperor
1519	Ferdinand Magellan sets out to circumnavigate the globe
1519	Hernán Cortés lands on the coast of Mexico
1521	Luther called before the Diet of Worms
1522	Ignatius Loyola begins *The Spiritual Exercises*
1525	German Peasant Revolt
1528	Castiglione's *The Courtier*
1529	Diet of Speyer
1529	Henry VIII summons the "Reformation Parliament"
1531	Zwingli dies in battle
1531	Francisco Pizarro sets out for Peru
1534	Henry VIII's Act of Supremacy
1534	Anabaptists seize Munster
1535	Sir Thomas More executed by Henry VIII
1536	Calvin publishes first edition of his *Institutes*
1540	Jesuits receive official papal sanction as religious order
1540	Henry VIII marries Anne Boleyn
1540s	Schmalkaldic War
1543	Copernicus publishes his *Concerning the Revolutions of the Celestial Spheres*
1543	Andreas Vesalius writes *De humani corporis fabrica* with its critique of the anatomical work of Galen
1545	Council of Trent convenes
1553	End of reign of Edward VI of England
1553	Michael Servetus burnt at the stake in Geneva
1555	Peace of Augsburg
1556	Philip II becomes King of Spain after Charles V abdicates
1558	Death of Queen Mary of England

Year(s)	Event
1558	Beginning of reign of Elizabeth Tudor
1559	Frederick III of the Palatinate converts to Calvinism
1559	Death of King Henry II of France
1559	Elizabethan religious settlement
1562	Beginning of the French Wars of Religion
1571	Battle of Lepanto
1572	St. Bartholomew's Day Massacre during the French Wars of Religion
1587	Execution of Mary, Queen of Scots
1588	Failure of the Spanish Armada to invade England
1589	Henry Bourbon becomes King Henry IV
1593	Henry IV converts to Catholicism
1598	Edict of Nantes
1600	Giordano Bruno burned at the stake
1602	First known performance of Shakespeare's *Hamlet*
1602	Dutch East India Company established
1603	James I becomes king following death of Elizabeth
1603	Michael Romanov begins new dynasty in Russia
1605	Cervantes publishes first part of *Don Quixote*
1607	Founding colony at Jamestown
1610	Assassination of Henry IV
1610	Galileo begins astronomical observations with his telescope
1613	Galileo publishes *Letters on Sunspots*
1616	William Harvey announces his discovery of the circulatory system
1618	Johannes Kepler reveals his third and final law of planetary motion
1618	Beginning of the Thirty Years' War
1620	Battle of White Mountain
1620	Founding of Plymouth Colony
1620	Francis Bacon publishes *Novum Organum*
1624	Cardinal Richelieu becomes Louis XIII's chief minister
1625	Charles I becomes king upon death of James I
1628	Petition of Right
1628	Murder of the Duke at Buckingham
1629	Edict of Restitution
1629	Personal Rule of Charles I begins and will last 11 years
1632	Gustavus Adolphus dies at the Battle of Lutzen
1632	Galileo's *Dialogue on the Two Chief Systems of the World*

Year(s)	Event
1633	Trial of Galileo
1633	Murder of Albrecht von Wallenstein
1637	Charles introduces the Book of Common Prayer into Scotland
1637	René Descartes publishes *Discourse on the Mind*
1640	Beginning of the reign of Frederick William (Great Elector)
1640	Charles forced to summon Parliament to deal with Scottish revolt
1641	Rebellion in Ireland
1642	Execution of the Earl of Strafford
1642	Issuing of Grand Remonstrance
1642	Beginning of English Revolution
1643	Five-year-old Louis XIV becomes King of France
1645	Execution of Archbishop Laud
1648	Peace of Westphalia

CHAPTER 4 KEY TERMS

The Renaissance: Overview

Georgio Vasari
"rebirth"
individualism
city-states
Northern Renaissance
Protestant Reformation

Italian City-States

Holy Roman Empire
popolo
Ciompi Revolt
the Medici
papal states
patrons

Humanism

humanism
Francesco Petrarch
"Dark Ages"
Pico della Mirandola, *Oration on the Dignity of Man*
Florentine Platonic Academy
Neoplatonism
civic humanists
Castiglione, *The Courtier*
Lorenzo Valla
Leonardo Bruni
Christine de Pisan

Renaissance Art

Filippo Brunelleschi
fresco
chiaroscuro
single-point perspective
High Renaissance
mannerism
Leonardo da Vinci, *Mona Lisa*
Raphael, *The School of Athens*
Michelangelo, *David,* the Sistine Chapel
Julius II

The Northern Renaissance

Christian Humanists
Desiderius Erasmus, *Adages; In Praise of Folly*
Sir Thomas More, *Utopia*
Albrecht Durer
Geoffrey Chaucer, *Canterbury Tales*
Boccaccio, *The Decameron*
Elizabethan Renaissance
Christopher Marlowe
Ben Jonson
William Shakespeare, *Hamlet; King Lear*
Johannes Gutenberg, the printing press

The Protestant Reformation

The Protestant Reformation
The Catholic Reformation
Black Death
anticlericalism
pietism
Great Schism
simony
John Wycliffe
Lollards
Jan Hus
Martin Luther, *95 Theses*
selling of indulgences
Albert of Hohenzollern
Johann Tetzel
Wittenberg
Pope Leo X
Diet of Worms
Charles V, the Holy Roman Emperor
transubstantiation
Protestantism
German Peasants' Revolt
priesthood of all believers
Ottoman Empire
Schmalkaldic War
Peace of Augsburg
Radical Reformation
Anabaptists
Antitrinitarians
Ulrich Zwingli

John Calvin
Calvinism
Huguenots

The English Reformation
Henry VIII, *The Defence of the Seven Sacraments*
Catherine of Aragon
Anne Boleyn
Reformation Parliament
Elizabeth Tudor
Jane Seymour
Act of Supremacy
Edward VI
Mary Tudor, "Bloody Mary"

The Counter-Reformation
Catholic Reformation (Counter-Reformation)
Index of Prohibited Books
papal Inquisition
Council of Trent
baroque
Society of Jesus (Jesuits)
Ignatius Loyola

The Portuguese and Spanish Empires
Prince Henry the Navigator
Bartholomew Dias
Cape of Good Hope
Vasco da Gama
Christopher Columbus
Ferdinand Magellan
Hernán Cortés
Aztec Empire
Tenochtitlán
Inca Empire of Peru
Francisco Pizarro
encomienda system
magnetic compass
sextant
Mercator projection
caravel
New World
Columbian Exchange

Development of Monarchical States
nation-states
bureaucratization
mercenary army

Italy
Treaty of Lodi
Ludovico il Moro
Charles VIII of France
Savonarola
Niccolò Machiavelli

England
Wars of the Roses
Henry Tudor (Henry VII)
Tudor dynasty
Queen Elizabeth (the "Virgin Queen")
Mary (Stuart), Queen of Scots

Spain
Ferdinand, King of Aragon
Isabella, Queen of Castile
Spanish Inquisition
Charles V
Philip
Battle of Lepanto
Council of Troubles
Don Juan
Spanish Armada
Cervantes
El Greco

The Holy Roman Empire
Golden Bull
Emperor Charles IV
Peace of Augsburg
Frederick III
The Thirty Years' War
Bohemia
Frederick, Calvinist Elector of the Palatinate
Albrecht von Wallenstein
Edict of Restitution
Gustavus Adolphus
Peace of Westphalia

France
Francis I
French Wars of Religion
Huguenots
Catherine de' Medici
Guises
Admiral Coligny
Prince of Conde
Henry of Navarre (King Henry IV)
St. Bartholomew's Day Massacre

CHAPTER 4 REVIEW QUESTIONS

Try these questions to assess how well you understood and retained the information covered in the chapter. Answers and explanations are in Chapter 8.

Questions 1 through 5 refer to the following.

"All these stadholders were commanders-in-chief of the military forces in their respective provinces. With the single exception of Count Egmont, in whose province of Flanders the stadholders were excluded from the administration of justice, all were likewise supreme judges in the civil and criminal tribunal. The military force of the Netherlands in time of peace was small, for the provinces were jealous of the presence of the soldiery. The only standing army which then legally existed in the Netherlands were the Bandes d'Ordonnance, a body of mounted gendarmerie, amounting in all to three thousand men, which ranked among the most accomplished and best-disciplined cavalry in Europe.

Besides these troops, however, there still remained in the provinces a foreign force, amounting in the aggregate to four thousand men…. Living upon the substance of the country, paid out of its treasury, and as offensive by their licentious and ribald habits of life as were the enemies against whom they were enrolled, these troops had become an intolerable burthen[1] to the people. They were now disposed in different garrisons, nominally to protect the frontier. As a firm peace, however, had now been concluded between Spain and France, and as there was no pretext for compelling the provinces to accept this protection, the presence of a foreign soldiery strengthened a suspicion that they were to be used in the onslaught which was preparing against the religious freedom and the political privileges of the country. They were to be the nucleus of a larger country, it was believed, by which the land was to be reduced to a state of servile subjection to Spain. A low, constant, but generally unheeded murmur of dissatisfaction and distrust upon this subject was already perceptible throughout the Netherlands, a warning presage of the coming storm."

Source: John Lothrop Motley, *The Rise of the Dutch Republic*, vol. 1, 1555–1559

[1] burden

1 ☐ Mark for Review

Bandes d'Ordonnance, a "body of mounted gendarmie," was probably drawn from

- (A) the priesthood of all believers
- (B) the peasantry
- (C) the merchant class
- (D) the aristocracy

2 ☐ Mark for Review

The "foreign force" mentioned in the passage is best described as a

- (A) conscription army
- (B) mercenary army
- (C) mounted cavalry
- (D) free infantry

3 ☐ Mark for Review

For the Netherlands, the result of the eighty-year-long conflict with Spain was

- (A) an era of restricted artistic freedom
- (B) a weakened political state and devastated economy
- (C) a period of economic and cultural power
- (D) a more united view of religion

4 ☐ Mark for Review

During the time of this passage, the Holy Roman Empire was controlled by

(A) the Hohenzollern

(B) the Habsburgs

(C) the Romanovs

(D) the Bourbons

5

"The coming storm" referred to in the final sentence most likely refers to

(A) the insistence upon divine monarchy

(B) the beginning of Lutheranism

(C) the Dutch Revolt

(D) the founding of the Dutch East India Company

Questions 6 through 10 refer to the following.

"Whereas the power of conferring Indulgences was granted by Christ to the Church; and she has, even in the most ancient times, used the said power, delivered unto her of God; the sacred holy Synod teaches, and enjoins, that the use of Indulgences, for the Christian people most salutary, and approved of by the authority of sacred Councils, is to be retained in the Church; and It condemns with anathema those who either assert, that they are useless; or who deny that there is in the Church the power of granting them. In granting them, however, It desires that, in accordance with the ancient and approved custom in the Church, moderation be observed; lest, by excessive facility, ecclesiastical discipline be enervated. And being desirous that the abuses which have crept therein, and by occasion of which this honourable name of Indulgences is blasphemed by heretics, be amended and corrected, It ordains generally by this decree, that all evil gains for the obtaining thereof,—whence a most prolific cause of abuses amongst the Christian people has been derived,—be wholly abolished….

[The Council] not only orders that bishops be content with modest furniture, and a frugal table and diet, but that they also give heed that in the rest of their manner of living, and in their whole house, there be nothing seen that is alien from this holy institution, and which does not manifest simplicity, zeal towards God, and a contempt of vanities. Also, It wholly forbids them to strive to enrich their own kindred or domestics out of the revenues of the church: seeing that even the canons of the Apostles forbid them to give to their kindred the property of the church, which belongs to God; but if their kindred be poor, let them distribute to them thereof as poor, but not misapply, or waste, it for their sakes: yea, the holy Synod, with the utmost earnestness, admonishes them completely to lay aside all this human and carnal affection towards brothers, nephews and kindred, which is the seed-plot of many evils in the church."

Source: The Council of Trent, 1564

6 ☐ Mark for Review

The Council of Trent is viewed as a reaction by the Catholic Church against which of the following?

(A) The Renaissance

(B) The Reformation

(C) The Scientific Revolution

(D) The Enlightenment

7 ☐ Mark for Review

The authors of the document display an attitude toward worldly possessions that is most directly at odds with which of the following?

(A) The principles of the Catholic catechism

(B) The beliefs of the lay piety movement in northern Europe

(C) The transatlantic transfer of animals, plants, and diseases during the Age of Exploration

(D) The splendor of St. Peter's Basilica in Rome

8 ☐ Mark for Review

The phrase "evils in the church" could be a reference to the abuse of the sale of indulgences by

(A) Martin Luther

(B) Pope Leo X

(C) Johann Tetzel

(D) Galileo Galilei

9 ☐ Mark for Review

The Council of Trent resulted in which of the following actions taken toward the Protestant Reformation?

(A) It restated the basic theological infallibility of the tenets of medieval Catholicism.

(B) It absorbed most Protestant ideas, with the intention of weakening its opponents' power.

(C) It agreed that the priestly caste was an unnecessary layer between the people and God.

(D) It sent papal armies to retake Protestant German villages by force.

10 ☐ Mark for Review

For the Catholic Church, the Council of Trent occurred at the beginning of a long period of

(A) artistic influence because of fewer options for artists to win commissions outside the church

(B) voluntary conversion of native people outside of Europe

(C) growth in political authority, particularly in western Europe

(D) decline in political authority, particularly in western Europe

Questions 11 through 15 refer to the following.

Vitruvian Man, Leonardo da Vinci, 1490

---

11 ◻ Mark for Review

In composing this drawing, da Vinci was most likely influenced by which of the following?

(A) Dadaism

(B) Classicism

(C) Romanticism

(D) Narcissism

12 ◻ Mark for Review

Which of the following statements is most closely associated with this work of art?

(A) I think; therefore, I am.

(B) Erasmus laid the egg that Luther hatched.

(C) A man has free choice to the extent that he is rational.

(D) Man is the measure of all things.

13 ☐ Mark for Review

Da Vinci's choice to depict the man in detail would seem to suggest all of the following EXCEPT

Ⓐ a desire to examine the human form in an analytical manner

Ⓑ a weaker sense of indecency

Ⓒ a need to win more commissions from the pope

Ⓓ a desire to improve his own artistic abilities

14 ☐ Mark for Review

In creating this drawing, da Vinci drew upon

Ⓐ Greek principles of number ratios

Ⓑ medieval theological principles

Ⓒ contemporary anatomical models

Ⓓ the scientific method

15 ☐ Mark for Review

The Renaissance began in the Italian peninsula for all of the following reasons EXCEPT

Ⓐ increased trade with Arab, Indian, and Chinese cultures

Ⓑ lack of connection to previous European civilizations

Ⓒ the presence of a wealthy and well-educated aristocratic class

Ⓓ the Black Death's force of a change in mentality of the people

Chapter 5
Units 3–5:
Monarchical States
to Napoleon
(c. 1648–1815)

FRANCE

Royal Absolutism

Until his assassination in 1610, Henry IV worked to revitalize his kingdom. With his finance minister, the Duke of Sully, Henry established government monopolies over a number of key commodities (such as salt) to restore the finances of the monarchy. He also limited the power of the French nobility by reining in its influence over regional parliaments. Despite this strengthening of monarchical power, Henry's assassination in 1610 and the ensuing ascension of his nine-year-old son, Louis XIII, made France once again vulnerable to aristocratic rebellion and the potential religious wars. Louis needed a strong minister, and he found one in **Cardinal Richelieu**. Richelieu defeated the Huguenots and took away many of the military and political privileges granted to them by the Edict of Nantes. He brought France into the Thirty Years' War—not as the defender of Catholic interests, but on the side of the Protestants—in order to counter the traditional French enemy, the Spanish Habsburgs.

The death of Louis XIII in 1643 once again left France with a minor on the throne; the five-year-old **Louis XIV** was unable to benefit from Richelieu's guidance because the great minister had predeceased Louis XIII by one year. Louis XIV's mother, Ann of Austria, selected **Cardinal Mazarin** to be the regent during the king's childhood. Mazarin had a less-sure political hand than Richelieu, and once again, France had to grapple with a series of rebellions known as the *Fronde* in the period between 1649 and 1652. These events scarred the young Louis XIV, who at one point during the rebellion had to flee from Paris. Following the death of Mazarin in 1661, Louis decided to rule without a chief minister and to finally grapple with the central issue that had dominated France for more than a hundred years—how to deal with an aristocracy that resented the ever-increasing powers of the French monarchy.

> **"I Am the State"**
> Although it is unclear whether Louis ever said the famous line *"L'état, c'est moi"* ("I am the state"), the statement does assert Louis's belief that no political or religious authority existed, either within or beyond the borders of France, that had any right to encroach on his sovereignty.

One way that Louis achieved this goal was to advocate a political philosophy that had been developing in France since the 16th century—**the divine right of kings**, or the notion that the monarch enjoyed certain divine rights. Using Old Testament examples of divinely appointed monarchs, Louis's chief political philosopher, Bishop Bossuet, wrote that because the king was chosen by God, only God was fit to judge the behavior of the king, not parliamentary bodies or angry nobles.

Louis built the palace of **Versailles** 12 miles outside of Paris as another way to dominate the French nobility and the Parisian mob. Although his grandfather had converted to Catholicism to appease the people of Paris, Louis felt he could safely ignore the people from the confines of his palace. Eventually, 10,000 members of the nobility and officials lived at Versailles, a palace so immense that its facade was a third of a mile long, with grounds boasting 1,400 fountains. While it cost a huge amount of money to maintain Versailles, Louis thought it was worth it. Instead of plotting against the king, the aristocrats were distracted by court intrigue, gossip, and ceremonial issues (such as who got to hold the king's sleeve as he got dressed). Those members of the aristocracy who did not live at Versailles were pleased with their tax exemptions as well as their high social standing.

To administer his monarchy, Louis made use of the upper bourgeoisie. No member of the high aristocracy attended the daily council sessions at Versailles. Instead, his most important minister was **Jean-Baptiste Colbert**, the son of a draper. Colbert centralized the French economy by instituting a system known as **mercantilism**. The central goal of mercantilism was to build up the nation's supply of gold by exporting goods to other lands and earning gold from their sale. To do this, Colbert organized factories to produce porcelains and other luxury items. He also tried to abolish internal tariffs, ultimately creating the **Five Great Farms**, which were large, custom-free regions.

Part of mercantilism was a reliance on foreign colonies to buy the mother country's exports. To that end, Colbert succeeded in helping to create France's vast overseas empire. By the 1680s, Louis controlled trading posts in India, slave-trading centers on the west coast of Africa, and several islands in the Caribbean, while the largest colonial possession was New France, the territory we know today as Quebec. Colbert particularly wanted to strike at the rich commercial empire of the Dutch, so he organized the **French East India Company** to compete with the Dutch. It enjoyed only limited success, partly as a result of excessive government control and a lack of interest in such ventures by the French elite.

Louis XIV touted religious unity in France as a means of enhancing royal absolutism. During the reign of his father, the rights of Huguenots declined due to the hostility of Richelieu, while the Edict of Nantes was still in effect. Louis decided that the time had come to eradicate Calvinism in France. In 1685, he revoked the **Edict of Nantes**, a fateful decision that would greatly weaken the French state. He demolished Huguenot churches and schools and took away their civil rights. Some remained underground, but as many as 200,000 were exiled to England and the Netherlands. The Huguenots were an important part of the French economy; by fleeing to enemy lands, they aided the two countries that were at war with Louis. For Louis, however, such economic considerations meant little in comparison to what he thought was the more important goal and the one most pleasing to God—the elimination of religious heresy from France.

> ### Rivals on the World Stage
> In the 1500s, France showed mild interest in exploring the Americas, mostly through a small presence in present-day Canada. England, however, showed even less appetite; after sponsoring John Cabot's excursions to North America in the late 1400s, it essentially gave up. Later, however, both countries realized just how dominant Spain and Portugal were becoming across the globe. By 1600, both governments had decided to step up their game. Samuel Champlain founded Quebec in 1608 and helped set up a series of small French outposts as far inland as present-day Chicago, while at the same time, England began to establish settlements in coastal Virginia and elsewhere. **[CED 1.7]**

During the reign of Louis XIV, France was involved in a series of wars as a means to satiate Louis's desire for territorial expansion. In the early part of his reign, this policy was quite successful, as France conquered territories in Germany and Flanders. This success lasted until 1688, when the English—in a move that marked the Glorious Revolution—replaced James II, the king who had received subsidies from the French, with a new monarch, **William of Orange**, who as leader of the Netherlands was committed to waging total war against Louis. After 1688, another series of wars erupted that lasted for 25 years, including the **War of Spanish Succession** between the French and the English and Dutch allies. This war lasted from 1702 to 1713 and concluded with the **Treaty of Utrecht**, which left a Bourbon (Louis's grandson) on the throne of Spain but forbade the same monarch from ruling both Spain and France. These wars ultimately resulted in the containment of Louis XIV's France but left the French peasantry hard pressed to pay the taxes to support Louis's constant desire for glory.

ENGLAND

The Stuarts

CED 3.3
Continuities and
Changes to Economic
Practice and
Development

When Elizabeth died childless in 1603, her cousin **King James VI of Scotland** inherited the throne, as promised. To a certain extent, James was ill-suited for the role of English king. The Scottish Parliament was a weak institution that did not inhibit the power of the monarch. James's interest lay in asserting his divine notion of kingship, which he had been exposed to by reading French writings on the subject. He told the English Parliament the following during the first session with them:

The state of monarchy is the supremest thing upon Earth: for Kings are not only God's lieutenants upon Earth and sit upon God's throne, but even by God Himself they are called gods. As to dispute what God may do is blasphemy, so it is sedition in subjects to dispute what a King may do in height of his power. I will not be content that my power be disputed on.

Such words could not have pleased his audience. In the relationship between the king and Parliament at the start of the 17th century, the monarch held the upper hand—only the king could summon a parliament and he could dismiss it at will. James did, however, have to consult the two-house English Parliament, the **House of Commons** and the **House of Lords**, when he needed to raise additional revenue beyond his ordinary expenses. This parliamentary control over the financial purse strings, in an age when the cost of governing was dramatically increasing, played a crucial role in Parliament's eventual triumph over royal absolutism.

Religious issues further complicated James's reign. (He was always suspected of being a closet Catholic.) The religious settlement worked out by Elizabeth in 1559 was no longer adequate in an age in which English religious passions grew increasingly intense. It failed to satisfy the radical Calvinist Protestants, known as **Puritans**, who emerged during the Stuart period. In 1603, most Puritans still belonged to the Church of England, although they were a minority within the Church. For the most part, what distinguished the Puritans was that they wanted to see the Church "purified" of all traces of Catholicism. Although raised in Calvinist Scotland, James, on his arrival in England, found the Church of England with its hierarchical clergy and ornate rituals more to his taste. He believed its Episcopal structure was particularly well-suited to his idea of the divine right of kings. In 1604, when a group of Puritans petitioned the new king to reform the Church of England, James met them with this declaration: "I will have one doctrine, one discipline, one religion, both in substance and in ceremony." He added words that would prove to be rather prophetic for his son: "No Bishop, No King," meaning that by weakening the Church, the monarchy in turn weakens. James's opposition to the Puritan proposal drove the more moderate of the Puritans—individuals who just wanted to rid the Church of England of its last traces of Catholic ritual—onto a more extreme track. Some Puritans even decided to leave England; one such group founded the colony of Plymouth, Massachusetts, in 1620.

James's three-part program—to unite England with Scotland, to create a continental-style standing army, and to set up a new system of royal finance—met with little support from Parliament. James's son, **Charles I** (r. 1625–1641), did not possess even the somewhat limited political acumen of his father. Like his father, Charles felt that the Anglican Church provided the greatest stability for his state, and he further enflamed passions by lending his support to the so-called **Arminian** wing of the Anglican Church. Arminius was a Dutch theologian of the early 17th century who argued in favor of free will as opposed to the Calvinist doctrine of **predestination**. In 1633, Charles named William Laud, a follower of this doctrine, his Archbishop of Canterbury. The Arminians, although certainly not pro-Catholic, refused to deny that Catholics were Christians; this philosophy greatly angered the Puritans. The Arminians further antagonized Puritan sentiment by advocating a more ornate church service.

The relationship between Charles and Parliament got off to a bad start when Parliament granted him **tonnage and poundage** (custom duties) for a one-year period rather than for the life of the monarch, as had been the custom since the 15th century. Charles, however, was committed to the war against Spain, so he cashed in his wife's dowry and sent an expedition to the Spanish port of Cadiz. The mission was a complete failure. To pay for these military disasters, Charles requested a forced loan from his wealthier subjects. Several Members of Parliament refused to pay this loan and were thrown in jail. Parliament was called in again in 1628, at which time it put forward a **Petition of Rights**, which Charles felt forced to sign. It included provisions that the king could not demand a loan without the consent of Parliament and that Parliament must be called frequently. The petition also prohibited individuals from being imprisoned without published cause and the government from housing soldiers and sailors in private homes without the owner's permission. Finally, it outlawed the use of martial law against civilians, which Charles had employed to collect his forced loan.

In August 1628, Charles's chief minister, the dashing but incompetent Duke of Buckingham, was murdered by an embittered sailor who blamed him for England's recent military disasters. Charles, on the other hand, blamed the leaders of the House of Commons, most notably John Eliot, for inflaming passions against Buckingham. When Parliament was again called in January 1629, both sides felt that the issue of exclusive rights would lead to a conflict between Parliament and the king. In March 1629, the issue came to the foreground when Eliot proposed three resolutions.

1. High churchmen and anyone suspected of popery (practicing Catholicism) should be branded as capital enemies of the state.
2. Any of the king's advisors who recommended that he raise funds without Parliament's approval should be tried as capital enemies of the state.
3. Anyone who paid tonnage and poundage, which the King was still illegally collecting, would be betraying the "liberties of England."

After hearing these demands, which he thought outrageous, the king summoned the Speaker of the House of Commons and ordered him to dissolve Parliament. Two Members of Parliament held the Speaker in his chair, a treasonable act because it disputes the right of the king to dissolve Parliament. Once Eliot's resolutions were passed, the king's messengers announced that he had dissolved Parliament.

For the next 11 years, what is known as the **Personal Rule of Charles** was the law of the land. Charles decided to govern England without calling a Parliament. Charles could have carried this off successfully and brought about the end of Parliament, as occurred in France during the same period of time. The major problem of how to raise enough revenue was solved by extending the collection of ship money throughout the kingdom, a politically explosive decision. Traditionally, certain coastal cities were responsible for raising funds for naval defense during times of national emergency. In 1634, Charles declared an emergency (although England was at peace), and two years later he extended this tax to inland cities and counties, areas that had never before paid ship money. This was such a substantial source of income that it could possibly have freed the king from ever having to call a Parliament.

By 1637, Charles was at the height of his power. He had a balanced budget, and his government policies and restructuring appeared to be effective. Yet within four years of this peak, the country would be embroiled in a civil war. Charles ultimately ruined his powerful position by insisting that Calvinist Scotland adopt not only the Episcopal structure of the Church of England, but also follow a prayer book based on the *English Book of Common Prayer*. The Scots rioted and signed a national covenant that pledged their allegiance to the king but also vowed to resist all changes to their Church.

The Case of John Hampden

The collection of ship money led to a famous legal case involving John Hampden, a Puritan Member of Parliament, who, having already challenged the legality of the forced loan, now questioned Charles's raising of ship money. While the judges found against Hampden by a vote of seven to five, he was viewed as having achieved a moral victory.

In 1640, Charles called an English Parliament for the first time in 11 years, because he believed it would be willing to grant money to put down the Scottish rebellion. This became known as the **Short Parliament** because it met for only three weeks and was dissolved after it refused to grant funds prior to Charles addressing their own grievances. Charles was still determined to punish the Scots; after he dissolved Parliament, he patched together an army with the resources he could muster. The Scots were the victors on the battlefield and invaded northern England. They refused to leave England until Charles signed a settlement and, in the meantime, forced him to pay £850 per day for their support.

To pay this large sum, Charles was forced to call another Parliament. This became known as the **Long Parliament,** because it met for an unprecedented 20 years. The House of Commons launched the Long Parliament by impeaching Charles's two chief ministers, the Earl of Strafford and Archbishop Laud (Strafford was executed in 1641, and Laud in 1645). Parliament abolished the king's prerogative courts, like Henry VIII's Court of Star Chamber, which had become tools of royal absolutism. Tensions grew even higher when a rebellion broke out in Ireland, which had been ruled with a strong hand since the time of the Tudors.

Parliament took the momentous step of limiting some of the king's prerogative rights. They supported what was known as the **Grand Remonstrance**, a list of 204 parliamentary grievances from the past decade. They also made two additional demands: that the king name ministers whom Parliament could trust and that a synod of the Church of England be called to reform the Church of England. In response, Charles tried to seize five of the leaders of the House of Commons, an attempt that failed, resulting in Charles leaving London in January 1642 to raise his royal standard at Nottingham. This marked the beginning of the **English Revolution**.

The English Revolution

During the initial stage of the English Revolution, things went poorly for Parliament. Their military commander, the Earl of Manchester, pointed out the dilemma when he noted, "If we beat the King 99 times, he is still the King, but if the King defeats us, we shall be hanged and our property confiscated." Individuals, such as **Oliver Cromwell**, who were far more dedicated to creating a winning war policy, soon replaced the early aristocratic leaders. It was Cromwell who created what became known as the **New Model Army**, a regularly paid, disciplined force with extremely dedicated Puritan soldiers. By 1648, the king was defeated, and in the following year, Cromwell made the momentous decision to execute the king, a move that horrified most of the nation.

From 1649 to 1660, England was officially a republic, known as **The Commonwealth**, but essentially it was a military dictatorship governed by Cromwell. Cromwell had to deal with conflicts among his own supporters, such as the clash between the **Independents** and the **Presbyterians**. The Independents, who counted Cromwell among their ranks, wanted a state church, but were also willing to grant a measure of religious freedom for others (although Catholics were to be excluded from this tolerant policy). On the other side of the divide were the Presbyterians, who wanted a state church that would not allow dissent. Cromwell also had to deal with the rise of radical factions within his army, groups such as the **Levellers** and the **Diggers**, who combined their radical religious beliefs with a call for a complete overhaul of English society. They touted a philosophy that included such radical ideas as allowing all men, not just those who owned land, to vote for members of the House of Commons.

Cromwell destroyed the Leveller elements in his army in 1649 after several regiments with large Leveller contingents revolted against his rule. In the following year, Cromwell led an army to Ireland, where he displayed incredible brutality in putting down resistance by supporters of the Stuarts.

Cromwell would find, as Charles I had earlier, that Parliament was a difficult institution to control. In 1652, he brought his army into London to disperse a Parliament that dared to challenge him, only to replace them with hand-selected individuals who still earned his displeasure within a matter of months. Over the next year, a group of army officers wrote the "Instrument of Government," the only written constitution in English history. This document provided for republican government (the Protectorate) with a head of state holding the title Lord Protector and a parliament based on a fairly wide male suffrage. Cromwell stepped into the position of Lord Protector, but still found Parliament difficult to control. Finally in 1655, Cromwell gave up all hope of ruling in conjunction with a legislature and divided England into 12 military districts, each to be governed by a major general.

By the time Cromwell died, an exhausted England wanted to bring back the Stuart dynasty. In 1660, the eldest son of the executed monarch became King **Charles II**. The return of the Stuarts turned back the clock to 1642 as the same issues that had led to the revolution against Charles's father remained unresolved: What is the proper relationship between king and Parliament? What should be the religious direction of the Church of England? These issues were not fully addressed during Charles's reign, although they came to the forefront during the reign of his younger brother, **James II**, who succeeded Charles on the throne in 1685.

> **CED 3.2**
> The English Civil War and the Glorious Revolution

Suspected of being a Catholic, like all previous Stuarts, James immediately antagonized Parliament by demanding the repeal of the **Test Act**, an act passed during Charles II's reign that effectively barred Catholics from serving as royal officials or in the military. (There was no law at this time barring Catholics from the monarchy.) James also issued a **Declaration of Indulgence**, which suspended all religious tests for office holders and allowed for freedom of worship. On the surface, James appeared to have been a champion of religious freedom, but this was deceptive. What James really wished to achieve in England was royal absolutism; however, the steps that he took to achieve this goal were illegal. The final stages of this conflict took place in 1688. Early in the year, James imprisoned seven Anglican bishops for refusing to read James's suspension of the laws against Catholics from their church pulpits, the usual way of informing the community of royal edicts in an age before modern communications. James also unexpectedly fathered a child in June 1688 and now had a male heir who would be raised as a Catholic, in contrast to his previous heir, his daughter Mary, who was a Protestant. These moves to create a Catholic England created unity among previously contentious Protestant factions within England. One faction of this political and religious elite invited **William, the Stadholder** of the Netherlands and the husband of Mary, to invade England. When his troops landed, James's forces collapsed in what was basically a bloodless struggle (except for in Ireland, where there was tremendous violence over the next several years), known as the **"Glorious Revolution."** James was overthrown, and William and Mary jointly took the throne.

> **What's a Stadholder?**
> In case you've never heard this term used before, a *stadholder* is a Dutch word referring to an office that primarily served a military function between the 15th and 18th centuries in the Netherlands.

What followed was a constitutional settlement that finally attempted to address the pervasive issues of this century of revolution.

The settlement consisted of the following acts:

- **The Bill of Rights** (1689) forbade the use of royal prerogative rights as Charles and James had exercised in the past. The power to suspend and dispense with laws was declared illegal. Armies could not be raised without parliamentary consent. Elections to Parliament were to be free of royal interference. The monarchs also had to swear to uphold the Protestant faith, and it was declared that the monarchy could not pass into the hands of a Catholic. Most importantly, Parliament's approval was now officially required for all taxation.
- **The Act of Toleration** (1689) was in many ways a compromise bill. To get nonconformists' (Protestants who were not members of the Church of England) support in the crucial months of 1688, Whigs and Tories (Whigs being the more liberal parliamentary faction than the Tories) promised that an act of toleration would be granted when William became king. The nonconformists could have achieved liberty of worship from James II's act of toleration, but an act from a popular Protestant monarch would prove to be a better safeguard to their liberties. The Act of Toleration granted the right of public worship to Protestant nonconformists but did not extend it to Unitarians or to Catholics. (Those two groups were also left alone, although legally they had no right to assemble to pray.) The Test Act remained, which meant nonconformists, Jews, and Catholics could not sit in Parliament, until the law was changed in the 19th century.
- **The Mutiny Act** (1689) authorized the use of civil law to govern the army, which previously had been governed only by royal decree. It also made desertion and mutiny civil crimes, for which soldiers could be punished during peacetime. But the act was only in effect on a year-by-year basis, which meant that a Parliament had to be summoned annually if for no other reason than to pass this act. Along with the Bill

of Rights' provision against standing armies in peacetime, the Mutiny Act brought the army under effective parliamentary control.

- **The Act of Settlement** (1701) was passed to prevent the Catholic Stuart line from occupying the English throne. In 1714, when Queen Anne, the second Protestant daughter of James II, died childless, the throne passed to George I, the Elector of Hanover, a Protestant prince and a distant relative of the Stuarts.
- **The Act of Union** (1707) marked the political reunification of England and Scotland, forming the entity known as Great Britain. This union was by no means a love match. In fact, it occurred primarily because relations between the two previously independent states were so bad that, on his deathbed, William III urged that union take place to forestall Scotland from going to war with England as an ally of France. As part of the agreement, Scotland gave up its parliament but was allowed to maintain the state-sponsored Presbyterian Church and its Roman-based legal system.

In short, after over a century of internal strife, England had successfully transitioned from a divine-based monarchy to a constitution-based monarchy. It was the first nation in Europe to begin to shift political power into the hands of the people, and this gamble would pay off handsomely in the next two centuries as Great Britain amassed the largest empire in the world (see Chapter 6).

THE NETHERLANDS

A Center of Commerce and Trade

The relative decline of Spain as an economic power was in part due to the growing competition from the Netherlands. The Netherlands had already achieved a central role in inter-European trade due to its geographic position and large merchant marine fleet. For example, it was the Netherlands that provided a connection between the raw material producers in the Baltic region and the rest of Europe. Beyond Europe, control over the lucrative spice trade in Asia was wrested from the hands of the Portuguese, a situation which was made worse when Spain took control over Portugal in 1580 and found itself without the resources to rival the Dutch in Asia.

> **CED 3.5**
> The Dutch Golden Age

Increasingly, it was the city of Amsterdam (the capital of the Netherlands), rather than the Spanish-controlled city of Antwerp, that became the center of commerce in northern Europe. The city of Antwerp further declined after it was sacked in 1576 during the **Dutch War for Independence**. Part of the Peace of Westphalia that followed the war included the permanent closing of the Scheldt River that led to Antwerp's harbor, which also aided Amsterdam in replacing Antwerp as an economic center.

Dutch dominance in part came from technological achievements such as the development of less-expensive but ocean-worthy cargo ships, but the Dutch also proved to be creative in their establishment of financial and commercial institutions. The **Bank of Amsterdam**, founded in the early part of the 17th century, issued its own currency and increased the amount of available capital, while also making Amsterdam the banking center of Europe. In 1602, the **Dutch East India Company** was established. The company operated under quasi-governmental control and was funded by both public and private investment. This kind of investment, used in the past but most successfully in the Netherlands, gave rise to the popularity of **joint-stock companies**. Such

CED 3.3
Continuities and
Changes to
Economic Practice
and Development

companies allowed risks and profits to be shared among many individuals. The large capitalization behind the Dutch East India Company allowed for the purchasing of more ships and warehouses. The Dutch also proved to be very nimble in business, so that when the prices of spices decreased due to oversupply, they quickly turned to other commodities, such as coffee, tea, and fabrics. However, by the beginning of the 18th century, Dutch commercial power would lose its preeminent place in Europe to the English, who in 1606 had started another joint-stock company, the Virginia Company, to develop the eastern coast of North America.

This **"Golden Age"** in the Netherlands produced a high standard of living, with wealth being more equally distributed than in any other place in Europe. The Netherlands also stood out from the rest of Europe for its tolerant attitude toward religious minorities, where Anabaptists, Catholics, and Jews fleeing the Spanish Inquisition could find a place among the majority Calvinist population.

Political Decentralization

Dutch exceptionalism also extended to the political realm because politically, the Netherlands didn't look like any other state in Europe. For most of the 17th century, it was politically decentralized, with each of the seven provinces retaining extensive autonomy. Wealthy merchants dominated the provincial Estates, which retained powers far more extensive than those of national Estates General, particularly in the area of taxation. Executive power, such as it was, came from the noble **House of Orange**, whose family members had achieved prominence for leading the revolt against Spain. The male head of this family held the title of *stadholder*, an office with primarily a military function; this wasn't just a formality, as the Netherlands switched from fighting for its independence from Spain to economic wars against the English and a long-term struggle for survival against France. During the struggle with Louis XIV's France, the power of the provincial Estates went into decline, while the authority of **William of Nassau**, the head of the House of Orange, increased tremendously, particularly when William became King of England after the Revolution of 1688.

Dutch Autonomy
Unlike other countries in Europe during the same period, the Netherlands did not have a centralized government. Rather, each of the seven provinces was politically autonomous.

A Golden Age of Art

Culturally, the 17th century proved to be a golden age as well. Dutch artists, reflecting the fact that the majority of the population was Calvinist, didn't receive large commissions to be placed in churches, although the Baroque style of painting penetrated the Netherlands through Catholic Flanders. Instead, Dutch artists painted for private collectors, who supported an incredibly large number of painters and a wide range of styles, including the production of a large number of landscapes. Like so much else in the Netherlands, pictures were treated as commodities, with prices at times reaching speculative rates.

The art market didn't just flourish in Amsterdam, as shown by the thriving career of Franz Hals (c. 1580–1666), the great portrait painter from Haarlem. Another gifted Dutch painter, **Jan Vermeer** (1632–1675), had initially thought of being a painter of historical scenes. But when he received no commissions, he turned to the carefully composed genre scenes of everyday Dutch life, for which he has become justifiably famous. The greatest genius of the Dutch golden age was **Rembrandt van Rijn** (1606–1669), whose paintings were initially influenced by the High Baroque style and more subtly painted later in his career, and are fraught with a deep emotional complexity. One of his most famous works, *The Night Watch* (1642), transforms a standard group portrait of a military company into a revealing psychological study.

ECONOMIC AND SOCIAL LIFE IN EARLY MODERN EUROPE

It's a little difficult to generalize about life in early modern Europe because conditions varied from region to region, but general trends do emerge for the period.

Economic Expansion and Population Growth

By the end of the 15th century, Europe was ushering in an age of economic expansion that sharply contrasted with the decline that had taken root in the 14th century with its disastrous famines and plagues. The key development in the period was the growth in population. To use France as a typical example, the population doubled from 10 million to 20 million from 1450 to 1550. This significant population expansion was very important for economic productivity, in an age in which labor power was still far more important than labor-saving technology. The expansion of Europe's population also provided for additional consumers, which meant that there was greater incentive to bring more food and other essentials to market.

The growth of population also had an impact on another important development: the significant increase in prices in the early modern period, which has become known as the **Price Revolution**. Initially, historians thought that this increase came from the influx of precious metals from the New World and the debasement of their coinage by money-hungry monarchs, but it is now apparent that it was population growth that put pressure on the prices of basic commodities, such as wheat. Grain prices increased 500 percent in the period from 1500 to 1650—a rate that doesn't seem surprising to modern consumers. Nevertheless, for a society that was accustomed to stable prices, an increase of this magnitude came as a shock. Historians have even tried to find ways of connecting the Price Revolution to the political and religious struggles of the age, based on the theory that periods of high inflation can be an important factor behind the development of social tensions.

Rural Life and the Emergence of Economic Classes

One way in which rural life was transformed in this period, in part due to the Price Revolution, was the emergence of a class of wealthy individuals, located socially below the aristocracy, who began to buy significant amounts of newly valuable landholdings. In England, this class of individuals, who often had their economic roots in fortunes made in towns and cities, were known as the **gentry**, and would play a major role in the political struggles that the English Parliament would wage against the monarchy in the 17th century. The land-buying habits of the gentry forced up the price of land. In addition, members of the gentry were able to use their social connections to get local authorities to accept the **enclosure** of lands for their own personal use, land that had previously been available for the grazing of animals by the entire community.

> **More Sheep**
> In Book 1 of *Utopia*, Sir Thomas More refers to the notion of sheep devouring men, a criticism of the displacement of the small farmer by valuable herds of sheep.

The problem of rural poverty became significantly worse in the early modern period, with many small farmers reduced to the role of beggars, spending their days tramping from one locale to another. Increasingly, the problem of poverty weighed on the political elite. In Catholic lands, the Church remained the major provider of social services, while in Protestant countries it became the task of the state to provide for the destitute, such as the first **English Poor Law** during the reign of Queen Elizabeth. Although rural overpopulation was a problem throughout most of western Europe, in eastern Europe, low population density was a much more serious problem, leading wealthy landowners to solve their labor shortages by binding the formerly free peasantry to the land in a process of enserfment.

Farm Life

For the majority of individuals in Europe, who lived in rural areas as small-scale farmers, life was fairly dismal and revolved around a constant struggle to find the resources to survive. Life centered on the small village, often fewer than 50 households, with most people never traveling a few miles beyond the location of their birth. Housing in rural villages offered little protection from the cold and wet winters. Homes were generally made of wood, had packed mud on the walls and straw on the floor, and lacked windows and adequate ventilation. For the most part, typical houses consisted of one main room with a stone hearth providing heat. The possessions that went into these houses were as simple as their surroundings. The worldly possessions of most rural households could fit in a single chest, which could double as a table and was easily carried in case the family had to flee during an emergency, such as the arrival of mercenaries looking for plunder.

The workdays were long during the summer harvests and shorter in the winter. Late winter offered the rural household the terrifying prospect of not having enough resources to tide them over until the coming of spring. Farming began to change by the end of the 17th century in the Netherlands and in England with the introduction of what we may refer to as scientific methods. However, for the most part, Europeans were farming in 1800 the same way they had farmed going back to the High Middle Ages (c. 1001–1300). The **three-field system** (in which crops were rotated across three pieces of land) was used in the north of Europe, while the two-field system (crops rotated on two pieces of land) predominated in the Mediterranean region. Farmland in most rural areas was set out in long strips, with individual peasant families owning a portion of land in each of the strips. Because animals such as cows and sheep needed copious amounts of food, common lands in each village were shared, although the wealthy rural elite was increasingly coveting this common land. Most of what was grown was used by the farmers for their own households, leaving very little to be brought to market. The diet of the average European peasant farmer was incredibly monotonous, with most calories coming from grain in various forms, ranging from dark bread to gruel and beer.

Life in the Cities and Towns

Although towns and cities held scarcely more than 10 percent of the overall population, they provided for some variation from what Karl Marx would call "the idiocy of rural life." Townspeople in general lived better than their rural counterparts, with better housing and a more varied diet, although urban poverty was also increasing in this period.

There was also a much greater variety of occupations, with an emphasis on specialization, with specific tasks such as baking or brewing taking place in specific quarters of the town. **Guilds**, which began to dominate the urban economy during the High Middle Ages, continued to play a role in the production of commodities down to the time of the French Revolution.

However, the guild method of production was being supplanted by a new means of production that was in part directed by the expansion of population and the growth of markets. Cloth was now produced on a much larger scale by a new group of **capitalist entrepreneurs** and required a large outlay of money to get started. These individuals would provide the money and the organizational skills, which they used to direct every stage of the production of broadcloth, beginning with the cleaning of the wool and ending with the weaving. This work provided a benefit in some rural households (where the various stages of production would now take place), adding an important source of revenue particularly during the long winter months.

For guild members, however, this new competition created great hardships. Also, for apprentices and journeymen, the dream of becoming a full-fledged guild master was becoming an increasingly rare occurrence. These men essentially became wage earners with little hope of rising up the economic and social ranks. Dissatisfied journeymen and apprentices would play an important role in the urban revolts of the period.

Family Life and Structure

Although we tend to assume that some notion of the extended family existed in the past, with several generations living under one roof, the family in the Early Modern period would not look significantly different from today's nuclear family. Family size was smaller than what one might have imagined for the period, with the average family consisting of no more than three or four children. The relatively small number of children was partly the result of fewer childbearing years resulting from later marriages, with women on average marrying at around age 25 and men at age 27. Traditionally, marriages were either arranged by the parents or at least formally approved, in part because even in the poorest of rural communities, marriage involved some transfer of property. Weddings were important community events, because the married husband and wife were now considered to be full-fledged members of society, and in general, single adults were looked on as potential thieves or troublemakers.

The Role of Men in the Family

In many ways, the family with the father as the patriarchal head served as a reflection of the larger hierarchical ordering of early modern society. In wealthier families, the father had to ensure that the family's wealth remained intact, which meant that the oldest male child inherited most of the estate (**primogeniture**). Younger sons were guided toward careers in the Church, military, or in the increased opportunities offered by the burgeoning administration of the early modern state. Among the poor, boys worked as early as age seven, as trade apprentices or as servants.

The Role of Women

The only claim that daughters would have on the parental estate would come with the **dowry** that they would receive upon marriage. Wives could usually determine who should receive their dowry upon their death, although during their own lifetimes their husbands would manage the dowry. For impoverished girls, domestic service was usually the only opportunity, and they were left with the difficult task of trying to raise their own dowries.

The Family as Economic Unit

Early modern families, whether rich or poor, can be seen as economic units. Before the late Industrial Revolution, child labor was accepted and commonplace. To some extent, jobs were gendered: men played a larger role in the "public" sphere, such as plowing, planting, and commerce, while women had responsibility over the home. However, in agricultural communities, everyone was expected to work in the fields; and among merchant classes, the "private" sphere might include bookkeeping and other administration of the family business while the men went on purchasing tours. In some cases, the main difference between women's work and men's work was that women's work included all the men's work, in addition to taking care of the house and the cooking. The strongest division between men's and women's roles was in the upper classes and the nobility. Only these very wealthy people could afford the luxury of an idle woman. This, combined with better diet, wet-nursing, and more sanitary conditions, was why wealthier families might see annual pregnancies (as opposed to every two or three years for poorer women), as well as why the wealthy had a much lower childhood mortality rate.

How the Protestant Reformation Changed Family Life

Although one can scarcely talk about a revolution taking place in family life in this period, the Protestant Reformation did usher in some changes. In Protestant lands, the household became the center of Christian life, rather than the church or monastery. Arguably, paternalism increased, as the father now assumed a spiritual role as the chief intermediary between the family and God, while also more strictly enforcing moral standards and the value of hard work. For women who wanted to avoid marriage and constant childrearing, the option of convent life came to an end. In some places, divorce was allowed, something that was anathema to the Catholic Church.

However, women in Protestant lands were conceivably freer in the sense that they were able, like any man, to directly communicate with God without relying on a male priest as an intermediary. However, those women who wanted to take a more active role by leading congregations and preaching—as seen in some of the more radical Protestant sects, such as the Anabaptists—were brutally persecuted.

EVENTS LEADING TO THE SCIENTIFIC REVOLUTION

In 1611, the English poet John Donne wrote *An Anatomy of the World*, in which he reflected on the multitude of ways that his world had changed as a result of the new discoveries in science.

CED 4.1
Contextualizing the
Scientific Revolution
and the Enlightenment

New philosophy calls all in doubt
The element of fire is quite put out;
The sun is lost, and th' Earth, and no man's wit
Can well direct him where to looke for it.
And freely men confesse that this world's spent,
When in the Planets, and the new firmament
They seeke so many new; then see that this
Is crumbled out againe to his Atomies
'Tis all in peeces, all coherance gone;
All just supply, and all Relation.

As Donne understood, the scientific discoveries of the 16th and 17th centuries brought about a fundamental change in the way Europeans viewed the natural world. To call this change a revolution may be misleading in light of the length of time over which it occurred, but the implications from these discoveries were truly revolutionary. Not only did it change the way Europeans viewed the world around them, but it also had significant implications in such areas as religion, political thought, and how they fought wars.

Why was it that 17th-century thinkers challenged the medieval view of the natural world? What possibly occurred in that age that led them to question ideas that previously had been readily accepted? The following are some possibilities.

Discovery of the "New World"

The period of exploration and conquest led to the discovery of new plant and animal life and possibly encouraged greater interest in the natural sciences. Also, the traditional link between navigation and astronomy and the great advances made by Portuguese navigators in the 15th century helped fuel an interest in learning more about the stars.

Invention of the Printing Press

Scientific knowledge could spread much more rapidly because of the printing press. By the second half of the 17th century, there were numerous books and newsletters keeping people informed about the most recent scientific discoveries. It is because of the printing press that Thomas Hobbes, sitting in England, was cognizant of scientific discoveries coming out of Italy.

Rivalry Among Nation-States

The constant warfare between the various nation-states may have pushed scientific development by placing an increasing importance on technology, or applied science. Further, Europe was a region with many powerful leaders who could fund scientific development. Columbus, an Italian, could find funding for his voyages from Ferdinand and Isabella of Spain after being turned down by John of Portugal. Compare this to the situation in China; with few technological competitors and a single ruler capable of canceling major projects, Chinese technological development slowed relative to that of Europe.

Reformation

The historian Robert K. Merton suggested a number of years ago that the English who professed Calvinist beliefs were somehow linked to those who were active in the new science. Even earlier than Merton, one of the founders of sociology, Max Weber, argued that the worldly asceticism found in Protestantism helped create capitalism, which in turn helped propel the Scientific Revolution. These theories, however, ignore the fact that much of the Scientific Revolution came from Catholic Italy. The telescope and microscope, for example, were Italian in origin, as was the rediscovery of botany. Nevertheless, the Protestant Reformation, by encouraging people to read the Bible, did help create a larger reading public. And although Luther, Calvin, and the like were not interested in challenging the traditional scientific worldview, their opposition to the religious hegemony of Rome did provide a powerful example of challenging established authority.

Renaissance Humanism

Humanist interest in the writings of the classical world also extended to the scientific texts of the ancient Greeks. Certain texts, such as Archimedes's writings on mathematics and Galen's anatomical studies, were rediscovered in the Renaissance. Although the Scientific Revolution ultimately rejected the ideas contained in such works, this basic familiarity with the past was a necessary stage in order for modern scientific thought to mature.

PRE-SCIENTIFIC WORLDVIEW

CED 4.2
The Scientific Revolution

The medieval worldview was based on **scholasticism**, a synthesis of Christian theology with the scientific beliefs of the ancient authors. The great architect of this synthesis was **Thomas Aquinas** (1225–1274), who took the works of Aristotle and harmonized them with the teachings of the church. Knowledge of God remained the supreme act of learning and was to be attained through both reason and revelation. The value of science, for those living in the Middle Ages, was that it offered the possibility of a better understanding of the mysterious workings of God. To view science without this religious framework was simply inconceivable in the Middle Ages.

Medieval "Science"
In the Middle Ages, people believed the world was made up of exactly four elements—earth, fire, air, and water—which in the human body were combined to make the four humours: yellow bile, black bile, blood, and phlegm. Mmm.

Influenced by the work of Aristotle, medieval people thought that the material world was made up of four elements: earth, air, fire, and water. Earth was the heaviest and the basest of the elements and therefore tended toward the center of the universe. Water was also heavy but lighter than earth, so its natural place was covering the Earth. Air was above water, with fire as the lightest element of all. It was this notion of the four elements that gave rise to the idea of **alchemy**, or the perfect compound of the four elements in their perfect proportions. Less perfect metals, such as lead, might be transformed by changing the proportion of their elements. The four-element approach also dominated the practice of medicine. The four elements combined in the human body to create what were known as the four humours: blood, phlegm, yellow bile, and black bile. An excess of any one of the humours produced one's essential personal characteristics.

People in the Middle Ages did not have a great interest in astronomy; the popular work of the Greek astronomer **Ptolemy** (c. 85–165 A.D.) was not questioned. The Ptolemaic, or Geocentric, system placed the Earth as a stationary object around which heavenly bodies moved, while the stars were fixed in their orbits. One problem with this system was addressed rather early: how does one explain the unusual motion of the planets in relation to the fixed stars? At times, planets even appeared to be moving backward. To cope with these problems, epicycles—planetary orbits within an orbit—were added to the system.

After Copernicus

The Earth-centered system would not go away that quickly. The Danish astronomer **Tycho Brahe** (1546–1601) tried to come up with a different Earth-centered system rather than just relying on the Ptolemaic system. Brahe had plenty of time on his hands to construct the best astronomical tables of the age, as his social life was nonexistent (this may be because he lost part of his nose in a duel and rebuilt it with a prosthetic made of silver and gold alloy). Brahe proposed a system in which the Moon and the Sun revolved around the Earth, while the other planets revolved around the Sun.

Brahe's student, **Johannes Kepler** (1571–1630), disagreed with his teacher concerning Copernicus's findings. Kepler ended up using Brahe's own data to search for ways to support Copernicus and eventually dropped Copernicus's "planets move in a circular motion" theory, instead proposing that their orbits were elliptical. However, it would take the greatest mind of the next age, **Isaac Newton**, to explain why this elliptical motion was in fact possible.

THE COPERNICAN REVOLUTION

In 1543, **Nicolaus Copernicus** (1473–1543), a Polish mathematician and astronomer, wrote *Concerning the Revolutions of the Celestial Spheres*. Copernicus was a cleric, and because he was afraid of the implications of the ideas contained in the work, he waited many years before he finally decided to publish. When he finally took that step, Copernicus cautiously dedicated the book to Pope Paul III and included a preface that claimed that the ideas contained in it were just mathematical hypotheses. Even the language of the work was moderate, as Copernicus merely suggested that, should the Earth revolve around the Sun, it would solve at least some of the problematic epicycles of the Ptolemaic system. However, since the Copernican, or **heliocentric**, system explains that the planets move in a circular motion around the Sun, it did not completely eliminate all the epicycles. Despite his book's famous reputation, Copernicus's ideas did not stir a revolution in the way in which people viewed the planets and the stars.

Galileo

The first scientist to build on the work of Copernicus was a Florentine by the name of **Galileo Galilei** (1564–1642). In 1609, he heard about a Dutchman who had invented a spyglass that allowed distant objects to be seen as if close up. Galileo then designed his own telescope that magnified far-away objects 30 times the naked eye's capacity. Using this instrument, he noticed that the Moon had a mountainous surface very much like the Earth. For Galileo, this provided evidence that it was composed of material similar to that on Earth and not some purer substance as Aristotle had argued. Galileo also realized that the stars were much farther away than the planets. He saw that Jupiter had four moons of its own. This challenged the traditional notion of the unique relationship between Earth and its Moon. Sunspots and rings around Saturn also put the whole Ptolemaic construct into doubt.

Galileo was also interested in the question of motion. He may not have really thrown a ten-pound weight and a one-pound weight from the top of the Leaning Tower of Pisa, but he did notice that heavier weights do not fall any faster than lighter ones. He also noticed that under ideal conditions a body in motion would tend to stay in motion. Therefore, it was relatively easy for him to deduce from this the possibility that Earth is in perpetual motion.

Following the publication of his *Dialogues on the Two Chief Systems of the World* (1632), the Catholic Church began to condemn Galileo's work. The church authorities warned Galileo not to publish any more writings on astronomy. Throwing caution to the wind, he wrote a book that compared the new science with the old; an ignorant clown Simplicio represented the old science. Pope Urban VIII thought the book was making fun of him, and he put Galileo under house arrest for the remainder of his life. This did not stop Galileo from writing, although he was forced to send his manuscripts to Holland, where the mood was more tolerant.

> **Giordano Bruno**
> Galileo proved to be far more fortunate than his fellow Italian, **Giordano Bruno** (1548–1600), a Dominican friar who was executed by the **papal Inquisition** in 1600 for arguing that there may be a plurality of worlds in the universe. The Church took this as an implication that there might be a multiplicity of redeeming Christs— an intolerable heresy.

Sir Isaac Newton

The greatest figure of the Scientific Revolution was **Isaac Newton** (1642–1727). Newton wanted to solve the problem posed by the work of Copernicus, Kepler, and Galileo: how do you explain the orderly manner in which the planets revolve around the Sun? Newton worked for almost two decades on the problem before he published his revolutionary work, *Principia*, in 1687. Galileo's work on motion influenced Newton, a sign of the intellectual link between southern and northern scientists. Newton wondered what force kept the planets in an elliptical orbit around the Sun, when theoretically they should be moving in a straight line. Supposedly Newton saw an apple drop from a tree and deduced that the same force that drew the apple to the ground may explain planetary motion. Newton finally posited that all planets and objects in the universe operated under the effects of gravity.

> Newton revealed his famous laws only after losing a bet to Edmund Halley and other scientists about the nature of planetary orbits— decades after he'd already worked them out!

It is important to remember that Newton was an extremely religious man. He often wondered why, when he delivered public talks, his audiences were more interested in his scientific discoveries than in theology. He spent a great deal of time studying alchemy and esoteric interpretations of the bible.

More importantly, he began to experiment with optics, thus making the study of light a new scientific endeavor. It was Newton who showed that white light was a heterogeneous mixture of colors rather than the pure light many believed it to be. Newton is also the founder of differential calculus (much to the regret of those of you who have to take it in high school). Finally, Newton also eventually became head of the British Royal Society, an organization committed to spreading the new spirit of experimentation.

THE IMPACT OF THE SCIENTIFIC REVOLUTION ON PHILOSOPHY

Among the philosophers affected by the new science was **Francis Bacon** (1561–1626). Bacon led an extraordinarily varied life. He was a lawyer, an official in the government of James I, a historian, and an essayist. The one thing he did not do in his life, it seems, was perform scientific experiments. What he did contribute to science was the experimental methodology. In his three major works—*The Advancement of Learning* (1605), *Novum Organum* (1620), and *New Atlantis* (1627)—Bacon attacked medieval scholasticism with its belief that the body of knowledge was basically complete and that the only task left to scholars was to elaborate on existing knowledge. Instead, Bacon argued that rather than rely on tradition, it was necessary to examine evidence from nature. Bacon's system became known as **inductive reasoning**, or **empiricism**. In France, this debate over the new learning method became known as the conflict between the ancients and the moderns, while in England it was known as the "Battle of the Books."

René Descartes

The French philosopher **Descartes** (1596–1650) can, in some ways, be seen as the anti-Bacon. For Descartes, **deductive thought** (also referred to as **rationalism**)—using reason to go from a general principle to the specific principle—provided for a better understanding of the universe than did relying on the experimental method. However, like Bacon, Descartes believed that the ideas of the past were so suffocating that they all must be doubted. In his famous quote, **"I think; therefore I am,"** Descartes stripped away his belief in everything except his own existence. This is the ultimate expression of **Cartesian doubt**, the system of methodical skepticism that defined his thought. ("Cartesian" refers to Descartes, minus the "Des-.") Another way that Descartes broke with the past was by writing in French rather than Latin, which had been the language of intellectual discourse in the Middle Ages. Descartes was also a highly gifted mathematician who invented analytical mathematics.

Descartes's system can be found in his *Discourse on Method* (1637). In the work, he reduced nature to two distinct elements: mind and matter. The world of the mind involved the soul and the spirit, and Descartes left that world to the theologians. The world of matter, however, was made up of an infinite number of particles. He viewed this world as operating in a mechanistic manner, as if in a constant whirlpool that provided contact among the various particles.

Blaise Pascal

Pascal (1623–1662) saw his life as a balancing act. He wanted to balance what he saw as the dogmatic thinking of the Jesuits with those who were complete religious skeptics. His life's attempt to achieve this balance is found in his *Pensées*, particularly in the idea that became known as **Pascal's Wager**, in which Pascal concluded that it was better to wager on the existence of God than not, because the expected value that comes from believing is always greater than the expected value of not believing. Pascal became involved with the Jansenists, a Catholic faction that saw truth in St. Augustine's idea of the total sinfulness of humankind and that, because we are predestined, faith is required to achieve salvation. These ideas were also followed by the Calvinists.

Thomas Hobbes

Thomas Hobbes (1588–1679) personally knew Galileo, Bacon, and Descartes, and was also friends with **William Harvey** (1578–1657), who, rather than relying on the writings of the Ancient Greeks, used dissections to show the role the heart plays in the circulation of blood through the body. His contact with the leading figures in the world of science influenced Hobbes to apply the experimental methods they used in the study of nature to the study of politics. Hobbes was horrified by the turmoil of the English Revolution and was convinced of the depravity of human nature; humans were like animals in that they were stimulated by appetites rather than by noble ideas. Hobbes wrote in his classic work, ***Leviathan,*** that life without government was "nasty, brutish, and short."

> **Science and Hobbes**
> Hobbes's willingness to think scientifically shows the way in which the world had changed from the time of Machiavelli, whose work reflects the world as it was before the Scientific Revolution.

Hobbes's view of the depravity of human nature led him to propose the necessity for **absolutism**. Man formed states, or what Hobbes called the great Leviathan, because they were necessary constructs that worked to restrain the human urges to destroy one another. Out of necessity, the sovereign has complete and total power over his subjects. The subjects are obliged never to rebel, and the sovereign must put down rebellion by any means possible. When the parliamentary side won the civil war, Hobbes went back to England and quietly went on with his life. He readily accepted any established power, and could therefore live under Cromwell's firm rule. His theories did not please traditional English royalists, because his brand of absolutism was not based on the divine right theory of kingship.

John Locke

Like Hobbes, **John Locke** (1632–1704) was interested in the world of science. His *Two Treatises on Government*, written before the Revolution of 1688, was published after William and Mary came to the throne, and served as a defense of the revolution as well as a basis for the English Bill of Rights. It also proved critical for the intellectual development of the founders of the United States. Locke argued that man is born free in nature, although as society gets more advanced, government is needed to organize this society. Because humans are free and rational entities, when they enter into a **social contract** with the state, they do not give up their inalienable rights to life, liberty, and property. Should an oppressive government challenge those rights, people have a right to rebel.

Locke was an opponent of religious enthusiasm. In his *Letter Concerning Toleration*, Locke attacked the idea that Christianity could be spread by force. His influential *Essay on Human Understanding* contained the idea that children enter the world with no set ideas. At birth, the mind is a blank slate or *tabula rasa*, and infants do not possess the Christian concept of pre-destination or original sin. Instead, Locke subscribed to the theory that all knowledge was empirical in that it comes from experience.

Scientists and Philosophers of the Scientific Revolution, 1450–1700

KEY DEVELOPMENTS IN 18TH-CENTURY LIFE

Urban Growth

Cities began growing rapidly in the 1700s. The population of Britain, for example, nearly doubled in that time, with most of the growth concentrated in urban areas. It wasn't only the overall population increase that led to the growth of the cities. Rural farmers found themselves out of work owing to the technological advancements of the time, so they moved to the cities in search of employment in factories and textile mills. In England, because of a mobile peasantry untethered to the land, that shift occurred more quickly than it did in continental Europe.

The new cities were not for the faint of heart, and many people from traditional rural communities found themselves in a dizzying new environment. In many quarters, the streets and alleys were filled with drunkards, prostitutes, and pestilence. Open gutters carried away human waste, horse manure, and animal entrails. Pollution was so bad that shopkeepers would sometimes light candles at midday. The smells were, by modern standards, horrific. Many travelers report smelling London long before reaching it.

CED 4.4
18th-Century Society and Demographics

On the positive side, a plethora of theaters, inns, taverns, and shops were open for enjoyment. A new craze, the urban coffee house, swept across Europe as people discovered the pleasant effects of caffeine on their nervous systems. Merchants and tradesman walked the streets, hawking their goods or services. Transportation consisted mostly of pedestrians, a few horse-drawn carriages, and—for the very wealthy—"sedan chairs" carried on the shoulders of servants. The older portions of the cities featured a medieval design, and so prevented many carriages from passing.

All these developments, especially the negative ones, presented many challenges to life and were impossible to ignore. As a result, city dwellers felt motivated to improve their surroundings. Slowly, over time, city governments began laying out new streets, cleaning existing ones, and installing streetlights, all to the great wonder of visitors. The very first police departments were created to manage the socially marginal groups of criminals and ne'er-do-wells. Finally, public health began to become a priority.

Medicine

The 1700s were responsible for some big leaps forward in the field of health. Scottish surgeons lifted the reputation of their field to a respectable science, especially through the efforts of **John Hunter**. An obstetrician, **William Smellie**, pioneered the use of forceps in childbirth, saving countless lives. More importantly, the practice of vaccination arrived in Europe in the 1720s via **Lady Mary Wortley Montagu**, an English aristocrat who had observed inoculations in Istanbul while her husband had been stationed there as the ambassador to the Ottoman Empire. Back in England, **Edward Jenner**, a country doctor, took this new concept and began injecting humans with the cowpox virus, the bovine form of smallpox. For centuries, this disease had been a scourge on humanity, and his innovation worked. The smallpox virus was eventually eradicated from the continent.

These advances, combined with the growth of new hospitals and an increased awareness of public health, led to a decrease in child mortality. Prior to this, it was accepted that half of all children died before reaching adulthood, but that percentage shrank dramatically during this century. This new expected lifespan caused a radical shift in thinking: children were no longer viewed as disposable. They now were regarded as valuable individuals who happened to be passing through a glorious period of innocence. As symbols of this new stage of life, children were celebrated as popular subjects of paintings. Publishers began issuing easy-to-read children's textbooks to help shape impressionable young blank-slate minds.

THE 18TH-CENTURY ENLIGHTENMENT

Although his response has become a bit of a cliché, there is no better answer to the question "What is the Enlightenment?" than that offered by the German philosopher **Immanuel Kant** (1724–1804). For Kant, the answer was clear: "Dare to know." By this, he meant that it was necessary for individuals to cast off those ideas of the past that had been

CED 4.3
The Enlightenment

accepted simply because of tradition or intellectual laziness, and instead use one's reason to probe for answers to questions on the nature of humankind. The ultimate reward, stated Kant, would be something that all previous generations had so woefully lacked—freedom. This freedom would extend to the political and religious realms and would also lead the writers of the Enlightenment to cast doubt on such ancient human practices as slavery. The broadest effect was to transform religion from something that was very outward, public, and political, into a private question that required privacy, consideration, and deliberation.

Overseas Enlightenment

Enlightenment principles extended all the way to the American colonies and provided the philosophical and political foundation of the United States. Because the U.S. Constitution has since been a model for so many others across the globe, it's safe to say that Enlightenment thinkers changed the world.

Traditionally, the Enlightenment has been associated with France, where they use the term *philosophes* to describe the thinkers of the age. These *philosophes* were not organized in any formal group, although many of the most prominent displayed their erudition at salons, which were informal discussion groups organized by wealthy women. Others would hang around the print shop putting the final touches on their pamphlets. No matter where their ideas were produced, French thinkers helped produce the so-called "Republic of Letters," an international community of writers who communicated in French. This Republic of Letters extended throughout much of western Europe and, of course, to the American colonies, where the ideas of the Enlightenment would play a significant role in the founding of the United States.

The direction of the Enlightenment changed over the course of the 18th century. The early Enlightenment was deeply rooted in the Scientific Revolution and was profoundly influenced by Great Britain, which appeared to continental writers as a bastion of freedom and economic expansion, while also providing the world with such inestimable thinkers as John Locke. Locke's idea that the individual is a blank slate at birth, expressed in his *Essay Concerning Human Understanding*, provided a powerful argument for the potential impact of education as well as for the inherent equality among all people. Locke also greatly influenced 18th-century thought through his contention that every person has the right to life, liberty, and property, and that there is a contractual relationship between the ruler and the subjects.

As the age of Enlightenment continued, it moved beyond the influence of Locke, who had refused to see how freedom could be granted to enslaved people in the Americas. Writers such as **Voltaire** and **David Hume** offered a powerful challenge to established religion. By the end of the century, people such as **Adam Smith** had veered into other areas, such as economic thought. **Jean-Jacques Rousseau** inspired people of the age to try to find truth not through the cold application of reason, but rather through a thorough examination of their inner emotions. Meanwhile, in places such as Russia, Prussia, and Austria, rulers sought to find ways to blend their royal absolutism with some of the ideas of the Enlightenment. However, little would come out of this attempt except perhaps a further enhancement of their absolute authority.

Voltaire

Perhaps the greatest of the *philosophes* was **Voltaire** (1694–1778). After writing a number of rather forgettable volumes of poetry and drama, Voltaire went to England on a trip that would forever change his life. He was struck by the relative religious tolerance practiced there, as well as the freedom to express one's ideas in print—far greater than that which existed in France. Voltaire was also struck by the honor the English showed Newton when the scientist was buried with great pomp at a state funeral. To Voltaire, England seemed to offer those things that allowed for the happiness of the individual, which seemed so desperately lacking in his own land of France. Although educated by the Jesuits, Voltaire hated the Catholic Church and despised what he thought was the narrowness and bigotry at the heart of all religious traditions. Voltaire, like many of his contemporaries, was a **deist**, one who believes that God created the universe and then stepped back from creation to allow it to operate under the laws of science. Voltaire felt that religion crushed the human spirit and that to be free, man needed to *Écrasez l'infame!* (Crush the horrible thing!)—his famous anti-religious slogan.

Voltaire became an intellectual celebrity across Europe following his involvement in the case of Jean Calas. Calas was a French Protestant who was falsely accused of murdering his son after learning that the son was planning to convert to Catholicism. In 1762, the Parlement of Toulouse ordered Calas's execution, and he was brutally tortured to death. In the following year, Voltaire published his *Treatise on Toleration* and pushed for a reexamination of the evidence. By 1765, the authorities reversed their decision, and while it was obviously too late to aid the unfortunate Calas, Voltaire was able to use the case as a linchpin in his fight against religious dogmatism and intolerance, one of the greatest legacies of the Enlightenment.

> ### Voltaire's Famous *Candide*
> Voltaire's most famous work is ***Candide*** (1759), which he was inspired to write following an earthquake that completely leveled the city of Lisbon in 1755. Voltaire was particularly struck by the story of a group of parishioners who, following the earthquake, went back into their church to give thanks to God for sparing their lives, only to have the weakened foundations of the church collapse on them. One of the false stereotypes concerning the Enlightenment is that it was fundamentally optimistic. *Candide* is a deeply pessimistic work, as young Candide and his traveling companions meet with one disaster after another. The book basically touts the idea that humans cannot expect to find contentment by connecting themselves with a specific philosophical system. Instead, the best one can hope for is a sort of private, inner solace, or as Voltaire put it, "one must cultivate one's own garden."

Montesquieu

Charles Louis de Secondat, **Baron de Montesquieu** (1689–1755), wrote what was perhaps the most influential work of the Enlightenment, ***Spirit of the Laws*** (1748). Montesquieu—who became president of the Parlement of Bordeaux, a body of nobles that functioned as the province's law court—was, like Voltaire, inspired by the political system found in Great Britain. He incorrectly interpreted the British constitution, and in the *Spirit of the Laws*, Montesquieu wrote of the English **separation of powers** among the various branches of government providing for the possibility of **checks and balances**, something that did not exist in the British system. In many ways, Montesquieu was a political conservative who did not believe in a republic—which he associated with anarchy—but rather wanted France to reestablish aristocratic authority as a means of placing limits on royal absolutism.

> **Montesquieu's View**
> Like Voltaire, Montesquieu believed that societies and their political institutions could be studied in a scientific manner.

In an earlier work, *Persian Letters* (1721), Montesquieu critiques his native France through a series of letters between two Persians traveling in Europe. To avoid royal and church censorship, Montesquieu executed a deeply satirical work that attacked religious zealotry, while also implying that, despite the differences between the Islamic East and the Christian West, a universal system of justice was necessary. Another aspect of Montesquieu's universal ideals was his antislavery sentiment; he deplored slavery as being against natural law.

Diderot and the *Encyclopédie*

The *Encyclopédie*, the brainchild of **Denis Diderot** (1713–1784), was one of the greatest collaborative achievements of the Enlightenment and was executed by the community of scholars known as the Republic of Letters. The *Encyclopédie* exemplifies the 18th-century belief that all knowledge could be organized and presented in a scientific manner. The first of 28 volumes appeared in 1751, with such luminaries as Voltaire, Montesquieu, and Rousseau contributing articles. Diderot, the son of an artisan, also had a great deal of respect for those who worked with their hands and included articles on various tools and the ways in which they made people more productive.

The *Encyclopédie* was also important for spreading Enlightenment ideas beyond the borders of France; copies were sent to places as far away as Russia, Scandinavia, and North America (Thomas Jefferson and Benjamin Franklin purchased their own sets). In various parts of Europe, the work was attacked by the censors—particularly in places like Italy, where the Catholic Church was highly critical of what it viewed as thinly veiled attacks on its religious practices. In France, the work was at various times placed under the censor's ban, because it was highly critical of monarchical authority. Ironically, Diderot had to turn to the throne for protection of his copyright when printers published pirated copies.

Rousseau and Romanticism

Rousseau helped set the stage for the Romantic Movement of the late 18th and 19th centuries. His pedagogical novel *Émile* (1762) deals with a young man who receives an education that places higher regard on developing his emotions over his reason. To achieve this, the character Émile is encouraged to explore nature as a means of heightening his emotional sensitivity. Rousseau also notably emphasized the differences between children and adults. He argued that there were stages of development during which the child needed to be allowed to grow freely without undue influence from the adult world.

Jean-Jacques Rousseau

Enlightenment thought did not consist of a single perspective. The work of **Rousseau** (1712–1778) provides one of the best examples of this fact. He lived a deeply troubled and solitary existence. At one point or another he antagonized many of the other leading *philosophes*, including Voltaire, who hated Rousseau's championing of emotion over reason. Rousseau was perhaps the most radical of the *philosophes*. Unlike many of the *philosophes* who believed in a constitutional monarchy as the best form of government, Rousseau believed in the creation of a direct democracy. Although during his lifetime his works were not widely read, following Rousseau's death, his ideas became far more influential, and many of the leading participants in the more radical stages of the French Revolution studied his work.

His greatest achievement, ***The Social Contract*** (1762), begins with this classic line: "All men are born free, but everywhere they are in chains." He once again differed from many of the other *philosophes*, however, in that he had little faith in the individual's potential to use reason as a means of leading a more satisfactory life. Instead, Rousseau explained that the focus needed to be placed on reforming the overall community, because only through the individual's attachment to a larger society could the powerless people hope to achieve much of anything. Sovereignty would be expressed in this ideal society not through the will of the king, but rather via the **general will** of the populace; only by surrendering to this general will could the individual hope to find genuine freedom.

Key Idea

During the Scientific Revolution, thinkers used reason to discover universal laws behind *the natural world*. During the Enlightenment, thinkers used reason to discover universal laws behind *human behavior*.

THE SPREAD OF ENLIGHTENMENT THOUGHT

Although originally rooted in France, over the course of the 18th century, the Enlightenment spread to other parts of Europe.

Germany

The greatest figure of the German Enlightenment was **Immanuel Kant** (1724–1804). In his 1781 book ***Critique of Pure Reason,*** he argued against the idea that all knowledge was empirical, since the mind shapes the world through its unique experiences. Like Rousseau, Kant emphasized that other, possibly hidden, layers of knowledge exist beyond the knowledge that could be achieved through the use of reason. This idea served to inspire a generation of Romantic artists who felt stifled by the application of pure reason.

Italy

In Italy, **Cesare Beccaria** (1738–1794), in his work ***On Crimes and Punishment*** (1764), called for a complete overhaul in the area of **jurisprudence**. For Beccaria, it was clear that those who were accused of perpetrating crimes should also be allowed certain basic rights. He argued against such common practices of the day as the use of torture to obtain admissions of guilt as well as the application of capital punishment. Beccaria's work can be seen as part of the overall theme of humanitarianism found in the Enlightenment, which extended from such areas as the push to end flogging in the British navy to the call for better treatment of animals.

Scotland

One of the most vibrant intellectual centers of the 18th century was Scotland, a place that hitherto had not been at the center of European intellectual life. The philosopher **David Hume** (1711–1776) pushed his thinking further than that of French deists and delved directly into the world of atheism. In ***Inquiry into Human Nature,*** Hume cast complete doubt on revealed religion, arguing that no empirical evidence supported the existence of those miracles that stood at the heart of Christian tradition.

Another Scottish author, **Edward Gibbon** (1737–1794), reflected the growing interest in history that was first seen during the Enlightenment with his monumental ***Decline and Fall of the Roman Empire***. His work criticized Christianity in that he viewed its rise within the Roman Empire as a social phenomenon rather than a divine interference. He also asserted that Christianity weakened the vibrancy of the Empire and contributed to its fall.

The Scottish Enlightenment also made a huge impact on economic thought through the work of **Adam Smith** (1723–1790), a professor at the University of Glasgow. In 1776, Smith published ***Inquiry into the Nature and Causes of the Wealth of Nations***, in which he argued against mercantilism, a term that refers to the system of navigation acts, tariffs, and monopolies that stood as the economic underpinnings for most of the nations of Europe. Smith became associated with the concept of ***laissez-faire,*** meaning to "leave alone," as he argued that individuals should be free to pursue economic gain without being restricted by the state. Rather than producing economic anarchy, such a system would be self-regulating, as if controlled by an **invisible hand,** which would lead to the meeting of supply and demand. Smith's thinking proved influential for both the Manchester School of economists in England and the Physiocrats in France.

WOMEN AND THE ENLIGHTENMENT

Women figured prominently in the Enlightenment; most of the Parisian **salons** were organized by women. At times, these wealthy and aristocratic individuals would use their social and political connections to help the *philosophes* avoid trouble with the authorities or perhaps aid them in receiving some sort of government position to allow them greater freedom to work. Perhaps surprisingly, given the great help that women proffered to the *philosophes*, these male thinkers for the most part were not tremendous advocates of the rights and abilities of women. The *Encyclopédie* barely bothered to address the condition of women, although the work may never have reached the reading public without the aid of the **Marquise de Pompadour**, Louis XV's mistress, who played a critical role in helping Diderot avoid censorship.

Some writers were more sympathetic to women's issues than others. Montesquieu, in his *Persian Letters*, included a discussion of the restrictive nature of the Eastern harem, which by implication was a criticism of the treatment of women in western Europe. Rousseau, on the other hand, while a radical on many issues, was an advocate of the idea that men and women occupied separate spheres, and that women should not be granted an equal education to men. By the end of the century, inspired partially by the French Revolution and partially by the Enlightenment, the Englishwoman **Mary Wollstonecraft** (1759–1797) wrote in her *Vindication of the Rights of Women* that women should enjoy the right to vote as well as to hold political office, the first openly published statement of such ideas.

THAT'S A LOT OF NAMES, HUH?

Many AP European History students struggle with the sheer volume of ideas and thinkers during the Age of Enlightenment. Check out this handy graphic to help you review who said what and hailed from where.

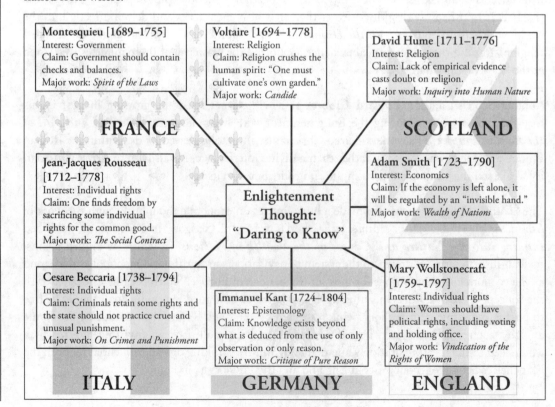

18TH-CENTURY ART, MUSIC, AND LITERATURE

CED 4.5
18th-Century Culture and Arts

Two hundred years after the printing press was invented, a publishing explosion occurred around Europe. Whereas buying books in the 1500s had been expensive for the peasantry, buying newspapers, magazines, and pamphlets in the 1700s proved far more affordable for the growing middle class. In particular, the Dutch took an early lead in the printed media business, owing to their total lack of religious or state censorship. As the century progressed, the French, Germans, and English developed equally large publishing cultures. All of them benefited from increasing literacy rates, and all of them used publishing to shape public opinion.

Through printed media, Europeans were exposed to new forms of thought. Novelists such as **Samuel Richardson** and **Daniel Defoe** wrote books that brought people into new modes of self-reflection. This was accompanied by the popularity of new types of private spaces in the home, such as offices, boudoirs, or sunrooms. Those spaces were decorated with new consumer items including mirrors, porcelain, and linens. This emphasis on home life was an obvious reflection of the growing dominance of the middle class. They were learning to draw a line between public and private spheres, which the Victorians would accomplish to a much greater degree a century later (see page 269).

Prior to the 18th century, the arts had been focused on royals and religion as subject matter. This occurred mostly to promote the image of a powerful state, and because the nobles or the clergy often served as patrons of the arts. Baroque composers such as **Frederic Handel** and **J. S. Bach** used music to stir religious feelings, or to celebrate the power of their respective royal families. Other baroque artists such as **Velazquez** or **Caravaggio** did the same in the visual arts. However, as the middle class grew, the Dutch once again took the lead in this field. **Rembrandt** introduced the European public to a wide variety of visual topics, including landscapes, mythological themes, and others, with many European painters subsequently following in his footsteps.

EUROPEAN POWERS IN THE AGE OF ENLIGHTENMENT

CED 4.6
Enlightened and Other Approaches to Power

The 18th century witnessed a number of significant developments for the European nation-states. Two major powers, Prussia and Russia, emerged over the course of the century, while Austria, France, and Great Britain adjusted to changing political, economic, and social circumstances.

The century would also be noteworthy for the monarchs who sought to govern using ideas taken from the writings of the French *philosophes*. Rulers such as Catherine the Great of Russia, Joseph II of Austria, and Frederick II of Prussia are generally referred to as "**enlightened absolutists.**" They could safely toy with the ideas of the *philosophes* without threatening their own power because most of the *philosophes* were not republicans but believers in monarchical authority (although they felt that the power of the monarchy should be wielded in a more rational manner). These monarchs found that the writings of the *philosophes* on economics and education could mesh with their own desires to enhance the power of their states within the community of European nations and their personal authority within the state. What was even more appealing for these enlightened absolutists was that their increase in power would be achieved at the expense of those elements in society, such as the nobility or the Church, that had previously stood in the way of this centralizing tendency.

Europe in 1715

Prussia and Austria

It is perhaps rather surprising that Prussia emerged in the 18th century as one of the dominant European powers and a rival to Austria for hegemony in Germany. In the 17th century, Prussia was a poor German state that was devastated by various marauding armies during the **Thirty Years' War**, although in the **Peace of Westphalia**, which marked the end of the conflict, Prussia did receive some minor territorial gains. Also, the threat from the Ottomans diminished with their defeat at the hands of the Austrians at the Battle of Vienna, ending their dreams of westward expansion. Nonetheless, relatively poor agricultural land and labor shortages led to the establishment of serfdom by the 16th century. This led to the state receiving some badly needed support from the Prussian nobility, the Junkers, who looked to the ruler to ensure control over their serfs.

The first ruler to tap into whatever potential the Prussian state possessed was **Frederick William** (r. 1640–1688), often referred to as the **"Great Elector"** because, in his capacity as ruler of Brandenburg, he served as one of the electors of the Holy Roman Emperor. Because his state consisted of three noncontiguous chunks of land without natural borders, Frederick William wanted to build an army. As he was without significant resources of his own, he worked out an agreement with the Junkers, according to which they would provide him with revenue in exchange for his acceptance of their control over the serfs. This was the beginning of a long and mutually beneficial relationship between the Prussian monarchy and the Junkers, who found that Frederick's expanded army offered them the opportunity to leave their poor agricultural lands and engage in more appealing careers as officers. The Great Elector left his son Frederick III (r. 1688–1713) a well-organized army, an expanded territorial base, and arguably the most efficient civil service in all of Europe. Frederick III was to take this inheritance and make Prussia into a kingdom in 1701, gaining the title of **King Frederick I**.

Prussian power would reach its zenith in the 18th century with the reign of **Frederick the Great** (r. 1740–1786). Frederick is often cited as an example of an enlightened absolutist because he was fascinated by the intellectual current from France. At his palace of Sans Souci, Frederick established a glittering intellectual center, where Voltaire would live for a time and where the king himself participated by writing philosophical tracts, which may have led Voltaire to make an early exit from the court. Frederick freed the serfs on the royal estates, though to ensure the continual support of the Junker class, he refused to emancipate the serfs living on private estates. He also brought an end to capital punishment and limited the use of corporal punishment on serfs, though he did not emancipate the Jews living within his kingdom.

> Frederick used the rational thought of the age as a tool for greater royal centralization and absolutism, rather than as a means of ensuring individual rights or establishing participatory political institutions.

A more thoroughgoing series of reforms inspired by the Enlightenment took place in Austria, where the Empress **Maria Theresa** pushed a series of reforms that removed some of the hardships that had been placed on the serf population. Her son **Joseph II** (r. 1765–1790) was impressed with the idea of religious toleration, mainly because he wished to reduce the power of the Catholic Church within his own domains. He viewed the Church as hostile to his plan for greater centralized authority. In 1781, he issued the first of a series of Edicts of Toleration granting Jews, Lutherans, and Calvinists freedom of worship. Civil liabilities were still left in place for Jews—while Protestants could enter into the Habsburg civil service, Jews were still barred and were forced to pay special taxes for the right to worship. Joseph antagonized his aristocracy by making them responsible for taxes and by abolishing serfdom. Following his death in 1790, his brother and heir, Leopold II (r. 1790–1792) was forced to back away from some of Joseph's enlightened policies in order to put an end to a series of aristocratic and peasant revolts.

Unfortunately, when they were not perusing the writings of the *philosophes*, the rulers of Prussia and Austria were often engaged in violent conflict. The roots of the **War of the Austrian Succession** (1740–1748) began during the reign of the Holy Roman Emperor Charles VI (r. 1711–1740). Because he lacked a male heir, Charles VI pushed the other European states to accept what was known as the **Pragmatic Sanction**, allowing for the assorted Habsburg lands under his control to remain intact under one ruler, and granting the right of a female heir to succeed to the throne of Austria if there was no direct male heir.

When Charles died without leaving a son, his daughter Maria Theresa came to the throne. While both France and Prussia had promised to respect the Pragmatic Sanction, both nations viewed the death of Charles as an opportunity to gain territory at the expense of the Austrians. Frederick immediately launched an attack to seize Silesia, the richest part of the Austrian empire at the northeastern border of Bohemia. Regaining Silesia was to prove impossible for Maria Theresa. But with the help of Hungarian nobility, which had agreed to the Pragmatic Sanction in exchange for recognition of Hungary as an independent kingdom, she was able to put down a dangerous revolt in Bohemia and remain on the throne.

The conflict became a general European war. Austria gained support from Russia, Sweden, Denmark, and eventually Great Britain, which feared French territorial gains in the Austrian Netherlands. Opposing them was an alliance made up of Prussia, France, and Spain. By the time the war came to a close in 1748 with the signing of the **Treaty of Aix-la-Chapelle**, the Austrian throne was ultimately saved for the Habsburgs. (Because women remained ineligible to head the Holy Roman Empire, Maria Theresa's husband was to hold that position as Emperor Francis I.)

One result of the war was that Prussia emerged as a German state and a major rival to Austria. Understanding that Prussia, under its aggressive King Frederick, would continue to be a threat, in 1756, Maria Theresa's able foreign minister, Count Kaunitz, worked out an alliance with France, the traditional enemy of the Austrian Habsburgs and a state that was increasingly wary of growing Prussian power. This became known as the **Diplomatic Revolution**, or reversal of alliances. France also demanded the Austrian Netherlands as their price for this alliance. Sweden and Russia signed on as part of an alliance that increasingly looked as if it would result in significant territorial gains at the expense of the Prussians.

The other side of this Diplomatic Revolution was that Great Britain broke off its ties with Austria and became allies with Prussia, and while the British did not contribute men to the war on the continent, their financial subsidies were vital in enabling Frederick to continue fighting. The Diplomatic Revolution led directly to the **Seven Years' War** (1756–1763), which started when Frederick launched an attack in 1756 in order to quickly put down his enemies before they had an opportunity to form a cohesive military plan to defeat Prussia. Initially, the bold Prussian plan paid off as Frederick first defeated a French and then an Austrian army, but disaster struck when a massive Russian army arrived from the east and took Frederick's capital of Berlin. Only the crowning of a new Russian tsar, **Peter III**, in 1762 staved off the complete destruction of the Prussian state, because Peter, an admirer of Frederick, wanted no part in the conflict and brought his army home. So Frederick, by preserving the Prussian state, was the clear winner on the continent, while overseas his British allies had won a series of tremendous victories against the French, particularly in North America, where the conflict was called the **French and Indian War** (because the French allied with the Indigenous peoples). Overall, the war spanned five continents, resulted in the confiscation of French colonies in Canada and India, and was called by Winston Churchill "the first world war."

At that point, England and France had fought each other in wars both large and small for 250 years. England was already on its way toward building the largest empire in the history of humanity, while France was about to be wracked by one of the bloodiest internal revolutions in the history of the continent—the French Revolution. Aside from a final skirmish during the Napoleonic era at the beginning of the 19th century, these longtime enemies more or less stopped fighting by 1763.

Russia

Until the 18th century, Russia remained largely closed off to western Europe as a result of the Mongol invasion of the 13th century. Some trade did exist; for instance, Elizabethan England imported Russian timber for the building of ships, but for the most part Russia was not affected by developments in the West, most notably missing out on the humanistic culture of the Italian Renaissance.

By the 16th century, the Duchy of Muscovy would emerge as the dominant state within the Russian steppe, an area that had absorbed a number of other rival states while pushing the Mongols back to the east. During the reign of the appropriately named **Ivan the Terrible** (r. 1533–1584), there was a significant expansion of the territory under the control of Muscovy, while Ivan also sought, often through staggeringly violent means, to gain control over a recalcitrant nobility. Following his death in 1584, Russia entered into the period known as the **"Time of Troubles,"** which lasted until the selection of a tsar from the **Romanov family** in 1613, the dynasty that would continue to rule Russia until the Revolution of 1917.

> **Off with Their Beards!**
> Peter famously forced his nobles to shave their beards, which was the style in the West, as his first step in Westernizing his state.

The individual who did the most to transform the Russian state into a major European power was **Peter the Great** (r. 1682–1725). As a young man, Peter traveled to the West where he became fascinated by the work done in Dutch shipyards and other examples of Western technology. Upon his return to Russia, Peter was determined to Westernize his state. Peter expanded the revenue available to the monarchy by imposing head taxes on Russian serfs, while also establishing monopolies on essential commodities such as salt. Peter used this expanded revenue to follow the lead of the absolutist states in Europe and establish a centralized bureaucracy. In order to ensure the loyalty of his nobility as well as use them for governance, Peter established a Table of Ranks, in which all positions in the state had graduated rankings, which also provided an opportunity for commoners to rise up the ranks and reach a coveted position as a noble. Just as in Prussia, members of the nobility were to be used as an essential tool of royal absolutism. In keeping with his desire to keep a **"window to the West,"** Peter established the eponymous city of **St. Petersburg** in 1703. The city was built on what seemed to be unpromising marsh land, and thousands of serf laborers would lose their lives in the building of a grand city with architecture that mimicked the newest styles from France.

> **CED 3.7**
> Absolutist Approaches to Power

At the start of World War I, many of the Russian officers had German names, as the descendants of the Western military experts that Peter invited to Russia to help him establish a standing army. To ensure that he had enough soldiers, Peter conscripted serfs to serve in his force for the interminable period of 20 years. Peter also built the first Russian navy. Peter used his army to greatly expand Russian territory, and in achieving this goal, he was fortunate that his state was becoming more powerful at the same time that the major states on his borders, the Ottoman Empire and the Kingdom of Poland-Lithuania, were in relative decline. Most notably, he defeated the Swedes in the **Great Northern War** (1700–1721), which marked the end of the brief period going back to the age of Gustavus Adolphus in the 17th century when Sweden was a great European power.

The westward outlook of Russia during the reign of Peter continued under his successors. Western thought, particularly the writings and ideas of French *philosophes* such as Montesquieu and Voltaire, would play a role in inspiring the reign of **Catherine the Great** (r. 1762–1796). Catherine began the process of revising and codifying Russian law, but for the most part, she only dabbled with bringing about actual reform. Once she became convinced later in her reign that enlightened thought could pose a challenge to her monarchy, she dropped the idea entirely. While few practical results stemmed from Catherine's infatuation with Enlightenment thought, it did help establish the primacy of French culture and ideas among the Russian aristocracy.

Spain

Before he ascended to the throne of Spain, **Charles III** (r. 1759–1788) was the well-regarded King of Naples. Having studied the essays of Benito Feijóo, Spain's foremost Enlightenment thinker, Charles embarked to bring about reforms that echoed Feijóo's challenges to the more orthodox teachings of the Catholic Church. One of Charles's first standoffs with the Church came in 1735 when Pope Clement XII refused to recognize Charles's legitimacy as King of Naples. Naples was seen by the Church as just another region under control of the papal states; accordingly, the Church considered the pope the one and only authority in this kingdom.

When Pope Clement died and was replaced by Pope Benedict XIV in 1740, Charles seized the opportunity to assert his firm belief that the Church should hold no special authority in his kingdom. Benito Feijóo's writings that rejected the harsh orthodoxy of the Church came into practice as Charles negotiated a concordat with Pope Benedict to tax church officials and hold them equal under the law.

Prosperity Under Charles

The prosperity of Charles's reign had much to do with Spain finally being viewed as a unified nation.

In 1759, Charles III ascended to the Spanish throne following the death of his brother. Charles was determined to continue his Enlightenment-inspired reforms, which included laws from banning bullfighting to protecting free trade to developing roads and canals. In Spain, Charles continued his goal of limiting the Church's power in his sovereign state. He was able to decrease the number of clergy members, who many Spanish felt were not contributing adequately to society. At the same time, because of the respect garnered by the Spanish Enlightenment philosophers, the Inquisition was increasingly viewed largely as an antiquated mission.

Russia: Catherine the Great (1762–1796)
Enlightened influence: Montesquieu and Voltaire
Enlightened actions: systemized laws, brought ideas of French philosophy to Russian aristocracy

Prussia: Frederick II (the Great) (1740–1786)
Enlightened influence: Voltaire
Enlightened actions: freed the serfs, supported academia, ended capital punishment

Austria: Joseph II (1769–1790)
Enlightened influence: Voltaire
Enlightened actions: issued the Edicts of Tolerance, weakened the Church

Spain: Charles III (1759–1788)
Enlightened influence: Benito Feijóo
Enlightened actions: weakened the Church, funded science and academia, kept peace

0   200   400 Miles
0   200   400 Kilometers

Enlightened Absolutists

Poland

The story of Poland in the 18th century consists of the complete eradication of a nation that had previously played a critical role in the affairs of central Europe. The traditional starting date for the history of Poland is 966, when Prince Mieszko, who was to be the founder of a dynasty (Piast) that would rule Poland for four centuries, accepted Roman Catholicism, firmly tying Poland to the culture of western Europe. Vulnerable to attacks because of a lack of natural borders, the Poles in the Middle Ages had to deal with threats from the Mongols from the east as well as the Teutonic Knights from the west. In order to deal with the threat from the crusading order, a new dynasty was established in 1385 (Jagiellon) through uniting Poland with Lithuania, when the Lithuanian Grand Duke Jagiello, the ruler of the last pagan state in Europe, married the Polish Queen Jadwiga. This newly created **Polish-Lithuanian Commonwealth** met its initial goal of defeating the Teutonic Knights by securing an important victory at the Battle of Grunwald (Germans refer to it as the Battle of Tannenberg.).

The fatal flaw for the Polish-Lithuanian state was the failure to create a strong, centralized government in the face of a recalcitrant nobility that feared the loss of authority. By the end of the 16th century, the nobles had greatly weakened the crown by making it an elective position and often selecting foreign princes to further ensure it would remain a weak title. This policy became increasingly dangerous in the 17th century, as new threats appeared from the Swedes and the Russians. The Polish-Lithuanian state still remained a significant player in Europe up until the end of the century, when King Jan Sobieski played a critical role in driving the Turks from the gates of Vienna in 1683, but by the middle of the 18th century, Poland was so weak that it maintained its independence only by the good graces of Russia. Eventually, Poland's luck ran out, resulting in the loss of a great deal of land.

When Stanislaw August Poniatowski became king in 1764, he displayed an independent streak that Catherine the Great did not expect from her former lover. This did not bode well for Poniatowski's attempt to move the nation's political system in a more centralized direction, an attempt that was met with displeasure by all of Poland's neighbors. In 1772, Russia, Prussia, and Austria forced Poland to accept a **partition** that cost Poland 30 percent of its territory. In some ways, this first partition provided the nudge for Poland to finally get its political house in order. Influenced by the ideas of the Enlightenment, in 1791, the Polish-Lithuanian parliament (*Sejm*) produced Europe's first written **constitution**. The constitution, which was never fully implemented (although it remained a beacon for later generations of Polish reformers), angered many nobles who saw their influence reduced as well as Poland's neighbors who feared a national revival. The anti-Poniatowski nobles applied to the Russians for assistance, and Catherine, with the aid of Prussia, was more than willing to intercede.

> **Love and Politics**
> Catherine didn't hesitate to mix love and politics. Her affair with Poniatowski resulted in not only his election as King of Poland-Lithuania but also the birth of Catherine's second child, Anna.

Russia and Prussia insisted on the removal of the constitution and also carried out the **Second Partition** in 1793. This led to the loss of vast lands in the eastern part of the nation and reduced Poland to a rump state (the remnants of a much larger state that has devolved). In a heroic, last-ditch effort to retain statehood, a Polish revolt broke out in 1794 under the military leadership of **Tadeusz Kosciuszko**, who had fought with distinction in the American Revolution. Overwhelmed by more powerful enemies, Poniatowski was forced to abdicate, and a **third and final partition** took place in 1795, wiping Poland off the map. Despite the best hopes of Polish nationalists throughout the 19th century, an independent Polish state would not be revived until the aftermath of World War I.

Great Britain

After the turmoil of the 17th century, Great Britain became the most stable nation in Europe in the 18th century. The triumph of Parliament in its struggle against Stuart absolutism put Great Britain in a position of political stability that would provide one of the critical foundations for the establishment of a vast overseas empire, as well as the industrial transformation that would begin by the middle of the century.

With the death of Queen Anne in 1714, the throne passed to **George I** (r. 1714–1721), the ruler of the German state of Hanover, whose sole qualification was that he was a Protestant cousin of the late queen. Like his son **George II** (r. 1727–1760), he was far happier spending time in Hanover, where he could reign as an unquestioned absolutist, rather than having to deal with the independent-minded British Parliament. While there is a historical debate over the strength of support within Great Britain for the Stuart cause, the 18th century did experience two pro-Stuart revolts, in 1715 and 1745, the latter one famous for the involvement of "Bonnie Prince Charles," who saw his dream of being restored to the throne dashed at the Battle of Culloden in 1746.

While it was clear that after 1688 the Houses of Parliament would dominate political life within the country, how that power was to be used in an efficient manner remained one of the significant questions in the early part of the 18th century. The most significant development in this regard was the evolution of the office of prime minister, which, while not officially recognized until 1905, became a political reality in all but name during **Robert Walpole's** tenure as Chancellor of the Exchequer from 1721 to 1741. The fact that both George I and George II were less than attentive to British domestic politics meant that Walpole had a free hand to mold the political system to his advantage. Walpole used a complex system of political patronage to maintain his control over the House of Commons. This support in the lower house became the vital component for ministerial power. When Walpole lost that support in 1741 over a conflict about the direction of British foreign policy, he resigned his post as Chancellor of the Exchequer even though he still enjoyed the support of George II.

Another development that shaped British politics in the 18th century was the formation of two parliamentary blocks: **Tories** and **Whigs**. While Tories stood for the prerogative rights of the monarch and support of the Church of England, the Whigs were more closely allied to the spirit of the Revolution of 1688 and the idea of religious tolerance. When George III (r. 1760–1820) came to the throne, he claimed that he wanted the throne to rise above party strife, though **Edmund Burke** in his *Thoughts on the Cause of the Present Discontent* (1770) argued that parties were essential to parliamentary government and were a fundamental component for political stability. George III's desire to choose his own chief minister during the first 10 years of his reign remained problematic until Lord North assumed the mantle of chief minister in 1770 and held the position for the next 12 years.

The Road to American Independence...

...is a topic we discuss in much greater detail in *AP U.S. History Exam Prep!* If you're taking AP U.S. History, check out our book for a thorough content review and lots of practice questions.

The problems stemming from the first 10 years of George III's rule were to have important consequences as the colonists in the 13 American colonies became increasingly restless, laying the groundwork for the American Revolution. The British government ended the Seven Years' War with a tremendous victory over the French but also with an enormous deficit. In order to pay for the increasing costs of administering their far-flung empire, the British government looked for new sources of revenue. The passage of the Stamp Act in 1765, during the ministry of George Grenville, was probably a mistake, because it ticked off the two groups in society you don't want to anger: publishers and lawyers. While the British government continued to assert its right to tax the colonists as it pleased, the colonists responded that without parliamentary representation, no taxes could ever be acceptable. By 1774, American anger at what was viewed as high-handed British policies led to the establishment of the **First Continental Congress**, with open hostilities breaking out the following year at Lexington and Concord in Massachusetts. The wars of the 18th century seemingly always brought about curious alliances, and the Americans were eventually to win their independence by 1783 with the help of France and Spain, with both states seeking to deliver a major blow to the British as payback for the Seven Years' War.

The struggle for independence by the American colonists also helped to inspire a movement for parliamentary reform in Great Britain. Voting in 18th-century Britain was primarily the prerogative of the landed classes, but there were plenty of anomalies in the system. For example, there was a fairly wide franchise in London, but in other areas there were "rotten" boroughs, such as Old Sarum, where no one had lived since the Middle Ages, but which still duly provided two members to the House of Commons. The parliamentary reform movement was to emerge as a significant factor in British political life in the 1780s. But by 1792, the advent of the French Revolution and, more specifically, its increasing violence and radicalism brought about a backlash against political reform in Great Britain, so that any expansion of suffrage would have to wait until the **Great Reform Bill** of 1832.

> ### Wilkes and Liberty
>
> In 1763, John Wilkes, a member of the House of Commons and part-time pornographer, was arrested for publishing a satirical attack on George III in his paper *The North Briton*. This event provided an outlet for those Englishmen, who, by shouting "Wilkes and Liberty" in the streets, saw the possibility of bringing about what they viewed to be much needed reforms in the political system, including greater freedom of the press and an expansion of suffrage.

France

Perhaps not surprising given the increased power of the throne during the reign of Louis XIV, a backlash against royal absolutism set in during the following century. Compared to its fellow absolutist states in central and eastern Europe, French absolutism seemed to hardly deserve the term at times, but for some Frenchmen, particularly those influenced by Enlightenment thought, the powers of the crown were seen as increasingly despotic.

An opportunity to challenge the throne came about at the middle of the century, when a papal decree attacked the Jansenists, a Catholic sect that held beliefs on predestination that were similar to the Calvinist point of view. **Louis XV** (r. 1714–1774) wished to support the papal decree and ban the group, but found himself blocked by the various provincial *parlements,* law courts primarily made up of nobles who had the prerogative right of registering royal edicts before they could be enforced. Many of those who sat in these *parlements*, while opposed to Jansenist teachings, also opposed registering the edicts because they felt it was emblematic of royal despotism.

During the long reign of Louis XV, the financial troubles of the monarchy increased, particularly as a result of the disastrous Seven Years' War, but once again, the *parlements* stood in the way of any significant reform in the revenue system. Finally, in frustration, Louis XV abolished the *parlements*, but Louis XVI (r. 1774–1792) felt forced to bring them back in an attempt to curry favor with the nobility. The recalcitrance of the *parlements* in allowing the establishment of a more rational revenue system was to play a significant role in bringing France to the point of revolution by 1789.

THE FRENCH REVOLUTION

Before 1789	Pre-revolutionary period (Ancien Régime)
1789–1792	Liberal phase (Constitutional Monarchy)
1792–1793	Moderate Republic (Girondins)
1793–1794	Radical Republic (Jacobins)
1795–1799	Directory (Moderate Republic)
1799–1804	Consulate
1804–1815	Napoleonic Empire

Background to the Revolution: The Ancient Régime

Under different circumstances, Louis XVI might have made a decent constitutional monarch. He possessed the two main qualities needed for success in that job—he was rather kind and not especially bright. Unfortunately, France at this time was an absolute monarchy, and Louis's personal limitations were significant. Louis was not helped by the tremendous unpopularity of his wife, Marie Antoinette, an Austrian princess who was extremely unhappy with her marriage to the sexually impotent Louis; theirs was an arranged marriage meant to aid relations between France and Austria. Rumors regarding acts of infidelity on her part continued to plague the monarchy and helped to widen the gap between the court and the rest of the country.

The major problem facing the monarchy was financial. France was not bankrupt in 1789, although the same could not be said for the French monarchy. Throughout the 18th century, the country had been at war, mostly with Great Britain, a conflict that dated back to the Glorious Revolution of 1688. The ignoble defeat of French forces in the Seven Years' War and the more successful involvement of French forces in the American Revolution helped exacerbate the financial difficulties facing the monarchy. The debt grew so large that interest and payments on the debt absorbed slightly more than half the annual budget. While all European nations in the 18th century had racked up large debts, and by comparison the French debt was not particularly onerous given the great wealth of France, the problem was that the French monarchy was unable to tap into the wealth of the nation.

In the 17th century, the French monarchy, in an attempt to pacify a potentially rebellious nobility, had basically granted the nobility freedom from most taxation. It would be the task of Louis XVI (r. 1774–1792) to try to convince the nobility to give up their cherished tax-free status. This meant that Louis, a weak man, would have to break the back of the Paris and regional *parlements*, royal law courts that claimed the right of judicial review of all royal edicts, therefore empowering them to veto any attempt to tax the nobility. These *parlements* had gained influence throughout the 18th century and were a bastion of aristocratic stubbornness on the taxation question.

Unpopularity with the Peasants

We'll never know whether Marie Antoinette truly said "Let them eat cake" when told that the people were starving, but the fact that she and her ladies-in-waiting enjoyed pretending to be peasants (for fun) at a specially created peasant village situated at Versailles points to her general insensitivity.

CED 5.4
The French Revolution

The Calling of the Estates General and the Demand for a National Assembly

By 1787, the financial situation grew so bad that Louis XVI called an **Assembly of Notables** made up of leading aristocrats and churchmen to see if they would willingly pay a new land tax that would apply to all, regardless of social status. The notables at the meeting refused to consider the tax and instead demanded that they be granted a greater share in governing the nation. This refusal by the nobility marks the start of the process by which France would be enveloped by the Revolution. Ironically, it is the nobles who set the stage for their own downfall with their demand for the **Estates General**, an institution from medieval times that consisted of a three-house body made up of clergy (the first estate), nobility (the second estate), and commons (the third estate). "Commons" referred to everyone from bourgeoisie to peasants who were neither clergy nor nobility. Traditionally, each house received one vote, so the clergy and nobility dominated the proceedings. The notables assumed that calling the Estates General, which had last met in 1614, would be an effective means of ensuring that the monarchy would not implement any economic reform that would place limits on their privileges. It also ensured that the bourgeoisie would not be able to limit the rights of the nobility.

By 1788, Louis XVI decided that in the following year he would call the Estates General. To the chagrin of the conservative nobles, the question of the assembly's voting structure immediately arose. Increasingly, writers began to declare that the **Third Estate,** consisting of all nonclergy and nonaristocracy (the majority of Frenchmen), was the true embodiment of the political will of the nation. Though members of the clergy were officially the **First Estate,** many simple parish priests felt more aligned with the Third Estate. Indeed, the most famous pamphlet from this period was written by the **Abbé Siéyès** (1748–1836), an obscure lower clergyman, who wrote:

> What is the Third Estate? Everything.
> What has it been in the political order up to the present? Nothing.
> What does it ask? To become something.

By the end of 1788, the king agreed to double the number of representatives to the Third Estate, which meant little, since voting would still be cast by each estate as a unit and not as individuals. A large portion of the 600 members of the Third Estate were lawyers. No peasants attended the sessions, which would be held in the very home of royal absolutism—Versailles.

This sense of wanting change but ultimately not knowing what direction this change should take can be seen in the thousands of *cahiers de doléances*, or lists of grievances, that were presented to the king by the various electoral assemblies at the start of the meeting of the Estates General. Many of these documents survive, and they reveal an assortment of grievances, such as the demand for a tax system that would be more equitable and the call for regular meetings of the Estates General (along with some more practical notions, such as the need to limit the size of sheep herds, whose bad breath was destroying French pastures). While many of the *cahiers de doléances* demanded a lessening of royal absolutism, all were loyal to the idea of monarchy and to the concept that the monarchy would continue to lead the French state. Many believed that abuses would be promptly rectified if only the king knew of them.

May 5, 1789, marked the first day of the meeting of the Estates General. Immediately, Louis XVI angered the members of the Third Estate by keeping them waiting for several hours as he formally received the credentials of members of the first two estates. Since it was clear that the king would not compromise on voting as individuals, the members of the Third Estate delayed formally submitting their credentials for several weeks. On June 17, in a momentous decision, the Third Estate declared that it would not meet as a medieval estate based on social status but instead would only assemble before the king as a national assembly representing the political will of the entire French nation, including representatives from all three estates.

From this point on, things moved rapidly. The First Estate, although it included great clerics like the Bishop of Paris who was a part of the nobility, also included those simple parish priests who saw themselves as having more in common with the members of the Third Estate. These parish priests voted to join the Third Estate and to meet as a national assembly. Rumors began to swirl that the king was preparing to take action against leading members of the Third Estate, who also found that their meeting hall was closed off. In one of the famous scenes from the Revolution, members of the Third Estate gathered at a tennis court on the grounds of Versailles and, in what became known as the **Tennis Court Oath**, promised to continue to meet "until the constitution of the kingdom is established and consolidated upon solid foundations." In response, the king granted a number of concessions, such as promising to periodically call the Estates General and to drop some of the more onerous taxes on the Third Estate. Just one year earlier, such acts would have been greatly welcomed, but by this point, the king's small concessions were "too little, too late." Finally, on June 27, a desperate Louis XVI formally agreed to the consolidation of all three estates into a new national assembly.

The Storming of the Bastille and the Great Fear

The implications from these momentous events would extend far beyond the confines of Versailles. Indeed, the Revolution was about to see the first incident of violence. In Paris, panic began to set in as people continued to try to cope with a shortage of food that many blamed on the rapacious nobility and the acts of hoarders. The populace believed the rumors that the king was not interested in meeting with the National Assembly and was instead organizing troops that would be used to scatter the National Assembly and to reestablish royal absolutism. This created a panic in Paris as people searched for weaponry to defend themselves against the royal troops.

The **Bastille** was a fortress prison in Paris famous as a symbol of royal despotism because it had held critics of the monarchy. There is an ongoing debate among historians as to whether the crowds that gathered around the Bastille were there spontaneously or whether they were organized by bourgeois (or middle class) elements. Regardless, the crowd of around 80,000 demanded the surrender of the fortress so they could confiscate the arms they believed were inside. Despite having promised safe passage to the small garrison inside, the crowd eventually surrounded them, cut off the head of the commander of the troops, and marched around the city with his head on a pike. When Louis heard about the storming of his fortress he asked, "Is this a revolt?" In response he was told, "No sire, it is a revolution."

Once again, Louis quickly made concessions. He sent away some of the troops that he had possibly planned to use to disperse the National Assembly. He formally recognized the **Commune of Paris**, the new municipal government that would come to play a pivotal role in the later stages of the Revolution. He also agreed to the formation of a National Guard under the leadership of the **Marquis de Lafayette** (1757–1834), who was already known as a champion of liberty because of his involvement in the American Revolution.

In the countryside, things also began to spiral out of control. Just as rumors had spurred on events in Paris, rumors in the countryside brought about further changes in the direction of the Revolution. For the peasants, the decade of the 1780s had been a period of poor harvests. This, combined with a crushing tax burden, had resulted in a resentful and fearful peasantry. A general panic set in known as the **Great Fear**, which consisted of rumors that the nobility was using the increasingly anarchical situation both at Versailles and in Paris to organize groups of hoodlums to steal from the peasants. In response, peasants began to attack some of the great noble estates, carefully burning documents that verified some of their old manorial obligations.

The Great Fear contributed to one of the most remarkable moments in the Revolution. On August 4, 1789, aristocrats in the National Assembly decided that the only way to halt the violence in the countryside was by renouncing their feudal rights. In a highly emotional scene, aristocrat after aristocrat stood up—some sincerely, others out of peer pressure—to renounce those rights that had made them a separate caste in French society. Peasants were no longer obligated to work on the local lord's land, nor were they barred from fishing in common streams or hunting in the forests, restrictions that the hungry peasantry found particularly onerous. As a result of the events of August 4, all the people of France were subject to the same laws and obligations to society.

The Constitutional Monarchy

Because there was no time to write a constitution, the National Assembly decided to put forward a document that would declare the rights of the new French citizen. Lafayette, aided by Thomas Jefferson, wrote the ***Declaration of the Rights of Man and Citizen***, one of the most influential documents in European history. Using the language of the Enlightenment, the work declared that political sovereignty did not rest in the hands of a monarch but rather in the nation at large. It also stated that all citizens were equal before the law and in their enjoyment of all rights and responsibilities of the society. Because all men were "born and remain free and equal in rights," they were entitled to enjoy freedom of religion, freedom of the press, and the freedom to engage in the economic activity of their choice. Befitting the bourgeois audience for whom this document was primarily intended, it also offered that property was inviolable and sacred.

Lafayette was being quite literal when he referred to the "Rights of Man." He, like most other men, believed that women were clearly not entitled to the same rights as men because their domestic role precluded the possibility of a life beyond the household. Nevertheless, the language of liberty tugged at women's sense of independence and by 1791, **Olympe de Gouges** wrote *The Rights of Women*, in which she argued that women should enjoy such fundamental rights as the right to be educated, to control their own property, and to initiate divorce. She did not, however, go so far as to demand full political rights for women. During this stage of the Revolution, women did gain certain rights over their property and the right to divorce, although these rights would be rolled back in the backlash that took place during the rule of the Directory and the reign of Napoleon. De Gouges herself would be executed during the Reign of Terror.

> **The Language of Liberty**
> De Gouges's book was the inspiration for Mary Wollstonecraft's *Vindication of the Rights of Women*.

The events of the summer of 1789 had left Louis XVI unsure as to how to respond. He hesitated to accept the dramatic changes posed by the renunciation of aristocratic privileges on August 4. Although Louis vacillated, events would once again overtake him. On October 5, a large crowd of women, angry over the shortage of bread in Paris, decided to go to Versailles to meet with "the baker, the baker's wife, and the baker's little boy" (referring to the royal family). At first, unsure of how to proceed, the crowd decided the surest way to hold the king to his promise to respect the decrees of the National Assembly was to escort him back to Paris where they could watch him more closely. This proved to be a pivotal decision; the king was now under the control of the people of Paris, whose revolutionary zeal far outstripped that of the rest of the country.

Another reason for the increasingly radical moves of the French revolutionaries was the steps taken by the National Assembly to control the Catholic Church in France. Part of the incentive for taking control of the Church was that the assembly now had to address the financial crisis that was initially the monarchy's undoing and was now their responsibility. To pay for the financing of the French debt, the assembly took the very risky step of confiscating and selling the property of the Church. The assembly decided to issue *assignats*, government bonds that were backed by the sale of Church lands.

Along with the confiscation of the Church's property, it was decided that the entire constitutional status of the Catholic Church needed to be altered. In July 1790, the king was forced, to his horror, to accept the passage of the **Civil Constitution of the Church**, legislation that basically made the Church a department of state. Bishops were to be chosen by assemblies of parish priests, who themselves were to be elected by their parishioners. Members of the clergy were now civil servants with salaries to be paid by the state. In addition, clergy had to swear an oath of loyalty to the French state and to uphold the Civil Constitution of the Church. While these measures might have seemed appealing to earlier monarchs seeking to consolidate their power at the expense of Rome, Louis would not be choosing them himself as a divine-right prerogative, making the idea much less palatable.

In response, **Pope Pius VI** denounced the Civil Constitution and the *Declaration of the Rights of Man*. This set in motion a major 19th-century conflict, the dispute between church and state. In France, these attacks on the privileges of the Church instigated a counter-revolutionary movement composed of people who were committed to undoing what they thought was the sacrilegious treatment of their church. Counter-revolutionary reaction, royalism, and Catholicism became associated in the public mind. With the king and the National Assembly safely ensconced in Paris, steps were taken by the National Assembly to establish a workable system of government. In 1791, a constitution for France was promulgated, creating a constitutional monarchy. The king had the right to delay legislation passed by the unicameral, or single house, legislature for at most four years, although the monarch retained significant powers, including control over foreign policy and command of the army. Because the framers of the constitution feared how popular influence would affect the political process, a complex system of indirect elections was set up. The men of France were split into two different categories: active and passive citizens. Only those men who paid taxes that equaled three days of a laborer's wages were allowed to vote for electors. Electors had to meet higher property requirements to qualify to vote for members of the assembly. Women were not given any sort of franchise. So, out of a population of roughly 25 million, only 50,000 qualified as electors.

Revolution in Haiti

The spirit of liberty in France extended to their colonies, including Haiti. The Haitian Revolution is the only slave uprising in history to have resulted in the formation of an independent state.

The National Assembly brought about other significant changes. The old French system of provinces was abandoned and replaced by 83 departments, which, making use of the rational spirit of the Enlightenment, were each roughly equal in size and still in use today. In a stunning development for the cause of religious liberty, Jews and Protestants were granted full political rights. Slavery, although still practiced in the colonies, was abolished in France. This led to a slave rebellion led by Toussaint L'Ouverture, a former slave, on the Caribbean island of Hispaniola. By 1794, slavery was abolished throughout the empire, although by that time, Haiti, the eastern half of the island of Hispaniola, had broken free from France and was the first independent Black state in the Caribbean.

The End of the Monarchy

By 1791, not only was there a growing counter-revolutionary movement within France, but on the borders of France resided thousands of nobles who had fled their country and were actively working to restore the *ancien régime* and their feudal privileges. The leader of these *émigrés* was the **Count of Artois**, the youngest brother of Louis XVI, and it was he who made the fatal decision to encourage his brother to flee France. On June 20, 1791, the royal family reached the French town of Varennes, on the border with the Netherlands, where the king was recognized and escorted back to Paris. Because the leaders of the National Assembly were still interested in maintaining the constitutional monarchy, they lied and said that the king had not fled Paris but instead had been abducted. Despite this attempt to keep Louis on the throne, the stage was set for the eventual collapse of the constitutional monarchy.

Although the new legislative assembly that was created out of the Constitution of 1791 stayed in existence for only one year, it was crucial for changing the course of the Revolution. The contentious debate within the assembly was matched by the factious debates that took place within the hundreds of political clubs that emerged throughout France. The most famous and popular of these clubs was the **Jacobins**, so named because they met in the Jacobin monastery in Paris. The Jacobins were represented in the National Assembly, although at this time, the **Girondins** faction primarily filled the leadership role in the assembly. The Girondins, named for the Gironde department in southwestern France where many in the faction came from, favored starting a revolutionary war to free from tyranny those people living in absolutist states, such as Austria and Prussia, the two nations on which France declared war in April 1792. This declaration of war ultimately sealed the fate of the royal family and helped further radicalize the Revolution.

Despite Girondin assurances that victory would be easy, the early stages of the war did not go well for France, which was forced to cope with an officer corps that was depleted by aristocratic defections. The war brought about an increasingly radical situation in Paris where the **sans-culottes** tried to deal with the scarce supply of bread and feelings of chagrin at being labeled passive citizens without the right to vote. They were also fearful following a manifesto issued by the Prussian commander, the Duke of Brunswick, which promised that he would destroy Paris if the royal family was harmed. In Paris, this helped create a political transformation that led to a demand for wider political participation and the establishment of a radical government, the Commune, in the city.

> **Cu-Whats?**
> *Culottes* were the fancy breeches worn by the aristocracy, so *sans-culottes* literally referred to those who did not wear them.

On August 10, a large mob of *sans-culottes* stormed the Tuileries palace, where the king and the queen were living, and slaughtered 600 of the king's Swiss guards. This was followed by another act of horrendous violence. In September, following a series of defeats by French armies, around 1,200 individuals who had been arrested as potential counter-revolutionaries were slaughtered by a frenzied mob that was reacting to rumors that the prisoners were about to escape and attack French armies from behind. The Paris Commune then forced the National Assembly to call for elections for a new legislative body using universal male suffrage. This body, known as the Convention, was given the task of drawing up a new constitution ending the constitutional monarchy. Meanwhile, the military acts that had spurred on these developments began to change. The threat to Paris, which had spurred on the September massacres, ended quickly when a French army, inflamed by revolutionary passion, stopped the combined Austrian and Prussian advance at the battle of Valmy. With the Revolution apparently saved from the combined threat of foreign armies and counter-revolution, France officially became a republic on September 21, 1792, and the royal family was placed under arrest. Following the discovery of a cache of letters that Louis XVI had exchanged with his brother-in-law, the Austrian Emperor, Louis was tried and, in early 1793, guillotined before a large crowd yelling for his blood.

CED 5.5
The French Revolution's Effects

European Reactions to the French Revolution

The French Revolution had a huge impact on the rest of Europe. For those on the continent who had been influenced by the ideas of the Enlightenment, the events in France seemed like a breath of fresh air, and they eagerly created radical political associations of their own in places like the Italian states and the German states. At first, Austria and Prussia thought that the Revolution would be useful for bringing about the eclipse of France as the major power on the continent. They soon came to regret their initial complacency and began to see the Revolution for its potential to spread to other areas and possibly to threaten their own thrones.

Burke's Conservatism

Only **Edmund Burke**, a leading British politician attached to the Whig faction, was cautious. In 1790, he wrote *Reflections on the French Revolution*, which expressed his opposition to the Revolution. Burke was not against reform; he himself had been interested in the reform of certain aspects of English political life. He feared, however, that once the traditional system of deference was removed, it would dramatically alter the role of such institutions as the monarchy and the Church and eventually force would rule. To that end, he predicted that the Revolution would take a more violent direction, something that was rather prescient considering he was writing in only 1790. Burke believed that reform could take place only by keeping the present political structure and seeking to achieve evolutionary rather than revolutionary change. His work serves as the foundation piece for modern political conservatism.

In Great Britain, the immediate reaction to the fall of the Bastille and the abolition of French feudalism, along with the establishment of a constitutional monarchy, was quite friendly. For many, it appeared as if the violent rivalry between the two nations would finally come to a peaceful conclusion. William Pitt the Younger, the British Prime Minister, stated, "The present convulsions in France must sooner or later culminate in general harmony and regular order and thus circumstanced, France will stand forth as one of the most brilliant powers of Europe. She will enjoy just that kind of liberty which I venerate." His chief political opponent, Charles Fox, was even more enthusiastic. He called the revolt "the greatest event that ever happened in the history of the world."

Britain was eventually brought into the Europe-wide war sparked by the Revolution. By the fall of 1792, French armies, following initial setbacks, were pushing the enemy back and began to occupy territories, such as the Austrian Netherlands. They also captured much of the Rhineland and the important city of Frankfurt. Wherever French armies went, they brought with them the ideas of the Revolution. Although the National Convention promised "fraternity and assistance to peoples who want to recover their liberties," the French armies soon became more of an occupying force than liberators.

THE REIGN OF TERROR

The King and I
Robespierre's anti-monarchical sentiments may have started at the age of 11, when a coach carrying the royal family splashed him with mud just as he was about to read some Latin verses he had written in their honor.

In the Convention, the Girondins and Jacobins continued to disagree over the direction of the Revolution. The radical Jacobins sat on the left side of the hall where the Convention met on a raised platform; this seating arrangement earned them the label "the Mountain." On the right sat the more conservative Girondins. This configuration was the origin of our modern political designations of left and right. In the middle of the hall sat those who were not directly tied to either faction; this section became known as "the Plain." It was this group that held the key to the Revolution, because whichever side they aligned with would ultimately triumph.

While both the Girondins and the Jacobins were considered republican, they had diverging opinions regarding some of the most pressing issues of the day. The

Girondins wished to make a clean break from the absolutist government of the previous decades, while still maintaining the democratic spirit of the revolution. Toward this end, they favored exile for the king (rather than execution). When creating policies for the new French government, the Girondins pushed to maintain a degree of local autonomy instead of allowing all authority to be centralized in Paris. They were also fearful of the political influence of the *sans-culottes* and hoped to stem their influence by maintaining a policy of voting rights based on property ownership. With regard to the economy, the Girondins favored *laissez-faire,* the idea that the government should not play an active role in regulating the economy.

In contrast, the Jacobins took a more radical stance. They believed that the king was a traitor and should therefore be executed. They also felt that the only way to maintain the spirit of the revolution was through a powerful centralized government in Paris. Economically, the Jacobins argued for selective regulation of industries like the wheat trade in order to fight against wild inflation. Their policies were not specifically antagonistic toward the common people of Paris. Therefore, they garnered the increasing support of the *sans-culottes,* a group that would be critical to Jacobin success in the next phase of the revolution.

The spring of 1793 marked the beginning of what became known as the **"Reign of Terror."** In part, it was inspired by the counter-revolutionary revolt that began in March in a western region of France known as the Vendée, a counter-revolution that was largely inspired by anger toward the restrictions placed on the Church. French armies met a major defeat that same month in the Austrian Netherlands, followed by the betrayal of their commanding officer, General Dumouriez, who fled to join the Austrians. In response to these provocations, the Convention created two committees, the Committee of General Security and the **Committee of Public Safety**; the latter assumed virtually dictatorial power over France throughout the following year. The leaders of the security committee included **Danton**, **Carnot**, and **Robespierre**, a lawyer. These men were associated with the Jacobin faction, which was becoming more influential at the expense of the Girondins. The Girondins were tainted by having made the traitor Dumouriez commander of French forces in the Netherlands and by their perceived lack of sympathy toward the Parisian masses.

The *sans-culottes* continued to be a useful tool for the Jacobins, and it was a mob of the former who stormed the hall where the Convention met and successfully demanded the expulsion of Girondin members. The Mountain further consolidated its control in July, when Charlotte Corday, a Girondin sympathizer, stabbed to death the radical journalist and *sans-culottes* hero, **Marat**, while he lay in his bath. To appease the *sans-culottes'* sensibilities, the Mountain-led Convention established a law of maximum prices, which placed limits on the price of bread and taxed the wealthy to pay for the war effort.

In August 1793, **Lazare Carnot**, the head of the military, issued his famous proclamation calling for a ***levée en masse***, drafting the entire population for military service. This marks the first time that all citizens of a nation were called on to serve their country. According to the proclamation, men were expected to go into battle; women should "make tents and clothing and...serve in the hospitals." Children were to "turn old linen into lint," and the old folks were to go to public places and "arouse the courage of the warriors and preach the hatred of kings and the unity of the Republic." The armies created out of this *levée en masse* proved to be surprisingly successful against the well-trained but unmotivated soldiers of Austria and Prussia, and the war once again began to turn in the French favor.

Once in power, the Jacobins worked to create what they considered to be a **Republic of Virtue**. To achieve this ideal, they felt that they had to obliterate all traces of the old monarchical regime. To that end, they came up with a new calendar based on 10-day weeks. The months were renamed to reflect the seasons, and 1792, the first year of the Republic, was labeled as year one. There was also an attack on Christianity and churches, and those in power forced the removal of religious symbols from public buildings. To move people away from what he thought was the corrupting influence of the Church, Robespierre established a **Cult of the Supreme Being**, turning the cathedral of Notre Dame into a Temple of Reason. Most of these steps proved to be quite unpopular and eventually led to a political backlash against the Committee of Public Safety.

From the summer of 1793 to the following summer, France was embroiled by the workings of the Reign of Terror. Because the Revolution was believed to be threatened by both internal and external enemies, courtesies such as the rule of law—or fair trials—were thrown out the window. The Committee of Public Safety first began by banning political clubs and popular societies of women. Next, they executed leading Girondin politicians who were accused of being traitors, and the **guillotine** became a symbol of the age. In the end, around 20,000 individuals were executed. Approximately 15 percent of these were nobles and clergy; the majority were peasants who had been involved in counter-revolutionary activities.

> Eventually, the Terror began to turn on those who had first set it in motion.

By March 1794, under the leadership of Robespierre, the Terror had an extreme radical faction known as the **Hébertists**, who were violently anti-Christian and wanted to see the government implement further economic controls. Soon afterward, Danton, one of the Jacobin committee leaders, and his followers were brought to the guillotine for arguing that it was time to bring the Terror to a close. The surviving followers of Hébert and Danton were joined by members of the National Convention who feared that they were next in line for the guillotine. The end was fairly anticlimactic: on 8 *Thermidor* (July 26, 1794), Robespierre spoke before the Convention about the need for one more major purge. Someone in the assembly shouted "Down with the tyrant," and for once, Robespierre seemed at a loss for words and left the building. The next day, he and his leading supporters were arrested by the **Thermidorians**, the label for those who were opposed to Robespierre, and after a quick trial that very same day, 100 leading Jacobins were escorted to the guillotine.

THE DIRECTORY (1795–1799)

Following the execution of the leading members of the Convention and the Committee of Public Safety, the Thermidorians abolished the Paris Commune, a hotbed of radical sentiment, along with the Committee of Public Safety. They produced a government known as the **Directory** because it was led by an executive council of five men who possessed the title of director. The new constitution provided for a two-house legislature, made up of a Council of the Ancients, which discussed and voted on legislation proposed by the second house, the Council of Five Hundred.

As part of the backlash against the radical republic established by Robespierre, the franchise was limited to those men who possessed property, and only those who possessed significant property were allowed to hold public office. In general, the Directory witnessed the triumph of men of property over the *sans-culottes*. One sign of this was the revival of ornate dress, which members of the *sans-culottes* had been proud to not possess, along with the removal of all price ceilings on staples such as bread. Another part of this backlash against the radical phase of the Revolution was the attack on Jacobin club meetings by wealthy young men whose families had grown rich by providing French troops with supplies or through the confiscation of church property.

The Directory also had to be concerned with the possibility of a royalist reaction, and on 13 *Vendémiaire* (October 5, 1795), a royalist rebellion did break out in parts of Paris. A young general named **Napoleon Bonaparte** was told to put down the rebellion, and with a "whiff of grapeshot," his cannon dispersed the rebels. The Directory had been saved, but soon it was to be destroyed by its savior.

NAPOLEON

Domestically, the Directory did little to solve the economic problems still facing the French nation, nor did it solve the ongoing conflict with the Catholic Church. Its armies, however, did meet with tremendous success on the battlefield. Among the rising generation of new French generals, the most important was Napoleon Bonaparte. Napoleon was born in 1769 to a family of minor nobles on the island of Corsica, which had been annexed by France the year prior to his birth. He attended a French military academy, and in 1785 he was commissioned as an artillery officer.

Had it not been for the French Revolution, Napoleon would have remained a junior officer for the remainder of his military career, owing to his relatively humble birth and Corsican background. However, the Revolution offered tremendous opportunities to young men of ability, and Napoleon became a strong supporter of the Revolution and was aligned with the Jacobin faction. In 1793, after playing a major role in the campaign to retake the French port of Toulon from the British, he was made a general. Napoleon was nothing if not lucky during his career, and while other Jacobins were dragged off to the guillotine during the Thermidor reaction, Napoleon was left unscathed.

> **CED 5.6**
> Napoleon's Rise, Dominance, and Defeat

Desperate for military victories that might take the people's minds off the dismal conditions at home, the Directory sent Napoleon to Italy. In a series of stunningly quick victories, Napoleon destroyed the combined Austrian and Sardinian armies, and before long, France controlled northern and central Italy. With the Austrians and the Prussians now out of the war, the only enemy was Great Britain. Instead of trying to cross the English Channel with an invasion force, a battle that Napoleon knew would have limited chance of success because of the powerful British navy, he decided to invade Egypt in order to cut Britain's ties with its colony of India. Napoleon succeeded in conquering Egypt (and ushered in a new age of appreciation for ancient Egyptian civilization, in part inspired by the discovery of the Rosetta Stone). He was unable to do much with his victories on land because a British fleet under the command of **Admiral Horatio Nelson** defeated a French fleet at the Battle of Abukir on August 1, 1798.

Seeing that the situation in Egypt was doomed, Napoleon abandoned his army and rushed back to France where he had received word that the Directory was increasingly unstable. On 19 *Brumaire* (November 10, 1799), Napoleon joined the Abbé Siéyès, who at the time was one of the five Directors, staged a *coup d'état*, and overturned the Directory. Siéyès, who thought Napoleon could be controlled, established a new constitution with a powerful executive made up of three consuls—Roger-Ducos (a sitting director), Siéyès, and Napoleon. One month after the coup, the politically ambitious Napoleon set up a new constitution with himself as **First Consul**. This structure granted universal male suffrage to satisfy republican sentiment but left Napoleon firmly in control over the real workings of the state. Using a technique that he would find increasingly useful, Napoleon staged a **plebiscite** (a vote by the people) for his new constitution to show popular support, and it was passed overwhelmingly.

Napoleon attempted to end some of the bitterness that had arisen out of the Revolution. A general amnesty was issued, and *émigrés* began to stream back to France. Since Napoleon required that public servants be loyal to him only, he was able to use the talents of those Jacobins and monarchists who were willing to accept his dominance over the French state. Napoleon treated those who were not willing with brutal cruelty. He established a secret police force to root out his opponents. Following a plot on his life, Napoleon purged the Jacobins, and he kidnapped and executed the Bourbon Duke of Enghien after falsely accusing the Duke of plotting against him.

Napoleon recognized that a major problem during the course of the Revolution was the ongoing hostility of French Catholics. He himself was not religious, but he recognized that religion could be a useful tool for maintaining political stability and that the Church would continue to be important for many French people. In 1801, Napoleon created a **concordat** with Pope Pius VII. Basically, the settlement worked to the benefit of Napoleon. The concordat declared that "Catholicism was the religion of the great majority of the French." The concordat did not, however, reestablish Catholicism as the official state religion, and it remained tolerant toward Protestants and Jews. The papacy would select bishops, but only on the recommendation of the First Consul. The state would pay clerical salaries, and all clergy had to swear an oath supporting the state. In addition, the Church gave up its claims to those lands confiscated during the Revolution. The Church was able to get Napoleon to do away with the calendar that had been established during the period of Jacobin dominance, which the Church particularly hated because it did away with Sundays and religious holidays.

Napoleon's Legacy
The Napoleonic Code provides the framework for the French legal system to this day.

Following a plebiscite in 1802 that made him Consul for Life, Napoleon set about to reform the French legal system. **The Civil Code of 1804**, commonly known as the **Napoleonic Code**, provided for a single unitary legal system for all of France, rather than the hundreds of localized codes that had been in existence under the monarchy. The code enshrined the equality of all people before the law and safeguarded the rights of property holders. Reversing the advances made by women during the Revolution, the code reaffirmed the paternalistic nature of French society. Women and children were legally dependent on their husbands and fathers. A woman could not sell or buy property without the approval of her father or husband, and divorce, while still legal, became much harder for women to obtain.

In 1804, Napoleon decided to make himself emperor. Once again, he held a plebiscite as a means of trying to show popular support, and again his wishes were overwhelmingly affirmed by vote. He invited the pope to take part in the ceremony, which took place in Notre Dame, rather than in Rheims Cathedral, the traditional place where French kings had been crowned. During the point in the ceremony at which the pope was about to place the crown on the Emperor's head, Napoleon yanked it out of the pope's hands and placed it on his own head and then took a second crown and placed it on the head of his wife, Josephine. Napoleon wanted to make it clear that he was Emperor of the French not based on the will of God or through accident of birth, but rather as a result of the weight of his own achievements. Napoleon also created a new aristocracy that was based on service to the state rather than birth. Members of the new aristocracy did not enjoy any special privileges before the law, nor could their titles be passed on to their children.

FRANCE AT WAR WITH EUROPE

Constant warfare was a hallmark of the reign of Napoleon. Although he is considered to be one of the geniuses in the history of warfare, in many ways his greatest skill was in taking advantage of certain developments that were taking place in 18th-century warfare. In 1792, with the *levée en masse*, French armies became larger than their opponents' forces, and Napoleon became an expert at moving these large armies to outmaneuver his opponents. In part, he could do this because he could trust his highly motivated citizen-soldiers, unlike his opponents, who employed unreliable mercenaries who were given little independence on the battlefield for fear of desertion. Napoleon certainly did not invent the new lighter artillery found in the 18th century, but he skillfully recognized that this new artillery could be fully integrated with the infantry and cavalry as a very effective fighting tool. Although Napoleon supposedly said that an army "moves on its stomach," he did little to feed those stomachs. He encouraged his men to live off the land, rather than using costly time to provide adequate provisions through the maintenance of a supply line, something that added to the great unpopularity of French occupying armies.

Although France was officially at peace with Great Britain as a result of the **Treaty of Amiens** (1802), Napoleon saw it only as a temporary measure while he sought for means to limit British influence. To antagonize the British, who had colonies in the Caribbean, he sent troops to Haiti—where a slave rebellion had created an independent republic—in an attempt to reestablish French control. After most of the French troops died from disease, Napoleon turned his interest away from the colonies and even sold the **Louisiana Territory** to the United States for the paltry sum of around $15 million. Napoleon refocused on Europe and readied plans to invade England, but first the powerful Royal Navy would have to be defeated. At the **Battle of Trafalgar** on October 21, 1805, Admiral Nelson died in the struggle that ultimately destroyed the French fleet and with it any hope of the French landing in England.

On land, however, Napoleon was in his element. Following the formation of the **Third Coalition**, in which Austria and Russia joined Great Britain, Napoleon set out to first destroy the Austrians, a goal which he achieved at the **Battle of Ulm** in October 1805. He then won his greatest victory over a Russian force at **Austerlitz**. Following these battles, Napoleon decided to abolish the Holy Roman Empire and created the **Confederacy of the Rhine**, a loose grouping of 16 German states that were placed under the influence of France. Ironically, just as in Italy, Napoleon's victories in Germany resulted in the redrawing of the map, although with long-term consequences not favorable to the French nation. When the Prussians, who had previously worked out a treaty with France, saw the extent of French control over German territories, they hastily joined the Third Coalition. To punish them, Napoleon quickly gathered his forces, and at the **Battle of Jena** he obliterated the Prussian army and occupied their capital city of Berlin.

Following the complete collapse of the Prussian army, the Russian Tsar **Alexander I** (r. 1801–1825) decided that it was necessary to make peace with France. He met with Napoleon on a raft on the Nieman River, and on July 7, 1807, the two monarchs signed the **Treaty of Tilsit**, with the Prussian monarch eagerly waiting on the shore to see what Alexander and Napoleon cast as the fate of his defeated kingdom. Because of the insistence of Alexander, Prussia was saved from extinction, but it was reduced to half its previous size and forced to become an ally of France in its ongoing struggle against Great Britain. Seeing that he could not defeat the British navy, Napoleon decided to wage economic war. He established the **Continental System**, an attempt to ban British goods from arriving on the continent. Rather than damaging Great Britain, however, the Continental System weakened the economies of those states that Napoleon had conquered and achieved little to advance French economic interests.

The Continental System and the resentment it caused throughout Europe helped galvanize support against French rule. Initially, wherever French troops went, they brought with them the ideals of the Enlightenment and the French Revolution. French troops arriving in Venice broke down the walls of the ghetto where Jews had been forced to live since the High Middle Ages and established full religious toleration. They also brought about the end of social distinctions wherever they went and imposed the Civil Code as the basic rule of law. Despite this, the French were still occupiers, and as time went on, increasingly harsh ones. Napoleon placed his family on the various thrones of Europe, essentially as figureheads, because all authority came from Paris.

THE DEFEAT OF NAPOLEON

Napoleon's eventual defeat came about for three reasons: the peninsula war in Spain, growing nationalism in French-occupied Europe, and the fateful 1812 invasion of Russia.

The War in Spain

In 1807, a French army passed through Spain on its way to conquer Portugal, an ally of Great Britain. The next year a revolt broke out against the incompetent Spanish King Charles IV bringing his son, the almost-as-incompetent Ferdinand VII (r. 1808–1833) to its throne. In response, Napoleon decided to take the opportunity to occupy Spain and place his brother Joseph on its throne. Almost immediately, the Spanish nation rose up in a nationalistic fervor to expel the French, who in turn used tremendous brutality against the Spanish people. Napoleon was eventually forced to leave 350,000 troops in Spain, where they were tied down in a costly struggle against Spanish patriots who fought with guerrilla tactics against the more static French troops.

Growing Nationalism in Europe

While Napoleon continued to struggle with what he called his "Spanish ulcer," stirrings of nationalism also began to churn in other parts of Europe. In the German states, intellectuals began to see that a struggle against the French might be just the tool to create that unified German state for which they longed. These writers looked to Prussia for leadership, while within Prussia, there were stirrings of reform as the nation began to grasp the magnitude of its defeat at Jena. Fortunately for Prussia, it was blessed with two administrators who possessed immense abilities: **Baron von Stein** (1757–1831) and **Count von Hardenberg** (1750–1822). These men were hardly democratic reformers; they wanted to see the continuation of monarchical power and aristocratic privilege. They did, however, bring about much-needed reforms, such as ending the Junker (Prussian noble) monopoly over the ownership of land and abolishing serfdom. To create an army of motivated soldiers led by competent leaders like the French model, Stein appointed some bourgeois officers and removed some of the more incompetent Junker officers. He also established a professional ministry of war. Stein eliminated some of the harsher elements of military discipline to encourage the peasant soldiers to fight loyally for the state, and he established a large reserve army made up of part-time soldiers.

The 1812 Invasion of Russia

Some of Napoleon's advisors warned him that the constant wars came at a high cost to the French nation. Napoleon, however, still looked for new lands to conquer. Russia seemed a suitable target, particularly because after the defeat of Prussia and Austria, only Russia was still standing as a strong continental rival. In June 1812, Napoleon took his **"Grand Army"** of 600,000 men into

Russia, where he fully expected to defeat the Russians in open battle. To his great annoyance, the Russians merely retreated within their vast landscape. When Napoleon took Moscow in September, he found the city a smoking ruin, with fires set by the retreating army of the tsar. Since there was no enemy to fight and few supplies left in the part of Russia occupied by French troops, Napoleon decided to withdraw his army in one of the most famous retreats in military history. The combination of Russian attacks and the brutal winter made the withdrawal a disaster; only 40,000 of the original Grand Army finally returned to France.

The Russian retreat marked the beginning of the end. In 1813, Russia, Prussia, Austria, and Great Britain formed a coalition to fight together until all of Europe was freed from French forces. While British forces under the **Duke of Wellington** pushed forward toward France through Spain, a combined Russian, Prussian, and Austrian force entered eastern France. By March of 1814, they were in Paris, and in the following month, after learning that the allies would not accept his young son on the French throne, Napoleon abdicated.

THE CONGRESS OF VIENNA, THE BOURBON RESTORATION, AND THE HUNDRED DAYS

In victory, the allies demanded the restoration of the **Bourbon monarchs** as outlined in the Treaty of Chaumont, which brought the Count of Provence, a brother of the executed Louis XVI, to the French throne as Louis XVIII. Meanwhile, Napoleon was exiled to the Mediterranean island of Elba, although the allies generously (and fearfully) paid off his debts and allowed him to maintain the title of Emperor and keep a small army on his tiny island state.

> **CED 5.7**
> The Congress of Vienna

To create a lasting peace and to try to put the revolutionary genie back in the bottle, the allies met at the **Congress of Vienna** beginning in September 1814. The four great powers, Great Britain, Austria, Prussia, and Russia, dominated the proceedings, although the great architect of the Congress settlement was the Austrian Chancellor, **Prince Metternich** (1773–1859). Metternich was aware that the social and political changes brought about by the French Revolution had been detrimental to his own state and that it was necessary to turn back the clock. Metternich and the other representatives wanted to make sure that such ideas emanating from the French Revolution, such as **nationalism** and **liberalism**, would have no place in a redrawn Europe. To that end, they made sure that Polish demands for a free and independent Poland went unanswered and gave the territory to the Tsar of Russia as the Duchy of Poland.

The great powers also wanted to ensure that no nation, least of all France, should ever dominate Europe again. To keep order in France and to ensure that the Bourbons' subjects would not greatly resent them, France walked away with rather generous peace terms, including the right to hold onto all territorial gains made prior to November 1, 1792. The great powers also erected a series of states that would serve as a barrier to future French expansion. They created the Kingdom of the Netherlands by incorporating the Dutch territory with the Austrian Netherlands to the south, gave Prussia important territories along the Rhine River to block future French expansion to the east, and gave Piedmont the territory of Genoa.

While the victors debated the future course of Europe, the past came back to haunt them. On March 20, 1815, Napoleon returned to Paris having escaped from Elba. He found many in the army and in the country at large willing to support him, particularly since the return of the

Bourbons had led to an unleashing of a violent **white terror** (white signifying the royalist flag and those loyal to the monarchy) against Jacobins and Bonaparte supporters. Louis XVIII was once again forced to flee his homeland as Napoleon was rapidly reinstalled as emperor. Although he promised France a liberal constitution and the end to foreign aggression, he knew that the other great powers would not allow him to maintain the throne, so once again he raised an army. At the **Battle of Waterloo** (June 18, 1815), Wellington, the British commander, aided by Marshal Blucher, the leader of the Prussian forces, defeated Napoleon. Following the **Hundred Days**, the name given to Napoleon's remarkable return, he was exiled once again, although this time to the distant island of St. Helena, in the middle of the Atlantic, where he died in 1821.

CHAPTER 5 TIMELINE

Year(s)	Event
1610	Assassination of Henry IV
1610	Galileo begins astronomical observations with his telescope
1613	Galileo publishes *Letters on Sunspots*
1616	William Harvey announces his discovery of the circulatory system
1618	Johannes Kepler reveals his third and final law of planetary motion
1618	Beginning of the Thirty Years' War
1620	Battle of White Mountain
1620	Founding of Plymouth Colony
1620	Francis Bacon publishes *Novum Organum*
1624	Cardinal Richelieu becomes Louis XIII's chief minister
1625	Charles I becomes king upon death of James I
1628	Petition of Right
1628	Murder of Duke of Buckingham
1629	Edict of Restitution
1629	Personal Rule of Charles I begins and lasts 11 years
1632	Gustavus Adolphus dies at the Battle of Lutzen
1632	Galileo's *Dialogue on the Two Chief Systems of the World*
1633	Trial of Galileo
1633	Murder of Albrecht von Wallenstein
1633	France enters the Thirty Years' War
1637	Charles introduces the Book of Common Prayer into Scotland
1637	René Descartes publishes *Discourse on Method*
1640	Beginning of the reign of Frederick William (Great Elector)
1640	Charles forced to summon Parliament to deal with Scottish revolt
1641	Rebellion in Ireland
1642	Execution of Archbishop Laud
1648	Peace of Westphalia
1649	Beginning of the Fronde
1649	Execution of Charles I and establishment of English republic
1653	Oliver Cromwell becomes Lord Protector
1659	Death of Cromwell
1660	Restoration of Charles II
1660	Thomas Hobbes publishes *Leviathan*
1661	Death of Cardinal Mazarin; Louis XIV becomes his own chief minister
1662	Royal Society is established by Charles II

Year(s)	Event
1664	Chartering of the French East India Company
1669	Louis XIV begins construction of the Palace of Versailles
1669	Posthumous publication of Pascal's *Pensées*
1682	Beginning of the reign of Peter the Great
1682	Rembrandt paints *The Night Watch*
1685	Revocation of the Edict of Nantes
1685	James II, a Catholic, becomes King of England
1687	Newton publishes his *Principia*
1688	John Locke's *Two Treatises on Government*
1688	Glorious Revolution
1689	Act of Toleration
1690	John Locke's *Essay on Human Understanding*
1701	Prussia becomes a kingdom
1701	Act of Settlement passed to bypass potential Catholic kings
1703	Cornerstone laid for the new city of St. Petersburg
1707	Act of Union brings about political unification of England and Scotland
1713	Treaty of Utrecht marks the end of the War of the Spanish Succession
1714	George I becomes first Hanoverian King of England
1721	End of the Great Northern War between Russia and Sweden
1721	Start of Robert Walpole's tenure as prime minister
1739	Hume's *Inquiry into Human Nature*
1740	Frederick the Great becomes King of Prussia
1740	Start of the War of the Austrian Succession
1746	Battle of Culloden
1748	Montesquieu's *Spirit of Laws*
1748	Treaty of Aix-la-Chapelle marks the end of the War of the Austrian Succession
1751	The first volume of Diderot's *Encyclopédie* appears
1755	Lisbon earthquake
1756	Maria Theresa carries out the "Diplomatic Revolution"
1756	Beginning of the Seven Years' War
1759	Voltaire's *Candide*
1762	Rousseau's *The Social Contract*
1762	Rousseau's *Émile* is published
1762	Start of the reign of Catherine the Great
1763	Voltaire pushes for reexamination in the trial of Jean Calas
1763	Peace of Paris marks end of Seven Years' War

Year(s)	Event
1764	Beccaria's *On Crime and Punishment*
1765	Stamp Act
1770	Burke writes *Thoughts on the Cause of the Present Discontent*
1770	Marriage of the future Louis XVI to Marie Antoinette
1774	Louis XVI becomes King of France
1774	First Continental Congress
1775	Fighting begins between American colonists and British
1776	Jefferson writes the Declaration of Independence
1776	The first volume of Edward Gibbon's *The History of the Decline and Fall of the Roman Empire* is published
1776	Adam Smith's *Wealth of Nations*
1778	France goes to war against Britain in support of the American colonies
1781	Kant's *Critique of Pure Reason*
1781	Joseph II of Austria issues Edicts of Toleration
1786	Calonne, finance minister to Louis XVI, informs him that the crown is bankrupt
1787	Assembly of Notables meets
1788	Louis XVI decides to call the Estates General
1788	Abbé Siéyès writes *What Is the Third Estate?*
1789	Estates General meets for the first time (May 5)
1789	Third Estate declares that it will meet only as a National Assembly (June 17)
1789	Tennis Court Oath (June 20)
1789	Storming of the Bastille (July 14)
1789	Lafayette selected as commander of the National Guard
1789	Great Fear (July–August)
1789	Renunciation of aristocratic privileges (August 24)
1789	*Declaration of the Rights of Man* is adopted by the Constituent Assembly (August 26)
1789	Women's march on Versailles (October 5)
1789	Jeremy Bentham's *Introduction to the Principles of Morals and Legislation*
1790	Civil Constitution of the Clergy
1790	Edmund Burke's *Reflections on the Revolution in France*
1791	Constitution adopted
1791	Revolt breaks out in the French colony of St. Domingue
1791	Louis XVI attempts to flee Paris (June 20)
1792	Mary Wollstonecraft's *Vindication of the Rights of Women*
1792	France declares war on Austria (April 20)
1792	Mob of *sans-culottes* storms the Tuileries Palace (August 10)

Year(s)	Event
1792	September Massacres
1792	Battle of Valmy (September 20)
1792	France becomes a republic (September 21)
1793	Execution of Louis XVI (January 21)
1793	Universal conscription for the French armies begins (February 24)
1793	Execution of Marie Antoinette (October 16)
1793	Britain enters the war against France
1793	Counter-revolution breaks out in the Vendee (March)
1793	Establishment of the Committee of Public Safety (April)
1793	Expulsion of Girondins from the Convention (June 2)
1793	Ratification of new republican constitution (June 24)
1793	Murder of Marat by Charlotte Corday (July 13)
1793	Napoleon retakes Toulon from counter-revolutionaries
1794	Execution of Danton (April 6)
1794	Festival of the Supreme Being (June 8)
1794	Fall of Robespierre and the Jacobins (July 27)
1795	Establishment of the Directory
1795	Napoleon puts down royalist revolt (October 5)
1796	Napoleon launches invasion of northern Italy
1798	Napoleon begins invasion of Egypt
1798	French fleet defeated at the Battle of the Nile (August)
1798	Thomas Malthus's *Essay on Population*
1799	Napoleon involved in coup overthrowing Directory
1799	Napoleon becomes First Consul
1801	Napoleon and Pope Pius VII sign concordat
1802	Plebiscite establishes Napoleon as Consul for Life
1802	Treaty of Amiens between Britain and France
1803	Napoleon sells Louisiana Territory to the United States
1804	Napoleon crowned Emperor
1804	Murder of the Duke of Enghien
1804	Promulgation of the Civil Code
1805	British victory over French-Spanish fleet at Trafalgar
1805	Defeat of the Prussians at the Battle of Jena
1805	Formation of the Third Coalition
1805	Defeat of the Austrians and Russians at Austerlitz

Year(s)	Event
1806	Abolition of the Holy Roman Empire
1807	Napoleon and Alexander I sign the Treaty of Tilsit
1807	Continental System implemented
1807	Invasion of Spain by French forces
1807	British Parliament votes for the end of the slave trade
1807	First passenger train line
1812	Napoleon's invasion of Russia
1812	Occupation of Moscow (September)
1813	Retreat from Russia
1813	Battle of Leipzig (October)
1814	Napoleon forced to abdicate and the reign of Louis XVIII begins
1814	Congress of Vienna convenes (September)
1815	Napoleon escapes from Elba (February 26)
1815	Battle of Waterloo marks end of the Hundred Days (June 18)
1815	Napoleon sent into exile on St. Helena
1821	Death of Napoleon

CHAPTER 5 KEY TERMS

France
royal absolutism
Cardinal Richelieu
Louis XIV
Cardinal Mazarin
divine right of kings
Versailles
Jean-Baptiste Colbert
mercantilism
French East India Company
Edict of Nantes
William of Orange
War of Spanish Succession
Treaty of Utrecht

England
Stuart dynasty
King James VI of Scotland
House of Commons
House of Lords
Puritans
Charles I
tonnage and poundage
Petition of Rights
Personal Rule of Charles
national covenant
Short and Long Parliaments
Grand Remonstrance
English Revolution
Oliver Cromwell
The Commonwealth
Independents vs. Presbyterians
Charles II
James II
Glorious Revolution
The English Bill of Rights
The Act of Toleration

The Netherlands
Dutch War for Independence
Bank of Amsterdam
Dutch East India Company
joint-stock companies
Golden Age
House of Orange
William of Nassau
Jan Vermeer
Rembrandt van Rijn

Economic and Social Life
Price Revolution
gentry
enclosure
English Poor Law
three-field system
guilds
capitalist entrepreneurs
primogeniture
dowry

Pre-Scientific Worldview
scholasticism
Thomas Aquinas
alchemy
Ptolemy

Copernican Revolution
Nicolaus Copernicus
heliocentrism
Galileo Galilei
Tycho Brahe
Johannes Kepler
Isaac Newton, *Principia*
Giordano Bruno

Impact of the Scientific Revolution

Francis Bacon
inductive reasoning, empiricism
René Descartes
deductive thought, rationalism
"I think, therefore I am"
Cartesian doubt
Blaise Pascal
Pascal's wager
Thomas Hobbes, *Leviathan*
William Harvey
absolutism
John Locke
social contract
tabula rasa

The 18th-Century Enlightenment

philosophes
Voltaire, *Candide*
deism
Baron de Montesquieu, *Spirit of the Laws*
separation of powers
checks and balances
Denis Diderot, *Encyclopedie*
Jean-Jacques Rousseau, *The Social Contract*
general will
Immanuel Kant, *Critique of Pure Reason*
Cesare Beccaria, *On Crimes and Punishment*
jurisprudence
David Hume, *Inquiry into Human Nature*
Edward Gibbon, *Decline and Fall of the Roman Empire*
Adam Smith, *Inquiry into the Nature and Causes of the Wealth of Nations*
laissez-faire
"invisible hand"
salons
Mary Wollstonecraft

18th-Century Life: Key Developments, Arts

John Hunter
William Smellie
Lady Mary Wortley Montagu
Edward Jenner
Samuel Richardson
Daniel Defoe
Frederic Handel
J. S. Bach
Velazquez
Caravaggio

European Powers in the Age of Enlightenment

enlightened absolutists
Thirty Years' War
Frederick II (the Great) of Prussia
Empress Maria Theresa
Joseph II of Austria
War of the Austrian Succession
Seven Years' War (French and Indian War)
Time of Troubles
Romanov family
Peter the Great
"window to the West"
St. Petersburg
Great Northern War
Catherine the Great of Russia
Charles III of Spain
Polish-Lithuanian Commonwealth
Partition of Poland
constitution
Tadeusz Kosciuszko
Robert Walpole
Tories vs. Whigs
Great Reform Bill
Louis XV

The French Revolution

Estates General
Third Estate
First Estate
Abbé Siéyès
cahiers de doléances
Tennis Court Oath
Bastille
Commune of Paris
The Great Fear
Declaration of the Rights of Man and Citizen
Olympe de Gouges, *The Rights of Women*
Civil Constitution of the Church
Jacobins vs. Girondins
sans-culottes
Edmund Burke

The Reign of Terror

The Reign of Terror
Committee of Public Safety
Danton
Robespierre
Republic of Virtue
Cult of the Supreme Being
guillotine

The Directory

The Directory
Napoleon Bonaparte

Napoleon; France at War with Europe

Admiral Horatio Nelson
First Consul
plebiscite
Napoleonic Code (Civil Code of 1804)
Louisiana Territory
Battle of Trafalgar
Third Coalition
Continental System
Grand Army
Duke of Wellington

The Congress of Vienna, etc.

Bourbon monarchs
Congress of Vienna
Prince Metternich
nationalism
liberalism
Battle of Waterloo
Hundred Days

CHAPTER 5 REVIEW QUESTIONS

Try these questions to assess how well you understood and retained the information covered in the chapter. Answers and explanations are in Chapter 8.

Questions 1 through 5 refer to the following.

"In France the formulation of a national commercial policy was largely the work of Colbert, who for twenty-two years, from 1661 to 1683, was Finance Minister to Louis XIV. Although France at that time was the most populous and wealthy country in Europe, the sea-borne trade of the world was largely in other hands. Consequently Colbert, in order to place his country in the premier position in all fields of economic activity, sought to wrest the supremacy in commerce from the Dutch and the English. Colbert's program was threefold, embracing the monopoly of overseas trade for the French marine, the improvement of domestic industry, and the erection of a protective tariff against the manufactures of foreign countries. This industrial and commercial program played such a vital part in the development of mercantilist policies that "Colbertism" and "mercantilism" are almost synonymous terms."

Source: Frank Arnold Haight, *A History of French Commercial Policies*, 1941

1 ☐ Mark for Review

Mercantilism, as an economic philosophy, seeks to increase state reserves of currency by

(A) instituting floating exchange rates

(B) escalating military conflicts against trade competitors

(C) favoring imports over exports

(D) improving a slightly positive balance of trade

2 ☐ Mark for Review

Colbert's attempt to bolster French industry is most evident in his support of

(A) weavers who had yet to unionize

(B) the domestic production of ceramics, glass, and textiles

(C) easing of tariffs

(D) the construction of a massive shipbuilding industry

3 ☐ Mark for Review

Despite Colbert's mercantilistic policies, the royal coffers continued to remain empty largely as a result of

(A) a series of expensive and fruitless wars

(B) a spendthrift king

(C) the rise of Spain as a naval power

(D) large peasant revolts that needed to be put down

4 ☐ Mark for Review

Opposite the ideas of economists who favored mercantilism and believed in the future of agriculture, this group was known as

(A) the Jacobins

(B) the Physiocrats

(C) the Utopians

(D) the Richilieus

5 ⌖ Mark for Review

Colbert and his policy of mercantilism could be viewed as part of the later philosophy of

(A) liberalism

(B) anarchism

(C) nationalism

(D) socialism

Questions 6 through 10 refer to the following.

"At the same time that this new revelation came, a crisis was going on in religion. The old Romish church was being uprooted, or, rather, a new system was being grafted upon its stock, for the links have never been broken. The saints were shortly to be tabooed by the large mass of the English folk; the festivals were already at a discount. Simultaneously with the prejudice against the very names of their saints and saintly festivals, arose the discovery of a mine of new names as novel as it was unexhaustible....

The Puritan rejected both classes. [The Puritan] was ever trotting out his two big 'P's—Pagan and Popish. Under the first, he placed every name that could not be found in the Scriptures, and under the latter every title in the same Scriptures, and the Church system founded on them, that had been employed previous, say, to the coronation day of Edward VI."

Source: *Curiosities of Puritan Nomenclature*, Charles Bardsley, 1888

6 ⌖ Mark for Review

In this passage, the author seems to be chiefly concerned with

(A) the failings of the church that led to a religious crisis

(B) describing all the names that the Puritans wanted to eliminate

(C) the revolutionary nature of the Puritan movement

(D) proving that Puritanism was promoted by the people, not the elites

7 ⌖ Mark for Review

Which of the following stands as the strongest expression of Puritan political power?

(A) The Puritan clergy who returned from exile when Mary I took the throne

(B) The calling of the Long Parliament under Charles I

(C) The rise of Oliver Cromwell

(D) The removal of James II from the throne

8 🔖 Mark for Review

Which of the following was NOT used to describe a faction of the seventeenth-century Protestant movement in England?

Ⓐ Palatines

Ⓑ Separatists

Ⓒ Dissenters

Ⓓ Diggers

9 🔖 Mark for Review

All of the following were reasons for the newfound popularity of direct Bible study among Puritans EXCEPT

Ⓐ the translation of the Bible into English

Ⓑ the invention of the printing press, which made it easier to distribute Bibles to the masses and increased literacy

Ⓒ a desire to perform acts of social justice

Ⓓ distrust of intermediaries such as priests and bishops

10 🔖 Mark for Review

As a professional historian who wrote two centuries later about the history of Puritan names, Bardsley most likely arrived at his conclusions through

Ⓐ confirmation of his preexisting biases

Ⓑ intense debate with other scholars about the veracity of their opinions

Ⓒ a thorough analysis of secondary-source material, such as encyclopedia summaries

Ⓓ original engagement with primary-source material, such as baptismal and county records

Questions 11 through 14 refer to the following.

Encyclopédie, illustrated plate, mid-1700s. Edited by Denis Diderot.

---

11 ⌖ Mark for Review

The illustration highlights what intellectual development that dominated the seventeenth century?

(A) Scholasticism

(B) Scientific Revolution

(C) Enlightenment

(D) Romanticism

---

12 ⌖ Mark for Review

By setting the work of artisans and laborers on equal footing with the work of clerics and rulers, the *Encyclopédie* contributed to what major event?

(A) The establishment of the Ancien Régime

(B) The French Revolution

(C) The Wars of Religion

(D) The construction of the Palace of Versailles

---

13 Mark for Review

Scientists of the eighteenth century saw the assembly and categorization of the natural world as

(A) the first step in the process by which one could arrive at universal laws

(B) a form of resistance against the tyranny of elite scientific thought

(C) a way to make money in an age marked by increased trade and commercialization

(D) an intellectual journey in which the collection of data was its own reward

14 Mark for Review

The figure who did NOT support the idea of inductive reasoning as seen in the *Encyclopédie* was

(A) Francis Bacon

(B) William Harvey

(C) René Descartes

(D) Thomas Hobbes

Chapter 6
Units 6–7:
Age of Revolutions
to World War I
(c. 1815–1914)

RESTORATION AND REVOLUTION

Following the final fall of Napoleon in 1815 and the restoration of the Bourbons to the throne of France, the rulers of Europe were faced with a daunting task—restoring stability to the relationships between the nations of Europe while also ensuring that the specter of revolution did not reappear within their domains. To aid in this task, one aspect of Napoleon's reign was widely copied throughout Europe—France's efficiency in controlling its population. In the period following the Napoleonic wars, states created larger and more efficient bureaucracies, secret police forces, and more efficient censorship offices. In an undeveloped nation such as Russia, these oppressive institutions were the only well-functioning part of the state.

States used another strategy to try to turn back the clock—attacking the legacy of the Enlightenment. No institution had suffered as much from the Enlightenment and the French Revolution as the Church. The German Romantic poet Novalis wrote in 1799, "Catholicism is almost played out. The old papacy is laid in the tomb, and Rome for the second time has become a ruin." Despite this prediction, the churches of Europe, both Catholic and Protestant, witnessed a remarkable recovery in the Restoration period (1815–1830). States viewed religion as a useful tool to aid in repression. In England, the Anglican clergy worked in the House of Lords to block parliamentary measures such as the bill in favor of Catholic emancipation and the Great Reform Bill. In Russia, the Orthodox clergy remained a bulwark of the reactionary policies of the state. The same was true in Catholic lands such as Spain, where the Inquisition was once again allowed to operate following its disappearance during the Napoleonic domination of Spain.

AN AGE OF COMPETING IDEOLOGIES

The Restoration period was a highly ideological period in which ideas inspired either from support or commendation of the French Revolution played a role in whether one was committed to the restored order that emerged after 1815 or wanted to see its demise. In fact, this era is sometimes referred to as "the age of -isms."

Conservatism

Modern conservatism is rooted in the writings of **Edmund Burke** whose ***Reflections on the Revolution in France*** (1790) was widely read throughout Europe. Two components of Burke's work were extremely popular in the Restoration period: his attack on the principle of the rights of man and natural law as fundamentally dangerous to the social order, and his emphasis on the role of tradition as the basic underpinning for the rights of those in positions of authority. Burke, a member of the English House of Commons, proposed a conservatism that was not reactionary in nature. He believed in the possibility of slow political change over the passage of time.

On the continent, however, a more extreme form of reactionary conservatism appeared in the writings of such men as **Joseph de Maistre** (1753–1821), an *émigré* during the French Revolution. The Church, argued de Maistre, should stand as the very foundation of society because all political authority stemmed from God. De Maistre advocated that monarchs should be extremely stern with those who advocated even the slightest degree of political reform and that the "first servant of the crown should be the executioner."

Nationalism

Nationalism is based on the idea that all people's identities are defined by their connection with a nation and that it is to this nation that they owe their primary loyalty, as opposed to their king or local lord. The roots of nationalism date back to the early modern period; however, nationalism emerged as an important ideology during the French Revolution. At this time, developments like national conscription, the calling of all young men for military service, helped create the idea of a citizen whose primary loyalty lies not to a village or province but to the nation instead.

Nationalism became important in other parts of Europe in reaction to the expansion in France. In the German and Italian states, the desire to rid their lands of French soldiers created a unifying purpose that helped establish a national identity. This growing national identity also had a literary component. Writers such as the Grimm brothers recorded old German folk tales to reveal a traditional German national spirit that was part of a common past, whether one lived in Bavaria, Saxony, or any of the other German states. Early 19th-century nationalism was often, though not exclusively, tied to liberalism because many nationalists, like the liberals, wanted political equality and human freedom to serve as the bedrock for the new state.

Liberalism

The foundations for 19th-century liberalism can be found in the writings of the philosophers of the Enlightenment, with their emphasis on the **individual's natural rights** and support for limits on political authorities through the writing of constitutions and the formation of parliamentary bodies. Liberalism was also connected to the events of the early stages of the French Revolution with the establishment of the constitutional monarchy and with Lafayette's *Declaration of the Rights of Man* serving as a basic foundational document. Liberals hoped to protect the rights of individuals by limiting the power of the state and by emphasizing the individual's right to enjoy religious freedom, freedom of the press, and equality under the law.

Besides being a political theory, liberalism was also a school of economic thought. The most important of the early liberal economists—individuals who collectively formed what became known as the **classical school**—was **Adam Smith** (1723–1790), who published his most important work, ***An Inquiry into the Nature and Causes of the Wealth of Nations***, in 1776. **Mercantilism** held that nations' wealth could be measured only in gold reserves and that foreign trade would necessarily hurt one side or the other. However, Smith realized a nation's true wealth was the goods produced by the labor of its citizens. Smith introduced two revolutionary ideas. First, specialists (whether individuals or countries) have natural skills and can produce their specialties better and faster than others. Trade could thus enrich everyone: France and Scotland would both be richer

> **Smith's *Laissez-Faire***
> The concept of *laissez-faire*, originated by Adam Smith, is the basis of free-market capitalism.

if they traded wine and coal, rather than the French mining in the vineyards and the Scots growing grapes in the highlands. Second, government price-fixing was unnecessary and counterproductive. Instead, governments should follow a ***laissez-faire*** policy and let individual businesses set their own prices and production levels. He argued that individual decisions, as though guided by an "invisible hand," would provide a balance between supply and demand, while also providing businesses an incentive to find cheaper ways to produce more goods, lower prices, and increase sales.

Economics is sometimes referred to as "the dismal science," because the classical economists—men such as **Thomas Malthus** (1766–1834) and **David Ricardo** (1772–1823)—reached conclusions that can only be viewed as deeply depressing. Malthus, a country parson, argued in his ***Essay on Population*** that the population was growing at a rate that would eventually outstrip the food supply. Factory owners were pleased to read in Malthus a justification for the payment of miserable wages to their workers because, according to Malthus, if they were better compensated, they would be more likely to produce more children, ultimately leading to only more misery as increasing numbers of workers competed for fewer jobs and less food. According to Ricardo, the only way factory owners could find an advantage over their competitors was by offering lower wages, resulting in a steady downward spiral in their earnings. This **"Iron Law of Wages"** must also have pleased factory owners because, once again, their thriftiness could be presented as if it were actually essential for the public good. Ironically, Malthus and Ricardo were both writing at a time when the dramatic expansion of production brought on by the Industrial Revolution was making their negative predictions obsolete.

Some writers, although we still apply to them the label of "liberal," began to question certain classical, liberal orthodoxies on the workings of the economy as well as the role of the state. **John Stuart Mill** (1806–1873) began as a disciple of **Jeremy Bentham** (1748–1832), who had provided a justification for an expanded role for government by suggesting that governments should seek to provide "the greatest happiness for the greatest number." Bentham's views, which are given the label of **utilitarianism**, were taken further by Mill, who wrote in his *Principles of Political Economy* that it may be necessary for the state to intervene and help workers achieve economic justice.

In some of Mill's later works, he began to move in a direction that brought him even closer to socialism, with his questioning of the absolute right to hold private property while also suggesting that there needed to be a more equitable way for societies to distribute their wealth. Mill's most famous work, *On Liberty*, was a clarion call for personal freedom. Although in the past the struggle for liberty involved placing constraints on monarchs, in Mill's day the danger was that in democratic governments, the majority could deny liberty to the minority, thus squashing the personal liberty that Mill cherished in the name of majority rule.

Unlike other male liberals who saw political liberty solely as a male domain, Mill was greatly influenced by the feminist thought of his wife, **Harriet Taylor** (1807–1856). Inspired by her, he wrote *The Subjection of Women,* arguing in favor of granting full equality to women.

Socialism

Socialism, like the other ideologies discussed above, was also partly rooted in the French Revolution. A number of radical Jacobins took the idea of political equality for all and moved it to the next step: economic equality for all through the common ownership of all property. The early socialist writers are sometimes given the label **"Utopian Socialists,"**

Early Socialists

The early Socialists provided no single answer to society's problems. **Henri de Saint-Simon** (1760–1825) argued that society needed to be organized on a scientific basis. He argued for the creation of a hierarchical society led by an intellectual class that improved society and, most important, the lot of those on the bottom of the social ladder. Contemporary events in Europe are currently heading in a direction that Saint-Simon imagined: he hoped to witness the rise of a community of European nations that would have a common currency, transportation, and a parliament, among other things.

Another Utopian Socialist was **Charles Fourier** (1772–1837), who created a blueprint for a cooperative community. The blueprint consisted of a self-contained group of precisely 1,620 people living on 5,000 acres of land. Fourier hoped to make the workday more satisfying by rotating tasks so that everyone would do the boring tasks but not exclusively—Fourier thought that because children liked to play with dirt, they should take care of the community's garbage.

Another individual who designed a planned community—and unlike Fourier, he actually built it—was **Robert Owen** (1771–1858), a self-made manufacturer. Like Fourier, he blamed environment for man's corruption and in response built New Lanark, a mill town in Scotland, where workers were housed decently and children received an education. These early Socialists had relatively little impact in comparison with Karl Marx's proletarian socialism, which came later.

a phrase coined by **Karl Marx**, who viewed these early writers with contempt because he felt they offered non-scientific, unrealistic solutions to the problems of modern society. Utopian Socialists believed that expansive possibilities were available to humankind and that poor environments corrupted human nature. The Utopians also believed that capitalism overemphasized production, underemphasized distribution, and possessed other serious flaws, such as unemployment and the suffering brought about by low wages.

POLITICAL RESTORATION AND REFORM

CED 6.5
The Concert of Europe and European Conservatism

France

The term *restoration* literally refers to the events in France when the Bourbons were restored to the throne following the final defeat of Napoleon at Waterloo. The throne that **Louis XVIII** returned to was different from the one his older brother had enjoyed up until 1789. The Charter of 1814—a hastily written constitution—contained many of the freedoms from the revolutionary period, such as freedom of religion, even though it was presented to the French people by the king and contained no notion of popular sovereignty. The charter angered many royalists by confirming land purchases made from nationalized Church property. Politically, it allowed for a constitutional monarchy with a chamber of peers and a chamber of deputies made up of a very restricted franchise. The king held the firm reins of power, however, because only he could introduce legislation, and ministers were responsible to him instead of to the assembly.

In 1820, the son of the younger brother of Louis, Duke de Berry, was assassinated. The ultra-royalists, individuals who wanted to see the revival of absolute monarchy, used the assassination to pressure the king to clamp down on the press and to give more rights to the aristocracy, including compensation for nobles who had lost land during the Revolution.

Political repression increased after the death of Louis XVIII in 1824. At that time, Louis's younger brother **Charles X** came to the throne. Charles felt more bitter about the Revolution than his brother Louis had. A year after taking the throne, he introduced a Law of Sacrilege, which ruled death as the penalty for any attack on the Church. In 1829, Charles appointed the Prince of Polignac as his chief minister, a man disliked throughout the country for being a leading ultra-royalist. In the following year, Polignac issued what became known as the **July Ordinances,** which dissolved the newly elected assembly, took away the right to vote from the upper bourgeoisie, and imposed rigid censorship.

That same month, revolution broke out in Paris. Leading liberals were afraid of the Parisian mob and wanted to avoid the creation of a republic because they associated republics with the violence of the first French republic dating back to 1792. Instead, they turned to Louis Phillipe, the Duke of Orleans, a liberal who had stayed in France during the Revolution. The **July Revolution** of 1830, which sparked revolutions throughout Europe, ended with the crowning of Louis Phillipe and the creation of what became known as the bourgeois, or **July monarchy**.

Revolutionary Movements

By the third decade of the century, people across Europe showed signs that it would be impossible to stem their desire for change.

Spain

In Spain, King Ferdinand VII had been restored to the throne following the collapse of French control in 1814. Ferdinand was restored on the condition that he honor the liberal constitution of 1812 drawn up by the Cortés, the Spanish parliament—which had met in Cadiz (in Andalusia, the southwestern coast of Spain), the one part of Spain that was not conquered by Napoleon. Once restored to his throne, Ferdinand dissolved the Cortés, and persecuted those liberals who had drawn up the constitution.

In 1820, a rebellion began among army divisions that were about to be sent to South America to put down the rebellions against the Spanish empire. The small Spanish middle class soon joined the army divisions in the rebellion. Although the king agreed to rule under the laws of the constitution to end the rebellion, Austria, France, Prussia, and Russia wanted to intervene to stem the tide of the revolt. The British, however, refused to directly intervene; they did not want the five great powers of Europe to be involved in putting down internal rebellions in other nations. Two years later, a French army acted unilaterally—although with the tacit support of Russia, Prussia, and Austria—and restored Ferdinand to absolute power.

Portuguese Power Play

A similar revolt took place in Portugal, where a group of army officers wanted to draw up a constitutional monarchy under John VI, who had fled to Brazil during the Napoleonic Wars.

Italy

A more serious revolt broke out in Naples, a revolt that the Austrian statesman Metternich labeled as the "greatest crisis" of his career. Similar to the situation in Spain, King Ferdinand of Naples had made promises while in exile to rule as a constitutional monarch, although once restored to the throne, he refused to give up any of his absolute powers. Neapolitan army officers, perhaps inspired by French ideas, joined with members of the bourgeoisie and began, with the assistance of secret nationalistic societies such as the **Carbonari**, to oppose the monarch. The revolt led to nationalistic stirrings throughout Italy and to another revolt in the Kingdom of Sardinia, which ultimately came to nothing.

Metternich wanted to put down the revolt in Naples, but once again, the British refused to participate in a joint attack. Metternich wanted the support of the other great powers, so he called the rulers of Austria, Prussia, and Russia to the Austrian town of Troppau to create what became the **Troppau Protocol**, which stated that the great European powers had the right to intervene in revolutionary situations. The following year, the rebellion in Naples was put down with the help of Austrian troops.

Greece

With the forces of repression everywhere triumphant, western European liberals looked to the Greek revolt of 1821 to free the "birthplace of democracy" from "Eastern despotism." This was also part of a thousand-year prejudice that claimed Turkish citizens lived and died at the whims of a tyrannical Emperor (an especially ironic claim in a time of resurgent absolutism in France, Prussia, Italy, and elsewhere). Some leading liberals even went to Greece to aid the rebels; the British Romantic poet Lord Byron (1788–1824), for instance, sent his own money to refit the Greek fleet and died amidst the struggle in Greece (not from battle, but from a fever). By 1827, Britain, France, and Russia organized a combined naval force to intervene on the side of the Greek revolutionaries, and in the following year, the Russians attacked the Ottomans on land. By 1832, Greece declared its independence from the Ottoman Empire—and became a monarchy with an imported Bavarian prince.

The Greek revolt was also tied to what became known as the **"Eastern Question"**—what should be done about the increasingly weak Ottoman Empire, appropriately nicknamed "the Sick Man of Europe." Like other multiethnic empires, the Ottoman Empire was breaking down after a series of rulers who could not keep the groups united. Europeans were also uncomfortably reminded of the threat the Ottomans had posed—the Ottoman Empire had most recently besieged Vienna less than 150 years earlier. As the Greeks were breaking away from the Ottoman Empire, so were the Serbians, who had established effective independence by 1830. The new Serbia was a small kingdom about the size of South Carolina, located north of Greece on the southern border of the Austro-Hungarian Empire. Ironically, this tiny kingdom would be a much greater threat to Austrian, and thus European, stability than the mighty Ottoman Empire ever was. The independent Serbian state strongly promoted nationalism in the Balkan regions of Austria, which ultimately led to the ethnic conflicts and revolutionary movements that started World War I.

> The Greek revolt was among the only revolts supported by the European powers—because it was directed against the Ottoman Empire!

Russia

Russia had emerged as a great European power as a result of the Napoleonic Wars, although in many ways, Russia was a much less developed nation than the other European countries. **Alexander I** (r. 1801–1825) had ruled Russia and at various times had toyed with the idea of political reform, although in the latter part of his reign he grew increasingly reactionary.

Alexander's death in 1825 produced confusion as to the succession; Constantine, the older of his two surviving brothers, turned down the throne, so **Nicholas I** (r. 1825–1855) stepped up. In the confusion, a small group of military officers decided to stage a revolt in support of Constantine, who they wrongly thought was in favor of a constitutional monarchy and had been unfairly removed from the succession. This **"Decembrist" revolt** was put down rapidly and with great brutality. In the following years, Nicholas ruled with an iron fist, making sure to stamp out any additional movements for reform within his vast empire.

Great Britain

The French Revolution and the wars against Napoleon had created a backlash against the idea of political reform in Great Britain. The governing elite were also wary of possible social unrest owing to the economic downturn that occurred following the end of the Napoleonic Wars. Such fears were realized in a catastrophe in 1819 when a large crowd of 60,000 people gathered in St. Peter's field in Manchester to demand fundamental political changes, including universal male suffrage and annual parliaments. Although those who attended the meeting were for the most part peaceful, the soldiers on hand shot 11 members of the crowd. This became known as the **Peterloo Massacre**, an obvious play on the Battle of Waterloo. Soon after this disgraceful event, Parliament passed the repressive **Six Acts**, which banned demonstrations, and imposed censorship.

The mood in Great Britain became more conducive to reform beginning in 1824 with the repeal of the **Combination Acts**, which had banned union activity. In 1829, restrictions dating back to the 17th century on the rights of Catholics to hold political office and government posts were lifted. In 1832, the **Great Reform Bill** was passed. The bill was hardly radical. Although it expanded the electorate to include those who had become wealthy as a result of industrialization, only one in five men in Great Britain could vote. It reduced, but did not completely eliminate, the number of so-called rotten boroughs, which were sparsely populated electoral districts. The bill succeeded in showing that political reform was possible in Great Britain without having to resort to the barricades as in continental Europe.

The new electorate created out of the Great Reform Bill undertook additional reforms. Although inspired by the middle-class Members of Parliament, they showed a new harshness toward the poor. The **Poor Law of 1834** forced the destitute to enter into workhouses where conditions were purposefully miserable to discourage people from seeking assistance.

On a more humanitarian level, in 1833 slavery was banned in the British Empire, and the **Factory Act of 1833** reduced the number of hours that children could work in factories and established government inspectors to ensure adequate working conditions. One sign that the new political order in Great Britain was now dominated by manufacturing interests as opposed to the old, landed class, was the 1846 elimination of the **Corn Laws**, which had imposed high tariffs on imported grain to support domestic growers. Manufacturers had long supported the end of the Corn Laws, believing that lower food prices would allow them to pay lower wages to their factory workers.

| CED 6.6 |
| Reactions and |
| Revolutions |

THE REVOLUTIONS OF 1848

On January 12, 1848, there was a rebellion in the Kingdom of the Two Sicilies against King Ferdinand II. This rebellion was to be the first of approximately 50 revolts that convulsed Europe in the first four months of that year. The rebellions were disjointed with very little cooperation or coordination between nations. However, there were a few key themes that ran through most of these contemporaneous upheavals. Primarily, widespread dissatisfaction with political leadership and an upsurge in nationalism motivated citizen demands for democratic government as well other liberal reforms. Following the revolutions of 1848, the Austrian Empire, now under the rule of **Emperor Francis Joseph** (r. 1848–1916), relied heavily on military force to subdue all forms of liberalism and nationalism. Magyars, Slavs, Italians, and Germans would have to wait to see nationalist reforms realized. The 1840s were a terrible decade for agriculture and have accordingly been labeled the "hungry forties." The Irish experienced the most terrible conditions, with the Irish **potato famine** of 1846 leading to the death of one million individuals and the emigration of an additional million out of Ireland.

France

There is an old saying that when France coughs, the rest of Europe catches a cold. In 1848, a rebellion in France created the spark for revolution throughout Europe. In France, the revolution of 1830 brought about only slight changes. The wealthy bourgeoisie dominated the July Monarchy, while the workers who had played such a pivotal role in the revolution of 1830 felt that they had received little for their efforts. Louis Phillipe's chief minister, François Guizot (1787–1874), believed that France had evolved politically as far as it should and that everyone who resented their lack of political rights should simply "get rich." With the rise of censorship and the banning of openly political meetings, opponents of the regime turned to the practice of holding banquets that were thinly disguised political meetings. Over the winter, there had been more than 70 of these banquets with the largest one scheduled for February 22, 1848, to honor George Washington, a great hero to continental liberals. On the day of the banquet, Guizot issued an order banning it, which resulted in four days of revolution in the streets of Paris. After the first day, Louis Phillipe forced the resignation of Guizot, which may have been enough to placate the liberals; however, the workers on the barricades were not satisfied until they forced Louis Philippe to flee to England.

Political disagreements between the liberals and the radicals plagued this revolution in France from the start, with the liberals focusing on political issues such as an expansion of suffrage. The radicals, led by socialist journalist **Louis Blanc** (1811–1882), spoke of the need for fundamental social and economic change. Blanc's supporters successfully pressured the provisional government to set up **national workshops** to provide jobs for the unemployed.

Outside of Paris, however, the nation was more conservative, as seen by the national assembly election held on April 23, which elected an assembly made up primarily of moderate republicans. The election, which had employed universal male suffrage, created a government run by a five-man executive committee comprised of moderates. In May, anger over the election results led to a **workers' revolt** in Paris that was quickly put down. In the following month, the government believed itself in a strong enough position to do away with the national workshops, which they had felt pressured to support.

The surprising outcome of this year of revolution came in December when the first election for president was held and the victor was **Louis Napoleon** (1808–1873), a nephew of the Emperor. Louis Napoleon was able to capitalize on the appeal of his name and made vague promises to aid the embittered workers.

> ### June Days and the French Second Republic
> The termination of the workshops led to what became known as the **"June Days,"** essentially a violent class struggle in the streets of Paris in which 10,000 people died. The June Days further strengthened the hands of the moderate republicans, and in November, they felt confident enough to create the French **Second Republic**, headed by a president who would be elected by a universal adult-male body of voters and who would not be responsible to the legislature.

After being elected, he created a rather conservative government, and by 1851, during a constitutional crisis, he assumed dictatorial powers. In 1852, seeking to emulate his famous relative, he made himself **Emperor Napoleon III**.

The German States

Events in France had huge repercussions in the German states. In Prussia, **Frederick William IV** (r. 1840–1861) had promised to promote moderate reform for many years, but he never implemented any changes. In March 1848, disturbances erupted in the streets of Berlin. Frighteningly, two shots rang out and struck two people. Horrified by the bloodshed, Frederick ordered his army to leave the city, which left him with no defense. The king then allowed an election for a constituent assembly, which would have the task of drawing up a new constitution for Prussia. Several months later, the king was confident enough to call back the troops, and the constituent assembly was dissolved. Nevertheless, in December 1848, the king did draw up his own constitution, which was rather close to what the assembly had planned. It allowed for personal rights such as freedom of the press, and it created a two-house legislature with adult-male universal suffrage for the lower house, although in the end, this provision was watered down by giving weighted votes to those who paid more taxes.

In Austria, news of the revolution in France inspired assorted nationalists to break free from the control of the Austrian monarchy. In Hungary, **Lajos Kossuth** (1802–1894) demanded a constitution that would provide for responsible government for Hungary. In Prague, a similar revolt called for the creation of a semi-autonomous Czech homeland. From May to October, Vienna was under the control of students and workers who demanded freedom of the press, an end to censorship, and the removal from office of the hated Metternich. As in Prussia, at first the emperor did not want bloodshed and called off his troops. By June, however, the revolt in Prague was put down by military force, and in November, the emperor was firmly in control in Vienna. However, he needed Russian help to put down the Hungarian rebellion.

The Frankfurt Parliament

Another notable event in 1848 was a concerted effort to establish a unified German state. On May 18, elected representatives from all the German states gathered in Frankfurt to participate in what they thought was going to be the birth of a nation. From the start, the **Frankfurt Parliament** was hampered by the political inexperience of its participants and by conflicting aims; while all wanted to see a unified German nation, major disagreements arose over whether it should be a monarchy or a republic.

A paralyzing dispute also emerged over the question of where to draw the borders of the new Germany. Those who favored the **Grossedeutsch** plan wanted to see all German lands, including German sections of Austria and Bohemia, united under German rule. **Kleindeutsch** supporters felt that the more realistic solution would be to include only Prussia and the smaller German states. Eventually, the delegates settled on the Kleindeutsch, and they offered the German Imperial throne to William IV, the King of Prussia. He responded that he did not want a "crown picked up from the gutter" and declined the offer.

This was a lost opportunity to build a German nation under a liberal parliament rather than by a militaristic Prussian state, as would be the case in 1871. Perhaps the future course of German history would have been very different had Germany united under a liberal parliament. The German liberals at Frankfurt, however, had proven to be quite militaristic when they helped put down a revolt in some of Prussia's Polish territories and had also been completely unconcerned with the rights of those Czechs who had no desire to see their lands included in the new Germany.

The Italian States

In the Italian states, the revolt that first broke out in Sicily led Ferdinand II to grant a liberal constitution. Eventually, similar revolts broke out and terrified monarchs granted charters in Tuscany and Sardinia. Even the pope granted a liberal constitution: the papal states, at the time still a substantial territory in central Italy under papal rule, also saw revolts. After the revolt, the territory was governed by a short-lived Roman Republic. In the north of Italy, revolts broke out in the Austrian-dominated provinces of Lombardy and Venetia. This led to a call by Italian liberals for a war of unification. **Charles Albert**, the ruler of the Kingdom of Sardinia, reluctantly took up the banner of Italian nationalists and attacked Lombardy, only to be easily defeated by the Austrians.

For Italy, the lesson for the future was that unification would not take place under the auspices of the papacy, as some Italian liberals prior to 1848 had assumed. On the other hand, the possibility of the Kingdom of Sardinia serving as the foundation for a unified state improved, because in the group of Italian states that were granted constitutions in 1848, only Sardinia governed via the constitutional monarchical course in the following years. A final important lesson had future ramifications: the Italians could not eject Austria from its possessions within Italy without the aid of another European power.

Russia and Great Britain

Two nations avoided the turmoil of revolution in 1848: Russia and Great Britain. Repression in Russia was so complete under the reign of Nicholas I that the nation passed the year with hardly a yawn. In Great Britain, the story was quite different, because 1848 marked the peak year for a movement known as **Chartism**, which dated back to the previous decade. Chartism centered on the belief that the problems of the working class could be corrected by changes in the political organization of the country. The **People's Charter of 1838**, from which the movement received its name, contained six points:

- universal adult-male suffrage (some Chartists did favor female suffrage as well)
- the secret ballot
- abolition of property requirements for Members of Parliament
- payment to Members of Parliament
- equal electoral districts
- annual parliaments with yearly elections

In many ways, working-class dissatisfaction with the House of Commons after the passage of the Great Reform Bill was a motivating factor behind the Chartist movement, because working-class citizens believed (correctly) that the reformed Parliament was completely unresponsive to their demands.

In April 1848, a mass meeting was scheduled in London for the presentation of the Charter to the House of Commons. If the petition were once again rejected by Parliament, the Chartist Convention planned to transform itself into a National Assembly that would take over the government of the country. The mood in the capital was apprehensive. One middle-class man wrote to his wife:

> London is in a state of panic from the contemplated meeting of the Chartists, 200,000 strong on Monday; for myself, nothing that happened would in the least surprise me: I expect a revolution within two years: there may be one within three days. The *Times* is alarmed beyond all measure. I have it from good authority that the Chartists are determined to have their wishes granted.

In London, there were preparations for a violent conflict, and Queen Victoria was sent out of London for safety. On April 10, the day of the mass meeting, the situation was tense as 200,000 individuals gathered to sign the petition. The petition was presented to the House of Commons, and basically, everyone went home peacefully. The House of Commons, however, refused to even debate the clauses contained in the petition. At this point, Great Britain appeared to be on the verge of revolution, but the country emerged far more fortunate than its continental counterparts. Reform did eventually come about in incremental stages; by the early 20th century, five of the six acts of the Charter (the annual parliaments didn't pass) were established parts of the British Constitution.

CED 6.2
The Spread of Industry
Throughout Europe

THE INDUSTRIAL REVOLUTION (1750–1850)

Historians had formerly placed the beginning of the Industrial Revolution in 1760, when a group of new inventors appeared from nowhere and began to develop factories, bringing an end to the **domestic system** of production that had guided manufacturing since the early modern period. Experts have modified this belief over the last several decades; some historians even avoid the term "Industrial Revolution," which they claim implies far too dramatic a change. We now know that technological progress did not begin in 1760; it had been occurring for centuries. This much is true: the second half of the 18th century saw a quickening of an age-old evolutionary process rather than a fresh break from the past. By the middle of the 19th century, particularly with the advent of the railroad, industrialization was beginning to reshape the European landscape and to dramatically alter the way in which people lived.

Great Britain's Industrial Lead

Great Britain was the first European nation to begin the process of industrialization. What motivated England to change so dramatically? Although numerous books and articles have dealt with this question, conclusive or definitive answers for queries of this sort are rare. Several possible factors may have contributed to England's role as the leader of the industrialization of Europe:

- In the years following the Glorious Revolution of 1688, Great Britain achieved a degree of **political stability** that created an environment friendly to economic investment.
- Compared to most other European states (the exception being the Netherlands), Great Britain permitted a much greater degree of **religious toleration**. For example, the Quakers, while closed off by law from parliamentary careers, had no such restrictions placed on their economic activities and were able to play a central role in the Industrial Revolution.
- **Expanding population**—which almost doubled in Great Britain over the course of the 18th century, due in large part to a lower death rate thanks to better diet and hygiene—is of particular importance to the Industrial Revolution. Britain's increased population size produced not only a large body of potential low-wage workers for the factories but also a steady supply of consumers.
- The **Agricultural Revolution** of the 18th century, initiated by men such as Jethro Tull, introduced scientific farming to Great Britain. Their observations led them to realize that continuous rotation of crops, instead of the traditional method of allowing land to lay fallow, allowed for an increase in crop yield while also leading to the growth of turnips and beets that could be used to feed larger quantities of animals during the difficult winter months.
- As a result of the Agricultural Revolution and the rise of cottage industries, England was already involved in **manufacturing industries**. Traditional manufacturing, like spinning and weaving, could be industrialized through labor-saving devices that improved production; it would be at least a hundred years before agriculture was industrialized to the same degree.
- The **Enclosure Acts** of the late 18th and early 19th centuries forced small-scale farmers into urban areas, both increasing the efficiency of the now larger farms and providing a low-paid workforce for the factories.

- The increased prosperity of English farms led to an **increase in capital** that could be used to invest in the new industries. Great Britain also had a central bank (the Bank of England, chartered in 1694) that encouraged the flow of money in the economy. Interest rates were lower in Great Britain than in any other part of Europe in this period.

- The 18th century witnessed a significant increase in Great Britain's **overseas trade**. Besides supplying additional investment capital, overseas trade provided the nation with the world's largest merchant marine. It is important to remember, however, that the 18th century also witnessed the height of the Atlantic slave trade, although the valiant efforts of individuals such as William Wilberforce finally paid off when Parliament brought the brutal trade to an end in 1807.

- **Transportation** within Great Britain was enhanced by the fact that the entire nation lies within close proximity to the sea. Internally, a network of navigable rivers and the creation of canals made water transport efficient. Turnpike trusts built new roads in Great Britain on a scale not seen since the end of Roman rule.

- Great Britain had available the two critical natural resources of the Early Industrial Revolution: **coal and iron.**

The first 18th-century technological advances occurred in cotton manufacturing. In 1733, **John Kay** (1704–1764) invented the flying shuttle, which greatly increased the speed at which weavers could make cloth. Kay's invention created a problem: cloth could be made so rapidly that it outstripped the supply of thread. By 1765, **James Hargreaves** (d. 1778) solved this problem by inventing the **spinning jenny**, a machine that initially spun 16 spindles of thread at one time, and by the end of the century, improvements allowed it to spin as many as 120 spindles at once. Kay's and Hargreaves's machines were small enough that they could still be used in the traditional location of cloth manufacturing—the home. Note that these labor-saving devices, including Arkwright's water frame (see inset), were in the field of cloth production. Labor-saving was useful because British cloth manufacturing was constrained by labor supply. Thanks to cotton imports (from the colonization of India and trade with the American South) and increased wool supply (due to enclosure and the agricultural revolution), labor savings actually resulted in more cloth to sell, giving factory cloth producers a strong price advantage over their competition. However, the cotton industry came at a cost: the cotton imports which fueled the Industrial Revolution were available only because of colonization and slavery.

> ### Arkwright's Water Frame
>
> If what was truly revolutionary about the Industrial Revolution was the displacement of domestic manufacturing by the factory system, then it was **Richard Arkwright's** invention of the **water frame** that marked the beginning of this development. The water frame was a huge apparatus that combined spindles and rollers to create a spinning machine to spin cloth. By 1770, Arkwright employed 200 individuals under one roof in what is known to be the first modern factory, and in so doing, made a half-million-pound fortune for himself.

The first factories were originally located along streams and rivers so that water could provide the energy needed to work the machinery. The invention of the **steam engine** made it possible to build factories in other locations. The ancestor of the steam engine was the steam pump, which was used to remove water from mines. **James Watt** (1736–1819) studied the steam pump and adapted it for use in industry. His invention was the first true steam engine, as opposed to a steam pump, because it worked by pushing steam into each end of a closed cylinder, resulting in the upward and downward movement of the pistons. A decade later, Watt invented an engine that turned a wheel. This made factories independent of waterpower and dramatically increased the pace of industrial change.

Another factor that increased the pace of industrialization was the greater ability to **smelt iron**. Traditionally, iron was smelted in extremely hot ovens fueled by charcoal, but by the 18th century, England was devoid of forests, and the resulting lack of charcoal seriously limited the production of iron. **Abraham Darby** (1677–1717) discovered a means of smelting iron using coal. Like the inventions discussed earlier, the economy experienced a multiplying factor as a result of Darby's invention, as more productive machines made of iron replaced those previously made from wood.

Iron and steam were the combination behind perhaps the most important invention of the 19th-century Industrial Revolution—the **railroad**. The first passenger railroad traveled between Liverpool and Manchester in 1830, and by the middle of the century, Britain was crisscrossed with railroad tracks that carried passengers and goods throughout the land. The railroads had an immense impact on the economy. Engines, tracks, stations, tunnels, and hotels for travelers were just some of the machines and structures that were connected with the railroads. It is estimated that by 1880, one in ten jobs in Great Britain was in some way connected either directly with the railroads or with services tied to rail transportation.

French Contributions to Industrialization

In certain industries, such as in the manufacturing of luxury goods, the French took the lead, and while their economic growth was not quite as dramatic as the British and Prussian models, it remained constant throughout most of the 19th century.

The British took the lead in manufacturing, but it wasn't long before methods pioneered by the British appeared on the continent. Belgium was the first to industrialize, possibly because, like Great Britain, it had a plentiful supply of coal and iron. Other nations industrialized with varying degrees of rapidity. The German states were hampered by numerous tolls and tariffs, making the transportation of goods extremely expensive. To aid in the spread of trade and manufacturing, Prussia in 1834 took the lead by creating the *Zollverein*, a customs union that abolished tariffs between the German states.

As certain German states, most notably Prussia, achieved significant industrial growth by the middle of the century, France lagged behind by comparison. Historians often make telling comparisons between Great Britain and France. Unlike Great Britain, France was wracked by political instability in the first half of the 19th century. France also lacked the centralized banking structure enjoyed by British entrepreneurs. Additionally, French population growth was only half that of the other European nations during this period. French peasants remained relatively content to stay on the land, unlike their British counterparts who had little choice but to go to the cities in search of low-paying factory jobs.

CED 6.2

The Spread of Industry Throughout Europe

In southern and eastern Europe, the Industrial Revolution was slower to take hold. There are two reasons for this. Southern Europe lacked the coal deposits and other resources that were necessary to drive the machines of the industrial era. Other regions, such as Romania, lacked a developed network of railroads or other forms of transportation infrastructure. England, by contrast, boasted both railroads and a wide network of canals and rivers, which made it easy to ship finished products by rail or by water. This explains why some areas of Europe, such as rural Spain, entered the 20th century with a mostly unchanged feudal system dominated by agricultural land-owning elites. The Industrial Revolution had passed them by.

The Impact of Industrialization

CED 6.4
Social Effects of
Industrialization

Industrialization dramatically changed life in Europe. Because the location of factories tended to be concentrated in certain areas, cities began to grow and develop rapidly. Industrialization, and the urban movement it spawned, replaced the **putting-out** (or domestic) **system**, in which raw materials were delivered to the homes of peasants and then the finished products were collected and sold by merchants. The change from rural manufacturing to bringing workers to a location significantly affected life in Britain.

By the middle of the century, Great Britain became the first nation to have more people living in the cities than in the countryside, one of the most dramatic transformations in the history of humankind. Unfortunately, the cities that grew from the ground up as a result of industrialization tended to be awful places for the working poor. Poor ventilation and sanitation led to conditions in which the mortality rates were significantly higher for urban dwellers than for those who resided in the countryside. Because people had to use a water supply that came into direct contact with animal and human feces, cholera became part of the early-19th-century urban landscape, killing tens of thousands of individuals. The European countryside was devastated in a different way by the slow-moving depopulation, since employers that remained in rural areas often couldn't find enough laborers or farmers when work opened up.

Industrialization greatly affected the family structure. The fact that the entire family was working was not new; the earlier domestic system had relied on the family as a cohesive working unit. What was different was that the family no longer worked together under one roof, with women and children now often working under conditions even more deplorable than the men's conditions, because factory owners thought they were less likely to complain. Great Britain's **Sadler Committee** exposed that children were being beaten in the factories. As a result, the House of Commons passed the Factory Act (1833), which mandated that children younger than 9 could not work in textile mills, that children younger than 12 could work no more than 9 hours per day, and that children younger than 18 couldn't work more than 12 hours each day. But the act provided for only seven inspectors to ensure compliance.

As the 19th century went on, the European middle class grew vast in size and began to develop differences with the working classes. One of these differences was in their interest in forming associations of all types—philanthropic, political, and social. Then and now, middle-class people maintained their status by pursuing a busy social calendar. Furthermore, they also reached across class lines by forming mutual aid societies with working-class brethren. This class divide was no secret, and generations of writers used it in novels and stage plays such as *Pygmalion*, by George Bernard Shaw (later adapted as *My Fair Lady*).

Working-Class Responses to Industrialization

At first, workers were befuddled as to how to grapple with the economic and social problems caused by industrialization. For some individuals, such as handloom weavers, complete economic dislocation ensued, and their traditional way of life was threatened by machinery. Some laborers tried to destroy the machines, which they blamed for their problems. Their fictional leader was Ned Ludd, and the term **Luddite** has stayed in the modern vocabulary in reference to those who refuse to embrace new technologies. Machinery also caused hardship for many laborers on the farms. They created an imaginary character known as Captain Swing, who righted the wrongs imposed on hardworking individuals by the advent of technology.

After these rather primitive means of dealing with industrialization proved to be ineffective, workers sought to create **cooperative societies**, small associations within a given trade that provided funeral benefits and other services for their members.

Despite government disapproval, workers in Great Britain in the late 18th century organized what first were known as "friendly societies," and these eventually evolved into full-blown unions once the ban on such activities was lifted in 1824. On the continent, it was not until the 1860s that unions were allowed to freely operate in France and in Prussia. Great Britain also took the lead in establishing the first unions that represented more than a single industry. In 1834, Robert Owen helped form the Grand National Consolidated Trades Union, which several decades later evolved into the Trade Union Congress, pulling together workers from disparate industries. Skilled laborers formed the first unions; by the end of the 19th century, however, unions were being formed by dockworkers and other non-skilled workers. Unions were a critical reason for the steady improvement in wages and factory conditions that took place in the second half of the 19th century.

While socialism and communism have the same aim—increased social and economic equality—they use different methods. **Socialism** attempts to redistribute wealth more evenly while preserving private property, but **communism** creates full equality by totally eliminating private property, even of minor things.

Socialism and Karl Marx

Some workers—particularly on the continent—found that although the unions' emphasis on gradual improvements in wages and hours worked, it was at best only a partial solution to the problems caused by industrialization. Many turned to socialism, believing that it offered a complete overhaul to an oppressive society. Socialism had early roots in the writings of such individuals as Saint-Simon, Robert Owen, and Charles Fourier; the most significant strand in socialist thought, however, was the so-called **scientific socialism** offered by **Karl Marx** (1818–1883).

Marx was born in the German city of Trier and eventually received a university education at Jena. As a young man, he became the editor of a Cologne newspaper, the *Rheinische Zeitung*, but he soon found that his political views were considered too radical by the authorities, who banned the newspaper, leading Marx to seek the freer intellectual climate of Paris. The French, however, quickly grew tired of Marx, so he left Paris for London where he spent the remainder of his life.

Marx and his colleague **Friedrich Engels** (1820–1895) organized a **Communist League** to link the far-flung German Socialists, many of whom, like Marx, were living in exile. In 1848, they teamed up to write a pamphlet that was to serve as a basic statement of principles for the organization. This document was ***The Communist Manifesto***, one of the most influential political tracts in history. The very first line contains Marx and Engels's view that all of history has been dominated by the struggle between social classes, an idea that was labeled as historical materialism, or the material dialectic. The origin of this idea can be found in the writings of the German philosopher Georg Wilhelm Friedrich Hegel, whose dialectic differed from Marx's in that he saw economic conditions emanating from ideas

Industrialization and Child Labor

Interestingly, many workers were against placing constraints on child labor. It was not that they were monstrous parents; it was simply that wages were so low that children were providing funds that were an essential part of the family budget. There has been a long-standing—and perhaps tired—historical debate about the wages earned by industrial workers and the type of life such wages provided. The "optimist" school on this standard-of-living debate argues that in the first half of the 19th century, wages did rise somewhat for workers while prices remained steady or in fact declined, thus allowing for improved living conditions. The "pessimists," on the other hand, claim that horrible working conditions and miserably low wages provided for an increasingly bleak existence for the working poor.

rather than the reverse. Hegel's thinking influenced Marx and many others, as it seemed to suggest a means toward analyzing historical events.

Marx posited that the feudal age was supplanted by the triumph of the **bourgeois** class in the 19th century. The development of capitalism led to the creation of a new class, the **proletariat** (the working class), who would one day arise and supplant those capitalists who had exploited them. In the beginning of this supplantation, the state would dominate in what Marx admitted would be a violent, though triumphant, struggle by the workers; eventually, the state would wither away when it was no longer needed as a result of the elimination of all other classes besides the proletariat. Marx is also known for ***Das Kapital***, an enormous treatise on capitalism that explains the mechanics by which capitalists extract profit from labor.

Marx brought a revolutionary dynamism to the class struggle, because he believed that the working class had to constantly prepare itself by organizing socialist parties. In 1864, he organized the **First International**, which Marx said was created to "afford a central medium of communication and cooperation" for those organizations whose aim was the "protection, advancement, and complete emancipation of the working classes." This First International was not a completely Marxist organization—Trade Unionists, Mazzini Republicans, Marxists, and Anarchists were all members. Internal conflicts eventually led the First International to dissolve in 1876. After Marx's death, Engels helped organize the **Second International**, a loose federation of the world's socialist parties heavily influenced by Marxism that met for the first time on July 14, 1889. It was, of course, no accident that this meeting took place on the hundredth anniversary of the storming of the Bastille—Marxists were consciously referencing the beginning of the French Revolution and calling for one of their own.

THE AGE OF NATIONAL UNIFICATION (1854–1871)

> **CED 7.3**
> National Unification and
> Diplomatic Tensions

Metternich once remarked that Italy was "a mere geographical expression." He could have said the same for Germany, because up until the second half of the 19th century, both lands consisted of a number of independent territories, a disunity that dated back to the Middle Ages. In the late Middle Ages (c. 1100–1500) and the early modern period (c. 1500–1789), the rulers of France, Spain, and Great Britain successfully expanded their authority. In France, this expansion resulted in the monarchy destroying the independence of the rulers of Normandy, Brittany, and Aquitaine and incorporating them into the domains of the French king. This process was not predestined: we could just as easily imagine a Europe where modern Spain is divided between a large nation of Portugal and a small Aragon; and as it happened, the process of consolidation did not take place in either the northern German territories or on the Italian peninsula. However, by the early 19th century, individuals in both the German and Italian states sought to create a nation-state that would unite all Italians or all Germans under one political banner because they shared either a common culture, or language, or a fear of foreign domination. This process of national unification would have a tremendous impact on the future course of European history.

The Crimean War (1854–1856)

The Crimean War was critical to the formation of centralized states in both Italy and Germany, though initially it was impossible to foresee such a result when the war began in 1854. Several factors led to the outbreak of hostilities, including a controversy over which nation would control access to the religious sites sacred to Christians in Jerusalem. The main issue, however, was the fear among British and French political leaders that Ottoman weakness was encouraging Russian adventurism in the Balkans and the possibility that the Russians might gain access to the Mediterranean by occupying the port city of Istanbul.

Following a naval defeat by the Ottomans, who had declared war on the Russians in 1853 with British encouragement, France and Great Britain declared war on the Russians. Most of the fighting took place in the Crimean region and was notable for the incredible incompetence of all participants. Most of the half-million casualties did not die in battle but perished because of disease in filthy field hospitals, something that inspired **Florence Nightingale** (1820–1910) to revolutionize the nursing profession.

The war came to an ignominious end after the fall of the Russian fortress of Sevastopol, Russia's chief port in the northern Black Sea and nearest access to the Mediterranean. Though reluctant to quit, the Russians were forced to reconsider when the Austrians threatened to enter the war on the side of the British and the French unless Russia accepted the offered peace terms. Russia was forced to cede some territories on the Danube River and to accept a ban on warships in the Black Sea region. This was a major blow to Russian ambitions of involvement in European politics. Since the time of Peter the Great, Russia had sought a warm-water port in the south which could provide access to the Mediterranean Sea through the Bosporus and the Aegean. Without power in the Black Sea or along the Danube, the Russian navy was trapped in ports along the Baltic, subject to Swedish and Danish tolls.

The real cost of the war, however, was that the **Concert of Europe**, the idea that the great powers (France, Prussia, Austria, Russia, and Great Britain) should work together—a concept that emerged from the Congress of Vienna—was finally shattered. This conflict was the first European war since the Napoleonic era. Previously, Russia and Austria had worked together to resist the trend toward nation-building. After all, both were large, multiethnic empires with much to fear from nationalist movements among ethnic minorities. During the Crimean War, the Germans and other Europeans had no sense of unity on such questions. Additionally, the British public was horrified by the course of events in the Crimean region; as a result, Great Britain became more isolationist regarding European affairs. This meant that when Austria stood in opposition to the building of states in Germany and Italy, it received no support from an embittered Russia, and when France found itself confronting Prussia in 1870, it would find little sympathy across the English Channel.

The Unification of Italy

The Unification of Italy

In 1848, Italian liberals made an aborted attempt to create an Italian state. Although the attempt failed, the dream for a state never disappeared. Following the collapse of the short-lived Roman Republic, **Pope Pius IX**—when his authority in Rome was restored—inspired increasingly reactionary policies. Liberals no longer saw any potential for the realization of a federation of Italian states headed by the pope. Although some liberals wanted nothing less than the creation of an Italian republic, an increasing number looked with hope to the Kingdom of Piedmont-Sardinia, the one Italian state that had preserved its liberal constitution since the year of revolutions.

The true architect of Italian unification, or what is referred to in Italian as the ***Risorgimento***, was not the King of Piedmont-Sardinia, Victor Emmanuel (r. 1849–1878), but **Count Camillo di Cavour** (1810–1861), his chief minister. Cavour was quite different from earlier Italian nationalists like **Giuseppe Mazzini** (1805–1872), who saw state-building in romanticized terms. Cavour was a far more practical individual who primarily sought ways to enhance the power of the Sardinian state.

Cavour realized that creating an Italian state would require the expulsion of Austria from the Italian peninsula. Events in 1848 foreshadowed the impossibility of succeeding in this expulsion without the aid of some other European state, so Cavour entered into a secret alliance with France. Cavour had set the groundwork for this relationship by cleverly entering the Kingdom of Piedmont-Sardinia in the Crimean War on the side of France and Great Britain, and although its participation was minimal, it earned Napoleon III's gratitude. Napoleon III was additionally interested in aiding the Sardinians because Austria was a traditional enemy of the French state. Napoleon III also periodically looked for foreign military adventures so that he could live up to his famous namesake, something that would eventually lead to his downfall.

What's the Kingdom of Piedmont-Sardinia?

This kingdom consisted of the island of Sardinia and Piedmont, a northern Italian territory that borders France and Switzerland. In some history textbooks, you may see this kingdom labeled as the Kingdom of Sardinia, or sometimes simply as Piedmont, though all these labels refer to the same state.

The war began in April 1859. The combined French and Sardinian forces won a series of battles against the Austrians, but Napoleon decided to bring the conflict to a close before expelling the Austrians from all Italian lands. He was horrified by the high number of casualties from the conflict (something that never seemed to bother his uncle) and was threatened by Prussia who was massing troops on the Rhine to come to the aid of the Austrians. Cavour was so angered over Napoleon's abortion of the war and his betrayal of the treaty with Sardinia that he resigned as prime minister, though a year later he resumed the office.

Both Cavour and Napoleon sought to create a state that would unite northern Italy. Napoleon did not want to see the entire Italian peninsula unified for fear that a large Italian state could be a threat to France. But to Cavour's and Napoleon's surprise, and to the latter's great displeasure, the war against Austria helped inspire popular rebellions throughout the Italian peninsula. In the Austrian-dominated regions of Tuscany, Parma, and Modena, revolts led plebiscites to join with Sardinia.

Meanwhile, one of the most intriguing characters in Italian history, **Giuseppe Garibaldi** (1807–1882), emerged in the south of Italy. Garibaldi was a link to the old romantic tradition of Italian nationalism; he had at one time been a member of Mazzini's Young Italy movement. Horrified by the terms of the treaty between Sardinia and France, which required Italy to hand over Savoy and Nice to the French, Garibaldi at first threatened to attack France over the loss of what he considered to be Italian territories. Cavour instead encouraged Garibaldi to invade the Kingdom of the Two Sicilies, thinking that it would be a suicide mission. To everyone's surprise, Garibaldi led his famous army of 1,000 **"red shirts"** and conquered this southern Italian kingdom, which had been ruled with great incompetence by the Bourbons. Garibaldi wanted to march on Rome and make it the new capital of a unified Italy, but this threat to papal control of the city would have greatly antagonized Napoleon III, who found it useful for his popularity among the French to portray himself as a defender of the Church.

Cavour was horrified by the idea that the vastly popular Garibaldi might seek to unify Italy under his own charismatic leadership rather than under Piedmont's control. To curtail this possibility, Cavour rushed troops to Naples to block Garibaldi from his march. Cavour was interested in the papal lands, however, and he shrewdly waited for a popular revolt in the papal states to commence, and only then, under the pretext of restoring order, moved Sardinian troops into all of the lands controlled by the pope except for the city of Rome. This was followed by the declaration of **Victor Emmanuel** as the first king of Italy on March 17, 1861. After the successful invasion of papal lands, only Venetia and Rome were not under the unified Italian flag. In 1866, after

Prussia's victory over Austria, the Italians used the opportunity of Austria's vulnerability to seize Venetia. Rome was added to Italy in 1870 and named as its new capital following the withdrawal of French troops from the city as a result of the **Franco-Prussian War**.

The new Italian nation was beset with problems and plagued by corruption and bribery. For more romantically oriented nationalists like Garibaldi, the new Italy was a cold bureaucratic state led by petty officials from Sardinia, inspiring little of the passion that they had felt for the cause of statehood. To this day, there is an economic divide between the north of Italy, which is highly industrialized, and the far less economically developed south. A major problem for the new state was the continuing hostility of the Catholic Church, which banned Catholics from participating in national elections, even though Catholics widely ignored this order. In fact, the Church would not fully reconcile with the Italian state until 1929 when Mussolini agreed to restore the sovereignty of Vatican City to the papacy.

German Unification

Although Italian unification had important implications for the rest of Europe, the rise of a unified German state in 1871 totally altered the balance of power in Europe, owing to the great military and economic strength of this new state. The story of German unification is rooted in the Napoleonic era. Napoleon's domination of large parts of Germany not only increased the demand among German patriots for the creation of a unified nation but also reduced the sheer number of independent German states, which eventually aided in the actual process of unification.

Following the fall of Napoleon, Austria and Prussia were the two dominant states within the German Confederation. In 1848, it appeared as if German unification would be achieved when the Frankfurt Parliament offered the crown to the Prussian king, but Frederick William's refusal delayed the process until it was achieved through means that the Prussians found more conducive to their interests.

Although it was not a foregone conclusion that it was to be Prussia rather than Austria that would take the lead in creating a unified Germany, Prussia did enjoy a number of significant advantages. Prussia, through its creation of the *Zollverein*, had achieved an economic preeminence over the other member states, while Austria was specifically excluded by Prussia for membership in the *Zollverein* customs union. By mid-century, Prussia had achieved a significant measure of industrialization, while Austria remained a primarily agricultural state. In addition, the Austrian Empire was a polyglot state made up of numerous nationalities, while Prussia was primarily a German state. Perhaps most important to its dominance, Prussia enjoyed the services of one of the most remarkable statesmen of the 19th century, **Otto von Bismarck** (1815–1898).

On taking the throne of Prussia, **William I** (r. 1861–1888) made the most important decision of his reign when he selected Bismarck as his prime minister. William was engaged at the time in a fight with his parliament over military reforms that he wanted in order to challenge Austrian supremacy in the German Confederation. To break the impasse, William turned to Bismarck, a Junker (Prussian noble), who was known for his arch-conservative views. Standing before the parliamentary budget commission, Bismarck delivered his **"Blood and Iron"** speech in which he said, "Germany is not looking to Prussia's liberalism but to her power…it is not by speeches and majority resolutions that the great questions of the time will be decided—that was the mistake of 1848 and 1849—but by iron and blood." Despite the colorful speech, the parliament still refused to vote in favor of the military budget. Never one to bother with constitutional niceties, Bismarck simply ignored parliament and proceeded to collect the taxes and implement the reforms. To their great discredit, the Prussian liberals did nothing to oppose this blatant disregard for their authority.

The key to his plan to create a unified German state was to modernize the Prussian army by giving it the latest weapons. The first stage in this plan took place in 1864 and involved an alliance with Austria against Denmark over the disputed territories of Schleswig and Holstein. After easily defeating the Danes (the **Danish War**, also known as the German-Danish War or Danish-Prussian War), Schleswig came under Prussian control while Holstein was run by the Austrians. Bismarck cunningly set up this system because he wanted the Danish dispute to help achieve his next goal—war with Austria.

By 1866, Prussia prepared for war by securing an alliance with Italy (which wanted to see the final removal of Austria from Italian lands) and securing a promise of nonparticipation from the French. Then, under Bismarck's orders, Prussia declared war on Austria, citing the petty dispute over the governance of Holstein as the reason for the attack. The modernization program undertaken by the Prussian army proved to be astonishingly successful, as Prussian forces brought about the defeat of Austria in a matter of seven weeks (the **Seven Weeks' War,** or Austro-Prussian War). Ignoring the advice of both his king and the generals who wanted to stage a victory parade through the streets of Vienna and to annex large pieces of the Austrian Empire, Bismarck wisely treated Austria with courtesy to keep it out of the next stage of his plan—a war with France.

After the defeat of the Austrians, Bismarck annexed those small German states in the north that had supported Austria in the conflict. Other northern German states were convinced to join Prussia in the creation of what became known as the North German Confederation. The states of southern Germany, while remaining independent, concluded a military alliance with Prussia in case of French aggression.

In 1870, the final stage of Bismarck's plan was set in motion when he provoked a war with the French (the **Franco-Prussian War**). Bismarck, with great cunning, made France the outward aggressor in a conflict that began when a prince, who was a relative of the Prussian king (a Hohenzollern), was invited to take the vacant throne of Spain. To Napoleon III, the thought of Hohenzollern rulers on two fronts was too much to contemplate. Napoleon III initially won a diplomatic victory when William I agreed to withdraw his cousin's name. However, Bismarck, who desperately wanted war, rewrote the so-called **"Ems dispatch,"** a telegram sent by the Prussian king to Bismarck informing him of what had transpired in the conversation between the king and the French ambassador, to make it appear as though the king had insulted France. Bowing to the demands of an outraged French public, Napoleon III declared war on Prussia. France, which many believed had the finest army in the world, was soundly defeated by Prussia following the decisive battle of Sedan. Using Prussia's newfound prestige earned by achieving this victory, Bismarck was able to either convince or bribe the rulers of the other German states to accept the creation of a Germany under Prussian leadership. On January 18, 1871, William I was proclaimed in the palace of Versailles as German emperor.

The creation of a German Empire completely changed the direction of European history. The following are some examples:

- The new German state created a bitter enemy of France, which lost the territories of Alsace and Lorraine and was forced to pay a huge indemnity to Germany for having started the war.
- The economic power of this new German state created rising tensions with Great Britain and helped set into motion the rush to build colonial empires in the last quarter of the 19th century. The mad scramble began when Bismarck encouraged the French to build an empire in Africa to distract from the loss of Alsace-Lorraine.
- Eventually, all the nations of Europe sought to create overseas empires. It was a means of furthering their political and economic interests within a Europe that was trying to adjust to the tensions that arose from the development of a powerful German state.

This new Germany was also not necessarily a very stable entity. Created by military might, its military commanders had a great influence over the nation at large, particularly following the forced retirement of Bismarck in 1890. Prior to being put out to pasture, Bismarck had worried about the internal dangers facing the new nation and therefore attacked two groups he deemed to be a threat to the internal cohesion of the Reich—the Catholics and the Socialists.

> The unification of Germany created what Bismarck called the Second Reich (or "regime"). The First Reich had been the so-called Holy Roman Empire, which had collapsed 60 years earlier after a thousand years of existence.

Fearful that Catholics owed an allegiance to a church that extended beyond nationalism to Germany, Bismarck responded with an attack on the Catholic Church in a conflict known as the **"Kulturkampf,"** in which he insisted on controlling all church appointments and on gaining complete supervision over Catholic education. Eventually, because of Catholic resentment toward such policies, Bismarck backed away from this struggle.

He turned to another perceived enemy—the Socialists—and in 1878, Bismarck called for the passage in the Reichstag of a ban on Socialists' right to assemble and to publish materials. Bismarck also attempted to limit the political appeal of the Socialists by establishing old-age pensions and other social benefits for all Germans. However, as in the case of the Catholics, Bismarck found that oppressing the German Social Democratic Party merely increased its appeal.

Despite his seemingly hostile nature, Bismarck was seen as having helped establish the glory of Germany and its peoples. His efforts to co-opt the appeal of socialism increased his prestige in his later years. However, he ultimately rose to power (and remained in power for more than 25 years) thanks to his careful manipulation of the press and the monarchs of Germany. Prussia (and later, Germany) was a conservative, aristocratic state. Bismarck ruled at the pleasure of the king, not the people; and his poor relations with Wilhelm II led to less-able leaders taking his place, jeopardizing his fragile peace with Russia, and ultimately sacrificing German stability for the sake of German glory.

France

France seemed to have a tortured existence throughout the 19th century as it continued to grapple with the legacy of the French Revolution. A measure of stability finally emerged with the rise of the **Third French Republic** (1870–1940), though it too had to deal with a past that still divided segments of the French public.

Following his victory in the December 1848 election, **Louis Napoleon** became the first and only president of the short-lived Second Republic. He used a tool developed by his uncle, Napoleon. Following a constitutional dispute with the legislature, he staged a plebiscite in 1851 that polled the people about whether to grant him dictatorial powers for a 10-year period. After winning this vote, Napoleon moved on in the following year to stage another plebiscite, this time on the question of whether to create a second French empire. Although there were numerous electoral irregularities, apparently large numbers of Frenchmen were perfectly content to see the revival of the empire in the hope of once again seeing France take the dominant position in Europe.

France prospered greatly during the first 10 years of the reign of **Napoleon III**. Cheap credit provided by the government allowed for a significant economic expansion during this period. The city of Paris underwent a remarkable transformation from a medieval city to a modern one under the guidance of **Georges Haussmann** (1809–1891), who cleared many of the slums of the city and in their place built the wide avenues that have become a hallmark of Paris. Besides making the city more attractive visually, this new Paris was a much cleaner place, with aqueducts to bring fresh water into the city and sewers to remove waste, resulting in the elimination of one of the great scourges of the earlier part of the century—cholera.

The New Paris

It's said that one British visitor told the emperor with a bit of sarcasm, "May it be said of you that you found Paris stinking and left it sweet."

Despite the economic improvements during the first decade of his reign, politically Napoleon III led an authoritarian regime. Beginning in 1860, Napoleon began to make a number of concessions, such as the easing of censorship, in part because of the unpopularity of his wars in the Crimean region and the Italian states. However, this liberalization had the opposite effect of what he intended; it led the people to openly display their disenchantment with his reign. Napoleon was, nevertheless, an effective politician, and he took a bold gamble in 1859 when he declared the creation of a "liberal empire," making his state a constitutional monarchy. This intriguing experiment never had the opportunity to succeed. Napoleon blundered into the Franco-Prussian War and was captured in battle. Eventually, he was sent into exile in Britain, where he soon died.

Following the collapse of the Second Empire, France created what became known as the **Third Republic**. Right away, the Republic had to deal with the daunting task of putting down a revolt in Paris, which resulted in the rise of the **Paris Commune**, a radical government created out of the anarchy brought about by the Franco-Prussian War. The republican government restored order in Paris only after winning an armed struggle that resulted in the massacre of 25,000 Parisians. By 1875, the republic was firmly established and consisted of a two-house parliamentary body, with a chamber of deputies, or lower house, elected by a universal male pool of voters and a senate chosen by indirect elections. The president, or head of government, was a relatively weak office, directly responsible to the chamber of deputies. The Third Republic would face its greatest challenge in 1889, when a *coup d'état* looked probable. What became known as the **Boulanger Affair** severely weakened the monarchist movement. Although it was marked by significant problems, such as tensions between the state and the Catholic Church and significant antisemitism, the Third Republic proved to be the most durable of all the French republics.

Great Britain

In contrast to France, Great Britain enjoyed remarkable stability and prosperity in the second half of the 19th century. A general sense of self-satisfaction pervaded in Victorian England. Nowhere was this more apparent than in the **Great Exhibition of 1851**, which boasted more than 13,000 exhibitors displaying the variety of British goods that were now available as a result of industrialization. To accommodate the exhibits and the millions of visitors, the architect John Paxton constructed a building with the greatest area of glass to date, which became known as the Crystal Palace. One contemporary wrote that because buildings represent the society that builds them, the Crystal Palace revealed "the aesthetic bloom of its practical character, and of the practical tendency of the English nation."

Politically, the nation was slowly evolving in the direction of increased democracy. The **Great Reform Bill of 1832** was only the first in a number of steps that were taken to expand the franchise. In 1867, under the direction of prime minister **Benjamin Disraeli** (1804–1881), one of the most remarkable men to ever hold that post, the **Second Reform Bill** passed, which extended the vote to urban heads of households. In 1884, during the Prime Ministership of Disraeli's great rival, **William Gladstone** (1809–1898), the vote was further extended to heads of households in the countryside. The rivalry between Disraeli and Gladstone was emblematic of another important aspect of Victorian politics—the evolution of a political system dominated by two political parties, in this case, Disraeli's Tory or Conservative party and Gladstone's Liberal party. The long reign of **Queen Victoria** (r. 1837–1901) saw a continuing deterioration in the political power of the monarchy, resulting in the crown's inability to play a significant role in the selection of a prime minister. This meant that, at times, Victoria had to live with Gladstone as her chief minister, even though she detested him and adored Disraeli, who knew how to flatter her vanity.

Russia

The stresses of war can show a nation at its best or they can reveal significant problems. For Russia, the poor showing in the Crimean War, fought in its own backyard, revealed the weaknesses of its society in comparison to the nations of western Europe. Although Nicholas I was far too reactionary to contemplate reform, his successor, **Alexander II** (r. 1855–1881), recognized that the greatest problem facing Russia was serfdom. In 1861, he issued a proclamation freeing the serfs, though the former serfs had to buy their freedom with payments that were to extend over 50 years (a practice that was stopped following the Russian Revolution of 1905). The peasants were also generally given the poorest lands by their former owners, which meant that life remained harsh for many agricultural laborers.

Administratively, to cope with a Russia that faced a burgeoning population throughout its far-flung empire, Alexander introduced *zemstvos*, or district assemblies, that had mandates to deal with local issues such as education and social services. The *zemstvos* were dominated by the local gentry and were hardly bastions of democracy, though some Russian reformers saw their existence as the potential for greater political freedoms. Alexander enacted further reforms, such as a revision of the legal system, although at heart he remained an autocrat and saw no need to implement fundamental changes like the introduction of a written constitution and parliamentary bodies. His inflexibility on these points led to a rise in revolutionary organizations such as the **People's Will**, which assassinated Alexander in 1881. The succession to the throne of his reactionary son Alexander III (r. 1881–1894) brought about a new round of repression and an attempt to weaken even the tentative reforms of Alexander II.

Austria

The 19th century was not kind to the Austrian Empire, a multinational empire in an age of growing nationalist sentiment. By 1866, the Habsburgs had lost all their territories in Italy, and their shattering defeat by the Prussians at the Battle of Sadowa made Austria no longer a factor in German affairs. In 1867, the government in Vienna found it necessary to sign an agreement with the Magyars in Hungary, creating a dual Austro-Hungarian Empire. Each state was to be independent but united under the mutual leadership of **Francis Joseph**, who became Emperor of Austria and King of Hungary. Perhaps not surprisingly, the Magyars, having achieved a measure of independence, turned around and did their best to ensure that the Croats, Serbs, Romanians, and other nationalities located within Hungary were denied any form of self-rule. As a result of a lessening influence in western Europe, Austria-Hungary attempted to become more influential in the Balkan region, ultimately with disastrous consequences.

The Ottoman Empire

Another multinational empire at the crossroads was the Ottoman Empire. Commonly referred to as "the sick old man of Europe," the Ottoman state attempted in the second half of the 19th century to implement a process of modernization. This reform program, which began during the reign of **Sultan Abdul Mejid** (r. 1839–1861) and was known as the *Tanzimat*, was an attempt to adopt Western methods of waging wars, to bring about a much-needed overhaul of the Ottoman economy, and to introduce such notions as equality before the law and freedom of religion.

The introduction of Western education played a significant role in forming a group of liberal intellectuals known as the **"Young Turks."** The Young Turks were eventually able to push reform further than the government had ever planned, and in 1876 helped establish the Ottoman state as a constitutional monarchy. However, when the brutal **Sultan Abdul Hamid II** (r. 1876–1909) came to the throne, the constitution was scrapped as part of his attempt to subjugate the non-Muslim peoples within his empire. His policies led to the deaths of thousands of Armenians (though they were only a precursor to the full-fledged Armenian Genocide that would take place under the Young Turks during the years following 1915). His policies also led to general repression throughout the state, although by the end of his reign, the Young Turks once again restored a measure of constitutional rule.

Ottoman weakness, however, continued to plague the empire up until it sided with the Central Powers in the First World War. The Ottomans could do little but sit idly by when, at the **Congress of Berlin** (1878), after another humiliating defeat at the hands of the Russians (the **Russo-Turkish War**), the other European powers recognized the independence of Serbia, Montenegro, Romania, and Bulgaria—all former Ottoman territories in the same Balkan region where the Austro-Hungarian Empire would soon have so much trouble.

CED 6.3 Second Wave Industrialization and Its Effects

THE SECOND INDUSTRIAL REVOLUTION

By the middle of the 19th century, Europe had undergone a dramatic process of economic expansion. These economic changes—sometimes referred to as the Second Industrial Revolution—had an impact on human lives that may have been even greater than what occurred during the initial stages of industrialization.

Steel

The label **"Age of Steel"** is an apt one for the second half of the century. Previously, steel production was expensive. In 1856, the Englishman **Henry Bessemer** (1813–1898) introduced a method that became known as the **Bessemer Process** that produced steel in far greater quantities without increasing costs. A few years later, **William Siemens** (1823–1883), a German, introduced an even better method of making steel that produced a higher-quality product at significantly reduced costs. Because of its strength and durability, steel became the metal of choice for buildings and ships, resulting in a revolution in architecture and shipbuilding.

Electricity

Few developments have affected the way people live their lives as significantly as the invention of the means to harness **electrical power**. In 1879, Thomas Edison invented the incandescent lamp. Two years later, the first electrical power station was built in Great Britain. Soon after that, European cities began to be lit after dark, and populations moved through the streets of the city more effectively with the introduction of electric tramways. Electric lights made cities far safer and even led to the expansion of nighttime activities in London and Paris, where the late 19th century saw a tremendous growth in the number of public opera houses and theaters.

Transportation

The second half of the 19th century witnessed many significant developments in all forms of transportation.

- Europe's rail network expanded dramatically. By the end of the century, well over 100,000 miles of track had been laid.

- In 1869, the French built the **Suez Canal**, though it was the British who gained control over the canal in 1875, eager to ensure their continued use of a waterway that almost halved the amount of time it took to travel from Great Britain to India.

- Speedy clipper ships began to set records for crossing the Atlantic Ocean, though by the end of the century they were to be replaced by steamships.

- Trains and steamships, using the ice-making machines that were introduced in the 1870s, were able to transport perishables around the world and made the United States, Australia, and Argentina major providers of European provisions.

- In 1885, Karl Benz invented an internal combustion engine powered by gasoline. Automobiles, however, would remain a plaything of the very wealthy until Henry Ford started producing his Model T in 1908.

- Finally, a whole new area of transportation was opened up when Orville and Wilbur Wright, brothers whose background was in bicycle building, launched the first successful airplane at Kitty Hawk, North Carolina, in 1903.

Communication and Education Advances

- In 1840, Britain was the first European nation to establish a national postal system, with users able to send a letter for a penny, affordable to almost all.

- The development of universal public education also meant that more people were inclined to communicate in writing.

- In 1844, the first telegraph line was completed, and by the second half of the century, Europe was covered with telegraph lines.

- In 1876, Alexander Graham Bell invented the telephone, and Germans were making 700 million calls per year by 1900.

- Some of those calls might have been to make social arrangements around the new entertainment options of the age, such as attending motion pictures, first shown publicly in the 1890s, while stay-at-home sorts could enjoy the phonograph, invented by the incredibly prolific Thomas Edison in 1877.

Other Scientific Developments

Science began to play an increasingly important role in industrial expansion. In particular, the second half of the 19th century produced a series of major developments. While this trend was to continue into the first decades of the 20th century, in many ways, the optimism that one could sense in the 1880s concerning the world of science was not to be found some 40 years later. Even before the First World War delivered a terrible blow to the belief in rational progress, scientists were revealing that nature was incredibly complex; many questions would remain unanswered while at least some of the basic assumptions concerning the workings of the universe were under attack.

- The introduction of synthetic dyes revolutionized the textile industry.

- The invention of synthetic fertilizers led to increased crop yields.

- The invention of dynamite by the Swedish chemist **Alfred Nobel** (1833–1896) made it possible to blast tunnels through rock and to remove those hills that nature had placed in inconvenient spots. Nobel, however, was horrified by the potentially destructive uses of his invention, and in his will he entrusted money for a prize to be given in his name to those who served the cause of peace.

Increasingly, the 19th and early-20th centuries witnessed greater specialization in the sciences, as scientists provided some of the key foundational work in areas such as physics and chemistry. Some of these developments include the following:

- Michael Faraday produced groundbreaking work on electricity and electromagnetism.

- Amateur scientist James Joule defined many of the laws of thermodynamics.

- In chemistry, Dmitri Mendeleev developed the periodic table, arranging the known elements by atomic weight while leaving empty spaces in his table for those elements then predicted but as yet unknown.

- In 1895, Wilhelm Röntgen made an accidental discovery of X-rays.

- In the following year, in another fortuitous accident, Antoine Henri Becquerel discovered radioactivity, although he did not follow this up with additional work. That task would be undertaken by the Curies—Marie and her husband, Pierre—who would spend their lives studying radioactivity. In 1910, four years after the death of her husband, **Marie Curie** isolated radium.

- In England, **Ernest Rutherford** laid the groundwork for an understanding of atomic structure by showing that atomic particles had a central core called the nucleus. Rutherford had once said (to paraphrase) that a theory in physics wasn't any good unless it could be explained to a bartender, yet his own work became part of an increasingly complex body of knowledge that left many ordinary people feeling alienated from the world as revealed by science.

- As a young student, **Max Planck** was told that there was nothing further to be discovered in physics, yet his work was to revolutionize the field. In 1901, he devised a theory based on the idea that energy did not flow in a steady stream, but rather was delivered in discrete units, or quanta. His quantum physics spelled an end to the dominance of the mechanistic interpretation of physics that stemmed from the work of Newton.

- Further undermining Newton's concept of the universe was **Albert Einstein's** special theory of relativity, in which time, space, and movement are not absolute entities but are understood to be relative in accordance with the position of the observer.

Philosophy

Just as scientific inquiry was revealing ideas and principles that appeared to be less than rational, philosophers such as **Friedrich Nietzsche**, for a time a professor of classical languages at the University of Basel, began to question and even to reject the ideas of the 18th-century Enlightenment. In Nietzsche's most influential work, *Thus Spake Zarathustra*, he argued that it was necessary to break free from traditional morality, which is why he famously proclaimed that "God is dead." It was necessary, according to Nietzsche, to "kill" God, because religion was at the center of a Western model of civilization that he despised. Nietzsche hated the Germany created by Bismarck and instead yearned for the emergence of the artist-warrior superman. Unfortunately, after his death in 1900, his pro-Nazi sister was in charge of his literary estate, and she edited his writings to make them supportive of Hitler's extreme nationalism and anti-semitism, two modern chauvinisms that he, in fact, despised.

Psychoanalysis

Sigmund Freud, the founder of psychoanalysis, took the methods of modern science and proposed to find a way to treat mental disorders by delving into the human subconscious, using what he referred to as the "talking cure." As he spelled out in *The Interpretation of Dreams*, Freud believed that dreams revealed the inner workings of a subconscious world and devised a list of Freudian symbols—items or events that appear in dreams that actually represent other items or events stored in the unconscious. In *Civilization and Its Discontents*, a book written in his more pessimistic later years, Freud questioned the very premise of continuous progress for the human race and instead posited that despite attempts to suppress it, violence lies at the very core of our being.

Advances in Medicine

The beginnings of modern Western medicine took root in the 19th century, marking the first time in history that going to the doctor was not such a bad idea.

- Surgery, previously dominated by practitioners who bragged about their ability to remove a leg in under 90 seconds, was transformed in 1846 when American dentist William Morton began to introduce anesthesia in the form of ether, followed by the use of chloroform anesthesia a few years later.
- Overall, the most significant change in medicine in the period was that the experimental method found in the sciences was applied to medicine. Applying the experimental method, **Louis Pasteur** discovered that microbes—small, invisible organisms—caused diseases.
- Pasteur also explained how vaccines, which had been in use since the 18th century to fight against smallpox, worked within the body by stimulating the immune system to produce antibodies after coming into contact with a weak form of the bacilli.
- The English surgeon Joseph Lister, building on Pasteur's discoveries, initiated the use of carbolic acid as a disinfectant during surgery.
- A Hungarian doctor, Ignaz Semmelweis, made childbirth much safer for women. He demonstrated that if doctors and nurses thoroughly washed their hands prior to delivery, it could dramatically reduce the number of women who died from what was known as "childbed fever."

Darwin

Few individuals had a greater impact on the intellectual world of the 19th century than **Charles Darwin** (1809–1882), an English naturalist who traveled on the *H.M.S. Beagle* to the Galápagos Islands off the coast of South America. Prior to Darwin, there were some, including his grandfather, who had challenged the biblical account of creation as a one-time event. (According to this view, species could never undergo a process of change—evolution—because God created the world in six days and then stopped.) In addition, geologists, like Charles Lyell (1797–1875), claimed that geological evidence proved that the Earth was much older than the biblical age of approximately 6,000 years.

CED 7.4
Darwinism, Social Darwinism

Although Darwin was not operating in an intellectual vacuum, he was the first to offer an explanation for the process of change. Darwin argued that certain members of a species inherit traits that, over time, may make them more successful in the struggle for survival. These traits are then passed down, while those members of the species who lack such characteristics ultimately do not reproduce. Darwin labeled this process **"natural selection"** in his important book *On the Origin of Species* (1859). It was not until more than a decade after the publication of his first book that Darwin, a cautious man, would take his idea to its natural conclusion. In *The Descent of Man* (1871), Darwin argued that humans were not exempt from this process of evolutionary change and that human beings have therefore evolved from simpler forms of life. The opposition to Darwin was swift and vehement, particularly from religious groups, who saw such ideas as a direct threat to the very basis of their beliefs.

Social Class and the Second Industrial Revolution

Far-reaching industrial developments played a significant role in changing the social dynamic in western Europe. One group in decline was the traditional aristocracy. The French Revolution created the concept of a meritocracy, thereby eliminating any special privileges based on birth. In Great Britain, the development of refrigerated railcars meant that less expensive agricultural products could be imported from the United States, Argentina, and Australia. This resulted in the propitious decline in the wealth of many of the great noble families, whose wealth was primarily based on land. The implementation of competitive examinations for civil service and military positions served to reduce the aristocracy's role in two of their traditional endeavors: government administration and command of the military.

The second half of the 19th century has sometimes been called the **"Age of the Middle Class."** Middle classes were not new. During the Renaissance, a different "middle class" was largely responsible for the changes that radically transformed society. That middle class consisted of wealthy, city-dwelling merchants, who lay somewhere between the three traditional classes, or "estates," of medieval society—the peasants, the priesthood, and the nobility. The money of these merchants, and their secular interests, contributed to the intellectual progress of the Renaissance.

In the late 19th century, however, the middle class was growing in size and importance. The merchants were joined by members of newly created professions (such as industrialists and engineers) and of newly wealthy ones (lawyers, journalists, doctors, and teachers). These people were "middle class" in the sense that they fell outside the earlier class system. On the whole, they were not middle-income; they were actually quite wealthy. The late 1800s were significant not because the middle class was new, but because it was larger than ever before.

Darwin's Followers and "Survival of the Fittest"

Darwin did attract a number of followers. Although Darwin was always calculating in his own speculative thought, many of his followers pursued his ideas with wild abandon. It was **Herbert Spencer** (1820–1903) who first used the phrase **"survival of the fittest,"** a phrase never in fact uttered by Darwin. For Spencer, such an idea provided justification for governments to abandon the poor; he believed that giving aid on their behalf would upset the natural order of survival. Such ideas, which received the label **"Social Darwinism,"** were used to justify the racist idea that Europeans were superior to Africans and Asians and therefore should dominate them. Across Europe, ardent nationalists used the concept of survival of the fittest to explain the constant state of tensions between nations and why some states thrived while others didn't. Social Darwinism also played a role in the heightened antisemitism found across Europe in the last quarter of the 19th century, as some argued that Jews were a lesser race and could never be integrated within the larger fabric of society.

A "Victorian" Morality

Another sign that the middle class enjoyed preeminence at this time was that its standards of behavior became the societal norms. In some instances, this trend produced positive results; for example, certain barbaric forms of popular entertainment, such as animal fights, ceased. Unfortunately, the middle class often obeyed a rather stuffy, or what we today refer to as "Victorian," morality. This sense of propriety also greatly affected middle-class women: Victorian sensibilities seemed to preclude them from living fulfilled lives. Women were excluded from the professions and from enrollment in institutions of higher education. The late Victorian period did witness the development in Great Britain, the United States, and, to a lesser extent, France and Germany, of a women's rights movement that sought to dramatically change the status of women.

The Beginnings of Anarchism

Another political ideology that began to attract some workers by the end of the century was anarchism. **Joseph Proudhon** (1809–1865), a self-educated typesetter, is often considered to be the founder of anarchism. In 1840, he wrote *What Is Property?*, and his answer to that question was simply that "property is theft." Proudhon, who was the first to use the term "**anarchist**," believed that the true laws of society had little to do with authority and came from the nature of society itself. Anarchism touted the idea that bringing these laws to the surface should be the ultimate goal of any society. Anarchists like Proudhon wanted workers to organize small groups of independent producers that would govern themselves without interference from the state, an institution that anarchists wanted to see abolished. Anarchism never gained the support of as many workers as socialism, but in certain regions, such as in the Spanish province of Andalusia, the movement had a significant following.

As a group, the middle class enjoyed new luxuries such as fresh running water and central heating. All families that were considered middle class had at least one servant, while wealthier families had large staffs to attend to their every need. Department stores began to cater to the increasing taste for consumer goods that became a hallmark of middle-class existence. Travel in the 18th century had been the preserve of the extremely wealthy, when it was considered an essential part of a young gentleman's education to go on a "Grand Tour" of the capitals of Europe. However, this too changed. **Thomas Cook** (1808–1892) popularized travel among the middle class when he organized day trips to the Great Exhibition in London, thus giving rise to the tourist trade. For those seeking less vigorous relaxation than seeing 10 countries in as many days, spas and resorts became common vacation destinations.

For workers, the Second Industrial Revolution brought about some improvements in their standard of living. One example of this is the development of popular entertainment such as dance halls and professional sports leagues, a sign that the working-class income was not entirely consumed by survival necessities, such as food and housing. Yet, for many workers across western Europe, the improvements were slight at best. Many still saw socialism as the best means to change their dreary existence. Socialism itself underwent some significant developments in the latter part of the 19th century. **Eduard Bernstein** (1850–1932), a German intellectual, challenged some of Marx's basic ideas in *Evolutionary Socialism* (1898). He and his followers, who were labeled "revisionists," argued that capitalism was not, as Marx claimed, about to collapse.

Because capitalism was firmly rooted in society, it was necessary for socialists to work toward the progressive improvement of working-class conditions within a capitalist framework rather than focus on revolutionary upheaval. Their more radical views had been mollified in part because of the development of parliamentary democracy and universal male suffrage in parts of western Europe, which led them to believe that socialism could be achieved through the ballot box.

Radicals, such as the German **Karl Kautsky** (1854–1938), held firm to the validity of Marx's "laws" and were harsh toward the revisionists, whom they considered heretics, although Kautsky himself in fact altered some of Marx's ideas. Unlike Marx, he claimed that the proletarian revolution would not be a bloody affair but a civilized process. A socialist movement could be a passive evolution because it was inevitable. Such views were in turn declared heretical by more extreme socialists such as Lenin and Rosa Luxemburg.

The meaning of the word *liberalism* underwent a change too. Economically, it had initially referred to a belief in free-market *laissez-faire*, but the excesses of industrialization made many liberals rethink that stance. Soon the word *liberalism* began referring to those who wanted to use the power of the state to intervene in society to stop the social abuses of capitalism. This found greatest expression in the reform movements that tried to clean up prisons, establish police forces, and initiate more public health reforms across the continent. This last change was compelled by the many cholera outbreaks that arrived on merchant vessels from abroad, prompting the creation of urban sewage and water systems. Public parks, public lighting, and even the first public housing also made an appearance in this century, thanks to the efforts of charity organizations and famous reporters like **Edwin Chadwick**. The reformers also demanded mandatory public education to maintain social order and promote national strength.

> **CED 6.9**
> Institutional Responses and Reform

SOCIAL AND CULTURAL DEVELOPMENTS

Religion

Religious beliefs and institutions made a significant recovery in the period after 1815, particularly considering the extent of the challenges posed to organized religion by the Enlightenment, the French Revolution, and the Napoleonic era. Secular rulers saw religion as an important fortification for the existing social order, with the revolutions of 1848 further spurring this trend toward state support of religion.

Catholicism

Spain, in 1851, declared Catholicism the only religion of the Spanish people, while in Austria, the reforms that Joseph II had imposed on the Catholic Church in the late 18th century over areas such as the training of priests were repealed.

Nowhere were the events of 1848 felt more than in Rome, where a revolution forced Pope Pius IX to flee his city. Restored to power with the help of French troops, he issued the encyclical ***Syllabus of Errors***, which listed liberalism as one of the errors of modern life. In 1870, Pius put forward the doctrine of **papal infallibility,** a controversial doctrine that alarmed moderate Catholics, as it posits that when making an official statement on matters of faith, the pope cannot be in error.

Perhaps inevitably, there was a backlash against religious institutions where they appeared to be standing in the way of change. Such criticism could be clearly expected from liberal circles, but even conservative politicians could be antagonistic toward religious bodies. In the newly unified Germany, Bismarck saw Catholicism as a force that could rip the nation apart, because Catholics were tied to a supranational institution that would be the object of their primary loyalties. To deal with this purported threat, Bismarck, with the support of German liberals, attacked Catholic institutions in what was known as the ***Kulturkampf*** (cultural war), taking control over Catholic schools and the appointment of bishops. After seeing that this was having little effect, Bismarck stopped this harassment in 1878.

In the last quarter of the 19th century, there was a growing sentiment among both Catholic and Protestant clergy that religion needed to address the social issues of the day. In 1891, **Pope Leo XIII** (r. 1878–1903) issued ***Rerum Novarum*** ("Of New Things"), and although the encyclical reaffirmed the right of private property and bashed socialism, it said that Christians in general and the Church specifically had a responsibility toward the poor. In primarily Catholic countries such as France and Italy, this message led to the establishment of the Catholic Social Movement, while in Protestant lands, churches expanded their efforts on behalf of the poor.

The Bible as History

In the German states in the early 19th century, a group of theologians began to study the Bible as history in search of the "historical" Jesus. A critical step in this effort was the publication in 1835 of *The Life of Jesus Critically Examined* by **David Friedrich Strauss** (1808–1874). For Strauss, the Bible consisted of a series of myths formulated by the early Christians, ultimately providing for a scripture that contained, in his famous phrase, a "Christ of faith, rather than the Jesus of history." The work of these German theologians was brought to England by Samuel Taylor Coleridge as well as by George Eliot, who translated Strauss's *Life* as well as Ludwig Feuerbach's (1804–1872) *Essence of Christianity*, which argued that God was a human-made device that reflected our own inner sense of the divine.

Religion for the Working Class and Peasants

The Lourdes Shrine
To this day, the grotto at Lourdes remains a place where those who are ill drink or bathe in the waters in the hope of being cured.

In Great Britain, a religious census taken in 1851 revealed that attendance at church (it assumed everyone was Christian) was much lower than expected and that the working class in particular had very little connection with organized religion. On the other hand, the 19th century was not without some interesting examples of the continuing strength of popular religious sentiment. One well-known incident dates back to 1858, when a young French peasant girl named Bernadette claimed she saw a vision of the Virgin Mary, and that it happened again 18 more times. The waters from the grotto at Lourdes, where she saw the vision, became an important religious shrine.

Judaism, Antisemitism, and Zionism

For Jews, the 19th century presented new opportunities as well as new pressures. The legal status of Jews improved throughout the century. In 1858, Jews were allowed to enter the House of Commons in Great Britain, and in the following decade, Jews received full political rights in Austria-Hungary and Germany. Despite their newly enhanced legal status, social discrimination remained endemic. Those Jews who wanted to rise in certain professions or in government often found the path blocked to them unless they converted.

CED 7.2
Nationalism

The last quarter of the 19th century was a period of increasing hardships for Jews. For many, Jews were seen as responsible for new and troubling trends in modern economic life, such as the creation of the department store, which put small shopkeepers out of business. The economic depression of 1873, which lasted for most of the remainder of the decade, led to an increase in prejudice. Economic resentment was combined with a new form of **antisemitism** (the word was first used in 1879) based on Social Darwinist notions of Jews as being part of a distinct and foreign race and not just members of a religious denomination.

Hitler's early years in Vienna were spent in a city governed by Karl Lueger (1844–1928), who was elected mayor of the city on an openly antisemitic platform. Antisemitic political parties formed in Germany, while in France, the **Dreyfus Affair** helped give rise to *Action Française*, a monarchist group that was also virulently antisemitic.

In Russia, the monarchy used attacks on Jews, or *pogroms*, as a tool for redirecting popular anger, which might otherwise have been directed toward the throne. Several million Jews left Russia at the turn of the century to escape the persecution that grew worse after the 1905 Revolution.

For many Jews, the optimism they felt at the middle of the century that the future would bring ever greater social acceptance was, by the end of the century, being destroyed by a wave of hatred. For some, this would lead to the conclusion that the only hope to live in peace would be through the establishment of a Jewish homeland. The leading advocate for **Zionism**, as this idea was called, was **Theodore Herzl** (1860–1904), an Austrian journalist who was horrified over the antisemitism that bubbled over the surface as a result of the Dreyfus Affair. In *The Jewish State*, he argued that Jews must have a state of their own and began to form a worldwide organization to achieve this goal, with the First Zionist Congress meeting in Switzerland in 1897.

The Rights and Role of Women

The role of the family changed in the 19th century, with one of the most significant developments being that families, which at one time operated as a cohesive economic unit, no longer functioned in such a manner. Increasingly, there were now separate spheres for both male and female endeavors, with men going off to earn the money that provided for the family's support. In the late 19th century, the rise of a sizable, wealthy middle class created new gender standards. Middle-class city-dwellers had the money and the energy to record their social views and set standards of taste for their nations. And, among those families who had the money, the new standard was for a man's place to be in the workforce and a woman's to be in the home, which was increasingly seen as a haven in an ever-changing world.

In the Victorian period, this idealization of the household and the female's place within it led to the rise of what is known as the **"cult of domesticity."** Among the well-off, women were expected to exhibit certain traits that were to make the home a blissful paradise. Submissiveness was one of the traits that women were expected to exhibit, along with sexual purity and religious piety, because women were expected to be responsible for the religious life of the family. Books were written to provide women with tips on running their households and raising their children. Standards were quite different for the poorer majority of the country. Working-class women worked just as hard as working-class men, whether in factories, or in forms of domestic labor (such as taking in laundry), or as servants. Many worked multiple jobs, and had little time or energy left to raise children, let alone read books on the subject. The working class would, nevertheless, sometimes receive visits from well-meaning but patronizing middle-class women offering to instruct them in the new ways of home economics.

> **Who Is Mary Mayson Beeton?**
> She wrote the most famous advice book for women during this period. Her *Book of Household Management* was second in sales in Great Britain only to the Bible.

Limits to Women's Education and Work

Keeping women in the home was in part ensured by outside institutions that limited the opportunities available to them. Higher education was generally reserved for men, although exceptions began to appear, with women being allowed to attend the University of Zurich by 1865 and the University of London in 1878. With the development of professional societies in areas such as medicine and law, women found an additional barrier, as the bylaws of these societies generally excluded women. For those middle-class women who did work outside the home, certain professions—such as primary school teacher, nurse, secretary, and librarian—became almost completely female, which also ensured that they were poorly paid jobs in comparison to those held by men.

Some women were able to move beyond the bounds of convention. Frances Power Cobbe (1822–1904) was one of the first women to make a living as a journalist and later became an active campaigner against medical vivisection, and Josephine Butler (1828–1906) challenged a basic Victorian prohibition simply by talking about sex publicly. Butler helped found the Ladies National Association in 1869, an all-female organization that fought against the Contagious Diseases Act, which allowed for women who were deemed to possibly be infected by sexually transmitted diseases to be dragged off the street for examination while men went unaccosted.

Women's Struggles for Increased Rights

As the century continued, a growing number of women began to criticize the civil disabilities under which they lived, such as the lack of right to divorce or to possess property. These women, who adopted the French word **"feminist"** to describe themselves, began to develop organizations to help bring about change. Even in unexpected places, such as in a conservative society like Greece, a feminist newspaper existed that advocated for both professional and civil rights, and it survived for more than 20 years with a circulation of 20,000.

Cross-national cooperation existed among the various feminist groups, and there were also transatlantic links with feminists in the United States. Although there was a general desire for cooperation, these first-generation feminists tended to split over the issue of whether the primary struggle should be for the vote or for the improvement of social conditions.

Some progressive women scorned feminism altogether, as was the case with the German Marxist Clara Zetkin (1857–1933), who saw socialism as offering women the only possibility for ending their oppression. In Great Britain, there was a split among those women who were working to achieve the vote. **Suffragists,** women who worked peacefully for the vote, were at times overshadowed in the public consciousness by the individuals who joined the **Women's Social and Political Union** formed by **Emmeline Pankhurst** (1858–1928). With her daughter Christabel (1880–1958) at her side, Emmeline and her followers (called **suffragettes**) pursued a militant campaign of heckling political speakers, breaking church windows, and committing arson. These were serious crimes, and there was no sense of mercy on account of their gender or their wealthy backgrounds (poorer women did not usually have the luxury of being involved in politics). On the contrary, suffragettes were punished severely for the significant threat they posed to the established social order: they were arrested for their actions and frequently beaten. They went on hunger strike in prison, only to be force-fed.

In 1918, women in Great Britain finally achieved the right to vote. There is ongoing historical debate regarding whether it was the suffragettes or the suffragists who ultimately deserve the credit for this momentous achievement. However, there is an additional factor that allowed women across Europe to achieve the vote in the early 20th century: the significant contribution that women made to the war effort during the First World War.

Cultural Changes

Meanwhile, there were cultural changes taking place that provided the foundations for the emergence of the so-called "new woman." **Maria Montessori** (1870–1952) exemplifies this new woman in Europe at the turn of the century. An Italian, Montessori became a famous educator and physician who was renowned for her teaching strategies. Factors such as the increased availability of birth control and greater educational and professional opportunities offered new horizons for women. For some men, this new woman was unsettling, with the British novelist D. H. Lawrence noting in an essay that women, who used to "see themselves as a softly flowing stream of attraction," were now "pointed and they want everything."

Emergence of the Social Sciences

History

In the 19th century, there was a new impetus to take the methodology established in the sciences and apply it to the workings of society. One result of this was the emergence of history as a modern academic discipline. One of the pioneers in the new historical methods was **Barthold Niebuhr** (1776–1831), who introduced the close examination of primary source documents into the writing of classical history. His *Roman History* influenced **Leopold von Ranke** (1795–1886) and led von Ranke to challenge the traditional way of looking at history as revealing some grand design, whether that design was the revealed work of God or led to a more secular purpose. Ranke felt that the historical texts of his day were unreliable and instead felt that it was necessary, like Niebuhr, to go to original sources.

Anthropology

Another social science, anthropology, was born out of the sudden expansion of European dominance over large parts of the globe as a result of the new imperialism. Across Europe, national anthropological societies were established, although unfortunately, due to the endemic "scientific" racism of the age, such societies often spent their time exploring the "inferiority" of non-Europeans.

Sociology

Sociology, the study of human social behavior, was in part inspired by the growing tendency of governments to keep statistics on the conditions of their citizenry. **Émile Durkheim** (1858–1917) held the first chair in sociology at the University of Bordeaux, an appointment that was met with skepticism by the more traditional faculty.

Archaeology

Scientific principles were also used in the field of archaeology, which in the 19th century still remained the preserve of dedicated amateurs such as **Heinrich Schlieman**, a German businessman who searched for the ruins of ancient Troy, and the Englishman **Sir Arthur Evans** (1851–1941), who excavated the Minoan culture of Crete.

The Arts

Romanticism began in the second half of the 18th century as a rejection of what was viewed as the cold rationalism of 18th-century Neoclassicism and instead placed a much higher value on the primacy of emotions and feeling.

Romanticism in Literature

CED 5.8
Romanticism

Part of the inspiration for Romanticism came from the writer **Jean-Jacques Rousseau**, who in his novel *Émile* proposed an educational program for a young man in which the education was derived from nature and not from rote memorization of facts.

Artists who worked in the Romantic tradition extolled both the beauty and mystery of nature. They also exhibited a great deal of interest in the supernatural, as for example in Goethe's *Faust*, which deals with a man who sells his soul to the devil in order to achieve worldly success.

Wolfgang von Goethe

The most important of the early Romantic writers is arguably **Wolfgang von Goethe** (1749–1832). In his *Sorrows of Young Werther*, an epistolary novel, young Werther kills himself when his love for a woman is not returned. The novel proved to be so popular that young men throughout Europe began to dress in clothes similar to Werther and, in some extreme cases, killed themselves. Goethe was the greatest figure of the ***Sturm und Drang*** (Storm and Stress) generation of German Romantic writers of the 1770s and 1780s. These writers were introduced to an interested French public by the author Madame de Staël (1766–1817), who was living in exile in Switzerland after angering Napoleon.

Romantics explored folklore and traditional peasant life because country people were idealized as living closer to nature. Romantics also found it necessary to break with the traditional styles of the past. In their jointly written *Lyrical Ballads*, the English poets **William Wordsworth** (1770–1850) and **Samuel Taylor Coleridge** (1772–1834) completely ignored the rules of punctuation, revealing their rejection of classical poetic forms.

Many of the artists who worked in the Romantic tradition became fascinated with the Middle Ages. Although their glorification of the medieval past, an age of theocratic kingship, would have seemingly pointed them into a more conservative direction, many of the Romantics were political liberals. **Sir Walter Scott** (1771–1832) and **Victor Hugo** (1802–1885) in many ways invented the popular image of the Middle Ages in novels such as *Ivanhoe* and *The Hunchback of Notre Dame*. Their influence can be felt when you look at almost any church in the United States from the second half of the 19th century; the odds are that it's built in the Gothic style.

Many in the Romantic movement not only rejected traditional literary and artistic styles, but also rejected the traditional political order. **Percy Bysshe Shelley** (1792–1827), an English Romantic poet, rebelled against the conservative values found in his country. In *Prometheus Unbound*, a lyrical drama, the mythical protagonist challenges the established order by stealing fire from the gods, and *Mask of Anarchy* was written as a political protest after the Peterloo Massacre. George

Gordon, **Lord Byron** (1788–1824), challenged the political status quo and ended up dying in Greece fighting in the rebellion against the Ottoman Turks. Amandine-Aurore Dupin (1804–1892), who wrote under the intentionally male-sounding pen name **George Sand,** challenged the endemic oppression that weighed down women. She was involved in a famous affair with Frédéric Chopin, who initially said about her to his family, "Something about her repels me." In *Indiana,* we have the story of a woman who is desperate for love but finds herself abused by both her husband and a selfish lover. Sand broke with stereotypes not only with her pen name but by smoking cigars, dressing like a man, and engaging in affairs with married men.

Music

In addition to its impact on literature and art, Romanticism influenced the world of 19th-century music. **Ludwig von Beethoven** (1770–1827) began to write compositions that broke with earlier classical forms by adjusting their length and doing unheard-of things, such as putting a vocal soloist toward the end of the last movement of a composition. Beethoven was able to break with tradition because he was the first composer to earn his living directly with proceeds from compositions and performances, earning enough to not have to rely on either aristocratic or religious patrons.

Other innovative composers include **Franz Schubert** (1797–1828), who invented the *lied*, or art song, which involves a solo voice performing a melody to piano accompaniment. **Hector Berlioz** (1803–1869) wrote pieces in which for the first time there was an attempt to tell a story without the use of singers and a written text, such as when he set Goethe's *Faust* to music. Some composers made use of traditional oral tales or folk songs: **Frederic Chopin** (1810–1849) was influenced by the music of the peasants of his native Poland, and **Franz Liszt** (1811–1886) wrote music based on traditional Romani music. At the turn of the century, a self-styled avant-garde sought to break with convention, so that when Sergei Diaghilev presented his ballet *The Rite of Spring* in 1913, the odd costumes, peculiar dancing, and jarring music by **Igor Stravinsky** seemed to be an utter rejection of every element of classical ballet. The artists were often well ahead of their skeptical audiences, and the premiere performance of *The Rite of Spring* was famous for the mayhem that ensued among the proper bourgeois crowd.

Art

Romantic artists became fascinated with what they deemed to be "exotic," and leading painters traveled to North Africa and to the Middle East in search of subjects. Also, like their literary counterparts, many artists rejected the political order in their works. For example, **Eugène Delacroix's** (1798–1863) *Liberty Leading the People,* painted one year after the overthrow of Charles X, captures the stirring events of the revolution in the streets of Paris.

By the mid-century mark, **photography** was beginning to have a significant impact on painting while also serving as a new art form in its own right. One of the pioneers was **Louis Daguerre** (1789–1851), who in 1835, accidentally discovered that he could produce an image when he put an exposed plate in a chemical cupboard where mercury vapor was present. It still took him several years to find a way to fix the image, a process that received the name of **daguerreotype.** Photography would enter into the mainstream with the introduction of celluloid film, and in the 1880s, **George Eastman** introduced flexible film and the first box camera, which made photography into something far less expensive that could be enjoyed by the masses.

> **Romanticism in Prayer**
> **John Wesley** was an Anglican preacher who traveled across Great Britain and Ireland, preaching to villages, organizing small religious societies, and appointing leaders to continue to work for social change after his departure. This revival movement became known as **Methodism**—a classic example of the Romantic style applied to religion.

The development of photography made it increasingly clear to painters that there would be less demand for realistic landscapes and portraits. Some artists began to look to new subjects and became known as **realists**, as they sought to paint the world around them without any illusions. In part inspired by the revolutionary upheavals of 1848, **Gustave Courbet** (1819–1877) began to paint works like *The Stone-Breakers* that rejected the romantic traditions of the day and instead focused on showing the world of the peasants in all its grim reality. **Jean-François Millet** (1814–1875) is most famous for *The Sowers*, which shows hardscrabble peasants who seem, like the wheat, to be growing out of the earth. Millet was himself from the peasant class and refused to paint them in an idealistic manner, nor did he seek to show that hard labor brought happiness. The artist **Honoré Daumier** (1808–1879) is best known for his cartoons that lifted the curtain on the corrupt politicians and legal system of the July Monarchy. In his later years, he turned to painting and sculpture, with one of his most famous works being *The Third Class Carriage*, focusing on a group of French peasants, their faces creased with the legacy of their difficult lives, sitting in the obviously uncomfortable setting of the railcar.

Realism in Literature

Realism was also an important movement in literature. Just as realist painters wanted to show the world the actual conditions of those on the bottom of the social order, so too did novelists like **Charles Dickens** (1812–1870), who used his brief experience in a blacking factory as the basis for his critique of industrialized society. In *Hard Times*, the noble workingman Stephen Blackpool struggles against forces over which he has no control. He can't divorce his drunken wife and marry his beloved Rachael because divorce is available only to the wealthy. Meanwhile, he's falsely accused of being a troublemaker at work and finds himself unable to make a living. Such works, although at times a shade maudlin, introduced many middle-class individuals in Great Britain to the hardships of working-class life.

Other realist authors focused on what they perceived to be the barrenness of middle-class domestic life and most notably the institution of marriage. One such writer was Mary Ann Evans (1819–1880), who wrote under the name **George Eliot**. In *Middlemarch*, her most important work, Eliot deals with English provincial life on the eve of the Great Reform Bill. Her main character, Dorothea Brooke, despite her own beauty, marries an unattractive older cleric named Casaubon in the failed hope that his scholarly ways will broaden her world. Although her second marriage, to Casaubon's young cousin, is a happy one, frustration still remains over her inability to realize her dream of improving the living conditions for their tenant farmers. Emma Bovary, the title character in **Gustave Flaubert's** (1821–1880) *Madame Bovary*, marries a mediocre village doctor only to find that reality is far different from the romantic notions of marriage she received from books. In search of excitement, she engages in a series of affairs, but the emptiness continues, and finally disappointment in love and financial failure lead her to commit suicide by taking arsenic. In **Leo Tolstoy's** (1828–1910) *Anna Karenina*, once again we have a beautiful but bored woman who engages in an affair that also meets with disastrous results.

History in Literature

Tolstoy's most acclaimed work, *War and Peace*, takes the grand events of Napoleon's 1812 invasion of Russia and reveals how ordinary people can get caught up in the swirl of events over which they have no control.

Tolstoy's fellow Russian, **Fyodor Dostoevsky** (1821–1881), was almost executed for his participation in an illegal political group, after which he was forced to spend 10 years in Siberia. The experience transformed him, pushing in a conservative direction both his politics and his interest in the psychological and moral obligations of man, an interest that was revealed in his classic novels, *Crime and Punishment* and *The Brothers Karamazov*.

Back in France, **Émile Zola** (1840–1902) found himself applying the social sciences to the novel. Using this "naturalistic" technique, he wrote a series of novels dealing with a family over several generations, showing how environment and heredity were the critical factors in explaining their moral and physical degeneration. Zola also defended Alfred Dreyfus from charges of treason in his open letter entitled *"J'accuse,"* which appeared on the front page of the French daily, *L'Aurore*.

Post-Realist Art: The Impressionists and Expressionists

Although some painters, such as **Édouard Manet** (1832–1883), were inspired by the realists, they wished to push their techniques in new directions. Manet's *Luncheon on the Grass* shows a rather peculiar picnic, with two fully clothed men and a nude woman. The work was in part startling to contemporaries because nudes were acceptable only if they were figures from classical mythology and not ordinary people. But besides the perplexing subject matter, Manet was changing the way we look at art. Dating back to the Renaissance and the introduction of single-point perspective, paintings served to open the window into another world. Now, however, Manet was inviting viewers to notice the surface of the canvas, something that was to be pivotal for the development of modern art.

Although Manet was a quiet man who was not looking to be controversial, he and other innovative artists of the day were to find themselves at the center of a controversy when they were not allowed to show their work at the official 1863 *Salon*, an annual public exhibition held in Paris. In response to the public outcry over the hanging committee's refusal to show these paintings, Napoleon III decided that the public should be given an opportunity to see them and make their own judgments, which led to the establishment of the **Salon des Refusés,** or "exhibition of the rejected."

Those artists who took the techniques of Manet are labeled **impressionists**, although the term was initially used as one of derision after a critic first used it in 1874 to blast a work by **Claude Monet** (1840–1926) entitled *Impression: Sunrise*. Instead of shying away from the label, painters embraced it, with the exception of Manet who refused to use it for his own work. Impressionists wanted to capture the shimmering effects of light, and to do this, they were the first to take their easels outdoors. They were aided in this desire to leave their studios by the invention of portable paint tubes. Monet would take the same theme, such as a haystack or the Cathedral of Rouen, and paint it at different times of day or different seasons to show how the impact of light would transform it. Although Monet is most famous for his landscapes, he didn't shy away from scenes of modern life, such as railroad stations. Other impressionists, like **Auguste Renoir** (1841–1919), captured everyday scenes such as couples flirting in a dance hall, or in the case of **Edgar Degas** (1834–1917), numerous works showing the behind-the-scenes world of the ballet.

By the end of the 1880s, impressionism, which had once seemed so revolutionary, had become widely accepted. Some artists, while acknowledging their debt to the impressionists, wanted to push things even further. **Paul Cézanne** (1839–1906) challenged traditional perspective, composition, and the use of color. His work had a great influence on 20th-century artists; he is therefore often referred to as the "father of modern art." Cézanne said that he wanted to make impressionism into "something solid and durable, like the art of the museums." Taking the forms of geometry that he believed were most commonly found in nature—the cylinder, sphere, and cone—he took the somewhat abstract technique used in his landscapes and applied it to numerous still lifes of fruit.

Cézanne became the inspiration for artists who would completely challenge the traditional three-dimensional picture frame. In fact, artists like Pablo Picasso said that Cézanne was his "one and only master." **Vincent Van Gogh** (1853–1890), on the other hand, influenced those 20th-century Expressionists who sought to put their deepest emotions on canvas. Van Gogh, a native of Holland, had a very brief 10-year career that ended by his tragic suicide. Although his dark early paintings, such as *The Potato Eaters*, reveal his deep sensitivity to those who were economically struggling, his style changed following a trip to Paris where he met a number of leading artists through his brother Theo's gallery. In Arles, in the south of France, he painted his most famous works, landscapes of sunflowers or cypress trees, using bright colors and broad brush strokes to provide them with a deep emotional intensity.

The Genius of Picasso

The most revolutionary artist of the 20th century was **Pablo Picasso**, who, with his nearly abstract *Les Demoiselles d'Avignon* (1907), made an irreparable break with the single-point perspective that had been central to Western art since the time of the Italian Renaissance. Later on, Picasso became famous as the co-founder (with Georges Braque) of cubism.

Painters such as the Norwegian **Edvard Munch** (1863–1944) also sought to reveal the emotions rather than portray the way things looked on the surface. In Vienna, one of the centers of the avant-garde movement, artists such as **Gustav Klimt** (1862–1918) saw themselves as rejecting the values of mass society and proceeded to find ways to shock their viewers through the vibrant use of color or by showing classical images in strange, unfamiliar ways. Munch's *The Scream* and Klimt's *The Kiss* are now two of the most notable works of Western art.

CED 7.6
New Imperialism: Motivations and Methods

The New Imperialism: Colonization of Africa and Asia

In the 1880s, the nations of Europe began an expansion into Africa and Asia that was unprecedented both for its speed and its scale. This period of conquest and the establishment of colonies is referred to as the **"new imperialism."** The term is used in part to separate the period from earlier periods of overseas conquest, such as the Spanish conquest of Central and South America, but also to denote the fundamental ways in which life was transformed in those regions that were now under the sway of Europeans.

- Breech-loading rifles, which allowed the user to fire from a prone position, offered a significant advantage over the muzzle loaders still in use by those Africans who had guns. Even greater firepower was provided by the introduction of rapid-fire weapons such as the Gatling gun.

- Steamships allowed for rapid transport across oceans without having to deal with the vagaries of wind power, and smaller steam-driven river boats allowed Europeans to penetrate into the heart of Africa. The construction of the Suez Canal, which was finished in 1869, significantly reduced the time it took to get to Asia.

- One of the most important technological developments for imperialism was the telegraph, which allowed for the exchange of messages between India and London over the course of a day—a dramatic decrease over the two years it took at the start of the century.

- The discovery in 1820 of quinine, a drug made from the bark of the cinchona tree, was an effective treatment for the great scourge of the tropics—malaria.

The new imperialism was built on a foundation of technological advances. Although technology was vital for the new imperialism, it would have made little difference without the various motivating factors that stirred Europeans to conquer foreign lands. One important factor was the search for profits that were assumed to be had from imperialism. With the establishment of higher tariff barriers in Europe in the last quarter of the century, nations began to look to colonies as potential free trade zones. Raw materials, such as the palm oil that was used as an industrial lubricant or precious metals such as gold and silver, led individuals to the African heartland.

Yet those imperialists who saw colonies as a source of unimaginable wealth were going to be disappointed, because many colonies lacked any economic value, or if they did, the extensive investments necessary to make them economically viable never arrived from Europe. The exception to this was India, where the British were able to extract enough wealth for it to be justifiably referred to as the "jewel in the crown."

Other motivating factors came from **social imperialists**, who viewed imperialism as a means of relieving certain domestic social problems such as overpopulation. This would also prove to be disappointing because, for example, in the case of Italy, those who left the country much preferred to go to the United States, rather than to an uncertain existence in the Italian colonies in East Africa.

Nationalism also played a major role in empire building. European states believed that the only way they could matter on a global scale would be through the establishment of colonies. For France, building an overseas empire was a way of showing it still mattered, even after its horrific defeat by the Prussians in 1870.

Religion also served as a motivating factor, and Christian missionaries were actually the first Europeans to penetrate central Africa. Some skeptics questioned the actual motivation behind the missionaries; a German political cartoon from the period shows an English preacher droning on while, behind a curtain, a businessman involves himself in the real business of the empire—financially squeezing the Africans.

Balance-of-power politics was perhaps the most significant reason for the acquisition of even unprofitable pieces of land. Nations wanted colonies so that other nations would not get them. Great Britain in particular, led by the adventurer **Cecil Rhodes**, attempted to gain colonial advantage from the Cape of Good Hope to Cairo.

In what has become known as the **"mad scramble"** for colonies, Europeans drew new borders that demonstrated their lack of concern for tribal and cultural differences with imperial territories. The Berlin conference ultimately set up rules for the establishment of colonies. Organized by Bismarck, nations had to prove that they established sufficient authority in a territory to protect existing rights, such as freedom of trade and transit. This set off the mad dash that left every square inch of Africa divided among the European powers, with the

Social Darwinism and the New Imperialism

Social Darwinism also influenced the new imperialism. There was a racist belief that white people were destined to have sovereignty over the peoples of Asia and Africa. Paintings would often show colonists with local children, the implied message being that all Africans were children who would benefit from the guidance of Europeans in the role of parents. Elements of this *noblesse oblige* can be found in Rudyard Kipling's (1865–1936) famous poem "The White Man's Burden," in which he writes that Europeans have a moral obligation to "bind your sons to exile/To serve your captives' need." The so-called moral imperative behind imperialism was also discussed at the **Berlin Conference** (1884–1885), ostensibly called to deal with the control of the Congo, where it was stated that one of the goals for the imperialist nations was "to care for the improvement of the conditions of their (the Africans') moral and material well-being and to help in suppressing slavery, and especially the slave trade."

exception of Ethiopia, which repelled an Italian invasion in 1896, and the small state of Liberia on the west coast of Africa, which remained independent as a result of its unique historical link to the United States.

British dominance over India began to take shape following the withdrawal of the French from the Indian subcontinent as a result of the Seven Years' War (1756–1763). As the 19th century continued, additional, formerly independent Indian territories fell under British control, with the last being the Punjab region in 1849. Following what the British refer to as the **"Indian Mutiny"** or **Sepoy Rebellion** of 1857, colonial control became more centralized with the establishment of an administrative structure to replace the British East India Company. By 1877, Prime Minister Disraeli went so far as to make Queen Victoria the Empress of India, thus flattering his queen while perhaps more importantly issuing a warning to the other European powers on the significance of India for Great Britain.

In China, Great Britain was the first European state to practice what is referred to as an **informal empire,** in which a state has significant influence over another nation's economy without actual territorial or political control. After fighting and losing a series of wars with assorted European powers in the second half of the century, China was forced to grant European states sovereign control over a series of treaty ports along the coast. In Southeast Asia, although Thailand was able to maintain its independence, the French seized control over **Indochina** with its vital rubber plantations.

Colonialist Violence

Violence was often a part of the colonial enterprise. The German explorer Carl Peters (1856–1914), whom Hitler admired, established a German colony in East Africa where he was referred to by the local population as the "man with blood on his hands." The most horrific example of colonial exploitation took place in the Belgian Congo. **King Leopold II** (r. 1876–1909), one of the pioneers in the scramble for Africa, personally established this massive colony many times the size of Belgium and expected the proceeds from this wealthy land to line his own pocket. Millions were enslaved, maimed, or killed in the crazed pursuit of profits. Eventually, there was an international outcry over these atrocities, including the publication of Mark Twain's sarcastic *King Leopold's Soliloquy*, forcing the king to concede control to the Belgian government, which corrected some of the worst abuses.

Other nations involved in colonialism in Asia included the Dutch, who controlled Indonesia, and the United States, which seized the Philippines in the aftermath of the **Spanish-American War**. Japan, which had imitated Britain and Germany in its economic transformation into an industrial power, would also mimic their taste for colonial expansion by seizing control over Korea in 1910 after the **Russo-Japanese War**.

Colonialism could also bring certain developments to the colonized nation. Again, the example of India stands out because here, the British made actual investments in infrastructure. Irrigation systems, railways, and cities were all byproducts of British rule. Concepts such as nationalism and political liberty, which were later to be utilized by colonized peoples as tools for their own liberation, were also European exports. It was those Africans and Asians who had the most contact with the West, often through study abroad in Europe, who were the most committed nationalists.

Views and Consequences of the New Imperialism

CED 7.7
Imperialism's Global Effects

In recent years, historians have asked whether imperialism was ever actually popular among the mass of population, and the question has not been fully answered. Newspaper editors, who enjoyed an increased readership in this age of growing literacy, apparently saw imperialism as a topic of interest to their readers because they filled their pages with colonial exploits. In Britain, the pro-imperial Primrose League had more than a million members, and in Germany, Italy, and France, similar organizations existed, although with far fewer members. In Great Britain, the Boer War (1899–1902) may have resulted in decreased popular support of the empire, although across Europe, the working class seemed to have little interest in such affairs.

Although some hoped that the building of colonies would lead to a diminishing of tensions on the European continent, the opposite was the case. Rivalries among the European powers led to further imperial expansion, as in the case with British establishment of a protectorate over Egypt and the Suez Canal in 1882 in order to ensure Britain's dominance over India. Both the British and Russians were involved in what was referred to as the **"great game"**—a struggle over the territory of Afghanistan—because for the Russians, British control over this region would put Russia's recent expansion into Central Asia in jeopardy, whereas the British were once again concerned for the security of India.

Also, Britain and France almost went to war over Fashoda in the Sudan in 1898, and France and Germany twice almost went to war over Morocco in 1905 and 1911. One of the problems that helped bring about the First World War was the sense among leading German political and military figures that their country did not have a colonial empire commensurate with its position in Europe. The problem dated back to Bismarck's lack of interest in colonies, which he once displayed by pointing to a map of Europe and stating, "This is my Africa" to show his true object of fascination. Bismarck's lack of interest was opposed by those Germans who joined the Society for German Colonization (1884). When Kaiser Wilhelm II pushed Bismarck into retirement in 1890, one of his reasons for removing the chancellor was his lack of interest in colonies, something by which the new kaiser simply couldn't abide.

Finally, it must be remembered that the colonized non-European peoples were far from submissive during this period. Members of those colonized societies, often the ones who had become educated in Western philosophy and values, began leading resistance groups against the colonizers. The first and most significant of these movements was the **Indian Congress Party**, which was founded in 1885 and later became the principal driver of Indian independence from the British Empire. Other nationalist movements of the period include the **Zulu resistance** to the British (in southern Africa), the **Boxer Rebellion** (in China), and the **Meiji Restoration** (in Japan).

CHAPTER 6 TIMELINE

Year(s)	Event
1717	Abraham Darby smelts iron using partially burnt coal
1733	John Kay's flying shuttle
1764	James Hargreaves's spinning jenny
1769	Richard Arkwright patents the water frame
1774	James Watt patents the first steam engine
1776	Adam Smith's *An Inquiry into the Nature and Causes of the Wealth of Nations*
1779	First iron bridge completed in Shropshire, England
1785	Power loom invented by Edmund Cartwright
1789	Jeremy Bentham's *Introduction to the Principles of Morals and Legislation*
1790	Burke's *Reflections on the Revolution in France*
1798	Thomas Malthus's *Essay on Population*
1807	British Parliament votes for the end of the slave trade
1807	First passenger train line
1815	Napoleon escapes from Elba (March 15)
1815	Battle of Waterloo marks the end of the Hundred Days (May 15)
1815	Napoleon sent into exile on St. Helena
1817	David Ricardo's *Principles of Political Economy*
1819	Peterloo Massacre in Great Britain
1819	Combination Acts ban union activity
1820	Troppau Protocol (agreement among Eastern Great Powers to oppose revolutionary states)
1820	Rebellion in Spain put down with French support in 1824
1821	Beginning of Greek revolt
1821	Death of Napoleon
1823	Revolt in Naples
1824	Charles X becomes King of France
1825	Decembrist revolt in Russia
1829	George Stephenson invents the early locomotive, the Rocket
1830	Charles X issues July Ordinances
1830	July Revolution topples the last French Bourbon monarch
1830s	Cholera outbreak in Europe
1831	Charles Darwin begins five-year voyage that will take him to the Galápagos Islands
1832	Sadler Committee looks into child labor in Great Britain
1832	Great Reform Bill

Year(s)	Event
1833	Slavery banned within the British Empire
1833	Factory Act
1833	English Poor Law
1834	Robert Owen establishes the Grand National Consolidated Union
1835	David Friedrich Strauss's *The Life of Jesus Critically Examined*
1835	Daguerreotype (early form of photograph) invented
1837	Beginning of the reign of Queen Victoria
1838	Beginning of the Chartist movement
1839	First in a series of Opium Wars between Great Britain and China
1840	Napoleon's body brought back to France for reburial
1840	Joseph Proudhon writes the anarchist tract *What Is Property?*
1842	British gain control over Hong Kong
1846	Repeal of the Corn Laws
1846	Irish potato famine
1847	Liberia established as independent African republic
1848	*The Communist Manifesto* by Karl Marx and Friedrich Engels (February)
1848	Overthrow of Louis Philippe (February)
1848	Unrest in various German states (March)
1848	Nationalist revolts break out throughout Austrian Empire (beginning in March)
1848	Charles Albert of Savoy goes to war against Austria (March)
1848	Meeting of the Frankfurt Parliament (May)
1848	"June Days" uprising in Paris
1848	Louis Napoleon elected president of the Second Republic (December)
1851	Louis Napoleon stages coup against the Second Republic
1851	The Great Exhibition at the Crystal Palace in London
1852	Development of the safety elevator
1852	David Livingstone begins exploring the African interior
1852	Commodore Perry arrives in Japan
1852	Establishment of the Second Empire by Napoleon III
1854	Charles Dickens publishes *Hard Times*
1854	Start of the Crimean War
1856	Development of the Bessemer process for manufacturing steel
1856	Synthetic dyes developed
1857	Flaubert publishes his acclaimed novel, *Madame Bovary*
1857	Indian Rebellion
1858	Jews allowed to enter the British Parliament

Year(s)	Event
1859	Darwin's *On the Origin of Species*
1859	France and Piedmont-Sardinia go to war against Austria
1859	Garibaldi invades the Kingdom of Two Sicilies
1861	Victor Emmanuel II becomes the first King of Italy
1861	Alexander II emancipates the serfs
1863	Opening of the Salon des Refusés (art rejected by the jury of the Official Paris Salon)
1864	Establishment of the First International in London
1864	Prussia and Austria go to war against Denmark
1866	Italians seize Venetia from Austria
1866	Austro-Prussian War
1867	Establishment of the Austro-Hungarian Empire
1867	Alfred Nobel patents dynamite
1869	Suez Canal completed
1869	John Stuart Mill's *On Liberty*
1870	Doctrine of Papal Infallibility
1870	Rome becomes the capital of Italy
1870	Franco-Prussian War
1870	French Third Republic created
1871	Establishment of the German Empire
1871	End of the French Second Empire
1871	Paris Commune
1871	Darwin's *The Descent of Man*
1874	Typewriters invented
1874	Claude Monet paints *Impression: Sunrise*
1875	Constitution establishes the French Third Republic
1876	Serbia becomes independent
1876	Alexander Graham Bell's telephone
1877	Thomas Edison's phonograph
1877	Queen Victoria becomes empress of India
1877	Russo-Turkish War
1878	Congress of Berlin
1879	Dual Alliance between Germany and Austria-Hungary
1879	Thomas Edison invents the incandescent lamp
1881	Assassination of Alexander II
1882	Great Britain seizes control over the Egyptian government

Year(s)	Event
1884	Berlin Conference
1885	Introduction of the internal combustion engine
1885	First meeting of the Indian National Congress
1885	Friedrich Nietzsche's *Thus Spake Zarathustra*
1887	Reinsurance Treaty between Germany and Russia
1890	Kaiser Wilhelm II forces Bismarck to retire as Chancellor
1890	Germany fails to renew Reinsurance Treaty
1891	Pope Leo XIII issues *Rerum Novarum*
1894	Beginning of the Dreyfus Affair
1894	Russo-Japanese War
1894	Russian-French alliance
1896	Italians defeated by the Ethiopians at the Battle of Adowa
1897	First Zionist Congress meets in Switzerland
1898	Eduard Bernstein publishes *Evolutionary Socialism*
1898	Spanish-American War
1898	France and Britain almost go to war over incident at Fashoda
1899	Start of the Boer War
1900	Sigmund Freud's *The Interpretation of Dreams*
1901	Max Planck introduces quantum physics
1902	J. A. Hobson's *Imperialism: A Study*
1903	Emmeline Pankhurst forms the Women's Social and Political Union
1903	First successful airplane flight by the Wright brothers
1904	Herero War
1904	British-French entente (Entente Cordial)
1905	Revolution in Russia leads to granting of a Duma
1905	First Moroccan Crisis
1905	Separation of church and state in France
1906	*HMS Dreadnaught* launched
1907	British-Russian entente
1908	Henry Ford's Model T
1908	Austria-Hungary annexes Bosnia
1910	Madame Curie isolates radium
1911	Agadir Crisis in Morocco (a.k.a. Second Moroccan Crisis)
1913	Sergei Diaghilev revolutionizes ballet with *The Rite of Spring*
1913	Socialists become the largest political party in Germany

CHAPTER 6 KEY TERMS

The Age of Competing Ideologies

conservatism

Edmund Burke, *Reflections on the Revolution in France* (see also Ch. 5)

nationalism

liberalism

individual rights

Adam Smith, *An Inquiry into the Nature and Causes of the Wealth of Nations* (see also Ch. 5)

mercantilism

laissez-faire (see also Ch. 5)

Thomas Malthus, *Essay on Population*

David Ricardo, "Iron Law of Wages"

John Stuart Mill, *On Liberty, The Subjection of Women*

Harriet Taylor

Jeremy Bentham

utilitarianism

socialism

Henri de Saint-Simon

Charles Fourier

Robert Owen

utopian socialists

Political Restoration and Reform

Charles X

July Revolution

Carbonari

"Eastern Question"

Nicholas I

Decembrist revolt

Great Reform Bill

Poor Law of 1834

Factory Act of 1833

Corn Laws (eliminated in 1846)

The Revolutions of 1848

Revolutions of 1848

Emperor Francis Joseph

potato famine

national workshops

Louis Napoleon (Emperor Napoleon III)

June Days

Second Republic

Chartism

People's Charter of 1838

The Industrial Revolution

domestic system

Agricultural Revolution

manufacturing industries

Enclosure Acts

increase in capital

John Kay

James Hargreaves

spinning jenny

Richard Arkwright

water frame

steam engine

James Watt

smelt iron

Abraham Darby

railroads

Luddites

cooperative societies

Karl Marx and Friedrich Engels, *The Communist Manifesto*

Karl Marx, *Das Kapital*

communism

bourgeoisie and proletariat

First and Second International

The Age of National Unification

Florence Nightingale
Concert of Europe
Pope Pius IX
Risorgimento
Count Camillo di Cavour
Giuseppe Mazzini
Giuseppe Garibaldi
"red shirts"
Victor Emmanuel
Franco-Prussian War
Otto von Bismarck
"Blood and Iron"
Danish War
Seven Weeks' War
Franco-Prussian War
Ems dispatch
"Kulturkampf"
Third French Republic
Paris Commune
Great Reform Bill of 1832
Benjamin Disraeli
Second Reform Bill
William Gladstone
Queen Victoria
Tsar Alexander II
Sultan Abdul Mejid
"Young Turks"
Sultan Abdul Hamid II

The Second Industrial Revolution

Second Industrial Revolution
"Age of Steel"
Henry Bessemer, Bessemer process
William Siemens
electrical power
Suez Canal
Alfred Nobel
Marie Curie
Ernest Rutherford
Max Planck
Albert Einstein
Friedrich Nietzsche
Sigmund Freud
Louis Pasteur
Charles Darwin, *On the Origin of Species*,
The Descent of Man
"natural selection"
Herbert Spencer
"survival of the fittest"
Social Darwinism
Age of the Middle Class
anarchism
Joseph Proudhon
Edwin Chadwick

Social and Cultural Developments

papal infallibility

antisemitism

Dreyfus Affair

pogroms

Zionism

Theodore Hertzl

cult of domesticity

feminism

suffragists

Women's Social and Political Union

Emmeline Pankhurst

Romanticism

Jean-Jacques Rousseau, *Emile*

William Wordsworth

Victor Hugo

Percy Bysshe Shelley

Wolfgang von Goethe

Ludwig von Beethoven

Frederic Chopin

photography

George Eastman

realists

Gustave Courbet

Charles Dickens

Fyodor Dostoevsky

Emile Zola, *"J'accuse"*

impressionists

Claude Monet

Vincent van Gogh

Pablo Picasso

The New Imperialism

new imperialism

Cecil Rhodes

"mad scramble"

Berlin Conference of 1885

Sepoy Rebellion, or "Indian Mutiny"

Russo-Japanese War

King Leopold II

CHAPTER 6 REVIEW QUESTIONS

Try these questions to assess how well you understood and retained the information covered in the chapter. Answers and explanations are in Chapter 8.

Questions 1 through 4 refer to the following.

CHRONOLOGICAL INDEX OF PATENTS APPLIED FOR AND PATENTS GRANTED

1. John Henry, of Friday Street, in the city of London, and Buchanan Street, Glasgow, in the County of Lanark, Manufacturer, for an invention for—"Improvements for weaving fabrics for ladies' dresses and petticoats."

    Provisional protection only.

2. James Murphy, of Newport, in the County of Monmouthshire, Civil Engineer, for an invention for—"Improvements in wheels used on railways."

    Complete specification: Letters Patent sealed.

3. Louis Joseph Arsène Brun, of Paris, in the Empire of France, Merchant, for an invention for—"Improvements in instruments for measuring angles, applicable to nautical and other purposes."

    Letters Patent sealed.

4. George Gorle, of Handsworth, in the County of Stafford, Plumber, for an invention for—"A new or improved service box for water-closets."

    Patent Office, London, England, 1858.

1 ☐ Mark for Review

The index implies which of the following?

(A) Great Britain's primacy in nineteenth-century European manufacturing

(B) The desire of English people to possess nice things

(C) A growth in the belief that technology would improve English life

(D) An increasingly heavy and unnecessary national bureaucracy

2 ☐ Mark for Review

The reference to "ladies' dresses and petticoats" serves to remind the reader that

(A) the Victorian era featured restrictive women's clothing

(B) women of the era demanded better-manufactured dresses

(C) layers of clothing kept women warm in the winter

(D) women were prohibited from creating their own clothing

3 ☐ Mark for Review

The source does NOT support which of the following conclusions about England in the mid-nineteenth century?

Ⓐ That the merchant class was supported

Ⓑ That entrepreneurship was encouraged

Ⓒ That government regulation was seen as necessary to the public good

Ⓓ That the sciences were more important than the liberal arts

4 ☐ Mark for Review

The Industrial Revolution, out of which grew these patents, did NOT benefit from the presence of which of the following unique traits?

Ⓐ A countrywide network of rivers and canals

Ⓑ Deposits of coal in the north of England

Ⓒ A tradition of peasant farming

Ⓓ A system of centralized banking that was willing to make loans

Questions 5 through 9 refer to the following.

"The history of every age proves that no people can attain a high degree of intelligence and morality unless its feeling of nationality is strongly developed. This noteworthy fact is an inevitable consequence of the laws that rule human nature.... Therefore, if we so ardently desire the emancipation of Italy—if we declare that in the face of this great question all the petty questions that divide us must be silenced—it is not only that we may see our country glorious and powerful but that above all we may elevate her in intelligence and moral development up to the plane of the most civilized nations.... This union we preach with such ardor is not so difficult to obtain as one might suppose if one judged only by exterior appearances or if one were preoccupied with our unhappy divisions. Nationalism has become general; it grows daily; and it has already grown strong enough to keep all parts of Italy united despite the differences that distinguish them."

Source: Count Cavour, 1846

5 ☐ Mark for Review

One way that the northern Italian nationalist movement differed from the southern Italian nationalist movement was the fact that

Ⓐ the northern movement relied upon the support of Austria, whereas the southern movement relied upon the power of the papal states

Ⓑ the northern movement had been attempting to unite Switzerland, but the southern movement hadn't regarded it as a proper part of Italy

Ⓒ the northern movement was mostly religious, but the southern movement was mostly financial

Ⓓ the northern movement was engineered by elite diplomatic action, but the southern movement was a primarily populist movement

6 ☐ Mark for Review

The process of national unification in Italy resembled the process of national unification in Germany in that both

Ⓐ trampled on the rights of minorities

Ⓑ provoked unnecessary wars to build a sense of unity in the people

Ⓒ increased tax rates upon the wealthiest citizens

Ⓓ tried to settle disputes with neighboring countries

7 ☐ Mark for Review

To achieve unification, Count Cavour manipulated and eventually co-opted which southern Italian revolutionary figure?

(A) Giuseppe Mazzini

(B) Giordano Bruno

(C) Giuseppe Garibaldi

(D) Benito Mussolini

8 ☐ Mark for Review

Nationalism did NOT necessarily rely upon a shared

(A) folklore

(B) custom

(C) language

(D) religion

9 ☐ Mark for Review

The nationalist movement weakened what other intellectual movement of the nineteenth century?

(A) Socialism

(B) Liberalism

(C) Anarchism

(D) Capitalism

Questions 10 through 14 refer to the following.

Mr. Matthew Crabtree, called in; and Examined.

"What age are you? — Twenty-two.

What is your occupation? — A blanket manufacturer.

Have you ever been employed in a factory? — Yes.

At what age did you first go to work in one? — Eight.

How long did you continue in that occupation? — Four years.

Will you state the hours of labour at the period when you first went to the factory, in ordinary times? — From 6 in the morning to 8 at night.

Fourteen hours? — Yes.

With what intervals for refreshment and rest? — An hour at noon.

When trade was brisk what were your hours? — From 5 in the morning to 9 in the evening.

Sixteen hours? — Yes.

With what intervals at dinner? — An hour.

How far did you live from the mill? — About two miles.

Was there any time allowed for you to get your breakfast in the mill? — No.

Did you take it before you left your home? — Generally.

During those long hours of labour could you be punctual; how did you awake? — I seldom did awake spontaneously; I was most generally awoke or lifted out of bed, sometimes asleep, by my parents.

Were you always in time? — No.

What was the consequence if you had been too late? — I was most commonly beaten.

Severely? — Very severely, I thought.

In those mills is chastisement towards the latter part of the day going on perpetually? — Perpetually.

So that you can hardly be in a mill without hearing constant crying? — Never an hour, I believe.

Do you think that if the overlooker were naturally a humane person it would still be found necessary for him to beat the children, in order to keep up their attention and vigilance at the termination of those extraordinary days of labour? — Yes; the machine turns off a regular quantity of cardings, and of course, they must keep as regularly to their work the whole of the day; they must keep with the machine, and therefore however humane the slubber may be, as he must keep up with the machine or be found fault with, he spurs the children to keep up also by various means but that which he commonly resorts to is to strap them when they become drowsy.

At the time when you were beaten for not keeping up with your work, were you anxious to have done it if you possibly could? — Yes; the dread of being beaten if we could not keep up with our work was a sufficient impulse to keep us to it if we could.

When you got home at night after this labour, did you feel much fatigued? — Very much so.

Had you any time to be with your parents, and to receive instruction from them? — No.

What did you do? — All that we did when we got home was to get the little bit of supper that was provided for us and go to bed immediately. If the supper had not been ready directly, we should have gone to sleep while it was preparing.

Did you not, as a child, feel it a very grievous hardship to be roused so soon in the morning? — I did.

Were the rest of the children similarly circumstanced? — Yes, all of them; but they were not all of them so far from their work as I was.

And if you had been too late you were under the apprehension of being cruelly beaten? — I generally was beaten when I happened to be too late; and when I got up in the morning the apprehension of that was so great, that I used to run, and cry all the way as I went to the mill."

Source: Transcript of an interview with Matthew Crabtree, given to the Sadler Committee, England, 1832

10 ⬚ Mark for Review

The themes in this passage are most similar to the themes in the fiction of

Ⓐ Lewis Carroll

Ⓑ Charles Dickens

Ⓒ Jane Austen

Ⓓ William Shakespeare

11 ⬚ Mark for Review

The argument against child labor was NOT weakened by which of the following facts?

Ⓐ Many children had also worked in agricultural jobs before the Industrial Revolution.

Ⓑ A child's income was often essential to the family's survival.

Ⓒ Textile mills often forced long hours and inhumane conditions upon the children employed.

Ⓓ Anglican ministers often believed that a child learned the value of effort and discipline through work.

12 ⬚ Mark for Review

One problem that children did NOT encounter in early-nineteenth-century English factories was

Ⓐ inadequate education

Ⓑ unfair contracts

Ⓒ poor health

Ⓓ sexual abuse

13 ⬚ Mark for Review

The socioeconomic and political inequalities of English industrial life were addressed by all of the following EXCEPT

Ⓐ Chartism

Ⓑ the Reform Act of 1867

Ⓒ the Corn Laws

Ⓓ Utilitarianism

14 ⬚ Mark for Review

The statement "if the overlooker were naturally a humane person" indicates that

Ⓐ by the time of the interview, establishing a more just civil society had become a concern for English society

Ⓑ the rationality of the Enlightenment had led to concern for the welfare of the downtrodden

Ⓒ the radicalism and violence of the French Revolution resulted in excessive attention to the poor

Ⓓ England's refusal to buckle under Napoleon's embargo had a lasting effect upon how the English people viewed domestic manufacturing

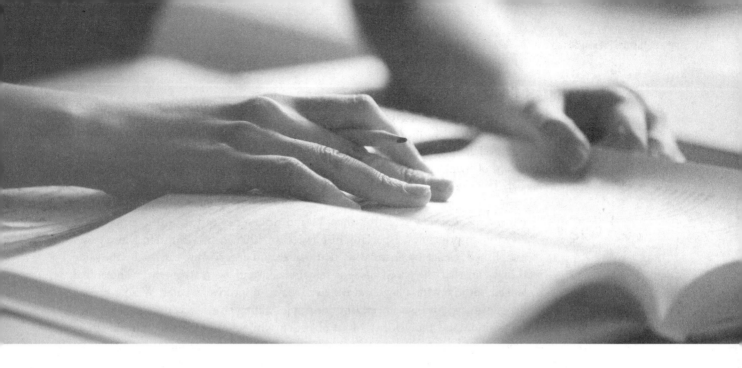

Chapter 7
Units 8–9:
Global Wars to
Globalization
(c. 1914–Present)

THINGS FALL APART

Until the 20th century, European philosophers generally believed that humankind was progressing toward a final form. Using logic, these thinkers reasoned that societies could be made perfect, especially through scientific progress. After all, the tools of science had produced a higher standard of living than had been known previously in Europe. Much of this faith in science was based on the discoveries of Isaac Newton, published over 200 years earlier.

CED 8.10
20th-Century Cultural, Intellectual, and Artistic Developments

However, some new scientific theories and discoveries called into question these Newtonian principles, especially in physics. In 1905, Albert Einstein flipped over established science by postulating that matter and energy were essentially the same thing, and that the speed of light remains constant no matter what. These challenged both Newton's laws and Maxwell's laws, respectively. Later, Werner Heisenberg advanced his own uncertainty principle, stating that it was impossible to measure both the position and the velocity of an object. Erwin Schrödinger used an imaginary experiment with a dead cat to illustrate how basic misinterpretations of quantum mechanics can result in ludicrous real-life outcomes. And Niels Bohr developed modern atomic theory, in which electrons circled a nucleus of an atom in different, unique orbits.

This change shattered people's faith in science and, in turn, themselves. There was a sense that nothing could be known for certain. The old methods of religion began to be challenged once again. In art, Georges Braque and Pablo Picasso, both painters trained in classic portrait style, shifted to Cubism, a style of painting that lacked a single perspective and appeared bizarrely broken.

This all continued to intensify during World War I. Europe was shellshocked, quite literally and emotionally. The population couldn't quite believe how the war had not only escalated but persisted across four horrific years of carnage.

THE FIRST WORLD WAR (1914–1918)

CED 8.2
World War I

Causes of the War

Although the Versailles Treaty, which marked the end of the First World War, stated emphatically that the Germans and their allies were responsible for starting the war, the reality is a bit more complicated. The following are some of the major reasons why Europe exploded in 1914, setting the stage for a conflict that would shatter the very foundations of the continent.

Political and Social Tensions in Europe

The first decade of the 20th century witnessed a number of political and social crises around Europe that may have led politicians to willingly pursue a foreign war, with the hope that it would divert attention from domestic issues.

Great Britain and Ireland

Great Britain faced the contentious issue of Ireland, which threatened to explode as Nationalist forces began to press for independence (a movement called **Home Rule,** with roots dating back to the 1860s), while their political opposites, the Unionists, expressed their increasingly determined desire to remain a part of Great Britain. These parties were associated with religious communities: the Nationalists were overwhelmingly Catholic, and hoped to break away from what they viewed as Protestant rule, while Unionists tended to be Protestant. Leading into World War I, Unionism grew around Protestant areas in the north of Ireland, most significantly in the province of Ulster. Great Britain was also shaken, as was France, by a growing number of labor conflicts that resulted from the overall stagnation of wages during this period.

France

In France, the Third Republic was in crisis over the **Dreyfus Affair,** which began in 1894 and involved a Jewish officer who was falsely accused of telling military secrets to the Germans. The incident revealed the virulence of French **antisemitism** while also showing the extent to which many in France despised the very idea of a republican form of government.

The "Affair" was also tied to another contentious issue splitting the French public—the question concerning the proper role of the Catholic Church in a democratic French state. Increasingly, by the end of the century, the individuals who governed France were openly hostile to the Catholic Church, which they considered to be anti-republican. These politicians worked to exclude the Church from French life by enacting laws such as one that eliminated the Church from primary and secondary education.

Russia

Russia rang in the 20th century with the **Russo-Japanese War** in 1904, which, when Russia lost once again, revealed the complete bankruptcy of the Tsarist state. This led to a revolution in the following year. Initially, the goal of the revolution was met—the creation of the **Duma,** or parliament—that would transform Russia into a constitutional monarchy. Tsar **Nicholas II** agreed to rule in conjunction with the Duma. Throughout the following years, the Tsarist regime recovered and once again functioned primarily as an unwieldy autocracy.

Germany and Austria-Hungary

The other imperial regimes, Germany and Austria-Hungary, also saw war as a possible means of escaping from a relatively bleak domestic political situation. In Germany, worker agitation was on the rise, and the kaiser and his inner circle dreaded the possibility of a Socialist revolution, although the threat did not really exist.

Austria-Hungary had to deal with its constant, seemingly insurmountable nationality problems. In the Hungarian part of the empire, the process of "Magyarization," the mandatory dominance of the Magyar language and culture, created great hostility among the other nationalities, who in fact made up the majority of the Hungarian population. As the Austro-Hungarian Empire lumbered from one crisis to the next, it appeared as though the union's demise was always just around the corner.

Entangling Alliances

In 1879, Bismarck created the **Dual Alliance**, a military treaty with the Austro-Hungarians. However, because Bismarck correctly foresaw that it would be fatal for Germany to face a war on two fronts, he signed the **Reinsurance Treaty** with Russia in 1887 in order to make it clear that the treaty with Austria-Hungary was purely defensive in nature and not meant to show possible hostile intent toward Russia. Unfortunately, once Kaiser Wilhelm II (r. 1888–1918), an inordinately pigheaded man, pushed Bismarck out of office, the Russians began to view the Germans with increased trepidation, particularly because Wilhelm didn't bother to renew the Reinsurance Treaty in 1890.

While France had remained diplomatically isolated after 1870, Germany's diplomatic missteps led the Russians to join the French in a military treaty that pledged that the two countries would fight together in the event of an attack on either state by the Germans. German fears of being encircled were enhanced when in 1904 Great Britain signed an **Entente Cordiale** with France, resolving certain contentious colonial issues. German fears were further increased when three years later Great Britain signed another entente with the Russians. This is why during the First World War, Britain, France, and Russia were referred to as the **Triple Entente.**

Increased Militarization

One of the worst decisions that the kaiser and his officers made was to build a high seas fleet in 1897. Britain and Germany were not necessarily natural enemies, with the British readily accepting the fact that Germany possessed the most powerful army on the continent. Navies, however, were a completely different matter for the British because they saw their fleet as their only means to protect their vast colonial empire. The British were particularly horrified given that the Germans took advantage of a revolution in battleship design and built powerful new ships known as dreadnoughts, thus making the British fleet suddenly obsolete. The rivalry between Great Britain and Germany now became far more openly hostile, as each side scrambled to enhance its fleets. In the end, navies were not particularly significant in the outcome of the First World War; the Battle of Jutland in 1916 was the only major naval battle of the war. Across Europe, the production of vast stores of weapons by the Great Powers dramatically increased tensions and played a critical role in the advent of the war.

Crisis in the Balkans

The immediate crisis that led to the war occurred on June 28, 1914, in Sarajevo, the capital of Bosnia. There, **Archduke Franz Ferdinand**, heir-presumptive to the Austrian and Hungarian thrones, was assassinated. Ferdinand was murdered by a Bosnian Serb who wanted to see Bosnia become part of an enlarged Serbian state.

The crisis in the Balkans had brought Europe to the brink of war in 1908, following the annexation of Bosnia and Herzegovina, previously Ottoman territories, by Austria-Hungary. The weakness of the Ottoman state allowed Bosnia and Herzegovina to be taken away from it. The Austro-Hungarians annexed these territories, not because they wanted more Serbs within their empire, but because they feared the lands would be taken by the Serbian state, a national state that the Austro-Hungarians saw as the greatest threat to their own survival as a multinational empire. Gavrilo Princip (1895–1914), the Archduke's assassin, had operated with the full cooperation of the **Black Hand**, a secret Serbian nationalist group with strong ties to Serbian officials in both the government and the army. Seeing that Serbian authorities were tied to the bloodshed, the Austrians issued an ultimatum that was clearly designed to provoke a Serbian refusal and achieve what the Austrians truly wanted—war with the Serbian state.

Europe on the Eve of World War I

The Course of the War

On July 28, 1914, Austria-Hungary declared war against Serbia, knowing that it risked setting off a larger European conflict. Russia had promised to protect the Serbs, but despite this pact, the Austro-Hungarians felt that they had to take the risk, or their multinational empire would collapse. Additionally, Austria-Hungary had the backing of Germany, the "blank check," which bears significant responsibility for the start of the war because it was the one power that could have possibly restrained the Austro-Hungarians from taking such an aggressive stance.

As a precautionary measure, Russia responded to the Austro-Hungarian declaration on Serbia by beginning the process of mobilization. Germany demanded that Russia stop the process, which the Russians refused to do, in part because they knew that their own mobilization would take much longer than that of the Germans. They also feared that if the war spread beyond just the struggle between Austria-Hungary and Serbia, they could be caught unprepared. The Germans, seeing the continuing of Russian mobilization, decided that they had to declare war on the Russians, which they did on August 1. The whole net of entangling alliances began to fall into place as France started to mobilize on that same day, which led the Germans to respond with a declaration of war on the French.

When the shelling began in August 1914, there was tremendous enthusiasm among the citizens of the combatant nations. To their great discredit, the parties of the Second International, which for years had claimed that they would not support a capitalist European war and spoke glowingly of international brotherhood, voted in each of their respective nations to support the war effort. One of the few Socialists who spoke out against the war was the idealistic leader of the French Socialist Party, **Jean Jaurès** (1859–1914). He was shot on the eve of the war by a fanatical French nationalist who hated Jaurès's pacifist posture. French Socialist leaders attended his funeral and on the same day voted in the Chamber of Deputies to support the government in the war with Germany and Austria-Hungary.

Part of the enthusiasm for war stemmed from the misbegotten belief that the struggle would be a short one. This premise was based on observations made from such admittedly quick conflicts as the **Austro-Prussian War** (1866) and the **Franco-Prussian War** (1870), both of which lasted only a matter of weeks. Unfortunately, the decades following those conflicts had witnessed the rise of new weapons that favored soldiers on the defensive, such as machine guns, barbed wire, land mines, and more powerful artillery shells, all of which created the eventual stalemate on the western front. Even the introduction of airplanes possibly made the war a more defensive affair because the planes were used for spotting the enemy's positions, making it harder to stage surprise offensives. Also, the economic expansion, industrial strength, and national wealth wrought by the Second Industrial Revolution allowed the participants to stay in the war much longer than before.

The Germans began the war by attempting to implement the **Schlieffen Plan**, which relied on a rapid advance through northern France, with the expectation that France would be knocked out of the war in six short weeks, allowing Germany's military power to be transported by rail to the east where it would be used to defeat the Russians. The German plan required the invasion of Belgium, a nation created in 1830 with the promise that its neutrality would be guaranteed by the major European powers. The German sweep through Belgium, which broke this guarantee, brought Great Britain into the war on the side of the French and Russians. The brutal German occupation of the small nation inflamed public opinion in the United States.

The German plan had succeeded in the early weeks of the war, although, with hindsight, the Belgians' spirited defense would prove very costly to the Germans, who were operating on a strict timetable. By the first week of September, German troops had threatened Paris, leading the French government to flee the capital. After the Germans crossed the Marne river, a French army under General Joffre (1852–1931) counterattacked and stopped the Germans at what became known as the **First Battle of the Marne**. For the remainder of the fall season, the various armies to the northern coast of Flanders made a mad scramble to see if either side could be outflanked. By the first winter of the war, both sides settled down to what now looked like a much longer contest. Both sides would hold positions that would remain virtually unchanged for the next three years.

Although everyone expected the war to be a glorious affair, trench warfare proved to be anything but glamorous. At first, the trenches were just rapidly dug ditches, but as the stalemate continued, huge networks of defensive fortifications were built. Life in the trenches was a series of horrors as the men had to deal with rats chewing on corpses, noise from artillery, and extreme boredom as the war dragged way past the time that soldiers had expected to be heading home. The soldiers were fairly well protected in their trenches, but unfortunately, both sides insisted on periodically sending their soldiers "over the top" into unoccupied zones to stage assaults on enemy trenches. These excursions often became little more than suicide missions, as soldiers got caught on the barbed wire or found that their artillery did little to break the fighting spirit of the opposing side.

The Horrors of Modern Warfare

In early 1915, **poison gas** began to be used by both sides. The Second Industrial Revolution had unleashed a new weapon on the battlefield, and while the introduction of gas masks cut down on the losses from these gases, it was another sign that modern warfare was an increasingly inhumane affair.

The war in the east was rather different from that in the west. At first, the Russians met with success against the Austro-Hungarians, but as the fighting began to stalemate in the west, German forces shifted to the east, where they began to pile up victories against the brave but poorly equipped Russians. The eastern front never became bogged down with trenches like in the west, in part because the huge size of the theater of war made it much easier to maneuver.

Attempting to break the stalemate in the east, the British decided to launch an attack on Türkiye, which had entered the war on the side of the central powers. **Winston Churchill** (1874–1965), who at the time was the First Lord of the Admiralty, organized the plan, which was such a disaster that it almost led to the complete obliteration of his political career. Churchill reasoned that knocking the Turks out of the war would allow the British to send supplies to the hard-pressed Russians through the Black Sea. In April 1915, five divisions landed on the beach of **Gallipoli**. Unfortunately for the soldiers, who were for the most part from Australia and New Zealand, the Turks were well dug in, and the attack failed. By January, the British withdrew after suffering withering losses.

The British were not the only ones who sought the pivotal breakthrough that would end the stalemate. In 1916, the Germans decided to launch a massive offensive against the French fortress of **Verdun**, a fortress that France would have to defend at all costs or risk creating a disaster in French public opinion. The Germans organized a huge number of artillery pieces, including some "Big Bertha" guns that fired shells weighing more than a ton. While it appeared as though the Germans might take the fortress, the French were able to put up a spirited defense under **General Philippe Pétain** (1856–1951). He survived the battle to later become the disgraced leader of the defeated Vichy French state following the German victory in 1940. While the Germans hoped to bleed France dry by attacking Verdun, in the end, both sides together lost 600,000 troops in one of the most costly battles of the war. The French and British, however, learned little from the failure of the German offensive. Each side was convinced that it held the secret to breaking the stalemate, and over the next year, both Entente powers launched wasteful and ineffective offensives, such as the **Battle of the Somme** and the **Battle of Passchendaele**, in an attempt to break the German lines.

THE END OF THE WAR

The year 1917 turned out to be the critical turning point in the war. The war in the eastern front came to a close as Russia became embroiled in revolution, and by December 1917, the leaders of the new Bolshevik state sued Germany for peace. For the Germans, this looked like it could be the turning point, enabling them to focus all their forces on breaking the impasse in the west. This German advantage was never to occur because of the entry of the United States into the war on April 6, 1917, a result of Germany's policy of unrestricted submarine warfare and the ill-considered **Zimmermann Telegram**, which was a secret note sent from Germany to Mexico asking for Mexico's support if the United States entered the war. In return, Germany promised to return to Mexico parts of the U.S. that had been sold off nearly a century earlier.

The unrestricted submarine warfare was just as influential in the U.S. decision to enter the war. In 1915, Germany declared that the waters around Great Britain were a war zone and warned that they would sink any ship—either British vessels or those from neutral lands—that tried to enter into British ports. Although this policy may appear to have been inhumane, at that time, the British were blockading German ports, but because of their powerful surface fleet, they did not have to rely on using submarines to indiscriminately sink ships. In May 1915, a German U-boat sank the *Lusitania,* a British passenger ship, stirring tremendous anger in the United States, from which 120 of the ship's passengers hailed. As a result of an American warning, the Germans agreed to end their attacks on neutral shipping, but as the war continued to drag on, the Germans decided in early 1917 to resume the practice.

Although it would take roughly a year for the Americans to make an impact in the war, their entry turned out to be a decisive factor. The Germans decided in 1918 that they had to move quickly if they hoped to achieve victory before the Americans could send in large numbers of fresh troops. Beginning in March, the Germans decided to gamble everything on victory. For four months, German troops met with the kind of success they had enjoyed in the first months of the war. Paris was once again evacuated, but Germany lacked the soldiers and raw materials to exploit its initial victory. By the summer, large numbers of Americans played a critical role in blocking any further German advance. By August, the German offensive was turning into a retreat, as Germany increasingly revealed how absolutely exhausted it was from the fighting.

After realizing that there was little it could do to block the Entente powers from marching all the way to Berlin, the German high command informed the kaiser that Germany had to sue for peace. A new German government, led by **Prince Max von Baden** (1867–1929), a man known for his moderate political views, contacted the American President **Woodrow Wilson** (1856–1924) and asked for an armistice that would be based on Wilson's **Fourteen Points**— an idealistic document that sought to reduce future tensions between nations by maintaining free trade and putting a stop to secret negotiations. Events in Germany, however, were spiraling out of control, and throughout November, soldiers and workers began to form soviets, or councils, and to demand that these loosely organized political debating societies be given authority to rule the state. Fearing that Germany would follow Russia's example and undergo a Bolshevik Revolution, the kaiser was convinced to abdicate, leading to the creation of a republic, which was empowered for the signing of the armistice that brought the war to a close on November 11, 1918.

The War on the Home Front

The First World War was the first armed struggle to witness the complete mobilization of society at large. This was total war—something that would be experienced again during the Second World War—in that no segment of the population within any of the participating nations could avoid its impact.

Total War
World War I was history's first total war, in which all of society was mobilized and affected by the war effort.

Once people realized that their initial expectation of a quick war was wrong, political leaders began to understand that they would have to mobilize all national resources. The war, therefore, was a major contributing factor to the increased role that government played in the 20th century. All aspects of the economy became regulated to support the war effort, including price controls, the banning of strikes, rationing, and the planned use of national resources such as coal. In Great Britain, the government regulated pub hours, ensuring that they closed in the afternoon to prevent factory workers from staggering back to work drunk.

Governments also began to play a larger role in trying to manipulate public opinion. Censorship became a basic task for all governments. They read and censored the letters soldiers sent home to shield the public from the full extent of the horrors of trench warfare. The governments believed that if the people realized the true nature of the war, support for it would rapidly diminish. Governments also set up **propaganda** offices to create films and posters to help boost morale. One reason so many Germans were later willing to believe Hitler's claims that Germany had not lost the war on the battlefield but had been "stabbed in the back" by Jews and other so-called enemies of the German people was that they had been told by their government, up until the day that Germany surrendered, that all was going well at the front and that victory was just around the corner.

The Versailles Treaty and the Costs of the War

It is impossible to determine a precise count of the human costs of the war. Around 9 million men lost their lives in battle, and approximately 23 million more were wounded. Many men who came home from the front were permanently affected by gas. Germany suffered about 6 million casualties (killed and wounded combined). France's losses were 5.5 million, proportionally much greater than Germany's losses, as France's prewar population had been less than two-thirds that of Germany's. Very few French families escaped losing a loved one, and today, if you travel to France, you'll find a memorial in every town to those lost in the war. Incredibly, the loss of life from the war was soon dwarfed by an outbreak of **influenza**, which claimed an estimated 30 million lives worldwide.

Besides the loss of lives, the economic costs of the war were unprecedented. Hundreds of towns and villages in France and Belgium were destroyed, and even today, occasionally a Belgian farmer is killed while plowing over an unexploded shell dating back to the trench wars in Flanders fields. Economically, both victors and vanquished were shattered. The nations of Europe, which had been the creditors to the rest of the world, were now heavily in debt to the United States, the only participant that still had a fully functioning economy. After the war, the Carnegie Endowment for International Peace attempted to discern the war's actual cost and estimated a figure of $338 billion. The wealth accumulated from the unprecedented economic growth of the Second Industrial Revolution dissipated in a matter of five years.

The terrible human and economic costs of the war must be considered when looking at the negotiations marking the end of the conflict. Five separate settlements were reached at the peace conference that took place in Paris. The first and most famous of them was the **Treaty of Versailles**, signed on June 28, 1919, in the Hall of Mirrors, the same place that the German Empire had been declared back in 1871. This event witnessed several competing visions on how to reshape the postwar world.

War and Civil Rights

War has a way of quickening long-term trends. In the United States, the Second World War helped pave the way for the civil rights movement, and the First World War helped bring about the greater emancipation of women. Prior to the war, Great Britain saw an expanding female suffrage movement. The Women's Social and Political Union, better known as the **suffragettes**, under the leadership of **Emmeline Pankhurst** (1858–1928), organized a militant campaign to win the vote. The suffragettes disturbed political meetings, destroyed stained-glass windows in historical churches, and set fires to draw attention to their cause. Once the war began, the suffragettes supported the war effort and encouraged women to do their share for the nation. By the end of the war, more than 5 million British women were employed, many in dangerous jobs, such as those in munitions factories. At the end of the war, British women were rewarded for their contribution to victory by being granted the **right to vote** in 1918. At the same time, in Germany, the Weimar Republic granted complete female suffrage as well.

Wilsonian Idealism

Woodrow Wilson is known for his political and diplomatic optimism. Perhaps the best example of this is the League of Nations, which was based on his hope for international cooperation and harmony.

CED 8.4

Versailles Conference and Peace Settlement

- Wilson wanted to reshape the world on the basis of the principles outlined in his **Fourteen Points**, a peace that would allow for national self-determination and an international body, the **League of Nations**, that would work to settle disputes between nations. Yet it was easy for an American president to be conciliatory, particularly because none of the fighting had taken place on American soil, and the loss of American lives, though significant, paled beside that of France and Great Britain.

- The French Premier, **Georges Clemenceau** (1841–1929), represented a completely different outlook from Wilson's. No nation had suffered during the war more than France, and Clemenceau had to satisfy a French public that wanted to ensure that Germany would never again be a threat.

- The third major participant, the British Prime Minister **David Lloyd-George** (1863–1945), while not as intransigent as Clemenceau, also wanted to see Germany punished. England was, as usual, interested in naval superiority and colonies. In the end, the treaty represented the triumph of Clemenceau's position over Wilson's.

To justify the demand for German payment of reparations, the victorious allies included Article 231 in the final treaty, which forced Germany to accept all responsibility for the outbreak of the war on behalf of itself and its allies. Although Germany may have had an additional measure of blame, all the nations of Europe bore some guilt, so Article 231 was quite unfair. Germany also had to pay a huge reparation sum of 132 billion gold marks to the Entente powers. Other clauses of the treaty included the return of **Alsace-Lorraine** to France and the occupation of French troops in those parts of Germany on the western bank of the Rhine and a strip of land on the right bank. These territories, while still German, were to remain demilitarized. France would maintain economic control over the coal and iron mines of the Saar border region for 15 years. Additionally, Germany was to have an army of no more than 100,000 men, was banned from having an air force, and could maintain only a tiny navy to protect its coastal waters.

Other treaties signed in Paris in 1919 reordered the map of Europe. With the demise of the Austro-Hungarian Empire and the reduction in size of Germany, new nations were recreated in central Europe.

Middle East and Africa Post–World War I

One place where nationalist sentiments were not satisfied was in the Middle East following the collapse of the Ottoman Empire. During the war, the British made numerous promises to both Arab Muslims and Jews to gain their support for the war effort. With the advent of peace, the British ignored these hasty wartime promises, and Great Britain and France divided the area into colonial spheres of influence. Also, despite the contributions that colonial soldiers made to the war effort, the French and British made no move to reward their African colonies with independence.

- Czechoslovakia was born, combining the lands of the Czechs and Slovaks and also including a significant number of Germans.

- Hungary became fully independent, though it was somewhat reduced in size.

- An independent Romania was also created out of former Austro-Hungarian lands.

- Serbia was rewarded with additional territories for being on the victorious side; the resulting enlarged state, Yugoslavia, was what the Serbs had dreamed of. This dream had been one of the root causes of the war.

- For the first time since the 18th century, there was an independent Poland.

- Finland and the Baltic states of Lithuania, Latvia, and Estonia were carved out of parts of the former Russian Empire.

- Although most of these states started as democracies, within a short time span, a host of problems, including economic and social issues, led all of them—with the exception of Czechoslovakia—to become dictatorships.

The Russian Revolution

Though it is hard to imagine, some Russian soldiers were thrown into battle during the First World War without guns, having been told to pick up rifles from their fallen comrades. This is just one way in which the First World War revealed the complete incompetence of the tsarist regime. Although it is hard to imagine any autocratic state functioning well during an unprecedented crisis like a world war, the problem was made more severe by the ill-advised actions of Russia's last tsar, **Nicholas II** (1868–1918), who decided during the second year of the conflict that he should emulate the warrior tsars of the past and assume personal command of the army.

In his absence, Nicholas left his wife **Empress Alexandra** in charge of the state. Alexandra turned out to be completely ignorant in matters of statecraft and was personally under the influence of a mystical Russian monk named **Gregory Rasputin** (1872–1916), who, she believed, had the power to control the bleeding of her son Alexis, who had hemophilia. Rasputin took advantage of Nicholas's absence to encourage the empress to place his friends in important state offices despite their obvious incompetence. With the war going badly for the Russians, false rumors began to spread that Alexandra and Rasputin were lovers and that the German-born empress was doing her best to make sure that Russia was defeated. (Similar rumors were spread about the British royal family, who also had German roots, leading them to change their family name from Saxe-Coburg to the more English-sounding Windsor.) Rasputin met his end in 1916 when he was killed by a group of arch-monarchists, who feared he was destroying the prestige of the throne. The problems in Russia, however, extended well beyond what could be solved by removing the monk from his position of influence.

The Provisional Government

Two revolutions occurred in Russia in 1917. The first was in March, when order collapsed in the capital city of Petrograd (formerly and currently St. Petersburg) as the population grappled with a severe shortage of food. Troops were called out to disperse the demonstrations, but instead of following their orders, the solders joined with the strikers. On March 14, the tsar abdicated. What became known as the Provisional Government took over authority. This government was made up of members of the **Duma**—the Russian parliament that arose out of the 1905 revolution—and was provisional because it was supposed to exist only long enough to establish a constituent body which would then write a constitution for the new Russian republic.

One sign of future trouble was that workers and soldiers continued to form soviets, as was the case in the revolution of 1905. These soviets consisted primarily of assorted Russian Socialists, with the majority belonging to the **Menshevik** and **Socialist Revolutionary** wings, while

CED 8.3
The Russian Revolution and Its Effects

only a minority belonged to the most extreme of the social groups, the **Bolsheviks**. Russian socialism had split into assorted factions back in 1903 when **Vladimir Lenin** (1870–1924) insisted that a small party of professional revolutionaries could seize power on behalf of the working class. His followers became known as the Bolsheviks. The group that insisted that Russia had to proceed through the proven historical stages before it could achieve an ideal socialist society, as Marx had mandated, became known as the Mensheviks. This led the Mensheviks, who dominated the Petrograd Soviet, to initially support the Provisional Government, because it fit their idea that a bourgeois revolution needed to precede a socialist revolution.

Tragically for the history of Russia, this short-lived republic faced problems of the greatest magnitude. One controversial decision was made when the Provisional Government decided to remain in the First World War rather than withdraw from the fighting. This decision stemmed partly from a sense of responsibility to the other Entente powers, but more important to this decision was the presence at that time of German troops on Russian soil. This presence led the Provisional Government to believe that a renewed war effort, led by a democratic regime, would inspire Russian support. The Provisional Government also decided to delay the redistribution of the great estates, which were supposed to be broken up to provide land for the peasantry. Seeing that their demands were not being met, the peasants acted on their own initiative and seized the great estates.

The Triumph of the Bolsheviks

In April, Lenin returned from exile in Switzerland, aided by the Germans who transported him through their territory in a sealed railcar. The Germans did this because they thought that Lenin would undermine the Russian war effort, never expecting that he would be able to seize power. Over the ensuing months, the Bolsheviks continued to build up their strength, particularly among the workers and soldiers in Petrograd. By the fall of 1917, the Bolsheviks were the largest party in the soviets.

As the situation in the city became more desperate and unrest continued, Lenin decided to seize the moment, and on November 9, new Bolshevik figurehead **Leon Trotsky** (1870–1940) rode the momentum of his party's electoral success to take over key positions in the city, including power stations and communication centers. The revolution came off without much violence as the Provisional Government simply collapsed. Much violence would ensue, however, over the next three years, as the Bolsheviks had to cope with a bloody civil war to maintain their power.

Lenin and his party operated under the assumption that the revolution in Russia was only the first in a series of Communist revolutions that would begin in Germany and then move on to the remainder of western Europe. Therefore, the Bolsheviks were willing to accept a draconian peace with Germany because they believed that Imperial Germany would shortly disappear, and the territorial settlements would no longer matter. By the end of 1917, the Germans and the new Bolshevik state had signed the **Treaty of Brest-Litovsk**, thus removing Russia from the war. The treaty was exceedingly harsh and involved German confiscation of huge tracts of Russian land (perhaps more unfair than what the Germans were punished with in the Treaty of Versailles). The Treaty of Brest-Litovsk was never fully implemented because of Germany's defeat in the war and the Allies' refusal to allow Germany to gain territories in the east. Much of the territory became Poland and the Baltics instead.

THE INTERWAR YEARS

The German Weimar Republic

The story of the German **Weimar Republic** is nothing short of tragic, though its ultimate failure should not be surprising given its problematic birth at the end of a disastrous war. It has sometimes been argued that the death of Weimar came not in 1933 with the triumph of Hitler and his Nazi Party, but rather in 1919, in the very early days of the republic, when its leaders were forced to sign the vastly unpopular Versailles Treaty.

Although forces from the extreme political right caused its final demise, in the first years of the republic, the far left was a much greater threat to its stability. The republic was created in November 1918 and was initially led by **Friedrich Ebert** (1871–1925), a moderate Socialist who served as its first president. To put down a rebellion led by radical Marxists like **Karl Liebknecht** and **Rosa Luxemburg** and to secure his republican regime, Ebert was forced to rely on the old imperial officer corps. Because the army was in no position to put down the rebellion alone, Ebert gave approval for the formation of "**Free Corps**," voluntary paramilitary groups that often held extreme right-wing leanings. In 1920, some of these Free Corps became involved in an attempt to overthrow the democratic state, but a general strike by workers put an end to what became known as the **Kapp Putsch**. However, by 1920, it was clear that although the threat from the left was eradicated, the far right had become an even greater danger to the long-term viability of the Weimar state.

By 1924, the republic had achieved some degree of stability, despite the continuing effects of the Versailles Treaty penalties. In the postwar years, Germany suffered from terrible inflation as a result of the government's wild printing of money to pay its reparations debt. This insanely high inflation, which eventually led to an exchange rate of 11 trillion marks to the dollar, shattered the German middle class who saw its life savings disappear overnight. In 1923, the Chancellor of Germany was **Gustav Stresemann** (1878–1929), the leader of the German People's Party, a conservative party that supported the Weimar Republic. Although this **hyperinflation** may have done more than even the Great Depression to damage the long-term possibility of success for the republic, in the short term, Stresemann was able to get the economy back on its feet. He was even able to work out a new agreement on reparations, making them less damaging to the German economy.

By 1925, Germany was slowly rebuilding its relations with the other nations of Europe. Germany signed the **Lucarno Agreement** with France, by which Germany agreed to accept the current borders between France and Germany (and therefore French control over Alsace-Lorraine). They also resolved other issues, such as initiating the withdrawal of French troops from the Rhineland. In the following year, Stresemann capped off these efforts by entering Germany into the **League of Nations**. By 1929, the republic appeared as though it was taking root within Germany, though the outbreak of the Great Depression would reveal how shallow German support for republican government truly was.

The Soviet Experiment

Following the Bolshevik Revolution of November 1917, Lenin and his tiny party ruled over a land that had been completely shattered. An indication of how little support they held within the nation can be seen by the elections for the constituent assembly that were finally held a few weeks after the Bolshevik Revolution. Despite attempts to intimidate voters at the polls, the best the Bolsheviks could garner was one-quarter of the seats in the assembly. With such a showing, it was not surprising that armed Red Guards dispersed the assembly at the end of its first and only meeting.

Over the next several years, the **Communists** (the name adopted by the Bolshevik party in 1919), worked to solidify their control over the vast Russian state. For three years they had to fight a life-or-death struggle against the **"White" forces**, a loose term for the various anti-Communist factions, including dedicated monarchists and ardent republicans. The Whites received support from a British and American contingent, who nominally were sent to protect supplies the Allies had sent during the war but were really in Russia to keep an eye on events. The Civil War provided justification for Lenin and Trotsky to launch a **"Red Terror"** against their opponents, some of whom were right-wing extremists and genuine enemies of the Bolshevik state; others were fellow Socialists, like the members of the Menshevik party, who feared the formation of a Communist dictatorship in Russia. By 1920, the Communists had defeated the various White armies and firmly established Bolshevik rule over Russia.

In the early days of the Soviet Union, there was still an expectation that the revolutionary tide would sweep across western Europe. To that end, in 1919, the Russian Communists founded the **Third (or Communist) International** to aid in the cause of revolution. The rise of this body, often referred to as the **Comintern**, had a major impact on the various Socialist parties of western Europe, as some Marxists turned to the new Soviet state for guidance. The majority of Socialists, however, were horrified by the obviously repressive nature of Lenin's regime. This led to a split across Europe between those who formed Communist parties and those who maintained their ties to the original Socialist parties. In Germany, this split within the ranks of the left played a major role in the eventual rise of the Nazis; the German Communists saw the Social Democratic Party as more of a threat to their eventual success than the Nazis. By 1920, when it was becoming clear that the revolutionary tide across Europe was barely a trickle, the Comintern shifted its focus more toward aiding the success of the one Marxist state, the Soviet Union, which filled all the leadership posts in the organization.

As the leaders of the Soviet Union increasingly turned their attention to internal questions within Russia, a debate ensued within the party concerning economics. During the Civil War, the party imposed "war communism," extremely tight control over all aspects of the economy. In 1921, anger over the harshness of this program led to a rebellion by the sailors of the Kronstadt Naval Base, which was once one of the primary strongholds of Bolshevik support. While the rebellion was crushed with stunning brutality, it did lead Lenin to replace war communism with the **New Economic Policy (NEP)**. This policy placed the "heights of industry" in government hands but also allowed a significant scope for private enterprise. Under this program, the economy made a quick recovery to prewar levels.

The question remained, however, as to how to build a socialist state. This debate became closely intertwined with the issue of who would succeed Lenin as the leader of the party after he died in 1924. One possible candidate for the post was Trotsky, who enjoyed immense prestige as the builder of the Red Army that had won the Civil War. Trotsky thought that the NEP was too much of an ideological compromise, and he envisioned the return of an economic structure more akin to war communism. Trotsky, as the leader of the "Left Opposition," also argued that it was necessary to focus on the spread of revolution to the industrialized nations of western Europe; he believed that communism could not survive unless it spread to other lands. His major opponent in this debate was **Nikolai Bukharin** (1888–1938), the "Right Opposition" leader who advocated continuing the NEP and building communism within the Soviet state.

Stalin

In the end, it was neither Trotsky nor Bukharin who took up the mantle of Lenin but **Joseph Stalin** (1879–1953) instead, a Georgian who had joined the party in 1902 but played a relatively minor role in the seizure of power in November 1917. Stalin was completely uninterested in ideological debates; he wanted to establish his own power within the Soviet system. To achieve this power, Stalin cunningly worked with Bukharin to maneuver Trotsky out of authority. In 1927, Trotsky and his ally Gregory Zinoviev (1883–1936) were expelled from the party. Stalin waited two years before he also ousted Bukharin. Eventually, beginning in 1936, Stalin launched a series of show trials in which his former opponents were tortured until they confessed to all sorts of crimes against the state.

While the complete story of Stalin's brutality will never be fully known, close to 10 million Russians were arrested in the late 1930s; several million were executed immediately or eventually died in the brutal detention camps that Stalin set up in Siberia. Stalin eventually decimated the ranks of the "Old Bolsheviks" who had joined the party prior to 1917; he destroyed the officer corps and anyone else he perceived as disloyal to the state or to him. In 1940, an agent sent by Stalin assassinated Trotsky, who had earlier been sent into exile.

Once in a position of undisputed authority, Stalin adopted the policy of the Left Opposition and its program to rapidly turn Russia into an industrial nation. To achieve this goal, in 1928 Stalin implemented the first **Five-Year Plan**, a comprehensive, centrally controlled plan for industrial expansion. To pay for this unprecedented economic growth, Stalin followed Trotsky's plan to extract the necessary money by squeezing the peasantry through the forced **collectivization** of Russian agriculture. The state waged an open war on the *kulaks*—the wealthy peasants—and sent party cadres to the countryside with the order to kill any peasant who refused to join the collective farm. Millions of *kulaks* were shot or died from starvation after they destroyed their crops and farm animals rather than turn them over to the hated Communist state. The human cost was staggering; perhaps 10 million people in the countryside died as Stalin moved the available crops to urban areas. The result, however, was that by the end of the 1930s, the Soviet Union emerged as a major industrial power, while the western nations were embroiled in a devastating economic depression.

The Great Depression

CED 8.5
Global Economic Crisis

Traditionally, we think of the Great Depression as beginning in October 1929 with the stock-market crash, which was soon followed by people hurling themselves out of windows (though there is little evidence such suicides took place). It should be understood, however, that the roots of the problem were deeper than just a crash of the financial markets, and the worldwide depression would not begin in earnest until the banking crisis in 1931.

In May 1931, the collapse of Vienna's most powerful bank, the Credit-Anstalt, created a domino effect. Banks throughout Germany and eastern Europe started to fail as citizens began to question banks' solvency. They withdrew their savings rapidly, which depleted

The 1920s: Perception vs. Reality

Our image of the 1920s is that of the **"Jazz Age,"** a glittering time chronicled in the novels of **F. Scott Fitzgerald**. The reality was far less festive. The war had been incredibly devastating to the worldwide economy. In places such as Great Britain, the 1920s remained a time of economic stagnation. Much of the postwar economic recovery in Germany was dependent on the availability of American bank loans, monies that the Germans in turn used to lend at higher interest to the newly emerging nations of eastern Europe. This led to what looked like solid financial gains in both the United States and Germany from 1924 to 1929, but in many ways it was a false prosperity. The decline in available credit brought on by the collapse of the American stock market caused the veneer of prosperity to rapidly fade.

available reserves until otherwise-healthy banks could not return depositors' money and were forced to fold. Meanwhile, in the highly uncertain economic environment, banks stopped making loans, and individuals started trying to save whatever money they could. This resulted in a major drop in demand for industrial goods. With the decline in demand came a corresponding decline in the number of available jobs, because there was less of a market for goods produced. However, rising unemployment only suppressed demand further, because unemployed workers had no money. Many countries worsened these problems by trying to remain on a **gold standard,** a fixed exchange rate between their currencies and gold. The gold standard prevented countries from using controlled inflation to help get out of the depression. Inflation, by increasing the amount of available money, allows individuals to meet their increased desire for savings while having some money left over to spend; it also discourages people from saving too much, because they realize their money will be worth less in the future than it is today.

The problems of the gold standard were made even worse by the common belief that the way to deal with an economic depression was to further tighten the supply of money, until all the "bad loans" went bust and "failed companies" went out of business (even though many of these were perfectly sound and were essentially innocent bystanders to the total economic collapse). Governments also tried to rein in their spending to balance their budgets, which only further suppressed the overall demand for goods (while also exposing unemployed workers to worse suffering, as social support programs, veterans' benefits, and so on, were cut). The English economist **John Maynard Keynes** (1883–1946) was almost a singular voice of dissent. He argued that because the problem was a lack of demand in the private sector, governments could best fix it through deficit spending, temporarily providing people with jobs and income again to enable a spending recovery and thereby restore the economy to health. This was known as "priming the pump," as this temporary increase in government spending in areas like public works would unfreeze the economy and get money moving again.

The depression worsened as governments took further misguided measures, such as raising tariff barriers to protect domestic manufacturing. The United States was the first to take this step when it raised the tariff wall in 1930. All the other nations of Europe soon followed, including Great Britain, where free trade was a doctrine held with almost religious intensity.

The depths of the depression were truly staggering. By 1932, the economies of Europe were performing at only half the 1929 level. The depression hit hardest in the United States and in Germany, where eventually almost one-third of the available workforce was unemployed. In the United States—a stable democracy—those embroiled in the depression elected **Franklin Roosevelt** as president and subscribed to his **New Deal**. In Germany—a shaky democracy at best—the crisis resulted in the death of republican institutions and the triumph of a political ideology that was anathema to the very spirit of democracy—**fascism**.

Fascism

CED 8.6
Fascism and
Totalitarianism

During the interwar years, as democracy appeared to be faltering, millions of people across Europe looked to fascism as a movement that offered the means to rebuild their shattered lives. Historians actively debate the definition of fascism; some claim that nothing really can be labeled as a fascist ideology outside the regimes of Hitler and Mussolini. Fascist parties emerged across Europe and in other parts of the world, including the United States. They did not all possess the exact same set of beliefs; there are certain ideas, however, they all hold in common, which can be useful in defining the movement.

The word *fascism* comes from the Latin term *fasces*, a reference to a small bundle of sticks the Romans carried as symbols of authority and community. These bound sticks were symbolic of one central goal of fascism—to destroy the notion of the individual and instead push for a common community. In some ways, this sounds similar to what the Communists wanted to achieve—a unified society devoid of class differences. But the fascist concept was not tied to an international identity, as communism was, nor did fascism advocate the end of class distinctions. Instead, fascism pushed for another identity, one that was rooted in both extreme nationalism and often in some mystical racial heritage, such as that found in the Völkisch Movement pursued by the German Fascists.

Volk is a German word that translates in English to "folk," but it more loosely means "nation" or "tribe," and is based on the idea of a common cultural tie that all German people share; it also implies that minority groups in Germany, such as Jewish people, are excluded from that German identity, and was used to justify the persecution of German Jews.

Fascists were deeply antagonistic to the idea of parliamentary democracy, which they viewed as anarchical and effete. Instead, fascism favored the idea of a strong leader; the Italian Fascists had ***Il Duce***, and the Germans had the ***Führer***, men who, in an almost mystical manner, represented all the desires and dreams of the nation. This antagonism toward democracy is interesting, because in the two nations where fascism triumphed, Italy and Germany, Fascist governments were created using the ballot box and not forced by an armed coup. Once in power, fascist regimes despised democracy and rejected many socialist ideas as well (though they shrewdly preserved a few popular ones). In short, fascists positioned themselves as the antidote to the Soviet collectivism, and this was a significant factor in their rise to power. Many middle-class individuals were fully aware that the Soviet regime had collectivized all private property and saw fascism as the only barrier to the triumph of the hated communism. While many Fascists, like Hitler, hardly bothered to contemplate a fascist economic program, Mussolini promised that an Italian fascist state would implement what he called **corporatism**—an association of employers and workers within each industry that would iron out all contentious issues regarding production and wages.

To a certain extent, fascism was antagonistic toward much of what is representative of the modern world. Fascists were against the political emancipation of women, they hated modern art, and they despised a religious faction that had become emancipated in modern times—Jews. **Antisemitism** was a key component in Fascist movements throughout Europe, except in Italy, in part because Jews were seen as standing outside the arch-nationalistic identity that was so dear to the heart of all Fascists.

Fascism in Italy

The first state to have a Fascist government was Italy, and because the empowerment of fascism occurred prior to the Great Depression of 1929, it was not this financial devastation that caused the movement. In Italy, fascism emerged partly out of a deep national dissatisfaction with its participation in the First World War. In 1915, Italy decided to enter the war on the side of the

Entente powers, in part because it was interested in extending Italian control over those areas of Austria-Hungary that were home to a significant number of people who spoke Italian as their first language. Italy's military participation was initially disastrous, leading to the almost total collapse of the Italian front in 1917, but Italy stayed in the war and played a role in the eventual triumph of the Entente powers. It was a costly victory, but many Italians thought it would be justified with the gains they would receive at the peace table. In the event, Italy got most of what it had been promised by the British and French, but with the collapse of the Austro-Hungarian state, many Italians believed that they should have been more generously rewarded for their participation.

Following the war, Italy underwent a marked political transformation. In 1919, the political system adopted proportional representation, whereby parties would be rewarded seats in the legislature on the basis of their percentages in the national vote. This new system favored the creation of mass parties such as Mussolini's Fascist movement. Italian politics were also transformed by events in 1919 and 1920, years that witnessed a series of factory occupations by angry workers who seemed to portend the advent of a Bolshevik state. This led many landowners and business leaders to turn against democratic politics. They began to look for another political solution and thought they had found it in fascism, a political movement that was just emerging in Italy.

The founder and leader of the Italian Fascists was **Benito Mussolini** (1883–1945). His father was a Socialist who named his son after the Mexican revolutionary Benito Juarez. Mussolini adopted his father's Socialist beliefs and became the editor of the party newspaper. Interestingly for a man who would eventually become an extreme nationalist, during his years as a Socialist, Mussolini wrote, "The national flag is a rag that should be placed in a dunghill." His views began to shift during the war when Mussolini broke with his fellow Socialists and supported Italy's entrance into the war, a war in which Mussolini eventually served but without any particular distinction, like Hitler.

Returning to civilian life, Mussolini founded a new party, the **National Fascist Party**. The party quickly formed paramilitary squads (the Blackshirts) to fight leftist organizations, thus earning them the gratitude of factory owners and landowners who filled the party coffers with much-needed cash. By 1921, the party had begun to seat members in the Italian parliament and emerge as a significant presence in Italian political life.

Although his party still had only a few seats in the legislature, by October 1922, Mussolini demanded that **King Victor Emmanuel III** (r. 1900–1946) name him and several other Fascists to cabinet posts. To provide support for his demands, Mussolini organized his Blackshirts to march on Rome and possibly attempt to seize power. If the king had declared martial law and brought in the army, there is little doubt that the Fascists would have been easily scattered. The king, however, was a timid man who was not altogether unsympathetic to the Fascist program, so he named Mussolini as prime minister. The Fascist march on Rome turned into a celebration instead of a possible coup.

Fortunately for Mussolini, there was very little opposition to his consolidation of political power. He played at being a parliamentary leader for only several months after taking over in 1922. He then implemented a number of constitutional changes to ensure that the niceties of democracy no longer limited his actions. Mussolini's grip on power in the early years was only shaken in 1924 when he and the party were involved in the murder of a Socialist politician. Mussolini, however, was able to take this crisis and turn it to his advantage: he further consolidated his power by basically banning all non-Fascist political activity.

Perhaps because of the nature of the land that he governed, Mussolini found it hard to recast Italy in his Fascist image. Rather than achieving the revolution that many of his followers wanted, he made peace with more established institutions, such as the Catholic Church, when in 1929 he signed the **Lateran Pact** with the papacy. For the first time, the papacy officially recognized the Italian state. In the latter part of the decade, Mussolini tried to implement the corporatist economic program that was supposed to be a hallmark of the new Italy, but in practice it never lived up to the promise. Italy did rebound economically in the late 1920s, but then again, so did the rest of the world economy.

German Fascism

A more thorough Fascist reordering of the state took place in Germany. While the Nazi regime in January 1933 marks the final stage in the collapse of the Weimar Republic, in many ways the failure of the republic dates back to the first years of the **Great Depression**. In March 1930, Hermann Müller (1876–1931), a government leader and Socialist, resigned over a crisis concerning unemployment insurance, which because of the depression was beginning to be an unbearable burden for the German government. This was the last truly democratic government in Germany until the end of the Second World War.

The long-term health of the Weimar Republic was shaky in that the president was **Paul von Hindenburg** (1847–1934). If there had been a genuine reordering of German society following the collapse of the imperial regime and the rise of a republic, then a bombastic general like Hindenburg would have been cast aside with scorn. Unfortunately, Weimar never really escaped its recent past. The republic had as its leader a dedicated monarchist, who in 1925, prior to running for the office of president, contacted his former emperor in exile in Denmark to ask the emperor's approval to run for office.

President Hindenburg took the opportunity of the resignation of the Socialist Chancellor to install a more authoritarian government. Hindenburg selected **Heinrich Brüning** (1885–1970), the leader of a middle-of-the-road Catholic party. Brüning proposed an economic program that would have done little to solve the economic crisis and simply led to increased political opposition by the left and the right. Because Brüning could not achieve a parliamentary majority, he took the terrible step of involving Article 48, an emergency decree within the Weimar Constitution that enabled him to govern under presidential decree.

For the remainder of his long life, Brüning would try to defend his next decision, which was to call for new parliamentary elections in September 1930, just as the economic crisis worsened. Brüning thought the electorate would back him on his austerity

Why the Nazis?

The rise of the Nazi Party seems bizarre in hindsight, but it made more sense to people who had not yet seen the horror of rampant nationalism in the form of the war and the Holocaust. Many Germans were still powerfully angry about the Treaty of Versailles, which the Nazis denounced as an affront to national pride (and a serious drain on resources). Many early Nazi supporters also believed in the *Dolchstosslegende* (stab-in-the-back legend), which was the claim that the German army lost World War I only because it was "stabbed in the back" by various hated groups: Jews, Communists, Weimar Republicans, big businesses, and so on.

Despite their conservatism, the Nazis were also one of the few groups to provide some coherent social support during the depression. While denouncing "Bolshevism," they championed certain moderate socialist rhetoric (such as increasing workers' wages and improving the common well-being), provided some support in the form of soup kitchens, and served free beer at political meetings. Most importantly, though, the Nazi Party indulged the people's desire for blame: the Nazis combined violent hatred of the Communists and the moderate Socialist party with denunciations of international capitalism as a "Jewish conspiracy" bent on war-profiteering and extorting workers, all while telling Germans that they were superior simply by virtue of being German. These positions were self-contradictory nonsense—but very appealing nonetheless.

measures. Instead, the **Nazis** emerged as the big winners. The election transformed the Nazis from a tiny party with only 12 seats in the Reichstag to a major force holding 102 seats.

With such a hostile Reichstag, Brüning continued to govern under Article 48. For the next two years, he attempted to implement his austerity program, which only served to deepen the economic crisis. By the spring of 1932, Hindenburg removed Brüning and put in his place Franz von Papen (1879–1969), a wealthy anti-parliamentary conservative. In the elections held in November, the Nazis became the largest party in the Reichstag with 196 seats, and in January 1933, Hindenburg, despite a certain measure of personal disgust for Hitler, asked him to become chancellor.

It was a remarkable achievement for the Austrian-born **Adolf Hitler** (1889–1945). As a young man, he had gone to Vienna to study at its Academy of Fine Arts, but unfortunately for the history of Europe, Hitler proved to have little talent as an artist and was rejected. It was while living in Vienna that Hitler developed his virulent antisemitism, although the roots of his hatred toward Jews are hotly disputed. Because he had little sympathy for the multinational character of the Habsburg Empire when war began in 1914, he volunteered to serve in the German army where he survived a poison gas attack.

In 1919, he joined the German Workers' Party, which was renamed the **National Socialist German Workers' Party**, one of the small extremist groups that formed in the early days of the Weimar Republic. By 1923, he thought the party was strong enough to seize power, so he launched the **Beer Hall Putsch** in Munich, falsely believing that it would set the stage for a revolt throughout Germany. Following this failure, he was put on trial but used this opportunity to stage a spirited defense before the court and to gain greater attention for himself and his movement. In prison, Hitler wrote *Mein Kampf* (*My Struggle*), outlining his extremist views, along with his desire, shared by Germans of assorted political persuasions, to overturn the Treaty of Versailles.

Following the Beer Hall failure in 1923, Hitler decided that in the future he had to use the existing political structure to achieve power rather than use extraordinary means like a coup. The Nazis, however, were not just a simple political party politely trying to convince the German electorate of the reasonableness of its views. Like Mussolini's Fascists, the Nazis enlisted a corps of armed goons to support their political rallies and to disrupt opposing groups' meetings. This helped lead to an increase in political violence in Weimar, as all political parties had begun to sponsor armed factions; street fighting became endemic in Berlin and other German cities. Ironically, even though the Nazis often instigated the violence, Hitler had strong appeal as a "law-and-order" candidate who would put an end to the brawls.

When Hitler was named chancellor in 1933, he rapidly sought to consolidate his power. On February 27, 1933, the Reichstag building in Berlin was set on fire, although to this day it is not entirely clear who set it. The Nazis, who may have set the fire themselves, blamed the Communists for the incident. By claiming that there was a Communist plot against the state, Hitler encouraged the Reichstag to vote to grant him emergency powers, allowing him to eliminate virtually all human rights while granting the executive branch of the government almost total authority. In the last election held in Germany until the end of the Second World War, the Nazis, despite having control over the state, received only 44 percent of the vote. Hitler followed the vote with an **Enabling Act**, which gave the party emergency powers to govern the state and combined the authority of the chancellor and the president into one with a new, non-republican sounding title—the *führer* (or leader). Finally, by the summer of 1933, Hitler banned all political parties except the Nazis and followed with an attack on the independent trade union movement.

Consolidation of power also meant that Hitler had to work out an arrangement with the one institution within the state that was still a threat—the army. The army was highly concerned about the growing size and power of the **S.A.**, the Nazi political army that had played such an important role in the party's rise to power. Once Hitler was in power, the S.A. was expendable. In June 1934, Hitler organized the **"Night of the Long Knives,"** in which he murdered his old ally Ernst Röhm (1887–1934), the leader of the S.A., who had wanted to make it the backbone of a new revolutionary army. Following the attack on the S.A., the members of the German army agreed to give their complete loyalty to the new German state and eventually would swear a personal oath to Hitler.

The Nazification of the German state soon proceeded apace. To create support for such a program, the Nazis put a great deal of effort into creating a Ministry of Propaganda under the leadership of **Joseph Goebbels** (1897–1945). German life had always been chock full of organizations like hiking groups and choral societies. The Nazis did their best to reorganize such groups along lines that the state could control, and huge organizations such as the **Hitler Youth** were established to indoctrinate the young. For those who refused to accept the new state of affairs, the Nazis organized a ruthlessly efficient police apparatus to silence political opposition and to intimidate anyone who even considered dissenting from the party line.

Western Democracies in Crisis

CED 8.7
Europe During the Interwar Period

Woodrow Wilson had promised that the First World War was fought "to make the world safe for democracy," and for a time it looked as if his vision was accurate. Democracies began to sprout throughout Europe in such places as the newly emerging nations of eastern Europe and in formerly monarchical states like Germany. Sadly, this democratic renaissance was to be short lived. By the 1930s, not only had democracy faltered in almost all the new states that had been born out of the Versailles Treaty (with the exception of Czechoslovakia), but it also appeared to be in crisis in western Europe, as France and Spain struggled with contentious political issues that threatened the very existence of parliamentary sovereignty.

Great Britain

Just as in the 19th century, Great Britain remained politically stable, though it certainly did not remain stagnant. One significant change was the emergence of the **Labour Party**, which supplanted the liberals to become Britain's second-largest political party. The First World War had revealed fundamental problems within the **Liberal Party**, which was much more comfortable with the trappings of the Victorian world, as opposed to the age of total war. Labour had achieved prominence by more effectively voicing the concerns of the working class. British Prime Minister **David Lloyd-George** had encouraged British soldiers and civilians to fight hard for the war effort by promising to make their country after the war a "land fit for heroes." Unfortunately, unless heroes happen to like high unemployment, urban slums, and a growing number of labor disputes, all of which were endemic in the 1920s and 1930s, they may have been rather disappointed, yet accurate, in thinking this new Britain was much like the old.

France

France had won an incredible victory in the First World War and had achieved such long-term goals as the recapture of Alsace-Lorraine and what she thought was the permanent reduction of the threat posed by Germany. However, just as in Great Britain, the war merely diverted attention from, but did not solve, the tremendous economic and social tensions on the eve of the war. Economically, France did grow in the 1920s, but it could hardly offset the tremendous impact of the Great Depression. The economic crisis helped spur the radicalization of French politics, as groups from the far left and far right gathered support. In February 1934, following a right-wing riot that looked like it was going to shake the French Republic to its core, a number of parties on the center and left began to work together to form a "**Popular Front**" to block the possibility of a Fascist victory in France as had occurred the previous year in Germany.

This "Popular Front" proved to be successful in May 1936, when a coalition of Communists, Socialists, and Radicals (the name belies the fact that this was a center-left party) won a majority in the Chamber of Deputies. They selected the leader of the Socialist Party, **Léon Blum** (1872–1950), to be Prime Minister. The new government worked to solve some of the labor issues that had plagued France for decades. In June, they put through the **Matignon Agreement**, allowing workers to collectively bargain with employers, reducing the work week to 40 hours, and granting the right to fully paid vacations. Attention to social problems, however, had to be delayed, as France had to now grapple with an issue that challenged the very existence of the Popular Front, the **Spanish Civil War**.

In the past few chapters, you have read a lot about the twists and turns of the French government. Let's review all of that in the following handy chart:

Brief History of French Governments from the Ancien Régime until WWII

Bourbon Monarchy

Constitutional Monarchy   (1791)
     Based on *Declaration of Rights of Man and Citizen*

First Republic   (Sept 1792)
     Reign of Terror
     Jacobins
     National Convention   (1792–1795)
     Directory   (1795–1799)
         Oversaw France's first bicameral legislature
         Marked by partisanship stemming from the Revolution
     Consulate   (1799–1804)
         Napoleon's coup d'état

First Empire   (1804–1814)
     Think of the painting of Napoleon as Emperor
     Ends with Hundred Days after escape from Elba

Bourbon Restoration   (1814–1848)
     Louis XVIII   (1814–1824)
     Charles X   (1824–1830)
         Experiences tide of revolutions common in Europe in 1830
         Bourgeoisie tired of his absolutist rule
     Louis-Philippe   (1830–1848)
         Takes power in bourgeoisie-led July Revolution
         Reign is called the July Monarchy (bourgeoisie friendly)
         Class tension—Workers call for a Representative Democracy

Second Republic   (1848–1852)
     Workers revolt in June (June Uprising)
     Louis-Napoleon elected leader (calls himself Napoleon III)

Second Empire   (1852–1870)
     Move to empire is approved on referendum
     Otto von Bismarck eventually removes Napoleon III from the throne
     Franco-Prussian War

Third Republic   (1870–1940)
     Strong bicameral parliament, weak president
     Conflict with Catholic Church
     Paris Commune   (1871)
     Radical movement arises during the vacuum created by Franco-Prussian War

The Spanish Civil War

Spain had become a parliamentary democracy only in 1931, following the fall of the Spanish monarchy in that year. The first elections in the Spanish republic brought about a victory for a coalition of liberals and Socialists. Unfortunately, the problems facing Spain were extremely severe, and the new government had trouble finding solutions. Many landless farm laborers waited in vain as the government failed to implement a promised land reform that would break up the vast estates of the rich. Increasingly, the failings of the government created more radical sentiments among the workers, which was matched by equally aggressive action from the parties of the far right.

In February 1936, a Popular Front coalition of the leftist parties—created to avert what they felt was a threat from Spanish Fascists—won a narrow electoral victory. This government attempted to achieve what the earlier socialist government could not, including significant reforms such as land redistribution. They still did not operate quickly enough to satisfy the disaffected masses who seized land and factories. This failure to maintain order was used by the far right to stage a coup to overturn the government.

In the summer of 1936, a group of army officers under the leadership of **General Francisco Franco** (1892–1975) took control of large parts of Spain. Their belief that the republic would simply collapse proved to be false, as republican loyalists bravely organized to defend the state against the nationalist insurgents. Spain was swept into an incredibly brutal civil war, which soon brought about the participation of German and Italian support for the nationalists.

Picasso's *Guernica*

As a reflection of his horror over the attack, the Spanish artist Pablo Picasso painted his most acclaimed work, *Guernica*, which he willed to Spain. The painting was to be handed over to the government only when the nation was once again a republic, something that happily occurred in the years following Franco's death in 1975.

The fascist states of Germany and Italy were interested in testing their new armaments, thus leading to one of the most brutal events in the war. On market day, in the city of **Guernica**, German and Italian planes bombed and strafed the civilian population. Guernica was not a military target in the least; it was targeted simply to instill fear among republican supporters. Although the Fascists willingly offered their support to those on the Spanish right, France and Great Britain refused to come to the aid of their fellow democracy. Instead of assistance, they promoted a nonintervention policy, which meant that the Spanish Loyalists had to make a Mephistophelean pact with the Soviet Union, whereby the Soviets would provide desperately needed arms in exchange for Spanish gold. Because of Soviet support, the Communists, who were initially a small faction on the Spanish left, began to play the preeminent role on the republican side.

Tragically, the Communists, having received their marching orders from Stalin, put as much effort into destroying their allies on the left as they did to defeating the nationalists. George Orwell wrote a fascinating firsthand account of these events in his story *Homage to Catalonia*, which details how the Communists destroyed the anarchist movement in Catalonia in June 1937. After reading Orwell, you will not be surprised to learn that by 1939, the nationalists had captured Madrid and triumphed over the republic.

The Road to the Second World War

CED 8.8
World War II

From the very beginning of his political career, Hitler had made clear his desire to overturn the Versailles Treaty. Once in power, he set about to keep that promise. In 1935, he openly began the rearmament of Germany, something that was prohibited by Versailles. Seeing that France and Britain did not respond to such an act of provocation, in the following year, the Germans remilitarized the Rhineland. While the French contemplated an aggressive response to this act, they knew that because they lacked British support, they would have to act unilaterally, and so they did nothing. Rather than satisfying Hitler, these steps convinced him of the weakness of the democracies, so he continued with his plans.

Germany Invades Austria

The very first sentence of *Mein Kampf* states Hitler's desire to absorb Austria into the larger **German Reich**. In March 1938, this became a reality as German troops moved into Vienna. Despite postwar claims by the Austrians that they were the first victims of Nazi aggression, the ***Anschluss*** was welcomed by a majority of Austrians who celebrated by wildly greeting Hitler on his arrival in the city and by attacking their Jewish neighbors.

> Hitler imagined his **Third Reich** (meaning "regime") as the historical successor to the earlier Holy Roman Empire and the German Empire (see Chapter 6 for more on these).

Germany Invades Czechoslovakia

Hitler next set his sights on Czechoslovakia. Czechoslovakia was the singular success story of eastern Europe; it was a thriving democracy, had a strong industrial base, and a relatively strong army. It was burdened with nationality problems, most particularly the animosity toward the state from the 3.5 million Sudeten Germans who lived in the western part of the nation. France had assured the Czechoslovak state that in the event of German aggression it would come to its aid. Unfortunately, these assurances, which also included guarantees for its security from the Soviet Union, ultimately came to nothing.

Great Britain Tries to Appease Germany

The British eventually settled on a policy known as **appeasement**. In 1937, **Neville Chamberlain** (1869–1940) became British Prime Minister and head of a conservative government. Chamberlain recognized that events in 1936 had been detrimental to British interests. These events included the German occupation of the Rhineland, the creation of the **Rome-Berlin Axis**, and even the Olympic games that had been held that year in Berlin, which were a propaganda victory for Germany. Chamberlain was not a fool, and he certainly had little sympathy for the brutality of the Nazi state, but he believed that it was impossible for Great Britain to fully rearm against the combined strength of Germany and Italy. As a result, he wanted to work out some sort of understanding with either Mussolini or Hitler.

Appeasement began with British recognition of Italy's annexation of Ethiopia. The British did nothing when Hitler annexed Austria. However, the policy of appeasement would stand a real test over the question of Czechoslovakia, which Germany threatened to invade unless the **Sudetenland**, the western part of the Czechoslovak state that was largely inhabited by ethnic Germans, was turned over to the Reich. In a radio address during this crisis, Chamberlain said it was "fantastic and incredible to be involved in a war because of a quarrel in a faraway country between people of whom we know nothing." In September, with Europe on the verge of war, Chamberlain flew to Munich to attend a four-power summit with France, Italy, and Germany to discuss the future of Czechoslovakia, whose leaders were not even invited to attend. At this summit, the powers signed the **Munich Agreement**, which led to the transfer of all Sudeten territories to Germany. In return, Hitler promised to respect the sovereignty of what remained of Czechoslovakia. Chamberlain returned home to London and was met by a huge crowd that roared with joy as Chamberlain announced that there would be "peace in our time." Rather than peace, his actions led to destruction in Czechoslovakia one year later, when the Germans ignored the Munich Agreement and seized most of what remained of the nation.

Before we are too quick to criticize the appeasers, we need to remember several things.

- First, politicians such as Chamberlain saw it as almost a sacred responsibility to remove the specter of war from Europe. The First World War was still vividly remembered by all who had lived through it.

- Also, from the British point of view, the Versailles Treaty was unjust, and part of what Hitler wanted appeared to be self-determination for nationalities, an idea that the respected President Wilson had promoted in his Fourteen Points.

- Finally, with hindsight, it is clear that Hitler never intended to maintain any of his promises. It may be unfair to have expected that the appeasers would have been able to foresee Hitler's intentions. In 1938, few individuals in Great Britain other than Winston Churchill fully understood that Hitler had to be stopped at all costs.

Germany and the Soviet Union Invade Poland

Following the dismemberment of Czechoslovakia, Hitler's attention was now drawn to the next contentious area—Poland. The Polish nation born out of Versailles included land that had once been part of the German Empire. To allow Poles access to the sea, the new nation was given a strip of territory that split East Prussia from the rest of Germany. Now that he realized Hitler's intentions following the complete occupation of Czechoslovakia, Chamberlain was determined to stop further German aggression. He worked out an arrangement with France whereby the two nations would respond in the event that Poland's borders were threatened.

At the same time, the Soviet Union was inquiring as to whether the British and French would consider forming a military alliance directed against the Germans. The British and French rebuffed the Soviets in part because, after Stalin's purge of the officer corps, they questioned the effectiveness of the Soviet military and they found little evidence that Stalin was any more a man of his word than Hitler. Once Stalin realized that he was getting nowhere with the British and French, he announced on August 22, 1939—to the shock of the rest of the world—that Germany and the Soviet Union had signed a **nonaggression pact**. The way was now open for Germany to invade Poland, while the Soviets were able to seize eastern Poland, Finland, and the Baltic states, all lands that Russia had lost in the First World War.

THE SECOND WORLD WAR (1939–1945)

The war began on September 1, 1939, with an attack on Poland. The Poles fought bravely; however, the Germans had learned critical lessons from the First World War and practiced *blitzkrieg* warfare, swift attacks using tanks and other highly mobile units, supported by warplanes. Within a month, the Polish army was routed and the British and French forces to the west maintained their defensive positions.

Over the winter of 1939–1940, little warfare occurred, earning the time period the nickname the **"Phony War."** This lull came to a shattering end in April 1940 when the Germans attacked Norway and Denmark to secure necessary iron ore supplies for Germany. In May, the Germans followed up these successes with an invasion of Belgium and the Netherlands before moving toward their ultimate goal, an attack on France. In six short weeks, the French army, considered after the First World War to be the finest in the world, was destroyed.

The Fall of France

Part of the problem for the French was that in 1940, their hearts were just not in the war. The *blitzkrieg* attacks in the east and the quick defeat of the Scandinavian countries bred tremendous pessimism among the French political and military leadership. The French were still following a military strategy that was tied to the way the First World War had been fought. During the inter-war period, they built the **Maginot Line**, a series of seemingly impregnable defenses to protect their soldiers during what they automatically assumed would be another war of stagnant positions. The Germans simply bypassed the fortifications, which were not extended to the Belgian frontier, and encircled the French armies. The British, seeing that France was about to fall, staged a heroic retreat from the Belgian beaches at **Dunkirk**, in which every available British ship, no matter the size, was used to take the British army back to Great Britain so that it might fight another day.

Following the military debacle, a new government was formed in France under the elderly Marshal Pétain, the hero of the Battle of Verdun. Pétain had been a bit of a defeatist in the First World War, and those pessimistic tendencies rose to the forefront once again as he decided to pull France out of the war and use the opportunity to create a more authoritarian French government. Pétain's **Vichy** regime brought to an end the Third Republic that was blamed for France's defeat.

Although almost the entire officer corps had been defeatists, one charismatic general, **Charles de Gaulle** (1890–1970), arrived in London and from there issued a call for French forces in the colonies to form a new French army to retrieve the national honor. Vichy authorities immediately labeled de Gaulle a traitor and began to happily assist the Germans. Nevertheless, a free French force did flourish under de Gaulle's leadership. On French soil, the *Maquis*, or French resistance, found itself fighting against both the Germans and the Vichy state.

Germany Against Great Britain

Hitler always believed that the British shared similar traits with the German Aryans. Because of such foolish racial theories, he thought that the British would see the folly of their ways after the fall of France and make peace with Germany. Great Britain, however, was gearing up for what would be the most dangerous moment in its history. Fortunately for the survival of the nation, it had an extraordinary leader in **Winston Churchill**, who had replaced Chamberlain as Prime Minister. Churchill committed the nation, which he inspired through a series of stirring speeches, to continue the war no matter what may come. In the House of Commons, Churchill declared,

"I have nothing to offer but blood, toil, tears, and sweat" and that the only goal for Britain was to "wage war against a monstrous tyranny, never surpassed in the dark, lamentable catalogue of human crime." In response to Britain's refusal to sue for peace, Hitler decided to attack.

The **Battle of Britain** was not the one-sided struggle that is often portrayed. It is true that the *Luftwaffe*, the German air force, had many more planes and trained pilots. But the British had radar, which had been developed at Cambridge University and could detect oncoming German attacks. The British Spitfires and Hurricanes were better planes than the German Messerschmits. Unbeknownst to the Germans, the British had also cracked the German secret military code. Furthermore, there was no comparison in terms of military leadership. Following the rapid fall of Poland and France, Hitler was convinced that he was a military genius, although fortunately for the eventual triumph of the Allies, that was clearly not the case. The German air force was led by the incompetent morphine addict **Hermann Göring** (1893–1946), who, after a token group of British planes dropped bombs on Berlin, decided to end the effective raids that had been staged on British air bases and directed the *Luftwaffe* to attack British cities. This strategy created tremendous suffering in the cities (the Blitz), but it also allowed the **Royal Air Force (RAF)** time to recover. By the end of September 1940, Hitler decided to drop the plan to invade Britain and move on to his ultimate dream, the defeat of the Soviet Union.

The Holocaust

CED 8.9
The Holocaust

The Holocaust, the slaughter of six million Jews, did not begin suddenly, nor is it clear at what point the Nazis decided to destroy European Jewry. Antisemitism had always been at the heart of Nazi ideology. Soon after taking power, the Nazis implemented the **Nuremberg Laws**, depriving Jews of citizenship and forcing them to wear a yellow Star of David on their clothing whenever they left their homes. Marriage and sex between Jews and Gentiles were also forbidden. While some Jews left Germany immediately after these restrictions were implemented, many refused to leave, thinking that things could not get any worse. Nevertheless, the following years would witness only a slow, steady decline for German Jews as they were forced out of all professions and had their stores boycotted and property confiscated. On November 9, 1938, the Nazis launched *Kristallnacht*, the "night of broken glass," so called because of the resonating sound of shattered glass from Jewish stores and homes that rung out throughout that night. The events of that night proved that the Germans were interested in eliminating the Jews, as several hundred people were killed and 30,000 Jews were shipped to concentration camps.

The "Final Solution"
Many historians argue that Hitler's fixation on eradicating the Jews ultimately hurt Germany's war effort, as valuable resources that could have been used to defeat the Russians were instead spent on killing the Jewish people.

One sign that demonstrates the Nazi obsession with the so-called **"Jewish Question"** is that when the Russians were putting up stiff resistance and Germany had not been able to defeat them, the Nazis still chose to direct resources that could have been used in the war effort to exterminate European Jewry instead. The conquest of Poland had placed the largest concentration of Jews in the world directly under German control. To deal with them, as well as with the large numbers of Jews from the other conquered territories, Hitler had his top lieutenants organize the **"Final Solution."** By the end of 1941, one million Jews had been slaughtered, most in mobile vans poisoned by carbon monoxide gas or machine-gunned by specially designated S.S. troops. This was not efficient enough for the Germans, however, and so in January 1942, the top leadership met in Wannsee, a suburb of Berlin, to plan a more efficient slaughter.

The Nazis organized a camp system throughout Poland, including concentration camps, where Jews from around occupied Europe were gathered, and extermination camps, the most notorious of these being **Auschwitz**. Upon arrival in the camps, the prisoners would be subject to a sorting process, in which S.S. doctors, including the notorious **Dr. Josef Mengele**, selected who would be sent to work camps and who would be sent immediately to die in the gas chambers. Besides Jews, the camps also contained Roma; gay, trans, and gender non-conforming people; Jehovah's Witnesses; Russian prisoners of war; Communists; and others considered by the Nazis to be "undesirables." Approximately 7 million such individuals were slaughtered, in addition to 6 million Jews.

One reason why two-thirds of European Jews were so effectively rounded up for slaughter was that the Nazis never lacked help among the conquered peoples of Europe to assist in this task. Yad Vashem, the Holocaust museum and memorial in Israel, has a special row of trees in honor of those Gentiles who risked their lives to help rescue Jews; however, a forest would be needed to represent the sheer number of people who aided the Germans in implementing the Holocaust. In France, Vichy officials rounded up Jews and turned them over to the Nazis before the Germans even asked for their help. In the Ukraine, Croatia, and other parts of eastern Europe, the local population set off on their own initiative to exterminate their Jewish neighbors. Antisemitic feelings obviously ran deep throughout European society in the early 20th century.

How Much Did the Allies Know?

There has always been a debate over what the Allies knew about the Holocaust and what they could have done to stop the German death machine. Although the S.S. took every precaution to hide the Final Solution, which was partly why the Nazis chose Poland as the site of the camps, word of the terror reached the West right from the beginning. Such reports were initially doubted. Who could believe such monstrosities were taking place? The sheer bulk of reports, many from eyewitnesses to the slaughter, however, made it clear that an unprecedented event in human history was happening. The debate on what could have been done will never be resolved. Many believe that attacks on the German rail network used to bring Jews to the camps could have possibly been of help, although Allied military leaders always claimed that the planes that could have been used for such raids were needed for more immediate military targets.

The Turning of the Tide

The Second World War had three critical turning points. The Battle of Britain was certainly one, as was the eventual entry of the United States into the war. The third turning point may be the most important of all—Operation Barbarossa, the German attack on the Soviet Union on June 22, 1941.

Germany Invades the Soviet Union

Initially, the attack went according to plan, as German forces drove deep into Russian territory. They caught the Soviet forces completely unprepared, even though Stalin had been warned by numerous sources, including his own intelligence agency, that such an attack was imminent. By the end of 1942, the Germans had reached the outskirts of Stalingrad and Leningrad, but both cities were held thanks to the Russian forces' dogged defense and the extraordinary sacrifices of the citizens of the Soviet Union. Because of their common enemy—Germany—Great Britain, the United States, and the Soviet Union were to form a rather unlikely alliance that would not only destroy the Third Reich but also shape the postwar world.

The War in North Africa

By 1941, the war had become a global conflict. The Italians under Mussolini had entered the war as allies of Germany just as France was about to collapse. The Italians also extended the war to North Africa, as they attempted to push the British out of Egypt. The Italians were hard-pressed to achieve this goal, forcing the Germans to come to their aid. The Germans had one of their best officers, **Erwin Rommel** (1891–1944), the "Desert Fox," positioned in this theater of the war. For a while he met with remarkable success, eventually proceeding within 60 miles of the Egyptian city of Alexandria. However, at the **Battle of El Alamein** in November 1942, a British army under the leadership of General Montgomery (1887–1976) pushed the German and Italian forces back to Tunisia.

U.S. Involvement

Following the Japanese attack on Pearl Harbor and Hitler's declaration of war on the United States in 1941, the United States became involved in the conflict with the Axis powers (Germany, Italy, and Japan). The entry of the United States into the war sparked a new energy to the war in the West, as the United States landed troops in Africa and joined with the British in pushing back the Germans and Italians. By 1943, the **Allies** had pushed the last of the **Axis forces** out of Africa and sent troops to Italy, the "soft underbelly" of the Axis. By 1943, Italy was knocked out of the war, although in many ways, the Italian campaign did not have a huge impact on the eventual course of the war.

Following a meeting between Stalin, Churchill, and Roosevelt in Tehran in November 1943, the decision was made that the British and Americans should stage an invasion of western Europe from Great Britain. On June 6, 1944, the Allies launched the **D-Day invasion.** While another year of brutal fighting was yet to be experienced, the landing of the Allied forces in Europe and the Russian counterattack following the lifting of the siege of Leningrad marked the beginning of the end for Nazi Germany.

On May 8, 1945, a week after the suicide of Hitler, Germany surrendered unconditionally. Japan had entered the Second World War with the goal of creating a vast empire in the Pacific where it would be able to exploit the natural resources of the conquered lands and use these territories as a market for Japanese manufactured goods. Such dreams of hegemony over the Pacific ended violently when the U.S. dropped the first **atomic bomb** on the city of **Hiroshima** on August 6, 1945, which was followed two days later by a second atomic bomb, this time on the city of **Nagasaki**. On August 14, the Japanese surrendered (signing the formal surrender document on September 2), thus bringing to an end the bloodiest conflict in human history.

The Aftermath

The Second World War was even more staggering in its destructiveness than the First World War. Civilian casualties—rather than military deaths—made up the majority of the 50 to 60 million people who lost their lives during the conflict. For the Soviet Union alone, although the precise numbers remain the subject of debate and will ultimately never be fully known, losses were upward of 25 million. Cities across the continent were leveled as brutal attacks on civilians, initiated with the German bombing of Warsaw in 1939 and followed by Rotterdam and London, eventually targeted the Germans. Allied attacks left 50,000 killed in the **firebombing of Dresden,** and almost every German target of any military, economic, or administrative value was brought to ruin. In Berlin and in other German cities, one found the *Truemmerfrauen*, or "rubble ladies," who in the absence of men and machinery began the slow process of removing the wreckage by hand.

In 1945, many Europeans had been displaced by conflict, especially Jewish people who had survived the death camps and found themselves living as refugees. Support for Zionism, or the concept of Jewish nationalism dating back to the 1800s, increased as much of Europe's displaced Jewish population sought to establish a Jewish state in the British-controlled mandate of Palestine, a region the British had taken control of after the First World War. Jewish migration to this region ultimately led to the establishment of the modern state of Israel in 1948, an important change in the Middle East's geopolitical situation as Israel's Arabic-speaking neighbors fought several wars against the fledgling state.

Russian POWs returned to the Soviet Union and immediately faced rearrest under the orders of Stalin, who thought their failure to die in battle might be an indication they were spies or had seen too much of life in the West to be satisfied with conditions in the Soviet Union. This was in spite of the fact that Soviet POWs had been treated with incredible brutality by the Germans, who saw them as subhuman.

Millions of Germans also poured west, fleeing from the forces of the Soviet Union, who were extracting their revenge through mass rape. Other Germans were forced from their homes in Poland and Czechoslovakia, as the civilians in those countries refused to tolerate living with ethnic Germans they blamed for the start of the war.

At the end of the First World War, cries of "Hang the kaiser!" could be heard in the capitals of the victors, but in the end, nothing was done to punish those individuals who were blamed for the war. However, by 1945, with the liberation of the Nazi death camps and the realization of the unspeakable scale of the slaughter, it was agreed by the Allies that Germany would not only have to undergo a process of **denazification,** but that the perpetrators of these crimes would have to be punished as well.

The new legal concept of **"crimes against humanity"** was applied to the defendants who took part in the first **Nuremberg Trial** that began on November 20, 1945, and ended on October 1, 1946. With the suicides of Hitler and Goebbels, the leading Nazi to stand trial was Hermann Göring, who escaped execution by swallowing poison that was smuggled into his cell, while 11 others were sentenced to death. Other trials were held for leading industrialists, military commanders, judges, and those involved in the Final Solution. Many Nazis escaped justice by fleeing to the Middle East and South America, such as the infamous Dr. Josef Mengele, while some, such as Gestapo officer Adolf Eichmann, were eventually brought to justice. Questions arose over what to do about the rank-and-file Nazi Party members, and although millions were investigated, relatively few received punishment. By June 1946, the Americans transferred responsibility for denazification to the German legal authorities, who quietly brought the process to a close.

> **Denazification**
> Following the end of the war, the Allies implemented the process of *denazification* in Germany, in which all remnants of Nazi ideology were removed from the German culture, and all Nazi Party members were removed from positions in the government. Any organizations associated with Nazism were disbanded.

In the years following the war, West Germans would refer to 1945 as **"Zero Hour,"** marking the darkest point in their national history. Many commentators thought that not only Germany but all of Europe would remain on its back, with minimal economic development and the renewed threat of war. Remarkably, Europe staged a thorough recovery over the next 20 years and in the process transformed the lives of people throughout the region and ushered in an age of political and social stability.

EUROPEAN STABILITY

The most important factor in European affairs in the period after 1945 was the emergence of political, economic, and social stability. Even while the war was raging, Allied political leaders began to think about ways of rebuilding Europe and creating lasting peace.

In 1941, President Roosevelt put forward the **Atlantic Charter**, advocating the establishment of an international organization to replace the ineffective League of Nations. Four years later, this dream became a reality when delegates from 50 nations met in San Francisco to formally create the **United Nations**. To ensure the participation of the United States, whose nonparticipation in the League of Nations doomed that body to failure, the new organization was to be based in New York. In July 1945, the U.S. Senate ratified the agreement (with others signing onto it in October), indicating that the United States was not going to return to its interwar isolationism and would instead remain committed to European recovery and stability.

Besides the significance of America's commitment to European affairs, other reasons help account for the development of stability in Europe. The level of destruction brought by Germany and Italy in a war they initiated and the extent of their atrocities against civilians led to a discrediting of Fascism as a political movement. *Revanchism*, a French word for revenge and often applied to the desire to regain so-called lost territories, was a major factor in destabilizing European affairs during the interwar period, as many nations—besides the most prominent example of Germany—sought to regain territories lost in the peace treaties following the Great War, or World War I. In part due to the mass expulsion of ethnic Germans from Poland and Czechoslovakia, *revanchism* became the cry of fringe groups in the postwar period rather than the stated policy of national governments.

Probably the most important factor in explaining postwar European stability was the emergence of democratic governments that were able to carry out policies that dramatically improved the economic conditions for their citizenry. Class conflict, which had been a destabilizing factor in the 1920s and 1930s, was replaced by a new social contract in which workers, in exchange for giving up their most extreme demands, received promises of full employment, living wages, and social welfare.

THE BEGINNING OF THE COLD WAR

There have been three major schools of thought on the causes of the Cold War.

1. For the **Traditionalists** (a position that emerged in the earliest days of the Cold War), the Soviet Union, under the brutal dictatorship of Joseph Stalin, was fundamentally responsible for the development of hostilities between the East and West.

2. Beginning in the 1960s (in part a reflection of the challenges that were being posed to all forms of established authority and anger over the Vietnam War), a new school of Cold War thought, known as **revisionism**, began to appear. For the Revisionists, fear of a postwar economic downturn (as was the case after 1918) meant that, in 1945, the United States was not seeking to make the world safe for democracy but was instead seeking to make it safe for American trade.

3. By the 1980s, a third position began to emerge, that of the **Post-Revisionists**, which perhaps not surprisingly took a middle ground. For the Post-Revisionists, even if the Soviet Union bore the brunt of the responsibility, the United States was more to blame than the Traditionalists might argue.

In many ways, the views of historians have not been altered all that fundamentally by the collapse of the Soviet Union and the opening, if at times tentatively, of their archives. What is often today referred to as the neo-Traditionalist point of view is currently in the ascendancy, although one can easily find in scholarly books and journals writings reflecting the other two traditions.

One can make the argument that the Cold War rivalry was largely inevitable. In an often-quoted passage, Alexis de Tocqueville, in *Democracy in America,* wrote:

> There are now two great nations in the world, which starting from different points, seem to be advancing toward the same goal: the Russians and the Anglo-Americans…Each seems called by some secret design of Providence one day to hold in its hands the destinies of half the world.

CED 9.3
The Cold War

When de Tocqueville wrote that passage in 1835, he certainly wasn't thinking about ideological differences, but such differences did emerge dating back to the establishment of the communist state in 1917, which was followed by limited Allied involvement in the Russian Civil War. Even during the war, although cooperation certainly existed, mistrust played a role in the relationship between the Soviet Union and its Western allies, ranging from Soviet anger over the delay in opening a second front to fears that the British and Americans were seeking to negotiate a separate peace with the Germans.

The Yalta Conference on the Future of Germany

Once the war came to an end and cooperation was no longer necessary for victory, mutual antagonism came out, beginning with the debate over the future of Germany. At **Yalta**, the Big Three—Churchill, Roosevelt, and Stalin—agreed to the temporary division of Germany, and in the aftermath of the war, Germany was divided into four zones (France was given a zone at the insistence of the British), with an Allied Control Council to make joint decisions. None of the Allies apparently wanted or expected dismemberment. Nevertheless, Yalta had provided each of the Allies with the opportunity to effect transformation in their own zone, with the end result that the Soviet Union would obviously transform its zone in a far different manner than the Western Allies. Ultimately, Germany would become a Cold War showcase for the rival ideologies.

The method chosen by the Soviet Union to gain control over political life in its zone was the subversion of a democratic structure it pretended to support. The Soviets began in their zone by allowing for the reestablishment of all non-right-wing parties that had existed in the Weimar Republic. **Walter Ulbricht**, the Soviet-selected leader of the German Communist Party (KPD), thought that because most Germans didn't want to go back to the world of Weimar and its capitalist crises, there would be genuine support for the KPD. The problem was that the widespread rape of German women by Soviet troops, dismantling of factories to be sent back to the Soviet Union, and the failure of land reform led to anger at the Soviets and their clients in the KPD. Seeing that no groundswell of electoral support would be forthcoming, Ulbricht brought about the forced merger of the KPD and the more popular Social Democratic Party (SPD) in 1946 and created a one-party state, a technique the Soviets were to find useful as they sought to gain control over other governments in Eastern Europe.

While these political developments were taking place, tensions were increasing over the issue of reparations. Neither the Americans nor the British were diametrically opposed to reparations, and an agreement had been reached at Yalta with an amount set at 20 billion dollars. At Potsdam, further negotiations led to the agreement that each occupying power would collect reparations in its own zone, with the hard-pressed Soviets receiving 25 percent from the amount collected by the other three.

The problem was that the Western Allies began to fear that carrying out a reparations program would leave the German economy prostrate, with the British and American public left paying the bill to feed the Germans. Even President Truman had been shaken by what he saw when he traveled to Germany for the Potsdam conference and noted, "Unless we do what we can to help, we may lose next winter what we won at such terrible cost last spring." On his own initiative, in May 1946, General Lucius Clay, the commander of the American zone, ended the collection of reparations, which was soon to be followed by the other two Western Allies, which meant that goods stopped flowing to the Soviet Union.

CED 9.4
Two Superpowers
Emerge

Increasing Tensions Outside of Europe

Tensions were also increasing between the Americans and Soviets in regions outside of Europe. Back in 1941, the Soviets and British jointly divided and occupied Iran, with an agreement that they would both leave at the end of the war. In 1945, the British promptly left, but the Soviets refused and demanded oil concessions. When Truman heard that Soviet tanks were heading to Tehran, the capital of Iran, he sent warships into the Persian Gulf, and Stalin responded by removing his troops.

Stalin also tried to intimidate Türkiye, which was neutral in the war, into granting the Soviets naval bases along the straits to give the Soviet fleet access to the Mediterranean, something Russia had long desired. To show the Turks he was serious, Stalin massed troops along their common border, and it was only when he understood that the United States would fight to protect Türkiye that he backed down and withdrew his forces.

American foreign policy toward the Soviet Union was in a state of flux in the immediate postwar period. In part, this reflected the replacement of Franklin Roosevelt, who felt that his good wartime relationship with Stalin could serve as the basis of postwar ties, with the no-nonsense Harry S. Truman, who saw Stalin in a more wary light.

American policy was also influenced by the writings of **George Kennan**, an official in the State Department. In 1947, Kennan wrote what became known as the **Long Telegram**, in which he indicated that the Soviets viewed the United States as an ideological enemy and would never seek to find the means for coexistence. In this and in articles that appeared under the pseudonym "X" in the journal *Foreign Affairs*, Kennan became the architect of the policy of **containment**, in which the goal of the United States needed to be the "long-term, patient but firm and vigilant containment of Russian expansive tendencies."

Containment and the Creation of NATO

Containment as an actual policy was first tested in Greece, where a Communist-led insurgency was fighting against the newly reestablished Greek government. Great Britain, which had assumed a watchdog position in Greece at the end of the war, informed the United States in 1947 that it lacked the economic resources to continue to support the Greek government. Seeing this as a major Soviet attempt to gain control over a strategically important nation (even though Soviet aid to the Greek Communists would later be shown to be quite minimal), Truman went before a joint session of Congress on March 12, 1947, and stated in what is known as the **Truman Doctrine** that, "it must be the policy of the United States to support free peoples who are resisting attempted subjugation by armed minorities or by outside pressures." He then proceeded to ask for money, which eventually reached the amount of $400 million to be given to the Greek and Turkish governments.

Containment was also going to figure into one of the most important decisions made by the United States in the postwar period. Rejecting George Washington's admonition in his farewell address to stay clear of permanent alliances with foreign powers, the United States decided to counter directly the threat posed by the millions of Soviet soldiers based in Eastern Europe by establishing the **North Atlantic Treaty Organization (NATO)** in 1949. Joining the United States as initial members were Great Britain, France, Canada, Denmark, Belgium, Iceland, Italy, the Netherlands, Portugal, and Norway, with Greece and Türkiye joining the alliance in 1952.

SOVIET DOMINANCE OVER EASTERN EUROPE

In 1944, seeing that Soviet troops were advancing through Eastern Europe, Winston Churchill traveled to Moscow to meet with Stalin. As Churchill recalled years later, after pushing a piece of paper in front of Stalin, "There was a slight pause. Then he [Stalin] took his blue pen and made a large tick upon it, and passed it back to us. It was all settled in no more time than it takes to set down." This document became known as the **Percentages Agreement**, because it divided the various nations of Eastern Europe into spheres of influence based on percentages, with for example, Soviet influence being at 90 percent in Romania and only 50 percent in Hungary. The agreement was seriously flawed, as Poland was left out of it entirely. The United States refused to accept the agreement.

With the war in Europe winding down, Stalin expected to be able to control the future of those areas liberated by the Red Army. With the enormity of Soviet losses in the war in mind and unwilling to see Roosevelt's Atlantic Charter as a source of future peace, Stalin wanted to establish a protective shield to protect the Soviet Union from any future invasion from the west. Meeting in Yalta, on the Crimean Sea, the British and Americans were able to get the Soviets to accept a high-minded **Declaration of Liberated Europe**, stating that in those countries that were Axis or liberated, governments were to be formed that were "broadly representative of all democratic elements in the population" and that free elections were to be held at the earliest possible time.

The Iron Curtain

Churchill, rushing to get an agreement signed in 1944, revealed his growing concern that Eastern Europe would become dominated by the Soviet Union and that there was not that much that the Western Allies could do to block this development. Several years later, it was Churchill who delivered his famous speech at Westminster College and used a metaphor that would represent Soviet control over Eastern Europe when he decried the fact that "From Stettin in the Baltic to Trieste in the Adriatic, an **iron curtain** has descended across the Continent."

Poland

On the question of Poland, Stalin was going to continue with his plans to establish a government dominated by Polish Communists; the only concession he granted was that an undetermined number of anticommunist Poles based in London would be added to this provisional government. This aspect of the Yalta Conference has proven to be very controversial, with Roosevelt being accused of selling out the Poles. The tragic reality was that the Soviets had troops on the ground in Poland, and there was little that the United States and Great Britain could do about it short of war. There was going to be a price for having the Soviet Union for an ally against Germany.

When the promised elections in Poland were finally held under conditions of intimidation in 1947, the Communists received 80 percent and proceeded to bring any sign of a multiparty state to an end. The Soviets understood that they would have to use force to maintain Communist control over Poland because they were hated in that nation—a loathing that grew worse when the role of the Soviets was revealed in the **Katyn Massacre**, the murder of 15,000 Polish officers in the forests of Katyn at the start of the war.

Elsewhere in Eastern Europe

Nevertheless, in the rest of Eastern Europe, the Soviets hoped that control could be achieved through less violent means. The Soviet Union seemingly had a number of advantages in this goal, including the economic and social failure of the states of Eastern Europe during the interwar period (with the exception of Czechoslovakia). This meant that few were advocating a return to the politics of the past, although in most of Eastern Europe, the Soviets were viewed as liberators from the horrors of German dominance. With the exception of Poland, the Soviet Union initially tried to establish "**People's Democracies**" in Eastern Europe. For the Communists, this was a go-slow program, with governments that were more proletarian than in the bourgeois West but were still not ready for a full-fledged Communist system as found in the Soviet Union.

In many ways, the push for tighter control over Eastern Europe came about in reaction to the offer of **Marshall Plan** money to all the nations of Europe. Stalin saw the Marshall Plan as a threat to informal Soviet control over countries like Hungary or Czechoslovakia, because by taking the money, those countries would automatically be drawn toward the capitalist West. So Stalin moved to assert more direct control. In Hungary, the Communists practiced "salami" tactics, in which intimidation and false plots against non-Communist political leaders sliced them away from the body politic. Using such tactics, the Hungarian Communist Party forced its competitor, the Smallholders' Party, out of existence by 1948 and in the following year won a tainted election with 95 percent of the vote.

Czechoslovakia

In Czechoslovakia, the situation was different. In the immediate postwar period, the government was dominated by men like President Eduard Benes. Although Benes was a non-Communist, he understood that it would be necessary to maintain a pro-Soviet foreign policy if Czechoslovakia were to retain its national independence. Also, the Czechs were more favorably disposed toward the Soviet Union, whom they gratefully saw as liberators, while feeling they didn't owe anything to the West, which had sold them out at Munich in 1938. This balancing act failed in the wake of Czech desire to accept badly needed Marshall Plan monies. To put pressure on Benes's government, the Czech Communists formed a "People's Militia," which intimidated Benes into forming a new government dominated by Communists.

When the body of Foreign Minister Jan Masaryk, the son of the founder of Czechoslovakia, was found outside his window—the result of either suicide or murder—it was clear that a multiparty Czechoslovak state was coming to an end. The Social Democrats were forcibly absorbed into the Communist Party, and in controlled elections in May 1948, the Communists won a complete victory and proceeded to set up a Soviet-style state.

Yugoslavia

The major exception to Soviet control over Eastern Europe took place in Yugoslavia. Initially, Yugoslavian resistance was based on a broad alliance against the brutal Croatian puppet government established by the Germans. As the war continued, however, a civil war broke out among the partisan groups with the Communists, led by **Josip Broz Tito**, fighting against the royalist Chetniks. The civil war ended with the triumph of Tito's Communists, but Stalin never trusted Tito, in part because of the assistance he received during the war from the British and Americans as well as the fact that Stalin never liked indigenous Communist movements that he couldn't directly control. Relations between the two states remained poor in the ensuing years, and by 1948, a formal break took place. Although Tito became the West's favorite Communist because of his independent foreign policy, at home he maintained a brutal, communist-style police state.

THE END OF IMPERIALISM

The British had hoped to maintain their vast empire following the war. The United States, however, was extremely reluctant to allow this, and Great Britain, which was dependent on American loans, was forced to concede the point. The beginning of decolonization took place on August 15, 1947, when India declared independence, initiating a domino effect throughout the rest of the Empire.

> **CED 9.9**
> Decolonization

Egypt and Africa

Great Britain maintained significant influence in Egypt, even though the latter had been an independent nation since 1922. This began to change when **Abdul Nasser** (1918–1970) became president. In 1956, he announced the nationalization of the Suez Canal, which the British still controlled. In response, Britain, France, and Israel planned a surprise attack on Egypt. The immediate outcry from the American and Soviet governments made it quite clear to Britain and France exactly who were the dominant powers in this postwar world. They bowed to the American and Soviet demands to withdraw.

Soon after, the British saw the writing on the wall, and they began the process of decolonization in sub-Saharan Africa. In 1957, the nation of Ghana declared its independence from Great Britain, and in the ensuing years Nigeria, Sierra Leone, Uganda, and Kenya followed Ghana's lead. Because these territories all contained few British settlers, independence came about without too much trouble. In Rhodesia, on the other hand, in 1965, the large number of British settlers formed their own white-supremacist government and declared their independence from Britain. Not until 1980 would Africans win control over that land, which they renamed Zimbabwe.

Indonesia, Vietnam, and Algeria

For nations such as France and the Netherlands that had a less-than-sterling military record in the Second World War, holding on to their colonies became an important part of restoring national honor. The Dutch maintained a costly and ultimately unwinnable struggle in the East Indies to keep the land they had first occupied in the 17th century. By 1949, the Netherlands reluctantly agreed to recognize Indonesian independence.

France almost ripped itself apart in its attempt to hold on to Algeria. This followed a bitter loss in Indochina (Vietnam), where a nationalist movement under the leadership of **Ho Chi Minh** (1890–1969) fought first against the Japanese during the Second World War and then against the French, as the latter attempted to restore its colonial authority. By 1954, France realized it was an impossible task and agreed to divide Vietnam into two states: a northern Communist-led nation and a republic in the south dominated by the United States.

Although the French could accept the loss of Indochina, Algeria was different; it had been a French possession since 1830, and more than a million native French lived in the territory. France almost erupted in civil war over the Algerian question in 1958, until de Gaulle took the helm of the French government and used his immense prestige four years later to grant Algerian independence.

THE CREATION OF A EUROPEAN UNION

In the aftermath of the war, there were several factors that contributed to the goal of establishing greater European cooperation. For the French in particular, pan-European cooperation would provide a means for keeping an eye on its traditional enemy, Germany. There was also a growing sense that economic rationalization and cooperation were needed to end wasteful competition and ease tensions between nations. Additionally, concern over the Soviet Union, which led to military cooperation through the establishment of NATO, aided the cause of European unity.

> **CED 9.10**
> The European Union

The first stage in this process took place in the realm of economic cooperation, with the establishment of the **Organization for European Economic Cooperation (OEEC)**, which had the task of handling the money provided by the United States through the Marshall Plan. The United States made it clear when providing the money that it did not want to see it used to revive unprofitable industries in order to salvage national pride, and the United States insisted that Europeans use the money in a cooperative manner. The OEEC also began the initial work on lowering tariffs and eliminating trade barriers among those states receiving assistance.

The next development was the creation in 1951 of the **European Coal and Steel Community (ECSC)**. The ECSC combined and administered the steel and coal resources of its member states: France, West Germany, Italy, Belgium, the Netherlands, and Luxembourg. The main architect of the ECSC, Frenchman Robert Schuman, stated that one byproduct of this form of economic cooperation was that "any war between France and Germany becomes not merely unthinkable, but materially impossible." The ECSC also provided certain models that were important for the future development of European unity, such as the establishment of a supra-national assembly to guide the ECSC (which was renamed the **European Parliament** in 1962), a court of justice, and direct income for the Community in the form of taxes.

In 1957, the original members of the ECSC signed the **Treaty of Rome**, establishing the **European Economic Community** (more commonly referred to as the **Common Market**). The members of the EEC, who were joined by Britain, Ireland, and Denmark in 1973 in the first expansion of the Community, lifted almost all trade restrictions among member states. In 1986, in the first major revision to the Treaty of Rome, the **European Single Act** provided for the free movement among member nations of capital, labor, and such services as banking and insurance.

The **Maastricht Treaty** of 1992 led to the establishment of a common currency, the Euro, with banknotes and coins going into circulation in January 2002, with the exception of Denmark, Sweden, and most significantly the United Kingdom, which refused to give up the pound. The Maastricht Treaty also introduced new areas where there was supposed to be increased cooperation, such as in defense, justice, and environmental affairs, which resulted in a name change from the EEC to the **European Union (EU)**.

Recent and Future Expansion of the European Union

The European Union has undergone a number of expansions in its list of member states (the largest crop of entrants joined in 2004), notably with nations that were formerly members of the Warsaw Pact or part of the Soviet Union, such as the Czech Republic, Estonia, Hungary, Latvia, Lithuania, Poland, Slovakia, and Slovenia. Bulgaria and Romania joined in 2007, and Türkiye entered into negotiations for membership back in 2005. Türkiye's European Union bid has been controversial for a number of reasons. Some EU officials doubt that Türkiye can meet economic targets required for membership, or they question Türkiye's commitment to human rights. Some have expressed concern about admitting a Muslim state into the EU with a large population second only to that of Germany.

EU expansion has also led to the desire to make it work more efficiently, which led to the writing of a **European Constitution**, the caveat being that all EU members had to approve the constitution for it to go into effect. France, however, a nation that has been at the forefront of European cooperation, voted "no" in May 2005 in a national referendum. Increased tensions and a resurgence of nationalism throughout Europe have made it clear that further European integration is on hold for the foreseeable future.

20TH-CENTURY CULTURAL CHANGES

The European Feminist Movement

European feminists of the 20th century stood on the shoulders of more than a century of female activists, known as first-wave feminism. These activists' efforts paid off immediately after the First World War, when women gained the right to vote—first in England, then elsewhere on the continent. Later, other feminist activists successfully opened up new avenues of access to education and professional careers. The same advances were made in the Soviet Union and its states through government mandates.

CED 9.8
20th-Century Feminism

The 1960s saw the beginning of second-wave feminism, a period during which the battle for the rights of women was extended to new realms. At this time, the invention of the birth control pill gave European women more control over their reproductive lives, as did increased access to abortion. Women could initiate divorce, which became commonplace. Some pointed their bullhorns toward persistent inequalities in the workplace and elsewhere, either guaranteed by law or practiced by custom. Scandinavia, the Netherlands, Germany, England, and Spain were all hotspots for this movement.

Politically, Europeans began to choose their first democratically elected female leaders, including Margaret Thatcher in the 1980s (Great Britain) and Mary Robinson in the 1990s (Ireland). At a less visible level, many parliaments and congresses found their number of female representatives growing as well.

Feminism wasn't the only social movement on the march, either. Having been persecuted by Nazi Germany and Francoist Spain, the gay and lesbian population worked for the rest of the century to expand their own civil rights. Today, 19 European nations have legalized same-sex marriage, with Western Europe consistently ranking as one of the most progressive regions of the world in this area.

CED 9.11
Migration and
Immigration

New Types of Immigrants

Europe's economic growth in the decades following World War II was a double-edged sword. As the continent recovered in the first half of the century, its industries began modernizing and transforming. To meet these needs, Europe needed more workers, and therefore attracted migrants from Africa, Asia, the Middle East, and elsewhere. Some came alone; others brought families.

This immigration brought about two significant outcomes. In terms of religion, the arrival of Muslims from Africa and the Middle East altered what had been a largely Christian (and Jewish) population, which stoked feelings of fear and distrust between faiths. Socially, the arrival of people who looked different and spoke differently gave populists the justification they were seeking to form radical-right, anti-immigrant European political parties such as the **French National Front** and the **Austrian Freedom Party**. Immigrant groups often became the target of working-class anger and frustration, especially during economic downturns.

Mass Consumerism and the United States

During World War II, the fruits of U.S. culture had begun to arrive in Europe in the backpacks of the thousands of American GIs who fought on the continent. In the decades after the war, these imports continued. American records (blues artists such as Muddy Waters), American books (*The Catcher in the Rye* by J. D. Salinger), and American beverages (Coca-Cola) flooded the European markets, along with the U.S. aid dollars provided to the European continent via the Marshall Plan. Furthermore, new ideas were transmitted quickly between the continents via international telephone lines, and new travels were made possible with the availability of mass-market international flights.

CED 9.13
Globalization

All of this provoked criticism from many European quarters, especially France, that traditional continental culture was being forgotten. Many intellectuals and students protested the new bourgeois lifestyle, which reached a peak in May of 1968 with nearly two months of civil unrest in France aimed against the forces of capitalism. Later, at the end of the century, this globalized consumerism was challenged once again in Europe by left-wing groups that urged sustainable development and local consumption.

Meanwhile, Europe was nonetheless adopting many of the same new economic advances in production and consumption that were sweeping much of the planet. These included the mass production of plastic, the use of polyester and other synthetic fibers for clothing and furnishings, and new ways of processing food for the masses.

As the economy recovered in the second half of the century, so eventually did the birth rate. France and Austria experienced significant baby booms post-World War II, as did most other northern European countries. These were spurred on by government policies encouraging the repopulation of a continent devastated by war. The Mediterranean countries didn't experience the same boom, however, since those governments didn't provide the same incentives.

Radicalism in Art and Religion

The early 20th century wreaked havoc on people's belief in reason and science, a trend that continued during and after World War II, particularly in the arts. The visual arts movement known as **postmodernism** included many smaller movements such as Abstract Expressionism and Pop Art. These groups differed widely, but they all rejected classical forms of traditional portraiture and landscape art. They encouraged individual self-expression in all its forms, with many of the artists portraying weird, very original interpretations of states of subconscious awareness that carried no clear meaning. Likewise, in architecture, the **Bauhaus school** was originally based in Germany and rejected the old beauty of form in favor of clean, simple functionality that didn't pretend to be part of any tradition. In literature, the same rejection of tradition continued with novelists such as **Albert Camus**, who in *The Stranger* struggled to express the inner life of a protagonist who was essentially dead inside, alienated from everything. French philosopher **Jean-Paul Sartre**, whose most famous work *Being and Nothingness* reflected the feeling of the postwar era, exemplified this literary movement of hopelessness known as existentialism.

CED 9.14
20th- and 21st-Century Culture, Arts, and Demographic Trends

The totalitarian changes that had arisen in Germany and the Soviet Union during the 20th century saw different responses from traditional Christianity. German theologians such as **Dietrich Bonhoeffer** tried to understand, explain, and urge resistance to the evil of Nazism; he was hanged by the regime just before its collapse. Pope Pius XI, however, failed to publicly condemn Nazi Germany for its atrocities against Jews, preferring to remain neutral even in the face of mass murder. Meanwhile, the Soviets had outlawed religion within their borders and persecuted Orthodox Christians and Jews, either murdering or condemning hundreds of thousands to death in Siberia. In the 1980s, **Pope John Paul II** publicly criticized communism, thus contributing indirectly to the fall of the Soviet Union. Prior to that, in the 1960s, the Catholic Church had undergone the **Vatican II Council**, a series of internal reforms designed to modernize its own doctrines and practices. This included changing the language of the mass from Latin to the vernacular.

POST-WWII DEVELOPMENTS IN WESTERN EUROPEAN STATES

Great Britain

The postwar period in Great Britain began with what at the time was considered to be one of the greatest political upsets in electoral history—the replacement of Prime Minister Winston Churchill and his Conservative Party with the **Labour Party** and its leader, **Clement Attlee.** It probably shouldn't have come as such a surprise, because although many in Britain were deeply grateful to Churchill for the steely leadership he provided during the war, there was a sense that he was not the man to lead them in times of peace.

Economic and Social Reforms

Even while the war was in full swing, a sentiment that many shared was that Britain had to move beyond the dismal economic and social conditions that had prevailed during the interwar years. **Sir William Beveridge**, a member of the Liberal Party, had produced in 1942 (at the request of the government) a report that recommended that all adults should pay a weekly contribution, and in return benefits would be paid to people who were sick, unemployed, retired, or widowed. For Beveridge, the benefit of such a system was that it would provide for a minimum standard of living "below which no one should be allowed to fall." The electoral triumph of the Labour Party was due to the belief within the British public that it was the party most committed to implementing this far-reaching plan for reform. With its victory in 1945, Labour began the establishment of a cradle-to-grave social welfare program—the highlight being the establishment of the **National Health Service (NHS)**, which provided for a comprehensive system of free health care.

CED 9.6
Contemporary Western Democracies

Such programs spread outwards from England, and soon many European countries were pursuing a system of government intervention in daily life that was intended to guarantee citizens a basic level of education, housing, and health care. However, this type of public spending is costly. Therefore, when Europe began to feel budgetary pressure at the end of the 20th century, these programs became a punching bag for many on the conservative side of the political spectrum, who complained not only of their expense but also of the weakened work ethic that they promote.

Nationalization of Industries

Attlee and the Labour Party were also committed to a program of nationalization of major industries. Beginning in 1945, the government took control of the Bank of England, the railroads, and the electric, iron, and steel industries. This was not as revolutionary as it might appear, because in many cases, these industries had already been placed under government control during the war years. Fair compensation was paid to the existing owners, and company management (which some of the more radical members of the Labour Party wanted to see handled by the workers through committees) remained in the hands of professional managers, in many cases the same individuals who had led the firm prior to the takeover.

Economic conditions remained fairly grim in the immediate postwar years. Britain was now a major debtor to the United States, because its own gold and foreign currency reserves had been depleted to save the nation from the Nazi onslaught. The Labour Party remained committed to sizable military expenditures, because Britain still had large military commitments overseas, and the advent of the Cold War also affected spending. Although the standard of living improved for many people in the immediate postwar years because of the increase in social services, this period, generally referred to as the **"Age of Austerity,"** lasted until 1954, when the wartime rationing of butter and sugar finally came to an end.

By the 1951 general election, the Labour Party and the public were fairly exhausted from the pace of change, which provided a renewed opportunity for Churchill's Conservatives. Aside from reversing the nationalization of the iron and steel industries, the Conservatives did not return the remaining industries to private hands and continued to support the social service network implemented by the Labour Party. This has come to be known as the **"Politics of Consensus,"** because although the two major parties may have differed on details such as funding levels, they were in general agreement on the need to provide social services and that government should play a large role in the management of the economy.

Economic Decline

Although one can refer to a postwar "economic miracle" in Germany and Italy, such talk for Great Britain would be wide off the mark. Britain's economic growth by the 1950s was clearly less than that achieved by the nations of Western Europe. The reasons for **Britain's economic decline** in the postwar period remain controversial, but one can generally see factors such as the reliance on older factories, whereas plants in places like Germany were rebuilt with the latest technology following the destruction brought by the war. Britain also lacked the central economic planning that was to prove to be critical for French economic growth, and Britain had to deal with aggressive unions that wanted higher wages without agreeing to produce gains in productivity. Some scholars have even looked to cultural reasons for Britain's decline suggesting, for example, that the study of the sciences in British universities took a back seat to the pursuit of the humanities.

> ### Violence in Ireland: Bloody Sunday
> During these same years, the situation in **Northern Ireland** worsened, with the British government sending troops into the troubled province in 1969. On January 30, 1972, thirteen Catholics were killed when British soldiers fired on civil rights marchers. The day became known as **Bloody Sunday** and led to a renewed surge of violence by groups such as the Irish Republican Army that were opposed to the British presence in Northern Ireland.

Following a period of Conservative dominance in the period after 1951, the Labour Party reemerged as the dominant political party in the period from 1964 to 1974. Although Prime Minister Harold Wilson was leading a party that would prove to be successful at the polls, he was not able to strengthen the position of Britain in the global economy.

Margaret Thatcher and the Post-Thatcher Years

In 1979, Prime Minister James Callaghan's Labour government proved unable to deal with a wave of strikes that negatively affected road transport and public services. This period was known as the "winter of discontent." This provided an opportunity for the triumph of the Conservative Party and its leader **Margaret Thatcher**, who became Britain's first female prime minister. Thatcher had made it clear that she wanted to break with what she viewed as the failed policies of the past and stated, "I am not a consensus politician, I am a conviction politician." **Thatcherism,** the eponymous term for her economic policies, included tight control over the money supply to reduce inflation, sharp cuts in public spending, and a cut in taxes, particularly for higher earners.

Thatcher sought to make Britain more competitive in the global market by reducing the power of the trade unions and by reprivatizing those parts of the British economy still under the control of the government. Thatcher was a very divisive leader, and her career might have come to an early end if it had not received a boost following the successful war that Britain fought with Argentina in 1982 over the **Falkland Islands**. Thatcher ran into trouble during her third term when she tried to introduce market principles into the running of the NHS and education system, and her hostility to working toward further European integration created dissent within her own party. In 1990, she resigned and was replaced by **John Major**. Major continued with most of Thatcher's domestic policies, though perhaps without the divisiveness that she had brought to British politics. Because he was more pro-European than Thatcher, he signed the Maastricht Treaty.

In 1997, after being out of government for 18 years, the Labour Party triumphed under its youthful leader **Tony Blair**. Blair, who had become the leader of his party in 1994, had moved Labour away from its socialist roots, creating what he referred to as "**New Labour**." Rather than renationalizing the economy, Labour under Blair focused on improving Britain's social services, reform of the House of Lords, and the devolution of power away from Westminster and toward regional parliaments in Wales and Scotland. Blair received a second term in 2001 and a third in 2005, although the margin of Labour's victory in the 2005 election was significantly reduced because of anger over Blair's support for the war in Iraq.

Blair resigned as Labour Leader in May of 2007, and Gordon Brown, who served as Chancellor of the Exchequer under Blair for many years, rose to become both leader of the Labour Party and prime minister of the United Kingdom. Brown served until 2010 when David Cameron (a Conservative Party leader) became prime minister. Cameron resigned in June 2016 after Britain voted in favor of Brexit (more on this in a bit), and Theresa May became leader of the Conservative Party and Prime Minister in July 2016.

France
France in 1945 had to deal with the grim aftermath of what one historian has termed the "Strange Defeat" of 1940. France largely chose to deal with the difficult Vichy years by propagating certain myths, including the idea that France was a nation of resisters against German occupation, that few supported Marshal Pétain and Vichy, and that the tragic fate of the Jews in France was entirely the responsibility of the Germans. Marcel Ophuls's powerful documentary *The Sorrow and the Pity* (1969) helped open the door to questioning these national myths, although it remained several years before French television was willing to show the film. Under **Jacques Chirac**, who served as president from 1995 to 2007, the nation finally began to address France's role in the deportation of 66,000 Jews to Germany, along with other issues involving collaboration activities during the war.

Charles de Gaulle, the leader of the French government-in-exile, expected to dominate political life in postwar France—but he stepped away from politics when the newly established **Fourth Republic** refused to establish the strong presidency that de Gaulle felt was needed if France was not going to repeat the mistakes of the politically contentious Third Republic. French political life was also transformed, if in a more positive manner, by the granting of the vote to women. It was left to the Fourth Republic to grapple with a series of colonial problems, including the disastrous defeat in Indochina in 1954 and a revolt that broke out in Algeria the same year.

The crisis in Algeria, which led to fears that a military coup would take place in France itself, brought about the return of de Gaulle to politics, and he led the vote for a plebiscite in 1958 establishing the **Fifth Republic**, which contained the powerful presidency whose office de Gaulle now held. Although his enemies saw him as dictatorial, de Gaulle was committed to restoring France to a leading place on the global stage. To do this, he committed France to taking a leading role in Europe, which meant vetoing Britain's attempt to enter the Common Market in 1962.

To ensure that it could provide for its own defense, France refused to sign the **Limited Test Ban Treaty** and exploded its first hydrogen bomb in 1968. France also maintained an independent foreign policy marked by its withdrawal from NATO's unified command in 1966 and its recognition, over the strong objections of the United States, of the Communist government in China.

Economic Struggles

France's economy in the 1950s and 1960s made significant strides from the serious economic difficulties it faced at the end of the war. In 1945, five million men returned home from Germany and needed jobs, the transport system was shattered during the heavy fighting in the last year of the war, and the country had limited supplies of coal and food. This dire situation favored the **French Communist Party**, which had a good wartime resistance record and appeared to offer answers to these economic problems. The party, however, turned against the German occupiers following the invasion of the Soviet Union. Although the Communists were part of the first postwar coalition government, they were pushed out of the coalition in 1947, in part with the support of the United States, which made it clear that economic assistance would not be forthcoming if the Communists remained in the government.

In that same year, France began the implementation of an economic program designed by **Jean Monnet**, who was also one of the founders of the European Community. The **Monnet Plan** established the *Commissariat Général du Plan* (CGP), which provided for nonpolitical technocrats to run the economy. With increased foreign investment and rational central planning, the French economy, which had traditionally lagged behind Germany and Great Britain, began to take off. This transformed life in France as newly prosperous consumers began to buy cars, televisions, and dishwashers. It also, however, created a sense that their unique way of life was being transformed by what its critics referred to as **Americanization**, embodied most directly by the newfound popularity of that most American of products, Coca-Cola.

By 1968, disenchantment among the young over what they considered to be the sterile course of French life—as well as anger over classrooms, laboratories, and libraries that were bursting at the seams as more students pursued higher education—led to student revolts at every major French university, with the most serious situation taking place in Paris. In May of that year, students forged an alliance with workers, but this soon petered out as the students' demand for a thorough reordering of French society clashed with the more limited demands of the workers for wage increases and better working conditions. Although de Gaulle survived this crisis, in the next year he resigned.

France continued to be led by members of the Gaullist party until the electoral victory in 1981 of Socialist leader **François Mitterrand**, the longest-serving president of France. A moderate within his party, Mitterrand focused on social reform programs and reducing unemployment rather than radical plans for the socialization of the French economy. Mitterrand, who was reelected in 1988, retired from politics in 1995 and was replaced in office by Jacques Chirac, the Gaullist mayor of Paris.

Chirac served two full terms as president of France for a total of 12 years, the second longest tenure in the job after Mitterrand. He ran on a platform committed to healing social ills (such as racism and labor strikes), providing tax cuts, and instituting job programs. Unfortunately, social unrest grew in his second term with some of the worst rioting seen in France since the late 1960s. Chirac also came under fire during his presidency for several instances of corruption that took place while he was mayor of Paris and for general wastefulness in spending, particularly concerning his own palace services.

Conservative **Nicolas Sarkozy** succeeded Chirac in May of 2007, winning a runoff against Socialist Segolene Royal. He vowed to implement a controlled immigration policy and an ambitious development plan to modernize the country. After Sarkozy, François Hollande of the Socialist party took office in 2012. In May of 2017, Emmanuel Macron was elected president under the banner of En Marche!, a centrist political party he had founded the previous year.

Italy

The fall of Mussolini's government in 1943 presaged a violent civil war that lasted until the end of the Second World War. Because the Italian monarchy was tainted by its association with the Fascists, a referendum in 1946 led to the establishment of a republic. The **Christian Democrats** became the party of government, dominating political life in Italy until the 1990s. In Italy, unlike the rest of Western Europe, the Communists remained a significant opposition party. In part, this was due to the influence of **Antonio Gramsci** (1891–1937), one of the founders of the Italian Communist Party, whose writings encouraged a measure of political flexibility that was certainly not found within the more doctrinaire French Communist Party.

Italy made outstanding economic progress in the 1950s and 1960s, to the point that it was referred to as the "economic miracle." In part, this progress was achieved through the large role played by the state in the Italian economy through the **Institute for Industrial Reconstruction (IRI)**, which was created in 1931 during the Fascist years. The IRI controlled shipbuilding, airlines, metallurgy, and the chemical industry, with the automaker Fiat being the only large manufacturer to remain in private hands.

Italy benefited from its early commitment to the Common Market, as well as from the cheap labor supply provided by the 6 million southern Italians who moved to the north in the 1960s. Attempts were made to address the longstanding poverty of the south, with an interest in the **"southern question"** emerging as a peculiar byproduct of Mussolini's exile of political opponents to the south. This meant that a number of postwar Italian political leaders had a firsthand acquaintance with the economic plight of that region. Land reform broke up the large estates, and money was pumped into the region through a series of five-year plans. But to this day, there is a significant economic gap between north and south.

By the 1970s, economic problems were increasing, including high unemployment, inflation, and the loss of a staggering number of workdays to strikes. The Christian Democrats limped on as the party in power, in part because, despite their own failings, there was seemingly no other option. A revival of the mafia took place in the south, while political terrorism from the extreme left led to frequent attacks on politicians, judges, and business leaders. The most brazen of these terrorist attacks took place in 1978 when the **Red Brigade** kidnapped former Prime Minster Aldo Moro and eventually murdered him when the government refused to negotiate his release.

Although Italy remains politically stable, frequent changes of government remain a part of the political landscape as do charges of corruption, which after years of being ignored, shook the Christian Democratic Party in the late 1990s. In 2006, questions regarding corruption led to the defeat of Prime Minister **Silvio Berlusconi**, a conservative media magnate who controls most of the major media outlets in Italy outside of government control. **Romano Prodi** of the Olive Tree party became prime minister in May of 2006, his second time assuming the position (the first was in 1996). Since then, Italy has had as prime minister Berlusconi again (2008–2011), Mario Monti (2011–2013), Enrico Letta (2013–2014), Matteo Renzi (2014–2016), Paolo Gentiloni (2016–2018), Giuseppe Conte (2018–2021), Mario Draghi (2021–2022), and Giorgia Meloni (2022–Present).

Germany

The first years after the war were extremely difficult in Germany, as the nation dealt with the sheer magnitude of its defeat and the incredible destruction from the war; in 1947, industrial production was still only half the prewar level. Adding to the problems was the reality that if there was one place in Europe where Cold War tensions could flare up into actual fighting, then that location was **Berlin**, a city that was divided, like the country at large, into four occupation zones.

A series of crises would periodically flare up over the divided city, the first taking place in June 1948, when the United States and Britain introduced a new currency into their occupation zones without seeking Soviet approval. Stalin retaliated by **blockading** the city of Berlin, completely cutting off the city from the west. Why Stalin took this step is not entirely clear, but perhaps he felt that this was a way to push for negotiations on the status of the city. An odd quirk from the negotiations at Potsdam was that although there was no written agreement on access to Berlin by rail, road, or water, there were three officially designated air corridors. Seeing this as an opportunity, U.S. General Clay once again showed personal initiative and began to send supplies by air, with President Truman soon offering his full support. The **Berlin Airlift** went on for ten-and-a-half months and came to an end in May 1949, when Stalin lifted the blockade with no preconditions.

A Divided Country: East and West Germany

Seizing on the momentum achieved by the successful airlift, in 1949, the United States, Great Britain, and France agreed to combine their zones to create the **Federal Republic of Germany**, with the city of Bonn as its capital. The Soviet Union responded several months later and decreed that its zone in eastern Germany would become the Communist-dominated **German Democratic Republic**. Possible reunification was suggested by Stalin in a note he sent in 1952 to the West German government, in which he implied that Germany could be reunified and exist as an unarmed and neutral state. There has been a historical debate over how sincere

Stalin was in his offer, though he may have been willing to allow for German unification because he desperately wanted to forestall West German rearmament. In any event, the offer was rejected, and West Germany rearmed and entered NATO in 1955.

Germany would remain at the center of the Cold War, with the city of Berlin as the critical hotspot. In 1958, Soviet Premier Nikita Khrushchev gave an ultimatum to the West saying that they could stay six months and then had to pull out all their troops and allow Berlin to become a free city with access controlled by East Germany. President Eisenhower refused to budge and made it clear that he would launch another Berlin Airlift if necessary.

The Building of the Berlin Wall

The next stage in the conflict over Berlin began at 2:00 A.M. on August 13, 1961, when East German border police began to string a barbed-wire barrier between East and West Berlin. This was followed over the next several days by the building of a concrete barrier, the infamous **Berlin Wall**. For the East German Communists, this was deemed to be necessary because they were suffering a serious brain-drain as the educated elite were leaving the country in droves, with more than 2.5 million having passed to West Germany by 1949.

The reaction of the Western Allies was fairly mild, because putting up the wall did not impact what the West thought was essential to its Berlin policy: the presence of Western troops, free access to the city, and political self-determination for West Berliners. President John Kennedy's critics said he should have done something when the barrier was just barbed wire, but short of war, there was little to be done. As proof that there may be something to the old adage "Good fences make good neighbors," the building of the Berlin Wall proved beneficial, in that it meant that the constant crises over Berlin would now come to an end with the acceptance by both sides of a divided city.

Political, Social, and Economic Reforms

The early years in the history of the Federal Republic of Germany were dominated by **Konrad Adenauer**, who served as chancellor from 1949 to 1963 as the head of the **Christian Democratic Union (CDU)** party. Adenauer, an anti-Nazi German conservative who had been mayor of Cologne in the Weimar Republic, greatly feared the Soviet Union and therefore preferred to see a West German state tied to the West rather than a unified Germany that was forced into neutrality. Adenauer's government also attempted to address the terrible crimes committed by the Germans during the Nazi period by paying compensation to Jewish victims of the Holocaust as well as making direct payments to the state of Israel.

Adenauer's government also ushered in a period of economic growth, aided in the immediate postwar years by the influx of millions of Germans who had fled west from Poland, Czechoslovakia, and East Germany. In the most dramatic example of a **postwar economic miracle**, the West German economy grew from $23 billion in 1950 to $103 billion in 1964. Equally significant, this newfound prosperity trickled down through the population so that workers experienced increased wages from higher productivity, which they used on hitherto-unimagined luxuries like new cars and foreign vacations. The main government architect of this economic boom, which was notably achieved without high inflation, was **Gerhard Ritter**, Adenauer's minister of economics and chancellor following Adenauer's retirement in 1961.

During the Adenauer/Ritter years, the **Social Democrats** looked like they were going to remain in a position of permanent opposition. Electoral success arrived through a combination of two elements: dropping the Marxist language of class struggle, which the party did in 1955, and the emergence of the charismatic **Willy Brandt** as the leader of the party. Brandt, who rose to national prominence as mayor of Berlin, became chancellor in 1969, the first time a Socialist led a German government since 1930.

Although remaining firmly tied to the West, Brandt felt it necessary to reach out to the Soviets and their satellite states in Eastern Europe. This policy of contact, known as *Ostpolitik*, led to the signing of treaties with the Soviet Union, Poland, and Czechoslovakia and provided for de facto recognition of the East German state. In a famous display of national contrition, Brandt, on a visit to Poland in 1970, knelt before a monument to those who fell during the Warsaw Ghetto Uprising. Despite the international acclaim that he received, including the awarding of a Nobel Prize in 1972, the end of Brandt's term as chancellor occurred swiftly in 1974, when a member of his staff was arrested as an East German spy.

Brandt's successor as chancellor was **Helmut Schmidt**, who despite having to face economic problems stemming from the oil crisis of 1973 was still able to lead the Social Democrats to an electoral victory in 1976. As in Great Britain and the United States, the early 1980s seemed to represent a surge in conservative politics, and in 1982, the CDU achieved an electoral comeback under **Helmut Kohl**.

German Reunification

It was Kohl, however, who would move with speed and determination to bring about **German reunification in 1990**. He also worked with French President François Mitterrand to promote the Maastricht Treaty, which created the European Union. Kohl's tenure as chancellor of Germany, at 16 years, was longer than that of any German chancellor since Otto von Bismarck. The aura surrounding him eventually wore off amid continuing problems in the newly reunified Germany, including high unemployment. In 1998, the German electorate turned once again to the Social Democrats under the leadership of **Gerhard Schröder**.

Schröder had promised more jobs during the 1998 election, and during his first term, unemployment did go down, only to rise back up to the level he had inherited from Kohl and later to a record-breaking level. After narrowly winning reelection in 2002, in large part because of his strong opposition to the looming U.S.-led invasion of Iraq, Schröder introduced several reforms that many perceived as a dismantlement of the welfare state. These reforms were very unpopular with the core constituency of the Social Democrats. In July of 2005, Schröder intentionally lost a vote of confidence in the Bundestag (German Parliament), paving the way for early elections in September of that year.

Angela Merkel of the CDU became the first female chancellor of Germany in November of 2005 after striking a coalition deal with the Social Democrats. This deal was brought about by the extremely close election in September of that same year whereby no party received a majority of seats in the Bundestag. Under Merkel, and until her resignation in 2021, the German economy boomed, and her approval rating was high.

THE COLLAPSE OF THE COMMUNIST BLOC

CED 9.7
The Fall of Communism

Having suffered two foreign invasions in the 20th century, the Soviet Union set as its priority the establishment of a system of satellite states in Eastern Europe. The Soviet Union created the Warsaw Pact in 1955 to establish military ties with its satellite states and the Council for Mutual Economic Assistance (COMECON) to link their economies. From the start, however, there was tension.

East Germany and the Berlin Wall

In 1953, East German workers went to the streets first to criticize the government's plan to increase productivity, and then later to demand greater political freedom. By 1961, life was so grim in East Germany that millions of individuals fled to the West, which led the Soviets to construct the **Berlin Wall**.

Reform in Hungary

In 1956, similar strikes in Poland set off an even more important movement for change in Hungary, where reform-minded Communists led by Imre Nagy took the helm of government and began a liberalizing process. The Hungarians wanted to create a multiparty system, pull themselves out of the Warsaw Pact, and reestablish Hungary as a neutral nation. By late 1956, the Soviets grew tired of such demands, which threatened the whole system of satellite states, and crushed the reform movement, killing thousands along the way.

Power Struggles in the Soviet Union

Within the Soviet Union, significant developments followed the death of Stalin in 1953. The winner of the power struggle for his replacement was **Nikita Khrushchev** (1894–1971), who, in a significant reversal from the previous regime, did not execute the losers in this political contest. At the Communist Party's 20th national congress in 1956, Khrushchev, standing before a secret session, made a speech in which he attacked the many crimes of Stalin. Khrushchev claimed that Stalin's government had deviated from the political program of Marxism-Leninism, rather than being a natural outgrowth of it, and that the only reforms that would be acceptable would be those that stayed within the guidelines offered by Marxism-Leninism. Although Khrushchev made a successful visit to the United States in 1959, tensions between the two nations were heightened in the following year when the Soviet Union shot down an American U-2 spy plane over Russia. By October 1962, the two nuclear superpowers nearly went to war when the Soviets placed missiles in Cuba. U.S. President Kennedy's skillful handling of the crisis, however, allowed both nations to avoid the specter of a nuclear nightmare.

The Fall of Communism in Eastern Europe

The relative liberalization of the Khrushchev years came to an end with his forced retirement in 1964. His successor, Leonid Brezhnev (1906–1982), did not reinstate the terror of the Stalin years, but he did seek to once again strengthen the role of the party bureaucracy and the KGB (the main security agency for the Soviet Union), and encouraged the further clampdown on reform in the satellite states.

By 1968, disaffection with this step backward led to the emergence of a reform movement in Czechoslovakia. The goal of this "**Prague Spring**" was to bring about a more humanistic socialism within certain limits, such as keeping the nation within the Soviet Bloc. Brezhnev still saw this as a threat to the entire Warsaw Pact and initiated what became known as the "**Brezhnev Doctrine**," declaring that the Soviet Union would support with all the means at its disposal (including military intervention) any established communist state in Eastern Europe that was threatened by internal strife. The reform movement was crushed and its leader, Alexander Dubček, was replaced by someone more to Brezhnev's liking.

Reform in Poland and Eastern Europe

The most significant challenge to the Brezhnev Doctrine came in Poland, a land whose people were deeply stirred when in 1978 Karol Wojtyla, a Polish Cardinal, was elected **Pope John Paul II**. Two years later, led by Lech Walesa, an electrician, a massive strike took place at the Lenin shipyard in Gdansk, where workers demanded the right to form an independent trade union. **Solidarity**, as the new union was called, survived the declaration of martial law and being outlawed by going underground, in part with the aid of the Catholic Church. By 1989, the Polish economy was in such a shambles that the government was forced to negotiate with Walesa and his union. Surprisingly, the negotiations resulted in the promise for multiparty elections, which, when they took place in that same year, resulted in the defeat of all Communist candidates.

When the reform-minded **Mikhail Gorbachev** (b. 1931) took charge of the Kremlin, he indicated his opposition to the "Brezhnev Doctrine." With reform looming overhead, 1989 proved to be one of the most remarkable years of the century, as Communist-led regimes peacefully collapsed in Hungary, Czechoslovakia, Bulgaria, and Albania. In East Germany, the collapse of the regime in that same year was followed in 1990 by the reunification of East and West Germany and the destruction of the Berlin Wall. Romania proved to be an exception to this peaceful transformation, as the violent dictator **Nicolae Ceausescu** (1918–1989) desperately tried to hold on to power. In the end, his government collapsed, and he and his wife, Elena, were executed on Christmas Day 1989.

The Collapse of the Soviet Union

As their satellite states underwent a complete political transformation, people within the Soviet Union expressed their desire for change. Disasters like the Soviet invasion of Afghanistan and the nuclear accident at Chernobyl revealed the deplorable state of affairs within the nation. Gorbachev wanted to limit the extent of this change. He accepted the need for *glasnost*, or openness in debate, as well as *perestroika*, an economic restructuring of the state, but he was no democrat and still wanted to see the Communist Party lead these reforms. Events, however, went beyond his control, and in 1990, the government was forced to allow the political participation of non-Communist parties. Nationalist movements throughout the Soviet Union also popped up, beginning with the declaration of independence by Lithuania, followed by the insistence of the Russian Republic, another Soviet state, that its laws superseded those of the Soviet Union.

By the end of 1990, Gorbachev appointed some hard-liners to government positions to make the prospect of future reform far less likely. Instead, the whole system collapsed. In part, this was the result of the rivalry between Gorbachev and **Boris Yeltsin** (1931–2007), who served as chairman of the Russian Parliament. In August 1991, hard-line communists decided that Gorbachev's policies were threatening the existence of the Communist Party and staged a coup while Gorbachev was on vacation, placing him under arrest in his Crimean home. This turned out to be the last gasp of the Soviet Union, as Yeltsin bravely defied the plotters when he stood on a tank outside the parliament building and led the resistance. The coup failed and with it any hope of preserving Communist control. One by one, the assorted republics left the Soviet Union, and by the end of 1991, the Soviet Union was dissolved. Soon after, Gorbachev resigned.

A New Russian Republic

In 1991, Yeltsin was elected president of the newly created Russian Federation with 57 percent of the vote amid heightened expectations among Russians following the end of the Soviet Union. Sadly, when he resigned from office in 1999, Yeltsin acknowledged that his time in office was a lost opportunity, and in his resignation speech, he went so far as to say to his nation, "I want to ask you for forgiveness, because many of our dreams have not been realized."

Beginning his first term in office, Yeltsin decided to move the economy rapidly from centralized state control to free-market capitalism, a policy strongly advocated by many foreign economists, including advisors from the International Monetary Fund. This policy, which both supporters and skeptics referred to as "shock treatment," was based on significant short-term economic dislocation followed by greater economic stability and expansion. Unfortunately, the pain proved even harsher than expected and was marked by the transfer of state assets to a handful of well-placed oligarchs and by hyperinflation, which created turmoil for millions of Russians who depended on fixed state pensions. Official corruption and the emergence of vast mafia-style criminal organizations also became mainstays of the new Russian state and greatly contributed to a diminishment of Yeltsin's popularity.

The transition to political democracy was equally troubled. Conflict with the Congress of People's Deputies (the Parliament of the Russian Federation) over Yeltsin's economic policies brought about a series of confrontations with Parliament, leading to a serious crisis in October 1993 when the Congress began impeachment proceedings against the president. Yeltsin responded by ordering tanks to shell the building where the Congress met and ordered the legislature to be dissolved. Without a recalcitrant parliament to block his plans, Yeltsin was able to impose a new constitution providing enhanced power for the presidency and the establishment of the **Duma**, a new parliamentary body.

In 1996, Yeltsin surprised many Kremlin observers by running for reelection, despite having suffered several strokes and also having appeared drunk during public appearances. When his reelection seemed about to be derailed by a growing electoral threat from a resurgent Communist Party, Yeltsin turned to the business oligarchs who agreed to fund a lavish campaign for him in exchange for greater access to the remaining state assets, and to prevent the election of a Communist government from hindering their economic activities. Yeltsin comfortably won reelection, but except for working out a peace treaty that brought a brief end to the fighting with separatists in Chechnya, there were few other significant accomplishments during his second term.

Just prior to his resignation in December 1999, Yeltstin chose the relatively unknown Vladimir Putin as his prime minister. A former officer in the KGB, one of Putin's first acts upon assuming the presidency was to protect Yeltsin and his family from prosecution for corruption. Because other possible presidential candidates were surprised by the rapid promotion of Putin and the resignation of Yeltsin, Putin had a tremendous political advantage over his rivals and was easily elected to his own term as president in 2000.

In sharp contrast with Yeltsin, Putin has garnered significant popular support among Russians and he would have been easily reelected in 2004 even without his control over most media outlets. Part of his popularity stemmed from a rise in worldwide oil prices, which provided a huge boost to the Russian economy, although once again, Russia is in danger of repeating the Soviet mistake of the 1970s when it became too dependent on the proceeds from this one commodity.

Democracy Under the Putin Presidency

Democracy, which never truly thrived under Yeltsin, has received further blows during Putin's presidency, such as in the aftermath of the Beslan massacre of September 2004, when Chechen terrorists seized control of a school leading to the death of more than 300 hostages. The tragedy was used by Putin as an excuse for enacting a law that ended the practice of popular elections for governors in Russia's provinces, with the spurious claim that it would be more efficient to fight terror with a more centralized government. The suspicious deaths of several Russian journalists and the poisoning in London of former spy and Putin critic Alexander Litvinenko has further chilled the political climate in Russia.

Ethnic Warfare in the Former Yugoslavia

Uncertainty has been the hallmark of the former Yugoslavia. Its former leader, Josip Tito (1892–1980), led a successful resistance force against the Germans during the Second World War and after the war helped establish a Yugoslav state that avoided being tied to the Soviet Bloc. His strong leadership limited the intense ethnic rivalries within the country, but after he died in 1980, Slovenia and Croatia broke away from Yugoslavia to create their own states.

In 1992, a majority of the Muslim and Croat populations living in the Yugoslavian province of Bosnia wanted to follow suit. Bosnia's Serbs, however, refused to allow themselves to become part of a Bosnian state in which they would be a minority. With the help of Yugoslavian President **Slobodan Milošević**, they carried out **ethnic cleansing**, the forced removal, and, at times, genocidal murder, of Muslims and ethnic Bosnians in certain regions under their control. One of the last great atrocities of a century that has known so many was the Serb shelling of the Bosnian capital of Sarajevo, particularly the firing of shells on market days, when more people would be out on the streets. Such horrors led to the American-brokered **Dayton Accords** of 1995, which provided for a precarious peace for a time.

The next stage of the conflict in the Balkans centered on the Yugoslav province of **Kosovo**, a territory that the Serbs saw as the cradle of their national identity, stemming from their defeat in the Battle of Kosovo against the Ottoman Turks in 1389. In 1998, Milošević ordered an assault on Kosovo, using as his justification the attacks made on Serbs living in the province by the Kosovo Liberation Army (KLA), a small militant group that wanted to see the creation of an independent Kosovo. When the Serbs refused to sign a treaty that would have granted the Kosovars greater autonomy, NATO in March 1999 launched an aerial bombardment on Serbia that lasted for 74 days. This was the first offensive action taken by NATO against a sovereign nation in the alliance's history and resulted in the withdrawal of Serbian troops from Kosovo.

For Milošević, this was the beginning of the end of his dominance over Yugoslavian politics. In 2000, he was forced to call new elections, which he lost to Vojislav Kostunica. While Milošević was reluctant to turn over the reins of government to Kostunica, his hand was forced when hundreds of thousands of Serbs went into the street to demand he honor the election results. Though initially President Kostunica said that he would not turn Milošević over to the **War Crimes Tribunal** in The Hague, he changed his mind in 2001 in order to receive badly needed economic assistance from the West—though the point wound up being moot when Milošević died of a heart attack while his trial was still ongoing in 2006.

In February 2007, the United Nations International Court of Justice (ICJ) found that there was no evidence linking Serbia under the rule of Slobodan Milošević to genocide and war crimes committed in the Bosnian War. However, the court did find that Milošević and others in Serbia did not do enough to prevent acts of genocide from occurring. Still today there is widespread disagreement and controversy over whether what occurred in this era was ethnic cleansing or genocide, or whether there is a significant difference between the two, and the ruling bodies (the International Criminal Tribunal of the Former Yugoslavia and the International Court of Justice) and courts have prosecuted numerous people involved in the warfare.

In January 2009, the European Parliament passed a resolution to commemorate July 11 as a day of remembrance and mourning of the 1995 Srebrenica genocide. That incident was a July 1995 killing, perpetuated by Bosnian Serb soldiers, of more than 8,000 Muslim men and boys and forcible deportation of nearly 25,000 women, children, and elderly.

The Rise of Far-Right Reactionaries and Brexit

In the first two decades of the 21st century, Europe found itself gripped by a rise in the popularity of far-right nationalism. This movement is marked by profoundly conservative social values, often aggravated by perceived slights from minority groups. It also features an ultra-nationalistic point of view, particularly in opposition to immigration from the Middle East, as well as explicit racism. A collection of these ultra-conservative parties has gained ground in various European parliamentary elections in recent years, including Marine Le Pen's **French Front National** (FN), Geert Wilder's Dutch **Party for Freedom** (PVV), and Nigel Farage's **United Kingdom Independence Party** (UKIP). These groups openly state that they would like to see the European Union dismantled.

Thus far, it has been in the United Kingdom where this dream has achieved real success. In the summer of 2016, the people of the British Isles decided, via a narrow 53–47 popular vote, to leave the European Union. This became known as the **Brexit vote** (the word is a mash-up of "British" and "exit"). Granted, the U.K. had always been a bit of an outlier in the EU. It had never adopted the euro, preferring its own pound sterling, and as an island nation, it has long kept a strong individual national identity separate from the European continent. Nonetheless, this came as a shock to the world, as it presented the first major retreat from the concept of a unified Europe that had been built for over 70 years. Negotiations over the withdrawal agreement grew tense, as UK leaders rejected the EU's terms of withdrawal three times. After much negotiation, in January 2020, the UK officially withdrew from the European Union. While the shape of the future relationship has yet to be determined, it is evidence that Western politics have taken a swing toward reactionary far-right nationalism.

CHAPTER 7 TIMELINE

Year(s)	Event
1914	Assassination of Franz Ferdinand (June 28)
1914	Austria-Hungary issues ultimatum to Serbia (July 23)
1914	Austria-Hungary declares war on Serbia (July 28)
1914	Russia begins mobilization (July 29)
1914	Germany declares war on Russia (August 1)
1914	Germany declares war on France (August 3)
1914	Germans defeat Russians at Tannenberg (August 26–30)
1914	First Battle of the Marne (September 5–10)
1914	Completion of the Panama Canal
1915	Gallipoli campaign begins (April 25)
1915	Sinking of the *Lusitania* (May 7)
1915	Germans begin attack on Verdun (February 21)
1916	British launch attack at the Somme (July 1)
1917	Zimmermann Telegram (January 19)
1917	Germany resumes unrestricted submarine warfare (February 1)
1917	Bolsheviks sign armistice with Germany (December 3)
1917	United States declares war on Germany (April 6)
1917	Provisional Government established in Russia (February)
1917	Bolshevik seizure of power (November)
1918	Worldwide influenza outbreak
1918	Female suffrage begins in Great Britain
1918	Germany Republic established after abdication of Kaiser Wilhelm II (November 10)
1918	Armistice brings the war to a close
1919	Treaty of Versailles
1919	Mussolini organizes first Fascist party
1919	Weimar Constitution established
1920	Formation of Communist International
1922	Mussolini becomes Prime Minister of Italy
1923	German hyperinflation
1923	Beer Hall Putsch
1924	Death of Lenin
1924	Dawes Plan
1925	Treaty of Lucarno
1928	First Soviet Five-Year Plan

Year(s)	Event
1929	Beginning of collectivized farms in Soviet Union
1929	Lateran Accord between Mussolini and the Catholic Church
1929	Young Plan
1929	Stock market crash
1930	Nazis make huge electoral gains
1931	Bank failures
1932	Hindenburg defeats Hitler for the German presidency
1932	Nazis become largest party in Reichstag
1933	Hitler becomes chancellor
1933	Reichstag fire
1933	Enabling Act
1933	Germany withdraws from League of Nations
1933	German boycott of Jewish businesses
1934	Beginning of the Great Terror in the Soviet Union
1934	"Night of the Long Knives"
1934	Hitler becomes führer after death of Hindenburg
1935	Germany openly begins rearmament
1935	Italian invasion of Ethiopia
1935	Nuremberg Laws directed against German Jews
1936	Berlin Olympics
1936	German remilitarization of the Rhineland
1936	Beginning of the Spanish Civil War
1938	Germany absorbs Austria in Anschluss
1938	Munich Agreement leads to dismemberment of Czechoslovakia
1938	*Kristallnacht* (November 9)
1939	Nazi-Soviet nonaggression pact
1939	Invasion of Poland
1939	Britain and France declare war on Germany
1940	Fall of France
1940	Winston Churchill replaces Chamberlain as prime minister
1940	Battle of Britain (July–October)
1940	Germans begin Blitz on British cities (September 1940 to May 1941)
1941	Germany launches Operation Barbarossa
1941	Japanese attack on Pearl Harbor
1941	30,000 Jews killed at Babi Yar over two days
1941	Atlantic Charter

Year(s)	Event
1942	German advance stopped at Stalingrad
1942	Battle of Midway (June)
1942	Wannsee Conference organizes the Final Solution
1943	Battle of Kursk
1943	Allies land in Italy
1943	Mussolini's government fails
1943	Warsaw ghetto uprising
1944	Percentages Agreement between Churchill and Stalin
1944	Allied invasion of Normandy, a.k.a. D-Day (June 6)
1944	Germans launch Battle of the Bulge (December 16)
1945	Yalta Conference (February 4–11)
1945	Hitler commits suicide (April 30)
1945	Victory in Europe Day (May 8)
1945	Victory of British Labour Party over Conservatives (July)
1945	Potsdam Conference (July 17–August 2)
1945	Atomic bomb dropped on Hiroshima (August 6)
1945	Victory over Japan Day (August 14)
1945	United Nations' charter is ratified (October)
1945	Nuremberg Trials for crimes against humanity begin (November)
1946	Establishment of French Fourth Republic
1946	Referendum establishes the Italian Republic
1946	Churchill delivers Iron Curtain speech at Westminster College
1947	George Kennan writes the "Long Telegram"
1947	Truman Doctrine
1947	Introduction of the Marshall Plan
1947	India and Pakistan become independent states
1948	Break between the Soviet Union and Yugoslavia
1948	Establishment of the State of Israel
1948	National Health Service established in Great Britain
1948	Soviet dominance in Eastern Europe solidified
1949	Formation of NATO
1949	Berlin Airlift leads to ending blockade after 11 months
1949	Establishment of the Federal Republic of Germany
1949	Establishment of Democratic Republic of Germany
1951	Establishment of the European Coal and Steel Community
1953	Death of Stalin

Year(s)	Event
1954	French suffer defeat in Indochina
1954	Algerian revolt begins
1955	Establishment of the Warsaw Pact
1956	Soviets send in troops to put down Hungarian uprising
1957	Ghana declares its independence from Great Britain
1957	Signing of the Treaty of Rome establishing the EEC
1958	French plebiscite leads to creation of the Fifth Republic
1961	East Germany begins construction of the wall dividing Berlin
1962	France vetoes Britain's attempt to join the European Community
1962	Cuban missile crisis
1968	Wave of student protests in Europe and the United States
1968	Prague Spring
1969	Willy Brandt becomes German chancellor
1972	Irish Troubles begin with the shooting of 13 Catholic peace marchers on "Bloody Sunday"
1973	Oil crisis
1978	Red Brigades kidnap and murder former Prime Minister Aldo Moro
1978	Papal election of John Paul II
1979	Margaret Thatcher becomes prime minister
1981	François Mitterrand elected president of France
1985	Mikhail Gorbachev becomes leader of the Soviet Union
1989	End of Communist rule in Eastern Europe
1990	Reunification of Germany
1991	End of Soviet Union Boris Yeltsin elected president of newly created Russian Federation
1992	Maastricht Treaty
1992	Beginning of a series of violent conflicts in the former Yugoslavia
1997	Tony Blair becomes prime minister of Great Britain and Northern Ireland
1999	Vladimir Putin becomes president of Russian Federation
2002	Introduction of the euro
2004	Entry into NATO of former Warsaw Pact nations
2008	Dmitry Medvedev becomes president of Russian Federation (Putin becomes prime minister)
2010	David Cameron becomes prime minister of Great Britain and Northern Ireland
2012	Medvedev and Putin switch positions; Medvedev becomes prime minister and Putin becomes president
2016	Great Britain votes to approve "Brexit"; Theresa May becomes prime minister

CHAPTER 7 KEY TERMS

The First World War

Dreyfus Affair

antisemitism

Russo-Japanese War

Duma

Nicholas II

system of entangling alliances

Entente Cordiale

Triple Entente

Archduke Franz Ferdinand

Schlieffen Plan

Winston Churchill

Gallipoli

poison gas

Verdun

General Philippe Pétain

Battle of the Somme

The End of the War

Zimmermann Telegram

Lusitania

Woodrow Wilson

Fourteen Points

propaganda

Treaty of Versailles

League of Nations

Alsace-Lorraine

Bolsheviks

Vladimir Lenin

Leon Trotsky

Treaty of Brest-Litovsk

The Interwar Years

Weimar Republic

Kapp Putsch

hyperinflation

League of Nations

Communists

"White" forces

"Red Terror"

New Economic Policy (NEP)

Joseph Stalin

Five-Year Plan

collectivization

gold standard

Jazz Age

John Maynard Keynes

Franklin Roosevelt

New Deal

fascism

Il Duce

Fuhrer

corporatism

Benito Mussolini

National Fascist Party

Great Depression

Nazis

Adolf Hitler

National Socialist German Workers' Party

Beer Hall Putsch

Mein Kampf

Joseph Goebbels

Hitler Youth

Labour Party

Popular Front

Spanish Civil War

General Francisco Franco

Guernica

Anschluss

Third Reich

appeasement

Neville Chamberlain

Sudetenland

nonaggression pact

The Second World War

blitzkrieg
Dunkirk
Vichy
Charles de Gaulle
Battle of Britain
Luftwaffe
Nuremberg Laws
Kristallnacht
Holocaust
Auschwitz
Dr. Josef Mengele
Allies
Axis forces
D-Day invasion
atomic bomb
Hiroshima
Nagasaki
firebombing of Dresden
denazification
Nuremberg Trial

European Stability

Atlantic Charter
United Nations
revanchism

The Cold War and Soviet Dominance

Cold War
Yalta
George Kennan
containment
Truman Doctrine
North Atlantic Treaty Organization
(NATO)
iron curtain
Katyn Massacre
Marshall Plan

The European Union

European Coal and Steel Community
(ECSC)
European Economic Community (Common
Market)
Maastricht Treaty
European Union (EU)

20th-Century Cultural Changes

French National Front
Austrian Freedom Party
Postmodernism
Bauhaus school
Albert Camus
Jean-Paul Sartre
Dietrich Bonhoeffer
Pope John Paul II
Vatican II Council

Post-WWII Developments

National Health Service (NHS)
"Age of Austerity"
Britain's economic decline
Northern Ireland
Bloody Sunday
Margaret Thatcher
Thatcherism
Falkland Islands
Jacques Chirac
Americanization
François Mitterrand
"southern question"
Berlin
blockading
Berlin Airlift
Federal Republic of Germany
German Democratic Republic
Berlin Wall
Konrad Adenauer
Christian Democratic Union (CDU)
postwar economic miracle
Helmut Kohl
German reunification in 1990

Collapse of the Communist Bloc
Berlin Wall
Nikita Khrushchev
"Prague Spring"
"Brezhnev Doctrine"
Pope John Paul II
Solidarity
Mikhail Gorbachev
glasnost and *perestroika*
Boris Yeltsin
Slobodan Milošević
ethnic cleansing
Brexit vote

CHAPTER 7 REVIEW QUESTIONS

Try these questions to assess how well you understood and retained the information covered in the chapter. Answers and explanations are in Chapter 8.

Questions 1 through 5 refer to the following.

"The Chain of Friendship," *The Brooklyn Eagle*, 1914

1 ☐ Mark for Review

Which of the following causes of World War I best describes the situation depicted in this cartoon?

Ⓐ Imperialism

Ⓑ Excessive military buildup

Ⓒ A system of entangling alliances

Ⓓ The assassination of the Archduke Franz Ferdinand

2 ☐ Mark for Review

The Treaty of Versailles that followed World War I did NOT force Germany to

Ⓐ suffer permanent exclusion from the League of Nations

Ⓑ accept official responsibility for starting the war

Ⓒ demobilize most of its German military

Ⓓ pay reparations for damage done

3 ☐ Mark for Review

The massive carnage that was created by the war was NOT caused by

Ⓐ new technology such as machine guns, mustard gas, tanks, and barbed wire

Ⓑ rampant disease in the trenches

Ⓒ a new military strategy that stressed mobility and evasion

Ⓓ the nearly four-year length of the war

4 ☐ Mark for Review

All of the following were root causes of the chain of relationships in the cartoon EXCEPT

(A) the wave of intense nationalism that Europe had been riding for seventy years

(B) a newly united Germany, in 1871, which had upset the old balance of power of Europe

(C) Britain's decision to abandon its role as a neutral negotiator and to instead enter into alliances

(D) a system of aristocratic marriages that had rendered the nobility of all European nations hopelessly intertwined

5 ☐ Mark for Review

The feeling among the Triple Entente (Russia, France, and Great Britain) that they were fighting a *moral* war against an over-militarized, hypernationalistic Germany is most supported by

(A) an increase in the number of widows and orphans

(B) total war's ability to transform European society

(C) the founding of the League of Nations

(D) the later rise of Adolf Hitler and the start of World War II

Questions 6 through 9 refer to the following.

"The Empress [Alexandra], like all stupid people, and her stupidity has not been denied, even by her best friends, believed that one could rule a nation by terror. She, therefore, always interposed herself whenever Nicholas II was induced to adopt a more liberal system of government and urged him to subdue by force aspirations it would have been far better for him to have encouraged. She had listened to all the representatives of that detestable old bureaucratic system which gave to the police the sole right to dispose of people's lives and which relied upon Siberia and the knout to keep in order an aggrieved country eager to be admitted to the circle of civilized European nations....She was at the bottom of every tyrannical action which took place during the reign of Nicholas II. And lately she was the moving spirit in the campaign, engineered by the friends of Rasputin, to conclude a separate peace with Germany.

...Though everyone was agreed as to the necessity of a change in the system of government of Russia, though a revolution was considered inevitable, yet no one wished it to happen at the moment when it did..."

Source: *Rasputin and the Russian Revolution*, Princess Catherine Radziwill, Polish aristocrat, 1918

6 ☐ Mark for Review

It can be assumed that the author's dislike for the Empress was motivated by

(A) the common knowledge that everyone in Russia hated Empress Alexandra

(B) investigative journalism, which was the author's strength

(C) the dislike of elites for one another

(D) the author's bias as a Polish princess against the Romanov family, which had partitioned Poland over a century earlier

7 ☐ Mark for Review

The author alludes to what massive event that racked Russia in the same year as the book's publication?

(A) Bloody Sunday

(B) The Bolshevik Revolution

(C) The Holodomor

(D) The Katyn Massacre

8 ☐ Mark for Review

The "detestable old bureaucratic" system's practice of "[relying] on Siberia" was

(A) continued by the Communists and even expanded under Stalin

(B) a national shame that was abolished by Lenin

(C) copied by other nations as an effective management tool

(D) the leading cause of Russia's lack of development

9 ☐ Mark for Review

All of the following contributed to the weakness of Nicholas II EXCEPT

(A) killing almost a hundred subjects in the Bloody Sunday demonstration

(B) the establishment of and subsequent poor relationship with the Duma

(C) his decision to sign the October Manifesto

(D) Russian involvement in World War I

Questions 10 through 13 refer to the following.

"The first morning in Madrid, as we looked out of the window of our room in the Hotel Ritz, one of the great and grand hotels of Europe, we faced the entrance of the Prado Museum. Along the top of the Museum steps nine women in blue work-dresses were ranged, back to us, on their hands and knees scrubbing the top while one woman stood in front of them directing their task with the peremptory manners of an army sergeant. Later in the day we sought in vain for any evidence that the place had been scrubbed.

In the Museum we were shocked, as we had been before, by the deplorable state of the paintings, the poor lighting, the haphazard groupings of many of the rooms and artists. It is one of the richest and most glorious collections of paintings in the world, yet hardly a picture had been cleansed of the varnish of the centuries. Professional friends of ours had tried in vain to get permission to have some of the dubious paintings X-rayed, to urge that others be cleaned, that a more logical arrangement be made, that a new wing be built to house the hundreds of paintings for which there is now no room.

This is Spain in 1960—the official neglect of art and culture, the backwardness and, in the case of the cleaning women, the waste of labor, yet the desperate need of women to work, the scrubbing by hand when one man with one machine could've done it better."

Source: Herbert Lionel Matthews, *The Yoke and the Arrows: A Report on Spain*, *Revised Edition*, 1961

10 ☐ Mark for Review

It is implied that the "official neglect of art and culture" and "the backwardness" noted by the author are the result of

(A) the long-term effect of the Moorish occupation

(B) a culture that had traditionally shown little interest in art

(C) decades of control by Franco's dictatorship

(D) the consequences of World War II

11 ☐ Mark for Review

If the author wanted to provide evidence of a national "waste of labor" like the one referred to in the third paragraph, which of the following would most accurately provide such evidence?

(A) A list of payments made by a corporation

(B) A table showing the ratio of the working population to national productivity

(C) A total number of workers employed in 1960

(D) A comparison of median salary to median age of Spanish workers

12 ☐ Mark for Review

The conflict that resulted in the decades-long neglect of the museum was primarily fought between

(A) Republicans and Nationalists

(B) Republicans and Democrats

(C) Democrats and Socialists

(D) Communists and Republicans

13 ☐ Mark for Review

The best explanation for why a museum such as the Prado escaped destruction in World War II is that

(A) the Nazis had deemed its treasures too valuable to destroy

(B) Franco hadn't taken sides during the war

(C) the Nazis had decided to use it as a headquarters

(D) the Allied powers had protected Madrid with troops and aircraft

Chapter 8
Chapter Review
Questions:
Answers and
Explanations

CHAPTER 4 REVIEW QUESTIONS

1. **D**   Standing armies of the 15th and 16th centuries were almost always drawn from the ranks of the nobility. There really wasn't much other choice—the merchant class barely existed, eliminating (C), the lower classes were deemed unteachable, (B), and the priests were exempt, (A). It wasn't until later that the middle class began to dominate—and in the case of Napoleon's army, the military became a tool of social mobility.

2. **B**   A mercenary army is a group of soldiers who are paid to wage war. They have no emotional, patriotic, religious, or legal reason to fight—their only motivation is financial. In fact, they don't even have to come from the society that they are fighting for. Mercenary armies were quite popular in Europe at this time, especially the Swiss Guard, who were favored by the French and eventually were hired to guard the pope.

3. **C**   After the 80 years of conflict with Spain petered to a halt, the Netherlands found themselves religiously divided. The southern portion of the Low Countries stayed Catholic and eventually became the nation of Belgium. The northern portion of the Low Countries became what we call the Netherlands. With a weakened Spanish Empire, an England wracked by civil war, and a France waging ineffectual wars in every direction—this new nation dominated shipping and trade for well over half a century.

4. **B**   The Habsburgs were one of the most powerful families in Europe for most of the 16th and into the 17th centuries. Through marriage, they obtained three pieces of land that were nowhere near one another—Spain, Austria, and the Netherlands—and waged a war on behalf of Catholicism.

5. **C**   Although the dates of the events in the passage are unknown, the phrase "the coming storm" indicates that it occurs just before the dawning of the 80 years of conflict that has become known as the Dutch Revolt (1568–1648). That span included the immensely deadly Thirty Years' War (1618–1648), which left millions dead across Europe for essentially no reason except religion and alliances. Following that, Europe stopped waging wars of religion.

6. **B**   Lasting nearly 20 years in the middle of the 16th century, the Council of Trent was one of the Catholic Church's most important ecumenical councils. It was initiated by several popes to investigate the reasons for its declining influence as the central power in Europe. The movement that was undermining the primacy of the Church, of course, was the Protestant Reformation.

7. **D**   Though the document orders that "bishops be content with modest furniture, and a frugal table and diet," it's impossible to forget that the church was in the process of building the biggest, most extravagant monument to itself in its entire history. Constructed over 120 years, the dome was finally completed in 1590, which was 26 years after the Council of Trent. Choices (A) and (C) are irrelevant to the attitude of the document. Choice (B), the lay piety movement, shared the belief in simplicity, even though it was Protestant.

8. **C**   Tetzel was a German Dominican friar who was tasked with the job of selling indulgences, which remitted a person's sins. No confession or ablution was required. Martin Luther, (A), attacked Tetzel for abusing church teachings. Choice (D), Galileo, is irrelevant. The trap answer is (B), Pope Leo X, who indeed supported the sale of indulgences, but did not sell them directly.

9. **A**   While the Council of Trent did agree upon many internal reforms as described in the document, its official external stance toward the Protestants was unbending. The Catholic Church reaffirmed its own teachings about God as being the one, the only, and the true. The other three choices never occurred.

10. **D**   The Renaissance and subsequent Reformation saw the beginning of the end of the strong political influence that the Catholic Church had wielded in medieval Europe. This occurred for many reasons, including the rise of science, the growth of centralized power under monarchs, and the continuing growth of Protestantism, particularly in the north.

11. **B**   The name da Vinci, along with the date, is a very big clue. Italians in the late 15th century were practically swimming in rediscovered classical texts—the philosophy of Aristotle and Plato, the plays of Aristophanes, and many more.

12. **D**   "Man is the measure of all things" is a famous statement by classical Greek thinker Protagoras. As one of the Sophists, his relativistic viewpoint perfectly encapsulated the central idea of humanism—that there is no absolute truth except what humans deem to be truth. This was used in the Renaissance as a rejection of the certainties of the medieval Catholic Church.

13. **C**   Da Vinci's choice to draw a nude human male, using proportions that had been borrowed from ancient Greek mathematicians, could be seen as an artistic rebellion against the Catholic Church of his day. At that time, church authorities commissioned all the copies of Mother and Child they could find, but little more—and certainly nothing based on the mathematical ideas promoted by long-dead heathens.

14. **A**   As an engineer, and as a student of the rediscovered classic texts that began arriving in Italy in his lifetime, da Vinci was undoubtedly acquainted with the numerical ratios described by classical Greek thinkers. This movement, in fact, was called Neoplatonism, and it was all the rage in his hometown of Florence throughout his life.

15. **B**   By contrast, Italy still maintained strong connections with the ghosts of the Roman Empire, particularly in the ruins of the aqueducts, arenas, roads, and even private homes. These things were constant reminders to Italians that a different civilization had existed prior to the overwhelming power of the Catholic Church.

CHAPTER 5 REVIEW QUESTIONS

1. **D** A positive balance of trade—meaning more exports than imports—was deemed essential for a healthy economy. Eliminate (C), since it describes the opposite. Eliminate (A), because floating exchange rates is a modern innovation. And (B) could potentially result in more currency, but waging war against a foreign nation in the 17th century was typically a way to lose currency.

2. **B** Colbert tried mightily to support the growth of domestic manufacturing, focusing mostly on production of glass, ceramics, and textiles. In fact, the famous blue-patterned French china that some people still use today is traceable back to his policies. He favored tariffs, so eliminate (C). Choices (A) and (D) are irrelevant.

3. **A** Sadly, all of Colbert's attempts to reform the economic system so that it served the state helped Louis XIV pursue a series of expensive and unnecessary foreign wars. These conflicts depleted the royal treasury just as quickly as it could be filled. This resulted in the extension of the system of punishing taxation that would lead to the massive French Revolution a hundred years later.

4. **B** The Physiocrats were a short-lived group of 18th-century French economists who believed that the value of land, and specifically the agriculture that grew upon it, was the primary way to measure the wealth of that nation. It made no allowance for the manufacturing of anything, which is maybe why it didn't last long as a school of thought. Still, Physiocracy was one of the earliest schools of economic thought.

5. **C** The purpose of mercantilism, according to Colbert, was to support the state with greater monies. Therefore, the support of the state could be viewed as allied with nationalism, certainly more than liberalism, anarchism, or socialism.

6. **C** By describing the ways that the common people had already abandoned the Catholic festivals, and the ways that the Puritans were eliminating names that had been featured under the Catholic Church, the author shows the extent of the desire for Puritans to remake English culture.

7. **C** Oliver Cromwell was the first and only Puritan to ever rule England during the Civil Wars period. He refused the title of king, preferring to be called Lord Protector, and wore all black. Choice (A) is the opposite of what really happened: the Puritan clergy was forced into exile when "Bloody Mary" began executing Protestants. Choices (B) and (D) are irrelevant.

8. **A** The Palatines were a German Protestant group that fled to England and Ireland at the beginning of the 18th century. The Separatists, Dissenters, and Diggers were all opposed in various ways to the Church of England.

9. **C** The translation of an English-language Bible and the printing press that made it available to the masses were the two most practical reasons for the renewed emphasis upon the Bible. Eliminate (A) and (B). Of the remaining two answers, recall that a major portion of the entire Protestant movement was *disintermediation*—a big word that basically means cutting out the intermediary, so that a believer can have a direct relationship with the Holy Spirit. Eliminate (D).

10. **D** Bardsley, like all professional historians, was trained to base his conclusions upon original research through primary-source materials. If he did his job correctly, he used all publicly available records to examine the patterns of names in England during this period of its history.

11. **B** The Scientific Revolution was the first time in human history in which people decided to collect data and draw general principles from that information. Under the Aristotelian method, which had ruled Europe for two millennia, a person could claim that women had fewer teeth than men, if it suited the person's premise and assumption. Aristotle did this, famously, and it presumably never occurred to him to open a woman's mouth to count her teeth.

12. **B** The French Revolution was the great leveling of society, remaking the structure of society not on inherited hierarchy but on meritocracy. The publication of the *Encyclopédie* was a reflection of this great egalitarianism. An entry on *potato farming* was presented in the same pages, and in the same manner, as an entry on *Louis XIV*.

13. **A** Recall the intellectual sea change that had occurred the previous century. The Scientific Revolution was so called because it had shaken off the dead-end deductive arguments that had slowed down European advancement. Instead, scientists adopted empirical thinking, or inductive reasoning, in which information is gathered first with the express purpose of drawing general principles. Today, this is known as the scientific method.

14. **C** Descartes was the odd duck in the Enlightenment. Unlike virtually every other figure of the time period, he stuck by the practice of using general principles to arrive at specific principles, also known as deductive reasoning (or rationalism). This system of abstract thought, unsullied by any real-world data, caused him to mentally doubt everything, including his own existence. This is how he came to his most famous realization: "I think; therefore, I am."

CHAPTER 6 REVIEW QUESTIONS

1. **C** Patents are official requests for ownership of a new mechanical idea. As such, this list of patents indicates that at least some portion of the English society believed that such inventions were useful, or at least profitable.

2. **A** Be careful on this question. There is very little we can say about what the reader thinks when they read the source, but you do know for sure that the reference to petticoats reflects the restrictive clothing of the era. The other answer choices go too far and are unsupported.

3. **D** Nowhere does this passage mention or even allude to the liberal arts, (D). Make sure not to choose answers that are unsupported by the passage. However, because this is a NOT question, the unsupported answer is the correct choice. Merchants, (A), entrepreneurs, (B), and government regulation, (C), were all hallmarks of the day.

4. **C** A tradition of peasant farming had been present in every country in Europe for thousands of years. It was not unique to England the way the other three answers were, and those three traits were the foundation upon which the Industrial Revolution was built.

5. **D** In the northern kingdom of Sardinia, King Victor Emmanuel and his prime minister, Cavour, used complicated schemes to turn European countries against one another to achieve their nationalistic aims. In the southern Kingdom of the Two Sicilies, Garibaldi led a charge of primarily young people, known as the red shirts, to unify the Italian peninsula.

6. **B** In northern Italy, Count di Cavour used French support to provoke a war with Austria, which controlled portions of northeastern Italy that he wanted to nationalize. In Germany, Bismarck used two different wars, the Austro-Prussian War and the Franco-Prussian War, to build a sense of unity among the fragmented German-speaking city-states that he was attempting to bring into Prussia's fold.

7. **C** Garibaldi was a passionate and inspiring revolutionary, but he wasn't wise in the ways of high-level cutthroat European diplomacy. (His previous job had been a high school math teacher in Uruguay, where he led a different rebellion, using the same red shirts that he later brought to Italy.) Cavour played him like a fiddle, sending Sardinian forces to Rome to intercept his forces, since an attack on the papal states would provoke war with France. He then engineered a plebiscite in which the people of the south agreed to join Sardinia.

8. **D** The romantic nationalist movement of the 19th century put much greater emphasis upon the shared literature, music, language, culture, and ethnicity than it did upon shared religion. For example, at the time of German unification in 1871, there existed both Roman Catholics and Protestants within the country's boundaries. The Jewish community in Germany was given complete emancipation and equal rights in that same year.

9. **B** The Revolutions of 1830 and 1848 had been expressions of pure liberalism—the desire of the people for more individual freedoms. Nationalists, on the other hand, were often willing to jettison those freedoms if it meant creating unity.

10. **B** Charles Dickens once called the factories of the early 19th century "dark satanic mills." Having worked in a shoe polish factory to save his family from starvation while his father was in debtor's prison, he was well acquainted with the dark side of child labor. Many of Dickens's books, from *Hard Times* to *Great Expectations*, explore this theme.

11. **C** It's true that child labor existed both before and after the early years of the Industrial Revolution, and many people have depended upon it to save their families, or to teach children the value of discipline. However, it's difficult to defend abnormally long hours or inhumane conditions.

12. **B** Contracts weren't a problem during the early years of the Industrial Revolution—the problem, actually, was the *lack* of contracts. Many employees would routinely arrive at the factory to find it closed, or would be dismissed with zero notice.

13. **C** The Corn Laws were a set of laws enacted between 1815 and 1846 that imposed taxes and tariffs on imported grain, which benefited domestic producers. However, this kept the cost of bread high, which caused the working poor to suffer.

14. **A** Choices (C) and (D) are far out of scope. The trap answer is (B), because the Enlightenment did feature people attempting to make their cultures more rational. However, this didn't often result in altruism, but instead self-interest. Adam Smith famously wrote that individuals who pursued their own interests may benefit society more than individuals who pursued actions intended to benefit society.

CHAPTER 7 REVIEW QUESTIONS

1. **C** While the other answer choices were certainly major causes of World War I, it was the system of defensive alliances that this cartoon best describes. On one hand were defensive agreements between Russia and Serbia, Russia and France, and England and Belgium. On the other side were agreements between Germany and Austria-Hungary. All were triggered by the assassination of Archduke Franz Ferdinand.

2. **A** Germany wasn't excluded permanently from the League of Nations. It entered in 1926, soon after it was allowed to stop paying reparations. It withdrew from the League in 1933. The other three answer choices were all famously punitive conditions of the Treaty of Versailles.

3. **C** The correct answer, (C), is quite the opposite of what occurred. World War I stressed a defensive strategy, which was in contrast to the 19th-century military strategy of all offense. This strategy led to the arrival of trenches, in which soldiers sat for months at a time. Some of the worst battles in the history of the war, such as the Battle of the Somme, were fought over just a few miles of land, with almost no movement.

4. **D** The practice of nobles marrying other nobles from other nations certainly had been typical throughout European history. However, this practice had been dying out in the 19th century, since the power of the aristocracy had been greatly weakened by the growing power of the middle class, representative democracy, and mass politics. By the start of the 20th century, and World War I, the aristocracy was no longer driving many European states.

5. **D** Some historians have characterized World War I and World War II as essentially the same war. There's some truth in that, since the same hypernationalistic drive to create a perfect Aryan race at all costs (exhibited by Hitler) was present in Germany prior to World War I as well, but to an obviously lesser degree. Choice (A) is a trap answer, since the number of widows and orphans was a result of the war, not a cause to enter it.

6. **D**   Poland had ceased to exist as a state more than a hundred years earlier, when Russia, Prussia, and Austria had carved it into three parts. Polish national pride was fierce, however, and the country was reestablished following World War I. It is very logical that an aristocrat widely known as a princess of Poland would hold resentment against the same Russian ruling family that occupied her homeland.

7. **B**   The Bolshevik Revolution, also known as the October Revolution, occurred in the winter of 1917–1918. It stands as the most radical change in the history of the country. The only other event that could compare would be the fall of the Soviet system that the Bolsheviks set into motion.

8. **A**   Princess Radziwill referred to "[relying] upon Siberia," which can be taken to mean sending political prisoners to die at wintry work camps. This had long been a favorite practice of the Romanov dynasty, and unfortunately the Communists continued the practice on a much grander scale. Joseph Stalin set up a system of forced-labor camps, called *gulags* (an acronym for the government department that controlled it). Estimates range that from 2 million to 17 million people passed through the system.

9. **C**   While the people grew fed up with Nicholas II's alternating weakness and pretensions at autocracy, he did accomplish one thing that made the people happy—he signed the October Manifesto. A response to the Russian Revolution of 1905, this manifesto established a parliament, the Duma, and promised to enact many civil rights. Granted, Nicholas signed the manifesto only after his chief general threatened to shoot himself if he didn't.

10. **C**   The date mentioned in the passage is significant. 1960 was more than 20 years after the end of the Spanish Civil War, and more than midway through Franco's dictatorship. It can be concluded that the general state of society after two decades is attributable to the policies of the Franco regime.

11. **B**   A waste of labor is one of those things that can be measured by modern economists. They love to analyze the productivity of nations over time, and comparing that productivity to the number of workers over time will provide a valuable snapshot of whether there is indeed a "waste of labor."

12. **A**   This question is alluding to the Spanish Civil War. On one side of the war were the Republicans, which were a coalition of leftist types who had triumphed electorally in 1931. On the other side were the Nationalists, centered in Madrid and led by Franco, who rested on the far right. The Nationalists won (with assistance from nationalists in other countries) and led Spain for approximately the next 35 years.

13. **B**   Spain never officially entered World War II. However, Franco had slight involvement in the war here and there. He supported Axis powers with some troops as a "thank you" for the support they showed him during the Spanish Civil War. At the same time, however, he posted troops in the Pyrenees to prevent German troops from entering Spain.

Part VI
Additional Practice Tests

Practice Test 2

AP® European History Exam

At a Glance

Time
55 minutes
Number of Questions
55
Percent of Total Score
40%

DISCLAIMER: The official AP European History Exam will be administered digitally. Instructions for the digital exam may differ from this practice test.

Instructions

Section I, Part A has 55 multiple-choice questions and lasts 55 minutes.

Each question in this part is followed by four suggested answers. Select the best answer to each question.

Indicate all of your answers to the multiple-choice questions on the answer sheet. Give only one answer to each question.

Use your time effectively, working as quickly as you can without losing accuracy. Do not spend too much time on any one question. Go on to other questions and come back to the ones you have not answered if you have time.

Your total score on the multiple-choice section is based only on the number of questions answered correctly. Points are not deducted for incorrect answers or unanswered questions.

At a Glance

Time
40 minutes
Number of Questions
3
Percent of Total Score
20%
Questions 1 and 2
Mandatory
Question 3 or 4
Choose one question

Instructions

Section I, Part B has 3 short-answer questions and lasts 40 minutes.

In this part, answer Question 1 and Question 2 and **either** Question 3 **or** Question 4.

In your responses, be sure to address **all** parts of the questions you answer. Use complete sentences; an outline or bulleted list alone is not acceptable.

You may pace yourself as you answer the questions in this part, or you may use these optional timing recommendations:

It is suggested that you spend an equal amount of time, approximately 13 minutes, on each question.

For this practice test, use scratch paper for notes and planning as well as writing your responses.

GO ON TO THE NEXT PAGE.

AP EUROPEAN HISTORY
SECTION I, Part A
Time—55 minutes
55 Questions

Directions: Each of the questions or incomplete statements below is followed by four suggested answers or completions. Select the one that is best in each case.

Questions 1 through 5 refer to the following.

"They have seen the French rebel against a mild and lawful monarch with more fury, outrage, and insult than ever any people has been known to rise against the most illegal usurper or the most sanguinary tyrant. Their resistance was made to concession, their revolt was from protection, their blow was aimed at a hand holding out graces, favors, and immunities. This was unnatural.

   Were all these dreadful things necessary? Were they the inevitable results of the desperate struggle of determined patriots, compelled to wade through blood and tumult to the quiet shore of a tranquil and prosperous liberty? No! nothing like it. The fresh ruins of France, which shock our feelings wherever we can turn our eyes, are not the devastation of civil war; they are the sad but instructive monuments of rash and ignorant counsel in time of profound peace."

Source: Edmund Burke, *Reflections on the Revolution in France*, 1790

1 ☐ Mark for Review

Burke's opinion of the recklessness of the French Revolution is most similar to which of the following?

(A) An Italian university student's opinion of the Revolutions of 1848

(B) A Russian noble's opinion of Peter the Great's attempts at modernization in 1700

(C) A Polish peasant's opinion of the Third Partition of 1793

(D) An English Catholic's opinion of the overthrow of King James II in 1688

2 ☐ Mark for Review

Following publication of the book, Burke most likely

(A) changed his opinion based on the newly peaceful revolt

(B) maintained his opinion based on worsening violence

(C) traveled to France to persuade the people to seek peace

(D) lost his position as a university lecturer

3 ☐ Mark for Review

Which of the following people in the nineteenth century would most likely have agreed with the sentiments in this passage?

(A) Giuseppe Garibaldi

(B) Benjamin Disraeli

(C) Prince von Metternich

(D) David Hume

GO ON TO THE NEXT PAGE.

4 ☐ Mark for Review

The political condition described in the passage did not stabilize until

(A) 1791

(B) 1795

(C) 1800

(D) 1830

5 ☐ Mark for Review

The passage clearly shows the influence of which of the following trends in eighteenth-century thought?

(A) Conservatism

(B) Rationalism

(C) Enlightened absolutism

(D) Neoclassicism

GO ON TO THE NEXT PAGE.

Questions 6 through 9 refer to the following.

"As far as this, after suffering great hardships, the Dutch, in recent times have progressed towards the top of the world, seeking unknown lands, and if there is any shorter way to China. Wonderful are their discoveries! Strange things have happened! Go on, O blessed progeny of Neptune, and add new honors to our race. You have begun ill if you stop here. It is a hard task, but endure. Do not yield to misfortune, but on the contrary be more daring. Fate will clear the way."

Source: Inscription on a Dutch globe manufactured by William Blaeu of Alcmar, 1599

6 ☐ Mark for Review

The impulse toward exploration was displayed most strongly by what other nation during this time?

(A) Italy

(B) Portugal

(C) France

(D) Austria-Hungary

7 ☐ Mark for Review

The ability of the Dutch to undertake such exploration was reflected by all of the following EXCEPT

(A) their status as the premier shipbuilders in Europe

(B) their invention of the telescope

(C) their usage of Mercator projection maps

(D) their Catholic work ethic

8 ☐ Mark for Review

Based on the passage, which of the following can be safely inferred about European explorers of the sixteenth century?

(A) No other country had suffered greater hardships than the Dutch in the sixteenth century.

(B) Only those who had personally sailed in exploration were allowed to design globes.

(C) The Dutch had gone further in their travels than any other nation.

(D) Christopher Columbus had been unsuccessful in finding a shorter path from Europe to Asia.

9 ☐ Mark for Review

Attitudes like the one found in Blaeu's inscription can be tied to the development of what major nineteenth-century intellectual trend?

(A) Nationalism

(B) Romanticism

(C) Socialism

(D) Liberalism

GO ON TO THE NEXT PAGE.

Questions 10 through 12 refer to the following.

Luddites, England, 1812 (Unattributed)

10 ☐ Mark for Review

The attitude exemplified by the illustration was most likely first influenced by which of the following?

(A) The invention of the power loom

(B) The growth of transnational corporations

(C) The guild system

(D) The Enclosure Acts

11 ☐ Mark for Review

The primary reason for the Luddites' violence was their view that

(A) the machines had eliminated their jobs

(B) less-skilled workers were being hired to run the machines

(C) automation was inherently wicked because it contradicted the Bible

(D) neither the king nor Parliament was hearing their demands

GO ON TO THE NEXT PAGE.

12 ▢ Mark for Review

Which of the following international events directly precipitated the Luddite movement?

(A) The Napoleonic Wars

(B) The French Revolution

(C) The modernizing reforms of Joseph II of Austria

(D) The War of the Spanish Succession

GO ON TO THE NEXT PAGE.

Questions 13 through 17 refer to the following.

"[By 1861] it could already be seen, from various external signs, that affairs in Russia were no longer the same as in Nicholas' time.... More newspapers were about, and in 1861 journals of all kinds were on sale at the railway stations, which had not been the case in 1857.

In 1857 it was absolutely necessary to put on evening clothes in order to be admitted into the picture-gallery of the Hermitage, for was not the Hermitage a palace? In 1861 this rule was no longer in force.

In 1857 smoking on the streets of St. Petersburg was forbidden. In 1861 it was permitted, or at least tolerated.

In the passport offices, the clerks of the year 1857 used to take bribes freely, in the form of paper money, conveniently folded in the document to which their signature was required. In 1861 I learned that it was neither considered necessary nor desirable, nor even, in some cases, polite to offer bribes at random."

Source: Henry Sutherland Edwards, *The Russians At Home and the Russians Abroad*, 1879

13 ☐ Mark for Review

Based on Edwards's account, it can be inferred that by 1861 Russia's leadership had been influenced by which of the following?

(A) Conservatism

(B) Liberalism

(C) Nationalism

(D) Anarchism

14 ☐ Mark for Review

One major political event that occurred in Russia in 1861 that might account for some of these changes was

(A) the establishment of the Duma

(B) the abolishment of serfdom

(C) the murder of the Romanov ruling family

(D) the limitation of corvée labor to three days a week

15 ☐ Mark for Review

Prior to 1861, the Westernization referred to in the passage had been attempted most extensively by which Romanov leader?

(A) Peter the Great

(B) Catherine the Great

(C) Nicholas I

(D) Nicholas II

16 ☐ Mark for Review

The change described in the passage found its best intellectual expression in which of the following works of the nineteenth century?

(A) *Le Politique,* Henri Saint-Simon

(B) *On the Genealogy of Morals,* Friedrich Nietzsche

(C) *The Communist Manifesto*, Karl Marx and Friedrich Engels

(D) *On Liberty,* John Stuart Mill

GO ON TO THE NEXT PAGE.

17 ⬚ Mark for Review

By the 1930s, the ideas concerning openness in Russian society reflected in the passage had undergone which of the following transformations?

(A) The ideas came to be regarded with suspicion by many European intellectuals.

(B) The ideas were enlarged by the addition of representative democracy in Russia.

(C) The ideas were regarded with increasing hostility by satellite states in eastern Europe.

(D) The ideas were largely rejected as being incompatible with Soviet doctrine.

GO ON TO THE NEXT PAGE.

Questions 18 through 20 refer to the following.

"When, after [Dreyfus's] arrival, I went to see the prisoner he was in a state of excitement impossible to describe—like a madman. His eyes were bloodshot, and he had upset everything in his room. I was able at length to quiet him. I felt that he was innocent....

On the 24th, in the morning, his mental state, bordering on insanity, seemed so serious that, anxious to screen my responsibility, I reported it to the minister of war and to the governor of Paris. In the afternoon I was summoned by General de Boisdeffre, and accompanied him to the war office. The general asked me my opinion. I replied without hesitation that Dreyfus was not guilty....

After the verdict Dreyfus was taken back to his cell, where I saw him about midnight. On seeing me he burst into sobs and said, 'My only crime is to be born a Jew.'"

Source: Major Forzinetti, as quoted in *Dreyfus and the Shame of France*, C.M. Stevans, 1899

---

18 ☐ Mark for Review

The beliefs of those who accused Dreyfus based solely on his religion are best expressed in which contemporary work?

(A) *The Protocols of the Elders of Zion*

(B) *J'Accuse*, Émile Zola

(C) *The Jungle Book*, Rudyard Kipling

(D) *Heart of Darkness*, Joseph Conrad

---

19 ☐ Mark for Review

The Dreyfus Affair did NOT demonstrate which of the following about France at the turn of the twentieth century?

(A) The persistence of antisemitism amongst the French public

(B) The demonstration of the growing power of the media and public opinion in an era of mass politics

(C) The efficiency with which the Third French Republic addressed civil issues

(D) The strengthening of French parliamentary democracy

---

20 ☐ Mark for Review

His coverage of the Dreyfus Affair inspired Austro-Hungarian journalist Theodor Herzl to

(A) urge Jews living in western Europe to continue assimilating themselves into Christian society

(B) plead for reconciliation between the different factions of the controversy

(C) call for the restoration of a Jewish state in its historic homeland of Israel

(D) condemn the growing Jewish separatist movement as undemocratic

GO ON TO THE NEXT PAGE.

Questions 21 through 25 refer to the following.

"What also is the cost of these fleets and garrisons which we have abroad to guard our interests and maintain our influence? I find that...after supplying the sums necessary to maintain these defences and guard these interests, there still remains a vast amount of public expenditure under these heads that is still unaccounted for.... But then a plausible objection may be taken—'You forget that the military and naval condition of England is, at the present moment, one of transition; that you are changing in this age of scientific discovery, and especially of scientific discovery as applied to armaments, your whole system of armaments, and that this leads to the vast expenditure which cannot be accounted for.'

...I believe I am right in saying that from the siege-train to the ambulance England was never so profusely and so effectively furnished as at the present moment. The conclusion we must come to when we find out that these armaments have been carried out so effectively and so completely, and apparently are so near entire fulfillment, is that the time has come... when a considerable reduction may be made in our naval and military expenditure without the least impairing our home defences or the efficiency of those forces which defend our interests abroad."

Source: Benjamin Disraeli, speech on Mr. Walpole's Resolution, 1862

21 ☐ Mark for Review

Disraeli's speech can be viewed as a call to resist which of the following?

(A) Imperialism

(B) Nationalism

(C) Militarism

(D) Industrialism

22 ☐ Mark for Review

According to the first paragraph, Disraeli's primary objection to England's military buildup was that

(A) it was technologically inferior

(B) it wasn't economically sound

(C) it had been opposed by his political enemies

(D) it had been undertaken during a period of transition

23 ☐ Mark for Review

Based on the speech, a modern historian might assume that military service in Britain had been increasingly portrayed as

(A) a horrific bloodbath to be avoided

(B) a noble calling to be pursued

(C) a largely intellectual exercise

(D) an expensive indulgence that would bankrupt the nation

24 ☐ Mark for Review

The increase in national armaments during the nineteenth century was NOT a major cause of which of the following?

(A) The Crimean War

(B) The scramble for Africa

(C) The Bolshevik Revolution

(D) World War I

GO ON TO THE NEXT PAGE.

25 ☐ Mark for Review

The English military differed from the Prussian military mostly in that

Ⓐ the English military focused primarily on building its naval forces, not its land forces

Ⓑ the English military occupied a significant part of the national budget

Ⓒ the English military benefited from the popular image of soldiers as heroes

Ⓓ the English military maintained a strict chain of command

GO ON TO THE NEXT PAGE.

Questions 26 through 29 refer to the following.

"Understanding from your letter to the Lord Cary that you approve my writings, I not only took it as a matter of congratulation with myself, but thought I ought to write and tell you how much pleasure it had given me. You are right in supposing that my great desire is to draw the sciences out of their hiding-places into the light. For indeed to write at leisure that which is to be read at leisure matters little; but to bring about the better ordering of man's life and business, with all its troubles and difficulties, by the help of sound and true contemplations—this is the thing I am at. How great an enterprise in this kind I am attempting, and with what small helps, you will perhaps learn hereafter...."

Source: Francis Bacon, "Letter to Casaubon," undated, seventeenth century

---

26 ☐ Mark for Review

A modern historian might interpret the phrase "out of their hiding-places into the light" as a reference to

(A) the forgotten scientific advances made by the Neoplatonists

(B) the popular oppression that faced ancient scientists when they presented their findings

(C) the dominance of the Aristotelian tradition in European intellectualism

(D) the secretiveness with which Bacon had to conduct his experiments

---

27 ☐ Mark for Review

By the nineteenth century, the type of thinking described by Bacon in the passage had led to which of the following in England?

(A) An acceleration in the innovation and adoption of technology

(B) A series of costly wars with continental Europe

(C) The development of the most feared army in the world

(D) The reestablishment of the divine power of the monarchy

---

28 ☐ Mark for Review

Despite Bacon's claim that he had only *small helps* to achieve his goals, all of the following figures could be viewed as his peers EXCEPT

(A) Tycho Brahe

(B) William Gilbert

(C) Johannes Kepler

(D) Voltaire

---

29 ☐ Mark for Review

Bacon did NOT make a great contribution to which of the following?

(A) The scientific method

(B) Deductive reasoning

(C) Inductive reasoning

(D) Empiricism

GO ON TO THE NEXT PAGE.

Questions 30 through 33 refer to the following.

Casa Pilatos, Seville, 1540

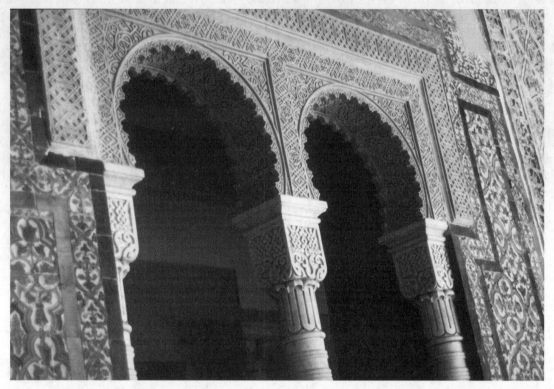

Detail of *ajimez* (paired horseshoe arch windows) with *alfiz* (rectangular surround) of carved stucco, and walls decorated with *azulejos* (glazed, patterned ceramic tiles) in geometric patterns.

30 ☐ Mark for Review

The creators of Casa Pilatos had primarily been influenced by whom?

(A) The French, whose cultural achievement was the highest in Europe

(B) The Portuguese, who were Spain's nearest neighbors

(C) The Moors, who occupied the Iberian peninsula for centuries

(D) The Habsburgs, who ruled both Spain and the Holy Roman Empire

31 ☐ Mark for Review

In sixteenth-century Spain, the religious sentiment that was reflected in the design of the building had been largely viewed as which of the following?

(A) Extremely inspirational, because the Spanish viewed all religious architecture as profound

(B) Overly intricate, because the Spanish preferred more streamlined design

(C) Highly technical and therefore worthy of emulation, especially in universities

(D) Undesirable, because the people who had inspired the design had been forced to either leave Spain or convert

GO ON TO THE NEXT PAGE.

32 ☐ Mark for Review

One of the things that made the Spanish Inquisition difficult to implement was the fact that

(A) many Jews and Muslims shared common ancestry with Christians

(B) the low levels of animosity toward Jews and Muslims were displayed by Catholic Church officials

(C) King Ferdinand and Queen Isabella disapproved of the oppression of minorities

(D) Jews and Muslims refused to renounce their religions

33 ☐ Mark for Review

One of the longest-lasting consequences of the expulsion of the Moors from Spain was

(A) a wealthier middle class as a result of increased trade

(B) economic inequality as a result of uneven distribution of reconquered lands

(C) stricter oversight of conquistadores' activities in the Americas

(D) faster adoption of customs from other parts of Europe

GO ON TO THE NEXT PAGE.

Questions 34 through 38 refer to the following.

"Somebody made a remark not very complimentary to Bismarck's enemies, to which [Bismarck] replied in a playful tone—
'Believe me, there is nothing some of my enemies find so difficult to forgive me as the crime of having become a rich man. Well, I suppose I must admit that I have been fairly successful in a material sense; even I wonder at it sometimes. For when I look back it seems to me that my wants were not extravagant. So long as I have a chair, and a table, and something overhead to keep the rain off, I am sure I could be happy.'

And in saying this he turned his face upwards and made a gesture—simulating an attitude of seeking protection from a threatened rainfall. Bismarck had been cruelly slandered by his foes, and there was an element of tragic pathos in the situation; yet it would've taken a bold man to offer condolence to one who, in his day, had so often smitten his enemies hip and thigh…. Kind as was the expression on Bismarck's face when he was comfortably seated at his own fireside, there were yet moments when his large, expressive eyes lit up with a threatening gleam. It was like sheet lightning shot across a landscape of a summer's eve, just sufficient to remind us amid an idyll that there are forces ever latent in men as in nature that need only be called into play to terrify us."

Source: *Personal Reminiscences of Prince Bismarck*, Sidney Whitman, 1902

---

34 ☐ Mark for Review

At the time of Whitman's visit, the political accomplishments of Otto von Bismarck were

(A) being vigorously lauded by European leaders across the continent

(B) regarded as part of a larger conspiracy against the spread of democracy

(C) part of the historical record, and irrelevant to the lives of his people

(D) in the past, but nonetheless viewed as integral to the strength of his nation

35 ☐ Mark for Review

Bismarck's foreign policy, known as realpolitik, culminated in which military action?

(A) The War of Austrian Succession

(B) The Schleswig-Holstein Affair

(C) The Austro-Prussian War

(D) The Franco-Prussian War

36 ☐ Mark for Review

Which of the following developments in German history is viewed as an obvious attempt by Bismarck to steal political support from socialist rivals?

(A) His waging of the Kulturkampf against Catholics

(B) His initial refusal to impose protective tariffs

(C) His "blood and iron" speech

(D) His creation of national health insurance, accident insurance, and pension programs

37 ☐ Mark for Review

Which of the following conclusions is best supported by Whitman's account?

(A) That Bismarck was capable of inflicting great cruelty upon his visitors

(B) That Bismarck had once been a powerful and effective politician

(C) That the modern nation of Germany was entirely Bismarck's responsibility

(D) That Bismarck was a simple man of humble origins

GO ON TO THE NEXT PAGE.

38 ☐ Mark for Review

At various times, Bismarck attempted to silence or restrain all of the following groups EXCEPT

(A) Junkers

(B) the media

(C) Socialists

(D) Catholics

GO ON TO THE NEXT PAGE.

Questions 39 through 41 refer to the following.

Paul Klee, *Untitled*, 1914

39 ☐ Mark for Review

The sense of dislocation seen in the painting was most profoundly reflected by what event?

Ⓐ The sudden adoption of the scientific method

Ⓑ The invention of the spinning jenny

Ⓒ World War I

Ⓓ World War II

40 ☐ Mark for Review

The underlying social forces that brought about Klee's painting did NOT produce which of the following?

Ⓐ Albert Einstein's theory of relativity

Ⓑ The Catholic Church's doctrine of moral absolutism

Ⓒ James Joyce's stream-of-consciousness novels

Ⓓ Germany's use of chemical weapons in World War I to cause mass death

41 ☐ Mark for Review

The painting is primarily an example of which of the following developments in European art?

Ⓐ Artists' abandonment of the figurative style in favor of more abstract ideas

Ⓑ Artists' embrace of overtly political metaphors in an age of war

Ⓒ Artists' sense of hopelessness in the face of a culture suspicious of innovation

Ⓓ Artists' understanding of asymmetrical design inspired by non-European cultures

GO ON TO THE NEXT PAGE.

Questions 42 through 45 refer to the following.

"Frenchmen! In commencing the War for maintaining the national independence, I relied on the union of all efforts of all desires, and the concurrence of all the national authorities. I had reason to hope for success, and I braved all the Declarations of the Powers allied against me. Circumstances appear to be changed. I offer myself sacrifice to the hatred of the Enemies of France. May they prove sincere in their Declarations, and have really directed them solely against my power. My political life is terminated; and I proclaim my Son, under the title of Napoleon II, Emperor of the French."

Source: Napoleon Bonaparte, declaration of abdication as Emperor, 1815

42 ☐ Mark for Review

Napoleon's reference to "the Powers allied against me" is best understood to refer to which of the following?

(A) The Catholic Church's opposition to his reign

(B) The coalition of European armies that had assembled to oppose his return to power

(C) The Portuguese forces that threatened his reign

(D) The economic sanctions that Europe had placed upon France while he was in power

43 ☐ Mark for Review

The "War for maintaining the national independence" is best interpreted as a reference to

(A) the Hundred Days

(B) the invasion of Russia

(C) the Peninsular War

(D) the Directory

44 ☐ Mark for Review

A modern historian would probably point to which of the following as strongest evidence of Napoleon's lasting influence in Europe?

(A) His dissolution of the Directory

(B) His unique naval military strategy

(C) His economic blockade of England via the Continental System

(D) His legal reform through the Napoleonic Code

45 ☐ Mark for Review

England resisted Napoleon's intrusions in all of the following ways EXCEPT

(A) the strength of its navy

(B) appeals to the power of the papacy to interfere

(C) subsidies to allies on the continental mainland who were affected by the blockade

(D) military support provided to Portugal during the Peninsular War

GO ON TO THE NEXT PAGE.

Questions 46 through 50 refer to the following.

Queen Victoria post office box, London, late nineteenth century

---

46 ☐ Mark for Review

Which of the following developments in late-nineteenth-century England was most responsible for the popularity of the postal system?

Ⓐ Better living conditions

Ⓑ Improved methods of steel production

Ⓒ Increased literacy rates

Ⓓ A decrease in leisure time for the middle class

---

47 ☐ Mark for Review

In late-nineteenth-century Europe, national postal systems were in most direct competition with what other form of communication?

Ⓐ Telegraph

Ⓑ Telephone

Ⓒ Radio

Ⓓ Television

GO ON TO THE NEXT PAGE.

48 ☐ Mark for Review

In Great Britain, the increased speed with which the postal system delivered items was mostly dependent upon which of the following?

(A) The network of trains and steamships that covered the island

(B) The invention of the internal combustion engine

(C) The first successful airplane launch

(D) The national system of electrical power stations

49 ☐ Mark for Review

The massive economic changes that gripped Europe in the nineteenth century, producing this postal box, are collectively known as

(A) the Scientific Revolution

(B) the Enlightenment

(C) the First Industrial Revolution

(D) the Second Industrial Revolution

50 ☐ Mark for Review

In the nineteenth century, economic thinkers used examples such as a postal system to argue for

(A) a return to conventional social order

(B) the greatest good for the greatest number of people

(C) a radical uprising to seize the means of production from the bourgeoisie

(D) the need for a strong sense of national unity

GO ON TO THE NEXT PAGE.

Questions 51 through 55 refer to the following.

"[Let us] return again unto our Courtier, whom in letters I will have to be more than indifferently well seen, at the least in those studies which they call Humanity, and to have not only the understanding of the Latin tongue, but also of the Greek, because of the many and sundry things that with great excellency are written into it. Let him much exercise himself in poets, and no less in orators and historiographers, and also in writing both rhyme and prose, and especially in this our vulgar tongue…. For truly it happeneth very seldom that a man not exercised in writing, how learned soever he may be, can at any time know perfectly the labor and toil of writers, or taste of the sweetness and the excellency of styles, and those inner observations that oftentimes are found in them of old time. And beside that, those studies shall make him copious, and, as Aristippus answered that Tiran, bold to speak upon a good ground with every man."

Source: *The Book of the Courtier*, Baldassare Castiglione, 1528

51 ☐ Mark for Review

The recommendation that Castiglione makes in the passage was regarded as which of the following?

(A) Irrelevant, because few people saw the usefulness of studying poetry

(B) Unusual, since only future scholars studied ancient Greek and Latin

(C) Typical, for the study of antiquity was seen as part of a well-rounded education

(D) Misguided, because becoming a writer wasn't seen as a path to fortune

52 ☐ Mark for Review

The system of *studia humanitatis* in sixteenth-century Italy insisted upon the study of Greek and Latin texts partly because of

(A) the frequent use of those languages in daily life on the Italian peninsula

(B) the plentiful number of those books in circulation

(C) the novelty of those texts, which had only recently been rediscovered through trade with Arabs

(D) the pope's decree that their study was mandatory

53 ☐ Mark for Review

Renaissance humanistic education of the type expressed in the passage did NOT include which of the following?

(A) Grammar

(B) Logic

(C) Economics

(D) Rhetoric

54 ☐ Mark for Review

One reason that Renaissance humanism began on the Italian peninsula was

(A) its frequent trade with northern Europe, which brought intellectual breakthroughs to the south

(B) its rural nature, which allowed uninterrupted study of new texts

(C) its unified political state, which enabled the quick spread of ideas

(D) its location on the Mediterranean as the center of exchange of both goods and ideas

GO ON TO THE NEXT PAGE.

55 ☐ Mark for Review

The changes in Italian Renaissance education can be best characterized as

- Ⓐ a reaction against the narrow ecclesiastical nature of medieval education

- Ⓑ a continuation of traditional perspectives on the value of religious education

- Ⓒ a rejection of all belief systems that had come before

- Ⓓ an affirmation of the idea that education was an elite pastime

GO ON TO THE NEXT PAGE.

AP EUROPEAN HISTORY
SECTION I, Part B
Time—40 minutes

Directions: Answer Question 1 **and** Question 2. Answer **either** Question 3 **or** Question 4.

In your responses, be sure to address all parts of the questions you answer. Use complete sentences; an outline or bulleted list alone is not acceptable.

Question 1 refers to the following.

"In the homes of the upper and middle classes Englishwomen suffer certain disadvantages in comparison with their poorer sisters, while they face other difficulties peculiarly their own. Physical brutality and drunkenness with the wretchedness of material surroundings they of course escape, but the domestic relations laws hang over them like the sword of Damocles, so that for the unhappily married woman of any class there is little hope of relief….

[Girls] are seldom given any practical education which would enable them to make their own livings, while primogeniture ensures the bulk of the family inheritance to the eldest son, that remaining for the daughters being usually a mere pittance…. Girls are consoled for their lack of advantages with the prospect of marriage, but their marriage is neither arranged nor are they given any adequate opportunity to achieve it for themselves…. There are thousands of homes today where the daughters can arrange neither their lives nor their friendships, but merely the flowers in their mothers' vases. All this is of course changing, and changing very rapidly in the middle class, but the home life of girls still remains on the whole seriously disadvantageous to their best interests."

Source: *What Women Want*, Beatrice Forbes-Robertson Hale, 1914

1 ☐ Mark for Review

Using the excerpt, respond to parts A, B, and C.

A. Describe one goal of the feminist movement in the early twentieth century.

B. Describe one method that women used to achieve this goal.

C. Describe one obstacle to the goals of feminism.

GO ON TO THE NEXT PAGE.

Question 2 refers to the following.

"I am speaking to you from the Cabinet Room at 10 Downing Street. This morning the British Ambassador in Berlin handed the German government a final note stating that unless we heard from them by eleven o'clock that they were prepared at once to withdraw their troops from Poland a state of war would exist between us. I have to tell you that no such undertaking has been received, and consequently this country is at war with Germany. You can imagine what a bitter blow it is to me that all my long struggle to win peace has failed…. [Hitler's] action shows convincingly that there is no chance of expecting that this man will ever give up his practice of using force to gain his will. He can only be stopped by force…"

Source: Radio address by British Prime Minister Neville Chamberlain, September 3, 1939

2 ☐ Mark for Review

Using the excerpt, respond to parts A, B, and C.

    A. Describe the actions of the prime minister toward the Nazi menace <u>before</u> this speech.

    B. Describe the actions of the prime minister toward the Nazi menace <u>after</u> this speech.

    C. Explain two advantages that the British enjoyed over Nazi Germany during World War II.

GO ON TO THE NEXT PAGE.

Question 3 or 4

Directions: Answer **either** Question 3 **or** Question 4.

3. Respond to parts A, B, and C.

    A. Describe one way that the enlightened despots supported reform movements in their societies in the eighteenth century.

    B. Describe one way that the enlightened despots undermined reform movements in their societies in the eighteenth century.

    C. Explain one significant cause of the changes in the relationship between European monarchs and the citizenry in the eighteenth century.

4. Respond to parts A, B, and C.

    A. Describe one significant continuity in the role of nationalism in Europe in the nineteenth century.

    B. Describe one significant change in the role of nationalism in Europe in the nineteenth century.

    C. Explain how the rise of nationalism affected the events of the twentieth century in European life.

3-4   🔖 Mark for Review

Choose a question to answer before you start writing.

○   **Answer Question 3**

○   **Answer Question 4**

END OF SECTION I

AP® European History Exam

SECTION II: Free Response

At a Glance

Total Time
1 hour, 40 minutes
Number of Questions
2
Percent of Total Score
40%

Question 1 (DBQ): Mandatory

Suggested Reading and Writing Time
60 minutes
Reading Period
15 minutes. Use this time to read Question 1 and plan your answer. You may begin writing your response before the reading period is over.
Suggested Writing Time
45 minutes
Percent of Total Score
25%

Question 2, 3, or 4 (Long Essay): Choose ONE Question

Answer either Question 2, 3, or 4
Suggested Time
40 minutes
Percent of Total Score
15%

DISCLAIMER: The official AP European History Exam will be administered digitally. Instructions for the digital exam may differ from this practice test.

Instructions

Section II has 1 document-based question (DBQ) and 1 long essay question, and lasts 1 hour and 40 minutes.

In this section, answer Question 1 (the DBQ) and **either** Question 2 **or** Question 3 **or** Question 4. After reviewing Questions 2, 3, and 4, choose the question that you are best prepared to answer. This section of the exam requires answers in essay form. Use complete sentences; an outline or bulleted list alone is not acceptable.

You may pace yourself as you answer the questions in this section, or you may use these optional timing recommendations:

For Question 1 (DBQ), it is suggested that you spend approximately 15 minutes reading the question and planning your answer, and then 45 minutes writing your essay. The suggested writing time for the long essay question is 40 minutes.

For this practice test, use scratch paper for notes and planning as well as writing your responses.

AP EUROPEAN HISTORY
SECTION II
Total Time—1 hour, 40 minutes

Question 1 (Document-Based Question)
Suggested reading and writing time: 1 hour

It is suggested that you spend 15 minutes reading the documents and 45 minutes writing your response.

Note: You may begin writing your response before the reading period is over.

Directions: Question 1 is based on the accompanying documents. The documents have been edited for the purpose of this exercise.

In your response, you should do the following:

- Respond to the prompt with a historically defensible thesis or claim that establishes a line of reasoning.
- Describe a broader historical context relevant to the prompt.
- Support an argument in response to the prompt using at least four documents.
- Use at least one additional piece of specific historical evidence (beyond that found in the documents) relevant to an argument about the prompt.
- For at least two documents, explain how or why the document's point of view, purpose, historical situation, and/or audience is relevant to an argument.
- Demonstrate a complex understanding of a historical development related to the prompt through sophisticated argumentation and/or effective use of evidence.

GO ON TO THE NEXT PAGE.

1 ☐ Mark for Review

Using the documents and your knowledge of European history, compare and contrast the relationship between England and both Spain and Portugal during the period 1421 to 1721.

Document 1

Source: Letter from King Alfonso V of Portugal to all English merchants in Portugal, 1443.

Through our good friendship and our ancient treaty with the King of England, our beloved brother, we secure all English merchants coming to our kingdom to trade, with their ships and the merchandise in them, so that they shall not be seized, nor be made to suffer any other harm or discomfort within our domain. Moreover we order the admiral and head captain of our fleet, and all the shipmasters and people of our kingdom, if they meet the English on the sea, coming to trade, not to rob, arrest, or spoil them, nor do them any other harm.

Document 2

Source: Peace of Utrecht, 1713.

[W]hereas the Most Serene and Most Mighty Lady Anne, by the grace of God, Queen of Great Britain, France, and Ireland, &c. and the Most Serene and Most Mighty Prince Philip the Fifth, by the grace of God, Catholic King of Spain, &c. wish for nothing more heartily, and endeavour nothing more earnestly, than that the ancient bonds of alliance and friendship between the British and Spanish nations should not only be renewed, but also more strongly knit together by fresh engagements of amity and interest on both sides, and transmitted indissoluble to all posterity....

Document 3

Source: Account of quantities of wine imported into London and Outports of England in sixteen years and a quarter, from Michaelmas 1696 to Christmas 1712.

LONDON.

Years.	France.			Portugal.			Spain.			Italy.			Rhenish.		
	Tons.	H.	G.	Tons.	H.	G.	Tons.	H.	G.	Tons.	H.	G.	Tons.	H.	G.
²1696 1697 }	184	0	18	4,260	0	61	6,935	0	10	332	0	0	396	2	62
1697 1698 }	1,439	0	34	3,621	0	29	5,931	2	60	775	0	0	693	0	45
³1698	136	1	43	812	0	49	801	1	33	136	0	40	29	2	55
1699	228	2	15	8,017	1	53	8,233	3	45	2,454	1	41	512	0	52
1700	570	0	23	6,584	0	18	9,788	3	26	2,050	3	34	591	0	61
1701	1,732	2	47	6,372	3	53	8,477	2	34	1,288	2	4	669	1	21
1702	1,297	1	62	5,069	0	55	5,849	1	39	932	1	30	632	1	15
1703	156	0	13	7,425	3	6	334	2	27	1,044	0	37	697	3	21
1704	391	0	27	8,164	1	5	980	1	55	1,931	1	58	590	2	52
1705	679	2	17	6,006	1	31	1,661	0	38	1,255	3	53	399	1	29
1706	186	2	11	3,094	2	28	1,623	0	7	205	3	3	299	1	29
1707	733	0	52	7,072	2	5	1,363	1	5	1,229	2	16	522	1	12
1708	119	3	38	7,515	2	41	1,414	3	36	1,670	2	3	524	1	10
1709	302	2	53	6,168	1	32	2,356	3	38	880	2	6	486	0	35
1710	149	2	40	5,427	1	48	4,664	2	13	2,459	1	50	411	1	43
1711	606	1	18	5,811	1	14	3,487	3	61	1,008	2	15	466	3	44
1712	698	1	36	5,647	2	62	3,625	0	62	827	3	4	433	0	18
Totals	9,613	3	43	97,071	1	22	67,530	0	21	20,484	0	24	8,356	0	37

GO ON TO THE NEXT PAGE.

Document 4

Source: "The Spanish Armada," Thomas Deloney, English balladeer, 1588.

The chiefest captain
    of this galleon so high,
Don Hugo de Moncaldo, he
    within this fight did die:
Who was the General
    of all the Galleons great;
But through his brains, with powder's force,
    a bullet strong did beat.
And many more,
    by sword, did lose their breath,
And many more within the sea
    did swim, and took their death.
There you might ace
    the salt and foaming flood,
Died and stained like scarlet red
    with store of Spanish blood.

Document 5

Source: Friedrich Schiller, *The History of the Thirty Years' War in Germany*, 1799.

Spain and Italy, from which Austria derived its principal strength, were still devoted to the See of Rome with that blind obedience which, ever since the days of the Gothic dynasty, had been the peculiar characteristic of the Spaniard. The slightest approximation in a Spanish prince to the obnoxious tenets of Luther or Calvin would have alienated forever the affections of his subjects, and a defection from the Pope would have cost him his kingdom. A Spanish prince had no alternative but orthodoxy or abdication.

Document 6

Source: Grant of privileges in Portugal to Nicholas Brown, an English merchant, 1448.

To all judges, etc.... Wishing to show favour to Nicholas Brown, an English merchant, bearer of this letter, we privilege and grant unto him that henceforth he shall be exempted from paying any of our special taxes, grants, excises, tallages, imposts, services, and all other charges that may be imposed by us or our council; nor shall he serve by sea or land in any part whatsoever, nor in any labours at walls, bridges, fountains, pavements, nor shall he keep arms nor a horse for our service… Moreover, we forbid that any person shall be lodged in his house, nor take his bread, wine, clothes, straw, wood, hens, cattle, nor his beasts of saddle or pack, nor any other of his possessions, under a penalty of 6 milreis…

Document 7

Source: Letter from William Stanhope to Sir Luke Schaub, Madrid, 1721.
Reprinted in *The History of Gibraltar and of its political relation to events in Europe*, Frederick Sayer, 1862.

"It is very unfortunate that our hands are tied as to Gibraltar, so as not to take advantage of this immoderate desire the King of Spain has to obtain it; for were it otherwise, notwithstanding the pretend promise of it, I am fully persuaded we might yet sell it for double its worth, in advantages to our commerce."

END OF DOCUMENTS FOR QUESTION 1

GO ON TO THE NEXT PAGE.

Question 2, 3, or 4 (Long Essay)

Suggested writing time: 40 minutes

Directions: Choose Question 2 **or** Question 3 **or** Question 4.

In your response, you should do the following:

- Respond to the prompt with a historically defensible thesis or claim that establishes a line of reasoning.
- Describe a broader historical context relevant to the prompt.
- Support an argument in response to the prompt using at least two pieces of specific and relevant evidence.
- Use historical reasoning (e.g., comparison, causation, continuity or change) to frame or structure an argument that addresses the prompt.
- Demonstrate a complex understanding of a historical development related to the prompt through sophisticated argumentation and/or effective use of evidence.

2. Evaluate the ways in which the modern notion of individualism was born on the Italian peninsula during the period from 1400 to 1550.

3. Outline the factors that led to England's role as the leader of the industrialization of Europe during the period 1760 to 1840.

4. Describe the causes of the Cold War.

2-4 ☐ Mark for Review

Choose a question to answer before you start writing.

○ **Answer Question 2**

○ **Answer Question 3**

○ **Answer Question 4**

WHEN YOU FINISH WRITING, CHECK YOUR WORK ON SECTION II IF TIME PERMITS.

STOP

END OF EXAM

_____

Practice Test 2:
Answers and
Explanations

PRACTICE TEST 2 ANSWER KEY

1.	D		29.	B
2.	B		30.	C
3.	C		31.	D
4.	B		32.	A
5.	A		33.	B
6.	B		34.	D
7.	D		35.	D
8.	D		36.	D
9.	A		37.	B
10.	C		38.	A
11.	B		39.	C
12.	A		40.	B
13.	B		41.	A
14.	B		42.	B
15.	A		43.	A
16.	D		44.	D
17.	D		45.	B
18.	A		46.	C
19.	C		47.	A
20.	C		48.	A
21.	C		49.	D
22.	B		50.	B
23.	B		51.	C
24.	C		52.	C
25.	A		53.	C
26.	C		54.	D
27.	A		55.	A
28.	D			

PRACTICE TEST 2: ANSWERS AND EXPLANATIONS

Section I, Part A: Multiple Choice

1. **D** The Glorious Revolution occurred in 1688 when King James II was removed from office by his daughter Mary. One of the reasons for this particular revolution was his growing movement toward religious toleration for all people, including Catholics. As a result, an immediate anti-Catholic bias was instituted across the nation, and Catholics were forbidden from sitting in Parliament for nearly a century. In fact, until the 21st century, it was prohibited for an English king to either be Catholic or marry a Catholic.

2. **B** In 1790, the French Revolution was barely a year old and had only recently passed out of its first stages. The worst violence was still to come, particularly Robespierre and his Reign of Terror, which saw the execution of nearly seventy thousand citizens and the imprisonment of hundreds of thousands more.

3. **C** Metternich was the last true conservative leader in European history. His control of the Congress of Vienna, and the stability that ensued, was the last time that any European leader relied upon the power of the people. After the rise of both liberalism and nationalism, the Revolutions of 1848, and particularly the arrival of mass politics, his distrust of the mob went out of style.

4. **B** The French Revolution passed through its worst days in 1793 and 1794 with the Reign of Terror. It wasn't until 1795 that the Directory assumed power with the backing of the military. Even though it lasted only five years, this brought stability to France that it had sorely lacked.

5. **A** Conservatism was a philosophy that had held sway for most of the previous three hundred years. Beginning in the 19th century, however, a whole host of other -isms began to take hold, including liberalism, nationalism, socialism, communism, and anarchism. The other three answers, while found in the 18th century, are unrelated to the passage.

6. **B** The three nations most deeply involved in the Age of Discovery were Spain, Portugal, and the Netherlands. (The English were also a minor player at this point, mostly through Francis Drake.) Spain was primarily interested in the Americas, but Portugal was the first to set up a global empire, arriving in South America, Africa, India, China, and even Japan.

7. **D** In 1599, like most of northern Europe, the Dutch had already transformed themselves into a solidly Protestant nation. This, in fact, was the root cause of the Thirty Years' War, which began about 20 years after the inscription was made. Furthermore, the famous work ethic was always attributed to Protestants, never to Catholics (though they clearly worked as well).

8. **D** The phrase *seeking unknown lands, and if there is any shorter way to China* reveals that Europeans were still seeking a shortcut to China. The trip around the southern horn of Africa could take months. Christopher Columbus had in fact been looking for a western route to China when he came upon the land mass that we now call North America.

9. **A** Blaeu's instruction to *[g]o on, O blessed progeny of Neptune, and add new honors to our race,* as well as the general go-get-'em attitude toward Dutch exploration, demonstrates his sense of a strong national identity. This prefigures the nationalist movement of the 19th century that, for example, sparked the revolutions of 1848 and eventually formed modern Germany and Italy.

10. **C** The guild system, which dated back to the medieval era, required skilled craftsmen to undertake years of study and apprenticeship in the pursuit of a single tradecraft. The machine revolutions of the Industrial Revolution ignored that long history by automating very complex processes. This phenomenon predates the other three answers.

11. **B** Luddites have been misunderstood in the public mind. They were largely composed of skilled laborers who were watching their own jobs being taken by unskilled workers. This was the target of their wrath, and they broke the machines in order to call attention to this inequity.

12. **A** Because Napoleon had been unable to conquer England, he placed the English under a strict embargo known as the Continental System. Because of these sanctions, English factory owners couldn't offer reliable employment to all of their workers. In this harsh economic climate—part of the short-lived Napoleonic Wars—the Luddites, as well as most English laborers, suffered greatly.

13. **B** The relaxation of strict social rules regarding public dress, a free press, and smoking is a hallmark of liberal social policies. The final paragraph, which describes the lack of need for bribery, is a sign of a less corrupt, more transparent state, which is a goal that is also aligned with liberalism.

14. **B** Promoted by Tsar Alexander II, the Emancipation Proclamation of 1861 abolished serfdom in Russia. This move was intended to promote and encourage the development of private property, free competition, entrepreneurship, and trade.

15. **A** While Catherine the Great had indeed paid lip service to Enlightenment ideas about equality, she failed to produce any political reforms on the scale of her predecessor Peter the Great. Peter had spent time in the Netherlands, France, and elsewhere in western Europe, even traveling incognito. As a result, he imported many Western social practices to his country, including the construction of a navy, the introduction of Western dress, and even the mandatory cutting of beards.

16. **D** Liberalism in the 19th century found its best expression in John Stuart Mill's book aptly titled *On Liberty*, which argued for the importance of individual civil rights, among other things. *The Communist Manifesto* reflected the ideas of the Bolshevik Revolution, which arrived much later.

17. **D** By the 1930s, the Soviet Union had been established in place of Russia. After the death of the revolutionary leader Vladimir Lenin in 1924, the new Soviet leader, Josef Stalin, displayed zero use for liberal policies. Under him, the Soviet state seized land, collectivized agriculture, and murdered millions of Russians by sending them to die in remote *gulags*.

18.   **A**   *The Protocols of the Elders of Zion* is a notorious antisemitic fictional document that originated in Russia in the first decade of the 20th century. It claims to document a Jewish conspiracy to dominate the world, and as conspirators against all modern states. It has been thoroughly discredited.

19.   **C**   The Republic's response to the Dreyfus Affair was anything but efficient, since it lasted nearly two decades and went through several different trials, which included both contradictory verdicts for Dreyfus. It culminated in his full pardon, and Dreyfus would go on to serve his country in World War I. Ironically, the French reactionary forces were ultimately weakened by the scandal, since the parliamentary democracy saw that justice was ultimately done, despite the length of time.

20.   **C**   Theodor Herzl began his journalistic career as a supporter of Jewish assimilation into European life, but the injustice of the Dreyfus Affair caused him to change his mind. Shortly afterward, he became the founder of the modern Zionist movement, which called for the establishment of a separatist Jewish state in the biblical homeland of Israel.

21.   **C**   Militarism characterized the period of Europe from roughly 1840 to 1917. During this time, there were relatively few wars—only a few minor ones—while the major nations exploited the fruits of the Industrial Revolution to create new, more deadly weaponry. While it's true that militarism was closely intertwined with nationalism and imperialism, those ideas weren't mentioned by Disraeli in this speech.

22.   **B**   Disraeli opens the passage by questioning *the cost of these fleets and garrisons.* Later, at the end of the paragraph, he discusses *the vast expenditure which cannot be accounted for.* This indicates that his primary concern was the spiraling costs of militarism.

23.   **B**   It stands to reason that if Disraeli were publicly pushing back against the massive power of the English military complex, then English society had also been selling the idea of military service to the citizenry as something that was desirable. That in fact was what had been happening. Cheap novels about the bravery of soldiers were all the rage in the Victorian era, and even the venerable Alfred, Lord Tennyson wrote a jingoistic poem about the glory of battle, "The Charge of the Light Brigade."

24.   **C**   While the increase in national armaments was the primary reason for wars during this era, it was also the primary driver behind the conquest of Africa. Fast boats powered by the steam engine, combined with new rifle technology, made the scramble for Africa happen, since Europeans could penetrate the so-called "dark continent" more easily. The Bolshevik Revolution, however, was largely caused by long-term factors specific to Russia that were unrelated to the buildup of armaments.

25.   **A**   The English navy was by far the largest and most powerful in the world during the 19th century. It was used to secure English trade routes and protect English economic interests in far-flung foreign ports. Prussia (and later Germany), while more militaristic by nature overall, focused primarily upon building an army on land, which was used to great effect during German unification, which occurred a few years after this speech was delivered.

26. **C** Europe had been under the thumb of the Catholic Church's Aristotelian tradition for more than a millennium and a half when the Renaissance, the Reformation, and the Scientific Revolution broke down the church doors. To a modern historian, Bacon's contribution to the third part of this sea change is what defines his life.

27. **A** Bacon's empiricism is the foundation of the scientific method, which in turn has given birth to our entire modern technological world. In the words of his 19th-century biographer, William Hepworth Dixon, "Bacon's influence in the modern world is so great that every man who rides in a train, sends a telegram, follows a steam plough, sits in an easy chair, crosses the channel or the Atlantic, eats a good dinner, enjoys a beautiful garden, or undergoes a painless surgical operation, owes him something."

28. **D** Brahe, Gilbert, and Kepler were Bacon's scientific contemporaries—Brahe and Kepler in astronomy, Gilbert in magnetism—but Voltaire lived in the 18th century. Also, he was primarily a writer, unlike Bacon, who served as a statesman, a jurist, and a scientist. However, it is true that Bacon's belief in a skeptical, methodical approach to data gathering influenced not only Voltaire, but the entire Enlightenment.

29. **B** The scientific method, inductive reasoning, and empiricism are all closely intertwined; they make up the intellectual backbone of the scientific, data-driven world that we now inhabit. Deductive reasoning, however, was viewed at the time as a relic of the medieval scholastic age, and was ignored by the new scientists for its lack of close observation of the world.

30. **C** The design of the building, and the description of the design, is classic Moorish. The Moors were the group of Muslims from Northern Africa who crossed the Mediterranean and occupied Spain (and Portugal) for hundreds of years, until the Christian rulers of Spain expelled them in the 15th and 16th centuries. Their design is famous for its repeated geometric patterns.

31. **D** The Moors had been forced to either leave Spain or convert to Christianity. This was part of Ferdinand and Isabella's efforts to unite Spain under their own banner, which was Christian. It stands to reason that the Moorish design would therefore be viewed as undesirable during this time period.

32. **A** In places like Córdoba, where Jews, Muslims, and Christians had mixed for years, it became difficult to differentiate between the different religious groups. This was especially true among the aristocracy, who took great effort to hide any non-Christian ancestry.

33. **B** As the Reconquista (reconquest) proceeded, the Christian rulers of Spain repossessed lands that had been owned by the Moors and handed them over to members of the nobility. This developed into a new feudalistic tradition of haves and have-nots, particularly in the south: a few wealthy landowners employed an enormous number of peasants to service the land.

34. **D** Bismarck's accomplishments were vast. He united most of the German-speaking people—minus Austria—through a combination of shrewd statescraft, maneuvering, outright lies, and powerful but quick wars against neighboring countries. The result was the modern nation of Germany.

35. **D** In his quest to unite the German-speaking people, Bismarck instigated a series of wars intended to gain the nationalistic fervor of German-speaking people who lay at the periphery of Prussia. This finally culminated in the Franco-Prussian War, which he began by editing a telegram from Louis Napoleon Bonaparte to make it look like the French had insulted the German people. After six weeks, the war was over, and Kaiser Wilhelm I was crowned German emperor in Versailles.

36. **D** National insurance programs of any kind are considered more on the socialist end of the political spectrum, and 19th-century Germany was no exception. Bismarck essentially swiped the legs out from under his socialist opponents by co-opting a few of the ideas that they believed in. However, he refused to institute restrictions on the number of hours that workers could be forced to labor, because he wanted the country to be as productive as possible.

37. **B** Always choose the safest possible answer when asked about conclusions. You don't know if Bismarck was capable of inflicting great cruelty upon his visitors, only that one visitor had the mere impression that his eyes *lit up with a threatening gleam*. Likewise, it's quite a stretch to claim that Bismarck alone was able to unite Germany, though he was obviously a principal force in the effort. Clearly, he was no simple man either.

38. **A** The Junkers were the ruling class of Prussia—the nobility—and Bismarck himself was part of this class. Therefore, the Junkers largely escaped his roving political eye and oppressive policies, unlike Catholics, socialists, and the media.

39. **C** World War I erupted in the same year as the painting was made, 1914, and there still is no event in European history that is comparable in the amount of wrenching change it caused. Wars had typically been rather brief until the arrival of the Great War. Everything about it was new—the length of the engagement, the variety of new weaponry, the shift of the perception of war from valorous to torturous, the sheer number of casualties, the amount of mobilization. The confusion this caused has never been equaled.

40. **B** Einstein's physics, Joyce's art, and the use of horrific chemical weaponry all reflected a profound change in European mentality. The old order, the old philosophies, the old traditions—all had changed, and something new and potentially horrifying was rising in its place. What had not changed, of course, was the doctrine of the Catholic Church, which has prided itself on its consistency for two thousand years.

41. **A** Until the 20th century, most of European fine art had been either figurative (human figures rendered exactly) or realistic (fields, still lifes, etc.) or both. That changed in the early years of the century, when artists like Paul Klee and Pablo Picasso began to break that mold. They expressed human figures and objects in a way that bore no resemblance to reality.

42. **B** Once Europe found out that Napoleon had escaped from exile in Elba with a ship of hundreds of men, the powers of Russia, Prussia, Austria-Hungary, and England immediately put 150,000 soldiers en route to France. Nonetheless, Napoleon managed to roll toward Paris, gathering supporters along the way. Once there, he reassumed power and sent an army to battle the coalition army at the Battle of Waterloo, but his army was defeated. He surrendered.

43. **A** Since Napoleon saw his own fate and the fate of France as one and the same, this *War for maintaining the national independence* can be interpreted as a battle for his own power. This last gasp of power that he seized is known as the Hundred Days, which was how long it took for him to escape Elba, reassume power, lose to the coalition of European armies, and abdicate again.

44. **D** All of Napoleon's political or military conquests fell apart the moment he left power. However, one lasting piece of influence that he had was through his reform of the French system of laws. The Napoleonic Code, as it's come to be known, has been adopted by colonies and nations all over the world.

45. **B** England never appealed to the power of the pope to interfere in Napoleon's plans. It did rely upon its command of the sea to defeat the French at the Battle of Trafalgar. Likewise, England did provide subsidies to European merchants whose trade was affected by Napoleon's forced embargo of England. And the Duke of Wellington did lead forces in Portugal against the French army.

46. **C** While the postal system was physically made possible by steel production, the popularity of letter-writing was only made possible by increased literacy rates. Also, middle-class women experienced more leisure time, not less.

47. **A** The telegraph was the most direct competitor with the postal service, since most of Europe was covered in telegraph lines in the second half of the century. The telegraph's shortcoming, however, was that it could send only short messages. The telephone was a plaything of the elite until the 20th century, and radio and television didn't make their appearances until much later.

48. **A** Britain's rail network was the best in Europe, since it was the first country to industrialize, and its steamships were the fastest in the world. Therefore, the delivery of letters was fast and reliable. The power stations were certainly important to other parts of English society, but not those two forms of transportation.

49. **D** The Scientific Revolution occurred in the 17th century and the Enlightenment in the 18th century. The First Industrial Revolution also occurred in the mid-18th century and included innovations like the spinning jenny and piecework completed in people's homes.

50. **B** *The greatest good for the greatest number of people* was the rallying cry of great economic thinker Jeremy Bentham, and a postal service is one small example of this philosophy. Much of the focus during this period of English history was upon methods of improving the standard of living for the rapidly growing cities of Great Britain. From a modern perspective, this makes a lot of sense, since the great technological advances of the 19th century (and the Industrial Revolution as a whole) had finally made such improvement possible.

51. **C** The great educational innovation of the Italian Renaissance was the trivium and quadrivium. In these courses, boys were educated in grammar, logic, and rhetoric (trivium), and arithmetic, geometry, music, and astronomy (quadrivium). The first part was humanistic, and involved the study of ancient Greek and Latin sources.

52. **C** The Italians had only recently rediscovered (in the 15th century) ancient Greek thinkers such as Aristotle. They had found these texts—their own texts—translated into Arabic, preserved by a totally different culture for centuries. Translated back into Latin, these philosophical works were viewed as the new—yet old—backbone of Western thought.

53. **C** Economics was never part of the Renaissance curriculum; it only became a popular field of inquiry beginning with the Physiocrats in the late 18th century. The other three answers were all part of the trivium.

54. **D** Frequent trade with Arabic cultures brought the Italians into contact with the long-lost philosophical texts of ancient Greece and Rome. Italy had neither a rural nature nor a unified political state. Likewise, the intellectual trade with northern Europe went the opposite way, with new humanistic ideas moving from Italy northward.

55. **A** Medieval education had been totally dominated by the Catholic Church, and as such, long debates were frequently held on such topics as "How many angels can dance on the head of a pin?" Italian humanists sought to broaden the educational scope by including philosophers that had typically been left out of the Catholic Church's official curriculum, including Neoplatonism and other more obscure threads of thought.

Section I, Part B: Short Answer

Question 1

A. The overriding goal of the early feminist movement was to earn women the right to vote. This was called the *suffrage* movement. Other possible answers include better educational opportunities and changes to domestic relations laws (both mentioned in the passage), but suffrage is really the best answer.

B. Various methods used by the feminist movement to reach their goals included gathering signatures for petitions, lobbying politicians, delivering speeches, and applying political pressure. More extreme methods included picketing and hunger strikes.

C. The primary goal of feminism at this time was enfranchisement, e.g., the right to vote. There were several obstacles holding them back from this:

- The lack of female representatives in English Parliament made it difficult to pass legislation granting women the right to vote. This was a chicken-or-the-egg problem.

- Middle-class women were often refused the right to work outside of the home, and this lack of independent funds hindered many women's ability to support feminist activism.

- The early European feminist movement failed to address the specific needs of women of color, Jewish women, and other minorities. Focusing solely on white Christian women, this dilemma persists even today (and has become addressed by the term *intersectionality*).

Question 2

A.   Neville Chamberlain is remembered in history as a proponent of the policy of appeasement—the idea that placating an aggressive foreign leader will somehow halt the march toward war. First he allowed Hitler to annex Austria, a move known as Anschluss. Then his policy of appeasement led to the signing of the Munich Pact, which allowed Hitler to annex Sudetenland (part of Czechoslovakia) with little consequence. Soon thereafter, Hitler took all of Czechoslovakia, with no repercussions. At last he invaded Poland in direct violation of the Munich Pact, which finally ended Chamberlain's policy.

B.   After this radio address, the British leadership's policy changed radically. Industry began to prepare for another total war, Chamberlain eventually resigned, and Winston Churchill became prime minister. Almost a year later, in July 1940, Hitler offered to make peace with England—a total role reversal—but Churchill turned him down, preferring to fight.

C.   The British used a plethora of unusual tactics to defeat the Germans. One was code-breaking—they were superior at intercepting and cracking the codes that German military commanders used to communicate with one another. Another was to lure German scientists (particularly Jewish ones) to England; at least 19 Nobel Laureates fled Germany for England during the war. A third was the British ability to buy weaponry from the Americans via the Lend-Lease Act, an advantage that the Germans obviously didn't have. Fourth, England enjoyed geographical superiority—the English Channel provided an excellent blockade against German ground forces, which never landed on the island.

Question 3

An enlightened despot used the principles of the Enlightenment to rule justly and respect the rights of the citizenry. Classic examples of enlightened despots include Joseph II of Austria, Catherine II of Russia, and Frederick II of Prussia.

A.   Joseph II of Austria believed in religious toleration. Frederick II of Prussia granted religious freedom, reduced censorship, improved education, reformed the justice system, and abolished torture. Catherine the Great reformed the Russian law code.

B.   Joseph II of Austria sought to reduce the autonomy of Hungarians in his empire. He also unilaterally restricted the power of the Catholic Church. Catherine II of Russia limited religious toleration and gave nobles full control over the serfs.

C.   Causes of these changes listed above included exposure to the ideas of the *philosophes*, the need to justify their absolute power given the movement toward constitutional republics, and the slow change from religion to science.

Question 4

A.   Nationalism grew in strength in the 19th century. Good examples to mention include the unification of Germany, the unification of Italy, Napoleon III's Second Empire, the industrialization of Russia, the loud agitation from the many ethnic groups inside Austria-Hungary, etc.

B.   Nationalism's biggest change was in its divorce from liberalism. At first nationalists were allies with liberals because love of homeland and individual civil rights were seen as one and the same. After the Revolutions of 1848, however, it became clear that nationalists were not as interested in liberalism as they once had been. Another possible answer is to describe the way that nationalism replaced the balance of power achieved under the Concert of Europe.

C.   Nationalism was without question a major factor in the events that sparked World War I. Without a strong system of interlocking nation-states—some of whom hadn't existed a few decades earlier—the total war that erupted simply wouldn't have. The assassination of Archduke Franz Ferdinand could possibly have remained a regional or local conflict in the Balkans.

Section II: Document-Based Question (DBQ)

The document-based question (DBQ) section begins with a 15-minute reading period. During those 15 minutes, you should 1) come up with some information not included in the given documents (from your outside knowledge), 2) get an overview of what each document means and the point of view of each author, 3) decide what opinion you're going to argue, and 4) write an outline of your essay.

The DBQ in Practice Test 2 concerns the issue of the relationship between England and the two countries of Spain and Portugal, respectively, from 1421 to 1721. You should be prepared to discuss how England's relationship changed over those three centuries, and how it stayed the same. You should also remember the famous PERSIA method of organizing characteristics of any historical time period—Political, Economic, Religious, Social, Intellectual, and Artistic. The first three tend to be more useful than the last three, so try to at least remember PER.

BEFORE YOU LOOK AT THE DOCUMENTS, first brainstorm for a minute or two. Try to list everything you know (from class or leisure reading or informational documentaries) about the issue of England's historical relationship with the Iberian peninsula. This list will serve as your reference to the outside information you must provide to earn a top grade.

Next, read over the documents. As you read them, take notes on your scratch paper, including which passages you are certain you will use in your essay. Make note of the opinions and position of each document's author. If a document helps you remember a piece of outside information, add that outside information to your brainstorming list. If you cannot make sense of a document or if it argues strongly against your position, relax! You do not need to mention every document to score well on the DBQ.

Here is what you might assess in the time you have to look over the documents.

The Documents

Document 1

This excerpt comes from a letter written by King Alfonso of Portugal in 1443 and is addressed to all English merchants. It clearly states that English merchants are friendly, and it pleads with all subjects to please allow them safe passage both inside and outside of Portugal.

This document clearly shows that the Portuguese king was trying to make nice with the English merchants. Try, however, to look under those words. What was Alfonso's interest in being nice to England? Well, given his position, and assuming that he was a responsible leader, you can probably guess that trade with England constituted an important part of his country's income.

Document 2

This document, a part of the Peace of Utrecht, dates from nearly 300 years after Document 1. In it, Queen Anne of England and King Philip V of Spain reaffirm the bond of friendship that had historically united England with Spain. Even if you don't remember the purpose of the Peace of Utrecht, the fact that it was called a *peace* means that the two countries had probably just finished some kind of war, as does language such as *the ancient bonds of alliance and friendship between the British and Spanish nations should ... be renewed*.

Document 3

This chart shows the quantity of wine imported from many European countries to England from the years 1696 to 1712. You can see that the total amount imported from Spain and Portugal dwarfs the total amounts imported from the other nations. This should indicate to you the economic nature of the bond between England and the Iberian peninsula—if nothing else, the English people depended upon Spanish and Portuguese wine.

Document 4

This portion of the poem, aptly titled "The Spanish Armada," ends with the words *died and stained like scarlet red/with store of Spanish blood*. The Spanish Armada, of course, set sail in 1588—the same year that the poem was written—when Spain decided to attack England by sea. It was totally destroyed by England's superior navy. Even if you didn't remember the Spanish Armada when brainstorming outside information, this document is your reminder to use it now.

Document 5

This document is our first glance at the religious nature of Spain. The author, a historian writing at the turn of the 18th century, made it clear that Spanish leaders had no choice but to remain Catholic. Phrases such as *the obnoxious tenets of Luther or Calvin* emphasize this opposition to the Protestant movement of northern Europe.

This document is an important one because it can be used as a springboard to discuss the religious nature of the Thirty Years' War, which both Spain and England were involved in.

Document 6

This document details how the Portuguese official body granted special rights to Englishman Nicholas Brown with regard to taxes, food, lodging, and other privileges. It demonstrates the length to which the Portuguese were willing to go to guarantee continued good trade with the English.

Document 7

This document is probably the most difficult to decipher, linguistically. In its meandering way, the author—William Stanhope, an Englishman—is writing to another Englishman that the king of Spain really wants to buy Gibraltar from the English and is willing to pay *double its worth*. This means that the English possessed Gibraltar (the big rock at the southern tip of Spain) in the year 1721. However, Stanhope goes on to say that *it is very unfortunate that our hands are tied as to Gibraltar, so as not to take advantage of this immoderate desire*—meaning that the English cannot sell it, for some reason.

To use this document in the essay requires a little ingenuity, but one possible way would be to point out that the English ownership of a large piece of land in the south of Spain is evidence of the deep relation that the two countries possess.

Outside Information

We have already discussed more than you could include in a 45-minute essay. Do not worry. You will not be expected to mention all of what we have covered in the section above. You will, however, be expected to include some outside information—that is, information not directly mentioned in the documents. Here are some examples of outside information that you might incorporate in your essay:

- Early in the era described, Spain and England had actually gotten along quite well, at least at the monarchic level. In 1509, Henry VIII of England famously married Catherine of Aragon (who was a Spanish ruler), though he later divorced her. In 1554, Philip II of Spain married Mary I of England. This resulted in him holding the Spanish, Portuguese, and English thrones all at the same time. Incredible! However, her death four years later ended Philip's political domination of England. After Mary died, Philip II tried to marry her successor, Elizabeth I. She rejected him, though they maintained cordial peace for many years. Until…

- The fighting began. This should definitely be analyzed in more depth in your essay. It would be good to put it in its context—the long and undeclared Anglo-Spanish War (1585–1604). It started with Queen Elizabeth I of England's offer of assistance to Protestants in the Netherlands who were resisting Catholic Spanish Habsburg rule. A few years later, Philip II of Spain answered that insult with the Spanish Armada, a 130-boat Spanish fleet that escorted a mercenary army from the Netherlands to England for the purpose of stopping the spread of Protestantism there. This famously failed. In fact, there were other armadas on both sides, lesser-known ones, in the years that followed. Finally the two sides made up with the Treaty of London, which was signed in 1604 by the two new leaders of the countries, James I of England and Philip III of Spain.

- This conflict played out on the high seas of the New World as well. During this same time, English explorer Francis Drake attacked the Spanish colony of San Juan, Puerto Rico. He failed in his attempt and was driven away. His partner, John Hawkins, died in the siege. Drake himself died a few years later from disease in Panama. Other English privateers routinely raided Spanish ships and settlements.

- England's role in the Thirty Years' War (1618–1648) was small—it only participated directly for less than four years, since the Protestant Stuarts preferred to stay out of the affairs of the European continent. However, Spain, being under Habsburg rule, was directly involved in the conflict, and was in fact one of its chief actors. That's why this essay would benefit from the inclusion of this conflict; it was an enormous event that indirectly pitted the two nations against one another. Note also that it occurred only a couple of decades after the undeclared Anglo-Spanish War.

- Leaping forward, the War of the Spanish Succession (1700–1714) was waged all because the Spanish king, Charles II, had no children. On his deathbed, he named his great-nephew, Philip, Duke of Anjou, to be his successor. The problem was that Philip was already in line to inherit the French throne, since he was also grandson of Louis XIV of France. This provoked alarm from other nations, since the growing power of the Bourbons was already a threat to the balance of power in Europe. England, the Dutch, Austria, the German states, and the Holy Roman Empire formed an alliance to challenge this inheritance. England called for a halt to the fighting when the Tories came to power. The Treaty of Utrecht formally ended the conflict, partitioning the Spanish Empire. Don't feel bad for Philip, Duke of Anjou. He renounced his claim to the French throne, true, but then sat on the Spanish throne as *Philip V* for the next 30 years.

- Shortly afterwards, the War of the Quadruple Alliance (1717–1720) occurred when Philip V decided to retake lands in Italy that he felt belonged to the Habsburgs. The rest of Europe disagreed, and an alliance between England, France, Austria, and the Holy Roman Empire (flashback to the last war!) defeated Spain soundly.

- Although it lay outside the time period of the question, it could be possible to bring in The War of Jenkins' Ear (1739 to 1748). It was a war between England and Spain that was fought mostly over lucrative trading contracts in the New World. The captain of the English merchant ship who had his ear cut off by the Spanish in 1731 saw himself turned into a cause célèbre eight years later, and his injury used as justification for national outrage against the Spanish.

- Other ideas from the Age of Exploration could be worked into this essay. You could discuss conquistadores such as Hernán Cortés, Francisco Pizarro, Hernando de Soto, Pedro de Alvarado, Vasco da Gama, and Prince Henry the Navigator—but only if you can think of a way to connect them to England. One way to do this might be to mention an English explorer of the same era, such as John Cabot or Martin Frobisher.

- Other possible terms from Spain's Golden Era include Ferdinand and Isabella, the Reconquista, the Inquisition, Miguel de Cervantes' *Don Quixote*, etc. Other ideas from the time could include the terrible inflation that struck Spain as a result of riches from its new colonies. Or the lack of a middle class. Again, all of these ideas would need to be connected with England.

- There is less outside information for Portugal, but you could mention the English Armada, which the English sent to Spain in the year 1589, after their defeat of the Spanish Armada. One of its purposes was to show support for the Portuguese independence movement, since Portugal was ruled by Spain at the time. Unfortunately, the Armada failed, but the intention was clear—English-Portuguese relations were strong.

Choosing a Thesis Statement

Continuity and change is always a good way to organize your response to an essay like this. In other words, things stayed the same in certain ways, while they changed in other ways. This allows a lot of wiggle room. However, the obvious structure would be a *compare and contrast*, since those words are literally in the prompt. The obvious answer here is to say that England's relationship with Spain has been volatile while its relationship with Portugal has been constant.

Planning Your Essay

Unless you read extremely quickly, you probably will not have time to write a detailed outline for your essay during the 15-minute reading period. However, it is worth taking several minutes to jot down a loose structure of your essay because it will actually save you time when you write. First, decide on your thesis and write it down on your scratch paper. Then, take a minute or two to brainstorm all the points you might put in your essay. Choose the strongest points and number them in the order you plan to present them. Lastly, note which documents and outside information you plan to use in conjunction with each point. If you organize your essay before you start writing, the actual writing process will go much more smoothly. More importantly, you will not write yourself into a corner, suddenly finding yourself making a point you cannot support or heading toward a weak conclusion (or, worse still, no conclusion at all).

The bad news about this particular DBQ is that there isn't much room for interpretation. It's clear from the documents that England's relationship with Portugal was based on stable economic trade. It's also clear that its relationship with Spain, on the other hand, began with stable trade but then devolved into several conflicts over religion and politics.

Of course, this rigidity could be viewed as good news too. The most obvious way to organize this essay would be to open with a brief examination of Portugal and then follow with a full examination of the more problematic Spain. Your grouping of documents might look like this:

Portugal
Document 1
Document 3
Document 6

Spain
Document 2
Document 3
Document 4
Document 5
Document 7

Within those groups, you have choices about ordering. One way to order them would be *chronologically*. (The documents are not often in chronological order, so you'd have to arrange them first.) This option is good for students who have the ability to briefly outline the full relationship of England and Spain. The order would look like this:

Portugal:
Document 1 (1443)
Document 6 (1448)
Document 3 (1712)

Spain:
Document 4 (1588)
Document 5 (1618–1648) The document is about the Thirty Years' War; remember that 1799
                          is outside the scope of the prompt.
Document 3 (1712)
Document 2 (1713)
Document 7 (1721)

The other way to order these documents would be by *category*. Using the PERSIA categories, you could divide the paragraphs into *political*, *economic*, and *other* categories. (Those three are a pretty standard way to order evidence for most historical essays.) This approach of course would mix both Portugal and Spain together, so this would be better suited for a compare-and-contrast thesis statement. Here's what that could look like:

Economic
Document 1—economic, political
Document 3—economic
Document 3—economic

Political
Document 6—political
Document 2—political
Document 7—political

Other
Document 4—literature
Document 5—religious

There are other ways to organize, but these are the most obvious two—and with only 45 minutes to write, it's often better to go the obvious route. Once you choose one of these structures, go down your list of outside information and think of ways to integrate each one into the essay. It won't always be possible, but every outside idea you can add will lend weight to your essay, as long as it can be fitted into your thesis statement. Remember that an obvious, desperate stretch will only hurt your score. However, history is by nature intricate, and the readers of your exam want to see that you respect the intrinsic complexity behind many historical events.

Section II: Long Essay

Because you have only 40 minutes to plan and write this essay, you will not have time to work out an elaborate argument. That's okay; nobody is expecting you to read three questions, choose one, remember all pertinent facts about your subject, formulate a brilliant thesis, and then write a perfect essay. Here is what you should do. First, choose your question: brainstorm for two or three minutes, and edit your brainstorm ideas. Then, number those points you are going to include in your essay in the order you plan to present them, just as you did for the DBQ. Last, think of a simple thesis statement that allows you to discuss the points your essay will make.

Question 2—Individualism in the Italian Renaissance (Option 1)

2. Evaluate the ways in which the modern notion of individualism was born on the Italian peninsula during the period from 1400 to 1550.

About the Structure of Your Essay

The nature of the Italian Renaissance is wide ranging, but one of its signature accomplishments is that it takes humanism a step further—toward the belief that individual humans are capable of great accomplishments. The more communal, group-oriented society and mentality of the Middle Ages was being replaced by a belief in the potential of the individual to make great achievements. One easy way to brainstorm is to divide into categories such as art, literature, science, and religion. Here are some points that you could mention in your essay:

- The great Leonardo da Vinci is emblematic of this time period. He was a painter, sculptor, architect, inventor, military engineer, and draftsman—the epitome of a "Renaissance man." With a curious mind and keen intellect, da Vinci studied the laws of science and nature, which greatly informed his work. You should mention *Vitruvian Man, Mona Lisa,* and *The Last Supper*. He also envisioned a helicopter, though he never built it.

- While medieval art was religious in tone, medieval artists commonly neglected lifelike details, making their art flat and lifeless. Faces and bodies were cartoon-like, having no individual features or anything approaching anatomical detail. Other features such as background, perspective, proportion, and individuality were all virtually unknown as well. Renaissance art, however, contrasted sharply with medieval art in all these respects. More paintings illustrated secular themes, and even religious paintings paid a great deal of attention to glorifying the individual human form and individual human accomplishments. A great example of this would be Michelangelo's *David*. Equally important to this essay, an individual point of view came into vogue in painting. In other words, the Renaissance resurrected the idea of perspective.

- The most famous manifesto of Renaissance individualism was delivered by Pico della Mirandola in the "Oration on the Dignity of Man." In this speech, he describes man as a dignified being, created by God to achieve his highest potential. Likewise, Baldassare Castiglione's *The Book of the Courtier* describes in great detail how such a Renaissance man would study humanities and carry himself with elegance and behave in accordance with virtue.

- The changes to educational curriculum contributed to the growth of individualism. The rise of the *studia humanitatis*, which consisted of rhetoric, grammar, poetry, history, and moral philosophy, was a major component of this.

- It would be possible to link other Renaissance figures to the prompt, such as Petrarch, who lived in the 14th century but whose rediscovery of Cicero's letters inspired both humanism and the individualism of the Italian Renaissance. Also, some of the political insights of Niccolo Machiavelli could be portrayed as individualistic, particularly in the use-or-be-used ethos of *The Prince*.

Question 3—England's Role in the Industrialization of Europe (Option 2)

3. Outline the factors that led to England's role as the leader of the industrialization of Europe during the period 1760 to 1840.

About the Structure of Your Essay

This essay is essentially asking you to outline the causes of the Industrial Revolution in England. There is certainly no shortage of material, and with basic preparation this should be fairly easy to knock out of the ballpark. Your only challenge will be how to organize the material, since there are so many options. As in the DBQ, you could arrange your points chronologically. You could divide the essay into the First Industrial Revolution and the Second Industrial Revolution. You could arrange the points according to agriculture, technology, etc. You could use PERSIA (though that might be difficult, since most of the points will be economic). Or you could get away with no obvious arrangement at all—as long as the paragraphs are well argued, a laundry list of various causes could serve you well. Here are a few ideas to get you started:

- The Agricultural Revolution of the 1700s set the stage for the Industrial Revolution. By increasing food production, the English population could be fed at lower prices with less effort than ever before, thus breaking the famous Malthusian trap. This surplus also meant that English families could use the money they saved to purchase manufactured goods.

- Peasants who had been fenced off from using previously public lands by the Enclosure Acts turned to the cottage industry, in which they made textiles at home. This ironically freed the population from its attachment to the land. As factories began to sprout up, this mobility made it easy for workers to relocate from the rural areas to the cities. In other countries, such as Russia, where the serfs were tied to the land, this mobility didn't exist.

- England already boasted a central bank to finance new factories. The profits it had enjoyed from the booming textile industries allowed investors to support the construction of these factories. Easy loans were made available by those banks to small business owners, facilitating the quick construction of new industry.

- The culture of economic risk-taking is often overlooked, but it was crucial at the time. The English revolutions of the 17th century had fostered a spirit of economic prosperity. Early industrial entrepreneurs were willing to take risks on the chance that they would reap financial rewards later.

- Some of it was geographical good fortune. England was lucky enough to have a vast supply of mineral resources, such as coal, that could be used to run industrial machines. England was also lucky enough to be located on a relatively small island, so these resources could be transported quickly and at a reasonable cost. England was lucky enough to be shot through with a network of rivers that made floating manufactured goods a breeze, which was vital before the railroad era. Where rivers didn't exist, canals were used.

- The government passed laws that protected private property and placed few restrictions on private business owners. For this, they could thank the philosopher John Locke, who lived decades earlier but who laid the basis.

- It would be worth mentioning various individuals and their technological inventions. James Hargreaves's spinning jenny in 1764 produced more yarn in greater quantities. In that same decade, James Watt's steam engine transformed the cotton industry. In 1787, Edmund Cartwright's power loom revolutionized the speed of cloth weaving. In the early 1800s, the locomotive was developed by various people.

- Lack of social reform. As the cities swelled with the poor, the dirty, and the oppressed, workers had zero representation at their factories and often arrived in the morning to find themselves suddenly unemployed. Child labor was common, a shameful phenomenon that was faithfully recorded by Charles Dickens. The social reformers eventually arrived, but production grew unchecked during this period of lack of oversight.

Question 4—Causes of the Cold War (Option 3)

4. Describe the causes of the Cold War.

About the Structure of Your Essay

As you can imagine, a conflict as large, long, and varied as the Cold War featured a lot of different causes. You can organize these causes in many ways, but one easy way is to rely again upon PERSIA (Political, Economic, Religious, Social, Intellectual, and Artistic). Of those six categories, the three most fruitful will be *political, economic*, and *intellectual*.

While there are many smaller causes to point to, here are some of the main ones that you probably want to hit:

Political:

- Many of the roots of the Cold War were political in nature. As far back as the Russian Revolution of 1917, the Soviets had devolved into a totalitarian political system with zero representation for the people. That, of course, is the opposite of the constitutional democracy that Western Europe, the United Kingdom, and the United States had all adopted.

- While the Western powers had political systems with multiple parties, the Soviet Union had a single-party system.

- During World War II, in his effort to defeat the Nazi menace, Josef Stalin had deployed millions of Soviet ground troops across Eastern Europe. At the close of the war, he left many of those troops in place, and they became de facto occupying forces. Winston Churchill and Franklin Roosevelt, at the Malta Conference, decided to allow him to do so, for the simple reason that neither the United Kingdom nor the United States had the political or economic will to oppose Stalin after such a long conflict.

Economic:

- The Soviet Union had a centralized communist economy in which private ownership of capital was forbidden. In this system, the communist central government owned all the means of production. The Western European powers, on the other hand, had (and still have) a capitalistic economy based on private ownership of capital.

- To help Europe recover from the tragedy of World War II, the United States began to offer massive financial aid packages to any nation willing to rebuild itself along the Western capitalist model. This was known as the Marshall Plan. Stalin, however, refused to allow the Soviet-occupied Eastern European nations to accept this financial aid.

Intellectual:

- Karl Marx and Friedrich Engels, the major influencers of communist ideology, are worth a mention here. Their book *The Communist Manifesto* set in motion the intellectual wheels of communism.

- The development of the atomic bomb. While the United States developed the bomb first—and used it in Japan in 1945—the Soviets were only a few short years behind. By 1949, the Soviets had reached that goal, which raised the stakes for the whole conflict for the next 40 years.

HOW TO SCORE PRACTICE TEST 2

Section IA: Multiple Choice

$$\underline{\hspace{3cm}} \times 1.090 = \underline{\hspace{3cm}}$$

Number Correct
(out of 55)

Weighted
Section I Score
(Do not round)

Section IB: Short Answer

Question 1: $\underline{\hspace{3cm}} \times 3.3333 = \underline{\hspace{3cm}}$

(out of 3)　　　　　　　　　　(Do not round)

Question 2: $\underline{\hspace{3cm}} \times 3.3333 = \underline{\hspace{3cm}}$

(out of 3)　　　　　　　　　　(Do not round)

Question 3 or 4: $\underline{\hspace{3cm}} \times 3.3333 = \underline{\hspace{3cm}}$

(out of 3)　　　　　　　　　　(Do not round)

AP Score Conversion Chart European History	
Composite Score Range	AP Score
107–150	5
90–106	4
73–89	3
56–72	2
0–55	1

Section II: Document-Based Question

Question 1: $\underline{\hspace{3cm}} \times 5.3571 = \underline{\hspace{3cm}}$

(out of 7)　　　　　　　　　　(Do not round)

Section II: Long Essay

Question 2, 3, or 4: $\underline{\hspace{3cm}} \times 3.750 = \underline{\hspace{3cm}}$

(out of 6)　　　　　　　　　　(Do not round)

Composite Score

$$\underline{\hspace{2cm}} + \underline{\hspace{2cm}} + \underline{\hspace{2cm}} + \underline{\hspace{2cm}} = \underline{\hspace{2cm}}$$

Weighted
Section IA
Score

Weighted
Section IB
Score

Weighted
DBQ
Score

Weighted
Long
Essay
Score

Composite Score
(Round to the
nearest whole
number)

Note: This score sheet is to help you estimate your approximate score for the official exam, not your actual score.

Practice Test 3

AP® European History Exam

At a Glance

Time
55 minutes
Number of Questions
55
Percent of Total Score
40%

DISCLAIMER: The official AP European History Exam will be administered digitally. Instructions for the digital exam may differ from this practice test.

Instructions

Section I, Part A has 55 multiple-choice questions and lasts 55 minutes.

Each question in this part is followed by four suggested answers. Select the best answer to each question.

Indicate all of your answers to the multiple-choice questions on the answer sheet. Give only one answer to each question.

Use your time effectively, working as quickly as you can without losing accuracy. Do not spend too much time on any one question. Go on to other questions and come back to the ones you have not answered if you have time.

Your total score on the multiple-choice section is based only on the number of questions answered correctly. Points are not deducted for incorrect answers or unanswered questions.

At a Glance

Time
40 minutes
Number of Questions
3
Percent of Total Score
20%
Questions 1 and 2
Mandatory
Question 3 or 4
Choose one question

Instructions

Section I, Part B has 3 short-answer questions and lasts 40 minutes.

In this part, answer Question 1 and Question 2 and **either** Question 3 **or** Question 4.

In your responses, be sure to address **all** parts of the questions you answer. Use complete sentences; an outline or bulleted list alone is not acceptable.

You may pace yourself as you answer the questions in this part, or you may use these optional timing recommendations:

It is suggested that you spend an equal amount of time, approximately 13 minutes, on each question.

For this practice test, use scratch paper for notes and planning as well as writing your responses.

GO ON TO THE NEXT PAGE.

AP EUROPEAN HISTORY
SECTION I, Part A
Time—55 minutes
55 Questions

Directions: Each of the questions or incomplete statements below is followed by four suggested answers or completions. Select the one that is best in each case.

Questions 1 through 4 refer to the following.

"The substitution of Plato for the scholastic Aristotle was hastened by contact with Byzantine scholarship. Already at the Council of Ferrara (1438), which nominally reunited the Eastern and Western churches, there was a debate in which the Byzantines maintained the superiority of Plato to Aristotle....Cosimo and Lorenzo de Medici were both addicted to Plato; Cosimo founded and Lorenzo continued the Florentine Academy, which was largely devoted to the study of Plato...The humanists of the time, however, were too busy acquiring knowledge of antiquity to be able to produce anything of value."

Source: Bertrand Russell, British philosopher, *A History of Western Philosophy,* 1946

1 ☐ Mark for Review

In what way does this passage best exemplify the view of twentieth-century philosophers and thinkers?

(A) Faced with an unprecedented number of social and technological changes, the twentieth century embraced innovation as one of the most valued characteristics of life.

(B) Overwhelmed by the unprecedented number of social and technological changes, the twentieth century sought refuge in the longstanding traditions of the past.

(C) After the devastation of World Wars I and II erased the possibility of finding a unified meaning to life, philosophers occupied themselves with finding small differences between the philosophies of past thinkers.

(D) Nihilists typically find ways to doubt the postulations of those who came before them.

2 ☐ Mark for Review

It can be inferred from the passage that the Council of Ferrara

(A) laid the foundation for the Florentine Academy

(B) permanently reconciled the differences between the Eastern and Western churches

(C) accelerated the rediscovery of classical philosophy in western Europe

(D) allowed the Byzantines to learn from Florentine scholarship

GO ON TO THE NEXT PAGE.

3 ☐ Mark for Review

According to the information in the text, the schools founded by the Medici family most favored a philosophy known as

Ⓐ Neoclassicism

Ⓑ Scholasticism

Ⓒ Renaissance humanism

Ⓓ Neoplatonism

4 ☐ Mark for Review

The cultural diffusion described by Bertrand Russell most directly influenced the composition of which text?

Ⓐ *Oration on the Dignity of Man*

Ⓑ *The Decameron*

Ⓒ *Handbook of the Christian Knight*

Ⓓ *Utopia*

GO ON TO THE NEXT PAGE.

Questions 5 through 9 refer to the following.

D-Day Statistics

Unit	Allies	Germans	Ratio
Ground Troops	1 million	700,000	1.43:1
Replacements	120,000	20,000	6:1
Other Men	1.75 million	780,000	2.25:1
Total	2.87 million	1.5 million	1.92:1

Unit	Allies	Germans	Ratio
Tanks	5,500	1,400	3.93:1
Artillery	4,800	3,200	1.5:1
Others	2,000	800	2.5:1

Air Force	Bombers	Fighters	Total
RAF	624	2,172	2,796
USAAF	1,922	1,311	3,233
Luftwaffe	400	420	820
Ratio	6.4:1	8.3:1	7.4:1

5 ☐ Mark for Review

The tables indicate which of the following about World War II?

(A) Rescuing Europe from the Germans was out of the question until the arrival of the American forces.

(B) Keen strategy was perhaps less important to military success than the amount of available resources.

(C) German replacements had slowed to an unacceptable level.

(D) The ratio of artillery to tanks didn't correlate with the eventual victory.

6 ☐ Mark for Review

In which unit did the Germans most closely match the Allies, according to the tables?

(A) Ground troops

(B) Tanks

(C) Artillery

(D) Air Force

7 ☐ Mark for Review

Which of the following statements about Germany could be supported by the data shown in the tables?

(A) What Germany's military lacked in ground troops, it made up for in replacements.

(B) Germany relied on its use of tanks more than it did any other unit.

(C) D-Day accounted for the worst losses Germany experienced during World War II.

(D) As opposed to aircraft producers in the Allied countries, Germany's aviation industry did not adequately meet the production needs requested by the generals.

GO ON TO THE NEXT PAGE.

8 ☐ Mark for Review

What might best explain the discrepancy between the number of fighter jets and bombers of the United States and the British?

- (A) The increased fuel efficiency of submarines at the time

- (B) A cultural preference for larger and smaller modes of transportation

- (C) The distance of North America from Europe versus the distance of Great Britain from Europe

- (D) Smaller production facilities in British factory towns

9 ☐ Mark for Review

The large difference in the number of tanks between the Germans and the Allies was most probably due to what?

- (A) The presence of the Russian army in the Allied forces

- (B) The German tendency toward quality, not quantity, in manufacturing

- (C) The enormous production capabilities of the United States

- (D) Japanese purchase of raw materials from Germany, limiting the available production

GO ON TO THE NEXT PAGE.

Questions 10 through 14 refer to the following.

Leonard Raven Hill, "Cannon-Fodder—and After," *Punch* Magazine, 1917

"And don't forget that your Kaiser will find a use for you—alive or dead."

10 ☐ Mark for Review

The concept of "total war" as practiced by the kaiser in the sketch included all of the following EXCEPT

(A) food rationing

(B) women moving into factory production

(C) propaganda

(D) attacks specifically targeting civilians

11 ☐ Mark for Review

The long-term impact of the event portrayed in the cartoon could best be seen through the

(A) proliferation of governmental regulation of industry throughout Europe

(B) end of European countries' imperial ambitions

(C) demilitarization of Germany

(D) end of the kaiser's rule in Germany

GO ON TO THE NEXT PAGE.

12 ☐ Mark for Review

One consequence that resulted from the situation depicted in the cartoon was

(A) a rise in unemployment

(B) a dramatic decline in food production

(C) the prohibition of cannon usage

(D) the decrease in funds available for the war effort

13 ☐ Mark for Review

The perspective of the cartoonist is most likely influenced by his

(A) experience in the kaiser's army

(B) experience working for the kaiser

(C) British citizenship

(D) German citizenship

14 ☐ Mark for Review

The cartoonist would be most likely to agree with which of the following statements?

(A) The kaiser's popularity was not limited to Germany.

(B) During a time of war, the kaiser was the best leader that Germany could hope for.

(C) The kaiser placed more value on the war effort than on the well-being of his people.

(D) The kaiser's immorality ultimately led to his downfall.

GO ON TO THE NEXT PAGE.

Questions 15 through 19 refer to the following.

"After all the slaves had been brought together and severally marked with the letter G, the emperor's fifths and then Cortés' were deducted before we were aware of it; and, besides this, on the night preceding, the finest of the Indian females had been secretly set apart, so that when it came to a division among us soldiers, we found none left but old and ugly women…. Another soldier asked Cortés if the division he had made of the gold in Mexico was not a sufficient imposition, for, at first, he had merely spoken of 300,000 pesos, but when we were obliged to retreat from the city, it was estimated at 700,000 pesos. And now he was going to deprive the poor soldier, who had undergone so many hardships, and suffered from innumerable wounds, of this small remuneration, and not even allow him a pretty Indian female for a companion…

[Later], when Cortés learnt that there were still a great many bars of gold among the men, and heavy gambling in consequence, (for, according to the old saying, gold and love cannot lie long concealed), he made known, under threats of severe punishment, that everyone should produce the gold he had obtained on the night of our retreat, of which one third was to be returned to him; but that anyone who refused to pay this, should have the whole taken from him. Many of our men refused downright to comply with this; yet Cortés managed to extort a good deal of it under the pretence of a loan..."

Source: *The Memoirs of the Conquistador Bernal Diaz del Castillo*, 1568

15 ☐ Mark for Review

As described by the author, the driving philosophy behind the *conquistadores*' search for gold was the economic policy known as

(A) protectionism

(B) *laissez-faire*

(C) mercantilism

(D) supply-side

16 ☐ Mark for Review

Upon the return of Cortés's expedition, which of the following was a consequence of the actions described in the memoir?

(A) A decentralized political state

(B) A strengthened agricultural sector

(C) An increased rate of inflation

(D) Less tolerance for Jews and Muslims

17 ☐ Mark for Review

The motivations described in the text are most similar to those of which explorer?

(A) Christopher Columbus

(B) Vasco de Gama

(C) Francisco Pizarro

(D) Bartholomew Dias

18 ☐ Mark for Review

The events described in the passage most likely occurred in which modern-day country?

(A) Argentina

(B) South Africa

(C) Mexico

(D) Peru

GO ON TO THE NEXT PAGE.

19 ▢ Mark for Review

The *encomienda* system, which is described in the text and was used during the colonization of the Americas to regulate the Indigenous people, was NOT ended by which of the following?

- (A) The protests of the Catholic missionaries against abuses of forced labor

- (B) The lack of new land to assign to well-connected Spaniards and conquistadores

- (C) The Spanish royal crown's desire to control the estates more directly

- (D) An increase in the number of mestizos, who by law were forbidden from working on the *encomiendas*

GO ON TO THE NEXT PAGE.

Questions 20 through 24 refer to the following.

"The Devilfish in Egyptian Waters," 1882

---

20 ☐ Mark for Review

The cartoon was created in reaction to Great Britain's ambitions following

(A) the Suez Canal Crisis

(B) the near war over Fashoda

(C) the completion of construction by the Suez Canal Company

(D) Russia's actions in the "great game"

---

21 ☐ Mark for Review

A similar cartoon could be made about each of the following countries prior to 1890 EXCEPT

(A) Netherlands

(B) France

(C) Belgium

(D) Germany

---

22 ☐ Mark for Review

Which was NOT a factor that led to the issue depicted in this cartoon?

(A) A natural system of internal waterways that facilitated transportation of raw materials and finished goods

(B) A natural barrier between England and possible invading armies from the European mainland

(C) A long tradition of technological innovation

(D) A top-down political system that implemented changes

GO ON TO THE NEXT PAGE.

23 ⬜ Mark for Review

The Primrose League's opinion of this cartoon would likely be one of

Ⓐ indifference, since they saw both the benefits and drawbacks of colonialism

Ⓑ displeasure at the cartoonists' critique of a noble pursuit

Ⓒ agreement with the criticisms offered by the cartoon

Ⓓ harsh condemnation for glorifying violent imperialism

24 ⬜ Mark for Review

This cartoon could be used as evidence to support the claim that

Ⓐ European lands were not immune to Great Britain's imperialism

Ⓑ Great Britain did not extend its imperial conquest to South Africa

Ⓒ the British Empire was limited to one hemisphere

Ⓓ Great Britain experienced little resistance to its colonial ambitions

GO ON TO THE NEXT PAGE.

Questions 25 through 29 refer to the following.

"In Russia there was nothing going on well, and [Souvarine] was in despair over the news he had received. His old companions were all turning to the politicians; the famous Nihilists who made Europe tremble—sons of village priests, of the lower middle class, of tradesmen—could not rise above the idea of national liberation, and seemed to believe that the world would be delivered—when they had killed their despot…

'Foolery! They'll never get out of it with their foolery.'

Then, lowering his voice still more, in a few bitter words he described his old dream of fraternity. He had renounced his rank and his fortune; he had gone among workmen, only in the hope of seeing at last the foundation of a new society of labour in common. All the sous in his pockets had long gone to the urchins of the settlement; he had been as tender as a brother with the colliers, smiling at their suspicion, winning them over by his quiet workmanlike ways and his dislike of chattering. But decidedly the fusion had not taken place.

His voice changed, his eyes grew bright, he fixed them on Étienne, directly addressing him:

'Now, do you understand that? These hatworkers at Marseilles who have won the great lottery prize of a hundred thousand francs have gone off at once and invested it, declaring that they are going to live without doing anything! Yes, that is your idea, all of you French workmen; you want to unearth a treasure in order to devour it alone afterwards in some lazy, selfish corner. You may cry out as much as you like against the rich, you haven't got courage enough to give back to the poor the money that luck brings you. You will never be worthy of happiness as long as you own anything, and your hatred of the bourgeois proceeds solely from an angry desire to be bourgeois yourselves in their place.'"

Source: Émile Zola, French writer, *Germinal*, 1885

---

25 ☐ Mark for Review

The conflict referred to in the final paragraph of the passage was best described in which book?

(A) *On Liberty,* by John Stuart Mill

(B) *The Communist Manifesto,* by Marx and Engels

(C) *Protocols of the Elders of Zion*

(D) *Looking Backward,* by Edward Bellamy

---

26 ☐ Mark for Review

The radical movement known as anarchism, alluded to in the first paragraph, had been related to all of the following EXCEPT

(A) the International Workingman's Association

(B) Pierre-Joseph Proudhon

(C) the Congress of Vienna

(D) the Paris Commune

---

27 ☐ Mark for Review

The passage displays the direct concern for the welfare of the working classes that was typically a part of which movement?

(A) Capitalist

(B) Scientific

(C) Communist

(D) Existentialist

---

28 ☐ Mark for Review

In European industry, the mining industry as discussed in the passage grew in importance following the invention of

(A) the water frame

(B) the spinning jenny

(C) the steam engine

(D) the internal combustion engine

GO ON TO THE NEXT PAGE.

29 ◻ Mark for Review

A nineteenth-century Russian historian evaluating this passage would probably be most interested in

Ⓐ the Russian interest in French culture

Ⓑ the spirit of camaraderie amongst the miners

Ⓒ the sense of continual class struggle

Ⓓ the need for *noblesse oblige*

GO ON TO THE NEXT PAGE.

Questions 30 through 34 refer to the following.

"In 1500 that work appeared which Erasmus had written after his misfortune at Dover, and had dedicated to Mountjoy, the *Adagiorum Collectanea*. It was a collection of about eight hundred proverbial sayings drawn from the Latin authors of antiquity and elucidated for the use of those who aspired to write an elegant Latin style. In the dedication Erasmus pointed out the profit an author may derive, both in ornamenting his style and in strengthening his argumentation, from having at his disposal a good supply of sentences hallowed by their antiquity. He proposes to offer such a help to his readers. What he actually gave was much more. He familiarized a much wider circle than the earlier humanists had reached with the spirit of antiquity.

Until this time the humanists had, to some extent, monopolized the treasures of classic culture, in order to parade their knowledge of which the multitude remained destitute, and so to become strange prodigies of learning and elegance. With his irresistible need of teaching and his sincere love for humanity and its general culture, Erasmus introduced the classic spirit, in so far as it could be reflected in the soul of a sixteenth-century Christian, among the people. Not he alone; but none more extensively and more effectively. Not among all the people, it is true, for by writing in Latin he limited his direct influence to the educated classes, which in those days were the upper classes.

Erasmus made current the classic spirit. Humanism ceased to be the exclusive privilege of a few. According to Beatus Rhenanus he had been reproached by some humanists, when about to publish the *Adagia*, for divulging the mysteries of their craft. But he desired that the book of antiquity should be open to all."

Source: Johan Huizinga, twentieth-century Dutch philosopher, *Erasmus and the Age of Reformation,* 1924

30 ☐ Mark for Review

Based on Huizinga's description of Erasmus's career, the contributions of Erasmus are most similar to those of

(A) Johannes Gutenberg

(B) Martin Luther

(C) Francesco Petrarch

(D) Christine de Pisan

31 ☐ Mark for Review

What was the primary impact of "Humanism ceas[ing] to be the exclusive privilege of the few"?

(A) The populace demanded rights from the state.

(B) People could begin to question the Church on a wider scale.

(C) Latin replaced many of the vulgar languages throughout Europe.

(D) European literature stagnated because of widespread interest in the writings of antiquity.

32 ☐ Mark for Review

Huizinga's apparent support of Erasmus's belief in the "book of antiquity" being "open to all" is most likely a product of

(A) the author's life as a member of twentieth-century Europe, which prized such characteristics

(B) the longevity of Erasmus's works

(C) the Dutch reverence for the works of Erasmus

(D) the typical unflinching support of one philosopher for another philosopher's work

33 ☐ Mark for Review

The type of humanism attributed to Erasmus in this passage is most similar to what Southern Renaissance movement?

(A) Neoplatonism

(B) Antitrinitarianism

(C) Pietism

(D) Rationalism

GO ON TO THE NEXT PAGE.

34 ☐ Mark for Review

According to Huizinga, Erasmus's legacy was more significant than that of earlier humanists because

(A) he had more support from the Church

(B) he wrote in a language that was understandable to the masses, unlike his predecessors

(C) he wrote exclusively about religious matters

(D) he valued educating the masses more than his predecessors had

GO ON TO THE NEXT PAGE.

Questions 35 through 39 refer to the following.

William Hogarth, *Gin Lane*, 1751

---

35 ☐ Mark for Review

Social reformers of the eighteenth century saw the exaggerations in Hogarth's work as reason to

(A) morally improve the living habits of the underclass

(B) feel deep revulsion against the working class everywhere

(C) take pleasure in seeing such joyfulness among the destitute

(D) return society to a more natural, unhurried state of life

36 ☐ Mark for Review

Hogarth primarily intended for this engraving to advocate for the passage of

(A) the Act of Toleration

(B) the Mutiny Act

(C) the Act of Union

(D) the Sale of Spirits Act

GO ON TO THE NEXT PAGE.

37 ☐ Mark for Review

This piece of art can be best categorized as

(A) Baroque

(B) Romanticism

(C) satire

(D) single-point perspective

38 ☐ Mark for Review

Which of the following would most directly have contributed to the scene depicted in the engraving?

(A) Enclosure Acts

(B) the Sadler Committee

(C) Poor Laws

(D) the Act of Settlement

39 ☐ Mark for Review

A modern art critic would most likely criticize Hogarth's work for all of the following reasons EXCEPT its

(A) emphasis on traditional portrayals of humans

(B) use of stereotyped characters

(C) attention to realistic detail

(D) typical portraiture composition

GO ON TO THE NEXT PAGE.

Questions 40 through 44 refer to the following.

"Buckingham Palace, 10th May 1839.

The Queen forgot to ask Lord Melbourne if he thought there would be any harm in her writing to the Duke of Cambridge that she really was fearful of fatiguing herself, if she went out to a party at Gloucester House on Tuesday, an Ancient Concert on Wednesday, and a ball at Northumberland House on Thursday, considering how much she had to do these last four days. If she went to the Ancient Concert on Wednesday, having besides a concert of her own here on Monday, it would be four nights of fatigue, really exhausted as the Queen is.

But if Lord Melbourne thinks that as there are only to be English singers at the Ancient Concert, she ought to go, she could go there for one act; but she would much rather, if possible, get out of it, for it is a fatiguing time....

As the negotiations with the Tories are quite at an end, and Lord Melbourne has been here, the Queen hopes Lord Melbourne will not object to dining with her on Sunday?"

Source: *The Letters of Queen Victoria, Volume 1 (of 3), 1837–1843:*
A Selection from Her Majesty's Correspondence Between the Years 1837 and 1861

---

40 ☐ Mark for Review

The long evenings of entertainment for Queen Victoria suggest what about the nature of the English monarchy in the nineteenth century?

(A) That true political power lay elsewhere

(B) That she was very fond of attending balls and concerts

(C) That important political progress could only be made by attending social events

(D) That with England's nineteenth-century economic success came more leisure time for the upper classes

---

41 ☐ Mark for Review

The phrase "negotiations with the Tories" suggests that what historical transition had been made complete?

(A) The switch from a liberal-dominated to a conservative-dominated Parliament

(B) The conversion from male-dominated politics to female-dominated politics

(C) The change from a divinely ordained monarch to a constitutionally approved monarch

(D) An end to war and the creation of a lasting peace

---

42 ☐ Mark for Review

A similar fondness for entertainment amongst the nobility was taken to its most outrageous degree in which of the following eras and places?

(A) Sixteenth-century Spain

(B) Seventeenth-century Netherlands

(C) Eighteenth-century France

(D) Nineteenth-century Prussia

---

43 ☐ Mark for Review

Modern historians are noted for their tendency to portray leaders and historical figures as merely human, even flawed. What might such a historian find most notable about the queen's letter?

(A) The odd capitalization of certain words

(B) Her sense of duty to support English singers

(C) Her referral to herself in the third person

(D) Admitting her exhaustion at having to attend so many social functions

---

GO ON TO THE NEXT PAGE.

44 ☐ Mark for Review

Apart from a grueling social calendar, which of the following most challenged Queen Victoria during her reign from 1837 to 1901?

Ⓐ An English potato famine in 1845

Ⓑ An unprecedented onslaught of industrial, social, cultural, political, and scientific change

Ⓒ Constant military attacks from mainland Europe

Ⓓ A rapidly shrinking number of overseas colonies

GO ON TO THE NEXT PAGE.

Questions 45 through 49 refer to the following.

The Soviet Union Before the Cold War

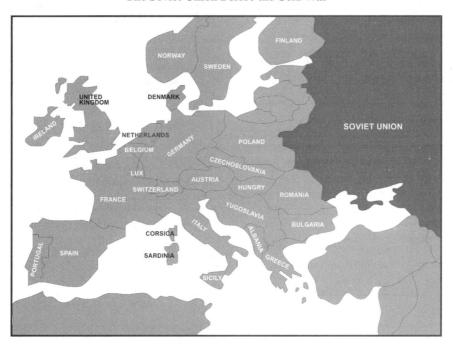

The Soviet Union During the Cold War

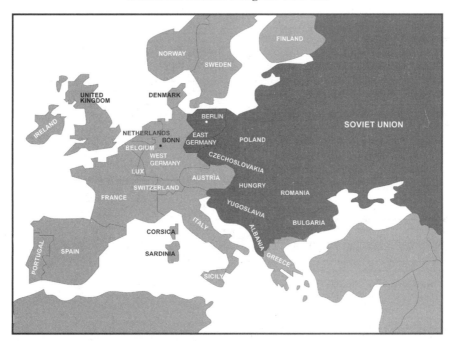

GO ON TO THE NEXT PAGE.

45 Mark for Review

The post–World War II geographic expansion of the Soviet Union began with

(A) the decision to expand to the Black Sea

(B) the ten-month-long blockade of Berlin

(C) the invasion of Afghanistan

(D) the decision at the Conference at Yalta to divide Germany into four different zones

46 Mark for Review

During the Cold War, Hungary was part of a treaty organization known as

(A) NATO

(B) the KGB

(C) the Warsaw Pact

(D) the Iron Curtain

47 Mark for Review

Which of the following statements about the Soviet Union's influence is consistent with the Cold War map's border?

(A) Stalin could not force his ideology on the Austrian president.

(B) Finland largely held on to a command economy.

(C) Greece and other Balkan nations maintained a strong alliance.

(D) Czechoslovakia was able to maintain a free economy.

48 Mark for Review

The only country in Eastern Europe that presented serious resistance to Soviet control was Poland. What was NOT a general reason for this?

(A) The popular perception that Western powers had abandoned them to the Soviets

(B) The questionable authenticity of the first postwar elections, in which communists won nearly all positions

(C) A general agreement with Soviet tactics during the war

(D) The reluctance to lose their identity as a country once again

49 Mark for Review

Which of the following is NOT true regarding the divided Germany shown on the second map?

(A) The capital of West Germany was located in East Germany.

(B) West Germany experienced a postwar economic miracle.

(C) Both East Germany and West Germany were allowed to rearm.

(D) France had occupied West Germany.

GO ON TO THE NEXT PAGE.

Questions 50 through 52 refer to the following.

Johannes Vermeer, *The Music Lesson*, 1665

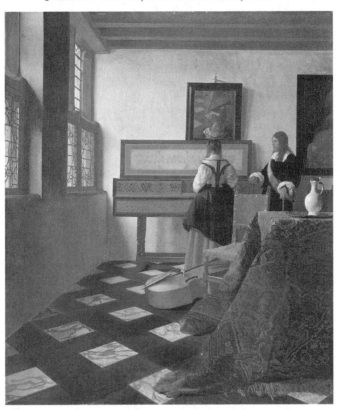

50 ☐ Mark for Review

How does the content of Vermeer's painting depict a lifestyle that is different from that of the Southern Renaissance?

(A) Works of art were often placed in homes, as they were commissioned by a new, wealthy merchant class, rather than by church officials.

(B) Music outside of the church was not central to Italian life, but was important to the Dutch middle class.

(C) Dutch architecture was more ornate than that of Italy.

(D) Dutch servants lived in the home, as opposed to the servants in southern Europe.

51 ☐ Mark for Review

The standard of living reflected in Vermeer's painting could be attributed to all of the following EXCEPT

(A) cheap energy available from windmills and peat

(B) Protestant and Jewish skilled craftsmen who immigrated to escape persecution in other lands

(C) a thriving fruit-and-vegetable export industry

(D) the establishment of the Dutch East India Company

GO ON TO THE NEXT PAGE.

52 ⬚ Mark for Review

The Music Lesson is indicative of the Golden Age of Dutch art, which often featured images of

- Ⓐ the ancient world

- Ⓑ royalty

- Ⓒ saints

- Ⓓ everyday life

GO ON TO THE NEXT PAGE.

Questions 53 through 55 refer to the following.

"XI. As the present sciences are useless for the discovery of effects, so the present system of logic is useless for the discovery of the sciences.

XIX. There are and can exist but two ways of investigating and discovering truth. The one hurries on rapidly from the senses and particulars to the most general axioms, and from them, as principles and their supposed indisputable truth, derives and discovers the intermediate axioms. This is the way now in use. The other constructs its axioms from the senses and particulars, by ascending continually and gradually, till it finally arrives at the most general axioms, which is the true but unattempted way.

XXII. Each of these two ways begins from the senses and particulars, and ends in the greatest generalities...

XXXVI. We have but one simple method of delivering our sentiments, namely, we must bring men to particulars and their regular series and order, and they must for a while renounce their notions, and begin to form an acquaintance with things."

Source: Francis Bacon, English philosopher and essayist, *Novum Organum,* 1620

---

53 ☐ Mark for Review

The method of inquiry elucidated by Francis Bacon in the passage is known as

(A) humanism

(B) deduction

(C) empiricism

(D) scientific socialism

---

54 ☐ Mark for Review

How does the approach outlined in *Novum Organum* differ from the studies of the Renaissance era that preceded it?

(A) The Renaissance was anchored in Italy; the scientific era was barely noticed there.

(B) The Renaissance revered the natural teachings of classical authority; Bacon's writings sought to overturn them.

(C) The Renaissance was sponsored primarily by the Church, whereas scientific societies were sponsored mainly by wealthy merchants.

(D) The Renaissance featured a wild spirit of discovery, but the scientific pioneers were much more cautious in their pronouncements.

---

55 ☐ Mark for Review

By the 1800s, the method of reasoning reflected in the passage had undergone which of the following changes?

(A) It had weakened to the point of irrelevance.

(B) It had become a core principle of European culture.

(C) It had been refined and changed by so many people that it had become unrecognizable to those such as Bacon who had pioneered it.

(D) It had stagnated to the point that the common person had begun to search for a new organizing principle of life.

GO ON TO THE NEXT PAGE.

AP EUROPEAN HISTORY
SECTION I, Part B
Time—40 minutes

Directions: Answer Question 1 **and** Question 2. Answer **either** Question 3 **or** Question 4.

In your responses, be sure to address all parts of the questions you answer. Use complete sentences; an outline or bulleted list alone is not acceptable.

Question 1 refers to the following.

1 ⬜ Mark for Review

Using the chart, respond to parts A, B, and C.

   A. Describe one similarity between the First Industrial Revolution and the Second Industrial Revolution.

   B. Describe one difference between the First Industrial Revolution and the Second Industrial Revolution.

   C. Describe one benefit that the Industrial Revolution, as a whole, provided to European society.

GO ON TO THE NEXT PAGE.

Question 2 refers to the following.

"As it ought to be, or … the ladies trying a contemptible scoundrel for a 'breach of promise'"
George Cruikshank, English illustrator, 1849

2 ☐ Mark for Review

Using the image, respond to parts A, B, and C.

A. Describe one socioeconomic factor <u>accelerating</u> the women's movement in England at the time of the drawing.

B. Describe one socioeconomic factor <u>restricting</u> the women's movement in England at the time of the drawing.

C. Explain one example of a political success <u>in the early twentieth century</u> enjoyed by the women's movement in England.

GO ON TO THE NEXT PAGE.

Question 3 <u>or</u> 4

Directions: Answer **either** Question 3 **or** Question 4.

3. Historians have praised many philosophers for ushering in the Enlightenment. These philosophers include

- John Locke
- Thomas Hobbes
- Adam Smith
- René Descartes
- David Hume

Respond to parts A, B, and C.

   A. Briefly explain why two of the thinkers on the list represent Enlightenment ideals.

   B. Briefly explain why one of the thinkers on the list does <u>not</u> represent Enlightenment ideals.

   C. Briefly explain how one thinker on the list influenced European life in the late eighteenth and nineteenth centuries.

4. Respond to parts A, B, and C.

   A. Describe one technological advance in medicine that had arrived by the end of the nineteenth century.

   B. Describe one technological advance in the arts that had arrived by the end of the nineteenth century.

   C. Explain one long-term effect of <u>each</u> of the above technological advances.

3-4 ☐ Mark for Review

Choose a question to answer before you start writing.

○ **Answer Question 3**

○ **Answer Question 4**

END OF SECTION I

AP® European History Exam

DISCLAIMER: The official AP European History Exam will be administered digitally. Instructions for the digital exam may differ from this practice test.

Instructions

Section II has 1 document-based question (DBQ) and 1 long essay question, and lasts 1 hour and 40 minutes.

In this section, answer Question 1 (the DBQ) and **either** Question 2 **or** Question 3 **or** Question 4. After reviewing Questions 2, 3, and 4, choose the question that you are best prepared to answer. This section of the exam requires answers in essay form. Use complete sentences; an outline or bulleted list alone is not acceptable.

You may pace yourself as you answer the questions in this section, or you may use these optional timing recommendations:

For Question 1 (DBQ), it is suggested that you spend approximately 15 minutes reading the question and planning your answer, and then 45 minutes writing your essay. The suggested writing time for the long essay question is 40 minutes.

For this practice test, use scratch paper for notes and planning as well as writing your responses.

At a Glance

Total Time
1 hour, 40 minutes
Number of Questions
2
Percent of Total Score
40%

Question 1 (DBQ): Mandatory

Suggested Reading and Writing Time
60 minutes
Reading Period
15 minutes. Use this time to read Question 1 and plan your answer. You may begin writing your response before the reading period is over.
Suggested Writing Time
45 minutes
Percent of Total Score
25%

Question 2, 3, or 4 (Long Essay): Choose ONE Question
Answer either Question 2, 3, or 4
Suggested Time
40 minutes
Percent of Total Score
15%

AP EUROPEAN HISTORY

SECTION II

Total Time—1 hour, 40 minutes

Question 1 (Document-Based Question)

Suggested reading and writing time: 1 hour

**It is suggested that you spend 15 minutes reading the documents and 45 minutes writing your response.
Note: You may begin writing your response before the reading period is over.**

Directions: Question 1 is based on the accompanying documents. The documents have been edited for the purpose of this exercise.

In your response, you should do the following:

- Respond to the prompt with a historically defensible thesis or claim that establishes a line of reasoning.
- Describe a broader historical context relevant to the prompt.
- Support an argument in response to the prompt using at least four documents.
- Use at least one additional piece of specific historical evidence (beyond that found in the documents) relevant to an argument about the prompt.
- For at least two documents, explain how or why the document's point of view, purpose, historical situation, and/or audience is relevant to an argument.
- Demonstrate a complex understanding of a historical development related to the prompt through sophisticated argumentation and/or effective use of evidence.

GO ON TO THE NEXT PAGE.

1 ☐ Mark for Review

Using the documents and your knowledge of European history, describe and evaluate the attitudes of those who saw Chartism as a revolutionary movement versus those who saw it as essentially moderate.

Document 1

Source: Minutes of the London Working Men's Association, May 15, 1838.

Resolved, That the Members of the Working Men's Association fully concurring in the great principles of Universal Suffrage, Annual Parliaments, the Ballot, and all the other essentials to the free exercise of Man's political rights—and hearing that a meeting is to be held at Glasgow on the 21st of May in furtherance of those objects do request our Honorary Members Mr. Thos. Murphy and the Revd. Dr Wade to present to that meeting our pamphlet entitled the 'People's Charter' being the outline of an act to provide for the just representation of the people of Great Britain in the Commons House of Parliament—embracing the principles of Universal Suffrage, No Property Qualifications, Annual Parliaments, Equal Representation, Payment of Members, and Vote by [secret] Ballot prepared by a committee of twelve persons, six members of parliament and six members of the Working Men's Association.

Document 2

Source: J.R. Stephens, in a speech at a Chartist Rally in Manchester, September 1838.

This question of Universal Suffrage was a knife and fork question after all; this question was a bread and cheese question, notwithstanding all that had been said against it; and if any man ask him what he meant by Universal Suffrage, he would answer, that every working man in the land had a right to have a good coat to his back, a comfortable abode in which to shelter himself and his family, a good dinner upon his table, and as much wages for that work as would keep him in plenty, and afford him the enjoyment of all the blessings of life which a reasonable man could desire.

Document 3

Source: Article from *The Chartist* publication, May 1839.

It is also upon all sides agreed that this is a fearful remedy, which, like hazardous, extreme, and painful operations in surgery, is only to be brought into action in very extreme cases, when all ordinary courses of treatment have failed. Physical force is a thing not to be lightly had recourse to; it is the last remedy known to the Constitution…

Document 4

Source: Thomas Cooper, from his poem "The Lion of Freedom," written in honor of Chartist leader Feargus O'Connor, 1841.

> …The pride of the nation, he's noble and brave
> He's the terror of tyrants, the friend of the slave,
> The bright star of freedom, the nobles of men,
> We'll rally around him again and again.
>
> Though proud daring tyrants his body confined,
> They never could alter his generous mind;
> We'll hail our caged lion, now free from his den
> And we'll rally around him again and again…

GO ON TO THE NEXT PAGE.

Document 5

Source: Excerpt from *Leeds Mercury,* August 1842.

Last evening, a Chartist tea party and ball, as previously announced by placard were given in the Carpenters' Hall, by 'The committee for the erection of Hunt's monument.' The room and gallery were densely crowded, and an amateur band was in attendance. John Murray presided. After tea, the Rev. James Scholefield entered the room, and announced that Mr. Feargus O'Connor was unable to attend, as he was, in conjunction with other Chartists, engaged in considering what measures were best to be adopted in the present crisis [the call for a general strike].

Document 6

Source: Address of the Female Political Union, a Chartist organization, to their fellow countrywomen, February 1839.

Year after year has passed away, and even now our wishes have no prospect of being realized, our husbands are over wrought, our houses half furnished, our families ill-fed, and our children uneducated—the fear of want hangs over our heads, the scorn of the rich is pointed towards us; the brand of slavery is on our kindred, and we feel the degradation. We are a despised caste, our oppressors are not content with despising our feelings, but demand the control of our thoughts and wants!—want's bitter bondage binds us to their feet, we are oppressed because we are poor.

Document 7

Source: Letter from a middle-class merchant to his wife, April 1848.

London is in a state of panic from the contemplated meeting of the Chartists, 200,000 strong on Monday; for myself, nothing that happened would in the least surprise me: I expect a revolution within two years: there may be one within three days. The Times is alarmed beyond all measure. I have it from good authority that the Chartists are determined to have their wishes granted.

END OF DOCUMENTS FOR QUESTION 1

GO ON TO THE NEXT PAGE.

Question 2, 3, or 4 (Long Essay)

Suggested writing time: 40 minutes

Directions: Answer Question 2 **or** Question 3 **or** Question 4.

In your response, you should do the following:

- Respond to the prompt with a historically defensible thesis or claim that establishes a line of reasoning.
- Describe a broader historical context relevant to the prompt.
- Support an argument in response to the prompt using at least two pieces of specific and relevant evidence.
- Use historical reasoning (e.g., comparison, causation, continuity or change) to frame or structure an argument that addresses the prompt.
- Demonstrate a complex understanding of a historical development related to the prompt through sophisticated argumentation and/or effective use of evidence.

2. Compare the extent to which the term "enlightened absolutism" applied to certain rulers in eastern Europe and Russia during the eighteenth century.

3. Compare the domestic problems faced by two of the great European powers in the decade immediately prior to the outbreak of the First World War.

4. Analyze the end of the imperialistic era after World War II in 2 of the following 3 countries:

> Great Britain
> France
> The Netherlands

2-4   ☐ Mark for Review

Choose a question to answer before you start writing.

○   **Answer Question 2**

○   **Answer Question 3**

○   **Answer Question 4**

WHEN YOU FINISH WRITING, CHECK YOUR WORK ON SECTION II IF TIME PERMITS.

STOP

END OF EXAM

Practice Test 3: Answers and Explanations

PRACTICE TEST 3 ANSWER KEY

1.	A		29.	C
2.	C		30.	C
3.	D		31.	B
4.	A		32.	A
5.	B		33.	A
6.	A		34.	D
7.	D		35.	A
8.	C		36.	D
9.	C		37.	C
10.	D		38.	A
11.	A		39.	D
12.	B		40.	A
13.	C		41.	C
14.	C		42.	C
15.	C		43.	D
16.	C		44.	B
17.	C		45.	D
18.	C		46.	C
19.	B		47.	A
20.	C		48.	C
21.	D		49.	A
22.	D		50.	A
23.	B		51.	C
24.	A		52.	D
25.	B		53.	C
26.	C		54.	B
27.	C		55.	B
28.	C			

PRACTICE TEST 3: ANSWERS AND EXPLANATIONS

Section I, Part A: Multiple Choice

1. **A** Innovation has become an accepted and desired part of life, but it wasn't always so. The world of tradition transformed itself in the last years of the 19th century and the first half of the 20th century, when massive world wars, radical scientific discoveries, and an utterly changed standard of living for all European people resulted in a new philosophy. Russell was radical in one other respect; he was one of Europe's first atheists as well.

2. **C** The text states that there was an emphasis on the relative importance of Plato as opposed to Aristotle. Such conversation, as well as the bridging of eastern European and western European cultures at the Council of Ferrara, created a venue for the Greek classics to enter the minds of western Europeans. Therefore, the correct answer is (C).

3. **D** The phrase *knowledge of antiquity* is a helpful clue. Neoplatonism developed concurrently with Renaissance humanism, but it was different—a mystical theology based on The One (think *The Matrix*), *nous*, the world-soul, numerology, and celestial hierarchy. None of this is covered by Renaissance humanism. Neoclassicism was an 18th-century movement, and scholasticism was medieval.

4. **A** According to the text, the *substitution of Plato for the scholastic Aristotle was hastened by contact with Byzantine scholarship*. Therefore, you should look for an answer that brings Plato to Italian culture. Italian Renaissance author Pico della Mirandola's *Oration on the Dignity of Man* provides a Platonic view of humanity by highlighting the potential of man. This is a perfect example of the cultural diffusion described by Bertrand Russell. The correct answer is (A).

5. **B** Process of Elimination combined with some test-taking logic will reveal that (A), (C), and (D) are unsupported. A glance at the tables tells you that, materially, the Allied forces outweighed the German forces in every possible way. The word *perhaps* in (B) also tells you that it's a good answer—the College Board does love a good weasel word, signifying possibility, but not certainty.

6. **A** The most straightforward way to determine which German and Allied units are most closely matched is to look at the ratios in the tables. The ratio of Allied to German ground troops is 1.43 to 1. This is closer than the ratio for tanks (3.93 to 1), artillery (1.5 to 1), and air force (7.4 to 1).

7. **D** It is clear from the table that Germany lagged far behind the Allies in terms of air force production. This data is consistent with the idea that German production lines did not keep up with the needs of the generals. Choice (D) is correct.

8. **C** Bombers were long-distance military planes. Given the distance from the United States to Europe—as well as the distance from our bases to various locations in the Pacific theater—it would be logical that the U.S. forces might have many more of those.

9. **C** Choice (A) is the trap. While the Soviets had an enormous military, they didn't quite have the same production capabilities as the United States. Furthermore, they didn't participate in D-Day, busy as they were with their own eastern front battle against the German menace.

10. **D**   During World War I, the German populace experienced rationing, the entrance of women into the factories (to replace the men who were called to duty), and much propaganda urging them to fight for their country. English citizens experienced all of these things, too. Total war, however, did not mean the total annihilation of all citizens of your opponent's country. While civilians were certainly killed, the primary aim of military attacks remained enlisted personnel and centers of production.

11. **A**   The cartoon depicts the German kaiser using all possible resources, including people, to win the Great War. (Remember to pay attention to the caption! This goes for any image on the exam that is accompanied by text.) This idea is referred to as "total war." In order to mobilize all resources, governments took control of certain industries. This action set the precedent in a number of countries for government regulation of industry—even during peacetime.

12. **B**   Because the cartoon is a commentary on the concept of total war, you should think about total war's consequences. One is that industries must focus their resources on winning the war and not necessarily domestic concerns. It was common for food shortages to arise on the home front because of this temporary change in priorities. Choice (B) is the answer.

13. **C**   The cartoon offers a critical view of the kaiser's commitment to total war. This is perhaps due to the fact that the creator of the cartoon is British, which matches (C). The clue here is the caption—*Punch* magazine was a famous British satirical publication, which suggests the nationality of the artist.

14. **C**   Indicating that he would use his people dead or alive is not a ringing endorsement for the kaiser's sense of empathy. The cartoon clearly intends to criticize this callous indifference, which aligns with (C).

15. **C**   The philosophy of mercantilism went through many phases, one of which was an early, primitive form known as bullionism. This holds one simple tenet—the more specie (gold and silver) your society possesses, the wealthier your society will be. This describes 16th-century Spain quite well. However, while this may seem superficially true, it doesn't take into account important variables, such as productivity, favorable balance-of-trade, individual rights, and so on.

16. **C**   High inflation was caused by the influx of gold and silver from the Spanish treasure fleet from the New World, especially the silver from Potosí, Bolivia. Basically, there were too many people with too much money chasing too few goods. While inflation has been a fact of life in the West for many decades, even centuries, back then it was a shockingly new phenomenon, and the poor felt even poorer as they could no longer afford to purchase goods.

17. **C**   This question requires you to have some knowledge about the individual goals and motivations of explorers during the Age of Exploration. According to the text, Cortés is motivated by the acquisition of gold. A similar motivation drove Pizarro, (C), to South America and into the Incan Empire. The primary goal of Columbus, da Gama, and Dias was to find better routes for the spice trade.

18. **C**   Hernán Cortés had briefly owned an encomienda in Hispañiola, but really is noted for conquering the Aztec Empire in modern-day Mexico. There is no other option that relates to his life. Be sure to associate Pizarro with the Incas, Cabral with Brazil, Diaz with the Cape of Good Hope, da Gama with India, and Magellan with circumnavigation.

19. **B** Given the vast amounts of land in South America, Central America, and the Caribbean, there was hardly any shortage of land. Most *encomiendas* were assigned to former conquistadores as the Spanish crown's way of both rewarding their loyalty (despite being essentially mass murderers) and organizing the people in newly conquered lands. Interestingly, though, the Spanish crown never intended them to be permanent, and by the end of the century had assumed direct control over the *encomiendas*.

20. **C** The title of the cartoon, "The Devilfish in Egyptian Waters," should indicate that it is referencing an event that took place in Egypt. This should eliminate (B) and (D), which involve Fashoda (in Eastern Africa) and Russia, respectively. This leaves (A) and (C), which both have to do with the Suez Canal. After the Suez Canal was completed in 1882, the British created a protectorate in Egypt to defend its pathway to its colonial holdings in India, which aligns with (C). The Suez Canal Crisis, (A), refers to an event that took place much later, during the Cold War.

21. **D** All of the countries listed in the answer choices except for Germany, (D), had significant imperial holdings. Germany, as you should recall, abstained from the imperial game because of Otto von Bismarck's indifference. He found European dominance much more appealing than imperialism.

22. **D** England, as the most advanced representative democracy in Europe, the first to convert to a constitutional monarchy, took the lead in decentralizing political authority. While there was still a king and queen, there had also been a prime minister since the early 19th century. Most other European countries retained harsher forms of centralized authority, and thus handicapped their own success.

23. **B** If you remember that the Primrose League advocated for British imperialism, then you should have guessed that they would not be happy with a cartoon such as this, since it portrays imperial Great Britain as a menacing creature. The correct answer is (B).

24. **A** As an old saying goes, "the Sun never sets on the British Empire." Great Britain had secured imperial holdings all over the globe, from India to Australia to Boersland (South Africa). Therefore, you can eliminate (B) and (C). The cartoon provides no evidence of countries either resisting or not resisting Imperial Britain, so (D) cannot be correct. The fact that the sea creature is holding on to Ireland should point you to (A).

25. **B** The word *bourgeois*, as well as the phrase *You will never be worthy of happiness as long as you own anything* were clues that the author is referring to redistribution of wealth via socialist means.

26. **C** The Congress of Vienna had existed to reorganize and stabilize Europe after the fall of Napoleon. Headed by Metternich, it was profoundly conservative by nature. That's a pretty far cry from anarchy.

27. **C** Communism primarily was concerned with overturning the traditional owner/employee model of societal organization. You could make the argument that capitalism also cares about its workers, but only indirectly, given the theories of the invisible hand and that a rising tide lifts all boats.

28. **C** The steam engine operated more efficiently on coal than on wood, and so with its invention, a new industry was created—coal mining. There were massive deposits in England, France, and Poland, and going down into the mines became the primary way for working-class people to make a living.

29. **C** Class struggle was on everybody's minds in the late 19th century owing to Marx and Engels. *Noblesse oblige* was a traditional way of taking care of the poorest in society, but that had been rejected a hundred years earlier. Choices (A) and (B) are off topic.

30. **C** Even though there are many similarities between Erasmus and Martin Luther, both of whom criticized the Catholic Church, the focus in this particular text is on Erasmus's ability to bring Latin and classical culture to the masses. The key sentence is at the end of the first paragraph: *He familiarized a much wider circle than the earlier humanists had reached with the spirit of antiquity.* In this regard, Erasmus is quite similar to Francisco Petrarch, whose fascination with classical culture inspired the civic humanists. Therefore, the answer is (C).

31. **B** When humanism ceased to be the exclusive privilege of the few, people could study the Latin Bible as well as ancient texts of the classical era. This newfound knowledge would eventually enable people to begin questioning the laws and interpretations of the Catholic Church. Thus, (B) is the answer.

32. **A** As a product of the 20th century, the author has consciously or unconsciously adopted the biases of his age, which include a predilection for universal education and openness to various different points of view.

33. **A** In the passage, Huizinga writes, *Erasmus introduced the classic spirit, in so far as it could be reflected in the soul of a 16th-century Christian, among the people.* It is evident that Erasmus understood classical texts to be consistent with his religion. Similarly, the Neoplatonists endeavored to use Platonic texts to better understand Christianity, making (A) the correct answer.

34. **D** According to Huizinga, *Until this time the humanists had...monopolized the treasures of classic culture.* However, he then goes on to contrast these humanists with Erasmus, who had *an irresistible need of teaching.* This indicates that, unlike earlier humanists, Erasmus made it a priority to spread his knowledge of classical culture. This best aligns with (D), which is the correct answer.

35. **A** The social reformers of the Victorian era were largely middle-class Christian women who decided that the lower classes lacked moral instruction, which alone would improve their lives. You can argue whether or not this was exactly true, but nonetheless it was in line with biblical teachings. It also reflected a new class-consciousness in England, as the middle class had ballooned to a previously unknown size and strength.

36. **D** The title *Gin Lane*, along with the destitute people pictured in the engraving, indicates that this piece of art comments on the problems associated with alcohol consumption. Since *spirits* refers to liquor, (D) is correct. Even if you have never heard of the Sale of Spirits Act, close analysis of the engraving coupled with Process of Elimination should help you get rid of the other answer choices, which have nothing to do with alcohol or destitution.

37. **C** Use question 35 to help you here, which established that the artist uses deliberate exaggeration for effect in this engraving. Deliberate exaggeration as an artistic device points to the piece's satirical purpose, which aligns with (C).

38. **A** The crowded city scene depicted in the engraving should bring to mind the Enclosure Acts, (A), which forced farmers off their lands and into the cities, resulting in overcrowding. This accelerated during the Industrial Revolution, as machines, rather than people, became a cheaper way for landowners to produce crops.

39. **D** Similar to what happened in the realm of science, 20th-century European art was marked by the rejection of pretty much every aspect of traditional art up until that time. This includes recognizable human figures, evident character, and attention to minute details. However, since Hogarth's work wasn't portraiture, (D) isn't applicable.

40. **A** Indeed, by this time in English history, the monarchy was well on its way toward becoming a titular head-of-state. The power of Parliament had already been well established, and the office of the prime minister had become (in the persons of Disraeli and Gladstone) a new center of political power.

41. **C** The Tories were (and are) one of England's political parties, which hints at the idea of democracy and greater egalitarianism. This transition had occurred back in the turbulent 17th century, as the members of the famous Stuart dynasty struggled with the rise of representative democracy. This ultimately ended with the forcible abdication of James II, and the official creation by William and Mary of a constitutional monarchy.

42. **C** For outrageous behavior amongst nobility, nobody can beat the French under Louis XIV. A quick tour of the pleasure grounds at Versailles will show you how vain, pompous, self-absorbed, and weak the nobility had become under his reign. That was all by design, of course. Distracting the nobles with endless free parties allowed Louis XIV to assume power in their neglected states, which contributed to his absolute power.

43. **D** There is nothing in this letter as ordinary—and, you could say, as touching—as when the queen complains of her exhaustion. We've all felt tired. Modern historians, and modern entertainment, have seized upon the "ordinary lives of the powerful" meme for quite a while. It's a sign of the deeply egalitarian ideals of our current society.

44. **B** With Britain enduring no military attacks from mainland Europe during this time period, and with the British Empire growing rapidly overseas, you can eliminate (C) and (D). There was a potato famine in 1845, but it was in Ireland, not England, so eliminate (A). You're left with the truth—in her 64-year reign, Queen Victoria had to navigate through an equally unprecedented number of changes to English society.

45. **D** At the conference at Yalta, Roosevelt and Churchill divided Germany into four zones—U.S., English, French, and Soviet. Since the Soviets had marched into the country from the East, it made sense that they would control that portion. This was the beginning of East Germany and the Iron Curtain, and it marks the first formal postwar expansion of their land.

46. **C** Hungary was one of the Eastern European countries that joined the Warsaw Pact, (C), an organization created as a direct answer to NATO. The Warsaw Pact was in part a Soviet military reaction to the integration of West Germany into NATO in 1955, but it was primarily motivated by Soviet desires to maintain control over military forces in Central and Eastern Europe.

47. **A** As indicated by the bottom map, while Eastern Europe fell under Soviet influence, Austria held its own (it is the lighter shade of gray). This observation is consistent with (A), as it suggests that Austria was able to resist Stalin. Since command economies are characteristic of communist systems, there is no evidence that Finland (also shaded the lighter gray on the map) had such an economy. Eliminate (B). Unlike the other Balkan countries on the map, Greece is a lighter shade of gray, so (C) can be eliminated. Choice (D) is also incorrect, as Czechoslovakia fell under Soviet influence (it is dark gray on the map) and therefore it's unlikely that it was able to maintain a free economy.

48.　**C**　Soviet tactics during World War II included rolling across Polish land, destroying its people, murdering 15,000 Polish officers in a forest (see Katyn Massacre), and generally behaving even worse than the Germans that were occupying the country. No Pole would support these methods.

49.　**A**　Although West Berlin, entrenched in East Germany, was technically a part of West Germany, West Berlin was not the capital. The capital of West Germany was actually Bonn, a city firmly situated in West Germany. Therefore, the answer is (A).

50.　**A**　Northern European churches did not place the same emphasis on art as did southern European churches. Therefore, churches in the Netherlands did not commission artists to create works. However, the Netherlands in the 17th century was a wealthy place. Private collectors were able to support the artists directly, so one could expect to see art on display in Dutch homes. The correct answer is therefore (A).

51.　**C**　Process of Elimination should help you choose the correct answer. Since the Dutch were dominant in trade in the 17th century, (D) should have stood out to you as being possibly true. The Netherlands was a haven of religious tolerance; indeed, the Puritans who first settled America spent several years in the Netherlands preparing for their journey. Thus, (B) can be eliminated. You should vaguely associate the Netherlands with windmills, so you can get rid of (A) as well. Choice (C) is the answer.

52.　**D**　The focus on the ancient world is more characteristic of the Italian Renaissance, so eliminate (A). Royalty commissioned art and thus increasingly became the subject of artwork when absolute monarchs began to rise, which is a bit later in European history than when this painting was created. Eliminate (B). The Dutch were not particularly concerned with religious imagery in art, so (C) does not work here. The mundane scene depicted in the painting should point you to (D), everyday life.

53.　**C**　The arrival of empiricism was the hallmark of the scientific era. Francis Bacon was one of its earliest proponents, and the book that this passage is taken from, *Novum Organum*, was his attempt to unseat Aristotle, whose body of work was called the *Organon*. It was intended to be a catalog of everything that could be sensed. Perhaps unsurprisingly, he never finished it.

54.　**B**　The Aristotelian worldview had been rediscovered by Italian traders as they entered into Arab lands. This sparked the accomplishments of the Renaissance. However, the scientists of the time considered ancient natural science to be antiquated and irrational, and a poor method of searching for truth. Therefore, the answer here is (B).

55.　**B**　The entire scientific explosion of the late 19th century—all the plodding laboratory work that was performed by Pasteur, Curie, and hundreds of other famous names—was based upon a belief in empirical thought. While (D) may have been tempting, the common person doesn't generally look for new organizing principles for life.

Section I, Part B: Short Answer

Question 1

A. Pinpoint the years from around 1760 to 1820 on the graph to locate the First Industrial Revolution, and 1840 to the late 19th century for the Second Industrial Revolution, to get a sense of the impact those revolutions had. Similarities abound between the two industrial revolutions, and you could've included any of the following:
- rapid technological advances
    - First revolution: Mention Richard Arkwright, flying shuttle, spinning jenny, etc.
    - Second revolution: steam engine, railroads, Henry Bessemer, etc.
- peasantry divorced from agriculture
- increased production, as evidenced by the graph
- continued rise of the merchant class
- improved health outcomes due to increased food production and medical innovations, as evidenced by the life expectancy data

B. Differences include any of the following:
- The Enclosure Acts and the putting-out system (or cottage industry) occurred in the first revolution. The peasants were reduced to doing piecework in their huts.
- The second revolution, by contrast, saw the massive movement of peasants into cities, and the beginning of work in factories.

C. The Industrial Revolution changed the very nature of modern life. It gave to modern life an assortment of new techniques, devices, inventions, and lifestyles.
- A system of indoor plumbing that contributed to a massive reduction in the spread of infectious disease. That one innovation singlehandedly helped extend the lifespan of the average European.
- A lower childhood mortality rate
- Better transportation options. In the eighteenth century, you could either travel by sailboat, horseback, or walking. By the end of the nineteenth century, your choices had expanded to steam-powered boats and railroads.
- Better medical procedures. Germ theory, stethoscopes, hearing aids, aspirin, antiseptics, and improved vaccines all improved daily life.
- Cheaper fabrics. Textile manufacturing was one of the first things to leap forward during this period. It enabled middle-class people to cover their homes in drapery and carpet.
- Electricity. Enough said.

This list merely scratches the surface. The process of technological innovation continues to this day.

Question 2

A. There are many possible answers to this question of what helped feminism. Bigger, more industrialized countries such as England and France did not have such oppressive governments as other countries did, which allowed early feminism to flourish. Another possibility: The expansion of the middle class in these countries brought greater leisure time to that part of the population, which used it to agitate for progressive causes such as feminism. Or the urbanization, media, and transportation that rose up in the cities created a more closely linked society, which shared news and built social movements much more quickly than rural parts of society could.

B.   Feminism was restricted by a system of Victorian principles that made a clear distinction between public and private spheres; men occupied the former while women occupied the latter.

C.   The obvious answer here would be the success of the women's suffrage movement, which was headed by the Pankhurst sisters. However, the entrance of women into the workforce during World War I is another possible answer.

Question 3

Here is a checklist of things you should have mentioned for each philosopher:

- Locke: strong individual = little government needed. The right to private property is sacred, *tabula rasa*, *Second Treatise on Government*.
- Hobbes: weak individual = strong government needed. *Leviathan*. Life in a state of nature is nasty, brutish, and short.
- Smith: invisible hand of the market guides society, *laissez-faire*, *Wealth of Nations*.
- Descartes: deductive reasoning, mind/body split, systematic doubt, "I think; therefore, I am."
- David Hume: empiricism, radical rejection of all religion, relentless systematic doubt, sensory experience is everything, early psychologist.

A.   The first three thinkers (Locke, Hobbes, Smith) are most likely to be chosen to be representative of Enlightenment thought.

B.   Descartes is most likely not to represent Enlightenment thought, but you can make a case for Hobbes or Hume too.

C.   Several of the thinkers, especially Locke, impacted the political life of Europeans through their insistence upon natural (a.k.a. civil) rights for all people. Known as liberalism, this philosophy was one of the demands made by many of the revolutions that followed—the French Revolution, the Revolutions of 1830, and the Revolutions of 1849. Locke's influences can also be found in the Napoleonic Code. Likewise, Descartes' system of doubt undermined the strength of political and religious authorities, which clearly contributed to the same revolutions.

One cornerstone of many modern European political systems is Thomas Hobbes' emphasis on individuals surrendering some of their freedoms to a strong central government in exchange for safety and security. Bismarck's government in the new nation of Germany, for example, asked this of its citizens during its founding in 1871.

In economics, Adam Smith's concept of *laissez-faire* capitalism was displayed in the excesses of the Industrial Revolution, particularly in Great Britain in the first half of the 19th century.

Question 4

A. The second half of the 19th century saw an explosion of new medical tools, techniques, and treatments. In no particular order:

    i. The stethoscope
    ii. Quinine (an anti-malarial agent)
    iii. Aspirin
    iv. Blood transfusions
    v. Surgical anesthetic
    vi. Antiseptic surgery (Joseph Lister)
    vii. Cholera vaccines
    viii. X-rays

B. There are several examples of 19th-century innovations in the field of the arts, particularly in visual arts.

    i. The most obvious would be the invention of photography. Louis Daguerre was the first, when he accidentally discovered how to imprint an image onto a plate exposed to mercury vapor. This became known as a daguerreotype.
    ii. Later, George Eastman refined the photographic process by introducing flexible celluloid film and a box around the aperture of the camera. This popularized the pursuit and made it affordable for the consumer.
    iii. At the end of the century, the moving picture camera was invented by the Lumiere brothers.

C. In medicine, the obvious effect of these inventions has been to save and prolong human life. The long-term effect of their use was an increase in the overall population of Europe. For painters, the invention of photography and film meant that the hyperrealistic mode of expressing oneself was dead, since a camera could do that better than any human. This freed artists to start experimenting with non-realistic methods of art such as impressionism, surrealism, cubism, and eventually modernism and post-modernism. Painters from all these eras are fair game to mention here, including names such as Monet, Picasso, Klee, Mondrian, Pollock, etc.

Section II: Document-Based Question (DBQ)

The document-based question (DBQ) section begins with a suggested 15-minute reading period. During these 15 minutes, you should do the following: (1) come up with some information not included in the given documents (your outside knowledge) to include in your essay, (2) get an overview of what each document means and the perspective of each author, (3) decide what opinion you are going to argue, and (4) write an outline of your essay.

This DBQ deals with the issue of Chartism and is asking you to determine whether Chartism should be viewed as a revolutionary movement or as a moderate movement. You will need to have some knowledge of British politics in the 19th century to handle this question and at least a little familiarity with Chartism, although don't be too concerned if your knowledge of Chartism is somewhat limited.

BEFORE YOU LOOK AT THE DOCUMENTS, first brainstorm for a minute or two. Try to list everything you know (from class or leisure reading or informational television programs) about both Chartism and British politics in the first half of the 19th century. This list will serve as your reference to the outside information you must provide to earn a top grade.

Next, read over the documents. As you read them, make notes on your scratch paper, including which passages you are certain you will use in your essay. Make note of the opinions and position of each document's author. If a document reminds you of a piece of outside information, add that information to your brainstorming list. If you cannot make sense of a document or it argues strongly against your position, relax! You do not need to mention every document to score well on the DBQ.

Here is what you might see in the time you have to look over the documents.

The Documents

Document 1

This first document lays out the six points of the Charter. They are as follows:

1. universal suffrage
2. no property requirement for Members of Parliament
3. annual parliaments
4. equal representation (meaning that all areas of the nation would be equally represented)
5. payment of Members
6. vote by secret ballot

You'll notice that the document refers to the idea of the Charter providing for the *just representation of the people of Great Britain,* an indication that the goal is the political inclusion of working-class individuals rather than the complete overhaul of the system.

Document 2

This excerpt from a speech by J.R. Stephens given at a Chartist rally addresses one of the central issues behind the rise of Chartism. For Stephens, the Charter is all about providing people with the basic needs of life, such as food and shelter. As a Chartist, Stephens believed that political rights were the means for British workers to achieve a better standard of living.

Document 3

This article, which appeared in a Chartist newspaper, appears to be aimed at those Chartists who were advocating the need for armed violence. While implying that it is within an Englishman's right to rebel and is, in fact, *the last remedy known to the Constitution,* the article strongly rejects the use of physical force as an option in the current situation.

Document 4

This document is a poem in honor of Feargus O'Connor. Besides noticing how nicely everything rhymes, you should be aware that the document refers to the earlier imprisonment of O'Connor, who, at the time the poem appeared in print, was free to continue with his labors on behalf of the Chartists.

Document 5

Document 5 contains a portion of a newspaper article detailing the events at a Chartist social gathering. It is important to note that the gathering consists of a tea party and ball, activities that clearly imitate the social activities of the upper classes and appear far from revolutionary. Feargus O'Connor (the same individual lionized in Document 4) was unable to attend the tea party because he and some of the other Chartists were busy debating whether to call for a general strike (certainly few middle-class tea parties were interrupted for similar reasons).

Document 6

While male Chartists split over the question of whether the right to vote should be extended to women, women were actively engaged in the Chartist movement, both as a source of support for male Chartists and as active participants in their own right. This document, from a female Chartist organization, should be viewed in conjunction with Document 2, because, like the earlier document, it focuses on the economic hardships of working-class life, rather than placing a specific emphasis on the political struggle or women's rights within the Chartist movement.

Document 7

Make note that the author of this letter is a middle-class man and that the letter reveals some of the fears that his class must have felt about a working-class movement that they neither understood nor sympathized with. Also, the source for his information is the *Times*, the most important newspaper of the establishment and again not necessarily a source for genuine understanding of the Chartist movement.

Outside Information

We have already discussed much more than you could possibly write in only 45 minutes. Don't worry. You will not be expected to mention everything or even most of what we have covered in the section above. You will, however, be expected to include some outside information, that is, information not mentioned directly in the documents. The following is some outside information you might have used in your essay.

- The ostensible goal of Chartism was the passage of the "People's Charter," a document that called for universal suffrage for all men over the age of 21, the end of property requirements for those holding seats in Parliament, annual parliamentary elections, equal electoral districts, and payment of those holding seats in Parliament. Chartists organized massive petitions that were presented on several occasions to the House of Commons, although the House of Commons did nothing to act on them. The largest and final petition was presented in 1848 with around 3 million signers.

- Five of the demands of the Chartists are today a part of the British constitution. The only one that has never been enacted was the idea of annual parliamentary elections, a radical idea that went back to the constitutional struggles of the 17th century. Today the maximum life of a parliament is five years thanks to the Fixed-Term Parliaments Act of 2011. Before the passage of this act, Parliament could be dissolved only by royal proclamation. The changes enacted in 2011 were part of the Conservative–Liberal Democrat coalition agreement which was produced after the 2010 general election.

- The late 1830s and the 1840s were a particularly difficult period, one known to historians as the "hungry forties." Economic difficulties may account for the rise of Chartism, particularly if the movement is viewed as one whose primary goal was the establishment of political rights for working-class individuals so that they could have some say over the economic conditions that ruled their lives. Economic conditions may also account for the decline of Chartism after 1848, since these were years of growing economic prosperity and therefore may have led to an easing of political demands.

- Working-class individuals were angered over the passage of the Great Reform Bill (1832), which provided political rights for middle-class individuals, but ignored the rights of the working class. Additionally, there was a tremendous amount of working-class frustration with certain bills passed by this new "reformed" Parliament, including the 1834 Poor Law, which treated those suffering from poverty with great harshness.

- 1848 was a year of revolutionary activity throughout Europe. In France, the monarchy was replaced by a republic and revolutions spread across Europe. You should know from your studies of this period, however, that England and Russia were the two European states that were exempt from revolutionary activity in that year.

- There were two dominant factions within Chartism. The majority can be labeled "moral force" Chartists; they wanted to peacefully campaign for the passage of the "People's Charter." "Physical force" Chartists were a smaller faction found primarily in the cities of Northern England; they advocated the possible use of violence should their demands not be met. William Lovell was the leader of the moral force Chartists, while Feargus O'Connor was the main figure in the opposing faction.

- Chartism as a movement declined rapidly in the years after 1848. Working-class men increasingly looked to labor unions as a source for economic change rather than mass political movements, though working-class political activity did not disappear. The British political system would prove to be more flexible than many had imagined, and in 1867 male working-class householders received the vote, while in 1884 their counterparts in the countryside received the same.

Choosing a Thesis Statement

This DBQ is asking you to take sides in a debate. On the basis of the documents, a much stronger case could be provided for taking the position that Chartism should be viewed as a movement for political change that was *not* fundamentally revolutionary. Keep in mind that while there are strong historical arguments for taking the other side (and a number of books and articles have taken the position that Chartism *was* inherently revolutionary), you must base your argument primarily on the documents provided on the exam. The documents provided truly lean toward the nonrevolutionary aspects of the movement. Your thesis statement could be as follows: Though it inspired passion among both upper and lower classes in England, Chartism was undoubtedly a nonrevolutionary movement.

Planning Your Essay

Unless you read extremely quickly, you probably will not have time to write a detailed outline for your essay during the 15-minute reading period. However, it is worth taking several minutes to jot down a loose structure of your essay because it will actually save you time when you write. First, decide on your thesis and write it down on your scratch paper. Then, take a minute or two to brainstorm all the points you might put in your essay. Choose the strongest points and number them in the order you plan to present them. Lastly, note which documents and outside information you plan to use in conjunction with each point. If you organize your essay in advance of writing, the actual writing process will go much more smoothly. More important, you will not write yourself into a corner, suddenly finding yourself making a point you cannot support or heading toward a weak conclusion (or worse still, no conclusion at all).

For example, to deal with the issue of whether Chartism was revolutionary, you might want to organize a brainstorm list like the following:

> *Political demands of the Chartists*
> *Six points of the Charter*
> *Economic issues*
> *Chartism and women*
> *Violence and nonviolence*
> *Hunger*
> *Actions taken by the Chartists*
> *End result of Chartist activities*

Next, you should figure out which of your brainstorm ideas could be the main idea of paragraph number one, which ones could be used as evidence to support a point, and which should be eliminated. You should probably begin your first paragraph with your thesis, and then discuss the specific political demands of the Chartists in an attempt to show that the Chartists were interested in being included in the British political system and were not seeking its destruction. You should mark the paragraph topic with a 1 to show that it's the theme of your first paragraph; then get more specific with a note if it's supporting evidence. In this case, your list might look like this:

> *Political demands of the Chartists*   *1*
> *Six points of the Charter*   *1-evidence*
> *Economic issues*
> *Chartism and women*
> *Violence and nonviolence*
> *Hunger*
> *Actions taken by the Chartists*
> *End result of Chartist activities*

If paragraph one is going to deal with the political demands of Chartism, you should certainly refer to Document 1 because it lays out the Chartist program. You might want to use your second paragraph to deal with the economic issues behind Chartism. This approach is a way to show that economic deprivation played a major role in leading working-class individuals toward political activity, not for the purposes of destroying British society, but to ensure that there was food on their tables. You could therefore make use of Documents 2 and 6, both of which deal with the economic deprivations behind Chartism. In this case your list would look like this:

> *Political demands of the Chartists*   *1*
> *Six points of the Charter*   *1-evidence*
> *Economic issues*   *2*
> *Chartism and women*   *2-evidence*
> *Violence and nonviolence*
> *Hunger*   *2-evidence*
> *Actions taken by the Chartists*
> *End result of Chartist activities*

Proceed in this way until you have finished planning your strategy. Try to fit as many of the documents into your argument as you can, but do not stretch too far to fit one in. Don't be concerned, for example, if you can't find a use for the poem in honor of Feargus O'Connor. An obvious, desperate stretch will only hurt your grade. Also, remember that history is often intricate and that the readers of your exam want to see that you respect the intrinsic complexity behind many historical events.

Section II: Long Essay

Because you have only 40 minutes to plan and write this essay, you will not have time to work out elaborate arguments. That's okay; nobody is expecting you to read three questions, choose one, remember all the pertinent facts about the subject, formulate a brilliant thesis, and then write a perfect essay. Here are the steps you should follow. First, choose your question, brainstorm for two or three minutes, and edit your brainstorm ideas. Then, number the points you are going to include in your essay in the order you plan to present them. Finally, think of a simple thesis statement that allows you to discuss the points your essay will make.

Question 2—Enlightened Absolutism (Option 1)

2. Compare the extent to which the term "enlightened absolutism" applied to certain rulers in eastern Europe and Russia during the eighteenth century.

About the Structure of Your Essay

In this essay, you should make a strong thesis statement, perhaps arguing that while those rulers who are labeled as *enlightened absolutists* often spoke about enlightened ideas, for the most part they failed to implement any substantive changes within their realms. On the other hand, you could list some of their actual achievements (such as in the area of religious toleration), while pointing out that powerful elements within their states, such as the Church or nobility, blocked any possibility for further reform. Most importantly, be sure to *compare* rulers of different countries and draw connections among them. The question makes it clear that comparison is the historical thinking skill you are being tested on.

Your essay should mention at least some of the following:

- Most of the leading writers of the Enlightenment, such as Voltaire and Diderot, wanted change to come about not through the advent of republics, but rather through "enlightened monarchs" who would seek to reform their ideas based on the concepts of enlightened reason.

- The monarchs whom historians are mostly referring to when using the term *enlightened absolutists* are Catherine the Great, the empress of Russia (1762–1796); Joseph II of Austria (1741–1790); and Frederick the Great, the king of Prussia (1740–1786).

- These enlightened absolutists certainly read the works of the leading writers of the Enlightenment. Frederick read Voltaire and was so impressed that he invited him to stay at his court. Catherine also read Voltaire, as well as Diderot, and when Diderot desperately needed money to get out of debt, Catherine bought his extensive library and then generously lent it back to him.

- Joseph of Austria was influenced by the Enlightenment's call for religious toleration. Joseph granted Jews the right to worship (though they had to pay special taxes for the privilege), while Protestants were given the right to hold positions at the court in Vienna. That spirit of tolerance didn't extend to all enlightened absolutists, as Frederick refused to grant similar rights to the Jews of his realm and Catherine did nothing to grant rights to religious minorities in Russia.

- Writers of the Enlightenment had discussed the need for humane treatment for the accused. Both Joseph and Frederick banned the use of judicial torture within their realms, while Frederick went so far as to ban capital punishment. Both rulers also relaxed the strict censorship that existed in their states, although at times they still banned works they considered critical of their rule.

- All three enlightened monarchs attempted to expand the number of individuals receiving an education, not to create freethinkers, but rather that they might have more trained individuals to serve as bureaucrats. Although none of the states implemented anything close to universal public education, they did greatly increase the number of individuals who went to school. These students, however, almost exclusively came from the higher classes.

- Frederick, in his youth, had toyed with the concept of enlightened statecraft based on just relations among states. However, when he saw the opportunity, he launched an unprovoked attack on the Habsburg territory of Silesia.

- Joseph of Austria ended the practice of owning serfs, although the newly freed peasants found that freedom came with the price of greatly increased taxes. Joseph discovered that further reform in the countryside was impossible because of the strong resistance of the nobility.

- None of these rulers took steps toward making their states constitutional monarchies. Catherine toyed with the idea of granting a constitution, but in the end, she and her fellow absolutists showed little interest in doing anything that would place actual limits on their power.

Question 3—Domestic Tensions on the Eve of World War I (Option 2)

3. Compare the domestic problems faced by two of the great European powers in the decade immediately prior to the outbreak of the First World War.

About the Structure of Your Essay

The years immediately prior to World War I were notable for the domestic problems faced by the great powers: Germany, Austria-Hungary, Russia, France, Italy, and Great Britain. Since the question is asking you to deal with two of these states, it would be to your advantage to quickly consider a list of domestic concerns for each of these states and then decide which two states on your list look most promising when it comes to writing your actual essay. Like question 2, this question requires you to compare the domestic problems of two countries, so be sure to draw explicit connections between them in the text of your essay.

Depending on which two nations you decide to focus on, your essay might mention some of the following points:

- On the surface, Germany was the great behemoth of Europe, possessing the strongest army, a growing navy, and an unmatched industrial base. Despite these apparent strengths, on the eve of the First World War, Germany was facing a potential political crisis, with more than one nationalistic politician stating that Germany needed a "blood cure" (war) to divert public attention. The constitution that Bismarck established for the new German state in 1871 did not create a constitutional monarchy along British lines. While the national Parliament, the Reichstag, was elected by universal male suffrage, its powers were severely restricted. The chief minister of the state, the chancellor, was selected by the kaiser and not dependent upon the support of the Reichstag.

  Despite being in many ways a conservative, militaristic society, Germany also had the largest Socialist party in all of Europe, and the Socialists were the single largest political party in the Reichstag by 1912. The problem was that while the party could bring hundreds of thousands of people out in the street for demonstrations and garner around a third of the popular vote, by itself it could not enact desperately needed political reform. The party rejected the revisionist Socialist views of Eduard Bernstein, who argued that a socialist state could be achieved without a violent revolution. Yet, the Socialist Democratic Party (SPD), while clinging to revolutionary rhetoric, became a parliamentary party rather than a revolutionary one. Kaiser Wilhelm, however, remained convinced that the party was committed to the destruction of his state and lived in dread of the eventual day when the Socialists would put their revolutionary rhetoric into action.

German Liberals, who perhaps should have been the leaders of the move to a genuine parliamentary system, found themselves split among a number of splinter parties as they argued over issues such as protective tariffs. Meanwhile, in the decade before the war, the right witnessed a surge in small parties that espoused beliefs that foreshadowed the program of the Nazi Party.

Germany faced other domestic problems on the eve of the war. Many Germans bemoaned the declining world of the independent farmers, who were being crushed by a decline in food prices, and of craftsmen, who were threatened by the rise of large industry. Small shopkeepers also were threatened by large department stores. All of these problems contributed to the rise of antisemitic parties, which deflected blame from the government and encouraged Germans to blame the negative changes that were coming to their lives on Jewish retailers and bankers. While not as considerable as that facing Austria-Hungary, Germany had its own nationality problem with many voicing concern that Polish families were buying farmland from impoverished Prussian Junkers, while the higher birthrate among Polish families portended a potential population explosion in the east. Meanwhile in Alsace and Lorraine, territories that Germany had seized as part of their victory in the Franco-Prussian War in 1871, a population that was ostensibly ethnically German would have preferred to substitute French rule for that of the heavy-handed Germans.

- In Austria-Hungary, the Emperor Franz-Joseph saw himself as the father of his people, but he couldn't have been a proud parent when considering the behavior of his "children." The emperor saw his throne as being above the nationality problem and to some extent affection for the emperor made this true. However, the aging Franz-Joseph (he was born in 1830) couldn't live forever, and there was a sense that his demise would soon be followed by the collapse of his empire. The establishment of the dual monarchy of Austria-Hungary in 1867 had not solved the nationality problem and, in some ways, had made it worse as other nationalities strove to match the status achieved by the Hungarians. Within Hungary, the Magyars, who made up half of the population, essentially ignored minority rights. With only five percent of the male population in Hungary allowed to vote, Magyar magnates controlled a political machine that ensured their dominance over the political and cultural life in the Hungarian kingdom. While there were those within the empire who were advocates of breaking the empire into a federation of nationalities, the grim reality in Hungary revealed that this would not solve the problem since each federation would have had its own nationality problem. The nationality question dominated all other issues within the empire and right on the eve of the war there was a major political problem in Bohemia over the question of whether to teach German or Czech in the public schools.

While the army and civil service were two institutions that were reasonably successful in providing some sense of common imperial identity, other attempts to match this success failed. Universal male suffrage, adopted in 1907, led to even greater conflict in the Austrian Parliament, the Reichsrat, as each nationality was represented by its various partisans. The institution itself was to become infamous for the unbelievably poor behavior of the parliamentary representatives as they cursed, threw things, and spit on their rivals. Eventually this tentative experiment in parliamentary rule was deemed a failure, and the emperor shut down the Parliament at the beginning of the war.

Of all the seemingly implacable problems facing Austria-Hungary, it was the South Slav issue that was most pressing on the eve of the First World War. The establishment of an independent Serbian state in 1878 out of a former piece of the Ottoman Empire was not a major problem for Austria-Hungary except for the fact that it was a state built on the issue of nationality, in this case, a Serbian national identity. At the same time the Serbian state was born, Austria-Hungary took administrative control over the province of Bosnia, a territory that had a significant ethnic Serbian population. Relations between the two states were amicable until 1903 when the pro-Austrian Serbian dynasty was replaced by a group of army officers who wished to see Serbia pursue a more nationalistic program and ally themselves with their fellow Slavs in Russia. Ensuing tensions between Austria-Hungary and Serbia led to the so-called "Pig War," an economic war in which Austria-Hungary refused to import Serbia's main export—pigs. In 1908, Austria-Hungary broke an earlier promise it had made to Russia and formally incorporated Bosnia into the empire. This step was undertaken not out of a desire to add more Slavs to their already polyglot empire, but rather to forestall a possible expansion of Serbian power into the territory. The step infuriated the Russians, who, because they were just recovering from their war with Japan and the Revolution of 1905, were unable to respond with vigor, though they vowed that next time they would not stand down if there was a similar Austro-Hungarian provocation in the Balkans. By the summer of 1914, tensions between Austria-Hungary and Serbia were at a fever pitch, with Archduke Franz Ferdinand on his way to Sarajevo to inspect the army divisions that would be used for a potential invasion and occupation of Serbia.

- In the years before the war, Russia remained something of an enigma in that it avoided all political modernization while making impressive economic advancement. The nation had begun to industrialize by the 1890s, and on the eve of the First World War, the potential size of its economy was becoming apparent. In 1914, Russia was the fourth-largest industrial power on Earth, having overtaken France. Rather than begin with smaller industrial concerns, Russian industrialization had occurred on a massive scale with gigantic factories sprouting up in the area in and around St. Petersburg, a city that was facing an acute housing shortage and sanitation problems. The booming economy in the years prior to the war also brought about a high rate of inflation and significant social tensions resulting from an exploited workforce, with a significant number of workdays lost to strikes. There was also serious unrest in the countryside, where many peasants continued to try to scrape by on inadequate land holdings and grappled with declining agricultural prices. Politically, the tsarist system of royal absolutism seemed incredibly anachronistic at the start of the 20th century. An unsuccessful war with Japan in 1904 revealed the numerous failings of the political system and helped bring about the revolution of 1905. The tsarist state survived, but just barely, in part because the army stayed loyal, while the opposition to the tsar was scattered among many different groups. As a concession to those clamoring for change, Nicholas II was forced to accept a parliament, or Duma, but he treated it with disdain and by 1907 had packed it with sympathetic representatives. In order to restore its popularity following the Revolution, the government turned to antisemitism and nationalism as unifying forces, but even these proved problematic. As an empire that stretched across two continents populated by numerous peoples with different languages and cultures, Russia had a serious national identity problem.

- It can be argued that of all the great powers, France was in the best shape domestically on the eve of the war. Even so, the Third French Republic did face some significant domestic conflicts prior to the First World War, including the fact that many Frenchmen still questioned the legitimacy of the republic itself. The Third Republic that was officially created in 1875 was in some ways conceived by accident when it became clear that restoring the monarchy, a move many Frenchmen would have preferred, was fraught with difficulties. In the years that followed, prime ministers came and went but no single party was able to dominate the legislature. Unlike that of the other great European powers, French economic output was fairly stagnant in the decade prior to the war. As a result of this lack of growth, France encountered significant labor unrest with the number of work days lost to strikes increasing every year leading up to 1914.

The fallout from the Dreyfus affair, in which a Jewish officer had been falsely accused of selling military secrets to the Germans, overshadowed life in the Third Republic even after Dreyfus's pardon in September of 1899. *Action Française*, a right-wing newspaper, continued to push an antisemitic agenda, something that received a favorable response among a significant portion of the French populace, particularly as France's Jewish population increased with refugees escaping from the horrors of tsarist Russia. Other religious issues were equally contentious, such as the question of the role of the Catholic Church. Although church and state were officially separated in 1905, that decision continued to rankle the more religiously inclined. In the years immediately prior to the war, the Third Republic also debated if it should maintain a three-year military service commitment for French conscripts (to keep up with Germany's vastly larger population) as well as the controversial question of whether to introduce an income tax to pay for larger military expenditures and a minimal system of old-age pensions.

- The Italian economy was growing at a nice clip in the years prior to 1914, but the economy still could not keep up with the needs of a rapidly growing population. The industrialized north suffered from a wave of strikes, which, due to the relative weakness of the Italian trade union movement in comparison with its German or British counterparts, provided an opening for extremist groups. One such group was the Syndicalists, a group whose mission was to transform capitalist society through action by the working class, who threatened to use the tool of the general strike to bring down the capitalist system. Meanwhile, in the largely agricultural south of Italy, life had hardly changed since the 18th century; it was still a land of great estates and a hardworking, impoverished peasantry. The desperate poverty of the region would eventually lead to entire villages packing up and emigrating to the United States.

  Parliamentary politics in Italy had never been a particularly enlightening sight, and, on the eve of the war, the entire system appeared to be breaking down. When Italy entered the war on the side of the Entente in 1915, the Parliament was not even consulted. As in France, there was a significant anti-clerical element in Italian politics. While the growing Catholic Center Party benefited from the papacy's continued refusal to recognize the Italian state, it came to realize that it would be useful to have a party that reflected Church desire in order to stop the passage of bills allowing for such things as divorce. As a possible way out of the political quagmire, the government turned its attention to imperial affairs, such as the worthless conquest of Libya in 1911. For more ardent Italian nationalists, this action was not enough, and they clamored for the conquest of *Italia irredenta* (unredeemed Italy)—that is, areas occupied by ethnic Italians living under Austro-Hungarian rule.

- Great Britain was facing a number of significant issues on the eve of the First World War. On the front burner in the decade prior to the First World War was the question of the extension of suffrage to women. In the first half of the 19th century, Liberals often argued that voting should be limited to men of property, but once the vote was granted to working-class male householders in the reform bills of 1867 and 1884, it opened up the possibility of further extensions to include women. In the second half of the 19th century, a number of women's suffrage societies emerged that worked for the vote through peaceful means, such as organizing petitions meant to influence Members of Parliament. By 1900, a new, more violent element emerged with the formation of the Women's Social and Political Union (W.S.P.U.), led by Emmeline Pankhurst. Pankhurst's group, often referred to as suffragettes, was quite different from the earlier suffrage societies in that the members felt justified in using means such as arson as a tool for bringing attention to the plight of women. When some suffragettes were arrested for violent acts, they staged hunger strikes in prison and brought negative publicity to the government of Liberal Prime Minister Herbert Asquith.

Great Britain struggled over the place of the unelected House of Lords in a nation that was increasingly heading toward democracy. The focal point for this struggle came in 1909 when the Liberals introduced a bill to provide for old-age pensions. In order to finance the plan, David Lloyd-George, the Chancellor of the Exchequer, proposed raising income taxes, raising death duties, and taxing landed wealth. The bill passed the House of Commons, but stalled in the House of Lords, where the Lords broke with tradition for the first time in more than 200 years and rejected a money bill. As punishment for this unprecedented behavior, the Liberal government pushed a bill to limit the House of Lords' power to a suspending veto lasting two parliamentary sessions. When the House of Lords refused to pass a bill that would effectively strip it of its powers, Prime Minister Asquith threatened to have the king instantly create several hundred new lords in order to stack the upper house of Parliament and pass the bill. With this, the House of Lords finally passed the bill.

Yet the most serious crisis facing the British government on the eve of the First World War was the question of Home Rule for Ireland. The Liberal Party had first broached the subject when Prime Minister William Gladstone introduced a Home Rule bill in 1884. The bill failed to win support among the party faithful and, in fact, led to a split within the Liberal Party that helped bring about a long period of Conservative dominance over British politics. By 1914, Asquith was ready to try again to bring about Home Rule. Fearing the domination of Catholics, the Protestants of Ulster began to take up arms to resist Home Rule, while the Catholic population began to arm in response. Civil war looked almost certain in Ireland, and to make matters worse, some British army officers indicated that they would refuse to obey if ordered to disarm the Ulster Protestants.

Question 4—End of Imperialism Post–World War II (Option 3)

4. Analyze the end of the imperialistic era after World War II in two of the following three countries.

> Great Britain
> France
> The Netherlands

About the Structure of Your Essay

World War II was expensive and damaging for all parties involved, and all European nations found themselves struggling economically in the years immediately following the war. This was the root cause for the colonial powers to shed their expensive overseas properties. Between 1945 and 1960, more than 35 different countries in Asia and Africa demanded, fought for, and won their freedom from European colonial powers.

Here are some points that you could include in your essay:

Great Britain: Definitely the hardest hit of the colonial powers, the mighty British Empire found itself forced to withdraw from many of its overseas properties as a condition of receiving American aid. These include the following:

- India. Thanks to individuals such as Mahatma Gandhi, the 150-year-long movement toward independence reached its end in 1947, when India successfully declared independence from Great Britain. This set off a chain reaction through the entire British Empire. The process wasn't smooth, however—the partition that occurred as India and Pakistan tried to define their border involved the largest human migration in history. Hindus, Sikhs, and Muslims all sorted themselves by religion, with most Muslims moving to Pakistan and most Hindus moving to India.

- Israel. In the same year, England announced that it would be removing itself from Palestine, the Arab territory in the Middle East that contained Jerusalem. Almost immediately, a new Jewish state called Israel was formed there—despite the protests of the Palestinians. To this day, the two groups have never agreed upon the nation's borders.

- Egypt. Great Britain had always maintained a strong interest in Egypt because of the Suez Canal, which shortened trade routes from Asia. For this reason, England owned the Suez Canal, together with France and eventually Israel. However, in 1956, the new Egyptian president Abdul Nasser declared the canal to be solely Egyptian property. The United States and Soviet Union supported this declaration, which forced Great Britain to withdraw.

- Other African nations. During the 1950s and 1960s, many British possessions in Africa were slowly divested from the dwindling Empire. Ghana was first, followed by Nigeria, Sierra Leone, Uganda, and Kenya. All proceeded smoothly, except for Rhodesia, which suffered a racially motivated war from 1965 as the white portion of the population attempted to claim itself as the rulers of an independent nation, so as to avoid majority rule by the Black population. By 1980, their efforts were defeated, a Black ruler named Robert Mugabe was elected by popular vote, and the nation's very British name was changed to Zimbabwe. Mugabe ruled for 37 years, until 2017.

France: Less extensive than the British Empire's colonial holdings, the French holdings were nonetheless important—and giving them up was undeniably more painful.

- Vietnam. As it tried to hold onto the colony, France faced the same nationalist rebellion, led by Ho Chi Minh, that the Japanese had faced during World War II. Ultimately France realized the nationalist movement was too strong, and so decided to divide the country into a North Vietnam (Minh's communist nation) and South Vietnam (dominated by the United States).

- Algeria. The nation of Algeria had been a French holding for 150 years, and the decision to let it go caused massive internal stress within France. President Charles de Gaulle ended the argument by granting it independence in 1958.

The Netherlands: Their holdings were just as farflung as those of Great Britain and France. They included:

- Indonesia. The Dutch presence in Indonesia dated back to the 17th century, when the Dutch East Asia Company locked down trading rights with the region. In 1945, led by Sukarno, Indonesians declared their independence. A bloody conflict ensued, and in 1949, the Netherlands relented.

- Suriname. This small colony, along the so-called "wild coast" of northeast South America, was granted independence in 1975. One-third of the population fled to the Netherlands, fearing what may come.

HOW TO SCORE PRACTICE TEST 3

Section IA: Multiple Choice

$$\underline{\hspace{4cm}} \times 1.090 = \underline{\hspace{4cm}}$$

Number Correct
(out of 55)

Weighted
Section I Score
(Do not round)

Section IB: Short Answer

Question 1: $\underline{\hspace{3cm}} \times 3.3333 = \underline{\hspace{3cm}}$

(out of 3) (Do not round)

Question 2: $\underline{\hspace{3cm}} \times 3.3333 = \underline{\hspace{3cm}}$

(out of 3) (Do not round)

Question 3 or 4: $\underline{\hspace{3cm}} \times 3.3333 = \underline{\hspace{3cm}}$

(out of 3) (Do not round)

AP Score Conversion Chart European History	
Composite Score Range	AP Score
107–150	5
90–106	4
73–89	3
56–72	2
0–55	1

Section II: Document-Based Question

Question 1: $\underline{\hspace{3cm}} \times 5.3571 = \underline{\hspace{3cm}}$

(out of 7) (Do not round)

Section II: Long Essay

Question 2, 3, or 4: $\underline{\hspace{3cm}} \times 3.750 = \underline{\hspace{3cm}}$

(out of 6) (Do not round)

Composite Score

$$\underline{\hspace{2cm}} + \underline{\hspace{2cm}} + \underline{\hspace{2cm}} + \underline{\hspace{2cm}} = \underline{\hspace{2cm}}$$

Weighted
Section IA
Score

Weighted
Section IB
Score

Weighted
DBQ
Score

Weighted
Long
Essay
Score

Composite Score
(Round to the
nearest whole
number)

Note: This score sheet is to help you estimate your approximate score for the official exam, not your actual score.

Completely darken bubbles with a No. 2 pencil. If you make a mistake, be sure to erase mark completely. Erase all stray marks.

1.

YOUR NAME: _____
(Print)   Last   First   M.I.

SIGNATURE: _____ DATE: ___ / ___ / ___

HOME ADDRESS: _____
(Print)   Number and Street

_____
City   State   Zip Code

PHONE NO.: _____

IMPORTANT: Please fill in these boxes exactly as shown on the back cover of your test book.

2. TEST FORM

_____

3. TEST CODE

	(A)	(J)	(0)	(0)	(0)	(0)	(0)	(0)	(0)	(0)
(0)	(B)	(K)	(1)	(1)	(1)	(1)	(1)	(1)	(1)	(1)
(1)	(C)	(L)	(2)	(2)	(2)	(2)	(2)	(2)	(2)	(2)
(2)	(D)	(M)	(3)	(3)	(3)	(3)	(3)	(3)	(3)	(3)
(3)	(E)	(N)	(4)	(4)	(4)	(4)	(4)	(4)	(4)	(4)
(4)	(F)	(O)	(5)	(5)	(5)	(5)	(5)	(5)	(5)	(5)
(5)	(G)	(P)	(6)	(6)	(6)	(6)	(6)	(6)	(6)	(6)
(6)	(H)	(Q)	(7)	(7)	(7)	(7)	(7)	(7)	(7)	(7)
(7)	(I)	(R)	(8)	(8)	(8)	(8)	(8)	(8)	(8)	(8)
(8)			(9)	(9)	(9)	(9)	(9)	(9)	(9)	(9)
(9)										

4. REGISTRATION NUMBER

6. DATE OF BIRTH

Month	Day		Year	

○ JAN
○ FEB   (0) (0)   (0) (0)
○ MAR   (1) (1)   (1) (1)
○ APR   (2) (2)   (2) (2)
○ MAY   (3) (3)   (3) (3)
○ JUN   (4)   (4) (4)
○ JUL   (5)   (5) (5)
○ AUG   (6)   (6) (6)
○ SEP   (7)   (7) (7)
○ OCT   (8)   (8) (8)
○ NOV   (9)   (9) (9)
○ DEC

5. YOUR NAME

| First 4 letters of last name | | | | | FIRST INIT | MID INIT |

(A) (A) (A) (A)   (A) (A)
(B) (B) (B) (B)   (B) (B)
(C) (C) (C) (C)   (C) (C)
(D) (D) (D) (D)   (D) (D)
(E) (E) (E) (E)   (E) (E)
(F) (F) (F) (F)   (F) (F)
(G) (G) (G) (G)   (G) (G)
(H) (H) (H) (H)   (H) (H)
(I) (I) (I) (I)   (I) (I)
(J) (J) (J) (J)   (J) (J)
(K) (K) (K) (K)   (K) (K)
(L) (L) (L) (L)   (L) (L)
(M) (M) (M) (M)   (M) (M)
(N) (N) (N) (N)   (N) (N)
(O) (O) (O) (O)   (O) (O)
(P) (P) (P) (P)   (P) (P)
(Q) (Q) (Q) (Q)   (Q) (Q)
(R) (R) (R) (R)   (R) (R)
(S) (S) (S) (S)   (S) (S)
(T) (T) (T) (T)   (T) (T)
(U) (U) (U) (U)   (U) (U)
(V) (V) (V) (V)   (V) (V)
(W) (W) (W) (W)   (W) (W)
(X) (X) (X) (X)   (X) (X)
(Y) (Y) (Y) (Y)   (Y) (Y)
(Z) (Z) (Z) (Z)   (Z) (Z)

1. (A) (B) (C) (D)
2. (A) (B) (C) (D)
3. (A) (B) (C) (D)
4. (A) (B) (C) (D)
5. (A) (B) (C) (D)
6. (A) (B) (C) (D)
7. (A) (B) (C) (D)
8. (A) (B) (C) (D)
9. (A) (B) (C) (D)
10. (A) (B) (C) (D)
11. (A) (B) (C) (D)
12. (A) (B) (C) (D)
13. (A) (B) (C) (D)
14. (A) (B) (C) (D)
15. (A) (B) (C) (D)
16. (A) (B) (C) (D)
17. (A) (B) (C) (D)
18. (A) (B) (C) (D)

19. (A) (B) (C) (D)
20. (A) (B) (C) (D)
21. (A) (B) (C) (D)
22. (A) (B) (C) (D)
23. (A) (B) (C) (D)
24. (A) (B) (C) (D)
25. (A) (B) (C) (D)
26. (A) (B) (C) (D)
27. (A) (B) (C) (D)
28. (A) (B) (C) (D)
29. (A) (B) (C) (D)
30. (A) (B) (C) (D)
31. (A) (B) (C) (D)
32. (A) (B) (C) (D)
33. (A) (B) (C) (D)
34. (A) (B) (C) (D)
35. (A) (B) (C) (D)
36. (A) (B) (C) (D)

37. (A) (B) (C) (D)
38. (A) (B) (C) (D)
39. (A) (B) (C) (D)
40. (A) (B) (C) (D)
41. (A) (B) (C) (D)
42. (A) (B) (C) (D)
43. (A) (B) (C) (D)
44. (A) (B) (C) (D)
45. (A) (B) (C) (D)
46. (A) (B) (C) (D)
47. (A) (B) (C) (D)
48. (A) (B) (C) (D)
49. (A) (B) (C) (D)
50. (A) (B) (C) (D)
51. (A) (B) (C) (D)
52. (A) (B) (C) (D)
53. (A) (B) (C) (D)
54. (A) (B) (C) (D)

55. (A) (B) (C) (D)

Completely darken bubbles with a No. 2 pencil. If you make a mistake, be sure to erase mark completely. Erase all stray marks.

1.

YOUR NAME: _____
(Print)   Last   First   M.I.

SIGNATURE: _____ DATE: ____ / ____ / ____

HOME ADDRESS: _____
(Print)   Number and Street

_____
City   State   Zip Code

PHONE NO.: _____

5. YOUR NAME

First 4 letters of last name				FIRST INIT	MID INIT
Ⓐ	Ⓐ	Ⓐ	Ⓐ	Ⓐ	Ⓐ
Ⓑ	Ⓑ	Ⓑ	Ⓑ	Ⓑ	Ⓑ
Ⓒ	Ⓒ	Ⓒ	Ⓒ	Ⓒ	Ⓒ
Ⓓ	Ⓓ	Ⓓ	Ⓓ	Ⓓ	Ⓓ
Ⓔ	Ⓔ	Ⓔ	Ⓔ	Ⓔ	Ⓔ
Ⓕ	Ⓕ	Ⓕ	Ⓕ	Ⓕ	Ⓕ
Ⓖ	Ⓖ	Ⓖ	Ⓖ	Ⓖ	Ⓖ
Ⓗ	Ⓗ	Ⓗ	Ⓗ	Ⓗ	Ⓗ
Ⓘ	Ⓘ	Ⓘ	Ⓘ	Ⓘ	Ⓘ
Ⓙ	Ⓙ	Ⓙ	Ⓙ	Ⓙ	Ⓙ
Ⓚ	Ⓚ	Ⓚ	Ⓚ	Ⓚ	Ⓚ
Ⓛ	Ⓛ	Ⓛ	Ⓛ	Ⓛ	Ⓛ
Ⓜ	Ⓜ	Ⓜ	Ⓜ	Ⓜ	Ⓜ
Ⓝ	Ⓝ	Ⓝ	Ⓝ	Ⓝ	Ⓝ
Ⓞ	Ⓞ	Ⓞ	Ⓞ	Ⓞ	Ⓞ
Ⓟ	Ⓟ	Ⓟ	Ⓟ	Ⓟ	Ⓟ
Ⓠ	Ⓠ	Ⓠ	Ⓠ	Ⓠ	Ⓠ
Ⓡ	Ⓡ	Ⓡ	Ⓡ	Ⓡ	Ⓡ
Ⓢ	Ⓢ	Ⓢ	Ⓢ	Ⓢ	Ⓢ
Ⓣ	Ⓣ	Ⓣ	Ⓣ	Ⓣ	Ⓣ
Ⓤ	Ⓤ	Ⓤ	Ⓤ	Ⓤ	Ⓤ
Ⓥ	Ⓥ	Ⓥ	Ⓥ	Ⓥ	Ⓥ
Ⓦ	Ⓦ	Ⓦ	Ⓦ	Ⓦ	Ⓦ
Ⓧ	Ⓧ	Ⓧ	Ⓧ	Ⓧ	Ⓧ
Ⓨ	Ⓨ	Ⓨ	Ⓨ	Ⓨ	Ⓨ
Ⓩ	Ⓩ	Ⓩ	Ⓩ	Ⓩ	Ⓩ

IMPORTANT: Please fill in these boxes exactly as shown on the back cover of your test book.

2. TEST FORM

3. TEST CODE

4. REGISTRATION NUMBER

⓪	Ⓐ	Ⓙ	⓪	⓪	⓪	⓪	⓪	⓪	⓪
①	Ⓑ	Ⓚ	①	①	①	①	①	①	①
②	Ⓒ	Ⓛ	②	②	②	②	②	②	②
③	Ⓓ	Ⓜ	③	③	③	③	③	③	③
④	Ⓔ	Ⓝ	④	④	④	④	④	④	④
⑤	Ⓕ	Ⓞ	⑤	⑤	⑤	⑤	⑤	⑤	⑤
⑥	Ⓖ	Ⓟ	⑥	⑥	⑥	⑥	⑥	⑥	⑥
⑦	Ⓗ	Ⓠ	⑦	⑦	⑦	⑦	⑦	⑦	⑦
⑧	Ⓘ	Ⓡ	⑧	⑧	⑧	⑧	⑧	⑧	⑧
			⑨	⑨	⑨	⑨	⑨	⑨	⑨

6. DATE OF BIRTH

Month	Day		Year	
◯ JAN				
◯ FEB	⓪	⓪	⓪	⓪
◯ MAR	①	①	①	①
◯ APR	②	②	②	②
◯ MAY	③	③	③	③
◯ JUN		④	④	④
◯ JUL		⑤	⑤	⑤
◯ AUG		⑥	⑥	⑥
◯ SEP		⑦	⑦	⑦
◯ OCT		⑧	⑧	⑧
◯ NOV		⑨	⑨	⑨
◯ DEC				

The **Princeton Review®**

1. Ⓐ Ⓑ Ⓒ Ⓓ
2. Ⓐ Ⓑ Ⓒ Ⓓ
3. Ⓐ Ⓑ Ⓒ Ⓓ
4. Ⓐ Ⓑ Ⓒ Ⓓ
5. Ⓐ Ⓑ Ⓒ Ⓓ
6. Ⓐ Ⓑ Ⓒ Ⓓ
7. Ⓐ Ⓑ Ⓒ Ⓓ
8. Ⓐ Ⓑ Ⓒ Ⓓ
9. Ⓐ Ⓑ Ⓒ Ⓓ
10. Ⓐ Ⓑ Ⓒ Ⓓ
11. Ⓐ Ⓑ Ⓒ Ⓓ
12. Ⓐ Ⓑ Ⓒ Ⓓ
13. Ⓐ Ⓑ Ⓒ Ⓓ
14. Ⓐ Ⓑ Ⓒ Ⓓ
15. Ⓐ Ⓑ Ⓒ Ⓓ
16. Ⓐ Ⓑ Ⓒ Ⓓ
17. Ⓐ Ⓑ Ⓒ Ⓓ
18. Ⓐ Ⓑ Ⓒ Ⓓ

19. Ⓐ Ⓑ Ⓒ Ⓓ
20. Ⓐ Ⓑ Ⓒ Ⓓ
21. Ⓐ Ⓑ Ⓒ Ⓓ
22. Ⓐ Ⓑ Ⓒ Ⓓ
23. Ⓐ Ⓑ Ⓒ Ⓓ
24. Ⓐ Ⓑ Ⓒ Ⓓ
25. Ⓐ Ⓑ Ⓒ Ⓓ
26. Ⓐ Ⓑ Ⓒ Ⓓ
27. Ⓐ Ⓑ Ⓒ Ⓓ
28. Ⓐ Ⓑ Ⓒ Ⓓ
29. Ⓐ Ⓑ Ⓒ Ⓓ
30. Ⓐ Ⓑ Ⓒ Ⓓ
31. Ⓐ Ⓑ Ⓒ Ⓓ
32. Ⓐ Ⓑ Ⓒ Ⓓ
33. Ⓐ Ⓑ Ⓒ Ⓓ
34. Ⓐ Ⓑ Ⓒ Ⓓ
35. Ⓐ Ⓑ Ⓒ Ⓓ
36. Ⓐ Ⓑ Ⓒ Ⓓ

37. Ⓐ Ⓑ Ⓒ Ⓓ
38. Ⓐ Ⓑ Ⓒ Ⓓ
39. Ⓐ Ⓑ Ⓒ Ⓓ
40. Ⓐ Ⓑ Ⓒ Ⓓ
41. Ⓐ Ⓑ Ⓒ Ⓓ
42. Ⓐ Ⓑ Ⓒ Ⓓ
43. Ⓐ Ⓑ Ⓒ Ⓓ
44. Ⓐ Ⓑ Ⓒ Ⓓ
45. Ⓐ Ⓑ Ⓒ Ⓓ
46. Ⓐ Ⓑ Ⓒ Ⓓ
47. Ⓐ Ⓑ Ⓒ Ⓓ
48. Ⓐ Ⓑ Ⓒ Ⓓ
49. Ⓐ Ⓑ Ⓒ Ⓓ
50. Ⓐ Ⓑ Ⓒ Ⓓ
51. Ⓐ Ⓑ Ⓒ Ⓓ
52. Ⓐ Ⓑ Ⓒ Ⓓ
53. Ⓐ Ⓑ Ⓒ Ⓓ
54. Ⓐ Ⓑ Ⓒ Ⓓ

55. Ⓐ Ⓑ Ⓒ Ⓓ

The Princeton Review®

Completely darken bubbles with a No. 2 pencil. If you make a mistake, be sure to erase mark completely. Erase all stray marks.

1.

YOUR NAME: _____
(Print)   Last   First   M.I.

SIGNATURE: _____ DATE: ____ / ____ / ____

HOME ADDRESS: _____
(Print)   Number and Street

_____
             City   State   Zip Code

PHONE NO.: _____

IMPORTANT: Please fill in these boxes exactly as shown on the back cover of your test book.

5. YOUR NAME

First 4 letters of last name				FIRST INIT	MID INIT
Ⓐ	Ⓐ	Ⓐ	Ⓐ	Ⓐ	Ⓐ
Ⓑ	Ⓑ	Ⓑ	Ⓑ	Ⓑ	Ⓑ
Ⓒ	Ⓒ	Ⓒ	Ⓒ	Ⓒ	Ⓒ
Ⓓ	Ⓓ	Ⓓ	Ⓓ	Ⓓ	Ⓓ
Ⓔ	Ⓔ	Ⓔ	Ⓔ	Ⓔ	Ⓔ
Ⓕ	Ⓕ	Ⓕ	Ⓕ	Ⓕ	Ⓕ
Ⓖ	Ⓖ	Ⓖ	Ⓖ	Ⓖ	Ⓖ
Ⓗ	Ⓗ	Ⓗ	Ⓗ	Ⓗ	Ⓗ
Ⓘ	Ⓘ	Ⓘ	Ⓘ	Ⓘ	Ⓘ
Ⓙ	Ⓙ	Ⓙ	Ⓙ	Ⓙ	Ⓙ
Ⓚ	Ⓚ	Ⓚ	Ⓚ	Ⓚ	Ⓚ
Ⓛ	Ⓛ	Ⓛ	Ⓛ	Ⓛ	Ⓛ
Ⓜ	Ⓜ	Ⓜ	Ⓜ	Ⓜ	Ⓜ
Ⓝ	Ⓝ	Ⓝ	Ⓝ	Ⓝ	Ⓝ
Ⓞ	Ⓞ	Ⓞ	Ⓞ	Ⓞ	Ⓞ
Ⓟ	Ⓟ	Ⓟ	Ⓟ	Ⓟ	Ⓟ
Ⓠ	Ⓠ	Ⓠ	Ⓠ	Ⓠ	Ⓠ
Ⓡ	Ⓡ	Ⓡ	Ⓡ	Ⓡ	Ⓡ
Ⓢ	Ⓢ	Ⓢ	Ⓢ	Ⓢ	Ⓢ
Ⓣ	Ⓣ	Ⓣ	Ⓣ	Ⓣ	Ⓣ
Ⓤ	Ⓤ	Ⓤ	Ⓤ	Ⓤ	Ⓤ
Ⓥ	Ⓥ	Ⓥ	Ⓥ	Ⓥ	Ⓥ
Ⓦ	Ⓦ	Ⓦ	Ⓦ	Ⓦ	Ⓦ
Ⓧ	Ⓧ	Ⓧ	Ⓧ	Ⓧ	Ⓧ
Ⓨ	Ⓨ	Ⓨ	Ⓨ	Ⓨ	Ⓨ
Ⓩ	Ⓩ	Ⓩ	Ⓩ	Ⓩ	Ⓩ

2. TEST FORM

3. TEST CODE

4. REGISTRATION NUMBER

6. DATE OF BIRTH

Month	Day		Year	
◯ JAN				
◯ FEB	⓪ ⓪	⓪ ⓪		
◯ MAR	① ①	① ①		
◯ APR	② ②	② ②		
◯ MAY	③ ③	③ ③		
◯ JUN		④ ④		
◯ JUL		⑤ ⑤		
◯ AUG		⑥ ⑥		
◯ SEP		⑦ ⑦		
◯ OCT		⑧ ⑧		
◯ NOV		⑨ ⑨		
◯ DEC				

3. TEST CODE / 4. REGISTRATION NUMBER bubbles

⓪	Ⓐ	Ⓙ	⓪	⓪	⓪	⓪	⓪	⓪	⓪
①	Ⓑ	Ⓚ	①	①	①	①	①	①	①
②	Ⓒ	Ⓛ	②	②	②	②	②	②	②
③	Ⓓ	Ⓜ	③	③	③	③	③	③	③
④	Ⓔ	Ⓝ	④	④	④	④	④	④	④
⑤	Ⓕ	Ⓞ	⑤	⑤	⑤	⑤	⑤	⑤	⑤
⑥	Ⓖ	Ⓟ	⑥	⑥	⑥	⑥	⑥	⑥	⑥
⑦	Ⓗ	Ⓠ	⑦	⑦	⑦	⑦	⑦	⑦	⑦
⑧	Ⓘ	Ⓡ	⑧	⑧	⑧	⑧	⑧	⑧	⑧
⑨			⑨	⑨	⑨	⑨	⑨	⑨	⑨

The Princeton Review®

1. Ⓐ Ⓑ Ⓒ Ⓓ
2. Ⓐ Ⓑ Ⓒ Ⓓ
3. Ⓐ Ⓑ Ⓒ Ⓓ
4. Ⓐ Ⓑ Ⓒ Ⓓ
5. Ⓐ Ⓑ Ⓒ Ⓓ
6. Ⓐ Ⓑ Ⓒ Ⓓ
7. Ⓐ Ⓑ Ⓒ Ⓓ
8. Ⓐ Ⓑ Ⓒ Ⓓ
9. Ⓐ Ⓑ Ⓒ Ⓓ
10. Ⓐ Ⓑ Ⓒ Ⓓ
11. Ⓐ Ⓑ Ⓒ Ⓓ
12. Ⓐ Ⓑ Ⓒ Ⓓ
13. Ⓐ Ⓑ Ⓒ Ⓓ
14. Ⓐ Ⓑ Ⓒ Ⓓ
15. Ⓐ Ⓑ Ⓒ Ⓓ
16. Ⓐ Ⓑ Ⓒ Ⓓ
17. Ⓐ Ⓑ Ⓒ Ⓓ
18. Ⓐ Ⓑ Ⓒ Ⓓ

19. Ⓐ Ⓑ Ⓒ Ⓓ
20. Ⓐ Ⓑ Ⓒ Ⓓ
21. Ⓐ Ⓑ Ⓒ Ⓓ
22. Ⓐ Ⓑ Ⓒ Ⓓ
23. Ⓐ Ⓑ Ⓒ Ⓓ
24. Ⓐ Ⓑ Ⓒ Ⓓ
25. Ⓐ Ⓑ Ⓒ Ⓓ
26. Ⓐ Ⓑ Ⓒ Ⓓ
27. Ⓐ Ⓑ Ⓒ Ⓓ
28. Ⓐ Ⓑ Ⓒ Ⓓ
29. Ⓐ Ⓑ Ⓒ Ⓓ
30. Ⓐ Ⓑ Ⓒ Ⓓ
31. Ⓐ Ⓑ Ⓒ Ⓓ
32. Ⓐ Ⓑ Ⓒ Ⓓ
33. Ⓐ Ⓑ Ⓒ Ⓓ
34. Ⓐ Ⓑ Ⓒ Ⓓ
35. Ⓐ Ⓑ Ⓒ Ⓓ
36. Ⓐ Ⓑ Ⓒ Ⓓ

37. Ⓐ Ⓑ Ⓒ Ⓓ
38. Ⓐ Ⓑ Ⓒ Ⓓ
39. Ⓐ Ⓑ Ⓒ Ⓓ
40. Ⓐ Ⓑ Ⓒ Ⓓ
41. Ⓐ Ⓑ Ⓒ Ⓓ
42. Ⓐ Ⓑ Ⓒ Ⓓ
43. Ⓐ Ⓑ Ⓒ Ⓓ
44. Ⓐ Ⓑ Ⓒ Ⓓ
45. Ⓐ Ⓑ Ⓒ Ⓓ
46. Ⓐ Ⓑ Ⓒ Ⓓ
47. Ⓐ Ⓑ Ⓒ Ⓓ
48. Ⓐ Ⓑ Ⓒ Ⓓ
49. Ⓐ Ⓑ Ⓒ Ⓓ
50. Ⓐ Ⓑ Ⓒ Ⓓ
51. Ⓐ Ⓑ Ⓒ Ⓓ
52. Ⓐ Ⓑ Ⓒ Ⓓ
53. Ⓐ Ⓑ Ⓒ Ⓓ
54. Ⓐ Ⓑ Ⓒ Ⓓ

55. Ⓐ Ⓑ Ⓒ Ⓓ

NOTES

NOTES

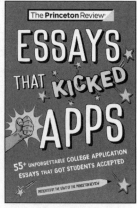